Sino-Soviet Relations,
1964–1965

Center for International Studies
Massachusetts Institute of Technology

Studies in International Communism

Sino-Soviet Relations, 1964-1965

Analyzed and Documented by

WILLIAM E. GRIFFITH

THE M.I.T. PRESS

Massachusetts Institute of Technology
Cambridge, Massachusetts, and London, England

Preface

This book is intended to analyze and document Sino-Soviet relations from November 1963 through November 1965, picking up where my *The Sino-Soviet Rift* left off. Like it, this account lays no claim to anything like definitiveness; rather, it is a brief, preliminary guide to the subject. Unfortunately, because of the flood of documentation and the constantly increasing complexity of the subject, there has been comparatively little recent systematic research on Sino-Soviet relations. I hope that this analysis may fill some of the gap and encourage more work in this field.

The analysis grew out of a paper presented at a conference on Sino-Soviet relations and arms control held by Harvard University and sponsored by the U.S. Arms Control and Disarmament Agency, at Airlie House, Warrenton, Virginia, August 30–September 4, 1965. I am grateful to the participants at the conference for their comments on the paper, and particularly to Professors Zbigniew Brzezinski and Richard Lowenthal. I expanded the paper to its present form at the suggestion of Mr. Roderick MacFarquhar, editor of *The China Quarterly* where it first appeared (No. 25, January March 1966, pp. 3–143). I am grateful to Mr. MacFarquhar for his willingness to publish so long a study and to have it reprinted here, and to Mr. Wolfgang Leonhard and Mr. Helmut Sonnenfeldt for comments on a draft of it. I have also profited at various stages of its composition from comments by Messrs. Donald L. M. Blackmer, James F. Brown, Kevin Devlin, Herbert Dinerstein, Christian Duevel, Fritz Ermarth, R. Rockingham Gill, Ernst Halperin, Morton H. Halperin, Joseph C. Kun, William McLaughlin, Uri Ra'anan. I owe the most gratitude for the help in research and editing given me by Dr. Robin Remington. The manuscript was edited by Dr. Remington and Mrs. Jean P. S. Clark, indexed by Mr. Peter Prifti, and typed by Mrs. Lila T. Rose. The manuscript and documents were prepared for the press by Miss Mary Patricia Grady and Mrs. Elizabeth G. Whitney.

Although the documents are primarily direct Sino-Soviet governmental or polemical exchanges, statements by other Communist parties have been included when (as with Togliatti's Memorandum of September

1964) they became a focal point for further polemics or when (as with the Rumanian Party Statement of April 1964) they aptly demonstrate the impact of Sino-Soviet differences upon the maneuverability of other parties within the international Communist movement. Whenever possible, the complete texts of documents have been reprinted. However, since problems of space made excerpting necessary in some cases, the excerpts were chosen so as (1) to illustrate a change in the level or tone of Sino-Soviet polemics and (2) to avoid duplicating a later, more extensive statement. The text first appeared in *The China Quarterly* without documents. The final document, a recent illuminating study by a leading Czech authority, Václav Kotyk, of the Institute of International Politics and Economics in Prague, reached me too late to be treated in the analysis.

Generally speaking, Soviet and Chinese documents have been reproduced as published in English translation; revisions have been necessary only with the Italian, Rumanian, and Czech ones. Chinese orthography has been revised to conform to the modified Wade-Giles transliteration rather than Peking's, for example, *Jen-min Jih-pao* instead of *Renmin Ribao, Hung Ch'i* rather than *Hongqi,* Ch'en Yi rather than Chen Yi. The standard transliteration of Russian names has in general been used, for example, Khrushchev instead of Khrushchov. Abbreviations have been standardized: CCP, CPR, USSR, and so forth. Soviet documents have been taken from Chinese sources only when not available in Soviet sources. Chinese references are primarily to the *Peking Review,* but references have also been given to the convenient Peking collection, *The Polemic on the General Line of the International Communist Movement* (Peking: Foreign Languages Press, 1965), 586 pp.

I am grateful to the Center for International Studies and to its director, Max F. Millikan, for their support in this study. Its publication has been made possible by a generous grant to M.I.T. by the Ford Foundation for research and teaching in international affairs. Neither the Center nor the Foundation, however, is in any way responsible for its contents; that responsibility is mine alone.

William E. Griffith

Cambridge, Massachusetts
March 18, 1966

Contents

vii

CONTENTS

DOCUMENTS

CONTENTS

CONTENTS

CONTENTS

ERRATA

Page 15 Note 13: Date of letter should read November 29, 1963.

Page 31 Note 68: Should be Mieczyslaw F. Rakowski.

Page 38 Text, 3rd line from bottom: Should read 26-party preparatory committee.

Page 40 Note 103: Source should read J. F. Brown.

Page 44 Note 116: *Peking Review* source is Vol. VII, No. 36 (September 4, 1964), pp. 8–9.

Page 60 Note 158, line 9: Should read Fürnberg.

Page 80 Note 241, last line: Title of article is "The Splitting Revisionist March 1 Meeting — A Great Plot Against Marxism-Leninism and International Communism."

Page 101 Note 327: Should read Kevin Devlin.

Page 132 Note 424: Quoted from pp. 5–6 and 36.

Page 142 Note 461: Should read "The International Duty of the Communists of All Countries"; quotations are from *CDSP,* Vol. XVII, No. 47 (December 15, 1965), pp. 3–5.

Sino-Soviet Relations,
1964 – 1965

I. Introduction

THE radical worsening of Sino-Soviet relations began in the spring of 1958 and the " point of no return " occurred at the latest in the summer of 1959. Indeed, since 1958 the public dispute has followed a cyclical course of escalation and partial détente. Each cycle has made Moscow-Peking relations worse than before and given other communist parties more autonomy from the Soviet Union. The apparent partial détentes have ostensibly been caused by Soviet and Chinese moves toward reconciliation, but these actually have been tactical maneuvers intended by each primarily to worsen the other's position and to gain support within other communist parties.[1]

The single most persistent dynamic characteristic of these cycles has been the greater assertion of national autonomy by communist parties and more generally by radical movements, particularly by the ones previously under predominant Soviet influence and, since late 1964, also by some who had previously moved from predominantly Soviet to

---

[1] The chronology of the Sino-Soviet dispute is too long and complex to summarize here, and its development up to the end of November 1963 has already been treated in detail. Several points about it, however, are especially important for understanding 1964–1965 developments. For 1962–1963, and for a fuller reconstructed chronology and analysis, with bibliography, on which this brief historical introduction is primarily based, see William E. Griffith, *The Sino-Soviet Rift* (London: Allen and Unwin; Cambridge, Mass.: The M.I.T. Press, 1964). For the earlier part of the dispute, see Donald S. Zagoria, *The Sino-Soviet Conflict, 1956–1961* (New York: Atheneum, 1964); William E. Griffith, *Albania and the Sino-Soviet Rift* (Cambridge, Mass.: The M.I.T. Press, 1963); G. F. Hudson, Richard Lowenthal and Roderick MacFarquhar, *The Sino-Soviet Dispute* (New York: Praeger, 1961); and Alexander Dallin, ed., *Diversity in International Communism* (New York: Columbia University Press, 1963). For an enlightening reconsideration of the historical background, see Klaus Mehnert, *Peking and Moscow* (New York: Mentor, 1964). See also Richard Lowenthal, " The Prospects for Pluralistic Communism," in Milorad M. Drachkovitch, ed., *Marxism in the Modern World* (Stanford, Cal.: Stanford University Press, 1965), pp. 225–274; Leopold Labedz, ed., *International Communism after Khrushchev* (Cambridge, Mass.: The M.I.T. Press, 1965); Robert A. Scalapino, ed., *The Communist Revolution in Asia* (Englewood Cliffs, N.J.: Prentice-Hall, 1963); Dennis J. Doolin, *Territorial Claims in the Sino-Soviet Conflict* (Stanford, Cal.: The Hoover Institution, 1965); and William E. Griffith, ed., *Communism in Europe*, Vols. 1 and 2 (Cambridge, Mass.: The M.I.T. Press, 1964 and 1966).

Chinese influence. Until the fall of Khrushchev and the American escalation of the war in Vietnam this cyclical development had also resulted in a steady decline of Soviet, and a rise of Chinese, influence. Since then, because the post-Khrushchev Soviet leadership has appeared to cut its losses and to accept autonomy of communist parties, while increasing weapons shipments to North Vietnam; and because, conversely, the Chinese, who have become increasingly less flexible in their stance, have also suffered a series of international defeats, Soviet influence has risen somewhat and Chinese influence has declined.

The Chinese, while protesting their opposition to a split and their desire to discuss and thus to solve the differences, have ideologically taken an increasingly adamant policy position and intensified their factional and splitting activity. This strategy was successful until Khrushchev's fall and, although it has since then contributed to a decline in their influence, they had not as of November 1965 substantially altered it. The Soviets, on the other hand, until the fall of Khrushchev tried to bring about the " collective mobilization " of other communist parties for expelling the Chinese, that is, formally to split the international Communist movement and thereby close off the possibility of neutralism or passivity and consequently preclude or at least limit the success of Chinese factionalist activities.

▶ The primary cause of the Sino-Soviet rift has been the determination of Mao and his associates that China should become a superpower and the determination of the Soviet leadership to prevent it.

To reach his goal, Mao had to undertake rapid economic development, acquire nuclear weapons (in our age the key symbol of superpower status), recover China's irredenta (notably Taiwan and the offshore islands but also, eventually, territories and spheres of influence lost by Imperial China to the Tsars), and become the dominant power in East and Southeast Asia. Because he could more easily have achieved these aims if Moscow had given him extensive economic and atomic aid and had supported him against the United States and India—his two main obstacles—Khrushchev's refusal to do so had convinced Mao by 1958–1959 that the policies of the Soviet leadership were a grave threat to China's vital and legitimate national interests and made it necessary for him to obtain his economic and nuclear goals by a labor-intensive, extremist domestic policy. Finally, Khrushchev's unsuccessful attempt at the economic blackmail of China, plus his support for opposition elements within the Chinese leadership (Marshal P'eng Teh-huai *et al.*), convinced Mao that Khrushchev was his deadly enemy. To Mao, as to any Marxist-Leninist " true believer," ideology and state interest should be, and are, indistinguishable. Thus Mao came to believe that the Soviet leadership was betraying Marxism-Leninism and therefore that

4

China must replace the Soviet Union as the head of a new, reformed communist movement centering in the underdeveloped world and committed to world-wide revolution, violent anti-Americanism, territorial revisionism, and ascetic fanaticism in domestic policy. Thereupon, because of the shared Marxist-Leninist ideology, conflict in state interests inevitably became translated into ideological polemics and universalized on the ideological plane.

To elaborate briefly on the more specific issues, Peking regarded the recovery of Taiwan, Quemoy, and Matsu, and more generally the expulsion of American power from the shores of Asia, as one of its vital interests. The post-Stalin Soviet leaderships have preferred a détente with the strategically more powerful United States to Sino-Soviet reconciliation (that is, they proclaim " peaceful coexistence " and the " noninevitability of war ") and, especially after the Cuban missile crisis of 1962, have been unwilling to accept the high level of risk-taking vis-à-vis Washington that Mao considered essential for the *Soviets* to accept so as to achieve Chinese vital interests. In this sense the United States has served as a divisive rather than unifying force.

The Chinese based their hopes of driving back the Americans on the revolutionary potential of the underdeveloped, colored areas (" the epicenter of the world revolutionary struggle "), and they insisted and continue to insist that Moscow must be willing to give priority to military aid for revolutions of national liberation over détente with the United States. To Moscow's reply that this falsely values the national liberation struggle above the " world socialist system " and moreover runs the risk of American escalation and therefore of general or nuclear war (that is, it is contrary to " peaceful coexistence "), the Chinese have retorted that the American " paper tiger " will eventually withdraw rather than either fight guerrilla wars indefinitely or escalate to general war.

Moreover, Khrushchev's refusal of massive economic and military aid to China, plus the failure of Mao's short-lived hundred-flowers experiment, had turned Mao from domestic relaxation to ascetic, extremist fanaticism. Conversely, Khrushchev and his associates remained determined to de-Stalinize in order to enable more effective exploitation of the Soviet industrial potential. Consequently, a sharp contrast developed between Moscow's and Peking's internal policies, with Mao considering Soviet internal relaxation a direct menace to China's maintenance of an ascetic, fanatical, labor-intensive police state.

A review of Chinese and Soviet policies in late 1963, and their evolution within the context of international political developments during the two years thereafter, will provide some general background for the detailed story of Sino-Soviet relations that follows.

Chinese Foreign Policy

Chinese foreign policy toward the Soviet Union as well as toward the United States is profoundly influenced by Chinese domestic policy. Since 1963 Peking's domestic policy has been characterized by an apparent paradox: a great intensification of political indoctrination and purge but a less extreme, more pragmatic line in industry and agriculture. The latter is a rational reaction to Chinese economic problems. The former seems to be motivated by an all-pervasive anxiety on the part of the aging Mao and the other veteran revolutionaries that their version of the good society for China—a vast, permanent, collectivist consensus—is menaced by human weakness, lack of ascetic fanatic dedication, and desires of younger cadres for some possibility to enjoy the fruits of their victories. As the Chinese ninth " Comment " put it:

> The question of training successors . . . is one of whether or not there will be people who can carry on the Marxist-Leninist revolutionary cause started by the older generation of proletarian revolutionaries . . . whether or not we can successfully prevent the emergence of Khrushchevite revisionism in China . . . a matter of life and death for our Party and our country.[2]

Therefore, Peking began intensifying pressure on what Mao apparently considered insufficiently fanatical cadres and intellectuals.[3] By mid-1964 the greatly intensified campaign was concentrated against the allegedly insufficient emphasis on " struggle " (the view that " two combine into one " rather than " one divides into two ") by the philosopher Yang Hsien-chen[4] and, as it spread throughout the country, reached unparalleled heights of adulation of Mao and fanatical collective indoctrination.

Can this fanatical revolutionary asceticism—the total primacy of revolutionary politics over economics—overcome indefinitely the tendency arising from modernization and industrialization toward rational bureaucracy? Mao, and presumably his immediate successors from his " Yenan generation," believe, like Stalin, that it can and must. (This is not a question of democratization but of rational versus revolutionary bureaucratic regimes.) The tension and conflict structurally involved in

---

[2] Quoted from *Peking Review*, Vol. VII, No. 29 (July 17, 1964), p. 26. For the above, see generally the penetrating analysis by Benjamin Schwartz, " Modernization and the Maoist Vision," *The China Quarterly*, No. 21 (January–March 1965), pp. 3–19.

[3] See Joseph Simon, " Ferment among Intellectuals," *Problems of Communism*, Vol. XIII, No. 5 (September–October 1964), pp. 29–37.

[4] See Donald J. Munro, " The Yang Hsien-chen Affair," *The China Quarterly*, No. 22 (April–June 1965), pp. 75–82. See also " The Purge," *China News Analysis*, No. 506 (February 28, 1964); " Yang Hsien-chen," *ibid.*, No. 535 (October 2, 1964); " Maoism Reimposed: On Reviews," *ibid.*, No. 559 (April 9, 1965); " The Purge in Action," *ibid.*, No. 561 (April 23, 1965); and " Chairman Mao and the Heretics," *Current Scene*, Vol. III, No. 13 (February 15, 1965).

this problem, plus the problems of Mao's aging, contribute much fanaticism of current Chinese internal policy.[5]

These considerations also contribute to current Chinese foreign policy, particularly vis-à-vis the Soviet Union, the basic tenets of which may be summarized as (1) economic and thermonuclear self-reliance as a precondition for becoming a superpower, (2) the primacy of the anti-American struggle, thus requiring independence from Moscow, which prefers détente with the United States, and an attempt to ally with Western Europe and Japan against Washington and Moscow, and (3) concentration on armed struggle in the underdeveloped world as the decisive area of conflict with America.[6]

Chinese foreign policy did not change significantly after Khrushchev's fall, nor has it as yet (November 1965) begun to adjust to its recent defeats.

Soviet Policy

In November 1963 the CPSU Presidium saw great dangers and limited opportunities in foreign policy, in large part because of its domestic problems. First, as is clear in retrospect, there were differences of view within it, and Khrushchev's ascendancy was not unquestioned. Second, the Soviet Union faced increasingly serious domestic economic problems, notably in agriculture and in its lagging rate of economic growth and these had to be given priority. Third, the resultant resource allocation problems were compounded by the continuing growth of American technological and strategic superiority and, particularly if American technological progress continued and Soviet-American tension rose, by the necessity for future expenditures for manned space military vehicles, for example, manned orbital laboratories (MOL), and for antiballistic missiles (ABM).

Although the partial test ban treaty had improved Soviet-American relations, it was uncertain to what extent the new American president would continue his predecessor's policies, in Vietnam and elsewhere; and, as it turned out, Johnson adopted a considerably more forward strategy, notably in Vietnam and the Congo. After the 1962 Cuban missile crisis, the watershed of recent international politics, the world had realized that the United States possessed, and was ready if necessary to use, decisive thermonuclear missile capacity and, except on the Eurasian land borders of Soviet Red Army, strength, superior

5 For the above, and for Chinese internal policy generally, see John Wilson Lewis, " Revolutionary Struggle and the Second Generation in Communist China," *The China Quarterly*, No. 21 (January–March 1965), pp. 126–147.
6 A. M. Halpern, " China in the Postwar World," *ibid*. pp. 20–45; Morton H. Halperin, *China and the Bomb*, and Morton H. Halperin and Dwight H. Perkins, *Communist China and Arms Control* (both New York and London: Praeger, 1965).

conventional (notably long-range air- and sea-lift) capacity as well. Moreover, as Khrushchev's withdrawal in Cuba showed, Moscow was not willing—at least raising the suspicion that it was not able—to challenge Washington's superiority.

American military superiority over the Soviet Union was a reflection of American economic and technological superiority, which was growing rapidly as a result of sustained American high growth rate caused by the Kennedy-Johnson neo-Keynesian economic policies. Western Europe's economic growth rate and consumer-oriented prosperity also remained high and, moreover, could be converted into a thermonuclear missile and conventional military power, a potential that Moscow considered particularly menacing with respect to West Germany. Conversely, Soviet and East European agriculture remained stagnant, and the decline in their growth rates, with the exception of Rumania, was such that drastic economic decentralization seemed rationally inevitable but politically dangerous.

With respect to Sino-Soviet relations, the collapse of the July 1963 Sino-Soviet negotiations in Moscow, the Chinese factional campaign, and the increasing challenge to Soviet authority of even such pro-Soviet parties as the Rumanian, Italian, and Cuban made some further action against Peking imperative.

Khrushchev, and after him Brezhnev and Kosygin, had many other foreign policy problems as well. Soviet heavy-handedness in Eastern Europe, notably in Rumania, had lost Moscow much influence; there, also, some attempt had to be made to stabilize the situation. Furthermore, Khrushchev's fury at the Chinese and his desire for a détente with the Americans had made him prepared practically to abandon East and Southeast Asia (except India) to Chinese predominance, although his successors tried to recover Soviet influence there.

In addition, Moscow was engaged in a world-wide struggle with Peking for influence in Africa, Latin America, the Middle East, and Southern Asia. There, although until October 1964 the Chinese continued to gain, Khrushchev's tactics of abandoning or using members of indigenous Communist parties to infiltrate native radical nationalist movements seemed to be showing some signs of success in Cairo and Algiers by 1964. However, after his fall, the November 1964 American-Belgian-South African suppression of the second Congo rebellion [7] showed that Moscow still lacks sufficient military and paramilitary capabilities to support guerrilla movements over long distances if the United States is prepared to use its air power against them.

In the light of these considerations, the new Soviet leadership

---

[7] Not that the United States and Belgium were allied with South Africa; but in fact all three worked toward the rebellion's suppression.

decided after October 1964 to readjust somewhat Khrushchev's priorities in foreign policy. Specifically they decided:

1. To move toward lowering the level of Sino-Soviet hostility, thus

(a) perhaps forcing the Chinese to do likewise and,

(b) in any case, thereby enabling the improvement of relations between Moscow and the recently pro-Chinese parties in North Vietnam and North Korea, as well as with Cuba, Rumania, and the Italian Communist Party.

Concretely, this involved

(c) transforming, after having first postponed, the international communist conference so that it would serve the best attainable, if partial, unity of the greatest number on the greatest number of practical issues; and, conversely, therefore abandoning the aim of collective mobilization for expelling or condemning the Chinese, at least for the present, since (1) it could not be achieved, and (2) its abandonment might improve the Soviet position.

2. To maintain the general line of détente with the United States, but restricting it more than Khrushchev had done in order to counter the Johnson administration's increased military activity.

(a) Specifically, with respect to Vietnam adopting a considerably more forward political and military policy, involving intensification of military aid to Vietnam while simultaneously utilizing the stepped-up military operations in the South and any eventual American air attacks against the North (for which Moscow, not Peking, could provide defensive weapons) as justification for suspension of collective mobilization to expel the Chinese, thereby hoping to influence North Vietnam to choose Moscow over Peking.

(b) Domestically pursuing the plans probably already laid by Khrushchev for creation of a significant Soviet long-range air- and sea-lift capacity, plus, insofar as possible, the acquisition of foreign bases so that eventually such American conventional and counterinsurgency operations as in Vietnam and the Congo could be deterred or prevented from crushing Soviet-aided guerrilla risings.

(c) Finally, with respect to Europe and disarmament, the revival of disarmament negotiations, thus (1) putting further strains on NATO and blocking German nuclear armament, multilateral or otherwise and (2) stalling if not preventing another leap forward in the arms race (MOL and ABM).

3. To reconsolidate the menaced Soviet position in Eastern Europe, among China's Southeast Asian allies, and in Cuba.

(a) In Eastern Europe this meant (1) readjusting Soviet–East European relations on the basis of a differentiated rather than monolithic alliance centering on geopolitical and military rather than on ideological factors, that is, giving priority to the area of minimum essential Soviet security interests: East Germany, Poland, and Czechoslovakia; (2) moving toward rapprochement with Rumania (essentially on Bucharest's terms); and (3) intensifying the rapprochement with Yugoslavia.

(b) With respect to Southeast Asia it involved countering Chinese influence by (1) the policy towards Vietnam just described, and (2) by the same means, improving relations with North Korea.

(c) As for Cuba, Moscow's policy included (1) improving relations by more economic aid, and (2) providing more financial and technical assistance—probably reluctantly—to stepped-up guerrilla operations in Latin America. In return for these concessions, Castro appears to have agreed (also probably reluctantly) to cease trying to supplant Latin American Communist leaderships thus hopefully—from the Soviet viewpoint—containing strife within these movements between Fidelistas and the Latin American Communist party leaderships.[8]

In sum, three developments have highlighted Sino-Soviet relations since January 1964. The first, in 1964, was the accelerated decline of Soviet influence in the Communist world, climaxed by the failure of the second Soviet attempt to mobilize its allies for collective action against China, and thereafter (as of November 1965) the (at least temporary) abandonment of this attempt. The second was the February 1965 American military escalation into North Vietnam and the commitment of major American air and ground forces to South Vietnam, and the subsequent Soviet decision not to risk a major military confrontation there with the United States because its own vital national interests were not directly involved and because the prime profiters from such a confrontation would be not Moscow but its enemies or unreliable friends in Peking and Hanoi. The third, which developed gradually between the October 1964 fall of Khrushchev and June 1965, was the abandonment by the new Soviet leadership of " collective mobilization " to expel the Chinese (that is, a Soviet-induced formal split in the international

---

[8] For Soviet military policy, including detailed discussion of forces levels, Vietnam, and air- and sea-lift capacity, see Thomas H. Wolfe, *Soviet Strategy at the Crossroads* (Cambridge, Mass.: Harvard University Press, 1964); " Trends in Soviet Thinking on Theater Warfare, Conventional Operations, and Limited War," RAND Memorandum RM-4305-PR, December 1964; " The Soviet Union and the Sino-Soviet Dispute," RAND Paper P-3203, August 1965; and " Soviet Military Policy Under Khrushchev's Successors," RAND Paper P-3193, August 1965. I have profited greatly from discussions with Drs. Wolfe and Herbert Dinerstein of the RAND Corporation and with my colleague Dr. Ernst Halperin.

Communist movement) for more flexible tactics allowing for national autonomy and neutralism by communist states and parties; and, on the part of the Chinese, the refusal to make a similar adjustment away from their ideological and organizational factionalism and fanaticism. This refusal, plus a series of Chinese losses in Africa and Latin America, in the Indo-Pakistani crisis, and in Indonesia, plus the reversal of the trend toward Viet Cong victory in South Vietnam resulted in a rise of Soviet, and a fall of Chinese, influence.

Most of this study will deal with the course and failure and aftermath of the second Soviet attempt to call a conference which began in early 1964, and, thereafter with the new Soviet leadership's shift to less extreme tactics, with more favorable results. First, however, general Soviet policy objectives and Moscow's unsuccessful first conference attempt, in September–October 1963, must be summarized.

II. THE SOVIET CONFERENCE PLAN RENEWED [9]

It is perhaps useful to review the first unsuccessful Soviet attempt at "collective mobilization." In July 1963, after the failure of the Sino-Soviet bilateral meeting and the Soviet signature of the partial test ban treaty, something like a Sino-Soviet schism occurred: Mutual polemics became explicit, general, and violent, and in September 1963 the Soviets moved toward calling an international communist meeting for the purpose of expelling the Chinese.

By so doing the Soviets and the Chinese had reversed their tactics, each now largely adopting the other's previous crisis management technique. Previously the Soviets had demanded a bilateral Sino-Soviet meeting while the Chinese had called for multilateral or all-party talks. By September 1963, however, the Chinese were demanding resumption first of bilateral, then of multilateral, and, last, of all-party talks, and stressing "adequate preparations," that is, delay. The Soviets, conversely, after having earlier used party congresses at anti-Chinese forums, by the autumn of 1963 demanded rapid reconvening of the November 1960 26-party editorial commission, to be followed soon by an all-party meeting.

This simultaneous reversal of tactics reflected the changing Sino Soviet balance of forces. As long as the Soviets thought that they could force the Chinese, if not to surrender, then to retreat by mobilizing international communist pressure against them, that is, by demonstrating that Chinese aims were unrealizable and that time would lead to Soviet gains (by forcing neutrals and reluctant allies off the fence), they wanted bilateral Sino-Soviet talks. The Chinese, on the other hand, wanted an

[9] Cf. Heinz Brahm, "Das Tauziehen um die dritte kommunistische Weltkonferenz," *Europa Archiv*, Vol. XIX, No. 16 (August 25, 1964), pp. 605–614.

all-party forum so that they could demonstrate to other Communist parties Chinese adamancy and rising influence, and thereby make them both fear a split and move away from Moscow. By mid-1963, however, the Soviets had clearly become convinced (a) that the Chinese would neither back down nor even retreat, (b) that Peking's factional activity was so dangerously successful that Soviet influence in the Communist world was declining, and Chinese influence rising, with increasing rapidity, and therefore (c) that speedy " political isolation " of the Chinese was necessary, that is, there must be a formal split whereby neutrals and recalcitrants could be forced into line and the decline of Soviet influence thereby halted if not reversed.

The Chinese meanwhile had become convinced that (a) Khrushchev was indeed preparing for a split and allying with Washington against them on all crucial foreign policy issues, (b) Chinese influence was rising and a formal split might slow down this rise, and therefore (c) formal international unity (that is, avoidance of split) plus stepped-up factional activity within international communism and alliance with all non-Communist powers outside it who were both anti-Soviet and anti-American offered Peking the best chance for further improving its position.

Within this context, and with these reversed tactics, Khrushchev began his first public attempt to convene an international conference to expel the Chinese in late September 1963. He did this by the " surrogate " method, that is, by reprinting resolutions of unconditionally pro-Soviet parties calling for such a meeting, by censoring less favorable parts of resolutions by other parties, and by strongly intensifying Soviet polemics against the Chinese. Privately the Soviet leadership brought strong pressure on pro-Soviet parties in order to force their public compliance with the conference plan.

But here as so often before the Soviet plan once again was foiled by their own tactical dilemma. They still had an assured majority of parties, including their most powerful allies, on the policy issues of the dispute, and in particular in favor of international détente and de-Stalinization. But their majority was rapidly declining as their decreasing authority and increasing record of failures emboldened their allies to assert their own interests on the organizational issue: the decrease of centralized (that is, Soviet) control over other Communist parties. The Soviet plan, unfolded in September and October 1963, called for an international conference, preceded by an editorial commission meeting, to undertake the formal revision of the November 1960 Moscow Declaration so as to declare that the Chinese Communist Party, not the Yugoslavs, was now the " main danger," that priority must be give to combating the CCP, and that therefore its " political isolation "

12

must be brought about. That is, a formal ban must be proclaimed (as Moscow had tried but failed to do in 1960) against factionalism in the international Communist movement, and neutralism on this issue must thus be precluded.

Even by early October several moderate, conditionally pro-Soviet parties were publicly opposing this Soviet plan. The Rumanians and Italians were the most active, the Norwegian, Swedish and British Communists were clearly also unenthusiastic, while the Cubans and even the Poles appear to have been opposing behind the scenes. The Rumanians probably refused, as they did in 1964 and 1965, to come to such a Soviet-arranged conference at all, and the Italian Communists probably refused to make a firm commitment to do so. Whether or not there were serious differences at that time within the Soviet leadership about Khrushchev's proposed conference remains unclear; some of his associates probably raised doubts about the wisdom of moving so rapidly toward such extreme goals when such important parties as the Rumanian and Italian were so recalcitrant. In any case, on October 25, 1963, Khrushchev called for an end to Sino-Soviet polemics and said that time would demonstrate which was correct, Moscow or Peking. This statement, plus his omission of any reference to a conference, indicated clearly that that Soviet plan had been postponed at least for the time being.[10]

Calm before the Storm (December 1963–April 1964)

The Soviets, who probably had never abandoned their conference plans, executed a temporary tactical retreat to regroup their forces. In public they refrained from anti-Chinese polemics, urged Peking to reciprocate, and reiterated their demonstrated desire to improve relations with China. In private they began a new conciliatory exchange of letters with the Chinese. Expecting to succeed in neither, they hoped that their apparent moderation would help dispel the fears of their reluctant allies that

10 This account is primarily based on Griffith, *The Sino-Soviet Rift, op. cit.*, pp. 207–230; for the Sino-Soviet territorial issue see also Doolin, *op. cit.*, pp. 31–33. I have since had the opportunity of reading an unfortunately still unpublished manuscript by Christian Duevel on this same episode, in which two additional important points are made: First, some time between September 12 and 24 there was passed for the press the annual yearbook of the Institute of World Academy and International Relations of the Soviet Academy of Sciences, in which a listing of the socialist countries, for the first and only time before or since (to my knowledge), omitted China, North Korea, and Albania (but not North Vietnam). Second, the November 1963 issue of *Problemy Mira i Sotsialisma* (passed for the press October 19, 1963) (*World Marxist Review*, Vol. 6, No. 11), which contained the article by Rumanian Premier Maurer opposing the conference, also reproduced excerpts from declarations by various parties calling for such a conference. Duevel deduces from this that the Soviets were unable to gain a majority in the editorial board of the journal to exclude the Maurer article, a fact that contributed toward, and indeed may have been primarily responsible for, Khrushchev's abandonment of the meeting; I would rather think it probably reflected some intermediate stage in Khrushchev's retreat from it. For the October 26 Chou Yang speech, see p. 16 and note 14.

13

Moscow would try to reimpose Soviet control over them once a split with Peking had occurred. Taking, therefore, a very pragmatic position concerning the style of Sino-Soviet negotiations, they proposed that both sides should agree on as many issues as they could and should postpone the consideration of undecided questions. In particular, they should cooperate against imperialism, that is, not go beyond Moscow's vital national interests in so doing. Consequently the Soviets offered a resumption of economic and technical (but not of military) assistance to China, although notably Moscow made no concessions on the Albanian and Yugoslav issues.

Many elements in this Soviet position appealed to those of Moscow's allies (Rumanians, Cubans, Italians, and others) who wanted the end of polemics, the deferment of unagreed issues, the end of Soviet use of economic and technical assistance as a means of pressure (but no nuclear aid to a militant China that might stumble into a nuclear war), and a more pragmatic Soviet position on the Yugoslav and Albanian issues. From these parties' point of view the Chinese could legitimately be expected to accept all these points, or at least to keep quiet about those they did not. Conversely, the Soviets had nothing to lose by making these proposals, since (a) they could feel quite sure that Peking would not accept them and (b) the subsequent Chinese refusal would help Moscow gain allies for relaunching the conference project.

The Chinese, on the other hand, continued to play a double game. They had helped foil the first Soviet attempt at a conference in part by deliberately creating a credible deterrent against it—that is, they had convinced reluctant Soviet supporters on the conference issue that Peking would so adamantly oppose compromise with Moscow that the Soviets would force a split in the international movement. Moreover, they did this while maintaining a public position against a split and in favor of prolonged negotiation—that is, delay.

Among the Soviet allies the Chinese were most likely to gain supporters on the organizational issue (independence from Moscow) and the least likely to do so, except from Castro, on such policy issues as priority for revolutionary struggle in underdeveloped areas, high risk-taking (by Moscow) vis-à-vis Washington, and anti-de-Stalinization. Peking therefore stressed the organizational and procedural issues and centered its secret exchanges with the Soviets on attacking the Soviet intention to compel it to surrender or to force a split, meanwhile declaring that the CCP preferred delay and was opposed to a split, like some Soviet allies (which was true), but simultaneously considerably intensifying their public ideological extremism. The Soviets, the Chinese presumably calculated, would soon again feel compelled to resume "collective mobilization," that is, to call a conference, thereby allowing the Chinese to abandon their private conciliatory position while still putting Moscow in the wrong with its reluctant supporters.

Soviet and Chinese Maneuvering

The interim conciliatory Soviet line was first outlined in a November 29 unpublished letter from the CPSU to the CCP Central Committee. Addressed also to Mao personally and signed by Khrushchev, it was not made public by Peking until May 8, 1964. Since Moscow must have assumed, correctly, that Peking would reject its overtures,[11] the letter's contents and the fact that Moscow did not publish it were primarily intended to appeal to the reluctant Soviet allies. The letter contrasted strikingly with the September–October 1963 Moscow conference plan and was reminiscent of, and probably influenced by, the PCI position. True, it reaffirmed Soviet support for an all-party conference, but this time for one that " will lead not to a split . . . but to genuine unity and solidarity." Polemics should be ended, but not "exchanges of view on questions of principle." Sino-Soviet relations must be improved primarily to benefit neither Moscow nor Peking but rather " the Communist movement," particularly those parties that, "forced to . . . struggle against imperialism in extremely difficult and complex circumstances . . . , rightly consider they require friendship with both the CPSU and the CCP." (The reference to such neutralist or only partially pro-Chinese parties as in Cuba, Rumania, North Vietnam, and North Korea was clear.) The pragmatic Soviet position was outlined:

> not to concentrate on . . . differences between us, but to let them wait . . . develop our co-operation . . . where favourable possibilities exist.[12]

particularly for peace and against imperialism. Specifically, the Soviet letter proposed (a) increased Sino-Soviet trade, (b) resumption of Soviet technical aid and the sending of specialists, particularly in the oil and mining industries, to China, (c) scientific, technical, and cultural Sino-Soviet cooperation, and (d) discussions on the delineation of the Sino-Soviet boundary, the historical nature of which, it stated, should be taken for granted and accepted.[18]

11 Moreover, despite the signing of a new trade protocol between Moscow and Peking in April 1965 (see *Pravda*, April 30, 1965), Sino-Soviet economic relations have apparently continued to worsen. The trade turnover in 1964 was 405 million rubles as compared to 540·2 for 1963. See *Vneshnyaya Torgovlya SSSR za 1964 god* (Moscow, 1965), pp. 228–236; j. c. k. [Joseph C. Kun], " Further Decline in Sino-Soviet Trade," Radio Free Europe, Munich, October 28, 1965; " History of Sino-Soviet Economic Relations," *China News Analysis*, No. 522 (June 26, 1964); and *The Times* (London), October 27, 1965.

12 The parallel to the agreed formulation for the second Soviet-Yugoslav rapprochement is striking. (See Griffith, *The Sino-Soviet Rift, op. cit.*, pp. 47 and 85–87.)

18 CPSU Central Committee to CCP Central Committee, November 28, 1963, quoted from *Peking Review*, Vol. VII, No. 19 (May 8, 1964), pp. 18–21, at pp. 19 and 21.

The Chinese ideological, and therefore political, position had already hardened—albeit this was then known only within the Chinese élite—by late October. On October 26, the day after Khrushchev publicly retreated from his conference plan, Chou Yang, Chinese agitprop deputy head, in a speech in Peking first provided the ideological imperative for Chinese factionalism. The speech reflected policy decisions by the Chinese leadership to intensify their factional activities and bring them into the open by the formal establishment of rival " Marxist-Leninist " communist parties, as well as to intensify intellectual repression domestically. The keynote of the speech, although Leninist in spirit, went far beyond anything that Lenin had ever explicitly proclaimed:

> Everything tends to divide itself in two. Theories are no exception, and they also tend to divide. Wherever there is a revolutionary, scientific doctrine, its antithesis, a counterrevolutionary, anti-scientific doctrine, is bound to arise in the course of the development of that doctrine.

" Political parties genuinely representing the revolutionary proletariat," that is, pro-Chinese, therefore " are bound to appear " everywhere. Conversely, the CPSU leadership's revisionism was leading it to forfeit " its place in the ranks of the vanguards of the international proletariat," a role that Chou implied would fall to China. Knowing that any increase of factionalism would not appeal to the reluctant Soviet allies, Chou Yang implicitly but clearly defended the Rumanian resistance to Soviet " neocolonialist theory." Finally, in order to strengthen its desired international image as organizationally conciliatory and pluralistic, even if ideologically adamant, Peking did not publish the Chou speech until December 27, by which time the Soviet resumption of their conference plan was again becoming clear, thereby making it seem that Moscow rather than Peking was pushing for an international split.[14]

Fitting theory to practice, the Chinese expanded and brought their factional activities more into the open. The subsequent weeks saw the official call for the founding congresses of two new " Marxist-Leninist " (that is, pro-Chinese) parties, in Belgium and Ceylon, and a " declaration

For the same generally conciliatory tone, but few of the November 29 letter's specific proposals, see " The Marxist-Leninist Program of the Communist Movement," *Kommunist*, No. 17, November 1963, pp. 12–24, and " For the Unity and Solidarity of the International Communist Movement," *Pravda*, December 6, 1963. Conversely, the November 17–December 3 National People's Congress session in Peking indicated that the Chinese neither intended to renew Soviet economic aid nor expected help (see *Peking Review*, Vol. VI, No. 49 [December 6, 1963], pp. 10–11), while Mao's January 12, 1964, statement on the U.S.-Panamanian crisis indicated an adamant CPR foreign policy stand (*ibid.*, Vol. VII, No. 3 [January 17, 1964], p. 5).

14 Chou Yang, " The Fighting Task Confronting Workers in Philosophy and the Social Sciences," *Jen-min Jih-pao*, December 27, 1963, quoted from *Peking Review*, Vol. VII, No. 1 (January 3, 1964), pp. 10–27, at pp. 12, 15, and 21–22. The first Chinese announcement concerning the Fourth Expanded Conference of the Department of Philosophy and Social Science of the Chinese Academy of Sciences, at which Chou Yang delivered the speech, mentioned his participation and gave the title but not the contents of his speech. See *ibid.*, Vol. VI, No. 49 (December 6, 1963), pp. 26–28.

of Marxist-Leninists " foreshadowing a third such party in Australia. In all three cases the Communist party concerned had formerly been pro-Soviet, and Chinese activity and Chinese financing had played a significant role in the split and the formation of the new pro-Chinese groups.[15]

Moreover, Chou En-lai's December 1963–January 1964 visit to Africa and Albania signaled not only Peking's continued support of Albania's intransigence [16] but also an increase in Chinese political, economic, and subversive activities in the Black Continent.[17]

That the Sino-Soviet conflict remained at a high level within international Communist-front organizations became clear at the November 28–December 3, 1963, Warsaw meeting of the World Peace Council, where a dissenting Chinese resolution was voted down by a pro-Soviet majority.[18] Furthermore, at the Jakarta preparatory meeting for the second Afro-Asian Conference (discussed below) Peking succeeded in vetoing the inclusion of the Soviets as full members.[19]

Nor were the Soviets inactive on the factional front. Pro-Soviet publications as early as January made it clear, if not explicit, that Moscow would not remain inactive in the face of Chinese factional activity.[20] In view of subsequent events one may assume that Moscow was already in active contact with Yoshio Shiga, who some months later, with Soviet support, began efforts to set up an anti-Chinese group (and eventually Communist party) in Japan.[21]

As for the Chinese, in mid-December 1963 Peking published their sixth " Comment " on the July 14 Soviet Open Letter, this time on peaceful coexistence. The article did not throw any substantially new

15 " Declaration of Australian Marxist-Leninists " (November 11, 1963), *ibid.* pp. 20–25; " To All Marxist-Leninists Inside the Ceylon Communist Party " (November 17, 1963), *ibid.*, Vol. VI, No. 50 (December 13, 1963), pp. 15–17; " Belgian Marxist-Leninists Decide to Rebuild Communist Party " (declaration of Brussels conference, December 22, 1963), *ibid.*, Vol. VII, No. 3 (January 17, 1964), pp. 26–27. For the 1963 CPR support of the dissident Brazilian Communist Party, see Griffith, *The Sino-Soviet Rift, op. cit.*, p. 128; for simultaneous ideological and political escalation (in Soviet-Albanian relations), see Griffith, *Albania and the Sino-Soviet Rift, op. cit.*, pp. 60–88.
16 *Peking Review*, Vol. VII, No. 3 (January 17, 1964), pp. 11–22.
17 William E. Griffith, " Africa," *Survey*, No. 54 (January 1965), reprinted in Labedz, *op. cit.*, pp. 168–189, at p. 187.
18 November 28 speech by Liao Cheng-chih, *Peking Review*, Vol. VI, No. 49 (December 6, 1963), pp. 12–15; " Two Different Lines at the Warsaw Session," *ibid.*, Vol. VI, No. 50 (December 13, 1963), pp. 13–15; *Pravda*, November 29–December 4, 1963 (excerpts in *Current Digest of the Soviet Press* [hereafter cited as *CDSP*], Vol. XV, No. 48 [December 25, 1963], pp. 29–31); and, re the protest against homage to the late President Kennedy by the Chinese and their allies, Reuters from Warsaw in *The New York Times*, November 29, 1963.
19 *Trud*, December 24, 1964; Khrushchev in *Pravda*, December 22, 1964.
20 One of the earliest indications was Václav Slavik, Norman Freed, and Mourad Kouwatli, " Unity Is the Guarantee of Success," *World Marxist Review*, Vol. 7, No. 1 (January 1964), pp. 3–8. See also the attack on " neutrality " by Jaime Perez, " The CPSU in the Vanguard of the World Communist Movement," *ibid.*, pp. 9–15.
21 See note 65.

light on the Chinese position, which remained one of advocating higher risk-taking in national liberation struggles. Like Peking's November 19 fifth "Comment," [22] it was so phrased as to counteract the Soviet denunciation of the Chinese as warmongers opposed to peaceful co-existence, while at the same time it appealed to all strongly anti-American communist parties by stressing Khrushchev's preference for a Soviet-American agreement.[23] The article was primarily significant for its reaffirmation, for the first time after the (then still not publicly known) November 29 Soviet letter, of the adamancy of the Chinese position. It made no reference to the organizational and procedural issues. The Albanians continued their vitriolic denunciations of Khrushchev, which the Chinese (at that time) regularly reprinted.[24]

That the Chinese position was becoming increasingly and explicitly more adamant became even clearer with the publication on February 4, 1964, of Peking's seventh "Comment," entitled "The Leaders of the CPSU Are the Greatest Splitters of Our Times." [25] This article made clear what the Chou Yang speech had implied: The Chinese now publicly and explicitly demanded nothing less than the complete reversal of Soviet domestic and foreign policy since Stalin's death, plus Moscow's eventual abandonment of its allies within the international Communist movement and the immediate abandonment of its attempts to block Peking's subversion of them. After reiterating the Chou Yang formu-lation that splits always occur in communist parties and that true Marxist-Leninists must struggle against revisionists even if the latter are in a " temporary " majority, the article declared that

> the leaders of the CPSU headed by Khrushchev have become the chief representatives of modern revisionism as well as the greatest splitters in the international Communist movement.

As evidence the article referred to, without explicitly identifying, Soviet policy toward Rumania; it discussed explicitly and at length Soviet coercion of Albania; it explicitly accused Khrushchev for the first time of conspiring with Marshal P'eng Teh-huai in 1959; and, finally, it ascribed the origin of Khrushchev's revisionism to "the lush growth of the bourgeois elements inside the Soviet Union " (a theme that the Chinese would soon extensively elaborate), and to " imperialist policy." The CCP was not anti-Soviet, the article continued, but

22 Griffith, *The Sino-Soviet Rift, op. cit.*, pp. 227–229.
23 " Peaceful Coexistence—Two Diametrically Opposed Policies. Comment on the Open Letter of the Central Committee of the CPSU, (6)," *Jen-min Jih-pao* and *Hung Ch'i*, December 12, 1963, and *Peking Review*, Vol. VI, No. 51 (December 20, 1963), pp. 6–18.
24 For example, " The Moscow Declaration—Invincible Banner of the Struggle Against Imperialism and Revisionism," *Zëri i Popullit*, December 6, 1963, reprinted in *Jen-min Jih-pao*, December 25, 1963 (SCMP 3129, December 31, 1963).
25 *Jen-min Jih-pao* and *Hung Ch'i*, February 4, 1964, quoted from *Peking Review*, Vol. VII, No. 6 (February 7, 1964), pp. 5–21, at pp. 9, 11 and 14.

Khrushchev was; by attacking him the CCP represented the true interests of the Soviet people. With respect to the head or vanguard position in the international Communist movement, the article declared that no headship is now possible since all parties are " independent and completely equal," but that in any case the CPSU has by its " revisionism and splittism . . . automatically forfeited the position of ' head.' " Thus the CCP explicitly and unilaterally revised the 1960 Statement, which had termed the CPSU the " vanguard," and the 1957 Declaration, which had termed it the " head." With respect to the Soviet position that the majority of all parties could bind all of them, the article not only again explicitly rejected it but declared that the Soviet majority was " false." With respect to the CCP's support of " Marxist-Leninist " (that is, pro-Chinese) parties, the article reaffirmed that this would continue and specifically endorsed the Belgian, Brazilian, Italian, Australian, U.S., and Indian pro-Chinese groups. Finally, the article reiterated the Chinese position against ending public polemics, gave the Soviets another detailed list of demands for their capitulation, and reaffirmed Chinese firmness and refusal to compromise.

Whether or not the Chinese knew when they published their February 4 article that Moscow was preparing a similar attack remains unclear. In any case the Chinese vow to resist to the end Soviet attempts to split the international movement was calculated to appeal to the parties who opposed a split, and to those who were not immediately menaced by Peking's announcement of intensified Chinese factional activities.

On February 12 the Soviets sent a letter to all but the pro-Chinese parties; although never published, its contents can be inferred from subsequent Austrian, Rumanian, Soviet, and Chinese Communist sources.[26] Moscow declared that Peking had not yet replied to the Soviet November 29, 1963 letter and was intensifying both polemics and factional activities. Therefore the forthcoming Soviet Central Committee plenum would discuss the situation fully, decide upon the required measures, and publish its proceedings. Moreover, the letter stressed that it was necessary to " give a rebuff " to the Chinese and take " collective measures to strengthen the unity " of the international Communist movement. This should be done through an international

[26] The most complete summary is in the report of Franz Muhri to the Austrian Communist Party Central Committee plenum of May 6, 1964, *Volksstimme* (Vienna), May 13, 1964 (JPRS 25,084, June 15, 1964, pp. 11–21, at pp. 14–15). A briefer Soviet summary is in the February 22, 1964, CPSU Central Committee letter, cited in note 34; and still briefer references are in the Rumanian Central Committee statement published on April 27, cited in note 71, and the February 20 CCP Central Committee letter, cited in note 32. Whether the CPSU Central Committee actually approved this letter is not clear; the only published reference to the letter's discussing Sino-Soviet relations is on February 15, when the CPSU Central Committee approved the resolution discussed below.

conference, the further postponement of which was being utilized by Peking only for Chinese splitting activities.

The subsequent violent Suslov report of February 14 to the Soviet Central Committee was primarily an organizational move. Suslov declared that the CCP leaders " have created the direct threat of a split," in that they

> have . . . encountered the general line of the international Communist movement with their own special line, which revises from positions of great-power chauvinism and petty-bourgeois adventurism the 1957 and 1960 Declarations.

Moreover, by their " schismatic activity " the Chinese leadership aims at

> forming under its aegis something in the nature of a special international bloc and counterposing it to the international Communist movement as a weapon for intensifying the struggle against it.[27]

Therefore, Suslov continued

> The policy and activities of the Chinese leaders today constitute the chief danger to the unity of the international Communist movement.

Suslov rehashed at length the Soviet version of the past course of the dispute; but unfortunately he revealed little or no significant new facts concerning it. He declared (truthfully) that the Chinese had by their actions rejected the Soviet proposals of November 29, 1963. He denounced the Chinese theory of an intermediate zone (a rapprochement with Japan and Western Europe directed against Moscow and Washington) and their attitude on the Yugoslav and Albanian questions. He attacked Mao's personality cult as comparable to Stalin's and simultaneously denounced " the anti-Party group of Molotov, Kaganovich, and Malenkov . . . who have been expelled from . . . our party "—the first public announcement of their expulsion and an implied threat to the Chinese position within the international Communist movement. He declared that the " filthy scheme " of the Chinese " to isolate Comrade Khrushchev from the Central Committee . . . is doomed to complete and shameful failure." In sum, condemning the totality of the Chinese positions, Suslov declared that Moscow would resume polemics against the " neo-Trotskyite " Chinese positions, that the struggle with them would be " serious and . . . prolonged," and that an international conference must be held so as to make possible

> collective efforts . . . to determine the necessary ways and means for preserving and strengthening the Marxist-Leninist unity of the Communist ranks.

Suslov said nothing about expelling the Chinese, but also nothing

---

[27] This probably was an eventual Chinese goal, but a more distant one than that of the Soviets of mobilizing their own bloc against Peking.

about omitting anything that would endanger unity; rather, particularly by declaring that the CCP was now the "main danger," he clearly implied that the 1960 Statement should be revised accordingly and (somewhat less explicitly) that organizational machinery for "strengthening unity" might be necessary.[28]

The Suslov report and the resultant Soviet Central Committee resolution were not published for nearly two months, on April 3. Why? Two explanations suggest themselves. First, there may have been resistance to them within the Soviet leadership that resulted in a compromise providing for postponement of publication. Second, the balance for postponement was tipped by the Rumanian mediation attempt. As to the first possibility, some reports to this effect circulated in Moscow after Khrushchev's fall.[29] That the Suslov report included the first public announcement of the expulsion of Molotov, Kaganovich, and Malenkov from the CPSU (a move that had probably been in dispute among the Soviet leadership at the Twenty-Second CPSU Congress) strengthens the credibility of these conjectures. As to the second, Bucharest has declared[30] (and Moscow has not denied) that the Rumanian protest came on February 14, the day Suslov gave his report, and that the Soviet reply agreeing to postponement reached Bucharest on that same day.

On the following day, February 15, the Soviet Central Committee adopted a resolution whose equivocal contents implicitly reflected the decision to postpone publication. Although, like Suslov's report, it was violent in tone and declared that "ideological exposure" (that is, resumption of polemics) and "a decisive rebuff to Chinese schismatic activities" were required, it did not mention an international conference, it did not officially "approve" Suslov's report but only "heard and discussed" it, and it stated, as Suslov did not, that the plenum

---

[28] *Pravda*, April 3, 1964; quoted (with a minor revision) from *CDSP*, Vol. XVI, No. 13 (April 22, 1964), pp. 5–16, at p. 5, and Vol. XV, No. 14 (April 29, 1964), pp. 3–17, at pp. 8 and 14–17. The late Otto Kuusinen declared at the same plenum that in China there was "no dictatorship of the proletariat and no leading role of the Communist Party; rather, there is a *dictatorship of the individual* [that is, Mao]." (*Pravda*, May 19, 1964, quoted from *CDSP*, Vol. XVI, No. 20 [June 10, 1964], pp. 3–4 and 10, at p. 4 [*Pravda's* italics].

[29] The plenum was very "expanded"; it was also attended by hundreds of other party and governmental officials (*Pravda*, February 11, 1964). Furthermore, the Suslov report was given in the larger Congress Palace rather than in the Supreme Soviet meeting place, where the plenum first met (Tatu from Moscow in *Le Monde*, February 18, 1964), and Moscow later declared that "6,000 activists" were present (CPSU Central Committee to CCP Central Committee, March 7, 1964, cited in note 39). In view of Khrushchev's October 2, 1964, expanded Presidium session, including some thousands (*Pravda*, October 2, 1964), one may perhaps speculate that Suslov also spoke to such large audiences that the Central Committee may have felt itself to have been packed.

[30] See note 71.

" expresses its readiness to exert further efforts toward normalizing the relations between the CPSU and the CCP." [31]

Simultaneously with their appeal to the Soviets, the Rumanians also appealed to the Chinese to end polemics and proposed a Sino-Rumanian bilateral meeting. On February 17 Mao agreed to such a meeting, adding that if it took place soon Peking would " temporarily " suspend polemics.

But Mao's apparent reasonableness was deceptive, as became apparent to Communist élites when they received copies of the (then unpublished) February 20 Chinese letter to Moscow. The optimal Chinese strategy, since predictably a renewed Soviet move toward an international conference was unavoidable and since the Chinese wanted neither split nor reconciliation, was to delay such a conference and thereby ensure its failure. From Peking's viewpoint it probably appeared desirable with respect to the reaction of other Communist parties not to reject flatly the ostensibly conciliatory Soviet November 29, 1963 letter. The Chinese therefore waited until the Soviets resumed their drive for a conference, thereby permitting them to accuse Moscow of once more desiring a " schismatic " conference while professing conciliation. The Rumanian move, which Peking made possible by its substantive adamancy, must have seemed to the Chinese an excellent contribution to their strategy. Tactically Peking was quick to seize upon the fact that the Soviets had circulated a " factional " letter against them without sending them a copy.[32] (In all likelihood it was " no accident " that on the same day, February 20, the Albanians seized the Soviet embassy buildings in Tirana.) [33]

The Soviets immediately and violently replied that they had not sent a copy to Peking because the Chinese had consistently refused to reply to their conciliatory démarches but had on the contrary continued to attack them and had intensified their " schismatic factional activity." [34] The Chinese thereupon challenged the Soviets to carry out their " empty threats," to tell them exactly what they proposed to do, to publish the Chinese views, and to send Peking a copy of the February 12 letter.[35]

On February 29, 1964, the day before the Rumanian delegation arrived in Peking, the Chinese sent the Soviets their then unpublished

31 " On the Struggle of the CPSU for the Solidarity of the International Communist Movement," resolution of plenum of CPSU Central Committee, adopted February 15, 1964, *Pravda*, April 3, 1964, quoted from *CDSP*, Vol. XVI, No. 13 (April 22, 1964), p. 4.
32 CCP Central Committee to CPSU Central Committee, February 20, 1964, *Jen-min Jih-pao*, May 9, 1964, and *Peking Review*, Vol. VII, No. 19 (May 8, 1964), pp. 10–11.
33 *Izvestiya*, February 25, 1964.
34 CPSU Central Committee to CCP Central Committee, February 22, 1964, *Peking Review*, Vol. VII, No. 19 (May 8, 1964), pp. 22–24.
35 CCP Central Committee to CPSU Central Committee, February 27, 1964, *ibid.*, Vol. VII, No. 19 (May 8, 1964), pp. 11–12.

reply to the Soviets' November 29, 1963 letter. Its contents made Chinese strategy clear. Ideologically the Chinese remained adamant and arrogant. As in their previous published articles and unpublished letters, they summarized uncompromisingly the issues in the dispute and dared the Soviets to do their worst. With respect both to specific Soviet proposals for renewed contacts and to the organizational issue of the international conference, they took a seemingly conciliatory attitude. Although they denounced the Soviets for alleged subversive activities in Sinkiang, they agreed to accept the " historic " Sino-Soviet border as a basis for Sino-Soviet border negotiations. (These negotiations in fact had begun in Peking on February 25 [36]; we know nothing of their course or outcome, but they were probably broken off without any results.) The Chinese position on Sino-Soviet economic relations was mixed. The letter rejected the return of Soviet experts on the ground that Moscow could not be trusted not to use them again as a political weapon, denounced the Soviets for having made the Chinese pay for the Soviet arms sent to China during the Korean War, and declared that Peking had proposed and Moscow had prevented an increase in Sino-Soviet economic exchanges. It added two points sure to appeal to the Rumanians. Moscow should cease trying to perpetuate lack of economic and industrial development in some socialist countries, and all socialist countries should be able to join a genuinely international CMEA (Council for Mutual Economic Aid). As to public polemics, the Chinese (correctly) pointed out that the Soviets had started them and had at first refused to agree to halt them, but now had reversed their position since the polemics were not to Moscow's advantage, that the Soviets continued to carry on some direct polemics [37] as did other communist parties (significantly, Poland and Rumania were omitted from the latter list—a clear indication of where Peking thought it might get support), and that suspension of polemics could only follow bilateral and multilateral consultations. Peking endorsed an international conference with " adequate preparations." For this purpose the Chinese proposed that bilateral Sino-Soviet talks should be resumed in Peking from October 10 to 25, 1964, to be followed by a preparatory meeting of seventeen parties—those in power (excluding Yugoslavia) plus Indonesia, Japan, Italy, and France.[38]

The specific Chinese proposal for resumption of negotiations looked reasonable on its face. Bilateral Sino-Soviet discussions would be resumed in the autumn (that is, within several months). They would be

---

[36] TANJUG in English, Belgrade, February 27, 1965 (text in Doolin, *op. cit.*, p. 37.)
[37] *Jen-min Jih-pao*, March 1, 1964, and *Peking Review*, Vol. VII, No. 10 (March 6, 1964), pp. 27–29.
[38] CCP Central Committee to CPSU Central Committee, February 29, 1964, *Jen-min Jih-pao*, May 9, 1964, and *Peking Review*, Vol. VII, No. 19 (May 8, 1964), pp. 12–18.

in Peking because the last such meeting had been in Moscow. The size and composition—a 17 instead of a 26-member preparatory committee (as in 1960)—could be justified as including 2 pro-Soviet and 2 pro-Chinese nonruling parties while eliminating *inter alia* those parties (Brazil, India, Great Britain, the United States, and Australia) in which pro-Chinese groups had already been constituted and either had been or probably would be constituted as parties, thereby preventing endless dispute over the committee's membership. Yet closer study makes clear that the Chinese had carefully stacked the procedure and participants in their favor. No specific date was set for the preparatory committee meeting, and it presumably could not meet until Sino-Soviet discussions had been successful, that is, unless China's terms were accepted by Moscow—in other words, never. If one adds to the 6 clearly pro-Chinese parties (Albania, China, North Korea, North Vietnam, Indonesia, and Japan) the 4 opposed either to an international conference or at least to expelling the Chinese (Cuba, Italy, Poland, and Rumania), the Chinese potentially had the support of 10 of the 17. Even if Poland finally voted with the Soviets, as it probably would, the result would be 9 to 8 in favor of Peking. So far had Soviet control slipped.

The March Sino-Rumanian discussions in Peking came to nothing. The Chinese would not agree to suspend polemics even during bilateral discussions about their suspension. While the discussions were taking place on March 7 the Soviet Central Committee answered the Chinese letters of February 27 and 29. The Soviet letter condemned the Chinese ideological deviations and factional activity as strongly as before. It dismissed the Chinese demand that the Soviets publish Peking's articles as a proposal actually for intensifying polemics. It declared that the Soviets continued to refrain from polemics and that the Chinese should do likewise and cease their factional activity. It reiterated that the general line for the international Communist movement could be worked out " only collectively," while stressing that Moscow anticipated and would work toward renewed international Communist unity. It (correctly) termed the Chinese February 29 letter a total rejection of the Soviet November 29, 1963 proposals. Finally, Moscow welcomed the Chinese endorsement of a conference; however, it declared (hypocritically) that the delay proposed by the Chinese was " inexplicable " and added that " we also fail to understand " why the Chinese proposed only 17 members for the preparatory committee. The Soviets proposed instead that bilateral Sino-Soviet discussions resume in Peking in May 1964, that the preparatory committee, composed of the same 26 parties as in 1960, meet in June–July 1964, and that the all-party meeting, " with the agreement of the fraternal parties," convene in the autumn of 1964.[39]

[39] CPSU Central Committee to CCP Central Committee, March 7, 1964, *Jen-min Jih-pao*, May 9, 1964, and *Peking Review*, Vol. VII, No. 19 (May 8, 1964), pp. 24–27.

After inconclusive discussions in Peking and thereafter in Pyongyang, the Rumanian delegation stopped in Moscow. There the Soviets at first insisted that they publish the February plenum material, but they then agreed that if the Rumanians could persuade the Chinese to cease polemics the Soviets would continue to do likewise. The Rumanians thereupon drafted an " Appeal," to be addressed to all parties by Moscow, Peking, and Bucharest, which they sent to the Soviets and Chinese on March 25. Moscow accepted it " in general "; Peking apparently did not reply, but on March 31 the Chinese published the eighth " Comment " on the Soviet Open Letter of July 1963, which in turn precipitated Soviet publication of the February plenum material on April 3.[40]

The eighth " Comment " added little of substance to Peking's position. Its primary significance lay in its total rejection of all Soviet approaches, thereby marking the end of the post-November 1963 public, if partial, détente and precipitating the resumption of open polemics by both sides. It was written " in more explicit terms than before," that is, more clearly directed against Khrushchev personally and more explicit in demanding his removal. It reiterated, without further development, the Chinese thesis that the social basis of Khrushchev's revisionism was " the capitalist forces that are ceaselessly spreading in the Soviet Union." It stressed violent revolution and declared that the Soviet line of peaceful transition had betrayed the revolutions in Cuba, Algeria, and Iraq. Finally, by describing Khrushchev as the revisionist successor of Browder as well as of Tito, it underlined the evils of the Soviet policy of rapprochement with Washington.[41]

Khrushchev's Second Conference Attempt (April–June 1964)

The April 1964 publication of the February Suslov report and the Soviet Central Committee resolution [42] signalled the beginning of a new phase: the second and a much more explicit, all-out Soviet attempt to mobilize other communist parties against the Chinese. Four aspects of

40 For the above, see the Rumanian April 27 resolution, cited in note 71.
41 " The Proletarian Revolution and Khrushchev's Revisionism—Comment on the Open Letter of the CPSU (VIII)," *Jen-min Jih-pao* and *Hung Ch'i*, March 31, 1964, quoted from *Peking Review*, Vol. VII, No. 14 (April 3, 1964), pp. 5–23.
42 The accompanying April 3, 1964, *Pravda* editorial, " Fidelity to the Principles of Marxism-Leninism," was only notable because it omitted any mention of an international conference, concerning which, however, Suslov's formulations were repeated in the long " For the Unity of the International Communist Movement on Principles of Marxism-Leninism," *Kommunist*, No. 5, March 1964 (signed to the press April 4, 1964), pp. 13–52 (JPRS 24,404, April 30, 1964). For Chinese reaction see *Peking Review*, Vol. VII, No. 18 (May 1, 1964), pp. 13–19. In March the CPSU Institute of Marxism-Leninism had (opportunely, to say the least) discovered Marx's and Engels' previously undiscovered 1872 amendments to the First International's rules, which provided for the suspension of national federations by the general council. See *World Marxist Review*, Vol. 7, No. 4 (April 1964), pp. 34–36.

this phase may be distinguished: (1) the maximum Soviet position, (2) the Chinese opposition to it, (3) the resistance of other communist parties opposed to Moscow's aims, and (4) the resultant Soviet retreat with respect to the purposes and tactics of the proposed international conference.

1. *The Maximum Soviet Position.* Once the Suslov report was published, a wave of anti-Chinese agitation swept Soviet supporters in the international Communist movement.[43] On May 15, Suslov declared that an international conference was " necessary." [44] (In his February 14 report he had said only that the CPSU " advocates " such a conference.) At the end of April Moscow announced that " more than 70 " parties favored such a conference.[45] On June 9 *Pravda* published an article by the head of the Paraguayan Communist Party calling for an " early " conference and declaring that delay would mean intensified Chinese factional activity and that indefinite postponement was " impossible." [46]

Moscow concentrated its attack on the nationalistic and anti-Soviet Chinese formulations, particularly on Mao's " intermediate zone " theory, the Chinese insistence that the basis of the world revolutionary struggle was the peasantry rather than the proletariat, Peking's demand to " re-examine and correct " the 1957 and 1960 Declarations, and the growing cult of Mao's personality. Moreover, the Soviets insisted (incorrectly) that the November 1960 conference had made majority decisions binding on all parties. They simultaneously attacked Chinese internal policies, denouncing the CCP's violation of its own statutes and its lack of a party program.[47]

The most important aspect, that of organized Soviet control over its communist allies, that is, the organizational goal of the maximum Soviet position, was made public only once, by Khrushchev in Budapest on April 3:

> The objective requirements of our economic development, as well as the necessity for struggling against all kinds of efforts to weaken the solidarity of the socialist countries, demand persistent work on the improvement of the entire system of our mutual relations. Apparently it would be expedient to think jointly about those organizational forms that would make it possible to improve the constant exchange of opinions and the co-ordination of foreign policy between the member

43 See *ibid.*, Vol. VII, No. 5 (May 1964), pp. 44–49.
44 *Pravda*, May 16, 1964.
45 See the *Kommunist* article cited in note 42.
46 *Pravda*, June 9, 1964. See also r. r. g. [R. Rockingham Gill], " A Conference Becomes Necessary " and " Problems of the Conference," Radio Free Europe, Munich, May 19 and June 10, 1964, respectively.
47 " Proletarian Internationalism Is the Banner of the Working People of All Countries and Continents," *Kommunist*, No. 7, May 1964 (signed to the press April 29, 1964); " On Certain Aspects of Party Life in the Communist Party of China," *Pravda*, April 28 and 29, 1964; " Marxism-Leninism Is the International Doctrine of the Communists of All Countries," *ibid.*, May 10, 11 and 12, 1964.

countries of the Council for Mutual Economic Aid, the participants in the Warsaw Pact.[48]

In other words, at least within East Europe some kind of formal political co-ordinating organ should be established, one in which Moscow would inevitably swing the most weight.

2. *The Chinese Response: Peking's Foreign Policy Made Explicit.* There is, surprisingly, no documentary evidence that the Chinese exploited the ominous implications of this Khrushchev declaration for those parties wishing to consolidate and extend their increased autonomy from Moscow. Nevertheless, the Chinese adamantly refused to attend an international conference, the calling of which, they declared, would cement a split. Conversely, they also reiterated that they did not desire a split. In sum, on the issue of postponing the conference or of emptying it of any real content, Peking's position was partially aligned with that of the reluctant pro-Soviet parties. A May 7 Chinese reply to the March 7 CPSU letter was until that time the clearest statement of Peking's preference for the indefinite delay of a conference, that is, for the continuation of a united international Communist movement in theory but for its paralysis in practice. It declared that the termination of the resumed Soviet polemics must be awaited before resuming bilateral Sino-Soviet discussions, for which Peking now suggested May 1965 instead of October 1964. It added that either Moscow or Peking could request still further postponement, thereby implying it would be still further postponed. As to the all-party meeting, preparations for it " may require four or five years, or even longer," that is, as far as Peking was concerned it was postponed *ad kalendas Graecas.* Finally, the Chinese immediately published this letter and all the previously unpublished correspondence dating from November 29, 1963, thus in effect ending any possibility of serious Sino-Soviet negotiations.[49]

Thereafter Chinese polemics against Moscow continued unabated. The Chinese accused the Soviets of subversion in Sinkiang,[50] while the Soviets accused the Chinese of border violations[51] and of profiting from British colonialism in Hong Kong.[52] The vehemence of Moscow and Peking was as usual exceeded in venom only by Tirana. At the end of May Hoxha declared that Khrushchev and his associates were criminals who had conspired to kill Stalin, and that " terror, murder, imprisonment, and concentration camps prevail in the Soviet Union."[53]

[48] *Pravda,* April 4, 1964, quoted from *CDSP,* Vol. XVI, No. 15 (May 6, 1964), pp. 7–8, at p. 7.
[49] *Jen-min Jih-pao,* May 7, 1964, and *Peking Review,* Vol. VII, No. 19 (May 8, 1964), pp. 7–10.
[50] NCNA, April 28, 1964, cited from Doolin, *op. cit.,* pp. 40–41, Document 10.
[51] Indian Information Service, April 4, 1964, and TASS in Russian, April 8, 1964, cited from Doolin, *op. cit.,* pp. 38–40, Documents 10 and 11.
[52] TASS, May 27, 1964, cited from Doolin, *op. cit.,* p. 41, Document 13.
[53] *Zëri i Popullit,* May 27, 1964 (in a speech delivered on May 24).

Peking presumably inspired, perhaps as a warning to wavering parties, a New Zealand Communist Party suggestion for a pro-Chinese international communist meeting,[54] but when no other parties endorsed it, the Chinese let the matter drop. Moscow, not to be left behind, accused Peking of financing its factional activities by a world-wide narcotics traffic.[55]

However, Peking's most extreme move arose out of its policy of considering the capitalist states of Western Europe and Japan as potential allies. This was made explicit by Mao himself in a July 10, 1964 interview with a group of Japanese socialists. This was the high point of Chinese attacks on the Soviet Union, then and since. Mao challenged the territorial integrity of the Soviet Union with respect to all its acquisitions during and after World War II as well as all the Tsarist acquisitions, for which "we have not yet presented the bill." He appealed primarily to Japanese and West German irredentist nationalism (with respect to the Kurile Islands and the former German territories east of the present Oder-Neisse East German–Polish frontier).

There are too many places occupied by the Soviet Union. In accordance with the Yalta Agreement, the Soviet Union, under the pretext of assuring the independence of Mongolia, actually placed the country under its domination. Mongolia takes up an area which is considerably greater than the Kuriles. In 1954, when Khrushchev and Bulganin came to China, we took up this question but they refused to talk to us. They [i.e., the Soviet Union] also appropriated part of Rumania. Having cut off a portion of East Germany, they chased the local inhabitants into West Germany. They detached a part of Poland, annexed it to the Soviet Union, and gave part of East Germany to Poland as compensation. The same thing took place in Finland. The Russians took everything they could. Some people have declared that the Sinkiang area and the territories north of the Amur River must be included in the Soviet Union. The Soviet Union is concentrating troops along its border.

The Soviet Union has an area of 22 million square kilometers and its population is only 220 million. It is about time to put an end to this allotment. Japan ocupies an area of 370,000 square kilometers and its population is 100 million. About a hundred years ago, the area to the east of [Lake] Baikal became Russian territory, and since then Vladivostok, Khabarovsk, Kamchatka, and other areas have been Soviet territory. We have not yet presented our account for this list. In regard to the Kurile Islands, the question is clear as far as we are concerned—they must be returned to Japan.[56]

54 NZCP National Committee resolution, " On the World Ideological Differences and a Meeting of the World Parties," July 26, 1964, in *New Zealand Communist Review,* August 1964, quoted from the full text in *Peking Review,* Vol. VII, No. 35 (August 28, 1964,) pp. 26–27.

55 Ovchinnikov from Tokyo in *Pravda,* September 13, 1964; " Has the *Pravda* Editorial Department No Sense of Shame?" *Jen-min Jih-pao,* September 21, 1964, and *Peking Review,* Vol. VII, No. 39 (September 25, 1964), pp. 13–14.

56 *Sekai Shūhō* (Tokyo), August 11, 1964, quoted from Doolin, *op. cit.,* pp. 42–44, Document 14, at pp. 43–44.

Seldom has Moscow been so menaced with so few words. The revelation (later confirmed by Moscow) that in 1954 Mao had demanded the return of Outer Mongolia indicated how far back his ambitions reached and how early Sino-Soviet relations must have been soured by those ambitions. The reference to " a part of Rumania " showed how he hoped to use Rumania's Bessarabian irredenta to pry Bucharest farther away from Moscow. The reference to the Polish and German boundaries—the most crucial issue in Europe—showed how Mao hoped to play Warsaw and Bonn against Moscow. His previous assertion that the Kurile Islands belonged to Japan closed the circle. Mao's " second intermediate zone " policy is in fact a *bouleversement des alliances*: Western Europe and Japan allied with China against Moscow and Washington. He accused Khrushchev of wanting to annex even more Chinese territory, and finally, by his assertion that " the Soviet Union is concentrating troops along its border," he intimated that military escalation, at least into extensive border conflicts, might occur.

The Mao interview was never published in China,[57] perhaps because it sounded so pro-Japanese (" The Japanese nation is a great nation "— exactly the same words General de Gaulle used in referring to the German nation!). Although it was briefly reported in Japan in mid-July [58] and in full in mid-August,[59] and Moscow must have known of it then, it did not become known throughout the world until *Pravda* republished it on September 2, along with a violent rejoinder of its own,[60] which added that the Soviets had tried to get Peking to repudiate the interview. However, Deputy Foreign Minister Wang P'ing-nan had only replied that " if Mao Tse-tung said so, he agreed with him." In addition, on August 1 Chou En-lai had given an interview to *Asahi* with " essentially . . . the same ideas." [61] *Pravda* then declared that through this interview Mao had made it clear that he was

> actually prepared to come to agreement with anybody for the sake of the struggle against the friends and allies of People's China—the Soviet Union and other countries of socialism.

Pravda did not attempt to conceal the seriousness of Mao's territorial

---

57 The NCNA news item, *Jen-min Jih-pao*, July 11, 1964 (SCMP 3258, July 15, 1964), only reported that the conversation had taken place.

58 *Asahi Evening News*, July 13, 1964 (Doolin, *op. cit.*, pp. 43–44).

59 *Sekai Shūhō* (Tokyo), August 11, 1964.

60 " Concerning Mao Tse-tung's Talk with Japanese Socialists," *Pravda*, September 2, 1964, quoted from *CDSP*, Vol. XVI, No. 34 (September 16, 1964), pp. 3–7.

61 Chou had also said in the same interview (which *Pravda* did not mention) that when he had been in Moscow in January 1957 he had " requested that the USSR make proper arrangements for the territorial issues covering Japan, China, the Middle East, and the Eastern European countries including Finland " but " could not get a satisfactory answer." See *Asahi Shimbun*, August 1, 1964, quoted from excerpts in Doolin, *op. cit.*, pp. 45–46, Document 16.

claims; on the contrary it set them forth in full and reaffirmed the historical validity of the present Sino-Soviet boundaries. To question them, it went on, would

> inevitably generate a whole series of mutual demands, claims, and insoluble conflicts among countries of Europe and Asia.

As to the Kuriles, *Pravda* hinted that if Japan were no longer an American base some agreement might be reached about them. It concluded by declaring that Mao's demand was reminiscent of those of his " predecessors " for *Lebensraum*—obviously Hitler.

In September Khrushchev replied to the Mao interview by declaring that

> the Chinese leaders are . . . all but proposing the division of the territory of the Soviet Union,[62]

that Moscow now had a weapon of unlimited destructive power (a declaration not reproduced in the Soviet text of the interview), and that Soviet frontiers were inviolable. As to Mao's interview, he stated:

> Mao Tse-tung calls himself a Communist, yet the philosophy he developed in his talk is alien to the people of labor; it cannot be the philosophy of a representative of the most progressive revolutionary doctrine—communism.

Repeating the theme of the *Pravda* editorial, he added that,

> given today's weapons of annihilation, it is especially dangerous, I might even say criminal, to seek wealth through the expansion of *Lebensraum*.

True, he continued, the Tsars had annexed territory, but so had the Chinese emperors:

> Take Sinkiang, for example. Have Chinese really lived there since time immemorial? The indigenous population of Sinkiang differs sharply from the Chinese in ethnic, linguistic, and other respects. It is made up of Uigurs, Kazakhs, Kirgiz, and other peoples. The Chinese emperors subjugated them in the past and deprived them of their independence.

The threat was clear: Moscow could stir up trouble for the Chinese in Sinkiang. (The Chinese have often charged the Russians with doing just this.)[63] The Soviets also submitted to the United Nations their previous proposal outlawing the use of force to solve territorial problems.[64]

---

[62] In a speech in Prague, September 4, 1964, in *Pravda*, September 5, 1964, quoted from *CDSP*, Vol. XVI, No. 36 (September 30, 1964), pp. 6–8, at p. 7.

[63] For the statement on a weapon of unlimited destructive power, see AFP from Moscow, *Le Monde*, September 17, 1964; for Khrushchev's declaration that he was misquoted, *Pravda*, September 22, 1964 (his speech to the World Youth Forum). Soviet text in *Pravda*, September 20, 1964, quoted from *CDSP*, Vol. XVI, No. 38 (October 14, 1964), pp. 3–7.

[64] TASS, September 23, 1964 (excerpts in Doolin, *op. cit.*, pp. 72–74, Document 27).

3. *Reaction to the Conference among Other Communist Parties.*
The unconditionally pro-Chinese parties continued to support Peking
completely [65]; of the conditionally pro-Chinese ones, Hanoi opposed the
Soviet call for a conference but called for resumption of bilateral
Sino-Soviet talks and did not mention polemics.[66]

Peking's moderate, conditional allies, such as the Indonesian Communist Party (PKI), were opposed to the conference for the same
reasons as the Italian and Rumanian Communists: It would split the
international Communist movement and therefore diminish their bargaining power vis-à-vis their major ally—for these Asian Communists—
China. The Japanese Communists, threatened by Soviet support of their
dissident minority, continued their anti-Soviet polemics.[67]

As for the pro-Soviet communist party leaderships, opposition to
the convening of an international conference continued because these
parties wanted more autonomy from the CPSU and therefore feared
that Moscow would try, as it had in 1957 and 1960, to use such a
conference to re-establish its control. This fear was made all the more
reasonable by Khrushchev's April 3 reference to " improving " CMEA
and the Warsaw Treaty Organization. Conversely, these parties probably
hoped, if Moscow's conference plan could be effectively delayed, that the
Soviets might give up the whole idea and accept their declining influence.
(Nor, it seemed by November 1965, were they wrong.) [68]

(1) *Rumania* was both the most opposed to the conference and in the
strongest position to resist it. Traditional anti-Russian feelings, the
Bessarabian irredenta, the determination of Rumanian Communists to
industrialize rather than remain a source of raw materials for CMEA,
rich resources salable on the world market (oil, grain and timber), a

65 For example, the April 8, 1964, declaration of the New Zealand Communist Party
and the pro-Chinese Belgian Communist Party leader Jacques Grippa's editorial, in
Peking Review, Vol. VII, No. 19 (May 8, 1964), pp. 35–36. In the case of the
Japanese Communist Party (JCP), Peking profited from Moscow's continued support
of the pro-Soviet Shiga splinter group. When JCP deputies Yoshio Shiga and Ichizo
Suzuki on May 15, 1964, voted in the Diet for ratification of the partial nuclear test
ban treaty, they were expelled by the pro-Peking majority. (*Akahata,* May 23, 1964,
in *Peking Review,* Vol. VII, No. 22 [May 29, 1964], pp. 17–21.) Thereupon first
Moscow (*Partiinaya Zhizn,* No. 14, July 1964, pp. 8–9) and then the JCP (*Akahata,*
August 8, 1964, and September 2, 1964, in *Peking Review,* Vol. VII, No. 37 [September
11, 1964], pp. 27–28, and Vol. VII, No. 38 [September 18, 1964], pp. 12–19)
published a long exchange of letters between the two, and polemics on both sides
intensified greatly.
66 Lao Dong Central Committee circular letter of April 21, 1964, to all communist
parties, *ibid.* p. 34.
67 I am grateful to Dr. Ruth McVey for discussions on the PKI. See a PKI Central
Committee resolution, " Marxist-Leninists of the World Unite, Continue to Smash
Revisionism," *Peking Review,* Vol. VII, No. 5 (January 31, 1964), p. 17. On the JCP,
see the exchange of letters with the CPSU cited in note 65, and " T. Timofeyev and
American Imperialism," *Akahata,* February 26, 1965 (JPRS 29,426, April 5, 1965).
68 For a perceptive communist analysis, see Mieczystaw F. Rakowski (editor of *Polytika*
and PZPR Central Committee candidate member) in *Kamena* (Lublin), No. 1/2,
January 31, 1965, pp. 1 and 10 (JPRS 29,309, March 26, 1965).

tightly knit and ruthless party leadership, and a skill at intrigue inherited from the Byzantines and Phanariots—all these enabled Gheorghiu-Dej to maneuver between the Russians and the Chinese to his, and Rumania's, advantage.[69] Bucharest had been largely responsible for the delay in the February 1964 Soviet attempt to summon a conference; it had openly opposed the September–October 1963 one; and it had gone the farthest in defiance of Moscow.

By April 1964 Rumania had successfully sabotaged Khrushchev's plan for supranational planning within CMEA.[70] Rumania's foreign trade pattern had been diversified so that the country was no longer so vulnerable to Soviet economic pressure. Bucharest was rapidly improving its relations with Western Europe and the United States and was de-emphasizing Russian and increasing Western cultural influence. Further, the Rumanians had clearly established a special posture in Sino-Soviet affairs: support for Moscow on the substantive policy issues (except for multilateral economic integration in CMEA), opposition to a split and to a pro-Soviet international conference, refusal to attack China publicly, and mediation between Moscow and Peking while simultaneously cementing good relations with the Italian, Polish and Yugoslav parties. Then at the end of April the Rumanian position was made explicit with the publication and wide distribution of a " Statement " endorsed by an enlarged Central Committee plenum.[71]

After detailing Rumanian attempts at mediation, the statement followed the Rumanian policy of taking the Soviet side on all the other substantive issues in the dispute. However, it condemned Moscow as well as Peking (although neither by name) for the violence of their polemics and for the attempts of each to remove the other's leadership. It censured Peking especially for the CCP thesis of the inevitability of splits and for its factional activities. Yet perhaps more important, with respect to the CMEA issue, the statement was clearly if implicitly anti-Soviet. It flatly rejected multilateral economic integration as incompatible with national sovereignty, and it declared that " distinctive national and state features " would continue " even when socialism has

---

[69] Griffith, *The Sino-Soviet Rift, op. cit.*, pp. 137–141 and 185–186, and *Communism in Europe, op. cit.*, Vol. 2, pp. 12–13 (both with bibliographic notes). Rumanian developments will be covered in detail in a forthcoming study by Stephen Fischer-Galati and John Michael Montias, *The New Romania* (Cambridge, Mass.: The M.I.T. Press, 1966).

[70] See, for example, the careful compromise formulas in Piotr Jarosiewicz, " The Council for Mutual Economic Aid—an Instrument of Cooperation Between Socialist Countries," *World Marxist Review*, Vol. 7, No. 3 (March 1964), pp. 3–8, and Stanisław Kuzinski, " Specialization of Production in the World Socialist System," *ibid.*, Vol. 7, No. 6 (June 1964), pp. 18–23.

[71] " Statement on the Stand of the Rumanian Workers' Party Concerning the Problems of the World Communist and Working-Class Movement," *Scînteia*, April 27, 1964, quoted, with revisions, from an official translation (Bucharest: Meridiane, 1964); hereafter cited as " Statement."

triumphed on a world scale or at least in most countries." All socialist countries, it went on, should be members of CMEA (a development that would add to Rumania's potential allies within the organization), and some kind of participation should be possible for underdeveloped countries (" the path of non-capitalist development "); that is, Rumania, like Yugoslavia, wanted to diversify its alliances.[72] Finally, after sharply criticizing Stalin for the great purges and for his break with Tito (that is, opposing any recurrence of either), the statement concluded with a call for the end of polemics and for bilateral Sino-Soviet discussions in order to set up a " commission . . . of representatives of a number of partics," and only after a " thorough preparation " should there be an international conference with " all " parties participating.[73] In effect the statement took the Chinese position on the preparatory committee and the conference and implied strongly that Rumania would not attend a Soviet-summoned international meeting. Therefore it was indeed a Rumanian declaration of independence from Moscow.[74]

During the summer and early autumn of 1964 Soviet-Rumanian relations worsened still further, and it became increasingly certain that the Rumanians would not participate in a Soviet-sponsored conference. Bucharest polemicized against Soviet articles and radio broadcasts [75] (whereupon Moscow retreated) [76] and censored the Rumanian edition of *Problems of Peace and Socialism.*[77] Frequent Soviet-Rumanian negotiations apparently came to nothing,[78] and even Tito's urging of Gheorghiu-Dej to be cautious did not improve the situation.[79] Rumania continued to expand its contacts with the West and its moves toward limited domestic liberalization (release of political prisoners, rise in

---

72 And it did: At the June 1964 Geneva UN World Trade Conference Rumania voted with and tried to join the group of 75 underdeveloped countries. See *East Europe*, Vol. XIII, No. 7 (July 1964), p. 47.

73 Quoted from " Statement," pp. 30–32, 52–53.

74 Even so, the strength and subtlety of Bucharest's position was demonstrated by the fact that Moscow evidently felt compelled to publish a carefully edited summary of the statement in *World Marxist Review*, Vol. 7, No. 7 (July 1964), pp. 60–64.

75 " Concepts Contrary to the Basic Principles Guiding Economic Relations Between Socialist Countries," *Viata Economica*, No. 24, 1964 (reprinted in *Jen-min Jih-pao*, July 26, 1964, and *Peking Review*, Vol. III, No. 31 [July 31, 1964], pp. 28–40), attacking E. B. Valev, " Problems of the Economic Development of the Danube Districts of Rumania, Bulgaria, and the U.S.S.R.," *Vestnik Moskovskogo Universiteta*, No. 2, March–April 1964, and the Fourth Congress of the Soviet Society of Geography, May 25–30, 1964; and (for radio polemics) Radio Moscow in Rumanian, May 30, 1964, and Radio Bucharest, June 5, 1964, and C. K. [Christian Kind], " Rumänische-sowjetische Meinungsverschiedenheiten," *Neue Zürcher Zeitung*, June 9, 1964.

76 O. Gobomolov, " Study in Greater Depth of the Problems of Cooperation among the Socialist Countries," *Izvestiya*, July 4, 1964.

77 " Les Roumains censurent la ' revue de Prague,' " *Est & Ouest*, Vol. XVI, No. 328 (October 16–31, 1964), p. 5.

78 For example, C. K. [Christian Kind], " Moskaus Werburg um Rumänien," *Neue Zürcher Zeitung*, May 29, 1964, and V. M. [Viktor Meier] from Moscow in *ibid.*, July 8, 16, 1964.

79 See a Vienna dispatch [by Dessa Bourne] in *The Times* (London), June 8, 1964.

wages, price cuts).[80] However, despite these Soviet-Rumanian differences, both Soviet and Chinese delegations attended the Bucharest liberation celebration in August.[81]

(2) *The Italian Communist Party's* effective resistance to the Soviet conference plan was a second blow to Moscow's position within the international Communist movement. The PCI's long-term goals are incompatible with Soviet domination of the Communist world. The Italian Communists want (a) an increase in electoral power, toward which they are working by professing (and increasingly, if not yet fully, becoming genuinely committed to) a revisionist program and by weakening the unpopular PCI alignment with Moscow, thereby decreasing its clash with Italian nationalism; (b) primacy in West European communism; and (c) a major role, not only in Western Europe but also in the underdeveloped world, in a pluralistic international Communist movement. To further these goals Togliatti used his great personal prestige, his experience in international communism, and all the *habilità* of Machiavelli.[82]

As early as January 1964, Togliatti said publicly that Tito joined him in expressing " many reservations " with respect to an international conference.[83] Just before the publication of the Suslov report, Mario Alicata declared that any attempt to " excommunicate " and " expel " a party would be " unacceptable to us." [84]

Later that same month Togliatti was even more specific:

> When talk arose of a new international meeting of all Communist parties, to examine and assess the attitude of the Chinese comrades . . . this . . . was likely to end in another excommunication . . . ; and, it appeared to us unnecessary and dangerous.

He made clear the basis of the PCI's fears:

> The method of official excommunication . . . may revive authoritarian and sectarian systems in the leadership of each party.

Rather, he declared, there should be " a series of bilateral or group

---

80 Reuters from Geneva, *Neue Zürcher Zeitung,* June 14, 1964; Geneva dispatch in *The New York Times,* June 7, 1964.
81 Bucharest, clearly at least as independent of Moscow as Belgrade, appeared by October 1964 to be moving toward even looser relations with the Soviet Union. The Chinese were of course jubilant, as well they might be. They had contributed toward the greatest blow to Soviet influence in East Europe since the Soviet-Yugoslav break in 1948.
82 See Griffith, *The Sino-Soviet Rift, op. cit.,* p. 179, and *Communism in Europe, op. cit.,* Vol. 2, pp. 33–34, Giorgio Galli, " Italian Communism," in Griffith, *Communism in Europe, op. cit.,* Vol. 1, pp. 301–384; and for more recent developments, Eric Willenz and Pio Uliassi, " Western Europe," *Survey,* No. 54 (January 1965), and Labedz, *op. cit.,* pp. 51–64, at pp. 58–64; Griffith, *Communism in Europe, op. cit.,* Vol. 2, pp. 34–36, and Kevin Devlin, " The Italian Position," " The PCI's Ideological Diplomacy," and " The Independent Italians," Radio Free Europe, Munich, May 6, 1964, July 17, 1964, and May 18, 1965, respectively.
83 Togliatti's press conference in Belgrade, *L'Unità,* January 22, 1964.
84 *Ibid.,* April 1, 1964.

meetings " (that is, a West European one, for example, with the PCI taking the lead), based on the conception of international communism as " a movement united by profound solidarity but open to necessary differences, to an exchange of ideas."

He concluded by summarizing his fears for the future and reaffirming his opposition to a meeting:

> As for the results the meeting may yield, our hesitation stems not only from a desire to avoid summary excommunication, but also from the fear that in a discussion at this level, inevitably too general in character, it may prove very difficult to make any serious advance in the creative elaboration of our policy. If things then go to the length of a rupture, the repercussions may be extremely grave for our whole movement. Once two opposed centres arise, we may be running the risk of all our future work being concentrated on a struggle between these two centres; it is almost inevitable that small pro-Chinese parties will appear in each country. Both sides will be more rigidly strict as to organisation and discipline than the present situation and present needs warrant, causing us almost inevitably to abandon the creative search for new development in all the major sectors and all fields of our activity.
>
> To sum up, we are not yet convinced that it is not worthwhile to continue the discussion and to work perseveringly for a correct political line and for the unity of the international movement in the present conditions, using methods which, as I have said, may at least give some hope of attenuating the political differences, establishing fruitful contacts, and gradually returning to complete unity.[85]

In June he called for an international communist *aggiornamento*:

> Autonomy, unless it is to develop into isolation, or still worse, into a centrifugal tendency, must postulate not only the diversity of position, but profound, reciprocal recognition, tolerance debate, and comparison, which, however, does not mean condemnation and breaking of relations at every turn . . . we can be effective in our struggle only by giving the entire movement a plan which is profoundly different from the traditional one.[86]

Furthermore, the PCI proposed " revising and expanding numerous parts " of the November 1960 Moscow Statement, particularly with respect to Yugoslavia and such national liberation movements as the new Algerian socialist party.[87] Finally, the PCI flatly rejected Khrushchev's proposed " new organizational forms ":

> We shall not combat effectively the myth of monolithism by seeking an agreement that would again render rigid the workers' movement at

---

[85] Togliatti to the PCI Central Committee, *L'Unità*, April 23, 1964, quoted from *Information Bulletin*, No. 11, June 6, 1964, pp. 41–63, at pp. 60–62.
[86] From an interview with Togliatti in *Rinascita*, Vol. XXI, No. 26 (June 27, 1964), p. 9 (JPRS 25,576, July 24, 1964, pp. 53–56).
[87] " Contro il dogmatismo," *L'Unità*, May 24, 1964 (JPRS 25,316, June 30, 1964, pp. 36–39).

precisely those points where it has started to advance toward renovation.[88]

Thus, although Togliatti reaffirmed his support of Moscow and his opposition to China on the substantive issues of the dispute, he was clearly not prepared to participate in Khrushchev's mobilization toward collective "political isolation" of the Chinese.

The PCI also continued to develop and expand its revisionist program. In April 1964 one of its major left-wing figures, Pietro Ingrao, declared that organized nonsocialist parties should exist after the PCI comes to power,[89] and in July another article in *Rinascita* went even further in rejecting Lenin's theory of the state.[90] Nor did the visits of several PCI delegations to Moscow change the Italian position.

In August, Togliatti himself went to the Soviet Union, where, after inconclusive discussions with Brezhnev and Ponomarev in Moscow, he prepared a memorandum for his scheduled talks with Khrushchev.[91] Before meeting with Khrushchev he was stricken with a fatal heart attack. In spite of Brezhnev's attempt at the funeral in Rome to persuade him not to, Togliatti's successor Luigi Longo, encouraged by the Yugoslavs, Poles, and Rumanians, decided to publish the memorandum, since generally known as the "Togliatti Testament."[92]

More than any other single document this marked the decline in Soviet power and influence in the international Communist movement. Not that it said anything strikingly new about the PCI's policies; rather, it was a codification of the accumulation of Italian Communist heterodoxy. But its publication under such dramatic circumstances, plus the fact that Moscow republished it and took issue with it only very indirectly, made clear to the world that Moscow was increasingly becoming a paper tiger.

Togliatti began by declaring that the PCI would "take part actively" in the proposed preparatory conference. Yet this was only a formal concession: He made it clear that the PCI would come to the conference to oppose (and, he implied, would refuse to accept) Soviet aims; more-

---

[88] Giancarlo Pajetta, "L'errore dei comunisti cinesi," *Rinascita*, Vol. XXI, No. 38 (September 26, 1964), pp. 1–2 (JPRS 27,635, October 22, 1964).

[89] Pietro Ingrao, "Democrazia socialista e democrazia interna di partito," *Rinascita*, Vol. XXI, No. 17 (April 25, 1964), pp. 3–6 (JPRS 24,751, May 26, 1964).

[90] Luciano Gruppi, "Le tesi di Lenin e di Engels sullo Stato," *Rinascita*, Vol. XXI, No. 30 (July 25, 1964), pp. 27–28.

[91] See an interview with his "compagna" Jotti, *L'Unità*, October 23, 1964.

[92] "Promemoria sulle questioni del movimento operaio internazionale e della sua unità," *Rinascita*, Vol. XXI, No. 35 (September 5, 1964), pp. 1–4; also in *L'Unità* and *The New York Times*, September 5, 1964; see Kevin Devlin, "From Memorandum to Testament," and "Togliatti's Testament: Challenge to Moscow," Radio Free Europe, Munich, both September 10, 1964; Kx. [Ernst Kux], "Togliatti's politische Testament," *Neue Zürcher Zeitung*, September 15, 1964; Robert F. Lamberg, "Das politische Testament Palmiro Togliattis," *Aussenpolitik*, Vol. XV, No. 12 (December 1964), pp. 849–856.

over, the PCI would advance its own position. The PCI, he went on, would prefer, first, "objective and persuasive" polemics with Peking, then a series of regional meetings during "a year or more," and only then an international meeting that, "if it were to appear necessary in order to avoid a formal split . . . one could also renounce." Furthermore, he continued, not nearly enough practical steps had been taken against Chinese factionalism. Communist parties should meet with noncommunist radical nationalist groups in underdeveloped countries for this purpose (a hint of the PCI's view that such groups should really be included in any unity conference).

The CCP should not be excluded from international communism, Togliatti maintained, if only because Chinese co-operation was necessary against imperialism, whose leader, the United States, was becoming more aggressive and dangerous. Moreover, a split would lead to much too great a concentration on the struggle against Peking. He flatly rejected "any proposal to create once again a centralized international organization." Rather, he postulated that "unity in diversity" should be obtained by

> rather frequent contacts and exchanges of experiences among the parties on a broad scale, convocation of collective meetings dedicated to studying common problems by a certain group of parties, international study meetings on general problems of economy, philosophy, history, etc.

plus objective "discussions," not personalized polemics (but not silence on existing differences).

Thus Togliatti voiced what had also been the Yugoslav position since Stalin's break with Tito: a Communist "commonwealth" with no more formally binding links than the British. He specifically indicated that he was opposed both to excessive nationalism and to "forced exterior uniformity" among communist states.

Togliatti's blow to Soviet authority was even greater, however, in that he sharply criticized Soviet internal affairs. He revived his 1956 thesis that not just Stalin's personality was responsible for Stalinism; he advocated "open debates on current problems" by leaders of communist states; and he took exception to Soviet "slowness and resistance" in returning to "a wide liberty of expression and debate on culture, art, and also on politics."

Nor did Togliatti's death bring any modification in the PCI's opposition to the Soviet conference objectives. On the contrary, the fact that Moscow and almost all other pro-Soviet parties published the Togliatti testament strengthened the Italian position.[93]

---

[93] *Pravda*, September 10, 1964. See Giuliano Pajetta, "Il dibattito internazionale sul documento di Yalta," *Rinascita*, Vol. XXI, No. 39 (October 3, 1964), p. 9, and

Togliatti's successor, Luigi Longo, reaffirmed the PCI's difference of views with Moscow on

> an Italian road to socialism based on . . . our realities and traditions in a multi-party system, with full respect for constitutional guarantees and for religious and cultural liberties. In this we separate ourselves from the methods followed in countries which . . . have already achieved socialism.[94]

Immediately before Khrushchev's fall, in a report to a PCI Central Committee plenum, Enrico Berlinguer proudly declared, " The prestige of the PCI is today greater than ever before in the past," and stressed the end of Soviet hegemony:

> The moment has come to realize that the situation has changed, to get rid of any nostalgia, to recognize that the kind of unity which we want to build tomorrow is and will have to be in the future a unity that recognizes differences as inevitable and accepts these differences without leading to any condemnations. . . .

Another speaker, Luciano Gruppi, one of the most revisionist PCI leaders, put the case for Italian (and for that matter, Chinese) " national communism " very precisely and in so doing took the same position against a ban on factionalism in the international movement as have the Chinese:

> One thing which we cannot accept is the principle of a majority which would be in a position to force the minority to accept its decisions; this principle was valid when there was an international organization but it can no longer be valid today when it would signify a limitation of the autonomy of the parties.[95]

(3) *Yugoslavia*, not surprisingly, was the first to reprint and endorse the Togliatti Testament.[96] The near-identity of Italian and Yugoslav Communist policy on the proposed international conference had been clear ever since Khrushchev first launched the idea in September 1963. Tito never endorsed it at any time.[97] Yet, for several reasons, Yugoslav statements on the issue were much fewer and less precise than Italian ones. First, Yugoslavia was not, since it had not been in 1960, a member of the 26-nation preparatory committee; it therefore did not need to take a position about either the committee meeting or its composition. Second, largely because of internal economic troubles and a rising

Luigi Longo, " The Italian Communist Party and Problems of the International Communist Movement," *World Marxist Review*, Vol. 7, No. 11 (November 1964), pp. 3-10.
[94] *L'Unità*, September 11, 1964, quoted from Kevin Devlin, " Moscow and the Italian CP," *Problems of Communism*, Vol. XIV, No. 5 (September-October 1965).
[95] *L'Unità*, October 15, 1964 (JPRS 27,299, November 5, 1964).
[96] *Politika*, September 5 and 6, 1964.
[97] Griffith, *The Sino-Soviet Rift, op. cit.*, pp. 182-183, and *Communism in Europe, op. cit.*, Vol. 2, pp. 9-11; Viktor Meier, " Yugoslav Communism," in *ibid.*, Vol. 1, pp. 19-64, and his running coverage in *Neue Zürcher Zeitung*.

nationalities problem, Tito was anxious to continue his post-1960 rapprochement with Khrushchev.[98] Consequently he was disinclined to take a clearly anti-Soviet position on the conference issue. Third, he could well afford to let the Rumanians and Italians express what was also his opposition, the more so since their success and the subsequent Soviet retreat had made clear by the summer of 1964 that Tito need not fear Soviet attempts to reimpose tighter controls on East Europe, which would endanger Yugoslav internal autonomy and external maneuverability. Fourth, Tito feared to attract Moscow's opposition to his still active goal (dating from 1945–48) of asserting Yugoslav influence in the Balkans. He therefore preferred that loosening of Soviet control, and the resultant greater opportunities for Belgrade, be initiated elsewhere. Indeed, during the summer of 1964 Tito appears to have feared that Gheorghiu-Dej might be risking Soviet intervention in Rumania, for after a hastily arranged meeting with Khrushchev in Leningrad, Tito reportedly conferred with Gheorghiu-Dej in order to caution him to go more slowly in asserting Rumanian independence.[99]

Poland's opposition to Khrushchev's conference plans was the most cautious of any Eastern European state that did not totally support the Soviet proposal.[100] Gomułka, like most Poles, remains convinced that *raison d'état* (the guarantee of the Oder-Neisse line against Germany) requires a Polish-Soviet alliance. Yet he wishes to prevent a renewed Soviet attempt to reimpose its control on Poland.[101] Moreover, as a convinced Communist—one of the few, as the Warsaw joke goes, in Poland—Gomułka is undoubtedly appalled by the disarray of the international Communist movement and strongly opposed to a Sino-Soviet split, the more so because he is so anxious to prevent factional strife in Warsaw.

Gomułka's real position became clear, if only between the lines, in his speech at the mid-June 1964 Fourth Polish Party Congress. There, after a long but relatively nonpolemical rejection of the Chinese views, he declared that not Peking but " a majority " of communist parties should determine when preparations for a conference should begin; that is, Poland would, like the Italian Communists, attend the conference.

---

98 For a significant pro-Yugoslav Soviet article see " Yugoslav Today," *World Marxist Review*, Vol. 7, No. 3 (March 1964), pp. 65–73.
99 AFP from Belgrade, *Le Monde*, June 27, 1964; Eric Bourne from Vienna in *The Christian Science Monitor*, June 23, 1964.
100 See Griffith, *The Sino-Soviet Rift, op. cit.*, pp. 184–185; Hansjakob Stehle, " Polish Communism," in Griffith, *Communism in Europe, op. cit.*, Vol. 1, pp. 85–176; and Griffith in *ibid.*, Vol. 2, pp. 15–16.
101 The small group of Polish Stalinists condemned at the Fourth PZPR Congress were not pro-Chinese, although they may have been in contact with the Chinese or Albanian embassies in Warsaw. See the excerpts from their clandestine pamphlet in *East Europe*, Vol. XIV, No. 3 (March 1965), pp. 7–15.

He went on:

> In the present situation it seems expedient to start in the very near future preparations for a conference with the participation of the parties representing the most important areas of the world. A committee composed of such parties would carry out preliminary discussions, which, having been discussed within individual parties and among parties, would be the basis of the future joint resolutions. . . .[102]

"The most important areas of the world"—who would represent East Asia, the CCP and its allies having refused to attend? Only the pro-Soviet Indian Communist Party led by Dange? Clearly Gomułka was trying to stall, as indicated by his elaborate procedure for discussions of drafts. Furthermore, the advance text of the speech released to correspondents contained a passage, which Gomułka did not deliver, to the effect that parties not attending the conference would "put themselves in the pale of the international movement." [103] Perhaps he cut it because he gave the speech on June 15, the same day that the Soviet letter of that date, explicitly calling for a conference, was dispatched. Contemporary accounts from Warsaw reported signs [104] that Gomułka and his associates were greatly disturbed by the pre-emptory tone of the letter. Not surprisingly, the subsequent PZPR congress resolutions contained no mention of the conference.[105] Clearly, Warsaw was giving only the most reluctant and minimal co-operation to Khrushchev's international conference plans.

Cuba's leader Castro was, like most Asian Communists, out of sympathy with Khrushchev on the key issues of peaceful versus revolutionary transition to socialism and of détente with the United States. Castro wanted to replace Moscow as the decisive influence over Latin American communism, despite his dependence on Moscow for massive and essential economic aid and his realization that a Communist Cuba could hope for none but Soviet military protection against Washington. His disagreement with Khrushchev's policy of détente became even clearer after the 1962 Cuban missile crisis and the Cuban refusal to sign the Moscow partial test ban treaty.[106] On the other hand, Castro's 1963-1964 visits to Moscow had brought the public Cuban position on the Sino-Soviet dispute still closer to Khrushchev's, presumably as the price for increased Soviet economic aid. Castro did not want a Sino-Soviet split; yet he could not afford directly to oppose Soviet desires. He therefore continued his ban on public discussion in Cuba

---

[102] *Trybuna Ludu*, June 16, 1964.

[103] J. F., "Eastern Europe," in Labedz, *op. cit.*, at p. 77, note 7.

[104] K. S. Karol, "Le nouveau drame de ' Wiesław ' Gomułka," *Le Monde*, July 3, 1964.

[105] *Trybuna Ludu*, June 25, 1964.

[106] For the above, see Griffith, *The Sino-Soviet Rift, op. cit.*, pp. 198-202, Ernst Halperin, "Latin America," *Survey*, No. 54 (January 1965), and Labedz, *op. cit.*, pp. 154-167.

of Sino-Soviet differences. In view of subsequent developments it seems probable that the Soviets and the Cubans were already engaged, along with the other Latin American communist parties, in the negotiations that led in late November, after Khrushchev's fall, to a major improvement in Soviet-Cuban relations. In any case, whether spurred by Soviet concessions or economic necessity, Cuban President Dorticós intimated in early October that Cuba would attend the proposed preparatory committee meeting.[107] By then, however, Castro hardly needed to worry that such a conference would produce the split he wanted to avoid.

(6) As for *the rest of the international Communist movement*, the British, Norwegian, and Swedish parties—small, threatened by affluence and major social democratic parties, and therefore increasingly revisionist and factionalized—were anxious to keep the Sino-Soviet dispute out of their ranks and consequently were notably unenthusiastic about the Soviet plans for a conference. However, their lack of size and influence made their wishes relatively unimportant in Soviet considerations.[108]

Khrushchev's Retreat (June–October 1964)

That Khrushchev would again abandon his international conference plans, as in October 1963, was most unlikely. With the publication of the Suslov report and the Central Committee resolution in April 1964 he had gone too far. But his retreat, although more concealed, was no less great; by mid-June he had clearly been forced to abandon his main objective of "collective mobilization" against the Chinese.

In early April Khrushchev had spoken of tightening multiparty ties within Eastern Europe in order better to combat Chinese factionalism and Rumanian obstreperousness.[109] By early June an *Izvestiya* article had already scaled this down to "a periodically functioning conference of ministers "[110]—typical of CMEA and the Warsaw Treaty Organization; while an article in *Partiinaya Zhizn* not only drew no organizational conclusions but also, although reaffirming the "Leninist principle of the subordination of the minority to the majority" and

---

107 In an interview in Cairo with Eric Rouleau, *Le Monde*, October 11–12, 1964.
108 Griffith, *The Sino-Soviet Rift, op. cit.*, pp. 179–182 (with bibliography); Willenz and Uliassi, *op. cit.*, pp. 50–54; running analyses by Kevin Devlin of Radio Free Europe, Munich, and his "Schism and Secession," *Survey*, No. 54 (January 1965), and Labedz, *op. cit.*, pp. 29–50; chapters on Nordic communism in Griffith, ed., *Communism in Europe, op. cit.*, Vol. 2; statements by Norwegian and Swedish Communist parties, April 1964, in *Information Bulletin*, No. 12, July 2, 1964, pp. 22–29.
109 See p. 26.
110 "On the Nature of Relations Between Socialist Countries: The Policy of Unity Against the Policy of Schism," *Izvestiya*, June 6, 1964, quoted from *CDSP*, Vol. XVI, No. 23 (July 1, 1964), pp. 5–7, at p. 6.

reiterating Khrushchev's favorite phrase that parties should "'synchronize watches,'" concluded by declaring only that

> if a party finds itself in isolation or in the minority on any question, the authoritative opinion of the majority must prompt it to self-criticism, to a careful rechecking of its positions. . . .[111]

In June, however, as an indication that Khrushchev's retreat was only partial and tactical, a Soviet propagandist hinted that Peking could not necessarily count on Moscow's support in any " terrible hour of trial." [112]

On June 15 Moscow sent a letter to the Chinese that was intended to gain the Soviets support among other parties. With respect to substantive issues it unequivocally declared that Peking was attempting to form its own bloc in order to split the movement, and it denounced Chinese great-power chauvinism. On procedural issues, it insisted that the " overwhelming majority " of communist parties favored an international conference "without delay ", that those parties with reservations had them only about the timing because of the Chinese position, that only the Chinese and Albanians were opposed *in toto* (a far from true statement), and that no one party could prevent the holding of such a conference. The letter indicated some willingness to compromise on the date but flatly rejected the Chinese proposal of a four- or five-year delay. The Soviets also rejected the attendance of pro-Chinese groups. With respect to the substance of the conference, however, Khrushchev's retreat was plain. The letter declared that Moscow wished to concentrate on what " unites " communist parties, on normalization rather than aggravation of differences. More significant, it admitted that the conference " will not immediately manage . . . to arrive at a common opinion on all questions " and declared that parties should nonetheless cooperate on positions held in " common " and " refrain in the future from any action that would aggravate the difficulties," thereby avoiding any chance of a split or worsening of differences. There was no more talk of a " collective rebuff " of the Chinese, nothing about tightening the ties between pro-Soviet parties; rather, its phrases reflected the Italian, Rumanian, and Yugoslav " exchanges of views " formulas instead of Khrushchev's April position.[113]

[111] " Against Splitters, For Unity of the Communist Movement," *Partiinaya Zhizn,* No. 11, June 1964, pp. 8–20, reprinted, slightly abridged, in *Pravda,* June 3 and 4, 1964, quoted from *CDSP,* Vol. XVI, No. 22 (June 24, 1964,) pp. 3–8, at p. 7. The full English text is in *Information Bulletin,* No. 17, August 25, 1964, pp. 5–19.

[112] Yury Zhukov, " The Chinese Wall," *Pravda,* June 21, 1964, quoted from *CDSP,* Vol. XVI, No. 25 (July 16, 1964), pp. 3–4, at p. 4.

[113] CPSU Central Committee to CCP Central Committee, *Kommunist,* No. 10, July 1964, pp. 9–20, and *Pravda,* July 17, 1964, quoted from *CDSP,* Vol. XVI, No. 30 (August 19, 1964), pp. 5–10, at pp. 5–6. See also the even more general article by Boris Ponomarev, " Proletarian Internationalism—a Powerful Force in the Revolutionary Transformation of the World," *World Marxist Review,* Vol. 7, No. 8 (August 1964), pp. 59–70, and the rejection of " excommunication " by Y. Tsedenbal and O. Vargas in *ibid.,* Vol. 7, No. 9 (September 1964), pp. 3–10 and 11–14.

Although the Chinese did not formally reject the Soviet June letter until a month thereafter, their publication on July 13, one year after the 1963 Soviet Open Letter, of their ninth " Comment " thereon made clear that their position was hardening. Entitled " On Khrushchev's Phony Communism and Its Historical Lessons for the World," it addressed itself to two general areas: the *embourgeoisement* of Soviet society and the future course of communism in China. Its importance transcends Sino-Soviet relations: It was Mao's political testament, his prescription for China's present and future Chinese domestic and foreign policy—the most important and authoritative contemporary Chinese Communist document we have.

Its treatment of the " restoration of capitalism " in the Soviet Union was in the best tradition of Machajski, Mosca, Trotsky, and Djilas. After having reiterated the Chou Yang thesis that the class struggle between bourgeois and proletarian elements and therefore the danger of the restoration of capitalism remained great during the " very, very long historical stage " of socialism, the " Comment " declared that the

> activities of the bourgeoisie . . . constantly breed political degenerates in the ranks of the working class and Party and government organizations, new bourgeois elements and embezzlers and grafters in state enterprises owned by the whole people and new bourgeois intellectuals.

and thus create the " social base of revisionism." But, the article continued,

> the gravity of the situation lies in the fact that the revisionist Khrushchev clique have usurped the leadership of the Soviet Party and state and that a privileged bourgeois stratum has emerged in Soviet society. . . .

This in turn has led to " an unprecedented danger of capitalist restoration " and to " an irreconcilable and antagonistic class contradiction " between Khrushchev and his privileged stratum and the masses of the Soviet people.

Given this Chinese view of Soviet " degeneration," the most extreme until that date, the article contrasted it with the most ascetic, grim, and fanatical view of China's future that Peking—and, in this instance, Mao personally, in fifteen points—has ever set forth. Transition to communism, Mao declared, will take " anywhere from one to several centuries." To prevent bourgeois degeneration during this long period, physical labor for cadres must be continued, incomes must be leveled, army, militia, and police must remain under strict party control, and above all great attention must be paid to

> the question of training successors for the revolutionary cause of the

43

proletariat . . . a matter of life and death for our party . . . for a hundred, a thousand, nay ten thousand years.[114]

On July 28 the Chinese finally replied to the Soviet June 15 letter. Moscow had "laid down a revisionist political program and a divisive organizational line" in order "arbitrarily, unilaterally, and illegally" to call an international meeting to bring about "an open split." After accusing Moscow of trying to subvert the Indian and Japanese Communist Parties, and declaring that unanimity was necessary for convening any international meeting, the letter concluded: "We firmly believe that the day your so-called meeting takes place will be the day you step into your own grave." [115]

Two days later, on July 30, the Soviets dispatched a circular letter to the 26 participants of the 1960 preparatory committee meeting, summoning them to meet in Moscow on December 15, 1964. The meeting would take place, the letter said, even if all parties summoned did not attend. Even more explicitly than in the previous June 30 letter, the Soviets stressed that the proposed meeting was not intended to lead to a split:

> The meeting will be called not to condemn anybody, to "excommunicate" anybody from the Communist movement and the socialist camp, to attach insulting labels, or to throw irresponsible charges.

The meeting would "enrich and develop" (that is, revise) the 1957 and 1960 declarations. Finally, the letter repeated the June 30 formulations about concentrating on areas of agreement and putting differences aside.[116]

The July 30 Soviet letter signified no slackening in the extent of Soviet hostility toward the Chinese, but only in method. Their lowered estimate of the chances of expelling them was made clear by the publication immediately thereafter of perhaps the most extreme anti-Chinese ideological diatribe the Soviets had ever produced: an article by the head of the CPSU Central Committee Agitprop section, Leonid Ilichev. A revised version of a lecture given in June, it was signed for

114 "On Khrushchev's Phony Communism and Its Historical Lessons for the World. Comment on the Open Letter of the Central Committee of the CPSU (9)," *Jen-min Jih-pao* and *Hung Ch'i*, July 13, 1964, and *Peking Review*, Vol. VII, No. 29 (July 17, 1964), pp. 7–28, at pp. 8, 9, 13, 15 and 26. *Cf.* An Tzu-wen, "Cultivating and Training Revolutionary Successors Is the Strategic Task of the Party," *Hung Ch'i*, No. 17/18, September 23, 1964, pp. 1–13 (JPRS 27,143, October 29, 1964).

115 *Jen-min Jih-pao*, July 31, 1964, and *Peking Review*, Vol. VII, No. 31 (July 31, 1964), pp. 5–11. Peking simultaneously published the June 15, 1964, CPSU letter.

116 Text only in *Peking Review*, Vol. VIII, No. 13 (March 26, 1964), pp. 19–20. The August 10, 1964, *Pravda* editorial, "An International Conference Is the Path to the Solidarity of the Communist Movement," which announced that the conference had been summoned, was much more polemic in tone than the letter, but it added nothing substantively new to it.

the press on July 31,[117] and it must have been considered by the international Communist movement, as Khrushchev probably intended it, to be equally as authoritative as the letter itself.

Ilichev's article was much more systematic and ideologically more complete than Suslov's February speech. It probably represented what Khrushchev would have liked to have obtained as a resolution of the scheduled December 15, 1964 meeting, and it may indeed have reflected a secret Soviet draft; at the very least, it must have been regarded as such in international Communist circles. Ilichev began by declaring flatly that

" Left " opportunism is becoming the chief danger in the international Communist movement.[118]

That is, he implied that the 1960 Statement must be revised. Furthermore,

No " Left " deviation in the past represented such a danger to the communist movement as present-day " Left " opportunism.[119]

because (a) the latter is now the " basis of political line " of China, (b) it is caused by Chinese " nationalism and great-power aspirations," and (c) Chinese factionalism is " subversive work on an international scale." [120] It rose objectively from Chinese economic backwardness, which in turn caused the Chinese Party to be based primarily on non-proletarian peasant and intellectual strata, that is, it is petty-bourgeois and therefore nationalist. Subjectively the CCP leadership is " Left opportunist " and " nationalist " because of Mao's personality cult, which in turn has led

to a situation when subjectivism and the personal whims of one man become an official policy, create fertile soil for unjustified experiments, absence of control, inordinate ambition, make for extremes, instability, adventurism, and nationalism . . . in a word, " neo-Trotskyism," which, unlike its predecessor, is " marked by strongly pronounced nationalism and great-power chauvinism, plus the ' ultra-revolutionism ' of the peasantry.[121]

This great-power chauvinism has been strengthened by an " imperial ideology," arising from Chinese traditions, of " China's special role in

---

117 Leonid Ilichev, " Revolutionary Science and Our Age. Against the Anti-Leninist Course of the Chinese Leaders," *Kommunist*, No. 11, July 1964 (signed to the press July 31, 1964), pp. 12–35. The article was a report delivered in June 1964 at a scientific session on the " Struggle of the CPSU for the Purity of Marxism-Leninism " sponsored jointly by the Academy of Social Sciences of the CPSU Central Committee's Institute of Marxism-Leninism and the Social Science Institutes of the USSR Academy of Sciences, " with some additions." It is quoted here from the text in *Information Bulletin*, No. 21, October 1, 1964, pp. 21–52. (The date of its publication in the latter would indicate that the Ilichev article remained the official Soviet position until a few weeks before Khrushchev's fall, that is, that Khrushchev had only organizationally, but not otherwise, scaled down his objectives.)
118 Ilichev, *op. cit.*, p. 23.
119 *Ibid.*, p. 24.
120 *Ibid.*, pp. 24–25.   121 *Ibid.*, pp. 29–30.

the history of mankind." All these factors have given rise to the "hegemonistic ambitions of the Peking leaders" in international communism.[122]

Ilichev then, after again cataloging the specific offenses of Peking much as Suslov had done, termed Chinese communism

> a conglomeration of "Left" opportunism, dogmatism and frankly revisionist ideas, fragments of revolutionary theory, Trotskyite theses, idealist opinions and sophistry of ancient Chinese philosophers, nationalistic and at times racialist ideas [123]

and Mao's philosophical views

> at best . . . a popular exposition which, moreover suffers from serious mistakes and oversimplification.[124]

At the end of his article, however, Ilichev implied, as had Khrushchev, that expulsion of the Chinese had been dropped:

> Social development, the entire course of events are increasingly laying bare the ideological poverty of the present-day splitters, the subjectivism and adventurism of their policy. The swiftly flowing stream of life, the irrepressible growth of the revolutionary forces will show the complete bankruptcy of the positions of the Chinese petty-bourgeois nationalists, "Left" opportunists and neo-Trotskyites. As for those who have taken a wrong stand because of delusion, insufficient maturity or lack of experience, the practical achievements of the Communist parties in applying the Leninist general line are bound to bring them back to the right road.

Yet the extent and gravity of his charges against the Chinese, and their publication in Russian on July 31 and in English on October 1, made clear that Khrushchev himself, however much tactical flexibility he might be forced to, was tied to a policy of total hostility to Peking.

The much more violent Chinese than Soviet reaction to the August 5 United States air action against North Vietnamese vessels in the Gulf of Tonkin [125] indicated the rising importance of the Vietnamese crisis as a factor worsening Sino-Soviet relations.

A month later, after charging Moscow with supporting the American attempt to intervene in Vietnam through the United Nations (the first clear signal of the growing importance of the Vietnamese issue in Sino-Soviet affairs), the Chinese replied on August 30 that

> the day in December 1964 on which you convene your drafting committee will go down in history as the day of the great split in the international Communist movement.[126]

[122] *Ibid.*, pp. 32–33. [123] *Ibid.*, p. 37.
[124] *Ibid.*, p. 40.
[125] *Pravda* and *Jen-min Jih-pao*, August 6, 1964. See *China News Analysis*, No. 530 (August 28, 1964), pp. 2–6.
[126] NCNA in English, Peking, August 30, 1965 (SCMP 3293, September 4, 1964, pp. 33–35), and *Peking Review*, Vol. VII, No. 36 (September 4, 1964), pp. 6–7. The Chinese simultaneously published the Soviet July 30 letter.

By September the Soviet attitude toward the conference had become increasingly ambivalent, perhaps reflecting some differences within the Soviet leadership concerning tactics about it. Although Moscow published the Togliatti Testament, it immediately, if esoterically (in theses on the hundredth anniversary of the First International), replied to its autonomist views by declaring that

> relations among the socialist states . . . cannot be limited merely to the principles of complete equality, respect for territorial integrity, state independence and sovereignty, and noninterference in one another's internal affairs, although they do presuppose the fullest and most consistent implementation of these principles. They also presuppose fraternal mutual aid and close cooperation among the socialist states.

Moreover, a new set of criteria for proletarian internationalism was set forth:

> In the activity of the International, along with certain historically transitory organizational forms conditioned by the then-existing stage in the development of the international workers' movement, there were expressed for the first time the most important organizational principles of proletarian internationalism. They are:
>
> —the duty to recognize the basic principles of the International on the part of all parties entering into it;
>
> —the duty to observe the decisions adopted within the framework of the International, with the subordination of the minority to the will of the majority;
>
> —the banning of factional schismatic activity within the ranks of the International.
>
> These principles retain their importance in our time as well.[127]

(Peking would reject all three principles, but the Italians and Rumanians would reject, and the Poles and others would oppose the second; therefore Moscow must either break with them as well or abandon the principle of democratic centralism, without which the Soviets could no longer enforce their will.)

Later that month, at the Moscow celebration of the centenary of the

---

127 Institute of Marxism-Leninism of the CPSU Central Committee, " 100th Anniversary of the First International: 1864–1964 (Theses)," *Pravda*, September 11, 1964, quoted from *CDSP*, Vol. XVI, No. 37 (October 7, 1964), pp. 3–11, at pp. 8 and 10. *Cf.* r.r.g. [R. Rockingham Gill], " Theses on the First International," Radio Free Europe, Munich, September 15, 1964. The extremely anti-Chinese September 1964 speech of Gus Hall, head of the CPUSA, which called for " a system of exchanges and international relations " among communist parties rather than " autonomy," can probably be explained by pressure on the CPUSA from pro-Chinese and Fidelista currents like the *Monthly Review* and the Progressive Labor Movement rather than as a reflection of any Soviet view. Hall's speech, curiously, appeared in *Information Bulletin* (Toronto), No. 27, December 17, 1964, pp. 39–51, that is, after Khrushchev's fall. For the CPUSA see the authoritative article by Joseph R. Starobin, " North America," *Survey*, No. 54 (January 1965,) reprinted in Labedz, *op. cit.*, pp. 144–153.

First International, Ponomarev declared, in another indirect reply to the Togliatti Testament, that

> The desire to interpret the independence of parties as a departure from the resolution of common international tasks, as some kind of "neutrality" in coping with common causes, cannot in the least be regarded as either a sign of independence or a sign of maturity.

However—and here the "objective" ambivalence became clear—he also reiterated the CPSU's July 30 conciliatory line:

> The goal of the new conference, as the CPSU Central Committee understands it, lies not in "excommunicating" anyone from it but in strengthening its unity, in continuing the creative resolution of the urgent problems of the world Communist movement.[128]

For the Western reader the Soviet dilemma may be clearer by an analogy (esoteric, that is) with the United Nations General Assembly [the international Communist movement]. There the United States [the Soviet Union] until recently had an assured majority, and the Russians [Chinese] therefore refused to accept Assembly decisions, but so did the French [the PCI]. But if the Russians [Chinese] or French [Italians] refuse to accept these decisions there is little the United States [the Soviets] can do about it, since the French [the PCI] and most other small nations [most of the pro-Soviet parties] so fear collapse of the United Nations [international Communist movement] that they will not vote for the Russians' [Chinese] or the French [the PCI] expulsion.

III. SINO-SOVIET POLICY AND THE "THIRD WORLD"

Chinese Policy

Communist Chinese foreign policy has always had extensive ambitions in underdeveloped areas. In 1936 Mao told Edgar Snow that

> . . . When the Chinese revolution comes into full power, the masses of many colonial countries will follow the example of China and win a similar victory of their own. . . .[129]

In 1946 Liu Shao-ch'i told Anna Louise Strong that Mao had created a "Chinese, or Asiatic," form of Marxism.[130] Given China's low level of economic, technological, and military development, its geographical position, its history of foreign, semicolonial subjection, and its strong awareness of the "colored" world as a distinct political unit, it was only natural that Peking turned to the underdeveloped countries. This

[128] "Proletarian Internationalism Is the Revolutionary Banner of Our Era," *Pravda*, September 29, 1964, quoted from *CDSP*, Vol. XVI, No. 40 (October 28, 1964), pp. 14–17, at p. 17. *Cf.* the similar Yuri Andropov, "Proletarian Internationalism Is the Battle Flag of the Communists," *Kommunist*, No. 14, September 1964 (passed for the press September 30, 1964), pp. 11–26 (JPRS 27,133, October 28, 1964).

[129] Quoted from Stuart R. Schram, *The Political Thought of Mao Tse-tung* (New York: Praeger, 1963), p. 256.

[130] Quoted from *ibid.*, p. 56.

trend was accentuated both by Soviet unwillingness to give priority to aiding violent revolutionary struggle in the "third world" over détente with the United States and by China's conflict with India, its rival for dominant influence in Asia. Once Mao had decided, probably in 1959 or 1960, to challenge Soviet leadership throughout international communism, he naturally intensified his drive in the underdeveloped, colored areas of Asia, Africa, and Latin America.

As the Sino-Soviet struggle increased, as simultaneously radical, anti-Western nationalism rose in the underdeveloped areas, and after Castro had turned into a self-declared Marxist-Leninist, both Moscow and Peking relativized their practices, and then their ideologies, with respect to cooperation with radical left-wing nationalists. In Chinese policy this process was even more pragmatic than its counterpart in Soviet doctrine and practice. Peking's ideology, although it remained more tied to the role of the proletariat,[131] and never adopted anything like the Soviet concept that the "world socialist system" could substitute for the missing domestic proletariat (that is, communist party), proclaimed that if a communist party became revisionist it could and would forfeit the leadership to "Marxist-Leninists inside and outside the party," [132] as the Cuban Communist Party had to Castro [133] and the Algerian Communist Party to the FLN.

Moreover, China's *raison d'état* was also behind its drive in the underdeveloped world. It hoped thereby to attack U.S. bases, investments, and influence, thus crippling its principal enemy's encirclement of China. Peking appears to have reasoned that most of the underdeveloped independent countries were unstable economically, socially, and politically, and that the physical power (army and internal security) of these states was so small that they were susceptible to *coups d'état* (for example, Zanzibar) and guerrilla warfare; the United States and the other Western powers would be unable or unwilling to combat these movements indefinitely, while the Soviet Union was already too affluent and too concerned about a détente with the United States to either assist in this process or prevent it. As for the role of the racist issue, particularly in Africa and (Peking hoped) in the United States itself—due to the weakness of the blacks and the power and determination of the whites—racial tensions would probably lead to

131 See Uri Ra'anan, " Moscow and the ' Third World,' " *Problems of Communism*, Vol. XIV, No. 1 (January–February 1965), p. 24.

132 Chinese Communist Party, " A Proposal Concerning the General Line of the International Communist Movement," June 14, 1963, quoted from Griffith, *The Sino-Soviet Rift, op. cit.*, p. 270.

133 See an interview with Chou En-lai in *Marcha* (Montevideo), December 13, 1963, p. 14 (JPRS 22,813, January 20, 1964). I owe this reference to Benjamin Schwartz, " The Polemics Seen by a Non-Polemicist," *Problems of Communism*, Vol. XII, No. 2 (March–April 1964), pp. 102–106, at p. 106.

protracted, bloody conflicts in which China could feed the flames and thereby gain.

Therefore China's expressed policies toward the underdeveloped areas were carefully designed to win friends and influence people. They stressed support for struggle against imperialism and neocolonialism and for totally independent and sovereign states. Chinese aid would be given without strings and on the most favorable terms possible, by means of technicians who would live at the indigenous standard of living, and its purpose would be to create diversified and self-sufficient economies with emphasis on agriculture and light industry. China would support peace, nonalignment, and the other Bandung principles, as desired by the underdeveloped nations themselves.

At the same time China considered its domestic policies to be a model for underdeveloped countries, conveniently so since Peking's emphasis on self-reliance fitted its limited resources.[134] Nevertheless, China did expend substantial sums on economic aid and on trips to Peking for influential Africans, Asians, and Latin Americans and with money and arms supported radical nationalist movements, both in and out of power.

Organizationally, by 1964 the Chinese were probably hoping to remove the forthcoming Second Bandung Conference, or the Afro-Asian Peoples' Solidarity Organization, from Soviet influence and to transform these organizations, either by purge or by split, into something like a new, fanatic, ascetic international organization of underdeveloped nations that would serve as a United Nations for the advancement of

[134] As an aspect of this general approach, Chinese economic policy toward the under-developed areas was further elaborated at a series of Afro-Asian Economic Seminars by their spokesman Nan Han-ch'en, who generalized the Chinese model of economic development for all underdeveloped countries. In a speech at the Second Seminar at Pyongyang on June 20, Nan struck the keynote:

> The fundamental way of developing an independent national economy is to carry on economic construction on the basis of self-reliance . . . to rely mainly on the enthusiasm, initiative and creativeness of the masses and . . . the internal resources and the accumulation of capital in the country. . . .

In other words, Peking recommended labor-intensive economic development, plus, as Nan added, mutual Afro-Asian economic assistance (without either Soviet or American economic aid). American economic aid, he continued, was given in order to plunder the Afro-Asian countries by keeping them underdeveloped and their raw material resources in foreign capitalist hands, by manipulating the terms of trade so as to keep prices of raw materials low and those of imported finished goods high, and by cooperating with the " modern revisionists " (that is, the Soviet Union) to " manipulate the United Nations or other world or regional economic organizations." See NCNA in English, Pyongyang, June 20, 1964 (SCMP 3245, June 24, 1964, pp. 26–29). See also *Peking Review*, Vol. VII, No. 27 (July 3, 1964), pp. 18–22, and a speech by Fang Yi at a June 16 Geneva meeting of the Economic Preparatory Meeting for the Second Afro-Asian Conference, *ibid.*, Vol. VII, No. 26 (June 26, 1964), pp. 8–10. For a Soviet reply see K. Dontsev, " Peking's False Tone," *Izvestiya*, July 12, 1964. For Chinese economic aid policy see Ai Ching-chu, " China's Economic and Technical Aid to Other Countries," *Peking Review*, Vol. VII, No. 34 (August 21, 1964,) pp. 14–18.

world revolution. They had increasing reason to hope for Indonesian cooperation in this, and they probably also hoped for Castro's help in bringing in Latin American radical movements.

This plan and Peking's support of radical nationalists highlighted the fact that Peking's bland theory contrasted throughout with its subversive practice, a contrast much sharper than that between Soviet theory and practice. Although China preached nonalignment, it constantly tried to line up underdeveloped countries against the United States, the Soviet Union, India, and Yugoslavia. To do so it was prepared to disrupt, paralyze, and, when it could not take over, split all varieties of Afro-Asian organizations. Although it talked peace, it practised nuclear testing, defied the Moscow partial test ban treaty, invaded India, and generally brandished its military power.[135] This aspect of Chinese practice was quite effective with many of the frightened smaller powers near it, as well as with those like Pakistan and Indonesia who were anti-Indian; however, it seemed not only irrelevant but positively dangerous to other African and Latin American underdeveloped nations. Finally, and for many leaders of underdeveloped nations most seriously, although China preached noninterference it in fact outdid Nkrumah and Nasser in its support of the most radical, subversive movements it could find.

Soviet Policy

After 1963 Moscow increasingly attempted to counter the Chinese challenge in underdeveloped areas, the more so because the opportunities offered by the increasingly radical and anti-Western policies of many of these states fed Moscow's appetite for expanding its influence among them. Basically Khrushchev, checked in Western Europe and Cuba, preferred to deal directly with radical nationalist movements, to gain their support by " aid without strings " and by dissolution of communist parties, to have individual Communists infiltrate them from within, and, most importantly, to convert their leaders, as Castro had been, to Marxism-Leninism. This tactic had the advantage of avoiding a military confrontation with Washington by acting through the intermediary of radical nationalist states.

Khrushchev had already intimated this to the Chinese in 1963, and after Peking had rejected his line (as well as the whole concept of " national democracy," which to the Chinese was objectionable because

---

135 The subject of Chinese atomic strategy and capacity is too complex to be treated within the limits of this study. Fortunately it has been authoritatively covered by Morton H. Halperin, *China and the Bomb, op. cit.*, and " Chinese Nuclear Strategy: The Early Post-Detonation Period," *Asian Survey*, Vol. V, No. 6 (June 1965), and *Adelphi Papers*, No. 18, May 1965; and by Halperin and Perkins, *op. cit.*, pp. 48–74.

it implied the peaceful instead of the violent road to socialism), he had reaffirmed it.[136]

Moreover, a Soviet writer in the authoritative *Problems of Peace and Socialism* had intimated in the summer of 1963 that the "non-capitalist way" could lead toward socialism, that the "socialist world system" would play the decisive role in this process, and that even non-Marxist socialist parties might become "mass parties of the Marxist-Leninist type" through the "growing working class" within them.[137] As a part of this policy *Pravda* in early December 1963 authoritatively, albeit not explicitly, had modified the November 1960 Statement's concept of "national democracy," in which the legalization of communist parties had been one of the preconditions (Nkrumah, Touré, and Keita had not permitted legalization, while Ben Bella had dissolved and Nasser had persecuted already existing communist parties).[138] *Pravda* substituted the new concept of "revolutionary democracy," or, more generally, of "non-capitalist development," which, *Pravda* declared, might occur without the existence of a communist party

> in countries where the proletariat has not yet taken shape as a class or where it has not yet become a sufficiently powerful force . . . , but then only by the influence of the world socialist system.

In sum, the Soviet Union was to take the place of the local communist party, and cooperation with the Soviet Union would guarantee socialist development.[139]

Later in the month Khrushchev made this even more explicit. Although Marxist-Leninists would prefer a "national democratic state" (that is, toleration of a legal communist party), he declared

> Of course this does not preclude other forms of development along the path of national liberation and social progress.

136 For this and subsequent developments in this area, when bibliographic citations are not given, see the penetrating analyses by Ra'anan in "Moscow and the 'Third World,'" *op. cit.*, and "Tactics in the Third World," *Survey*, No. 57 (October 1965), pp. 26–37. See also Richard Löwenthal, "Die Haltung der Sowjets zu den Einparteisystem der Entwicklungsländer," *Aus Politik und Zeitgeschichte* (Beilage, *Das Parlament*), June 16, 1965 (hereafter cited as Löwenthal "Haltung"), republished in *Entwicklungsländer zwischen Ost und West* (Schriftenreihe des Forschungsinstituts der Friedrich-Ebert-Stiftung) (Hannover: Verlag für Literatur und Zeitgeschehen, 1965), and Elizabeth Kridl Valkenier, "Sino-Soviet Rivalry and the National Liberation Movement," in Labedz, *op. cit.*, pp. 190–204.

137 Mikhail Kremnyov, "Africa in Search of New Paths," *World Marxist Review*, Vol. 6, No. 8 (August 1963), pp. 72–76, at pp. 75–76, cited in Löwenthal, "Haltung," p. 10, *q.v.*, pp. 10–11, for citation of pro-FLN Algerian Communist declarations.

138 See Klaus Westen, *Der Staat der nationalen Demokratie* (Cologne: Verlag Wissenschaft und Politik, 1964).

139 "For the Unity and Solidarity of the International Communist Movement," *Pravda*, December 6, 1963, quoted from *CDSP*, Vol. XV, No. 47 (December 18, 1963), pp. 15–19, at p. 17. See C. Duevel, "Moscow on the Defensive," Radio Liberty, Munich, December 11, 1963.

He prescribed only one condition:

> Socialism cannot be built on positions of anticommunism, opposing the countries in which socialism has won the victory and persecuting the Communists.[140]

That is, to "build socialism" (and get Soviet support) a radical nationalist regime must ally itself with the Soviet Union, and, although it may ban the existence of a communist party, it must not imprison or persecute individual Communists but rather must allow them to participate in the ruling élite. Khrushchev hoped that these regimes would thereafter pass through "noncapitalist development" to the "construction of socialism" and eventually to a "people's democracy," perhaps even, as Cuba had, by the élite itself declaring that it was "Marxist-Leninist."

In practice one of the best examples of the extension of this principle into political life was the changing nature of Soviet policy toward Algeria. The Soviet view of the Algerian governing party, the FLN, had been becoming more favorable since late 1962 as the FLN had moved to the left and as Khrushchev's policy of improving relations with radical nationalist movements had gotten under way.[141] Moscow stopped classifying the FLN leadership as "national bourgeois," individual Algerian Communists gained influence within the FLN *apparat,* and Soviet aid to Algeria increased. By the spring of 1964, when Ben Bella arrived in Moscow on a state visit, Algeria had become the most favored Soviet example of a radical nationalist movement in power. The final communiqué referred to Ben Bella, to whom Khrushchev awarded the title "Hero of the Soviet Union," as "Comrade" and announced the establishment of "fraternal relations between the CPSU and the FLN." Shortly thereafter a "prominent Algerian Marxist" (that is, Communist), Bashir Hajj Ali, declared in a statement [142] later endorsed by Moscow [143] that the FLN, a "vanguard party," had been built "in the course of the revolution launched by the proletariat of town and country" rather than having "preceded the revolution" (that is, as the Algerian Communist Party had). Moreover, although the FLN's "socialist road" did not involve "the adoption of Marxist

---

140 "Replies of N. S. Khrushchev to Questions of Editors of *Ghanaian Times, Alger Républicain, Le Peuple,* and *Botataung," Pravda* and *Izvestiya,* December 22, 1963, quoted from *CDSP,* Vol. XV, No. 51 (January 15, 1964), pp. 11–16, at p. 13. See Ra'anan, "Moscow and the 'Third World,'" *op. cit.,* pp. 22–31, which outlines similar but less explicit early 1963 developments.

141 See "Algeria: A 'Fruitful Dialogue,'" *The Mizan News Letter,* Vol. 6, No. 2 (February 1964), pp. 1–7 (with full bibliography) and Löwenthal, "Haltung," pp. 10–11. See also Griffith, "Africa," *op. cit.,* pp. 183–185.

142 *L'Unità,* June 30, 1964.

143 By being reprinted in the *World Marxist Review* supplement, *Information Bulletin,* No. 16, August 18, 1964, pp. 18–22.

philosophical principles as a whole," it was advancing toward socialism by creating the objective conditions for socialist construction. Finally, he had remarkably favorable words for Islam (which in fact the recent FLN congress,[144] in a move generally interpreted as a shift away from Marxism, had strongly endorsed), declared that " the Algerian masses are marching to socialism with the Koran in one hand and *Capital* in the other," and concluded by proclaiming that "Algeria will be the center of revolutionary radiance in Africa, in the Maghreb, and all over the Arab world." Clearly the Algerian Communist Party and the Soviets hoped that the FLN could be infiltrated from within and influenced by Moscow from without, with the eventual aim of having Ben Bella declare himself a " Marxist-Leninist." [145]

Since the spring of 1963, however, there had been signs of differences of opinion within the Soviet leadership on policy toward underdeveloped areas, centering on how favorable an attitude to take toward such " revolutionary democratic " leaders as Ben Bella and Nasser and on the extent to which the wishes of Middle Eastern Communists should be subordinated thereto. Particularly after his May 1964 visit to Cairo, Khrushchev increasingly adopted the priority for the radical nationalist leaders evident in the views of a group of young intellectuals in the Moscow Institute for World Economy and International Affairs, while Suslov, Ponomarev, and those responsible for dealing with communist parties tended to support the communist parties in those countries.[146]

---

[144] Which, however, the *L'Unità* interviewer referred to as " keynoted by ideas of scientific socialism."

[145] Another, if less clear-cut, example may be seen in Soviet policy toward the UAR. Detailed accounts of Nasser's relations with the communist world include Wolfgang Berner, " Nasser und die Kommunisten," *Europa Archiv*, Vol. 20, No. 15 (August 10, 1965), pp. 569–578; Reinhard Kapferer, " Nassers Schwierigkeiten mit ' positiven Neutralismus ' und ' arabischen Sozialismus,' " *ibid.*, Vol. 19, No. 20 (October 25, 1965), pp. 759–766; and Peter Meyer-Ranke, " Nasser am Tor des sozialistischen Lagers," *Aussenpolitik*, Vol. 16, No. 3 (March 1965), pp. 153–162. For the general Soviet rapprochement with the Arab world, and controversies among Soviet and Arab Communists concerning it, see Ra'anan, " Moscow and the ' Third World,' " *op. cit.*, and " The Union Between the Forces of Socialism and the National Liberation Movement," *Kommunist*, No. 8, May 1964, pp. 3–10; also " The USSR and the Middle East Arab States in 1965," *Mizan*, Vol. 7, No. 4 (April 1965), pp. 1–13 (with bibliographic citations).

[146] For a penetrating and detailed analysis, with bibliographic citations, particularly from the Institute's journal *Mirovaya Ekonomika i Mezhdunarodnyie Otnosheniya*, see Ra'anan, " Moscow and the ' Third World,' " *op. cit.* See also " New Thoughts on the New States," *The Mizan News Letter*, Vol. 6, No. 6 (June 1964), pp. 1–7; " Soviet Reappraisal," *ibid.*, Vol. 6, No. 8 (September 1964), pp. 1–9; " Khrushchev and the Developing Countries," *ibid.*, Vol. 6, No. 9 (October 1964), pp. 1–5. The same eclectic position was increasingly taken toward European social democracy. See A. Chernyayev, " Communists and Socialists: Prospects for Cooperation," *Kommunist*, No. 7, May 1964, pp. 107–118. For the explicitly anti-CCP aspects of the Khrushchev position see Fuad Nassar and Aziz al-Hajj, "The National Liberation Movement and the World Revolutionary Process," *World Marxist Review*, Vol. 7, No. 3 (March 1964), pp. 9–15, and W. Sheppard, " The One-Party System and Democracy in Africa," *ibid.*, pp. 86–90. For a summary, with quotations, of

In part as a consequence of these differences within the Soviet leadership, Moscow's maneuvering within the "third world" was tempered by caution. Khrushchev's early January 1964 proposal for the renunciation of force in territorial disputes, which was probably in considerable part aimed at making Sino-Soviet border incidents less likely and at forestalling Peking's claims to Soviet territory,[147] also may well have been intended to limit Moscow's risk that its aid to national liberation movements might result in dangerous military escalation arising from border conflicts.

This Soviet caution was clearly indicated in Moscow's reaction to the 1964 "rebellion" in the Congo. Largely tribal in character, the Congo uprising furthered social dislocation and economic decline. The leadership was mediocre and often pathological, and it was lacking in both strategy and sufficient external support. Although the rebellion became more antiliteracy and racist as it developed, it was never ideological in character or centrally directed. The Soviets, restrained by the memories of their failures in Guinea in 1959 and in the Congo in 1960, might well have continued their initial reserve toward it had not Peking supported the rebel leaders Mulele, Gbenye, and Soumaliot from its enclaves of influence in Bujumbura, Brazzaville, and elsewhere. Thereupon the Soviets could no longer resist both opportunity and Chinese competition. Even so, they carefully did not commit themselves openly or completely to the "rebellion": They sent arms via Algiers and Cairo, and when Tshombe crushed the rebellion with African white mercenaries, American airplanes, and exiled Cuban pilots, they quietly ended their support. Meanwhile, although the Chinese had been thrown out of Bujumbura and were meeting increased Soviet competition in Brazzaville, rising unrest in Tanzania and Uganda continued to tempt Peking.[148]

Moreover, in the underdeveloped world the Soviets faced competition stemming from the increasingly differentiated activities of other at least tacitly pro-Soviet communist parties. Such activity, made possible by their increasing autonomy from Moscow, was particularly characteristic of the Italian and Cuban parties. Cuba focused on trips by Guevara and others that were intended to mobilize support against Washington and to propagate the Cuban model of national liberation struggle, while the PCI was active particularly in North Africa, where

Khrushchev's visit to the UAR, see *The Mizan News Letter*, Vol. 6, No. 5 (May 1964), pp. 57–66.
[147] Khrushchev in *Pravda*, January 4, 1964; see also "Why Mislead?" *ibid.*, January 30, 1964. The Chinese press did not mention Khrushchev's proposal (Doolin, *op. cit.*, p. 20).
[148] See especially M. Crawford Young, "The Congo Rebellion," *Africa Report*, Vol. X, No. 4 (April 1965), pp. 6–11, and Russell Warren Howe, "The Eastern Congo's Phony Rebellion," *The Reporter*, March 11, 1965, pp. 35–36.

its relations with the FLN were especially close,[149] and also in Asia and Latin America. As Togliatti's Testament clearly showed, the PCI's autonomist attitude with respect to international Communist unity *inter alia* extended that concept to include such revolutionary national liberation movements as the FLN; that is, the PCI abandoned the requirement for unity composed exclusively of communist parties for a larger one including revolutionary movements of all kinds. The PCI was clearly sympathetic to Khrushchev's views, and Togliatti in his Testament went out of his way to endorse them. (In fact, so did the Chinese—another illustration of how organizational autonomists relativize ideology from no matter what substantive position.) [150]

Organizational Rivalries

Sino-Soviet organizational rivalries in the underdeveloped world centered around the Afro-Asian Peoples' Solidarity Organization and the preparations for the Second Afro-Asian Conference (" Second Bandung "). Peking continued its efforts to set up and develop new Afro-Asian organizations from which Moscow would be excluded. The 1963–65 negotiations on the Second Afro-Asian Conference threw light on all aspects of Soviet and Chinese policies toward the " third world " and on the Sino-Soviet conflict with respect to it. Exhaustive treatment of this problem is impossible within the space limits of this study; it can be only briefly summarized.

Given the general course of the Sino-Soviet dispute and the diverging policies and increasing rivalry of both Moscow and Peking vis-à-vis the underdeveloped world, plus the increasing disunity of the latter, it was inevitable that the question of a second Bandung conference would become at once one of the points of polarization not only for Sino-Soviet relations but for rivalries within the underdeveloped world as well. This was the more true because of the effect of the Chinese attack on India in October 1962 and because of the increasingly radical Indonesian domestic and foreign policy.

The Indian defeat in October 1962 and the Soviet successes vis-à-vis China on the nuclear test ban treaty issue made a Second Afro-Asian Conference attractive to China as a forum within which Peking could move further against India and intensify its rapprochement with Pakistan; counteract the warlike image given China by its opposition to the test ban treaty; further cement its alliance with Indonesia, which had always wanted another Bandung conference to enhance its own role and to lower India's; openly humiliate the Soviet Union by success-

---

149 See especially Luigi Longo, " La rivoluzione algerina verso il socialismo," *Rinascita*, Vol. XXI, No. 4 (January 25, 1964), pp. 12–13 (the " vanguard " FLN " constructing socialism ").
150 Yugoslav activity became less significant as CPSU-LCY rapprochement intensified.

fully excluding it from the conference; and in general move as much of the Afro-Asian world as possible (that is, the " New Emerging Forces "—NEFO's) toward a more radical course like Indonesia's Furthermore, with a second nonaligned conference scheduled for 1964, from which China and Pakistan were excluded, both wanted another Afro-Asian gathering even more.

The Soviet Union did not want the Afro-Asian conference to meet unless it could participate. India's lack of enthusiasm was due to its fear that its decreased prestige would become more evident, that it would be forced into taking a more extreme position than its fundamental policy of maintaining good relations with Washington and Moscow would justify, and that the conference would help its three major enemies—Pakistan, China, and Indonesia. Rather than have any of these dangers occur, it preferred to have the conference not meet at all and hoped it would fail if it did.

China lobbied strongly (notably by Chou's 1964 trip to Africa) for convening the conference, and Indonesia and Pakistan did the same. Even so, the April 1964 Jakarta preparatory meeting was attended by only twenty-one nations (Japan, for example, refused to come), and India and the U.A.R. tried hard to postpone the conference indefinitely.[151]

As it turned out, India agreed on April 1965 as a date, but in return it was able to have the site moved to Africa, thus depriving Sukarno of having it again in Indonesia and thereby dramatizing his NEFO concept as opposed to the United Nations. Moreover, in a move that eventually torpedoed the conference, it proposed that the Soviet Union and Malaysia be invited. China adamantly refused to accept the former, and Indonesia the latter, as India had calculated. (Pakistan tried to be neutral on both invitations.) In particular, although the majority of participants would probably have accepted Soviet participation, Indonesia and China had succeeded in having the principle of " unanimity through consultation " adopted, and China, by threatening to walk out, was able to postpone the question of Soviet admission—indefinitely Peking insisted, but, as it turned out and as the Indians had maintained, until the plenary meeting.[152]

[151] For Soviet exclusion at Jakarta, see Chung Ho, " Triumph of the Bandung Spirit," and the Djarkarta communiqué, *Peking Review*, Vol. VII, No. 17 (April 24, 1964), pp. 5–7. For Sino-Soviet exchanges see the Soviet April 24 government statement (to the CPR) on the Jakarta meeting, *Pravda*, May 5, 1964; a May 30 CPR statement, *Peking Review*, Vol. VII, No. 23 (June 5, 1964), pp. 6–8, with accompanying *Pravda* and *Jen-min Jih-pao* editorials; " Splitters' Maneuvers," *Pravda*, July 11, 1964; and " In Whose Interests? " (re the Pyongyang Second Asian Economic Seminar), *ibid.*, August 18, 1964. For background see W. A. C. Adie, " China and the Bandung Genie," *Current Scene*, Vol. III, No. 19 (May 15, 1965).

[152] For the above see particularly the penetrating study by Franklin B. Weinstein, " The Second Asian-African Conference: Preliminary Bouts," *Asian Survey*, Vol. V, No. 7 (July 1965), pp. 359–373; for background, Adie, " China and the Bandung Genie," *op. cit.*

Ben Bella succeeded in having Algiers designated as the meeting place, and, in part because of slowness in constructing a lavish site for the meeting, it was postponed first until May and then until June 1965. By June 1964, however, at another preparatory meeting in Geneva, the question of Soviet participation was still clearly the major divisive point. Shortly thereafter Khrushchev apparently decided that, since it was uncertain whether or not enough nonaligned nations would push Soviet participation through at the risk of a Chinese boycott, it would be more prudent for Moscow " voluntarily " to withdraw. (This decision also reflected his general desire to concentrate on radical nationalist movements favorable to him as well as on a détente with the United States; another aspect of this was his disengagement from Southeast Asia.)

IV. THE AFTERMATH OF KHRUSHCHEV'S FALL

Khrushchev was removed as First Secretary and Chairman of the Council of Ministers on October 14 by the CPSU Central Committee as a result of a conspiracy carried through against him by his designated successors, Brezhnev and Kosygin. That he did not " resign," as the official announcement indicated, because of age and ill health is certain; the probable cause of his fall must be deduced from what material is available.

The primary causes for Khrushchev's fall, in my view, were internal and bureaucratic in character: the crisis in the Soviet economy and agriculture, and his apparent determination to attempt to surmount them and to increase his personal power by going over the heads of the Presidium and the Central Committee to acquire support from élite public opinion.[153] Foreign policy issues probably played some role in Khrushchev's fall, although, in my view, not a decisive and probably not even a major one. Press reports from Moscow indicated [154] that

---

[153] See Zbigniew Brzezinski, " Victory of the Clerks," *The New Republic*, Vol. CLI, No. 20 (November 14, 1964), pp. 15–18; Robert Conquest, *Russia after Khrushchev* (New York and London: Praeger, 1965), pp. 109–123; Myron Rush, *Political Succession in the USSR* (New York and London: Columbia University Press, 1965), pp. 208–214; Richard Löwenthal, " The Revolution Withers Away," *Problems of Communism*, Vol. XIV, No. 1 (January–February 1965), pp. 10–16, and comments in the two subsequent issues; Peter Reddaway, " The Fall of Khrushchev," *Survey*, No. 56 (July 1965), pp. 11–30; a series of articles in *Osteuropa*, Vol. XIV, No. 11 (November 1964), pp. 777–813 (by Richard Löwenthal, David Burg, and Herman Achminow), and Vol. XIV, No. 12 (December 1964), pp. 877–902 (by Günther Wagenlehner and Erich F. Pruck); and especially a series in *Osteuropa* by Boris Meissner, " Chruschtschowismus ohne Chruschtschow," Vol. XV, No. 1/2 (January–February 1965), pp. 1–15, Vol. XV, No. 3 (March 1965), pp. 138–165, and Vol. XV, No. 4 (April 1965), pp. 217–227.

[154] See the obviously inspired press agency dispatches from Moscow in *The Times* (London), *Le Monde*, and *Neue Zürcher Zeitung*, October 31, 1964. The most detailed account of the " 29 points " was in a Moscow dispatch in *Paese Sera* (Rome), October 30, 1964; as to their doubtful authenticity, see a denial by Pancaldi from Moscow in *L'Unità*, October 30 and 31, 1964 (JPRS 27,590, November 30, 1964).

Khrushchev's intention to attempt a rapprochement with Bonn was probably one of the more important foreign policy issues. At any rate it was the position his successors most rapidly and completely reversed. Khrushchev's failure either to force the Chinese to retreat or to mobilize effective collective action against them was, as has been shown earlier, sufficiently clear to have made this an obvious charge against him, and press reports indicate it may well have been so used. Nevertheless, all available evidence and the course of Sino-Soviet relations thereafter indicate that Khrushchev's successors at most objected to some of his tactics against Peking but shared with him a refusal to agree to the fundamental Soviet capitulation that Peking demanded.

There had been particularly violent Chinese attacks on Khrushchev in August [155] and October [156] for allegedly " creating border incidents " and " harboring wild ambitions " with respect to Sinkiang. On October 1, Saifudin, the Chairman of the Sinkiang Uighur Autonomous Region, even went so far as to declare that

> If the Khrushchev revisionists dare to stretch out their evil hands to invade and occupy our territory, they will certainly be repulsed. . . . Their evil hands will be cut off as relentlessly as were those of the Indian reactionaries when they invaded China.[157]

The Strategy of the Post-Khrushchev Leadership

The overthrow or death of a dictator is usually followed by a struggle for power; and even though there are as yet few clear signs of such a struggle among Khrushchev's successors, it is probably under way. The current Soviet leaders not only have been preoccupied with the serious domestic economic and agricultural situation but also, like any collective leadership, are less capable than a dictator of pursuing a clear-cut, decisive course. Consequently, and since Moscow's relations with Washington were at the time of Khrushchev's ouster still relatively smooth, the Soviets tried at once for a partial détente in the Sino-Soviet crisis.

Yet their maximum objective can hardly have been anything like a Sino-Soviet reconciliation. Peking had demanded total capitulation from Khrushchev. Khrushchev had fallen. However, the new Soviet leaders were anxious to gain domestic popularity, which they could get only by further liberalization at home and détente abroad: exactly the

---

[155] Irhali, chairman of the Ili Kazakh autonomous *chou*, on August 26–29, 1964, in *Peking Review*, Vol. VII, No. 37 (September 11, 1964), pp. 5 and 26 (excerpts in Doolin, *op. cit.*, pp. 65–66, Document 24).

[156] Radio Urumchi, October 1, 1964, in Doolin, *op. cit.*, pp. 75–76, Document 29.

[157] *Ibid.*, p. 76. I do not, however, share the view of some scholars that this indicates that Khrushchev was preparing to either invade Sinkiang or bomb the Chinese atomic facilities there and was therefore removed by his associates; there does not seem to me, at least as yet, to be sufficient evidence to make this conjecture probable.

opposite of the Chinese demands. The Central Committee resolution announcing Khrushchev's " resignation " had reaffirmed the validity of the Twentieth and Twenty-Second CPSU Congresses, thus automatically cutting off any possibility of total agreement with Peking. Moreover, with Khrushchev gone, Mao aware of the lack of authority of his successors, and Peking having exploded its first nuclear device, the new leaders could hardly expect that the Chinese would soften their attitude toward the Soviets.

What the new Moscow leadership wanted from the Chinese was much less: cessation of polemics, détente in Sino-Soviet relations, the containment if not decline of Sino-Soviet competition throughout the world, cooperation on such foreign policy issues as Vietnam—an agreement to disagree and a pragmatic armistice. To obtain these ends, the new Soviet leaders appeared ready to resume extensive economic and technical assistance to China, and, unlike Khrushchev, to postpone indefinitely the scheduled international Communist conference.

The reaction to Khrushchev's removal among hitherto pro-Soviet parties, with the exception of the French and Bulgarian, had been far from satisfactory from the Soviet viewpoint. Even the East Germans and the Czechs, as well as the Poles, Hungarians, Yugoslavs, and Italians, had expressed praise for Khrushchev's merits, thus going contrary to Moscow's indirect criticism of him; and only after they had sent delegations to Moscow for " explanations " did they, with the exception of the Italians, endorse Khrushchev's replacement. The Italians defiantly reasserted their criticism, including criticism of other Soviet internal policies. The Austrian Communist Party did the same, although with more reserve. The Rumanians, on the other hand, gave only minimal notice to the fall of their hated enemy.[158] Soviet authority and influence had clearly been dealt another blow, one that did not escape notice by the Chinese.

Post-Khrushchev Chinese Aims

These were, if possible, more extreme than before. The fall of their chief opponent, which they had long demanded and predicted, had

[158] Marchais and Waldeck-Rochet in *L'Humanité*, November 9, 1964 (JPRS 27,590, November 30, 1964); *Neues Deutschland*, October 18, 1964; *Rudé Právo*, October 20, 1964, and Frankel from Prague in *The New York Times*, November 1, 1964; *Trybuna Ludu*, October 29, 1964, and Frankel from Warsaw, *The New York Times*, November 8, 1964; *Népszabadság*, October 25, 1964; *L'Espresso*, November 15, 1964; interview with Berlinguer, *Der Spiegel* (Hamburg), November 11, 1964, statement by Berlinguer upon his return from Moscow, *ibid.*, November 4, 1964, and his press conference, *Avanti!*, November 4, 1964 (all in JPRS 27,590, November 30, 1964); Fürneberg to the Austrian Communist Party Central Committee, *Volksstimme* (Vienna), November 6, 1964 (JPRS 27,590, November 30, 1964); Bucharest dispatches [by Dessa Bourne] in *The Times* (London), November 14 and 16, 1964; and for a roundup of reactions, Salisbury in *The New York Times*, October 21, 1964. See also *Osteuropa*, Vol. XV, No. 4 (April 1965), pp. 228–240, for PCF, PZPR, and Rumanian Communist Party reactions.

finally occurred, largely, Mao probably thought, because of Chinese pressure. And on that same day they had exploded their first nuclear device [159] in spite of Moscow's having cut off all nuclear, military, and economic aid. Chinese influence had been steadily rising as Soviet influence steadily declined. Was this trend now not likely to accelerate still further? Finally, Chinese success had been accompanied by, and in large part, as Peking must have been convinced, caused by, the flat refusal of Peking to yield an inch.

Having succeeded in delaying for some time the international conference, was it not now likely that if they continued on the same course, partially concealed by apparently conciliatory moves, the conference would be postponed still further, perhaps canceled, thus further increasing Chinese and decreasing Soviet prestige? Moreover, Peking also had to pay attention to its allies, many of whom (the Japanese Communists, for example, as well as the Albanians) had exposed themselves greatly vis-à-vis the Soviets. Any sign of Chinese concessions to the Soviets would have imperiled Peking's support within the international Communist movement and made it the more difficult to reactivate its alliances when and if—and most likely when—Sino-Soviet relations worsened again. It would have been surprising if Mao had changed his tactics after such a victory; and, as it soon became clear, he had not.

Not that Peking wished to appear totally inflexible; it wanted to improve, or at least not worsen, its relations with parties such as the Rumanian that were opposed to an international conference for their own reasons and wanted a decline in Sino-Soviet hostility. (The signs of disquiet in East Europe over Khrushchev's fall made this consideration even more attractive.) But, as the previous period had demonstrated, it had been the Soviets rather than the Chinese who felt compelled to move toward a formal international split in order to cut their losses. Peking could therefore safely afford to return to its former tactic of *suaviter in modo, fortiter in re*: to respond with formal politeness to any Soviet overtures but to reassure its supporters and ensure the revival of Soviet hostility by continuing its refusal to make any substantive concessions.

Chou En-lai in Moscow and Late 1964–Early 1965 Developments

Direct Soviet polemics against the Chinese ceased with Khrushchev's fall and Peking also ceased explicit polemics against the Soviets. Whether this was a unilateral Soviet initiative reciprocated by the Chinese or whether it was accompanied by some formal exchange of

---

159 CPR statement, October 16, 1964 in *Jen-min Jih-pao*, October 17, 1964, and *Peking Review*, Vol. VII, No. 42 (October 16, 1964), pp. ii–iii; see "The Savior of Mankind," *China News Analysis*, No. 538 (October 23, 1965), pp. 1–3.

letters between Moscow and Peking we do not know. The former seems more likely. Moreover, the new Soviet leadership hinted that it might modify its attitude on the international conference and on Soviet economic aid to China.[160] Moscow invited a high-level Chinese delegation to the October Revolution celebrations in Moscow, and on November 6 Peking sent Chou En-lai, Ho Lung (another Politburo member), and among others, K'ang Sheng and Wu Hsiu-ch'üan, both participants in the July 1963 Sino-Soviet bilateral discussions. That Moscow also invited a Yugoslav government and party delegation but not an Albanian representative, and that it invited Yoshio Shiga, the head of the pro-Soviet Japanese Communist group,[161] was a clear sign that no decisive Soviet concessions were in the offing. Conversely, Albania began attacking Khrushchev's successors soon after he was removed, a move that Peking may not have initiated but one that must not have been totally unwelcome to the Chinese; and the late October 1964 Budapest WFTU meeting saw the Chinese as adamant as ever.[162]

The celebrations demonstrated that Sino-Soviet substantive differences remained as great as ever. Brezhnev's November 6 speech amounted to a complete rejection of the Chinese views. He emphasized the production of consumer goods over heavy industry; he lifted restrictions on collective farmers' private plots; he reaffirmed the validity of the 20th CPSU Congress. He reiterated the Soviet line of peaceful coexistence; he specifically endorsed the partial test ban treaty, the CPSU Party Program, and the "state of the whole people"; and he listed Yugoslavia as a socialist country. He appealed to the Chinese only to improve interstate relations and to tolerate differences in methods of socialist construction, with effectiveness being the test of correctness. (This was substantially the June 15, 1964 Soviet position.) Brezhnev's most hostile statement, from Peking's viewpoint, must have been his declaration that the time was "obviously ripe" for an international Communist conference to serve "cohesion" and "unity." [163]

---

[160] ". . . duty . . . of wide cooperation in all spheres of economic . . . life . . . an international conference of *all* communist parties [my italics—W.E.G.]," in "Unshakeable Leninist General Line of the CPSU," *Pravda*, October 17, 1964, quoted from *CDSP*, Vol. XVI, No. 40 (October 28, 1964), pp. 3 and 6, at p. 6.

[161] *China News Analysis*, No. 542 (November 27, 1964), p. 2.

[162] Spiro Koleka in *Zëri i Popullit*, October 23, 1964; "The Fall of Khrushchev Did Not Entail the Disappearance of Khrushchevian Revisionism," *ibid.*, November 1, 1964; and "Let Us Raise High the Victorious Banner of the Ideas of the Great October," *ibid.*, November 7, 1964.

[163] *Pravda*, November 7, 1964, quoted from *CDSP*, Vol. XVI, No. 43 (November 18, 1964), pp. 3–9. The conference call was repeated in "In the Vanguard of the Struggle for Communism and Peace," *Pravda*, November 10, 1964. The first post-Khrushchev reaffirmation of Soviet support for a conference of "all" communist parties was much more general and made no reference to timing. See "Soviet Progress Reviewed on the Eve of the 47th October Revolution Anniversary," *Kommunist*, No. 15, October 1964 (passed for the press October 26, 1964), pp. 3–9 (JPRS 27,466, November 20, 1964).

The Soviet plan, then, was to improve Sino-Soviet state relations on a pragmatic basis. To this end the October Revolution slogans were somewhat more anti-American,[164] and there were some earlier indications that Moscow might be willing to make minor concessions to Chinese views about strategy toward the United States.[165]

The Chinese response was substantively at least as negative as before Khrushchev's fall. Although Peking's October Revolution anniversary message to Moscow was cordial,[166] and the Chinese reprinted some *Pravda* editorials and Brezhnev's speech, P'eng Chen's October Revolution speech and the November 7 *Jen-min Jih-pao* editorial repeated, firmly albeit politely, the major Chinese theses: revolutionary violence, dictatorship of the proletariat (that is, no " state of the whole people "), " unanimity through consultation " in the international Communist movement (that is, Chinese factionalism), a violent anti-United States policy, 13 socialist states (that is, not including Yugoslavia), modern revisionism as the " main danger," and the Chou Yang thesis of the inevitability of splits within individual parties.[167]

Compared to this restatement, the reference to " temporary " Sino-Soviet difficulties that could be " gradually dissolved " was not so significant. Finally, the editorial declared that " Khrushchev revisionism " would be " spurned by the people . . . in the past, . . . in the present, . . . and in the future "—a clear warning to Brezhnev and Kosygin.[168] Moreover, even before November 7, Albanian, West European, and Asian pro-Chinese parties and groups were already denouncing Khrushchev's successors.[169]

Chou En-lai made his continued disapproval of Soviet policies publicly clear in Moscow. When Brezhnev welcomed the Yugoslav delegation, he alone did not applaud,[170] and he laid a wreath on Stalin's tomb as he had in 1961. On November 13 there was a formal meeting

---

164 *Pravda*, October 18, 1964. They did not refer to the partial test ban treaty or to international détente.)

165 For example, the Soviet-Cuban communiqué of October 18 (*ibid.*, October 19, 1964), which listed the anti-imperialist struggle before the reinforcement of peace. (See Michel Tatu, " La politique soviétique sans M. Khrouchtchev, II. Vers une reprise de contact avec la Chine?" *Le Monde*, November 4, 1964.) The same was true of " Foreign Policy and the Contemporary World," *Kommunist*, No. 3, February 1965 (passed for the press February 22, 1965), pp. 3–14, but it also reaffirmed (in italics) a view Peking rejected, that "The question of peace has been and remains the overriding issue of all contemporary life."

166 *Jen-min Jih-pao*, November 7, 1964 (SCMP, 3335, November 12, 1964, pp. 27–28).

167 For the Chinese position see j.c.k. [Joseph C. Kun), " The Pros and Cons of Reconciliation," Radio Free Europe, Munich, November 9, 1964, and *China News Analysis*, No. 542 (November 27, 1964), pp. 2–3.

168 *Jen-min Jih-pao*, November 7, 1964, quoted from *Peking Review*, Vol. VII, No. 46 (November 13, 1964), pp. 14–17.

169 See Kevin Devlin, " Pro-Chinese Factions Intensify Struggles," Radio Free Europe, Munich, November 19, 1964.

170 Radio Belgrade in Serbo-Croat, November 6, 1964, 1830 GMT.

between the Soviets and Chinese to which the Soviet communiqué referred as "frank" and "comradely" but to which the Peking communiqué did not deign to apply any adjective at all.[171] Chou later said [172] that he had unsuccessfully tried to get the Soviets to abandon the conference project, but he had succeeded only in getting it postponed. Still later Peking declared that the new Soviet leadership then

> told the members of the Chinese Party and Government Delegation to their faces that there was not a shade of difference between themselves and Khrushchev on the question of the international communist movement or of relations with China.[173]

On November 13 the rising Albanian hostility was again evidenced by the publication, allegedly postponed since mid-October, of a long Tirana attack on the Italian Communist Party. It was mainly devoted to outlining and rejoicing over the differences between the Soviet and the Italian "revisionists." More significant for Sino-Soviet relations was its flat statement that "the present Soviet leadership . . . resolutely pursues the revisionist line of the 20th, 21st, and 22nd CPSU Congresses" and its call for "defending, . . . helping, . . . and . . . supporting unreservedly . . . new parties and Marxist-Leninist revolutionary groups"—that is, the intensification of pro-Chinese factional activity.[174]

On November 21, with the publication of an exultant and defiant *Hung Ch'i* editorial, "Why Khrushchev Fell," the Chinese position was once again in the open. Peking maintained that Khrushchev's fall, which was inevitable because of his "revisionist general line," had been long foreseen. In twelve points the editorial summed up and rejected the totality of Soviet foreign and domestic policies and all of the Soviet moves against Peking. The article concluded with a barely veiled warning to the new Soviet leaders:

> The course of history will continue to be tortuous. Although Khrushchev has fallen, his supporters—the U.S. imperialists, the reactionaries and the modern revisionists—will not resign themselves to this failure. These hobgoblins are continuing to pray for Khrushchev and are trying to "resurrect" him with their incantations, vociferously proclaiming his "contributions" and "meritorious deeds" in the hope that events will develop along the lines prescribed by Khrushchev, so that "Khrush-

---

[171] *Pravda*, November 14, 1964; *Peking Review*, Vol. VII, No. 47 (November 20, 1964), pp. 5–6 (SCMP 3393, November 18, 1964, p. 39).

[172] In an interview with K. S. Karol in Peking in late March 1965 (*The New Statesman*, March 26, 1965).

[173] "Refutation of the New Leaders of the CPSU on 'United Action,'" *Jen-min Jih-pao* and *Hung Ch'i*, November 11, 1965, quoted from *Peking Review*, Vol. VIII, No. 46 (November 12, 1965), pp. 10–21, at p. 12.

[174] "The Testament of P. Togliatti, the Crisis of Modern Revisionism, and the Struggle of Marxists-Leninists," *Zëri i Popullit*, November 13, 1964. Not reprinted by the Chinese; see Griffith, *Communism in Europe, op. cit.*, Vol. 2, Appendix to Chapter 1.

chevism without Khrushchev " may prevail. It can be asserted categorically that theirs is a blind alley.

Different ideological trends and their representatives invariably strive
to take the stage and perform. It is entirely up to them to decide which
direction they will take.[175]

This defiant Chinese article may well have encouraged the new
Soviet leadership to dispatch on November 24, 1964, a circular letter
summoning the postponed drafting committee meeting for March 1,
1965. Not surprisingly, China and her allies again immediately refused
to attend,[176] for the Soviet letter, although conciliatory in tone, in fact
marked the Soviet decision to resume—under far less favorable conditions—its " collective mobilization " against the Chinese.[177]

Simultaneously *Jen-min Jih-pao* began reprinting comments on
Khrushchev's fall by pro-Soviet and pro-Chinese parties, among them
a violent November 1 Albanian editorial entitled " Khrushchev's Fall
Did Not Entail the Disappearance of Khrushchevian Revisionism,"[178]
and a declaration by PKI leader Aidit that Khrushchev's removal was
not " the end of the struggle to smash modern revisionism " and that
Moscow should amend the 20th, 21st, and 22nd Congress resolutions.[179]

In January 1965 Mao told Edgar Snow that there was " possibly
some but not much . . . improvement in Sino-Soviet relations."[180]
Then by late January, Peking was reprinting much more bitter anti-
Soviet articles, for example, a Japanese Communist attack denouncing
the new Soviet leadership for " disruptive activities " within the Japanese
party [181] and an Albanian one specifically calling for an end to the truce
in explicit Sino-Soviet polemics, which, allegedly, " the present revisionist Soviet leadership " were only using to " restore all the links
and agreements maintained by Khrushchev with the imperialists."[182]

175 " Why Khrushchev Fell," *Hung Ch'i*, Nos. 21/22, November 21, 1964, quoted from
Peking Review, Vol. VII, No. 48 (November 27, 1964), pp. 6–9. The reference to
" contributions " is to East European Communist leaders' statements about
Khrushchev, but it implied that the new Soviet leadership took the same view. For
analysis see *China News Analysis*, No. 542 (November 27, 1964), pp. 3–7.
176 See, for example, the December 1 PKI refusal in *Peking Review*, Vol. VII, No. 52
(December 25, 1964), pp. 17–18.
177 *Pravda*, December 12, 1964, quoted from *Peking Review*, Vol. VIII, No. 13 (March
26, 1965), pp. 21–22. The letter also contained the information that China, North
Korea, North Vietnam, and Albania had previously refused to participate in any
international meeting, that the Japanese and Indonesian parties had " requested
further information " (and, in fact, did not participate), and that Rumania refused
to participate unless all others did—that is, in fact refused. See also the implicitly
anti-Chinese " The State of the Whole People," *Pravda*, December 6, 1964.
178 *Zëri i Popullit*, November 1, 1964. See also j.c.k. [Joseph C. Kun], " Khrushchev's
Fall—As Seen From Peking," Radio Free Europe, Munich, November 21, 1964.
179 *Peking Review*, Vol. VII, No. 48 (November 27, 1964), pp. 18–19.
180 *The New Republic*, Vol. CLII, No. 9 (February 27, 1965), p. 17–23, at p. 21.
181 " On a Series of New Attacks on Our Party by Prokharov and Others," *Akahata*,
December 28, 1964, reprinted in *Jen-min Jih-pao*, January 20, 1964.
182 " Revolutionary Marxism Will Triumph in Europe," *Zëri i Popullit*, January 6, 1965,
reprinted in *Jen-min Jih-pao*, January 21, 1965.

Peking also renewed its attacks on India [183] and publicized extensively the first congress of the pro-Chinese Indian Communist Party.[184]

Moreover (as Tirana made public in early February), Poland, at the beginning of January, presumably on Moscow's behalf, had invited Albania to the January 19–20 Warsaw meeting of the Warsaw Pact Political Consultative Committee. The Albanian reply was a long violent demand for a total and humiliating Soviet capitulation as the price of its attendance, by far the most extreme Albanian demand ever made on Moscow. Not only did the Albanians demand that the Soviets publicly renounce their Albanian policy and make economic and military reparations to Tirana but they also insisted on the end of Soviet military aid to Yugoslavia and India, the immediate signature of a separate peace treaty with East Germany, the immediate denunciation of the partial nuclear test ban treaty by Moscow and all other Warsaw Pact members, and a collective commitment that all socialist countries would receive nuclear weapons (presumably given by Moscow) " as a countermeasure " [185] if West Germany were admitted to the MLF or otherwise got nuclear arms. One wonders if all this was Chinese-inspired; perhaps, given the fact that Peking did not reprint any of these articles, the Albanians were trying to overcommit Peking. This was the second time Moscow had reluctantly made an overture to the Albanians, and the second time Tirana had violently rejected it.[186]

V. THE RETURN TO NEUTRALITY IN HANOI AND PYONGYANG

North Vietnam

From March 1963 until Khrushchev's fall in October 1964 North Vietnam, previously neutral in Sino-Soviet relations, had been moving closer to the Chinese position.[187] Just before the fall of Khrushchev its statements reached hitherto unparalleled pro-Chinese heights.

---

[183] "Another Glaring Exposure of the Indian Government's Reactionary Features," *ibid.*, January 17, 1965, and *Peking Review*, Vol. VIII, No. 4 (January 22, 1965), pp. 5–6.

[184] *Ibid*. pp. 17–18.

[185] *Zëri i Popullit*, February 2, 1965, which included: the texts of a January 5, 1965 note from Warsaw to Tirana and a January 15 Tirana reply with a long letter to the Warsaw Pact meeting; a Warsaw Pact Political Consultative Committee decision of January 20; and a final brief Albanian note of January 29 to the Warsaw Pact. (As it was not reprinted by the Chinese, this may well, like other Albanian moves, have been somewhat more extreme than Peking desired.

[186] For the March 1963 incident, see Griffith, *The Sino-Soviet Rift, op. cit.*, pp. 117–118.

[187] P. J. Honey, *Communism in North Vietnam* (Cambridge, Mass.: The M.I.T. Press, 1963); Ernst Kux, " Nordvietnam," in Ernst Kux and Joseph C. Kun, *Die Satelliten Pekings* (Stuttgart: Kohlhammer, 1964), pp. 25–189; John C. Donnell, "North Vietnam: A Qualified Pro-Chinese Position," in Scalapino, *The Communist Revolution in Asia, op. cit.*, pp. 140–172; King Chen, "North Vietnam in the Sino-Soviet Dispute, 1962–1964," *Asian Survey*, Vol. IV, No. 9 (September 1964), pp. 1023–1036; and Griffith, *The Sino-Soviet Rift, op. cit.*, pp. 128–130 and 192–193. See also P. J. Honey's regular " Quarterly Survey " in *China News Analysis*.

Yet Hanoi had always been careful not to cut entirely its bridges to Moscow; rather, the North Vietnamese preferred to avoid taking a stand (to the extent possible) and to work toward containing if not reconciling the dispute. For the Lao Dong leadership was rent with division on the question, and Ho Chi Minh had no easy time in maintaining a shifting, balancing line.

To review briefly the history of the DRV's position: Hanoi's main concern was the guerrilla war in South Vietnam, and since its main enemy was, therefore, the United States it was adamantly opposed to a Soviet-American détente. In 1962 a series of events had influenced Hanoi in favor of Peking and against Moscow. First, after the July 1962 Geneva accords on Laos, Khrushchev had decided to abandon any active policy in Southeast Asia and had therefore refused to increase Soviet military and economic aid to Hanoi. Second, India, Moscow's friend and Peking's enemy, had voted with Canada against North Vietnam in the International Control Commission when North Vietnam was forced to take a position—inevitably a negative one—on the Moscow partial test ban treaty. Finally, when Khrushchev pushed his collective mobilization against the Chinese, the balance of forces in the Lao Dong Politburo had shifted increasingly toward China. Still Hanoi neither attacked the Soviet Union by name nor echoed the Chinese line on factional and splitting activity and, in spite of Moscow having cut aid to North Vietnam, signs continued that the pro-Soviet group in the Lao Dong Politburo, while restrained, was still at work.

Although it was the new Soviet leadership that took the initiative to improve relations with Hanoi, the majority of the Lao Dong leadership, as events later showed, was willing to go along, primarily after the course of the war in South Vietnam brought increased American military intervention, this time not only in the South but also directed against the North.

Uncertainty about American intentions undoubtedly played its role in this shift. The rapid, sharp reaction of Washington in July 1964 to the Gulf of Tonkin incident had shown that the Americans could be provoked to reprisals. On the other hand, Washington had not reacted, probably because of the impending presidential election, to a Viet Cong raid on an American base at the end of October. Yet even so, Hanoi's need of Soviet military aid might well become imperative. Moreover, the new Soviet leadership, as will be seen, was in the process of coming to terms with Castro, which involved some step-up in Soviet aid to South American guerrilla operations. Moscow's public pronouncements in general indicated some cooling of relations with Washington. Finally, Brezhnev and Kosygin were clearly undertaking an attempt to contain polemics and dignify their relations with China. Therefore collective mobilization in its initial sense would at least be postponed if not, as the North Vietnamese probably gathered from the Italian and Cuban Communists, in the long run suspended indefinitely.

The abrupt withdrawal, immediately after its distribution, of the November 1964 issue of the Lao Dong theoretical monthly *Hoc Tap* in order to remove a strongly pro-Chinese and anti-Soviet article was the first sign that Soviet–North Vietnamese relations were beginning to improve. Thereafter attacks by Hanoi on Soviet policies ceased, and favorable references to Moscow increased, although Hanoi made it clear—by favorable references to Albania [188]—that it did not accept all aspects of the Soviet policy position. Simultaneously Soviet statements about Hanoi also became warmer and Kosygin publicly promised Hanoi assistance if America attacked it. Moscow also authorized the National Liberation Front of South Vietnam (NLFSV) to set up a permanent mission in Moscow.[189] Then at the end of January 1965 Kosygin's visit to Hanoi was announced—a clear sign that a major improvement in Soviet-North Vietnamese relations was impending.[190] Yet, as the Chinese revealed in November 1965, Moscow had in January—perhaps in the hope of avoiding escalation—transmitted to Hanoi a request by Washington that the Soviet Union use its influence to persuade Hanoi to end its military supply of the Viet Cong and have the Viet Cong stop its attacks on South Vietnamese urban areas. (Hanoi must have rejected this American proposal.) [191]

The Kosygin Visit, American Escalation, and Sino-Soviet Relations

On February 7 Soviet Premier Kosygin and a Soviet delegation, including several high-ranking military officers, arrived in Hanoi. Kosygin had stopped over in Peking on February 6, where he was correctly but coolly received by Chou En-lai. On that same day American bombers carried out the first of a series of raids on North Vietnam. (Kosygin stopped again in Peking on his way back, and he was received by Mao on February 11.) Since then Sino-Soviet relations have been increasingly influenced by the Vietnam crisis. With the brief and partial exception of the 1962 Cuban missile confrontation, this was

---

[188] For example, Ho Chi Minh to Hoxha, VNA in English, November 28, 1964, 1918 GMT.

[189] See an interview with its head, Dang Quang Minh, in *Sovetskaya Rossiya*, April 27, 1965. Yet the Soviet representative at the NLFSV mission's arrival was low level (TASS, April 23, 1965).

[190] For the above, see the detailed analysis, with bibliography, by P. J. Honey, " Cross Purposes in Hanoi," *China News Analysis*, No. 555 (March 12, 1965).

[191] " Refutation of the New Leaders of the CPSU on ' United Action,' " p. 15. (Judging by past Chinese statements the revelations in this article are probably true in general, but not the whole truth.)

the first time since the 1958 Quemoy-Matsu crisis that the action of a major noncommunist power—in all three instances the United States—exercised a major influence on Sino-Soviet relations. (As in 1958 [192] and 1962 [193] Sino-Soviet relations had been worsening again, after a temporary improvement, before American action influenced them significantly, but also, as in the two previous instances, this worsening was considerably accelerated by Washington's position.)

For some years Viet Cong guerrilla activity had been increasing in South Vietnam, and the Saigon government's control of the country weakening. The Viet Cong's political organization, the National Liberation Front, was substantially and increasingly under Hanoi's control [194] and became more confident, as did Hanoi (itself increasingly pro-Chinese) and Peking, that Washington would eventually withdraw from Saigon.

Concomitantly, United States support of South Vietnam had increased. After the overthrow of Ngo Dinh Diem, a series of Viet Cong victories, and a series of *coups d'état* in Saigon, President Johnson decided that direct American military intervention was necessary to prevent a neutralist coup in Saigon, redress the military balance so that negotiations with Hanoi might not result in its absorption of the South, and, more generally, contain Chinese expansionism and demonstrate that " national liberation wars " could not defeat American power. The American decision to begin continuous bombing of North Vietnam and to put American air and ground forces into combat in South Vietnam was apparently taken around the turn of the year; a Viet Cong attack on an American installation at Pleiku, and perhaps Kosygin's visit to Hanoi as well, provided a convenient opportunity to begin it.[195]

---

[192] See Zagoria, *The Sino-Soviet Conflict, op. cit.,* pp. 200–224.
[193] See Griffith, *The Sino-Soviet Rift, op. cit.,* pp. 60–63.
[194] The Viet Cong will be treated at length in a forthcoming book by Douglas Pike, to be published by the M.I.T. Press. For its control by the People's Revolutionary Party, a branch of the Lao Dong, see the evidence cited by Seymour Topping, *The New York Times,* July 31, 1965.
[195] For the role of Hanoi in the Sino-Soviet dispute, see Honey, *Communism in North Vietnam, op. cit.,* and Griffith, *The Sino-Soviet Rift, op. cit.,* pp. 128–130. For general views on Vietnam and American policy with respect to it, see Honey, " The New Phase of the War," *China News Analysis,* No. 568 (June 11, 1965) (*North Vietnam Quarterly Survey,* No. 16), " The New Situation in Vietnam," *China News Analysis,* No. 588 (November 12, 1965), and " Vietnam Argument," *Encounter,* Vol. XXV, No. 5 (November 1965), pp. 66–69; Zbigniew Brzezinski, " Peace, Morality and Vietnam," *The New Leader,* Vol. XLVII, No. 8 (April 12, 1965), pp. 5–6; Griffith, " Containing Communism—East and West," *The Atlantic Monthly,* Vol. 215, No. 5 (May 1965), pp. 71–75; George McT. Kahin and John W. Lewis, " The United States in Vietnam," *Bulletin of the Atomic Scientists,* Vol. XXI, No. 6 (June 1965), pp. 28–40; Hans Morgenthau, " Vietnam: Shadow and Substance," *New York Review of Books,* September 16, 1965, pp. 3–5; Alexander Dallin, " Moscow and Vietnam," *The New Leader,* Vol. XLVII, No. 10 (May 10, 1965), pp. 5–8; an anti-U.S. policy symposium in *Dissent,* Vol. XII, No. 4 (Autumn 1965), pp. 395–404; and Richard Löwenthal, " America's Asian Commitment," *Encounter,*

Soviet Policy on Vietnam

American military escalation in Vietnam presented an unavoidable but exceedingly embarrassing problem for Moscow. Khrushchev had come close to disengaging the Soviet Union from Vietnam and Laos; however, Kosygin's visit to Hanoi was a sign that the new Soviet leadership was attempting to re-establish some Soviet influence in Hanoi. Given its decision to postpone but eventually to summon the international Communist conference, Moscow wanted Hanoi's neutrality, if not support, for this move. More importantly, even before the American escalation, the deepening crisis in Saigon confronted the Soviets with great dangers and considerable opportunities vis-à-vis Peking's allies. If Washington were eventually to withdraw rather than escalate (as Moscow, Hanoi, and Peking expected in late 1964), Moscow could not afford to have been inactive during such a major Chinese victory and American defeat. On the contrary, the Soviets had to participate in the victory to limit China's gains. Thus, the move toward a rapprochement with Hanoi and transmission of the American proposal stemmed from Moscow's desire to establish some measure of Soviet control over a situation that potentially threatened to drag the Soviet Union *nolens volens* into a confrontation with Washington. On the international level, the Soviets wanted: first, negotiations, which they hoped would prevent or limit American escalation; second, moves toward neutralization; and third, progress toward the absorption of South Vietnam by a Hanoi no longer under predominant Chinese influence.

After the American escalation the Soviets were in a much worse dilemma. Admittedly Moscow was more able than Peking to offer Hanoi modern (surface-to-air—SAM) antiaircraft defenses to limit the bombing. Thus by February 1965 Hanoi was actually more dependent on Moscow than before and therefore more amenable to Soviet influence. Also, given the continuing if temporarily latent Sino-Soviet hostility and Soviet determination to cut its losses within the international Communist movement, Moscow could not afford to give other communist parties the impression that it would entirely sacrifice its "proletarian international" obligations to Hanoi for its overriding interest in avoiding a confrontation with the strategically superior United States; to do so would be playing into Peking's hands. In sum, Moscow had both more reason and more opportunity to try to recover control over Hanoi, but its fear of a confrontation with Washington not only required it to favor some sort of negotiation, but also precluded it

Vol. XXV, No. 4 (October 1965), pp. 53–58. For U.S. policy see particularly an interview with President Johnson by Roscoe Drummond, *The Washington Post*, August 30, 1965.

from giving Hanoi the active Soviet military assistance that alone would have made possible the restoration of complete Soviet control. Even so the Soviets probably hoped they could use Hanoi's need for SAM's and other advanced military technology that only Moscow—not Peking—could supply, to recover some of the lost Soviet influence in North Vietnam.[196]

Chinese Policy on Vietnam

Peking's objectives in Vietnam were quite different from Moscow's. True, both shared a desire to avoid a direct military confrontation with the United States; indeed Mao himself [197] and his associates [198] have consistently been careful to make it clear that they will not attack the United States unless Washington first attacks China. Nevertheless, as the course of the Sino-Soviet dispute has indicated, there was a basic difference between the Soviet and the Chinese assessment of American policy when confronted with a " national liberation struggle." Mao was convinced, contrary to the Soviet leaders, that protracted guerrilla struggle would make American escalation unlikely and, if and when it occurred, both limited and unsuccessful.

Although the Chinese originally must have delighted in the embarrassment to the Soviets inherent in the United States attack on North Vietnam, Peking too faced an increasingly dangerous situation. Ideally, if the United States did not defeat the Viet Cong or attack China itself, and if Hanoi remained recalcitrant, the resultant protracted U.S.–Viet Cong struggle would raise China's prestige as a prophet of imperialist intentions both within and outside the communist movement. It would also justify an extremist domestic policy in China, and finally would force Moscow to abandon its priority for détente with Washington for a more militant posture that could only justify Chinese policy and improve Chinese security. However, if the United States appeared to be winning, then Peking faced the unpleasant prospect of seeing Hanoi move closer to Moscow as a result of practical necessity, and suffer a loss of prestige stemming from China's inability (in part a result of North Vietnamese unwillingness to be aided by Chinese troops) to step in and turn the tide. In short, although a prolonged stalemate that would bleed the Viet Cong but not actually amount to a United

---

[196] For detailed treatment of recent Soviet pronouncements on Vietnam see " Soviet Comment on the Vietnam Situation," *The Yuva Newsletter*, Vol. IV, No. 4 (July 1965) pp. 1–6.

[197] In an interview with Edgar Snow in Peking in January 1965, *The New Republic*, Vol. CLII, No. 9 (February 27, 1965), pp. 17–23, at p. 22.

[198] Lo Jui-ch'ing, " Commemorate the Victory Over German Fascism! Carry the Struggle Against U.S. Imperialism Through to the End!" *Peking Review*, Vol. VIII, No. 20 (May 14, 1965), pp. 7–15.

States victory was to China's advantage, real American military gains would make not only the Soviets but most of all the Chinese appear to be a paper tiger.

As for Hanoi [199]: combining guerrilla communism with Vietnamese nationalism, anticolonialism, and determination to reunify Vietnam, Ho Chi Minh had defeated the French. The Viet Cong seemed well on the way to victory. Why should he retreat, despite American escalation? He did need and want more Soviet support, and he had never wanted a Sino-Soviet split; rather, his own security interests demanded joint Sino-Soviet support for Hanoi against Washington. Therefore, at least unless and until American escalation was to wreak major damage in North Vietnam or American ground forces were to defeat the Viet Cong in South Vietnam, or both, he wanted to continue the war. The same was even truer of the National Liberation Front, to whom victory must have seemed within reach and who had no desire to return to the North, as they had in 1954, to wait for a better day.

The February 10 Soviet–North Vietnamese communiqué, cordial in tone, included a Soviet commitment to "strengthen the defense capacity of the DRV," [200] and shortly thereafter construction began around Hanoi for Soviet ground-to-air antiaircraft missiles.[201]

Thus the Kosygin visit to Hanoi, the simultaneous beginning of the American bombing of North Vietnam, and the subsequent beginning of Soviet military and technical aid, particularly of SAM's, to North Vietnam in response to the American bombing (reportedly after a brief delay due to a temporary Chinese refusal to let Moscow ship them overland), further improved Soviet-Vietnamese relations.[202]

In a subsequent secret letter to the CPSU the Chinese declared that they had never obstructed the transit of Soviet military material to

---

199 For the most extreme (and pro-Chinese) Hanoi position see two articles by Truong Chinh, " Let Us Raise High the Creative Marxist-Leninist Banner and Hold Fast to the Party's Military Line," *Quan Doi Nhan Dan* (Hanoi), February 4, 1965, and another article in *Nhan Dan*, September 2, 1965, summarized in Honey, " The New Situation in Hanoi," *op. cit.* Although Hanoi's position has been moderately and conditionally pro-Chinese since May 1963 (see Griffith, *The Sino-Soviet Rift, op. cit.,* pp. 128–130 and 192–193), a December 1963 Lao Dong Central Committee communiqué (*Nhan Dan*, January 21, 1964, and *Jen-min Jih-pao*, January 23, 1964) carefully distinguished between " the Tito revisionist clique, a lackey of imperialism," and " . . . a mistaken people within the international Communist movement . . . who commit the error of revisionism or right-wing opportunism [that is, the Soviets]." The former are to be exposed and opposed, the latter struggled with " for the sake of unity." See j.c.k. [Joseph C. Kun], " North Vietnamese Still on the Fence," Radio Free Europe, Munich, January 27, 1965.

200 *Pravda*, February 11, 1965, quoted from *CDSP*, Vol. XVII, No. 6 (March 3, 1965), pp. 9–11, at p. 9.

201 UPI dispatch from Saigon in *The New York Times*, February 17, 1965.

202 This became particularly clear as a result of Le Duan's April 1965 visit to Moscow. See Kx. [Ernst Kux], " Höhere Einsatz Moskaus gegen Peking," *Neue Zürcher Zeitung*, April 20, 1965.

Vietnam but that they had rejected a Soviet request to send four thousand Red Army troops to North Vietnam, to " occupy and use " one or two airfields in southwestern China (a move involving the stationing of five hundred Red Army troops there), and, finally, to grant Moscow free transit over an air corridor to be established through China between the Soviet Union and North Vietnam.[203] (As of mid-November 1965 this Chinese statement has been neither confirmed nor denied by Moscow.)

Improvement in Soviet-Vietnamese relations remained partial. Hanoi rejected Kosygin's February 16 proposal for a conference on Indochina without preconditions. Hanoi's differences with Moscow were also reflected in occasional attacks on Tito[204] particularly for his friendship with India, denunciations of India vis-à-vis Pakistan, and other pro-Chinese statements.[205] Yet the extent to which Moscow-Hanoi relations had improved was indicated by the (pro-Soviet) North Vietnamese Prime Minister Pham Van Dong's support in April 1965 for " joint action " against the Americans[206] (the post-Khrushchev Soviet line, which the Chinese termed betrayal of Hanoi) and his statement that Moscow was aiding Hanoi.[207]

It is unclear whether Pham's position also reflected some increased desire in North Vietnam for negotiations. It does appear that Hanoi (presumably with Moscow's encouragement) may have indicated this indirectly to Washington in April and May.[208]

In sum, the lack of any effective Chinese help against the American bombings and North Vietnam's continued need for Soviet antiaircraft missiles to protect Hanoi and Haiphong in case Washington extended the bombing, Moscow's already extensive aid and China's attempt

---

203 Edward Crankshaw in *The Observer* (London), November 14, 1965, p. 5. Crankshaw gives extensive quotations from a CCP letter replying to an April 17 CPSU one; but, with the exception of the above (and one other point—the April 3 Soviet proposal for a USSR-CPR-DRV summit meeting), they add nothing of significance to " Refutation of the New Leaders of the CPSU on ' United Action,' " *op. cit.* For China's rejection of the Soviet air base proposal, see also Liao Cheng-chih at a press conference in Peking, July 15, 1965, reported by Radio Tokyo, July 15, 1965, 1000 GMT; Richard Hughes from Hong Kong, *The Sunday Times* (London), July 25, 1965. By April 1965 Soviet weapons were moving through China to North Vietnam (*The New York Times*, April 2, 1965).
204 For example, *Nhan Dan*, March 18, 1965.
205 For example, " Let Us Heighten Our Revolutionary Ardor and Advance toward Winning New Successes," *Hoc Tap*, February 1965; the Lao Dong Central Committee message to the PKI, VNA in English, May 23, 1965, 0545 GMT; *Nhan Dan* endorsement of the Chinese position on the Indo-Pakistani conflict, VNA in English, September 23, 1965, 0555 GMT.
206 Radio Hanoi in Vietnamese, April 13, 1965, 1300 GMT.
207 VNA in English, April 28, 1965, 0150 GMT.
208 See the report by Eric Sevareid on his August 12, 1965, conversation with Adlai Stevenson in his " The Final Troubled Hours of Adlai," *Look*, November 30, 1965, pp. 81–86, at p. 84, and Washington dispatches in *The New York Times*, November 16 and 17, 1965.

to stop or discredit Soviet aid have all pushed Hanoi toward a position of neutrality in which it shows occasional signs of some slight favor toward Moscow but continues alignment with Chinese policy positions vis-à-vis the United States.[209] Hanoi cannot afford to antagonize Peking, from whom it still obtains most of its small arms and ammunition and whose troops, if only as a deterrent to American extension of the war, are of great potential value.[210] Even so, in the present stage of the war Moscow, not Peking, delivers the crucial aid.[211] Moreover, Moscow has suspended the collective mobilization that Hanoi disliked, and the Soviets have improved relations with Pyongyang, Bucharest, and Havana. (On the occasion of the July 1965 Rumanian party congress Hanoi warmly endorsed Rumanian " self-reliance " but was otherwise carefully neutral.)[212] Finally, in summer and autumn 1965 China suffered a series of foreign policy reverses that made her even less attractive, and Moscow more attractive to Hanoi.

Sino-Soviet Polemics on the Vietnam Issue

It is not surprising therefore that the February 8 Soviet and Chinese governmental declarations on the American bombing[213] differed, and these differences intensified thereafter. Both of course condemned it strongly. But while Moscow, with careful imprecision, spoke only of being

> forced, together with its allies and friends, to take further measures to safeguard the security and strengthen the defense capability of the Democratic Republic of Vietnam.

Peking declared that

> all the other socialist countries have the unshirkable international obligation to support and assist it with actual deeds.

Moreover, Peking's attack on the United States was considerably more violent than Moscow's.

[209] See, for example, the USSR–DRV communiqué, *Pravda*, April 17, 1965 (" unity of action . . . of the socialist countries "), and the April 20, 1965, *Nhan Dan* editorial; for a relatively pro-Chinese statement see Hoang Van Hoan in NCNA, Peking, July 13, 1965; for neutrality, Ho Chi Minh speech, VNA in English, April 16, 1965, 0838 GMT, and his interview in *Pravda*, June 19, 1965; and Le Duc Tho at the Rumanian Communist Party congress, VNA in English, July 18 and 19, 1965.

[210] See, for example, the appointment as foreign minister of (presumed pro-Chinese) Nguyen Duy Trinh (*The New York Times*, April 8, 1965).

[211] By early April 1965 Soviet aid was moving uninterrupted through China (*ibid.*). Another indication of how Hanoi now gauges its relations with socialist countries on the basis of its aid requirements was the deterioration of Rumanian–North Vietnamese relations subsequent to Rumania's cutting down its exports to Hanoi. See j.c.k. [Joseph C. Kun], " Strained Rumanian-Vietnamese Relations," Radio Free Europe, Munich, July 5, 1965.

[212] VNA in English, July 18 and 19, 1965, cited from j.c.k. [Joseph C. Kun], " Vietnamese, Korean Delegates Demonstrate Neutral Attitude," Radio Free Europe, Munich, July 23, 1965.

[213] Texts in *The New York Times*, February 9, 1965.

That Kosygin's conversations in Peking did not stem the worsening of Sino-Soviet relations, in spite, apparently, of Kosygin having renewed the previous Soviet offers to expand economic and technical co-operation,[214] soon became clear. About Kosygin's discussions with Mao and the other Chinese leaders only Chinese evidence is available.

Peking declared in November 1965 that Kosygin had then " stressed the need to help the United States ' find a way out of Vietnam,' " but, when the Chinese " expressed the hope that the new leaders of the CPSU would . . . not make a deal with the United States on . . . Vietnam," Kosygin declared that they would " not bargain with others [that is, Washington] on this issue." [215] (The Chinese are probably right, however, in declaring that Moscow did just the contrary.)

It appears that Mao simultaneously propounded to Kosygin a new and more extreme Chinese thesis: Sino-Soviet unity can be, as it surely will be, restored only in case of a war with the United States. (Kosygin ascribed this view to " certain people " in May 1965 [216]; Matern, the leader of the Communist Socialist Unity Party of East Germany denounced this thesis at the 19-party Moscow meeting in March 1965,[217] and Novotný did the same in Moscow in September 1965.[218] Since the thesis had not been referred to before, and clearly was a Chinese one, it would seem likely that Mao announced it to Kosygin in February.) In sum, then, the conversations were clearly unsuccessful.

Although the mid-February Soviet and Chinese messages on the occasion of the fifteenth anniversary of the Sino-Soviet alliance were cordial in tone, their substantive differences were even clearer than in the February 8 statements, particularly with respect to the United States.[219] Shortly thereafter Chinese Foreign Minister Marshal Ch'en Yi declared that peaceful coexistence with the United States was " impossible " and that

> only by concrete action against U.S. imperialism and its followers can the Sino-Soviet alliance be tested and tempered and can Sino-Soviet unity be consolidated and developed.

---

214 See Kosygin's speech after his Hanoi trip, *Pravda*, February 27, 1965 (CDSP, Vol. XVII, No. 9 [March 24, 1965], pp. 3–6); *Borba*, February 21, 1965.

215 " Refutation of the New Leaders of the CPSU on ' United Action,' " *op. cit.*, pp. 15–16.

216 " Certain people assert that only a new world war will lead to the consolidation of the socialist camp and the international Communist movement. We resolutely reject such a point of view." (*Pravda*, May 8, 1965, quoted from *CDSP*, Vol. XVII, No. 19 [June 2, 1965], pp. 4–7, at p. 6.)

217 " The point of view according to which the unity of the socialist camp and the international Communist movement would be restored only in case of a war is in our view not only an expression of the theory of spontaneity but damaging and dangerous for the cause of peace and socialism." (*Neues Deutschland*, March 28, 1965, tr. from text in *SBZ Archiv*, Vol. XVI, No. 8 [2. Aprilheft], pp. 127–128, at p. 128.)

218 *Pravda*, September 15, 1965.   219 *Pravda* and *Jen-min Jih-pao*, February 14, 1965.

He also demanded the withdrawal of all U.S. troops from Vietnam as a precondition for peace there.[220] Kosygin, on the other hand, while he also demanded U.S. withdrawal, referred to this problem only as an " obstacle." [221]

As usual this contrast reflected a sharp Sino-Soviet policy difference. The Chinese later charged [222] that Kosygin on February 16, the day after he returned to Moscow, proposed the " convening of a new international conference on Indochina without prior conditions," that is, without the prior withdrawal of U.S. troops. Hanoi (the Chinese said) rejected this.

By the end of February, reports from Paris indicated that Moscow had told the French that it would support General de Gaulle's plan for a negotiated settlement in South Vietnam.[223] (The Soviets have since denied this but the Chinese have confirmed it.) Peking and Hanoi, on the other hand, again rejected negotiations.[224] In addition, just before the March 1 opening date of the preparatory committee for an international conference, the Chinese declared that Moscow was supporting " a vicious scheme of the United States to promote neo-colonialism "— the establishment of a United Nations peacekeeping force.[225] In another sign of the new storm to come, Peking again began explicitly attacking Soviet publications and accused Moscow of resuming polemics.[226]

North Korea

Since the 1953 Korean truce North Korea's policy, like that of Rumania, has been primarily characterized by nationalism. The history of Korean communism has always been of factional strife. Although its leader since 1945, Kim Il-song was himself put into power by the invading Red Army, by 1958 he had succeeded in purging, in turn, the native Korean Communists, the pro-Chinese " Yenan group," and the pro-Soviet Communists. (In 1956 he barely survived an attempt, with Soviet and perhaps also Chinese support, to purge him.)

220 *Jen-min Jih-pao*, February 16 and 19, 1965, and *Peking Review*, Vol. VIII, No. 8 February 19, 1965), p. 12, and Vol. VIII, No. 9 (February 26, 1965), p. 4.
221 *Pravda*, February 17, 1965.
222 " Refutation of the New Leaders of the CPSU on ' United Action,' " *op. cit.*, p. 16. Note the simultaneity of dates between public Soviet and Chinese declarations and private Soviet and Chinese moves. For a detailed analysis of this simultaneity of public ideological declarations and secret political and economic moves, see Griffith, *Albania and the Sino-Soviet Rift, op. cit.*, pp. 60–88.
223 Paris dispatch in *The Times* (London), February 25, 1965; Henri Pierre from Moscow in *Le Monde*, February 26, 1965; and " Refutation of the New Leaders of the CPSU on ' United Action,' " *op cit.*, p. 16.
224 André Fontaine in *Le Monde*, February 27, 1965, and *Jen-min Jih-pao*, February 19, 1965.
225 *Ibid.*, February 25, 1965 (SCMP 3407, March 2, 1965).
226 *Jen-min Jih-pao*, February 26, 1965 *et seqq.* For a summary see *China News Analysis*, No. 567 (June 4, 1965), pp. 3–4.

Angered at the lack of Soviet support in the Korean War and determined to get out from under the dependence on China that arose from Chinese intervention, in the mid-1950s, against Soviet wishes, Kim concentrated on building up North Korea's heavy industry, attacked indiscriminate emulation of the Soviet Union, and emphasized "independence and self-reliance." In 1958 Kim, like Mao, instituted a "great leap forward"—the "flying red horse campaign."

These developments illustrated certain policy objectives that Kim had in common with Mao: rapid economic development toward economic self-sufficiency, preferably with extensive Soviet aid, but, since that was not possible, by labor-intensive policies; and hostility toward the United States which blocked the reunification of Korea under Kim (as it did Mao's absorption of Taiwan). Both were also disappointed by Soviet economic aid, and both therefore stressed self-sufficiency. Finally, Khrushchev probably attempted to bully Kim into line, as he did Mao, Hoxha, and others. He failed to overcome Kim's (or Mao's) nationalism.

From 1956 until 1960 Kim, although ideologically leaning increasingly toward Peking, avoided taking sides in the Sino-Soviet dispute. Then in 1960 and 1961 Kim refused to condemn the Albanians or to endorse the Soviet rapprochement with Yugoslavia. In 1962 he took the Chinese view on the Sino-Indian and Cuban crises, and by 1963 the North Koreans were openly siding with the Chinese and being denounced by the Soviets for attacking Soviet policy in almost all respects, without, however, naming Moscow or Khrushchev specifically. The North Koreans emphasized "some people's" (that is, Khrushchev's) pressure on other communist parties, and they clearly defended the Rumanians. In 1964 Pyongyang explicitly refused to attend Khrushchev's planned conference, defended the Chinese splitting policies, and by September 1964 was attacking Moscow explicitly for Soviet economic policies toward North Korea and Soviet interference in North Korea's internal affairs.[227]

As in North Vietnam, anti-Moscow polemics ceased in North Korea with Khrushchev's fall. Thereafter North Korea constantly stressed the need for "unity" of the socialist camp.[228] Pyongyang made clear that it continued to differ with Moscow and agreed with Peking

---

227 Chong-Sik Lee, "Stalinism in the East," in Scalapino, *The Communist Revolution in Asia, op. cit.*, pp. 114–139 (the most recent and authoritative analysis); Joseph C. Kun, "Nordkorea," in Kux and Kun, *Die Satelliten Pekings, op. cit.*, pp. 190–253; and j.c.k. [Joseph C. Kun], "North Korea's Neutral Course," Radio Free Europe, Munich, August 25, 1965. For bibliography see also Griffith, *The Sino-Soviet Rift, op. cit.*, p. 192, note 56.
228 For example, Kim Il-song at a banquet for Sukarno, KCNA in English, November 1, 1964, 1234 GMT, and DPRK telegram to USSR, KCNA in English, November 6, 1964, 1032 GMT.

on policy toward the United States, on revisionism (including support for the pro-Chinese parties and opposition to their pro-Moscow opponents), on Albania [229] (with which cordial relations were still maintained), and on " self-sufficiency," independent all-round industrialization, and Rumania.[230] It had not forgotten Khrushchev's pressure and blackmail, and its policy toward Moscow would be primarily gauged on the extent of the latter's support through " actual deeds " (that is, it must do more) against the United States and aid to North Vietnam and other areas of revolutionary struggle.[231] Soviet–North Korean and East European–North Korean economic relations also improved, and Moscow sold Pyongyang some commercial airplanes.[232] In February 1965 Kosygin visited Pyongyang after Hanoi. His and Kim's speeches and the final communiqué stressed unity of the socialist camp, strengthening of Soviet–North Korean party and state relations, and common struggle against American imperialism. Kosygin must have agreed to give more military aid to Kim, as he had to Ho [233]. A Soviet–North Korean agreement providing for Moscow " strengthening further the defensive capabilities " of North Korea was signed at the end of May 1965.[234] The North Koreans were careful, however, to remain cordial to the Chinese [235] and to maintain neutrality in the Sino-Soviet dispute,[236] and they supported Peking's position on the Indo-Pakistani conflict.[237]

The Soviets were apparently willing to be satisfied for the present with North Korean organizational neutrality, combined with ideological

[229] Kim to Hoxha, KCNA in English, November 28, 1964, 1618 GMT.

[230] *Minju Choson*, December 30, 1964 (KCNA in English), December 30, 1964, 0526 GMT.

[231] " Strengthen the Unity of the International Communist Movement and Intensify the Anti-Imperialist, Revolutionary Struggle," *Nodong Shinmun*, December 3, 1964 (KCNA in English, December 3, 1964, 0550 GMT). See also *Nodong Shinmun* on Lenin, April 22, 1965 (KCNA in English, April 22, 1965, 0515 GMT); and especially Kim Il-song to the PKI Aliarcham Academy of Social Science, Djakarta, April 14, 1965 (KCNA in English, April 19, 1965, 1013 GMT) (for which see also j.c.k. [Joseph C. Kun], " North Korea: Back in the Middle?" Radio Free Europe, Munich, May 7, 1965), and Kim against the pro-Soviet Yoshio Shiga in an interview on June 18, 1965, with *Akahata* (KCNA in English, June 19, 1965, 0608 GMT).

[232] j.c.k. [Joseph C. Kun], " Soviet–North Korean Trade Protocol for 1965," Radio Free Europe, Munich, December 3, 1965, citing Radio Moscow, December 1, 1965.

[233] Kosygin at Pyongyang, *Pravda*, February 13, 1965; Kim, KCNA in English, February 11, 1965, 1615 GMT; joint communiqué, *Pravda*, February 15, 1965.

[234] TASS in Russian, May 31, 1965, 1526 GMT.

[235] For example, the celebration of the fourth anniversary of the Korean-Chinese friendship treaty, KCNA in English, July 9, 1965, 1648 GMT.

[236] Kim Kwang-hyop at the Rumanian Communist party congress, Agerpres, July 21, 1965, quoted from j.c.k. [Joseph C. Kun], " Vietnamese, Korean Delegates Demonstrate Neutral Attitudes," Radio Free Europe, Munich, July 23, 1965.

[237] For example, Pak Mun-song in *Nodong Shinmun*, September 17, 1964 (KCNA in English, September 17, 1965, 0516 GMT), and a North Korean–Indonesian parliamentary delegations' communiqué, KCNA in English, September 28, 1965, 1720 GMT.

support for the Chinese. The Chinese, however, were not: The mid-August celebrations of the twentieth anniversary of the liberation of North Korea revealed more clearly than any other single event that Mao at least as yet was not as prepared to adjust to a decline in his influence among other communist parties as Khrushchev's successors were. Although the Soviet delegation was headed by A. N. Shelepin, member of the CPSU Presidium and Secretariat and the rising young man in Moscow, China sent only Wu Hsin-yu, deputy secretary-general of the National People's Congress Standing Committee, who is not even a Central Committee member, and the Albanians sent no delegation at all.[238]

Thus North Korea, even more than North Vietnam, because it is not so immediately dependent on both Moscow and Peking, has not only returned to neutrality in the Sino-Soviet dispute but also, like Rumania, has become at least for the present a truly "national communist" regime determining its own policies, furthering its own influence, and balancing skillfully between the two communist giants.[239] Moscow has been the winner thereby, but only because it has been prepared to adjust to Korean desires; China, up to now, has been the loser.

VI. The March 1965 Moscow 19-Party Meeting

Soviet-Cuban Developments

Developments on the organizational issue from Khrushchev's fall until the 19-party meeting on March 1 confirmed the accelerating decline of Soviet influence. Both the membership and the character of the meeting became less favorable from the Soviet viewpoint.

Cuba's attendance became certain only shortly before the meeting; and, although this indicated that Soviet-Cuban relations had improved, a communiqué of a late 1964 meeting of Latin American Communist parties in Havana [240] had shown that Moscow had made some concessions to Castro concerning the revitalization of violent struggle in

---

238 j.c.k. [Joseph C. Kun], "Peking Snubs North Korean Anniversary," Radio Free Europe, Munich, August 13, 1965, and l.z. [Louis Zanga], "Albania Snubs North Korean Liberation Anniversary," *ibid.*, August 17, 1965. For the Chinese greeting message, less enthusiastic than in 1964, see NCNA in English, August 14, 1964 (SCMP 3282, August 19, 1964, p. 31), and a Hong Kong dispatch in *The New York Times*, August 17, 1964. The DPRK also took the Chinese side in the Indo-Pakistani and Indonesian crises.

239 For North Korea's furthering its own influence, see j.c.k. [Joseph C. Kun], "North Korea's Drive for Recognition in the Developing World," Radio Free Europe, Munich, December 11, 1964, and "The Kim Visit: North Korean Diplomatic Offensive," *ibid.*, April 12, 1965.

240 *Pravda*, January 19, 1965. The communiqué took pro-Soviet and implicitly anti-Chinese positions on the international conference issue, cessation of polemics, and

Latin America and that Cuba continued to oppose any Sino-Soviet split.[241]

As has been pointed out, Khrushchev was engaged before his fall in recementing relations between Moscow and Havana.[242]. Events in Latin America had been working in favor of his purpose. Castro's influence there had been declining ever since the 1962 Cuban missile crisis, when it became clear to the radically anti-American extreme Left that, should they take power, they could not count on Soviet military support against American intervention. The failure of the Venezuelan guerrilla movement to prevent the election of Leoni, the victory of Frei in Chile, and the overthrow of Goulart in Brazil had all been blows to Castro's expectations. But they were also indications that the peaceful ascent to power by communism in Latin America, the course Moscow and the Latin American Communist leaderships had

other points. It was, however, more favorable to the Fidelista advocacy of armed struggle than the Moscow-oriented Latin American Communist parties previously had been. See A. Ferrari, J. M. Fortuny, P. Matta Lima and L. Ferreto, "The Cuban Revolution and the Anti-Imperialist Struggle of the Latin American Peoples," *World Marxist Review*, Vol. 8, No. 1 (January 1965), pp. 29–35. Yet Fidelista versus pro-Soviet Communist party tension still exists in Latin America; see, for example, the antiguerrilla article by the Argentinian Ernesto Judisi, "The Revolutionary Process in Latin America," *ibid.*, Vol. 8, No. 2 (February 1965), pp. 15–22; Ernst Halperin, *The Peaceful and the Violent Road: A Latin American Debate* (Cambridge, Mass.: Massachusetts Institute of Technology, Center for International Studies, September 1965); a Guatemalan Communist Party appeal against the "Trotskyite" guerrillas led by Yon Sosa, *Information Bulletin*, No. 56, October 20, 1965, pp. 41–47; and Luis F. de la Puente Uceda, "The Peruvian Revolution: Concepts and Perspectives," *Monthly Review*, Vol. 17, No. 6 (November 1965), pp. 12–28, and James D. Cockcroft and Eduardo Vicente, "Venezuela and the FALN since Leoni," *ibid.* pp. 29–40.

[241] See the March 13 Castro speech, reprinted by *Pravda* on March 18, which by implication criticized Soviet lack of aid to Hanoi but which contained sharp if implied criticism of Peking for its "splittism" and its spreading of Chinese propaganda in Cuba. See Fritz Ermarth, "Fidel, the Giant Killer," Radio Free Europe, Munich, March 20, 1965. "The Communiqué testifies to a triumph of the revisionist Togliattist theses and tactics, clearly outlined in the 'Testament' of P. Togliatti, which came out against the monocentrist line of the Soviet leadership." ("The Splitting Revisionist Meeting of One Man," *Zëri i Popullit*, March 18, 1965.)

[242] For the following see, in addition to the treatment (with bibliography) of the pre-November 1963 period in Griffith, *The Sino-Soviet Rift, op. cit.*, pp. 60–62, 198–202, the following subsequent material: Theodore Draper, *Castroism Theory and Practice* (New York, Washington, and London: Praeger, 1965); Ernst Halperin, *Nationalism and Communism in Chile* (Cambridge, Mass.: The M.I.T. Press, 1965) and *The Peaceful and the Violent Road: A Latin American Debate, op. cit.*; Boris Goldenberg, *The Cuban Revolution and Latin America* (New York: Praeger, 1965); and a series of articles by Branko Lazitch, "Retouches à la politique soviétique au sein de l'internationale," *Est & Ouest*, No. 344 (June 16–30, 1965), pp. 7–9; "Tactique 'chinoise' et obédience soviétique. L'exemple du Guatemala," *ibid.*, No. 336 (February 16–28, 1965), pp. 10–12, "Le Parti Communiste Vénézuélien et le conflict sino-soviétique," *ibid.*, No. 335 (February 1–15, 1965), pp. 1–7, and "Les répercussions de la querelle sino-soviétique dans les partis communistes d'Amérique latine," *ibid.*, No. 333 (January 1–15, 1965), pp. 3–10.

been advocating, was unlikely. Conversely, the instability of the Caribbean area and the growth of guerrilla activity in Guatemala, Peru, and in Colombia had shown that the "violent road" might have some chances. However the splits among the Guatemalan guerrillas, the growth of tension not only between the old-line pro-Soviet Latin American Communist leaderships and the Fidelistas, and the splitting activities of the Chinese had indicated that neither the violent nor the peaceful road could succeed without greater external support and less factionalism. Finally, Castro's economic problems were endemic, and only Moscow could give him the economic aid and deterrence vis-à-vis American intervention that he needed. Moreover, Khrushchev's scaling down of the objectives of the preparatory committee meeting— that is, his abandonment of collective mobilization for expelling the Chinese—made it possible for Castro to agree to participate in such a meeting while not taking a totally anti-Chinese position.

The fall of Khrushchev greatly facilitated the Soviet-Cuban rapprochement. First, the new Soviet leadership's decision to improve relations with a whole series of defiant parties, not only pro-Soviet ones like the Italian one but also such pro-Chinese ones as the North Vietnamese and North Korean and neutral parties like the Rumanian, made it likely that an intensified rapprochement with Cuba would also be undertaken. Second, Brezhnev and Kosygin had decided to limit and partially to reverse the détente with the United States, *inter alia* and to resume a more forward policy in Southeast Asia vis-à-vis the United States, for the most part by increased military support to the North Vietnamese. It was only logical, therefore, that they should do the same with respect to Latin America.

For Castro, who probably had never forgiven Khrushchev's abandonment of Cuban interests in October 1962, the new Soviet leadership in itself as well as its policies offered an opportunity to gain more support for his goals in Latin America. He could accept the Soviet desire for coordination between Havana, Moscow, and the Latin American Communist parties (but not necessarily implement it in practice) because the Chinese factionalism in Latin America was even less to his liking than it was to Moscow's.

The result was the convening in Havana in November 1964 of a conference of 22 Latin American Communist parties. A Soviet representative participated, but the Chinese did not. The conference's communiqué, published first in *Pravda* on January 19, 1965, represented a three-way compromise among Moscow, Havana, and the Latin American party leaderships. It stressed the necessity of unity in the international Communist movement, the end of public polemics, and the condemnation of factionalism—all fully in accord with the Soviet leadership's new line. Moreover, its reference to an international conference was sufficiently general that, given Moscow's postponement of the preparatory meeting, it would not bind Castro if Brezhnev were to return to the original interpretation of collective mobilization. Finally, Castro in return got a Soviet commitment for " active aid " to the " freedom fighters " in Venezuela, Colombia, Guatemala, Honduras, Paraguay, and Haiti, that is, an increase in material aid to the guerrilla operations within Latin America. On the other hand, the condemnation of factionalism indicated that Castro had promised not to subvert or split the orthodox Latin American Communist leaderships, and that he condemned Chinese splitting policies.[243] In a speech on March 13, 1965 that was clearly directed against Peking, Castro advocated that Cuba " drive from our country, from the ranks of our people, these disputes, these Byzantine feuds." [244]

This Soviet-Cuban rapprochement probably also included a Cuban commitment to come to an international meeting provided that it was not one of collective mobilization to expel the Chinese. However, Castro could rely on the PCI to reject such a meeting in any case. Indeed relations between the Cuban and Italian Communists improved greatly and both sides probably cooperated before and during the March 1965 Moscow meeting.[245]

It is convenient at this point, even at the risk of getting ahead of our story, to survey briefly subsequent Soviet-Cuban relations until November 1965. The rapidity and massiveness of the American intervention in Santo Domingo in April 1965 produced, on balance, a loss of American influence in Latin America in general and Santo Domingo in particular. In this sense, therefore, its result could be considered favorable to Moscow and Havana.[246] Nevertheless, it also demonstrated that Washington would not tolerate, and would prevent by military force, a communist or Fidelista government, at least in the Caribbean and perhaps in Latin America as a whole. Thus the intervention limited Castro's possibilities and reminded him that the United States could, and might, overwhelm him as well—and that Soviet support was essential to deter this danger.

There was considerable disagreement within the Cuban leadership about the policy to follow on the Sino-Soviet rift. After the Havana meeting Castro sent Guevara to Peking, but the sharp decline in Chinese coverage of Cuban affairs, plus a sharp attack against Castro on July 2,

---

[243] The Albanians attacked the November 1964 Havana meeting as one organized " with diabolic aims " by the " Soviet revisionists " for " their anti-Marxist plans." (*Zëri i Popullit*, February 16, 1965.)
[244] Reprinted in full in *Pravda*, March 18, 1965.
[245] See especially the PURS-PCI communiqué in *L'Unità*, June 9, 1965.
[246] See Griffith, *Communism in Europe, op. cit.*, Vol. 2, p. 4, note 4.

1965, in *Le Drapeau Rouge* (Brussels), the organ of the pro-Chinese Grippa group, indicated that Peking-Havana relations had worsened markedly. Guevara, whose views had always been closer to the Chinese than those of the other Cuban leaders, publicly criticized Soviet and East European policies in March 1965 [247] in Cairo and then disappeared from public sight. His whereabouts, and indeed whether or not he is alive, remain uncertain. Castro announced in October 1965 that Guevara had left Cuba in April 1965 to carry on his revolutionary activities elsewhere,[248] in a context that implied that he and Che had come to a parting of the ways—*inter alia*, it seems fair to assume, on the Sino-Soviet issue. In any case, after November 1964 the Cuban position remained pro-Soviet, but reservedly so; indeed, shortly after the November 1964 meeting signs again appeared of continuing differences between the orthodox Latin American Communist leaderships and the Fidelistas.[249] Moscow nevertheless, however reluctantly, probably did help Castro to step up his financial and other support to guerrillas in the Caribbean, as was most strikingly evidenced by the arrest in Caracas of an Italian Communist carrying over 300,000 dollars —presumably for the Venezuelan guerrillas.

The Importance of the Italian Communists

Rumania refused to come to the March meeting. The British Communist Party almost did not attend (its one representative arrived a day late)[250] and emphasized its opposition to the meeting itself and its refusal to cooperate in the originally specified purposes.[251]

Yet the position of the Italian Communist Party was perhaps most important in changing the character of the meeting. After Khrushchev's fall, with respect to which the PCI reiterated Togliatti's criticisms of Soviet internal affairs,[252] the Italian Communists intensified their attempts to influence other parties to support their views concerning

[247] In an interview with *al Tali'ah* (the Cairo theoretical journal of the Arab Socialist Union), April 1965, summarized (with extensive quotations), in William McLaughlin, " Guevara on Factionalism in Cuba and Economic Revisionism in East Europe," Radio Free Europe, Munich, July 29, 1965.

[248] *Hoy and Revolución*, October 4, 1965.

[249] See Ernst Halperin, *The Peaceful and the Violent Road, op. cit.*

[250] *Pravda*, March 2, 1965.

[251] *Daily Worker* (London), January 11, 1965; excerpts in *Peking Review*, Vol. VIII, No. 4 (January 22, 1965), pp. 19–20; and *The Sunday Times* (London), February 28, 1965.

[252] Bufalini and Berlinguer upon their return from Moscow, in *L'Unità*, November 8, 1964. See also the questioning of the extent of the leading role of the CPSU in Giuseppe Boffa, " La funzione del PCUS nella società sovietica," *Rinascita*, Vol. XXI, No. 44 (November 7, 1964), pp. 11–12, and Amendola's request for limitations on criticism of the Soviet Union, *ibid.*, pp. 3–4.

the international conference,[253] structural reform, autonomy of individual communist parties, the Vietnam crisis, and policy toward underdeveloped areas. The main right-wing leader, Giorgio Amendola, made a major new domestic proposal: the formation of a unified working-class party that, like radical national liberation movements, would be based "neither on social democratic nor on communist positions," and that would encourage "the most advanced currents of modern thought"—not only those of Marx, Lenin, Labriola, and Gramsci but also "other philosophical and cultural positions." Amendola explicitly advocated the end of democratic centralism and the allowing of factions:

> One cannot pretend to create a unitary party on the ideological positions occupied by the communist avant-garde. The communists will continue, naturally, their Marxist struggle within the unitary party, in a permanent, democratic debate of ideas.

True, this meant communist "infiltration from within"; but perhaps as important was his justification for his proposals: the communist as well as the social democratic parties had failed to realize a "socialist transformation of society." [254] Amendola's proposals were not at first endorsed by his associates, but nevertheless the PCI rejected [255] Soviet criticism of them.[256] In mid-February the PCI made clear that it would attend only if the preparatory meeting were consultative in character.[257]

On February 22, after the first American bombing of North Vietnam, the first authoritative and comprehensive ideological statement of the new Soviet leadership's foreign policy was sent to press. It showed if only by negative evidence, the Italian victory with respect to the consultative nature of the proposed meeting.

The Soviet statement made clear that Moscow was not changing its general line. Peaceful coexistence was given absolute priority:

253 Mario Alicata, "Il dialogo del PCI con i partiti fratelli," *ibid.*, Vol. XXI, No. 40 (October 10, 1964), pp. 5–6; Enrico Berlinguer's rejection of PCF leader Leroy's criticism of the Togliatti Testament, especially concerning the conference, in *L'Unità*, October 24, 1964, and *Rinascita*, Vol. XXI, No. 42 (October 24, 1964), pp. 7–8 (JPRS 27,299, November 10, 1964); and three Radio Free Europe, Munich, analyses: j.c.k. [Joseph C. Kun], "Italian Party Delegation to Hanoi," April 11, 1965, William McLaughlin, "French Left Looks at Italian Communism," May 13, 1965, and Kevin Devlin, "The PCI's Ideological Diplomacy," May 18, 1965.
254 Giorgio Amendola, "Ipotesi sulla riunificazione," *Rinascita*, Vol. XXI, No. 47 (November 28, 1964), pp. 8–9.
255 g.c.p. [Giancarlo Pajetta], "Pubblicita del dibattito," *ibid.*, Vol. XXII, No. 5 (January 30, 1965), p. 13.
256 "Italian Communist Party Discusses the Creation of a Single Party of the Working Class," *Kommunist*, No. 1, January 1965, pp. 97–104 (JPRS 28,914, February 26, 1965).
257 Berlinguer to the PCI Central Committee, *L'Unità*, February 19, 1965 (JPRS 29,136, March 16, 1965), and the PCI Central Committee resolution, *ibid.*, February 20, 1965 (JPRS 29,215, March 22, 1965). The initial PCI reaction to Moscow's December 1964 postponement of the meeting had been noncommittal (*Rinascita*, Vol. XXI, No. 50 [December 19, 1964], p. 2).

The question of peace has been and remains the overriding issue of all contemporary life.

Moreover, its attitude toward the United States was less favorable but not wholly negative. The "wild men" in Washington "have become more active and persistent of late"; however, there are also "sober voices." The American administration, although not leading the "sober circles" as Kennedy did, "vacillates between the 'wild men' and the 'moderates'" but, as "events of recent days [the bombing of North Vietnam] have shown, . . . is increasingly veering in the direction of the 'wild men.'"

With respect to the international Communist movement, this statement was primarily notable for what was *not* said: There was no mention of collective mobilization, no attack on revisionism, no mention of the forthcoming conference, no attacks on the Chinese even implied—indeed, reading it, one might feel that there were no problems at all between Moscow and Peking. Emphasis was put on progress in the "solidarity and unity" of the socialist countries, as exemplified in the Warsaw Pact and CMEA ("on a multilateral and bilateral basis . . . in full conformity with the principles of equality, respect for sovereignty, and national interest"—that is, the rapprochement with Rumania), and on the "greater mutual understanding and reinforced cooperation" arising from the Kosygin visits to Peking, Hanoi, and Pyongyang. With respect to China the USSR-CPR friendship treaty (that is, interstate relations) was stressed; and with respect to Vietnam the promise was reiterated that Moscow would render "the necessary aid and support . . . to strengthen the defense capacity" of North Vietnam. All in all, then, the statement reflected as uncontroversial a Soviet agenda as possible for the March meeting.[258]

In December Moscow had referred to the meeting as the "first session of the editorial commission,"[259] that is, identifying it with the preparatory meetings prior to the 1960 conference. Now, in late February, they termed it only a "consultative meeting."[260] Thus the meeting was emptied of all effectively anti-Chinese content before it ever began.[261]

258 "Foreign Policy and the Contemporary World," *Kommunist*, No. 3, February 1965 (signed to the press February 22, 1965), pp. 3–14, quoted from JPRS 29,538, April 12, 1965.
259 *Pravda*, December 12, 1964.
260 *Ibid.*, February 28, 1965. For earlier indications of Soviet retreat, see François Billoux, "Some Urgent Problems of the International Communist Movement," *World Marxist Review*, Vol. 8, No. 1 (January 1965), pp. 9–14. The Japanese Communist Party has stated that it was "orally" informed on February 26 that the meeting would not be a "drafting committee" but a "consultation." See *Akahata*, April 13, 1965, cited from William McLaughlin, "China's 'Vanguard,'" Radio Free Europe, Munich, May 19, 1965.
261 See in general C. Duevel, "March 1 Conference Overshadowed by Pending Ideological Blast from Peking," Radio Liberty, Munich, March 2, 1965.

The " consultative meeting " of 19 parties (including one " observer " delegation, of the United States Communist Party) met in Moscow from March 1 to 5. The meetings were secret, and the only major published documentation on its discussions available by late 1965 was the speech of the chief Italian Communist delegate, Enrico Berlinguer.[262] The fact that the PCI published it, and a comparison of it with the conference communiqué (summarized below), demonstrates clearly how great a victory the PCI won at the conference.

Berlinguer stated frankly that the PCI's views at this meeting, on which a " consultative character has been opportunely conferred, on some points are different from those of other comrades." After quoting and endorsing Togliatti's Testament's views on a conference, including the criticism of the slowness of democratization in socialist countries, Berlinguer rejected " the myth of an immediate and world-wide solution " of Sino-Soviet differences in favor of " gradual construction " of unity. This would include close contacts with radical revolutionary movements, in order, after the " liquidation of outlived schemes and methods " among communist parties, to create " the basis of a world-wide unity of the whole revolutionary movement." After declaring that the PCI was not professing nationalist and regional views and that the PCI had " no objection in principle " to international meetings, he then declared that the PCI refused to accept Soviet objectives for such a meeting. The two-year attempt to convene one, he said, " could not be judged entirely positively." It had divided parties into " supporters and opponents of a conference."

> The practical result of this . . . was that the conference, long considered imminent, did not take place.

because of the risk of a split. At the present conference " the fundamental part of the revolutionary forces of a whole continent like Asia " is absent. He then flatly declared:

> Our view point is summed up in the conviction that it is right to recognize that the conditions for a new, useful international conference of all the fraternal parties have not yet matured.

Not, he went on, that the idea of such a conference should be abandoned: It should remain a " perspective " but not the immediate goal. However—and here the PCI veto became clear and detailed:

> We are opposed to putting in motion an organizational mechanism before the necessary political conditions have matured, one which would in any case be contrary to the purely consultative character of our meeting. We are absolutely in agreement with those comrades who have excluded any eventuality in which this meeting could adopt

262 Enrico Berlinguer, " La posizione del PCI all' incontro di Mosca," *Rinascita*, Vol. XXII, No. 11 (March 13, 1965), pp. 3–5.

decisions or formulate propositions relative to the date of the conference or the date of the other meetings which may be prepared, as well as to the themes of discussion and its course. We are not in agreement with the views of certain comrades that we should consider the dates and places of the next meetings. I add also, with all explicitness, that we are totally opposed to any proposals which would tend to give organizational continuity, in whatever form, to this meeting. We can in no sense give the impression of constituting an organizing committee for the conference or for an eventual preparatory meeting of the 81 parties.

Probably the British and Cubans, and to some extent the Poles, supported Berlinguer's views, while the Soviets, Bulgarians, French, and the pro-Soviet factions of the three split parties (Australian, Brazilian, and Indian) favored a stronger anti-Chinese stand than actually emerged from the conference.[263]

The Communiqué

The meeting (at least initially) was a fiasco for Moscow. The final communiqué made clear that the participants had only "held consultations" and "exchanged opinions." Only once, in reaffirming the 1960 Statement in favor of international communist conferences, was it specifically stated that the participants "unanimously" agreed. The formulations on international politics reflected the hardening Soviet line against the United States, but an accompanying statement on Vietnam was couched in very general terms. "Unity of action in the struggle against imperialism" was advocated, "even given the existence of disagreements concerning the political line and many important problems in theory and tactics"—that is, it was tacitly admitted that Sino-Soviet disagreements would continue for a long time. The passages concerning further "collective efforts" made clear that the Italian view had prevailed over the Soviet. Despite his death months before, Togliatti was the victor at the conference.

Although the desirability of an international conference was "unanimously" affirmed, it was thereafter so qualified that in fact it was indefinitely postponed. No date was set for such a conference; it was to meet "as a suitable time." Not only was it to be "carried out with the observance of the principles of full equality and the independence of each party" but also it had to be "thoroughly" prepared. Specifically it was to be prepared not by a preparatory committee (a body that the meeting implicitly dissolved) but by a "preliminary consultative meeting" of all the 81 parties that met in Moscow in 1960. Consultations were to be carried out with "all" these parties in order to

263 The hypotheses as to the line-up represent deductions from the positions of these parties before and after the meeting.

"solve the question" of calling the preparatory meeting, and "joint efforts were to be actively exerted to create favorable conditions for participation in its preparation by all the fraternal parties." Thus not only the Italians but presumably also the Chinese could delay even the 81-party preparatory consultative meeting for a long time to come. Finally, the communiqué, like Togliatti's Testament, called for the end of open polemics, the continuation of a comradely "exchange of opinion," and the end of "the interference of some parties in the internal affairs of others." [264]

What was *not* in the communiqué was perhaps an even clearer indication of the Soviet losses than what was in it. There was no mention of collective mobilization or of a "firm rebuff" of the Chinese, indeed no reference to the Chinese at all except the very indirect one about "unfriendly and offensive" polemics, no mention of dogmatism as "the main danger" (and no mention of the Yugoslavs) and no mention of majority decisions being binding on all parties. Indeed, by its emphasis on independence and equality and by its definition of the meeting as consultative, the communiqué implicitly recognized that unanimity was necessary for any pronouncement. Moreover, the reactions of various West European parties to the communiqué showed that the meeting had reinforced their drift away from Moscow,[265] and a subsequent *Pravda* editorial went even farther than the communiqué in emphasizing the necessity for "new" ways and approaches to unity.[266]

The Chinese Response

If the participants in the Moscow 19-party meeting had any illusions left about Peking's response to their efforts, these must have been swept away by the violent March 4 demonstration by Chinese and Vietnamese students against the United States embassy in Moscow. In view of its timing and subsequent developments, it is most probable that this demonstration was staged by the Chinese embassy in Moscow on orders

---

264 " Communiqué on the Consultative Meeting of Representatives of Communist and Workers' Parties in Moscow," *Pravda*, March 10, 1965, quoted from *CDSP*, Vol. XVII, No. 9 (March 24, 1965), pp. 7-8; " Statement on Events in Vietnam by Participants in Consultative Meeting of Communist and Workers' Parties," *Pravda*, March 4, 1965. See Christian Duevel, " First Class Funeral for World Communist Conference," Radio Liberty, Munich, March 10, 1965; r.r.g. [R. Rockingham Gill], " Not with a Bang, But a Whimper," Radio Free Europe, Munich, March 10, 1965; and " United about What?" *The Economist* (London), March 13, 1965.

265 *Daily Worker* (London), March 15, 1965; *De Waarheid* (Amsterdam), March 10, 1965; *L'Unità*, March 10, 1965; see William McLaughlin, " West Europe CP's and the Conference," Radio Free Europe, Munich, March 23, 1965.

266 " An Important Step toward the Consolidation of the World Communist Movement," *Pravda*, March 11, 1965. See also " The Ideological Weapon of the Party," *Kommunist*, No. 4, March 1965, pp. 3-14, and "A Vitally Necessary Matter," *ibid.*, No. 5, March 1965, pp. 3-15.

from Peking. (It bore many resemblances to the 1963 Naushki incident.) [267]

On March 4 several hundred Chinese students led Vietnamese and other students in storming Soviet police lines before the United States embassy. Serious fighting broke out, and many were injured on both sides; Soviet mounted police, in scenes reminiscent of Cossack charges under the Tsars, unsuccessfully rode into the students in order to disperse them and only when several hundred Red Army soldiers arrived did the students disperse.[268] Peking violently protested, alleging that Soviet police had tortured Chinese students and that Soviet hospitals had refused to treat them, and demanding that the Soviet government " admit its errors," " apologize to the students," and " severely punish " the Soviet police involved.[269] The Soviets rejected the protest, termed the demonstration a " premeditated provocation," declared that any similar ones would be " resolutely cut short," and stated that international law required the Soviets to protect foreign embassies.[270] The Chinese on March 16 sent another note, again demanding that Moscow " admit its mistakes " and apologize to the students, and added sarcastically:

> How ruthless you were to the demonstrators against U.S. imperialism, and how abjectly subservient you were to the U.S. imperialists! [271]

When the injured Chinese students returned to Peking they were received with all honors,[272] whereupon Moscow declared (probably with considerable justification) that they were faking their injuries and that the Chinese were concocting a " propaganda farce." [273] The violence of the Chinese response and the genuinely provocative nature of the demonstration and its aftermath fundamentally reflected the grave deterioration in Sino-Soviet relations then under way.

Although the first official Chinese commentary on the conference did not appear until March 22, the Peking press had made clear by reprinting alleged Soviet attacks on China [274] and articles from pro-

---

[267] See Griffith, *The Sino-Soviet Rift, op. cit.*, pp. 174–176.
[268] *The New York Times*, March 5, 1965.
[269] CPR note, *Jen-min Jih-pao*, March 7, 1965, quoted from *Peking Review*, Vol. VIII, No. 11 (March 12, 1965), p. 16.
[270] Soviet note, *Pravda*, March 13, 1965, quoted from *CDSP*, Vol. XVII, No. 10 (March 31, 1965), pp. 4–5,
[271] *Jen-min Jih-pao*, March 17, 1965, quoted from *Peking Review*, Vol. VIII, No. 12 (March 19, 1965), pp. 7–8.
[272] *Ibid.* pp. 8–9.
[273] *Pravda*, March 21, 1965, quoted from *CDSP*, Vol. XVII, No. 10 (March 31, 1965), p. 6.
[274] *Peking Review*, Vol. VIII, No. 10 (March 5, 1965), pp. 27–31, and Vol. VIII, No. 11 (March 12, 1965), pp. 11–12. The Albanians again signaled the Chinese position. On March 18 they declared that the March Moscow conference " of hardened conspirators . . . decisively tore the mask from the present Soviet leadership. . . . Alongside N. Khrushchev and with him, they are the greatest plotters and splitters the history of the international Communist movement had known, revisionists and incorrigible renegades of Marxism-Leninism, allies and auxiliaries of imperialism." (*Zëri i Popullit*, March 18, 1965.)

Chinese parties that in Peking's view the conference represented "Khrushchevism without Khrushchev" and that Moscow was conspiring with Washington to sell out the DRV's and the Viet Cong's interests.[275] On March 20, in publishing the Moscow meeting communiqué, Peking spoke of "a schismatic meeting illegally convoked by the CPSU leadership."[276]

Then on March 22 Peking published "A Comment on the March Moscow Meeting," a programmatic statement that marked the public death sentence for any Sino-Soviet reconciliation and signaled the opening of a major Chinese campaign against the new Soviet leadership. The meeting, it declared, was "illegal and schismatic . . . quite small and most unseemly . . . a gloomy and forlorn affair"—that is, a fiasco. It was "rent by contradictions and disunity": some "wholeheartedly" supported Moscow, some "half-heartedly" [for example, the Italians], some were only a "claque"; and "still others [the Cubans?] may have temporarily fallen into the trap from naïveté." The new Soviet leadership, the article continued, was continuing "Khrushchevism . . . , revisionism, great-power chauvinism, and splittism." They had removed Khrushchev only because he was too "odious" and "stupid":

> All their fine words only amount to selling horsemeat as beefsteak. . . . They are saying one thing and doing another. . . , they are still bent on deepening the differences, wrecking unity, and . . . openly splitting the international Communist movement.

The meeting's proposal for "concerted action" against the imperialists was also a "swindle," for "they continue to adhere to Khrushchev's reactionary policy of Soviet-U.S. cooperation for the domination of the world"—that is, they will not break with Washington and support Chinese policy. Specifically, the article went on, Moscow is willing to compromise on the United Nations Article 19 controversy and to join with Washington to set up a U.N. peacekeeping force; the Soviets want negotiation instead of struggle in Vietnam; they are continuing their attempts to subvert the Japanese, Indonesian, and Burmese Communist parties; and they continue Khrushchev's "erroneous" policies toward Albania and their alignment with Tito. Finally,

> To sum up, what the new leaders of the CPSU have been doing can be described as "three shams and three realities": sham anti-imperialism but real capitulation, sham revolution but real betrayal, sham unity but a real split. They are still doing what Khrushchev did . . . "four alignments with and four alignments against": alignment *with*

---

[275] *Jen-min Jih-pao*, March 9, 10, 12 and 13, 1965. See also the introduction to the third volume of Khrushchev's works, *Peking Review*, Vol. VIII, No. 10 (March 5, 1965), pp. 11–12.

[276] NCNA in English, Peking, March 19, 1965 (SCMP 3423, March 24, 1965).

imperialism *against* socialism, alignment *with* the United States *against* China and the other revolutionary countries, alignment *with* the reactionaries everywhere *against* the national-liberation movements and the people's revolutions, and alignment *with* the Tito clique and renegades of all descriptions *against* all the fraternal Marxist-Leninist Parties and all revolutionaries fighting imperialism. . . .

Polemics cannot be ended, for the modern revisionists must be refuted publicly, even if it takes "ten thousand years." Moreover, the Moscow meeting created "new and serious obstacles" for an international meeting, the preparation for which will now take not four or five years but "twice as long, or even longer"—that is, China will indefinitely refuse to participate. As a precondition for "concerted action against the enemy and unity against imperialism," Moscow must publicly repudiate the meeting as well as "Khrushchev's revisionism, great-power chauvinism, and splittism," the 20th and 22nd CPSU Congresses, and "all the words and deeds of the leaders of the CPSU against China, Albania, the Japanese Communist Party, and the other Marxist-Leninist parties." As for China, the article concluded—and this was its most important point—the Moscow meeting has given the "Marxist-Leninist parties . . . the right to take the initiative":

> We have not given enough support to the revolutionary Left in some countries and henceforth must greatly intensify our endeavors in this respect.

In these words Peking defied the new Soviet leadership, refused to cooperate with it on the Vietnamese or any other issue, and announced the intensification of its anti-Soviet factional activity throughout the international Communist movement.[277]

VII. After the Moscow Meeting: The Further Worsening of Sino-Soviet Relations

Sino-Soviet relations have continued to worsen since the March meeting. Peking has intensified its offensive against Moscow and has continued to center its attack on the Vietnam issue. Although the Chinese propaganda position has been made more difficult by the further hardening of Soviet policy in face of increased American willingness to negotiate in Vietnam, Peking has stubbornly maintained that Moscow continues to plot with Washington to sell out Hanoi. Thus

---

[277] "A Comment on the Moscow Meeting," *Jen-min Jih-pao* and *Hung Ch'i*, March 22, 1965, quoted from *Peking Review*, Vol. VIII, No. 13 (March 26, 1965), pp. 7–13 (italics in original). See j.c.k. [Joseph C. Kun], "Chinese to Increase Factionalism and Continue Polemics," Radio Free Europe, Munich, March 22, 1965. It was preceded on March 18 by a similar *Zëri i Popullit* editorial, "The Splitting Revisionist Meeting of 1 March—A Great Plot Against Marxism-Leninism and International Communism."

each time that Moscow has tried to diminish, although not eliminate, its differences with Peking by increasing Soviet hostility toward Washington, Peking has toughened its line still more. This Soviet response has paralleled Washington's reduction of most of the conditions it had previously attached to negotiations centering on Vietnam, a step that in turn has made the Soviet position more difficult.

On April 3 Moscow secretly proposed a summit conference of the Soviet Union, China, and North Vietnam; Peking rejected the proposal,[278] while Hanoi's response is unknown.

One point of caution must be made: At the level of military policy, where events in Vietnam are increasingly determined, both Moscow and Peking have continued their caution in the face of extended American bombing of North Vietnam and, beginning in April 1965, the increased commitment of American ground troops to South Vietnam. Although in April Moscow for the first time explicitly stated its willingness, in principle, to send Soviet volunteers to North Vietnam, the commitment was carefully qualified and made clearly applicable only to a future contingency, not present policy: "If . . . U.S. aggression is intensified, . . . if need be, and if the DRV government so requests. . . ." [279] Similarly, in early May Peking's army chief of staff Lo Jui-ch'ing, in an otherwise belligerent article, repeated Mao's January formulation that "we will not attack unless we are attacked." [280]

President Johnson's April 7 offer of " unconditional negotiations " [281] was answered by DRV Premier Pham Van Dong the following day, April 8, with a four-point program unacceptable to Washington: (1) immediate and total American withdrawal from South Vietnam, (2) no foreign troops in either North or South thereafter (that is, no U.N. or other peacekeeping force), (3) South Vietnamese affairs to be settled without foreign intervention according to the NLF (Viet Cong) program, and (4) peaceful unification of Vietnam with no foreign intervention.[282] (It therefore seems doubtful that Hanoi then intended serious negotiations with Washington.) True, Moscow also rejected Johnson's proposals and endorsed Pham's,[283] but it did so with little enthusiasm. Peking, on the other hand, continued to insist on the one point Johnson was unwilling to concede: that Washington could negotiate only with

278 Edward Crankshaw, *The Observer* (London), November 14, 1965, p. 5.
279 See the joint USSR-DRV communiqué, *Pravda*, April 18, 1965, quoted from *CDSP*, Vol. XVII, No. 16 (May 12, 1965), pp. 14–15, at p. 13. See also the Kosygin speech, *Pravda*, April 20, 1965. Brezhnev had earlier (*ibid.*, March 24, 1965), apparently in response to a March 22 NLF request for volunteers, hinted that Soviet volunteers might be sent.
280 Lo Jui-ch'ing, " Commemorate the Victory Over German Fascism! " *op. cit.*
281 *The New York Times*, April 8, 1965.
282 Text in *ibid.*, April 14, 1965.
283 " What's All the Fuss about? " *Pravda*, April 10, 1965.

the NLF.[284] Moreover, although Moscow's attitude hardened and in mid-March the Soviet government refused to join London in proposing a cease-fire in Vietnam,[285] China reportedly at least temporarily held up Soviet aid going to Hanoi,[286] refused (as did Hanoi) to allow a visit from London's special envoy Patrick Gordon-Walker,[287] declared that " Khrushchev's successors are pursuing the Khrushchev line to form an anti-Chinese alliance with Nehru's successors," [288] exploded a second atomic bomb,[289] denounced the 17-nation nonaligned appeal as one " masterminded and created . . . by the Tito clique," [290] and sabotaged the attempt—to which the Soviets had agreed—to reconvene the Geneva conference in Cambodia as a means of beginning informal negotiations on Vietnam.[291]

Meanwhile, Peking's polemics became constantly sharper. Perhaps the most substantively significant was a long article by Chief of Staff Lo Jui-ch'ing. By declaring that the Maoist strategy of " active defense should not have the holding or capturing of territory as its major objective " and by reaffirming the superiority of men and revolutionary fervor over weapons and nuclear bombs, he seemed almost to be implying that Hanoi should accept maximum American bombing and continue fighting indefinitely. More generally, he pointed to Soviet caution in its support of Hanoi (because of its interest in avoiding a confrontation with Washington) as evidence of the wrong nature of Soviet policy:

> Countries which have won victory should support and help the revolutionary struggles of those countries and people that have not yet won victory. The socialist countries should serve as base areas for the world revolution. . . . Whether or not a country which has won victory dares to serve as a base area for the world revolution and to support and

[284] See Chou En-lai's message, via Algiers, to U Thant, *The New York Times*, April 7, 1965, and Ch'en Yi's interview with K. S. Karol, *Peking Review*, Vol. VIII, No. 23 (June 4, 1965), pp. 14–15.
[285] Henri Pierre from Moscow in *Le Monde*, March 19, 1965, and *The Times* (London), March 17, 1965.
[286] Henry Tanner from Moscow in *The New York Times*, March 29, 1965.
[287] Anthony Lewis from London in *ibid.*, April 13, 1965.
[288] " Observer," " What Shastri's Soviet Trip Reveals," *Jen-min Jih-pao*, May 27, 1965, quoted from *Peking Review*, Vol. VIII, No. 23 (June 4, 1965), pp. 17–19, at p. 19.
[289] Communiqué of May 14, 1965, in *ibid.*, Vol. VIII, No. 21 (May 21, 1965), p. 6.
[290] " A Comment on the 17-Nation Appeal," *Jen-min Jih-pao*, April 22, 1965, quoted from *Peking Review*, Vol. VIII, No. 18 (April 30, 1965), pp. 10–12, at p. 12.
[291] Cambodia had originally requested the convening, but only to guarantee its neutrality, on March 15; of the two cochairmen, Moscow agreed on April 3 and London on April 26. By that time London was hoping to use the conference to negotiate on Vietnam, whereupon Moscow hesitated, and Sihanouk, presumably under Chinese pressure, on April 24 declared that not Saigon but the NLF must represent South Vietnam, thus ending the whole affair. See Tanner from Moscow in *The New York Times*, April 15, 28, 1965; *The Times* (London), April 27, 1965; and a CPR government statement of May 2, 1965, in *Peking Review*, Vol. VIII, No. 19 (May 7, 1965), pp. 11–12, a commentary on a May 1 Cambodian government statement.

aid the people's revolution in other countries is the touchstone of whether or not it is really for revolution and whether or not it really opposes imperialism.[292]

As has so frequently happened in the course of the Sino-Soviet dispute, Tirana preceded Peking in the public accusations. Although the Chinese did not reprint the Albanian denunciation, one may assume that Peking had already made the charge privately and that the only decision that remained for the Chinese was when to publicly accuse the Soviets on this score. On April 20 the Albanians declared:

> The diabolical aim of the . . . Brezhnev-Kosygin-Mikoyan-Suslov group . . . is to get the Democratic Republic of Vietnam into their snare by undertaking an operation allegedly to send arms and volunteers into that country. . . . This action . . . is accompanied by American bombings, which decrease only with the conclusion of the Soviet operation—that is, when so-called Soviet " volunteers," as alleged experts, rocket technicians, etc., have occupied key places in Vietnam.
>
> Thus, the Soviet revisionists . . . hope and endeavor to create a favorable, relatively calm situation for negotiations with the Americans, and to turn Vietnam and Indochina into a base for plots and threats against the Chinese People's Republic.[293]

In the spring of 1965 there were intensified Sino-Soviet propaganda battles at various international Communist-front organization meetings in Algiers [294] and Winneba, Ghana,[295] and conflicts between the pro-Chinese Japanese Communist Party and Soviet-supported Japanese Communist dissidents and the pro-Soviet left wing of the Japanese Socialist Party.[296]   The Chinese protested against Soviet expulsion of Chinese students in Moscow [297] and the prevention of a North Vietnamese

---

292 Lo Jui-ch'ing, " Commemorate the Victory Over German Fascism! " *op. cit.* For other anti-Soviet attacks see " A Great Victory for Leninism," *Hung Ch'i*, No. 4, April 1965, and *Peking Review*, Vol. VIII, No. 19 (May 7, 1965), pp. 7–10; " The Historical Experience of the War Against Fascism," *Jen-min Jih-pao*, May 9, 1965, and *Peking Review*, Vol. VIII, No. 20 (May 14, 1965), pp. 15–22; and statements by Ch'en Yi and P'eng Ch'en in a Hong Kong dispatch in *The New York Times*, May 30, 1965.

293 " The Traitorous Group of Soviet Revisionists Supports American Imperialists in the Aggression Against Vietnam," *Zëri i Popullit*, April 20, 1965. See Griffith, *Communism in Europe, op. cit.*, Vol. 2, Appendix to Chapter 1.

294 At the Afro-Asian Economic Seminar, February 22–28, 1965, and the Fourth International Teachers' Conference, April 8–18 (NCNA in English, April 21, 1965, 1901 GMT).

295 At the April 15–21 WFDY meeting (NCNA in English, May 2, 1965, 2041 GMT) and the May 4 AAPSO conference (NCNA in English, May 9, 1965, 1905 GMT, and May 18, 1965, 2200 GMT); " Hold Still Higher the Afro-Asian People's Revolutionary Barrier of Solidarity Against Imperialism," *Jen-min Jih-pao*, May 19, 1965 (SCMP, 3464, May 25, 1965, pp. 22–23); speech of Liao Cheng-chih, *Peking Review*, Vol. VIII, No. 21 (May 21, 1965), pp. 14–17; resolution, *ibid.*, pp. 17–19; Hsien Pien, " Success of the Fourth Afro-Asian Peoples' Solidarity Conference," *ibid.*, Vol. VIII, No. 22 (May 28, 1965), pp. 13–15; and resolution on Vietnam, *ibid.* pp. 15–16.

296 *Akahata*, April 2 and 14, 1965.

297 In an April 13 Chinese Foreign Ministry memorandum to the Soviet embassy in Peking (NCNA in English, May 5, 1965, 1741 GMT).

student protest in Leningrad.[298] Simultaneously Peking continued its efforts to exclude the Soviet Union and Malaysia from the second Bandung conference scheduled for late June in Algiers (see Part X).[299]

In late May and mid-June, Peking picked up the Albanian accusation that Moscow was plotting with Washington to the disadvantage of both North Vietnam and China. It was used first in a speech by P'eng Chen at the PKI Higher Party School[300] and then, even more extensively and authoritatively, in a long editorial on June 13, 1965.[301]

The June 13, 1965, article began by reiterating the thesis of the ninth " Comment," [302] that Khrushchev's social base was " the new privileged bourgeois stratum." This same stratum, the article added, " got rid of Khrushchev " because he was " too stupid and disreputable " and therefore " endangered their dominant position." His replacements, the article continued, have been Khrushchev's closest associates, were fundamentally associated with his whole revisionist line, and, like him, represent the " privileged bourgeois stratum " and therefore " can only act in conformity with the interests of that stratum and pursue a revisionist line. . . ." (In other words, the new Soviet leadership must be revisionist.) They are " old actors who face the . . . awkward and difficult problem of how to deck themselves out as new ones." Therefore they face an insoluble contradiction: They profess revolution but practice " Soviet-U.S. cooperation " against revolution. Their method is, therefore, ". . . compared to Khrushchev, a more covert, more cunning, and more dangerous revisionism. . . ." P'eng Chen went even further, implicitly applying to the new Soviet leadership the formulation of Lenin and of the 1949 Cominform Resolution:

> Objectively they are a political detachment of the bourgeoisie . . . its agents in the labor movement,

clearly implying that they are even worse than Sukarno and Norodom Sihanouk:

> They really cannot be compared with the anti-imperialist and revolutionary representatives of the national bourgeoisie in Asia, Africa, and Latin America, nor even with the anti-imperialist and patriotic representatives of royal families and the nobility.

The article accused the new Soviet leadership of continuing

298 NCNA in English, May 6, 1965, 1301 GMT. Hanoi did not make any reference to the incident.
299 For example, Peter Grose from Moscow in *The New York Times*, June 13, 1965.
300 P'eng Chen in *Peking Review*, Vol. VIII, No. 24 (June 11, 1965), p. 20.
301 " Carry the Struggle Against Khrushchev Revisionism Through to the End," *Jen-min Jih-pao* and *Hung Ch'i*, June 13, 1965, and *Peking Review*, Vol. VIII, No. 25 (June 18, 1965), pp. 5–10.
302 See p. 43.

Khrushchev's anti-Albanian and pro-Indian policies and of trying to subvert the Japanese and Indonesian Communist parties. Worse,

> while making some gesture of aid to Vietnam, they have divulged their "aid" plans to the Americans in advance and have been busy in Washington, London and Paris trying to bring about peace negotiations, in a painstaking effort to find a "way out" for the U.S. aggressors.

The article then turned to a Soviet argument that, one suspects, has probably been causing the Chinese some trouble: "unity against imperialism." The Soviets, the article declared, preach "unity," in spite of having disrupted unity by "brazenly calling the schismatic March meeting." Moreover,

> they have a despicable aim . . . to capitalize on the aspirations of the people of the world for . . . closer unity . . . in the face of the U.S. imperialists' rabid aggression.

The article concluded:

> We therefore must continue our triumphant pursuit and firmly carry forward the fight against Khrushchev revisionism to the very end.[303]

The Soviets had long been patient in the face of the rising post-March 1965 Chinese polemics, but, predictably, their patience—or was it perhaps their hesitation to act—gave way. P'eng Chen's speech proved too much for Moscow to bear, and upon their departure to the PKI's forty-fifth anniversary celebration the Soviet delegation issued a statement accusing P'eng of having made "provocational and slanderous" attacks on CPSU policy and the Soviet government expressed regret that such a "memorable" occasion should have been used by the Chinese for their "schismatic ends."[304]

Yet despite this brief outburst, the Soviets were not anxious to resume either public attacks on the Chinese or collective mobilization designed to expel Peking from the international Communist movement, or at least formally to condemn its conduct. As the March 1965 19-party Moscow conference demonstrated, the new Soviet leadership had initially been less successful than Khrushchev in aligning pro-Soviet communist parties in favor of condemning the Chinese. However, as has been pointed out earlier, the new leadership was less committed to these kinds of collective mobilization, more doubtful of their success,

---

303 P'eng Chen, in his speech at the PKI Higher Party School (*op. cit.*, p. 18), modified this conclusion somewhat (but presumably only for tactical purposes) by prefacing the same statement with: "We still place some hope in the leadership of the CPSU, and will welcome the day when they admit and rectify their mistakes. . . . But it seems that this day is still far off."

304 *Pravda*, June 7, 1965, quoted from *CDSP*, Vol. XVII, No. 23 (June 30, 1965), pp. 19–20.

and therefore more able to accept and cope with the consequences of their failure.

Where their policy not only differed from Khrushchev's but was in my view more successful than his, was in their acceptance of the failure of collective mobilization as originally perceived by the Soviets (that is, either expulsion or condemnation of the Chinese) and their subsequent attempt to salvage from it what they could and, by making a virtue of necessity, to profit from their defeat by improving relations with those parties that had opposed collective mobilization, including North Vietnam and North Korea. These parties had previously been pro-Chinese but would, Moscow had reason to hope, because of the scaled-down Soviet objectives, more rapidly turn to a neutral position between Moscow and Peking.

This was a gradual, prolonged development in Soviet policy. As the drive to condemn the Chinese declined, the drive for rapprochement with the dissidents intensified. How the new Moscow leadership had begun immediately after Khrushchev's fall to mend their fences with Havana, Hanoi, and Pyongyang has already been described. The beginning of the American bombing of North Vietnam in February had greatly speeded up the improvement of Moscow's relations with Hanoi and Pyongyang and the American intervention in Santo Domingo in April probably further strengthened Soviet-Cuban relations because of the threat it implied to Cuba.

After the March meeting, Soviet policy within the international Communist movement concentrated on general approval of the documents of the consultative meeting as a step in the direction of unifying the movement. The policy theme was " joint action " against the imperialists, particularly by aid to North Vietnam.[305] The call for convening a new international conference was not silenced, but it was certainly toned down. For example, of the twenty-three *Pravda* summaries of Communist and workers' parties' resolutions, communiqués, and speeches supporting the March meeting between March 13 and May 30, 1965, only eight explicitly referred to a new international conference.[306] This was particularly remarkable because the full texts of

[305] See " On Results of the March 1–5, 1965 Consultative Meeting of Representatives of Communist and Workers' Parties—Resolution of Plenary Session of the CPSU Central Committee Adopted March 26, 1965," *Pravda*, March 27, 1965 (*CDSP*, Vol. XVII, No. 11 [April 7, 1965], pp. 5 and 13).

[306] French Communist Party Politburo communiqué, *Pravda*, March 13, 1965; declaration of the Presidium of the Central Committee of the Czechoslovak Communist Party, *ibid*., March 19, 1965; Finnish Central Committee resolution, *ibid*., March 25, 1965; CPSU Central Committee plenum resolution, *ibid*., March 27, 1965; resolution of the plenum of the French Communist Party, *ibid*., April 3, 1965; National Council of the Communist Party of India resolution on the Moscow meeting, *ibid*., April 7, 1965; the Greek Communist Party Central Committee resolution, *ibid*., April 9, 1965; and the French-Portuguese Communist communiqué, *ibid*., May 14, 1965.

seven of the fifteen documents that in *Pravda*'s summary versions did not contain specific support for a new world conference did in fact approve of the project, if in some cases with reservations.[307]

Moscow gave indications that the Soviets had far from entirely given up the conference project—for example, they published a strong Portuguese resolution in June.[308] But *Pravda* did not reprint either the U.S. Communist Party's demand for preparation for a new world conference to be held at the earliest possible moment [309] or that of the South African Communist Party, which not only specified that the new conference should be held at " the earliest possible moment " but stated that

> unwillingness or refusal of any section of the movement, however important, to join in consultations should not be allowed to prevent those who are willing to meet together from doing so.[310]

The South African Communist Party's appeal made explicit the willingness to exclude Peking and its allies implied in the Portuguese acceptance " in principle " of an 81-party consultative meeting. It appeared, as did the British Communist Party resolution opposing a meeting of the 81 parties at the present time [311] and the Italian position, that " the eventual international conference should not be seen as a prerequisite for but as the culmination of a gradual process of restoring unity," [312] in the *Information Bulletin* of the *World Marxist Review*. It was, therefore, difficult to determine whether the South African appeal indicated stepped-up Soviet pressure for the conference or the *Information Bulletin*'s current policy of presenting diversified views. Yet signs that Soviet support for a new international conference was gradually increasing during the course of the summer made it likely that publication of the South African appeal suited Moscow's purposes in any case.[313] Certainly, although the Soviets had been careful not to

---

307 Uruguayan Communist Party editorial on the Moscow meeting, *Pravda*, March 14, 1965, and *Information Bulletin*, No. 42, May 13, 1965; Communist Party of Germany, *Pravda*, March 18, 1965, and *Information Bulletin*, No. 47, July 6, 1965; statement by the Eleventh Congress of the Communist Party of Norway, *Pravda*, March 29, 1965, and *Information Bulletin*, No. 43, June 3, 1965; thirty-first plenary meeting of the Central Committee of the Communist Party of Colombia, *Pravda*, April 6, 1965, and *Information Bulletin*, No. 46, June 30, 1965; statement of the Communist Party of Spain, *Pravda*, April 10, 1965, and *Information Bulletin*, No. 43, June 3, 1965; Czechoslovak Communist Party plenum, *Pravda*, April 25, 1965, and *Information Bulletin*, No. 44, June 4, 1965; and Canadian Communist Party Secretary-General's report to the National Committee, *Pravda*, April 29, 1965, and *Information Bulletin*, No. 48, July 16, 1965.
308 *Pravda*, June 13, 1965.
309 *The Worker*, May 9, 1965, and *Information Bulletin*, No. 47, July 6, 1965.
310 *Ibid.*, No. 52, August 26, 1965.
311 *Daily Worker*, March 15, 1965, and *Information Bulletin*, No. 39, April 23, 1965.
312 *L'Unità*, March 10, 1965, and *Information Bulletin*, No. 38, April 21, 1965.
313 See the French-Bulgarian communiqué, *Pravda*, July 7, 1965, and the resolution of the Brazilian Communist Party, *ibid.*, August 27, 1965.

give the impression that the CPSU was reactivating collective mobilization in its former sense of expulsion or condemnation of Peking, the
round of bilateral meetings conducted by Soviet leaders during the
summer and fall of 1965 served as a form of the "consultations" called
for by the March meeting communiqué.

In September Brezhnev underlined both the importance and the
extent of these visits.[314] He did not call for a new international conference or refer to the Moscow March meeting. However, in the
Czechoslovak-USSR joint communiqué[315] and the GDR-USSR joint
communiqué,[316] both parties had expressed the opinion that conferences
such as the June meeting in Brussels of the communist parties of the
capitalist countries of Europe "create favorable conditions for the
calling of an international conference of all Communist and workers'
parties in the future."

The high-level Czechoslovak, Rumanian, and East German delegations' visits to Moscow in September represented Soviet attempts to
consolidate their remaining authority in Eastern Europe. Moscow made
substantial economic and political concessions in that generous trade
agreements followed, and the Soviets recognized formally the principles
of equality of rights, independence, national sovereignty, mutual aid,
and noninterference in each other's affairs, combined with socialist
internationalism, as a basis for relations among socialist states.[317]
These Soviet concessions were not without price. As Brezhnev made
quite explicit,

> Our friendship fosters the further development of mutually advan-
> tageous collaboration in the fields of politics, economics, and culture.
> The more such actual accomplishments there are, the stronger the
> fraternal ties that unite us. The closer our friendship, the broader the
> possibilities for collaboration for accelerating our common progress
> forward.[318]

Moreover, the September meetings demonstrated that although

---

[314] For example, the CPSU-Chilean Communist Party communiqué, *Pravda*, July 10,
1965 (*CDSP*, Vol. XVII, No. 28 [August 4, 1965], p. 26), stressed that both parties
considered the Moscow March meeting an important step in the direction of
unity without referring to a new international conference or the proposed preliminary
meeting of 81 parties. Considering that an earlier Chilean-Bolivian declaration
(*Pravda*, June 3, 1965) had specifically endorsed the initiative for convening a
consultative conference of the 81 Communist and workers' parties, the omission was
clearly Soviet inspired. Moreover, the CPSU-Chilean communiqué followed by only
a few days the French-Bulgarian communiqué, stating that "the organization of a
new conference of the international Communist and workers' parties fully corresponds
to the interests of the international Communist movement."
[315] *Pravda*, September 30, 1965.
[316] *Ibid.*, September 16, 1965, and *Neues Deutschland*, September 28, 1965.
[317] Content note on trade agreements, also Soviet-Rumanian joint comuniqué, *Pravda*,
September 14, 1965 (excerpts in *CDSP*, Vol. XVII, No. 37 [October 6, 1965],
pp. 19–21.)
[318] *Pravda*, September 11, 1965 (*CDSP, ibid.* p. 17).

Soviet pressure for a new international conference was temporarily scaled down, Moscow appeared to be renewing Khrushchev's drive of the preceding April for "perfecting" the Warsaw Treaty Organization. At the Czechoslovak-Soviet friendship rally on September 15 Brezhnev reminded Novotný and in effect warned other East European Warsaw Treaty members that

> The present day situation puts on the agenda the task of further perfecting the organization of the Warsaw Treaty, this powerful instrument of peace.[319]

That the Czechoslovak leader viewed this proposition somewhat unenthusiastically may be seen from Novotný's response that Czechoslovakia was

> fully aware of the importance of strengthening our defense capabilities and our armed forces, in keeping with our obligation as members of the Warsaw Treaty Organization.[320]

Nor did the final communiqué contain Brezhnev's formulation; rather, both delegations noted

> that the security of Czechoslovak Socialist Republic boundaries are reliably guaranteed by the Treaty of Friendship, Mutual Aid, and Postwar Cooperation between the two countries and also by the Warsaw Pact.[321]

Earlier the Soviet-Rumanian communiqué had referred to the need for strengthening the might and defense potential of the Warsaw Pact member states "and all socialist countries"—surely a concession to Rumania's self-proclaimed neutrality in the Sino-Soviet dispute. The GDR-USSR joint communiqué that followed did not mention the organizational issue but emphasized that if the NATO states gave West Germany nuclear weapons, the "GDR and the Soviet Union, together with the rest of the Warsaw Pact member states," would be forced to "take measures" to ensure their own security.[322]

That the Soviets had not substantially retreated, however, became obvious with Brezhnev's September speech when he underlined that recent discussions had taken place among socialist states on

> the question of improving the activity of the Warsaw Pact Organization and the need to set up within the framework of that pact a permanent and prompt mechanism for considering pressing problems.[323]

But the Soviets were, if anything, in basically the same dilemma as before. The Portuguese Communist Party resolution called for an

[319] *Pravda*, September 15, 1965 (*CDSP, ibid.* p. 22).
[320] *Pravda, ibid.* (*CDSP, ibid.*).
[321] *Pravda, ibid.* (*CDSP, ibid.* p. 24).
[322] GDR-USSR joint communiqué, *op. cit.*
[323] *Pravda*, September 30, 1965.

international conference [324] yet simultaneously tried to accommodate reluctant Soviet supporters within the international Communist movement by indicating that no new international organizational form should be set up and that formally decisions of an international conference are not binding on its members, quoting Lenin to the effect that

> The moral significance of the decisions of an international conference is such that non-observance is an exception in practice.[325]

Moreover, the Portuguese resolution both supported the conclusions of the March 1 meeting and stressed that:

> It is known that Communist and workers' parties differ in their views as to the forms and methods of overcoming the existing differences, the resolution says. In the majority of cases this difference reflects the striving of each party to make its own constructive contribution toward the restoration and consolidation of the unity of the international Communist movement.

Meanwhile, the head of a PCI delegation had declared upon his return from Hanoi:

> The Vietnamese Party of Labor is one of the parties which did not take part in the Moscow Conference, and disagrees with the CPSU and, in fact, with us as well, on the advisability of participating in this conference; but we found a common ground, and what seemed important to us and which should be recorded here as well, is that they not only expressed their interest, their sympathy—as the party secretary put it—with the last words Comrade Togliatti left us, but that they consider the watchwords stressed in Togliatti's testament—unity in diversity—to be a watchword which should be adopted by the whole Communist movement and which in any event the Party of Labor accepts as a watchword, as a direction which had value for it.[326]

The same note was struck in the Cuban-Italian communiqué repeating of Berlinguer's March formulations about

> new forms of unity, solidarity, and cooperation for the whole world revolutionary and working-class movement, based on equality, independence of judgment and respect for the norms that should regulate relations between all the Marxist-Leninist parties.[327]

Peking, to whom any opposition to a Soviet-staged conference was welcome, could only be pleased. As for Moscow, perhaps the most uncertain factor in Sino-Soviet relations throughout the summer of

---

[324] *Ibid.* June 13, 1965.
[325] Ye. Bugayev in *Partiinaya Zhizn*, No. 7, 1965 (quoting Lenin, *Sochineniya*, Vol. XIII, pp. 66–67), cited from r.r.g. [R. Rockingham Gill], " B and K Against a Second Cominform," Radio Free Europe, Munich, June 1, 1965.
[326] Giancarlo Pajetta in *L'Unità*, May 20, 1965, quoted from JPRS 30,437, June 7, 1965, pp. 1–14, at p. 5.
[327] PURS-PCI communiqué, Havana, June 4, 1965, in *L'Unità*, June 9, 1965, quoted from Kevlin Devlin, " The Rome-Havana Entente," Radio Free Europe, Munich, June 12, 1965.

1965 was the question of whether the Soviets had given up, suspended their attempt at collective mobilization to expel the Chinese, or changed the fundamental character of collective mobilization by exchanging the Soviet goal of expulsion for a call to " joint action," thereby making it acceptable to their previously reluctant supporters.

VIII. Soviet and Chinese Changing Relations toward the " Third World "

The New Soviet Leadership

In retrospect it seemed as of November 1965 that the new Soviet leadership by the spring of 1965 at the latest had undertaken a significant reappraisal of its policy toward underdeveloped areas in general and toward Nasser and Algeria in particular. Several factors were probably involved in this decision: First, Soviet aid commitments, both economic and military, to underdeveloped areas had been roughly 500 million dollars in 1963 and had risen to approximately 800 million in 1964. Given Soviet domestic economic and resource allocation problems, the step-up in Soviet economic and military aid to North Korea and North Vietnam, and, probably, increased Soviet general military allocations, this aid had to be cut. (Moreover, in some countries, notably Indonesia, Soviet military aid was coming dangerously close to the thermonuclear threshold.) Second, the new Soviet leadership probably felt that the underdeveloped areas had proved themselves increasingly intractable for Soviet purposes. Ben Bella and Nasser were not becoming other Castros. The 1964 crushing of the Congo rebellion had demonstrated that Moscow could not match Washington's long-range air- and sea-lift capacity. The Afro-Asian bloc was increasingly split, and by both its own dissensions and those caused by the Chinese and their Indonesian allies. That is, as in Cuba in 1962, Khrushchev's forward policies in North Africa and elsewhere had resulted in gains not commensurate with the risks and expenditures involved. Third, the Arab Communists, and particularly their most influential one, the Syrian leader Khaled Bagdash, were strongly opposing the Khrushchevian policy of dissolving communist parties and trying to infiltrate and convert radical nationalist movements. In view of the general decision by the new Soviet leadership to cut Khrushchev's losses in the international Communist movement and the danger that Arab Communists might drift toward Peking, it must have seemed desirable to Brezhnev and Kosygin, particularly because of Bagdash's membership in the 26-party preparatory committee, to veer back toward Khrushchev's point of view.

Moscow therefore apparently decided to concentrate on only very selected targets, to cut down aid allocations, to stop giving aid without strings, to concentrate on areas of common interest, and to put relations with radical nationalist movements more on a state-to-state than an ideological basis.[328]

Initially Brezhnev and Kosygin still seemed to be feeling their way, and contradictory tendencies appeared in Soviet policy. However the coup deposing Ben Bella in Algeria was certainly one of the more important events contributing to Moscow's disillusionment with the policy of rapprochement and infiltration of radical nationalist movements.

Early in the morning of June 19, 1965, Algerian army troops under the orders of Defense Minister Boumédienne surrounded Ben Bella's villa in Algiers, arrested him, and transported him to an unknown place of imprisonment. Boumédienne took over the government, purged many of Ben Bella's associates, including all the extreme left-wing, Marxist, and Communist ones, and set up what amounts to a military dictatorship of a radical nationalist, Moslem, xenophobic, anti-Western, and anti-Communist character.

The background of this coup is still far from clear but it appears that Ben Bella was preparing to purge some of Boumédienne's associates, and Boumédienne in turn had become suspicious of Ben Bella's relations with secular Marxists at home and Soviet, French, and Italian Communists abroad. Since Boumédienne had the monopoly on armed force he succeeded easily, the more so—and this is perhaps the key point of Soviet as well as PCI and PCF miscalculation—since Algerian communism was always a weak sect composed primarily of Europeans and without any roots in the population at large: the equivalent of the Jews in East European communism. Moreover, the Algerian revolution in general, and the FLN in particular, had always been much more radical nationalist than Marxist and Boumédienne's coup was in a sense the last purging of European influence.

Communist reaction to the Boumédienne coup was markedly diverse. The Italian and French Communists attacked Boumédienne strongly, particularly when he began arresting Algerian Communists. (Boumédienne continued Algeria's excellent relations with General de Gaulle.) The Soviets and East Europeans remained officially silent, but by

---

[328] I have profited greatly in writing the above from conversations with Mr. Ra'anan and with Professor Marshall Goldman. See also A. H. [Arnold Hottinger], " Moskaus Einfluss in der arabischen Welt," *Neue Zürcher Zeitung*, February 28, 1965, and " Die Strategie der Kommunisten im Mittleren Osten," *ibid.*, September 3, 1965; and, for ideological formulation, Polyansky's October Revolution anniversary speech in *Pravda*, November 7, 1965, and " The Supreme International Duty of the Country of Socialism," *ibid.*, October 27, 1965, both discussed later. (Although the 1963 and 1964 figures were higher in part because of long-term commitments for steel mill construction in India and Iran, the 1965 decline in aid commitments was still very substantial.)

reprinting PCI and PCF attacks, and by other means, Moscow indicated how surprised and displeased it was. Castro denounced the coup in an emotional outburst, primarily caused, one may assume, by his close personal relations with Ben Bella. The Chinese and the Albanians, conversely, endorsed Boumédienne immediately, and Tirana and the pro-Chinese Belgian Communists denounced Ben Bella as an ally of the Khrushchev revisionists.[329]

By the autumn of 1965, however, Algiers' relations with Moscow were improving, but Boumédienne continued his repression of Algerian Communists.[330] In August 1965, an authoritative Soviet ideological pronouncement had stressed that

> the Communists welcome any social forces that sincerely aspire to socialism, but do not dissolve into them, rather occupying their own place, expressing the interests of the most advanced and revolutionary class of our time, the working class. . . . The Communists say to the representatives of the non-communist currents of socialism: You are for socialism; very well, we sincerely rejoice at this. But we do not conceal the fact that we are striving to introduce into any revolutionary movement a genuinely scientific theory and practice of socialism.[331]

Moscow subsequently made it clear that the Boumédienne coup in Algeria and the Indonesian crisis had limited Soviet-Algerian and Soviet-Indonesian relations to the state level in contrast with the continuing more cordial relations with such still " revolutionary democratic " states as the UAR, Guinea, Ghana, Burma, and Mali.[332]

China's Position

In general, Chinese influence in the underdeveloped world, after having risen in 1964, declined considerably in 1965. Its influence in East and Southeast Asia declined largely as a result of the 1965 American military escalation in Vietnam and the Indonesian crisis. Its influence

[329] See *L'Unità*, *L'Humanité*, and *Pravda*, June 20, 1965, *et seqq.*; Castro on Radio Havana, June 26, 1965; *La Voix du Peuple* (Brussels), pro-Chinese, June 25 and July 2, 1965; *Zëri i Popullit*, July 10, 1965; and NCNA, June 20, 1965. The best analytical treatment of communist reaction to the coup is in a series of Radio Free Europe, Munich, papers: Kevin Devlin, " The Communists and the Coup," June 27, 1965; and William McLaughlin, " The Irrelevant Communists," June 30, 1965, and " Algeria and the Sino-Soviet Rift," July 14, 1965. See also Charles F. Gallagher, " The Franco-Algerian Agreements," American Universities Field Staff Reports, North Africa Series, Vol. XI, No. 1 (August 1965).

[330] See Philippe Herreman, " Les origines de la campagne anti-communiste," *Le Monde*, October 10–11, 1965.

[331] Fedor Burlatsky, " The Liberation Movement and Scientific Socialism," *Pravda*, August 15, 1965, quoted from *CDSP*, Vol. XVII, No. 33 (September 8, 1965), pp. 3–5, at p. 5. See also Fritz Ermarth, " Who Has the Patent on Socialism?" Radio Free Europe, Munich, August 20, 1965, and V. Midtsev, " Guinea on a New Path," *Kommunist*, No. 12, August 1965, pp. 85–93.

[332] See the October Slogans (*Pravda*, October 23, 1965); Christian Duevel, " Comparison of October Slogans, 1964–1965," Radio Liberty, Munich, *Daily Information Bulletin*, No. 2112 (October 27, 1965); and Polyansky, *op. cit.*

in Latin America, seen in the creation of new splinter communist parties in Colombia, Ecuador, and Peru, declined, primarily because of the Soviet-Cuban rapprochement and the consequent worsening of relations between Peking and Havana. It was also due to the general decline of the extreme Left in Latin America, which was exemplified in the failure of the Venezuelan guerrilla movement to disrupt the Acción Democrática government, the victory of Frei in Chile, and the overthrow of Goulart in Brazil, plus, in the short run (in the long run its effect may well be the opposite), the American military intervention in Santo Domingo.[333]

The decline of Chinese influence was the most striking in Africa, which Peking considered to be in the center of the liberation struggle.[334] Although Chou En-lai's two visits there, in February 1964[335] and June 1965, gained China some influence in Tanzania and Mali, probably, when coupled with a series of events in Africa itself, they were a net loss to Peking. Chou's repeated declaration that "the revolutionary situation in Africa is excellent" reminded most African leaders that the Chinese were supporting plotters against themselves. This impression was strengthened by the coming to power of extreme, pro-Chinese radicals in Brazzaville and the Chinese support for the unsuccessful Congo rebellion (the American-Belgian-South African repression of the rebellion hardly helped American prestige by associating Washington with mercenaries from Pretoria but it demonstrated that Chinese support would bring in effective Western countermeasures), the instability in Burundi that resulted in the expulsion of the Chinese, the unsuccessful Chinese operations in Kenya, and the unsuccessful coup in the Niger, whose participants had had Chinese support and training. In general, African unity declined during the period. The political climate moved sharply to the right as a result of the defeat of the Congo rising, the Kenyan turn against both China and the Soviet Union because of their support to Odinga and other extreme radicals, and the building by Houphouet-Boigny of a French-speaking coalition against Nkrumah and the radical African states. Moreover, most African states were unfavorably impressed by the Chinese willingness to sacrifice everything to their struggle against the Soviet Union in the Afro-Asian Peoples' Solidarity Organization and the Algiers conference

---

[333] Ernst Halperin, *Nationalism and Communism in Chile*, op. cit., and *The Peaceful and the Violent Road*, op. cit.; and Joseph J. Lee, "Communist China's Latin American Policy," *Asian Survey*, Vol. IV, No. 11 (November 1964), pp. 1123–1134. See also Griffith, *Communism in Europe*, op. cit., Vol. 2, p. 4, note 4.

[334] It was so stated in the secret Chinese military publication *Kung-tso T'ung-hsun* (*Bulletin of Activities*), quoted by John Wilson Lewis, "China's Secret Military Papers: 'Continuities' and 'Revelations,'" *The China Quarterly*, No. 18 (April–June 1964), pp. 68–78, at p. 78.

[335] W. A. C. Adie, "Chou En-lai on Safari," *ibid.* pp. 174–194.

preparations. In sum, then, Chinese influence in Africa by the end of 1965 seemed largely confined to Brazzaville and Tanzania.[336]

Moreover, although at the beginning of 1965 China's desire to form a new, revolutionary, United Nations–type organization received a great push forward from Sukarno's withdrawal from the United Nations and his proposal to form a new, " revolutionary " one, the necessary support from the rest of the third world was not forthcoming. Both Peking and Jakarta probably envisaged a second Bandung conference as a major step in this direction. Even so, the Chinese were cautious in their support of Sukarno's step and avoided any firm commitment to his proposal,[337] presumably because they realized that they could not as yet persuade many underdeveloped states to withdraw from the only organization where their votes are not overshadowed by their lack of political and military power.[338] But that Peking was committed to paralyzing the United Nations, even if it did not hope that it could soon destroy it, became clear in mid-February when the Albanian General Assembly delegate almost succeeded in forcing a vote on the Article 19 issue (compulsory assessment for United Nations peacekeeping activities) and thus wrecking the efforts for a Soviet-American compromise on it. Although Moscow and Washington eventually succeeded in foiling this plan, several African states demonstrated their opposition to great-power domination by endorsing the vote or abstaining.[339]

IX. Impact of International Crises on Sino-Soviet Relations, 1965

Vietnam, Summer–Autumn 1965

" Political power," Chairman Mao once remarked, " grows out of the barrel of a gun." [340] Although like the Soviets and the North Vietnamese,

[336] For Chinese activities in Africa see Robert A. Scalapino, " Africa and Peking's United Front," *Current Scene*, Vol. III, No. 26 (September 1, 1965), and " Sino-Soviet Competition in Africa," *Foreign Affairs*, Vol. 42, No. 4 (July 1964), pp. 640–654; John K. Cooley, *East Wind Over Africa* (New York: Walker, 1965); Donald W. Klein, " Peking's Diplomat in Africa," *Current Scene*, Vol. II, No. 36 (July 1, 1964); " China and Africa," *The Mizan News Letter*, Vol. 6, No. 9 (October 1964), pp. 15–19; Jan S. Prybyla, " Communist China's Economic Relations with Africa 1960–1964," *Asian Survey*, Vol. IV, No. 11 (November 1964), pp. 1135–1143; Griffith, " Africa," *op. cit.*, pp. 168–189, at pp. 185–189; and j.c.k. [Joseph C. Kun], " Chinese Frustration in East Africa," Radio Free Europe, Munich, July 28, 1965, and " Chinese Troubles in Mali?" *ibid.*, September 29, 1965.

[337] See Chou En-lai's January 24, 1965 speech and Ch'en Yi's January 26 one in *Peking Review*, Vol. VIII, No. 5 (January 29, 1965), pp. 5–7, and a Chinese-Indonesian communiqué of January 28, 1965, and " New Page in Sino-Indonesian Comradeship in Arms," *Jen-min Jih-pao*, January 30, 1965, and *Peking Review, ibid.* pp. 7–9.

[338] For Afro-Asian reluctance to leave the United Nations see Radio Algiers, January 25, 1965, and Radio Accra, January 26, 1965.

[339] Hamilton from the United Nations in *The New York Times*, February 17–19, 1965, and *Zëri i Popullit*, February 17–20, 1965.

[340] Mao Tse-tung, " Problems of War and Strategy," *Selected Military Writings of Mao Tse-tung* (Peking: Foreign Languages Press, 1963), p. 272.

he was probably surprised by the arrival of massive American air, sea, and ground military reinforcements in Vietnam [341] he may have understood something of its significance, as the most important factor in international relations in general, and in Sino-Soviet relations in particular, since the 1962 Cuban missile crisis.

In the fall of 1962 and the winter of 1964/65 the Viet Cong shifted from guerrilla warfare to a main forces offensive, which in turn implied even greater military dependence upon, and control by, Hanoi. North Vietnam probably took this decision after it had been assured in November 1964 by the post-Khrushchev Soviet leadership that Soviet SAM's would protect Hanoi and Haiphong against any American air retaliation. Hanoi anticipated that its move into the main forces stage would soon make Washington decide to abandon the war.

The contrary occurred. By the summer and autumn of 1965 as Bernard Fall (an observer unsympathetic to the Johnson Administration's policy), wrote in October 1965 after his return from a trip to South Vietnam, the massive injection of American military power had made the South Vietnam war, in the short run, militarily "unlosable." [342] This was particularly true of American air power which had begun to diminish the effectiveness of North Vietnam's communications and logistic routes to the South and which in the South itself, more importantly, had disrupted Viet Cong military installations and rest areas, thereby diminishing the effectiveness of their guerrilla attacks. This led in turn to a steady rise in Viet Cong defections, a decline in defections from the South Vietnamese army, stabilization of the political situation in Saigon, and an increasing worldwide realization that Washington could and would hold on in South Vietnam. Meanwhile, American air and port installations in South Vietnam were being built on so large a scale as significantly to improve American military containment of China.

As of November 1965 neither side was yet winning in South Vietnam; indeed there were some signs that Hanoi was again intensifying military operations, this time with regular North Vietnamese troops, in an attempt to reverse the American gains, and Hanoi gave no indication of preparing to negotiate.[343] But the point was that South Vietnam and the United States were no longer losing. The defeat of the Viet Cong's attempt to move into the main force phase had

---

341 Hanson W. Baldwin, "Vietnam: New Policy in the Making," *The Reporter*, Vol. XXXIII, No. 3 (August 12, 1965), pp. 16–20.
342 Bernard Fall, "Vietnam Blitz," *The New Republic*, October 9, 1965, pp. 17–21, at p. 20.
343 Max Frankel in *The New York Times*, August 27, 1965, and Joseph C. Harsch, "Another Round," *The Christian Science Monitor*, October 26, 1965.

transformed the military and political picture [344]—and not only in Vietnam. What did this mean to Hanoi, Peking, and Moscow, and what were its effects on Sino-Soviet relations?

First, all three could no longer assume that a Viet Cong victory was highly probable. Peking and Hanoi probably still believed in November 1965 that the Americans would eventually get tired and go home, and anti-Vietnam war demonstrations in the United States may well have reinforced this belief [345]; but all public opinion polls indicated that American popular support for the Johnson policy was rising constantly, probably because the military tide seemed to be turning in Johnson's favor, because Hanoi, Peking, and Moscow had neither agreed to negotiate nor intervened in force in South Vietnam, and because American power was continuing to pour into South Vietnam.[346]

Second, Sino-Soviet discord had increased. Hanoi, no longer winning in the South, needed more and, this time, decisive aid; but both Moscow and Peking were deterred from giving it, the former because it saw no more advantage than before in becoming involved militarily with Washington, the latter because it feared American bombing of China would result. Each was therefore the more anxious to blame the other for what both in fact did, preferring their own *raison d'état* to running high risks of American attack by stepping up aid to Hanoi. Moreover, while many in the Viet Cong were probably increasingly dissatisfied with Moscow, Peking, and even with Hanoi, they were the more dependent on all three because of current defeats.

As a result of the Chinese decision in March for all-out anti-Soviet polemics and, conversely, the Soviet one to limit them to the minimum and to stress " joint action," the summer and autumn of 1965 saw a flood of violent Peking assaults on Moscow and very few Soviet replies. At the beginning of June Chinese Foreign Minister Ch'en Yi declared that " a certain north European nation [that is, the Soviet Union] once asked People's China to persuade the Vietnamese People's Republic to negotiate peace," but that Peking had refused.[347] In late June all the Chinese atomic scientists who had been working at the Dubna Joint

---

344 The above is primarily based on discussions with and publications by two experts on Southeast Asia who were in Vietnam in the summer of 1965: my colleague, Professor Lucian W. Pye, and his interview in *U.S. News and World Report*, October 18, 1965, pp. 76–81, and P. J. Honey and his " Vietnam Argument," *op. cit.*, and " The New Situation in Vietnam," *op. cit.* See also Fall, " Vietnam Blitz," *op. cit.*, whose analysis of the change in the military situation is similar.

345 James Reston, " Washington: The Stupidity of Intelligence," *The New York Times*, October 17, 1965.

346 Stewart Alsop, " What the People Really Think," *The Saturday Evening Post*, October 23, 1965, pp. 27–31 (with Oliver Quayle public opinion polls). The Gallup and Harris polls showed the same results.

347 *Tokyo Shimbun*, June 2, 1965. The Chou En-lai interview in *Al-Musawwar* (Cairo), June 3, 1965, declaring that China did not want Soviet aid in a war with the United States, was probably propagandistic.

Nuclear Research Institute in the Soviet Union returned to China.[348]
Then in July Peking declared that the Chinese army was "in battle
array" against the United States.[349] Nevertheless, Ch'en had also
stressed that "China will never launch a war unless attacked from
without," [350] and this theme, which Mao had launched in January, continued to be reiterated, indicating Peking's hope to deter any American
attack on China.

Shortly thereafter Peking sharpened its attack on Moscow on the
Vietnam issue and accused the Soviets of conspiring with the United
States to sell out Hanoi so as to counteract the impression of American
military successes, of Soviet, not Chinese, technological military aid to
North Vietnam, and of Soviet gains in international communism. The
Chinese reiterated, in a sharpened form, their post-March view of the
new Soviet leadership:

> The followers of Khrushchevism without Khrushchev are now serving
> U.S. imperialism in more covert and cunning ways. They are doing
> not less but more harm than Khrushchev did. It is therefore necessary
> to expose their dual tactics and hypocrisy and smash the Krushchev
> revisionist line of Soviet-U.S. cooperation for world domination in
> order to lead the struggle against U.S. imperialism to still greater
> victories.

They then denounced the post-Khrushchev leadership's more conciliatory
line in international communism:

> They are using more cunning tactics, known as the soft tactics, in
> handling Marxist-Leninists and all other revolutionaries . . . and are
> trying hard to mingle with the revolutionary ranks in the world so as to
> gain breathing space and political capital.

Finally, after stressing once again that the United States is a paper
tiger, they came to the point concerning Soviet policy on Vietnam:

> They profess support for the fraternal socialist countries but, when it
> comes to deeds, they betray their interests.
>   Their double-faced trick is particularly conspicuous in the Vietnam
> question now. On the one hand they loudly proclaim that they support
> the Vietnamese people, while on the other hand they have spilled
> the blood of students from Vietnam and other countries in the
> Soviet Union for staging anti-U.S. demonstrations in Moscow and
> Leningrad. On certain occasions they make the gesture of demanding
> the withdrawal of U.S. troops from South Vietnam while on other
> occasions they keep complete silence on the matter. On the one hand
> they give miserly aid to Vietnam, while on the other they divulge in

348 NCNA in English, June 23, 1965 (SCMP 3486, June 28, 1965.) North Vietnamese
    scientists remained there (Radio Moscow in Vietnamese to Vietnam, September 18,
    1965, 1030 GMT).
349 *Jen-min Jih-pao*, July 13, 1965, and *Peking Review*, Vol. VIII, No. 29 (July 16, 1965),
    pp. 6–7.
350 *Tokyo Shimbun*, June 2, 1965.

advance particulars about this aid to the Americans. They profess opposition to U.S. imperialist aggression against Vietnam but at the same time they embrace and sing in chorus with such faithful lackeys and precious pets of U.S. imperialism as Tito and Shastri and advocate " peace talks " so as to find a way out for U.S. imperialism. . . .

Their real aim is to bring the Vietnam question into the orbit of " Soviet-U.S. cooperation for world domination " and stamp out the Vietnamese people's struggle against U.S. aggression.[351]

On September 2 the twentieth anniversary of the defeat of Japan gave the Chinese leadership a favorable opportunity for stepping up still further the fury of their anti-American and anti-Soviet propaganda. In three declarations—by Defense Minister Lin Piao,[352] chief of the army general staff Lo Jui-ch'ing,[353] and a *Jen-min Jih-pao* editorial [354] the more intensified line was authoritatively set forth.[355]

China was already increasingly in the grip of war hysteria. Peking propaganda emphasized the long guerrilla war against Japan. Peking underlined political control of the army and went so far as to abolish all insignia of rank. Travelers reported that air raid drills, construction of shelters, and even some evacuation of cities was occurring, particularly in Southern China.[356]

Lin Piao's speech, by far the longest and most complete, caused large-scale Western comment, most of which regarded it as a near-Hitlerite pronouncement perhaps foreshadowing massive Chinese entry into the Vietnam war. On closer examination, however, it and the other two declarations were probably more correctly viewed as a continuation of the July *Ta Kung Pao* article's propagandistic compensation for the increasingly unfavorable military situation in Vietnam and, in addition, as an argument that North Vietnam, even after it had failed to enter

351 Fan Hsiu-chu, " The Struggle Between the Two Lines over the Question of Dealing with U.S. Imperialism," *Ta Kung Pao*, July 27, 1965 (SCMP 3509, August 3, 1965, pp. 27–33, at p. 32).

352 Lin Piao, " Long Live the Victory of People's War!" *Jen-min Jih-pao*, September 2, 1965, quoted from *Peking Review*, Vol. VIII, No. 36 (September 3, 1965), pp. 9–30.

353 Lo Jui-ch'ing, " The People Defeated Japanese Fascism and They Can Certainly Defeat U.S. Imperialism Too," *Jen-min Jih-pao*, September 2, 1965, quoted from *Peking Review*, Vol. VIII, No. 36 (September 3, 1965), pp. 31–39.

354 " U.S. Imperialism Can Be Defeated As Well," *Jen-min Jih-pao*, September 2, 1965 (SCMP 3533, September 8, 1965).

355 For other analyses, see Donald S. Zagoria, " China's Strategy—A Critique," *Commentary*, Vol. 40, No. 5 (November 1965), pp. 61–68; Wolfgang Leonhard in *Die Zeit*, September 21, 1965; Kx. [Ernst Kux], " Pekings Kampfansage an die Welt," *Neue Zürcher Zeitung*, October 1, 1965; " A Plea for People's War," *Current Scene*, Vol. III, No. 28 (October 1, 1965); and " Fear of War," *China News Analysis*, No. 580 (September 10, 1965).

356 *Ibid.*, Richard Halloran, " Red China Sets Defenses for U.S. Air Raids," *The Washington Post*, September 3, 1965; " Democratic Tradition of Chinese People's Liberation Army," *Hung Ch'i*, No. 8, 1965 (JPRS 31,360, August 20, 1965); decree abolishing formal military ranks and insignia (NCNA, May 24, 1965 [SCMP 3466, May 27, 1965]); Ho Lung, " The Democratic Tradition of the Chinese People's Liberation Army," *Hung Ch'i*, August 1, 1965, and *Peking Review*, Vol. VIII, No. 32 (August 6, 1965), pp. 6–16.

the main force stage, should continue fighting rather than, as Moscow preferred, begin to negotiate. One cannot of course exclude the possibility that these pronouncements foreshadowed Chinese military intervention against the United States and one does get the feeling that they reflected Chinese fear of an American attack and therefore stressed the necessity of war preparations. However, Chinese leaders continued to stress that they would not attack the United States unless they were attacked by Washington first—that is, they continued their low-risk policy.[357] More basically, though, these statements seemed to be attempts to overcome the impression produced by the American military escalation in Vietnam, that the Viet Cong could not win and therefore that the Chinese strategy of national liberation wars could not succeed. They therefore stressed that American power, although great, is overextended and that if America invades China it will be swallowed up and eventually destroyed.

All three expanded at great length, as did many other articles at that time, on the lesson of the protracted struggle with Japan: A "people's" guerrilla war can overcome massive conventional military might—that is, they returned to the glorious victory of the past to gain sustenance for national unity and for popular support of the present Maoist strategy.

Lin Piao reviewed at length Mao's guerrilla strategy and summarized it as follows:

> To rely on the peasants, build rural base areas and use the country-side to encircle and finally capture the cities—such was the way to victory in the Chinese revolution.[358]

He stressed Mao's caution in guerrilla warfare:

> Revolutionary armed forces should not fight with a reckless disregard for the consequences when there is a great disparity between their own strength and the enemy's,

and also his emphasis on "wars of annihilation"[359]: to annihilate the enemy we must adopt the policy of "luring him in deep and abandon some cities and districts of our own accord."[360] In speaking of the necessity of self-reliance in war, Lin implied that the Viet Cong should fight on even if it not only lost some of its territory by the Maoist tactics previously described but also that it should not "lean wholly on foreign aid—even though this be aid from socialist countries which persist in

---

[357] For example, a Ch'en Yi statement in *Tokyo Shimbun*, June 2, 1965; a Chou En-lai interview with *Al-Musawwar* (Cairo) in an AFP Cairo dispatch, *Le Monde*, June 4, 1965; *Jen-min Jih-pao*, July 13, 1965 (NCNA in English, July 13, 1965, 0300 GMT).
[358] Lin Piao, *op. cit.*, p. 15.
[359] *Ibid.* p. 18.
[360] *Ibid.* p. 19.

revolution [that is, China, not the Soviet Union]" but that, rather, it should

> adhere to the policy of self-reliance . . . and prepare to carry on the fight independently even when all material aid from outside is cut off.[361]

That is, Hanoi should fight, not negotiate, even if China could not protect it from an American attack. (The same, of course, would apply to China, which, Lin implied, should fight the United States even if the Soviet Union did not aid it.) After all, "in diametrical opposition to the Khrushchev revisionists, the Marxist-Leninists and revolutionary people never take a gloomy look of war." [362] (Lin was probably polemicizing with those in Hanoi who did take a "gloomy view" of the lack of Chinese, and Soviet, aid.)

The part of the Lin Piao article that excited the most interest abroad was his explicit adaptation of the Maoist guerrilla strategy to the world-wide scene:

> Taking the entire globe, if North America and Western Europe can be called "the cities of the world," then Asia, Africa and Latin America constitute "the rural areas of the world." . . . In a sense, the contemporary world revolution also presents a picture of the encircle-ment of cities by the rural areas.[363]

Yet considering the Chinese setbacks in the underdeveloped world in 1965, this statement reads more like whistling in the dark than a realistic analysis of the situation. After reiterating previous Chinese charges against the "Khrushchev revisionists," Lin concluded on a note of intense emotional defiance of an American invasion:

> The vast ocean of several hundred million Chinese people in arms will be more than enough to submerge your few million aggressor troops. . . . If you want to send troops, go ahead, the more the better. We will annihilate as many as you can send, and can even give you receipts.[364]

Lo Jui-ch'ing argued in more detail why the United States could not win:

> (1) the world balance of forces has drastically changed . . . the United States is now beset by all the revolutionary peoples waging anti-imperialist struggles; . . .

[361] *Ibid.* p. 22.
[362] *Ibid.* p. 28.
[363] *Ibid.* p. 24. This was not new; Aidit had said substantially the same in December 1963. See D. N. Aidit, *Set Afire the Bandung Spirit! Ever Forward, No Retreat!* (Peking: Foreign Languages Press, 1964), and P'eng Ch'en, quoted in his May 25, 1965, Djakarta speech, *op. cit.* See "A Plea for Peoples' War," *Current Scene, op. cit.* See also Paul Wohl in *The Christian Science Monitor,* November 15, 1965, citing Branko Lazitch of *Est & Ouest.*
[364] Lin Piao, *op. cit.,* p. 29.

(2) the counter-revolutionary military alliances rigged up by the United States are in the process of disintegrating. . . .
(3) since U.S. imperialism cannot frighten the people with its war blackmail, how can the Khrushchev revisionists succeed in frightening them by propaganda about the horrors of a nuclear war?

But war will be necessary, he continued:

through their protracted war against aggression, the Chinese people came to realize the truth that liberation involves bloodshed and death. Bloodshed and death can only be curtailed by not being afraid of them. It is only through the sacrifice of the blood and lives of the few that the vast majority can avoid the sacrifice of their blood and lives.

Finally, he echoed Lin's defiance of any American attack:

We Chinese people love peace but we have never been afraid of war. If U.S. imperialism insists on imposing war on us, there is nothing terrifying about that. The more men it throws in, the better—whether by air, by sea or by land, whether in tens of thousands, hundreds of thousands or millions. And if it chooses to dispatch all its troops, that will be better still. We will wipe them out if they come; the more they come, the more we will wipe out; if the whole lot of them come, we will wipe out the whole lot. The U.S. aggressors have already become irretrievably bogged down in South Vietnam by a war of the entire people. If U.S. imperialism should dare to send its troops to invade China, the fate awaiting it can be none other than complete destruction.

Foreign Minister Ch'en Yi even managed to intensify this frenetic line:

If the U.S. imperialists are determined to launch a war of aggression against us, they are welcome to come sooner, to come as early as tomorrow. Let the Indian reactionaries, the British imperialists and the Japanese militarists come along with them! Let the modern revisionists act in coordination with them from the north![365] We will still win in the end. . . .

For sixteen years we have been waiting for the U.S. imperialists to come and attack us. My hair has turned grey in waiting. Perhaps I will not have the luck to see the U.S. imperialist invasion of China, but my children may see it, and they will resolutely carry on the fight. Let no correspondent think I am bellicose.[366]

Meanwhile, Soviet policy on Vietnam continued relatively unchanged. Soviet leaders continued to denounce American policy there [367] and were not responsive to American attempts to get their support for arranging negotiations.[368] Furthermore, the Soviet military build-up in North Vietnam continued,[369] and several American planes were shot

---

[365] That is, the Soviet Union—W.E.G.
[366] In his September 29, 1965, Peking press conference; quoted from *Peking Review*, Vol. VIII, No. 41 (October 8, 1965), pp. 7–14, at p. 14.
[367] Kosygin at Riga, *Pravda*, July 18, 1965.
[368] Max Frankel in *The New York Times*, June 20, 1965.
[369] Hanson W. Baldwin in *ibid.*, July 4, 1965.

down over North Vietnam by Soviet-supplied SAM installations,[370] in return for which the United States bombed a few such installations. Yet in other areas the new Soviet leadership indicated its desire to limit the deterioration of its relations with Washington: The Harriman visit to Moscow in July went off relatively well, the Soviets resumed disarmament negotiations at Geneva (probably primarily in order to worsen U.S.–West German relations but also as a signal to Washington that the détente would not be abandoned), and, most importantly, Moscow cooperated closely with Washington in the Indo-Pakistani conflict. Even so, and although Moscow had certainly gained, and China lost, in Hanoi and Pyongyang, Soviet prestige had suffered generally from its demonstrated unwillingness to risk a confrontation with Washington to prevent the United States bombing of a " fraternal socialist country."

By November 1965, in spite of some few signs that Hanoi if not the Viet Cong [371] was less hostile to negotiations than Peking, there was little indication that negotiations would soon begin. Yet implicitly the course of the war itself was a part of the negotiating process [372]; indeed, there might well be no formal negotiations at all.[373] In the meantime China had lost and Washington had gained, while Moscow had both gained and lost from the crisis.

The Indo-Pakistani Conflict (August–September 1965) [374]

The brief, undeclared, limited Indo-Pakistani war over Kashmir in August and September 1965, although not as crucial for Sino-Soviet relations as the American military escalation in Vietnam, was a major example during 1964 and 1965 of events outside the communist world worsening Sino-Soviet relations. Soviet policy toward India had been one of Peking's main complaints against Moscow. Soviet neutrality between China and India in 1959 and again in 1962 had gravely worsened Sino-Soviet relations.

After 1962 the United States had greatly increased its military commitments to India and the Soviet Union, fearing that Pakistan would

---

[370] *Ibid.*, August 13 and 26, 1965.
[371] Specifically as to whether prior U.S. troop withdrawal was a precondition for negotiation: For example, a Moscow Viet Cong spokesman reportedly hinted it was not. See Vera Stovickova on Radio Prague, October 21, 1965, 2100 GMT, reporting on a Helsinki press conference by Moscow NLFSV representative Nguyen Van Dong. See also *The Economist* (London), October 30, 1965, pp. 474–475; Paul Wohl in *The Christian Science Monitor*, October 29, 1965; and, for earlier indications, Bernard Fall, " North Vietnam: A Profile," *Problems of Communism*, Vol. XIV, No. 4 (July–August 1965), pp. 13–25, at pp. 24–25. In late November 1965 a report, denied by Washington, indicated that Rumania was attempting to mediate between Washington and Hanoi (*The New York Times*, November 22 and 23, 1965).
[372] Fred Charles Iklé, " The Real Negotiations on South Vietnam," *The Reporter*, June 3, 1965, pp. 15–16.
[373] Pye, *op. cit.*
[374] I have profited greatly from discussions with my colleague Professor Myron Weiner.

fall under Chinese influence, had attempted to improve its relations with both India and Pakistan. This type of political juggling was made increasingly difficult by the outbreak of violence, for states are far from immune to the philosophy that the friend of my enemy is my enemy. Conversely, China carried on a rapprochement with Pakistan.

Although the immediate cause of the 1965 Indo-Pakistani conflict was the infiltration in early August of Pakistani irregulars into Kashmir, the long-term cause was India's hardening refusal to contemplate a plebiscite for Kashmir even though an eventual plebiscite had been called for by the United Nations.

The conflict itself can be briefly summarized.[375] The Indian army immediately intervened against the Pakistani infiltrators and, in order to show its determination and to gain more favorable positions, crossed the Kashmir cease-fire line into Pakistani occupied territory. Thereupon the Pakistan army, as it presumably had always planned, attempted to cut off Kashmir from India by a major tank assault in the Chamb sector. China, meanwhile hoping to encourage Pakistan to prolong the war and thus create confusion in the subcontinent and further lower India's prestige and contribute toward its fragmentation, on September 16 sent India an ultimatum to evacuate its border posts in Sikkim.[376] India, however, sure of American and perhaps of Soviet support, held firm, in spite of some minor concessions,[377] and China, warned by Washington that America would retaliate if China attacked India,[378] first postponed [379] its ultimatum and then in effect withdrew it. Simultaneously the Indian army drove toward and succeeded in cutting off Sialkhot, the major Pakistani communications center for its Kashmir drive, and also threatened Lahore, thus preventing Kashmir from being cut off. Thereupon, as the Indians had hoped,[380] parallel Soviet-American pressure through the United Nations, plus the Anglo-American suspension of military and economic aid to both sides and Pakistan's

[375] See "How the Kashmir War Began," *The Times* (London), September 13, 1965 (from their Delhi correspondent).
[376] Text in *Peking Review*, Vol. VIII, No. 39 (September 24, 1965), pp. 8–9.
[377] The Chinese declared (*ibid.*, Vol. VIII, No. 40 [October 1, 1965], pp. 16–17) that the Indians had torn down their own advanced border posts; India (*Boston Herald*, September 22, 1965) denied it. India did agree, although it had previously refused, to joint inspection; see its note of September 17, to Peking, *Peking Review*, Vol. VIII, No. 39 (September 24, 1965), pp. 11–12.
[378] This was apparently conveyed at a U.S.-Chinese ambassadorial meeting in Warsaw. See a Warsaw dispatch in *The Observer* (London), September 19, 1965. That it was not unwelcome to Moscow was indicated by a Prague radio comment: "It appears that a warning delivered to Peking by the U.S. government stated that a large-scale action against India could result in extensive U.S. retaliation. . . . Damage that the U.S. army and, above all, the U.S. air force could inflict on China would be very considerable and severe." (Milan Weiner on Radio Prague, September 26, 1965, 1200 GMT.)
[379] CPR note of September 19 (text in *Peking Review*, Vol. VIII, No. 39 [September 24, 1965], pp. 9–11).
[380] J. Anthony Lukas from New Delhi in *The New York Times*, October 5, 1965.

understandable reluctance to break with Washington and Moscow [381] and throw itself into the hands of an unreliable and militarily weak China, brought about a cease-fire. The resultant Indian refusal to negotiate on Kashmir and the likelihood that the great powers in the United Nations would not, even if they could, force her to do so, made Pakistan frustrated and bitter.[382] Conversely, Indian nationalism reached new heights.

China's verbal support of Pakistan was, of course, total,[383] and it was echoed by North Korea, North Vietnam, Indonesia, and Albania. It is doubtful, however, that Peking ever intended to use serious military force against India, the more so because Pakistan was too fearful of U.S. intervention against Peking (and therefore in support of New Delhi) to accept major Chinese assistance. In any case, in the short run China's withdrawal of its ultimatum hardly gained Peking much prestige, particularly within the context of the Chinese loss of influence in North Vietnam and in the Afro-Asian bloc.

Yet the Indo-Pakistani war will certainly cause both New Delhi and Rawalpindi to concentrate on armaments rather than economic development, and China's long-term hopes for increasing instability on the subcontinent are therefore not without basis. From the Chinese point of view there is, however, the less attractive alternative that India may have been brought closer to both Moscow and Washington by the crisis—and that reviving nationalism may well impel New Delhi toward a nuclear capability, thus weakening China's position as the only nuclear power in Asia.[384]

China was enraged by what it correctly perceived to be Soviet-American cooperation toward ending the war, thereby foiling Peking's chances of gaining from its continuance while simultaneously maintaining Soviet and American influence in both countries of the subcontinent. As *Jen-min Jih-pao* put it on September 18:

> Who are their [the "Indian reactionaries"] backers? One is U.S. imperialism, the other the revisionist leadership of the Soviet Union, . . . [which] is not one whit inferior to U.S. imperialism. . . .
>
> The Soviet leaders are pursuing Khrushchev revisionism without Khrushchev. In order to carry out their general line of U.S.-Soviet cooperation to dominate the world, they always oppose the revolutionary

---

[381] Hanson W. Baldwin, "Barrier to a Long War," *ibid.*, September 9, 1965.

[382] *The Economist* (London), October 23, 1965, p. 383.

[383] See, for example, a September 7 CPR governmental statement, *Peking Review*, Vol. VIII, No. 37 (September 10, 1965), pp. 6–7.

[384] See Roderick MacFarquhar, "China and the Cease-Fire," *The New Statesman*, September 24, 1965, pp. 323–324, and "Thanks for Muffing It," *The Economist* (London), September 25, 1965, pp. 1177–1179. For support of the CPR by Pyongyang see a DPRK-Indonesia communiqué (KCNA in English, September 28, 1965, 1720 GMT), and by Hanoi, *Nhan Dan*, September 23, 1965 (VNA in English, September 23, 1965, 0555 GMT).

struggles and wars of the peoples and thereby help U.S. imperialism and its flunkeys. They brazenly supported the Indian reactionaries in attacking socialist China and are now brazenly supporting them in committing aggression against Pakistan. This shows clearly the extent to which the Khruschev revisionists have degenerated. . . . The revisionist leadership of the Soviet Union can only reveal once again its shameful features as the willing pawn of U.S. imperialism.[385]

The *Soviet Union*'s tactics in the Indo-Pakistani conflict were necessarily even more complex than Washington's, and certainly more so than Peking's. Moscow wanted: to increase its influence in India; to maintain at the least its newly won rapprochement with Pakistan; to prevent China from profiting from the conflict; to prevent or at least limit Washington from profiting as well; and, finally, to maintain good relations with China's neighbors and former allies, but now increasingly "neutralist," North Korea and North Vietnam. Moscow's minimal objective was the containment of both Peking and Washington; its maximum aim was to detach India from Washington and Pakistan from Peking while moving both closer to Moscow, and, finally, to improve relations between the Indians and Pakistanis so that together they might devote their energies to containing China rather than to fighting each other. This final objective is shared by Moscow and Washington, and it is sufficiently important for both to make each willing to settle for Indian and Pakistani neutrality vis-à-vis themselves—the more so because this is what India and Pakistan want.[386]

Moscow therefore from the beginning of the crisis stressed its interest in the area, reiterated appeals for a cease-fire,[387] which culminated in Kosygin's invitation to Shastri and Ayub Khan to meet in Tashkent,[388] and, at first in veiled tones and later explicitly if indirectly, criticized the Chinese for throwing fuel on the flames.[389] Moscow greeted the cease-fire warmly and thereafter, as before, cooperated in the United Nations with the United States first to obtain it and then to enforce it.

The Soviets can be quite satisfied with the results of their policies during the conflict. While Peking's threat had again brought home to India that it could not do without American military power in case of a Chinese attack, the lack of Chinese military action indicated that Peking was probably effectively deterred by Washington from attacking India. Moreover, in order to maintain its freedom of action India had

385 " Who Backs the Indian Aggressor?" *Jen-min Jih-pao*, September 18, 1965, quoted from *Peking Review*, Vol. VIII, No. 39 (September 24, 1965), pp. 13–16.
386 For a perceptive analysis of Soviet policy in this context, see Dev Murarka from Moscow in *The Spectator*, September 24, 1965.
387 For example, a TASS statement, September 7, 1965, 1841 GMT.
388 *Pravda*, September 20, 1965.
389 For example, a " news review " in *ibid.*, September 22, 1965.

to accept Soviet aid to have a counterweight against American influence. China had been unsuccessful in the short run—a Soviet gain—while Peking's allies North Korea and North Vietnam, although supporting the Chinese position, had not echoed Chinese criticism of Moscow. Pakistan, because of its continuing desire to remain on good terms with China and the United States as well as the Soviet Union, did not adopt an increasingly favorable attitude toward Moscow. Finally, these gains occurred without Moscow undertaking any new major military or economic commitments. Thus the Soviets succeeded in maintaining the policy of cutting down foreign expenditures.

All in all, then, China was probably something of the loser, and Moscow certainly one of the gainers, in the Indo-Pakistani conflict. That Washington had also gained somewhat, by its effective threat to China, could not please Moscow, but this was counterbalanced by the resultant loss to Peking.

Coup and Countercoup in Indonesia, September–October 1965

In view of the extent to which Sukarno and the PKI had become among China's most important foreign allies in 1964 and 1965, the September coup in Jakarta led to the single most serious and most dramatic recent reversal of Chinese influence.

The Sino-Indonesian rapprochement in 1963–1965 resulted from a mutual coincidence of revolutionary aims vis-á-vis Malaysia, Great Britain, and the United States, plus a shared rivalry with India. It resulted in Sino-Indonesian cooperation in opposing the United Nations, Moscow, and Washington and in attempting to set up a new international organization—the New Emerging Forces—to take over or split the various Afro-Asian groupings. It was reported that China might give Indonesia an atom bomb. The friendship was strengthened by the shift in allegiance from Moscow to Peking, which became public in 1961 over the Albanian issue and intensified continually thereafter. Given Sukarno's rapprochement with Peking, the nationalist orientation of the PKI (similar to that of North Korea, with which it had particularly close relations) and Indonesian Communist hopes to merge with and eventually take control of Sukarno's regime or his successor's by peaceful means, it is not surprising that after Khrushchev's fall the PKI did not revert to neutrality as did North Korea and North Vietnam. Rather, it carefully maintained its contacts with Moscow, while, since Indonesian communism is not menaced by the United States directly and therefore not in need of Soviet assistance, it simultaneously remained moderately pro-Chinese.[390] At home, in 1964 and 1965 it intensified its attempts to

---

[390] Compare the PKI-CCP communiqué (" a complete unanimity of positions and views ") in *Peking Review*, Vol. VIII, No. 33 (August 13, 1965), p. 5, and Aidit

infiltrate the armed forces, to obtain the arming of a people's militia open to its influence, and to push Sukarno closer to Peking.[391]

To what extent, if at all, the PKI leadership was involved in the coup on the night of September 30 is still not known. Whether, as the coup's leader Untung reportedly told Sukarno, his coup was a countermeasure against a planned coup by the army generals is uncertain. It is true that the generals were alarmed by Sukarno's increasing politicization of the army, and they have always been anti-PKI because they are extreme nationalists and therefore anti-Chinese and because Moscow and Washington, not Peking, can furnish them advanced weaponry. That the generals actually planned a coup, however, seems doubtful. More likely the antiarmy palace guard and air force, plus quite possibly Sukarno himself, were involved.

The coup was striking both for its brutality (six generals were murdered) and for the incompetence of its perpetrators. When General Nasution, chief of staff of the armed forces, escaped (although his young daughter was killed), he and his associates quickly quelled the uprising. Whether or not some PKI elements had been involved in the coup attempt, the PKI organ *Harian Rakjat* was so imprudent as to endorse the coup on October 2 just before it was quelled. Thereafter the PKI urged support for Sukarno's fruitless efforts to restrain the army's moves against Indonesian communism.

Subsequently, while protesting loyalty to Sukarno, who wished to keep the political situation as unchanged as possible in order not to be dependent solely on the army, Nasution and the army proceeded to ban and to attempt to destroy the PKI. (Some reports indicated that the

statements against imperialism and modern revisionism (*ibid.*, Vol. VIII, No. 23 [June 4, 1965], pp. 8–12) and in favor of continuing polemics (*ibid.*, Vol. VIII, No. 35 [August 27, 1965], pp. 23–24) with a PKI-CPSU communiqué (" exchange of opinions "), *Pravda*, August 1, 1965 (*CDSP*, Vol. XVII, No. 31 [August 25, 1965], p. 19).

391 See Ruth T. McVey, " Indonesia," *Survey*, No. 54 (January 1965), reprinted in Labedz, *op. cit.*, pp. 113–122, and her forthcoming book, to be published by the M.I.T. Press on the PKI and the Sino-Soviet rift; Justus van der Kroef, *The Communist Party of Indonesia* (Vancouver : University of British Columbia Publications Center, 1965), " Indonesian Communism and the Changing Balance of Power," *Pacific Affairs*, Vol. XXXVII, No. 4 (Winter 1964–1965), pp. 357–383, " The Vocabulary of Indonesian Communism," *Problems of Communism*, Vol. XIV, No. 3 (May–June 1965), pp. 1–9, and " The Sino-Indonesian Partnership : Its Origins and Implications," *Orbis*, Vol. VIII, No. 2 (Summer 1964), pp. 332–356; Donald Hindley, *The Communist Party of Indonesia, 1951–1963* (Berkeley and Los Angeles: University of California Press, 1965) and " The Indonesian Communist Party and the Conflict in the International Communist Movement," *The China Quarterly*, No. 19 (July–September 1964), pp. 99–119; " Peking and Indonesia," *China News Analysis*, No. 551 (February 12, 1965); Griffith, *The Sino-Soviet Rift*, *op. cit.*, pp. 23–26, 35–36, 102–103, 122–123 and 207–210; j.c.k. [Joseph C. Kun], " Will Sukarno Get the Bomb? " Radio Free Europe, Munich, July 29, 1965; and William McLaughlin, " Mr. Aidit's Holiday," *ibid.*, August 6, 1965. I am grateful to Dr. McVey for comments on an earlier draft of this section.

PKI might be reorganized with a new, nationalist—that is, not pro-Chinese—leadership.) Sukarno's efforts to stop the army were ineffective. The PKI headquarters were burned, the Communist Party and its organizations forbidden, and when Sukarno's chief deputy, the radical leftist Subandrio, tried to stem the tide the army turned on him too.

Anti-Chinese demonstrations also occurred, notably on October 16 when the Chinese embassy in Jakarta refused to lower its flag to half-staff in memory of the slaughtered generals. (Allegedly the Cuban embassy also refused.) [392]

More importantly for our purposes, the countercoup was a major and perhaps deadly blow to the Sino-Indonesian entente as well as to China's ally the PKI. After Peking's postcoup efforts to urge Sukarno to resist the triumphant anti-PKI and anti-Chinese army leadership had failed (Sukarno probably could not have done so anyway), China finally broke its public silence on October 20 by publishing a stiff protest note to Jakarta. It declared that

> Since October 1, lies and slanders about China and anti-Chinese clamours have continuously appeared in Indonesia and all kinds of threat and intimidation have been made against the Chinese diplomatic missions in Indonesia.

Moreover, the note went on, the Indonesian government, despite Chinese requests for protection, had " all along been condoning the increasingly unruly anti-Chinese activities," and on October 16 Indonesian soldiers had invaded a Chinese embassy building, searched and questioned embassy personnel, and "even pushed and struck Chinese Commercial Attaché Li Ching-tang, behaving in a most uncivilized way." The note demanded that Jakarta apologize, punish " the culprits and their instigators, and guarantee against similar incidents in the future." [393] *Jen-min Jih-pao* simultaneously published a long report on Indonesian developments, which was intended to demonstrate that Nasution and the army were terrorizing " Communists and other progressives " and instigating anti-Chinese demonstrations. It quoted Aidit's condemnation of the generals and implied that Moscow had endorsed not only Sukarno but Nasution as well and had condemned the PKI. [394]

The Soviet position was much more complicated. Moscow wanted to cut down Chinese influence in Indonesia and replace it with its own. Moscow did not condemn the PKI, because of general ideological

---

[392] For the events of September 30 *et seqq.*, only journalistic accounts were available as of November 1965. See particularly the dispatches from Djakarta by John Hughes in *The Christian Science Monitor*, notably his reconstruction of the coup of October 10, 1965, and by Seth S. King in *The New York Times*, notably two of October 31, 1965, pp. 1 and E3.

[393] Quoted from *Peking Review*, Vol. VIII, No. 43 (October 22, 1965), p. 5.

[394] *Ibid.* pp. 6–14.

reasons, because of its desire to maintain close ties with the PKI's allies in North Korea and North Vietnam, and because it hoped that the PKI might be re-formed on a pro-Soviet basis. The Soviets also wanted to reestablish their ties with Sukarno, the more so because he might then again become a Soviet rather than a Chinese ally in the Afro-Asian bloc. Finally, Moscow did not want to break off all ties with Nasution, to whose armed forces Moscow had given so much aid; rather, it wanted to restrain him vis-à-vis the PKI and move him, like Sukarno and the PKI, back toward Moscow.

By the end of October Moscow had formulated a careful complex position. *Pravda* wrote on October 26 that even if

> certain members of leftist organizations, giving way to provocations, had some kind of connection to the events of September 30,

this did not justify repression of the PKI. After strongly endorsing Sukarno's line of maintaining the unity of the nation (that is, if not persecuting the PKI), the article implied that the Chinese were responsible for the whole affair:

> political adventurism, putschism, and sectarianism are alien to Marxism-Leninism.[395]

Although lack of evidence prevents a definitive evaluation of the events in Jakarta, several points are already clear. First, the PKI's position has been greatly weakened and perhaps even smashed, Sukarno's prestige and power have been greatly diminished and the Indonesian army seems dominant. Second, because the army remains radically nationalist and expansionist, particularly on the Malaysia issue, a turn by Indonesia toward the West can be excluded. Third, the military victors in Jakarta are radical, Moslem, and xenophobic nationalists, much like Colonel Boumédienne in Algeria; in both instances internal and foreign communist influence have lost by their coming to power. Fourth, the main external loser has clearly been China because of the loss of influence of both the PKI and Sukarno—Peking's supporters in Indonesia—and because China will probably lose Indonesian support on the international scene in general and in the Afro-Asian bloc in particular. Fifth, the Soviet Union has therefore profited considerably and may hope to restore some of its influence in Jakarta, yet the blow to the PKI may be so great that a reassertion of Soviet influence may not be worth much. Sixth, the greatest gainers of all have been Great Britain, the Netherlands, and, indirectly, the United States. For London it means that *konfrontasi* in Malaysia, whose prospects had seemed greatly improved by the breaking away of Singapore and the resultant instability in North Borneo, will probably be weakened for

395 *Pravda*, October 26, 1965.

some time. For Washington it means a major blow to its enemy China and a weakening of the forces in Indonesia for whom the United States was the main enemy. Finally, the amazingly rapid rapprochement between Jakarta and the Hague will most likely now accelerate even more, since the PKI was less enthusiastic about it than the non-Communists.

More generally, the Jakarta crisis once again showed the intractability, instability, and unpredictability of the "third world." It thereby furthered tendencies in Moscow as well as in Washington to confine ties with underdeveloped countries to those that directly profit Soviet, or American, interests. How China will adjust its losses in Jakarta, and those elsewhere, remains to be seen.

X. Pluralism in the Communist Bloc and the "Third World"

When one looks at only bilateral Sino-Soviet relations in 1965, one tends to get the feeling that China was losing as rapidly as the Soviet Union was gaining influence. That China was losing is true, but the gains of the Soviet Union vis-à-vis China were somewhat offset by two facts: Chinese losses were also in a sense gains for Moscow's enemy, the United States, while the increasingly pluralistic tendencies within international communism and the increasing instability of the underdeveloped world also sapped at Soviet authority. The latter development can best be illustrated by two examples: pluralism within international Communist-front organizations as seen in the October 1965 Warsaw congress of the World Federation of Trade Unions (WFTU) and the postponement of the Algiers Afro-Asian conference in June and October 1965.

The World Federation of Trade Unions

The thousands of pages of reports on debates between the Soviets and the Chinese at international Communist-front organization meetings during 1964 and 1965 in general offer arid and repetitive reading. Only rarely do they furnish indicators otherwise not available for the state of Sino-Soviet relations or throw light on pluralism within international communism in general; rather, they usually reflect only the level of Sino-Soviet tension at the time and thus add somewhat, but not decisively, to that tension itself.

The World Federation of Trade Unions was an exception. Composed of national trade-union organizations, which, unlike other international front organizations, had other than primarily propaganda purposes, the WFTU reflects national differences much more clearly and thus showed the shifting alliances within an increasingly pluralistic

122

communist movement, most notably in the roles of the Rumanians, Cubans, and Italians.

The desire for increasing organizational independence of the Italian trade-union federation (Confederazione generale italiana del lavoro—CGIL), which had first become clear at the December 1961 Moscow WFTU congress, was pushed hardest by the minority Nenni Socialist (PSI) representatives in the CGIL, but it also gradually grew stronger in the PCI majority. The main CGIL aims in the WFTU were (1) its depoliticization through disassociating it from the communist parties and regimes, thus making it more effective in the underdeveloped areas, (2) greater autonomy for national federations, (3) a more flexible and favorable policy toward unity with the ICFTU and the Christian trade unions (a reflection of PSI and PCI policies in Italy), and (4) a more constructive attitude toward structural reform in general and the European Common Market (with which the CGIL finally set up its own liaison office in Brussels early in 1963 when it failed to persuade either the WFTU or the CGT to do so jointly) in particular.

At the late October 1964 WFTU General Council meeting in Budapest, the first Sino-Soviet face-to-face confrontation after Khrushchev's fall, the conciliatory Soviet line and the defiant Chinese one (backed by North Korea, North Vietnam, and Albania) indicated that Sino-Soviet relations would remain hostile. Moreover, the Chinese then threatened to withdraw their financial support from the WFTU. In early 1965 they did so, thereby forcing a curtailment of its activities. Moreover, for the first time the meeting saw the emergence of something like a "neutralist" group. The Italians, Cubans, and Rumanians abstained from voting on the final resolution, while the Rumanian representative demanded that voting be by unanimity only.

At the July 1965 Prague WFTU Executive Committee meeting the revised statute drafts were opposed by the Chinese and their supporters plus the Rumanians and Italians (the Soviet-Cuban rapprochement presumably had made the Cubans more amenable).

By then the PSI delegation within the CGIL had demanded withdrawal from the WFTU altogether and the PCI majority, although it voted this down, demanded that the WFTU be broken down into regional federations. Italian pressure had some effect; the WFTU secretariat made some concessions to the CGIL's aims, but it did nothing organizationally decisive.

At the October 1965 Warsaw WFTU Sixth Congress, however, Sino-Soviet battling reached new heights, with the Soviets and most of their European allies demonstratively leaving the hall during Chinese attacks. Significantly, the Italians, Rumanians, and Poles stayed behind. (Warsaw had been showing some, but only partial, sympathy for the

CGIL position.) The Chinese, Albanians, Indonesians, and Rumanians demanded " unanimity through consultations." The North Vietnamese were less completely aligned with the Chinese than they had been before. The Soviets were relatively conciliatory, although less so than previously, but the Chinese remained rigid, both stances reflecting Sino-Soviet general positions in the dispute.

In summary, the Rumanians thus made it clear that they would neither accept nor implement WFTU decisions with which they disagreed. The Poles criticized the overpoliticization of the WFTU and the lack of emphasis on trade-union problems. The Yugoslav observer delegation proposed a new, all-inclusive world trade-union organization with national trade-union autonomy. The Italians were relatively quiet at the meeting, but some progress was made on their proposals for changes, and the French CGT took a more pro-Italian line in this respect.

The Italian and Rumanian positions were sufficiently opposed to Soviet objectives so that whatever Moscow gained at the WFTU congress because of Chinese rigidity was outbalanced by its losses to increasingly pluralist tendencies. In fact, Soviet control of the WFTU and especially of the European delegations in it seemed, after the congress, to be a thing of the past.[396]

The Second Afro-Asian Conference: Pluralism, Postponement, and Sino-Soviet Rivalry

As you are aware, new tensions and conflicts have occurred between certain Afro-Asian countries during this period, and even now there exist among Afro-Asian countries differences, which cannot be solved for the time being, over a series of questions of key importance to the success of the Second African-Asian Conference.[397]

It will be remembered that in April 1964 the Chinese had succeeded in preventing Soviet participation in the forthcoming Second Afro-Asian Conference and that, probably within the context of his general dis-

---

[396] For the WFTU I have drawn primarily on a lecture by Kevin Devlin of the Columbia University Research Institute of Communist Affairs, delivered at the Columbia Faculty Seminar on International Communism on October 26, 1965. See also Kevin Devlin, " Chinese Reject Soviet Overtures at Budapest Meeting," Radio Free Europe, Munich, October 26, 1964, and " Disunity in the WFTU: Storm Signals for Warsaw Congress," ibid., July 26, 1965; l.z. [Louis Zanga], " Yugoslav Trade Union Chief Calls for Greater WFTU Autonomy," ibid., October 5, 1965; and Williams McLaughlin, " WFTU Embarks on Collision Course," ibid., October 7, 1965. For the October 1965 Warsaw WFTU congress see the running coverage by PAP, NCNA, TASS, L'Unità, and Le Monde; Luciano Lama, " Fatto nuova alla FSM," Rinascita, Vol. XXII, No. 43 (October 30, 1965), pp. 3-4; and especially William McLaughlin, " WFTU: End of the Affair," Radio Free Europe, Munich, October 25, 1965. The best sources on WFTU activities are L'Unità and Avanti!

[397] Premier Chou En-lai's letter to leaders of Afro-Asian countries, quoted from Peking Review, Vol. VIII, No. 44 (October 29, 1965), pp. 6-7 at p. 7.

engagement from East and Southeast Asia, Khrushchev in August had indicated that he no longer desired to participate.

After Khrushchev's fall his successors decided to attempt to regain Soviet influence in East Asia and in Cuba. After they had had considerable successes in Havana, Hanoi, and Pyongyang, after the violence of the Chinese assault on them had antagonized some Afro-Asian leaders, and after Chinese influence in Africa was beginning to decline, the new Soviet leadership undertook an extensive lobbying operation to assure itself support in this aspect of its " joint action against the imperialists " line. Then publicly at the beginning of June 1965, the Soviets announced their desire to participate in the conference because

> forces have emerged within the Afro-Asian movement that are trying to split, and chiefly, isolate it from the socialist countries and the international workers' movement.[398]

Meanwhile the Algerians were trying to get Latin American participation, which would also have diluted Chinese influence (the more so because of the Moscow-Havana rapprochement).[399] However, Algeria refused to invite South Korea and South Vietnam and thus antagonized some moderate Asian states. Moreover, nine French-speaking African states, headed by Houphouet-Boigny of the Ivory Coast, refused to participate because of their hostility toward Algeria, Ghana, the Chinese, and the Soviets.[400] To add further to the confusion, the Chinese were prepared to sacrifice Indonesia's desire to keep Malaysia out for votes to keep the Soviet Union out, whereupon Indonesia decided to sacrifice its opposition to Moscow in favor of keeping out Kuala Lumpur.

Thereupon, just before the conference was scheduled to open, Boumédienne overthrew Ben Bella. Indeed, the coup occurred at that time to prevent Ben Bella's prestige from rising because of the meeting and to foil Ben Bella's plans to dismiss some of his opponents, who would be hindered from resisting the dismissals by the conference being in session.

Boumédienne's Foreign Minister, Bouteflika, wanted the conference to meet in order to improve the new regime's prestige. However, those powers who never had wanted it now seized upon this pretext to postpone the meeting. None of them wanted to take sides in the Sino-Soviet dispute: Pakistan did not want to take sides on the Malaysian issue;

---

398 " Observer," " The Soviet Union and the Afro-Asian Forum," *New Times*, No. 22, June 2, 1965, pp. 7–8. See Henri Pierre from Moscow in *Le Monde*, June 8, 1965, and, for Chinese opposition in January 1965, PTI (Bombay) Moscow dispatch, February 5, 1965.
399 Philippe Herreman in *Le Monde*, March 31 and June 4, 1965.
400 On the OCAM and Houphouet-Boigney see Victor D. Du Bois, " The Search for Unity in French-Speaking Africa," American Universities Field Staff Reports, West Africa Series, Vol. VIII, Nos. 3, 4 and 5 (June and July 1965).

Ghana, the East African states, and others were anti-Algerian, particularly since the Boumédienne military coup; and India, Malaysia, and Japan were against the conference in any case. Nasser first tried to postpone the conference, and by the end only five states insisted on having it: Algeria itself, China, North Korea, North Vietnam, and Indonesia. (China had immediately recognized Boumédienne, hoping thereby to get Algerian support against Soviet participation.) Hanoi and Pyongyang did not follow the Soviet line on these kinds of issues but continued to support the Chinese, without, however, publicly criticizing the Soviets. Nasser's initial inclination to postpone the conference, in part because he hoped that the Boumédienne coup might be reversed, changed as soon as he realized that Boumédienne was firmly in the saddle and insisting on the conference. Nasser therefore temporarily shifted in favor of it, but thereupon all the African states demanded its postponement. Nasser then shifted again, whereupon, with as much face-saving as possible for the Algerians and without postponing it indefinitely, as the Indians were urging, the conference was postponed until November. Chinese Foreign Minister Ch'en Yi fought until the end for convening it. Although the postponement was certainly a Chinese defeat, in the sense that the Soviets were thereby for the time being unable to achieve their publicly announced objective of participating, it was something of a defeat for them as well. Finally, by demonstrating that splits, Sino-Soviet and otherwise, within the underdeveloped world made it impossible to agree even on having the conference, the postponement also lowered the prestige of the "third world" in general.[401]

By September, when negotiations on the postponed conference got under way again, the world situation had changed considerably. The use of American military power in North and South Vietnam had demonstrated that Washington would not be driven out of Southeast Asia. The crushing of the Congo rebellion had demonstrated Chinese (and Soviet) impotence in black Africa when faced with even minimal Western military power. Sino-Soviet differences had increased even further, in part due to the Vietnam crisis. The Indo-Pakistani crisis was under way and was helping Moscow and, if anything, hurting Peking. The maneuvering over the Accra African summit conference had indicated the decline in influence of such potential Chinese allies as Nkrumah and other African radical leaders and the rise of the anti-Chinese and also anti-Soviet Houphouet-Boigny and the moderate OCAM states. Finally, Chinese intransigent opposition to negotiations on Vietnam, to

[401] For the conference postponement see G. H. Jansen, " Postponement of the ' Second Bandung,' " *The World Today*, Vol. XXI, No. 9 (September 1965), pp. 398–406; Guy J. Pauker, " The Rise and Fall of Afro-Asian Solidarity," *Asian Survey*, Vol. V, No. 9 (September 1965), pp. 425–432; and the running coverage in *Le Monde*.

the United Nations, and to the June postponement of the conference had all lowered Peking's influence. Moreover Chinese and Indonesian attempts to prevent the participation of some of the more moderate Afro-Asian states, notably India, got nowhere, particularly in the face of UAR (and Soviet) opposition.[402]

At Algiers in June, the Chinese risked a good deal of prestige and suffered a tactical defeat in order to bring about the convening of the conference. Until some time in September their position continued to be the same. Chinese Foreign Minister Ch'en Yi toured Africa to gather support for the conference, for the Soviet exclusion from it, and for a strong declaration against the United States.[403] (His lack of success was indicated by the fact that no joint communiqués were published.)

But by early September the Chinese position had already worsened considerably. Peking's policy in the Indo-Pakistani conflict had antagonized many underdeveloped nations who feared any kind of increased military conflict. The apparent change of the military situation in Vietnam in favor of the United States had both decreased Peking's prestige and convinced many underdeveloped countries that a too strong condemnation of " American imperialism " would be inopportune, since it might hinder a negotiated peace in Southeast Asia. Finally, Soviet successes plus Moscow's appearance of reasonableness when compared with Peking's rigidity had improved Moscow's prestige, and, significantly, Nasser, who needed Soviet support after his Yemen defeat, had publicly favored Moscow's participation in the conference,[104] whereupon Ch'en Yi ostentatiously did not stop at Cairo on his African trip.

Realizing that Peking's chances of using the conference against either Moscow or Washington, to say nothing of both, were no longer good, and determined not to participate in a conference that China could not dominate, Chou En-lai on September 8 declared that Moscow not only had reversed its July 1964 waiver of participation in the conference but was now " sabotaging " it, and that Soviet nonparticipation was for China " a question of principle " concerning which " the Chinese Government will carry the struggle to the end "—that is, if necessary, refuse to attend any conference in which Moscow would participate.[405] At the end of September Ch'en Yi declared that China would not accept anything less than a total condemnation of American imperialism and cancellation of U Thant's invitation to the conference.[406]

---

402 AFP from Cairo, *Le Monde*, July 1, 1965.
403 *Jeune Afrique* (Algiers) September 23, 1965.
404 USSR-UAR communiqué, *Pravda*, September 2, 1965.
405 In an interview with the UAR Middle Eastern News Agency (MENA), published by NCNA in English, September 12, 1965, 0659 GMT, quoted from *Peking Review*, Vol. VIII, No. 38 (September 17, 1965), pp. 8–9, at p. 9.
406 *Ibid.*, Vol. VIII, No. 41 (October 8, 1965), pp. 7–14, at pp. 10–11. See also the Sino-Cambodian communiqué, *ibid.*, pp. 17–18.

China's position on postponement was supported by North Korea,[407] North Vietnam,[408] Tanzania, Cambodia,[409] Pakistan, Guinea, Mali, and the Congo (Brazzaville). However, given the renewed "communist neutralism" of North Korea and North Vietnam, Pakistan's fear of pro-Indian sentiment at such a conference, the general leftist policy of Tanzania, Guinea, Mali, and the Congo (Brazzaville), and their desire not to take sides against China, and Cambodia's generally pro-Chinese policy, in no case did support mean total adherence to the Chinese position. Indonesia did not endorse postponement after Chou's interview, even before the September 30 coup,[410] and thereafter Sukarno, although he requested that Moscow withdraw its bid for participation, supported the Algerian policy in favor of the meeting.[411] India, in contrast, immediately came out for holding the conference at all cost in the hope of thereby hurting Chinese prestige. The Soviets (less openly) did the same; and some of the moderate Africans who had refused to attend indicated they would come after all if China did not. All attempts by Algeria and others to persuade the Chinese to change their stand failed.[412] Thereupon both the Algerian hosts, who by then had sufficiently demonstrated their good will and their diplomatic respectability, and the great majority of the other noncommunist delegates (who opposed an open split such as the Chinese were clearly prepared to provoke) voted for indefinite postponement of the conference.

The Chinese thus won a tactical victory but suffered a strategic reverse, because they were clearly unable, contrary to their April 1965 victory in Jakarta, to exclude the Soviets and still have the conference meet. True, the Chinese have always been prepared to split organizations they could not control. The dilemma of many underdeveloped nations confronted by Chinese intransigence,[413] and their resentment

---

407 Letter to Chou from Kim Il-song, KCNA in English, October 27, 1965, 1630 GMT, and DPRK statement, ibid., 1640 GMT.
408 "It Is Necessary to Postpone the Second Afro-Asian Conference," Nhan Dan, October 28, 1965 (VNA in English, October 28, 1965, 0541 GMT).
409 Norodom Sihanouk, "Bandung and Algiers," Sangkun, No. 1 (Radio Pnom Penh, September 7, 1965, 0700 GMT.)
410 ". The Second Afro-Asian Conference," Indonesian Herald, September 17, 1965.
411 Interview with Sukarno, Nihon Keizai (Tokyo), October 20, 1965, and Indonesian draft resolution cited in note 412.
412 For an October 22 circular letter by Chou En-lai, an October 26 CPR statement, and other Chinese material, plus an Indonesian draft resolution, see Peking Review, Vol. VIII, No. 44 (October 29, 1965), pp. 5–12; for the attempts in Algiers see Brahem from Algiers in Le Monde, October 30, 1965.
413 It should be noted that just before the conference was postponed Ch'en Yi denounced the United Nations more violently than Peking ever had before, and he demanded that its condemnation of the CPR and the DPRK be replaced by condemnation of the United States and that "all imperialist puppets should be expelled" from it—that is, Peking was hardening rather than modifying its line. (See the September 29, 1965 Ch'en Yi press conference, Peking Review, Vol. VIII, No. 41 [October 8, 1965], pp. 7–15, at p. 12.) After the conference was postponed Peking reiterated its call for a reorganization of the United Nations or a "revolutionary" United Nations "to replace it." (See ibid., Vol. VIII, No. 42 [October 15, 1965], p. 11.)

of it, was aptly expressed by a high Algerian press spokesman just before the postponement:

> Algeria has great friendship for China. It will do everything to remain on good terms with her.
> But this matter raises a question of principle. Can a great power, even if it represents 45 per cent of the population of Asia, impose its will on fifty smaller ones? In order to fight imperialism and have a chance to survive, must the latter align themselves with certain anti-imperialist countries? Are not fifty votes worth one vote? [414]

The Soviets won somewhat, by the demonstration of the increased support for them, but the fact that they and the Indians could not bring about a conference without the Chinese, plus the votes for postponement by the North Koreans and North Vietnamese as well as the Pakistanis, Guineans, and Tanzanians, showed that their influence, too, was limited. Finally, the Afro-Asian world in general lost, not only by its inability to convene a conference but by being forced to postpone the gathering indefinitely.[415]

More generally, the October postponement made it clear that Afro-Asian solidarity was indeed a myth and that national rivalries, relations with the great powers, and stages of economic and political development were far more powerful divisive influences than the unifying memory of colonialism or general anti-imperialist sentiments. (At present it seems doubtful that the scheduled January 1966 Afro-Asian-Latin American Solidarity Conference in Havana, even if it actually meets, will alter this estimate.) Finally, it was clear that neither Moscow nor Peking could predominate in the Afro-Asia world but, like the Western powers, could only exercise varying degrees of influence upon weak and divided but essentially nationalistic and opportunistic new states.

XI. CONCLUSIONS

East Europe

Within the context of, and in considerable part because of, its suspension of attempts to expel or condemn the Chinese, the new Soviet leadership made considerable progress in the summer and autumn of 1965 in preventing further losses, even recouping to some extent its position in

---

[414] Quoted from *Le Monde*, October 27, 1965, p. 1.
[415] In addition to the previous specific bibliographic references, see the excellent *Le Monde* coverage, notably Philippe Herreman on October 17–18 and November 3, 1965, and j.c.k. [Joseph C. Kun], " Sino-Soviet Maneuvering over Algiers Meeting," Radio Free Europe, Munich, September 15, 1965, " Peking Seeks Postponement of Afro-Asian Meeting?" *ibid.*, September 30, 1965, and " Peking's Failures in the Afro-Asian Arena," *ibid.*, October 26, 1965.

European communism.[416] It did so by accepting its losses, relying upon geopolitical rather than ideological ties and simultaneously refining its ideological position.

The Soviet-Yugoslav rapprochement intensified still further during Tito's June visit to the Soviet Union. Yugoslav internal nationality and economic strains, plus a revival of ideological revisionism, all of which remained among the main reasons for Tito's more pro-Soviet position since 1962, were becoming more serious, while the disunity and impotence of the "third world" made him inclined to move closer to Moscow. Moreover, for the present he did not need to fear either a Sino-Soviet rapprochement or a Soviet return to hegemonic practices. However, Yugoslavia's internal problems, combined with its weakened position in the West and the "third world," made Tito's rapprochement with Moscow less valuable to the Soviets than it might have been previously.[417]

In Bulgaria, Zhivkov's regime seemed to have overcome the after-effects of the abortive April 1965 coup. Yet Moscow's suspension of "collective mobilization" and even more the new Soviet leadership's acceptance of the Rumanian deviation could not but encourage the autonomist tendencies, however, weak, still alive in Sofia.[418] Indeed, Zhivkov may be tempted to avert future opposition by himself taking a more nationalistic position. However, Bulgaria's geography and history give its alliance with Moscow a stronger base than in any other East European country, and the alliance bids fair to continue.

The new Rumanian leadership, headed by the young, native Communist Nicolae Ceauçescu, in July 1965 staged a party congress that demonstrated its consolidation both at home and abroad. Ceauçescu made clear that he intended to pursue Gheorghiu-Dej's autonomous course, and he succeeded in preventing Peking, Moscow, Belgrade, and Tirana from polemicizing at the congress. His September 1965 visit to Moscow signalled at least a partial normalization of Soviet-Rumanian relations, and one almost entirely on Bucharest's terms. Moscow committed itself to abandon any interference in Rumanian internal

---

[416] The following brief summary of post-June 1965 developments in Soviet relations with European Communist parties and states is largely based on my "European Communism, 1965," in Griffith, *Communism in Europe, op. cit.*, Vol. 2, pp. 1–39, *q.v.* for extended analysis and full bibliographic citations.

[417] *Ibid.* pp. 9–11, and more recently the penetrating survey by Viktor Meier, "Jugoslawien in Prozess des Umdenkens," *Neue Zürcher Zeitung*, September 14, 21, 30, and October 3, 1965. As as been indicated, Albania, in spite of some indications that Peking did not identify totally with its policies, remained in the Chinese sphere. See Griffith, *Communism in Europe, op. cit.*, Vol. 2, pp. 8–9.

[418] *Ibid.* p. 12, and note 13, V. M. [Viktor Meier] from Sofia, " Bulgarien als freiwillinger Satellit," *Neue Zürcher Zeitung*, October 16 and 20, 1965; Paul Lendvai, " Bulgaria Steers a New Course," *East Europe*, Vol. 14, No. 10 (October 1965), pp. 26–29; and the Rumanian-Bulgarian communiqué, *Scînteia* and *Rabotnichesko Delo*, September 19, 1965.

affairs, and although Rumanian-American relations had cooled somewhat because of the Vietnam crisis, as had Rumanian-West German
contacts because of political developments in Bonn, Ceauçescu gave no
sign of abandoning his general policy of improving relations with the
West as well as with the underdeveloped areas. Bucharest also moved
to improve its relations with Belgrade, Sofia, and even with Budapest,
and revived, to Moscow's displeasure, its Balkan "zone of peace"
proposal. Moreover, the independent Rumanian position at the October
1965 Warsaw WFTU congress and continued Rumanian departures
from Moscow's United Nations voting patterns demonstrated that
Bucharest would continue to oppose Soviet and Chinese policies alike
when it deemed it desirable, particularly on the issue of national
independence.[419]

Czechoslovakia continued to support Soviet policies, in spite of
some reports of Soviet-Czechoslovak economic differences, but internal
liberalization, although slow, continued apace and did not bode entirely
favorably for permanent alignment with all of Moscow's policies.[420]

The increased international tension arising from the Vietnam crisis
and Bonn's bowing to Washington's stand against the establishment of
a West German trade mission in Peking (thereby making it more difficult for the Chinese to play with Bonn against Pankow) both contributed
to keeping Soviet-East German relations close. However, this was in
part because Ulbricht had never favored a Sino-Soviet break and
probably was pleased by the suspension of Soviet efforts toward that
end.[421]

The West European Communist Parties

In West European communism the new Soviet policy of suspending
efforts toward expulsion or condemnation of Peking greatly improved
Moscow's relations with the Italian Communist Party, whose policy in
this respect the Soviets had in fact adopted. Moreover, although the
French Communist Party probably would have preferred continuation
of the previous Soviet line, its desire for a popular front in France plus

---

[419] Griffith, *Communism in Europe, op. cit.*, Vol. 2, pp. 12–13; V. M. [Viktor Meier],
" Aktivierung der rumänischen Aussenpolitik," *Neue Zürcher Zeitung*, October 17,
1965; *The New York Times*, November 22, 1965; and Philippe Ben from New York
in *Le Monde*, November 28–29, 1965.

[420] Griffith, *Communism in Europe, op. cit.*, Vol. 2, pp. 16–21, note 17, and, for reported
USSR-CSSR economic differences, V. M. [Viktor Meier] from Vienna in *Neue
Zürcher Zeitung*, October 11, 19, and 30, 1965, and a Radio Free Europe, Munich,
analysis, October 29, 1965; Chauvier in *Le Drapeau Rouge* (Brussels), October 14,
1965 (JPRS 32,800, November 10, 1965), pp. 24–26.

[421] Griffith, *Communism in Europe, op. cit.*, Vol. 2, pp. 21–24. I have omitted any
reference to Polish and Hungarian developments because of their lack of significance
for Sino-Soviet relations. See *ibid.* pp. 14–16, and, for an indication of deviant
Polish U.N. voting, Philippe Ben from New York in *Le Monde*, November 28–29,
1965.

its traditional pro-Soviet orientation prevented it from opposing Moscow on that issue.

In the long run, however, Italian communism remained too independent and revisionist for Soviet tastes, and the June 1965 endorsement of Amendola's *partito unico* concept by Longo and the Central Committee (despite some public negative votes from the left wing, followed by continuing opposition led by Ingrao), plus the continued independent Italian course within the WFTU, were bound to have effects on European communism that could not further Soviet interests. Moreover, although Moscow probably welcomed PCI assistance in the cultivation of Hanoi and Havana, in the long run this kind of free-wheeling PCI diplomacy was hardly desirable or reliable from the Soviet viewpoint. Finally, the fall of Ben Bella had been a greater defeat for the PCI and the PCF than for Moscow, which could always recoup somewhat with Boumédienne on the state level but whose efforts to do so could hardly be entirely pleasing to the French and Italian Communists.[422]

In the smaller West European parties Soviet influence continued to decline, but this was a loss Moscow could easily afford, the more so since the loss also was limited by the suspension of collective mobilization.[423]

Recent Soviet Maneuvering

The October celebrations of the thirtieth anniversary of the Seventh Comintern Congress served both as a focal point for Soviet maneuvering on the organizational issue and as an opportunity for Moscow to furnish historical precedent for its " unity of action " line. Pomelov's major article about it did not mention the proposed international conference or explicitly criticize the Chinese. It did, however, stress that

> the achievement of the unity of the workers' movement, as the Marxist-Leninist parties rightly emphasize, demands giving up the attitude of seclusion on the part of the Communists.

and quoted the resolution of the Seventh Comintern Congress to the effect that

> the actual implementation of a united front demands of the Communists . . . that they overcome smug sectarianism within their own ranks, which at present is already in a number of cases no longer an " infantile disorder " of the Communist movement but an entrenched vice.[424]

[422] Griffith, *Communism in Europe, op. cit.*, Vol. 2, pp. 31–36, and, in addition, for PCI internal disunity, Nobécourt from Rome in *Le Monde*, November 2, 1965, p. 14, and a Milan dispatch in *Neue Zürcher Zeitung*, November 7, 1965.
[423] Griffith, *Communism in Europe, op. cit.*, Vol. 2, pp. 24–29, 36–37.
[424] " Strategy of Unity of Anti-Imperialist Forces," *Pravda*, August 20, 1965, quoted from *CDSP*, Vol. XVII, No. 33 (September 8, 1965), pp. 6 and 36.

Significantly, however, major Soviet pronouncements came not during the actual anniversary, which would have been in July and August, but during October, first at a conference in Moscow devoted to the occasion and then at a celebration in Prague. On October 4 Suslov reiterated that the CPSU " like other Marxist-Leninist parties " favored holding an international forum of Communists after " careful and thorough preparation "—the first direct Soviet call for such a conference since the CPSU Central Committee resolution on the March meeting. Yet he carefully did not refer to the timing of such a meeting, praised bilateral meetings among Communists, and gave Moscow plenty of room to retreat by underlining that

> Communists have always subordinated organizational forms to fundamental political tasks of the workers' movement that stem from the specific features of the concrete situation.[425]

As for the " differences " within the communists' ranks, Suslov re-emphasized Soviet good faith in attempting to overcome them, and he made no mention of the Chinese.

However, when Ponomarev spoke at the Prague meeting commemorating the anniversary,[426] he not only reiterated that

> the CPSU and other Marxist-Leninist parties believe that a carefully prepared world-wide forum could well serve the cause of overcoming differences and rallying the communist movement on the basis of Marxism-Leninism.

but coupled this Soviet support for an international conference with direct, if somewhat restrained, criticism of Peking's rejection of the path to unity:

> Our party is firmly holding its course at rallying the socialist community according to the principles of Marxism-Leninism and socialist internationalism. The CPSU Central Committee has taken all possible measures to normalize relations with the Chinese Communist Party. As is known in the international Communist movement, however, these measures of ours have not led to positive results.[427]

Ponomarev too praised bilateral meetings among Communist leaders.

That opposition, and in all likelihood decisive opposition, to the conference plan still existed within the international Communist movement became clear when there was no mention of the project either in the major *Pravda* October 27 editorial (only five days after Ponomarev's speech) or at the November 7 celebration of the forty-eighth anniversary of the October Revolution.

The PCI had already flatly stated in July that it thought such a

[425] *Pravda*, October 5, 1965, quoted from CDSP, Vol. XVII, No. 40 (October 27, 1965), p. 23.
[426] *Pravda*, October 23, 1965.
[427] *Ibid.*

gathering could lead to no good. Mario Alicata, although endorsing "unity of action" as the way to lay the foundation for new forms of solidarity of the international Communist movement, explicitly stated:

> We must concentrate the attention of our movement on discovering concrete initiatives for peace and against imperialist aggression. For developing unity of action a new way must be found to lay the foundations for new forms of solidarity, of cooperation, and of unity in our movement. This reaffirms our position, which is against returning, at this time, to a concentration of attention on the part of the Communist and workers' parties on the problem of a new international conference. We understand the negative reactions, the nervousness, and the impatience of those who see—and even we see it clearly—the harm resulting from the division existing today. But this does not induce us to change our position. On the contrary, we are convinced that to delay efforts to reconstruct the unity of our movement in new ways does not favor the demand and the implementation of initiatives toward unity.[428]

Moreover, PCI Secretary-General Luigi Longo, after the Ponomarev speech, pointedly reiterated to the PCI that he considered an international conference to be both harmful and dangerous, and that " all measures which could aggravate the existing ruptures and divisions in the communist movement should be rejected." [429]

Nor was opposition among generally pro-Soviet parties limited to the Italians. Despite the broadening Soviet-Cuban rapprochement throughout the summer, Cuba maintained studied silence not only on the question of an international conference but on the March Moscow meeting. Moreover, although when the Rumanian delegation was in Moscow, Ceauçescu had endorsed international meetings as at least potentially useful, there was no official reaction to Ponomarev's suggestion from Bucharest.

As to Peking's former allies on this issue, North Korea and North Vietnam presumably remained opposed, and indeed in all likelihood more effectively so, because the Soviets' desire to encourage their shift toward neutrality in Sino-Soviet matters made Moscow increasingly sensitive to their wishes. Interestingly enough, as of November 11 there had been no public Albanian reaction.[430] The desperate situation of the Indonesia Communist Party made the PKI's stand less important than formerly.

What actually took place at the Prague meeting, which *Pravda* termed " an international meeting " of " almost 40 parties," [431] remains

[428] *L'Unità*, July 9, 1965.
[429] Quoted from j.c.k. [Joseph C. Kun], " Opposition to International Conference," Radio Free Europe, Munich, October 28, 1965.
[430] Based on review of *Zëri i Popullit* by Peter Prifti from October 23 through November 11, 1965.
[431] *Pravda*, October 22, 1965.

unclear. Yet the gathering was certainly significant for both its composition and its published speeches.[432] Of the East European states Rumania was conspicuously absent. The PCI attended; however, Cuba and Yugoslavia did not and, not surprisingly, neither did North Vietnam or North Korea. The Polish representative, Jarosinski, stressed that "under present conditions no international center of the world Communist movement is in existence."[433] He was not explicitly contradicted but Koucky, as host, pointedly referred to the Soviet Union as the "main force" of the socialist system.[434]

However, the Soviets had come a long way since Khrushchev's heavy-handed attempts to force collective mobilization against the Chinese. *Pravda*'s excerpts of other speeches at the Comintern anniversary celebration made no mention of the conference project,[435] although a subsequent Soviet reference to the "exchange of opinion among representatives of almost 40 Communist parties in Prague"[436] plus its coupling of this meeting with that of the Latin American Communist parties in November 1964 and the Brussels conference of West European Communist parties in June of 1965, indicated that Moscow was trying to give the anniversary celebration the status of at least a partial international conference.

Yet the organizational issue was also excluded from reports on Soviet bilateral discussions with Bulgarian, Polish, and Mongolian delegations between October 25 and 30. This silence on the conference project must have been at Moscow's request for the Soviet-Bulgarian communiqué reaffirmed:

> During the exchange of opinions, the two sides noted the complete identity of views between the CPSU and the Bulgarian Communist Party and the Soviet and Bulgarian governments in assessing the present international situation and the situation in the international Communist movement.[437]

It was undoubtedly no accident that this communiqué appeared in the same issue of *Pravda* as the most authoritative pronouncement of Moscow's post-Khrushchev leadership position within the international Communist movement to date—the editorial entitled "The Supreme International Duty of the Country of Socialism."[438]

[432] Radio Prague referred to "representatives of 35 Communist and workers' parties" (CTK in English, October 21, 1965, 1305 GMT.)
[433] *Trybuna Ludu*, October 23, 1965.
[434] *Rudé Právo*, October 24, 1965.
[435] *Pravda*, October 24, 1965. Entitled "The Great Forces of Internationalism," these excerpts included comments by high-level Hungarian, Polish, East German, Bulgarian, Czechoslovak, and Mongolian representatives.
[436] "The International Duty of Communists of All Countries," *ibid.*, November 28, 1965.
[437] *Ibid.*, October 27, 1965, quoted from *CDSP*, Vol. XVII, No. 43 (November 17, 1965), pp. 6–9.   [438] *Ibid.*

Although the editorial did not mention the conference project,[439] it strongly reaffirmed Moscow's primary role in the world revolutionary movement without so much as mentioning the Chinese. This role was said to be shared with other socialist countries:

> We know that in the past the center of the world revolutionary movement shifted from one country to another. This shift was linked with the upsurge and subsequent decline of the revolutionary wave in various countries. . . .
> In Russia, which at the beginning of our century became the vanguard of the world liberation struggle, victory came not only to the bourgeois-democratic but also to the socialist revolution, and socialism was built. Our country thereby became the stable center of the world revolutionary movement. After World War II socialist revolutions were victorious in a number of countries of Europe and Asia, which, together with the Soviet Union, created a powerful socialist camp. Thereafter the socialist revolution was victorious in Cuba. The socialist camp is now the center of the world revolutionary movement.

The editorial was careful to qualify this commonwealth-like formula, however, by insisting that

> we are thereby in no way belittling the gigantic importance of the national liberation movement and the struggle of the working people of capitalist countries in the contemporary revolutionary process.

(That is, it was careful not to reject the Italian and Cuban desire for a " camp " composed of radical nationalist movements as well as communist states and parties.) Professing a wish to avoid abstract discussions on the question of " the center," it posed and answered the crucial question:

> Who is bearing the chief brunt of the struggle against imperialism, who is shackling its main forces? This is done by the socialist countries, and first of all by the strongest of them, the Soviet Union.

In other words, the Soviet geopolitical and military strength would replace the Soviet ideological monopoly as criteria for Soviet leadership of the " camp of socialism," and Moscow would thus still remain dominant. Again, referring to aid for revolutionary movements, the editorial blandly asserted that it was impossible to name a single important revolutionary movement that did not receive " every possible support " from the socialist countries, " first and foremost, the Soviet Union."

Yet in fact the editorial went much farther than any Soviet pronouncement had before in stressing the primacy of Soviet domestic

---

[439] It was subsequently revealed that after Suslov's speech and before Ponomarev again endorsed the conference plan, Moscow had agreed that " the present time would not be favorable for calling an international conference." See Franz Muhri's interview on his discussion in Moscow, *Volksstimme* (Vienna), October 14, 1965 (JPRS 32,800 [November 10, 1965], pp. 16 and 17).

developments over foreign policy obligations, not only vis-à-vis the Vietnam war but more generally vis-à-vis all communist countries, and the decline in Soviet willingness to give massive economic and military aid. The coming of socialism in developed and underdeveloped countries will be primarily the result of the efforts of " the peoples of those countries "; and, conversely,

> the socialist countries . . . cannot substitute for other detachments of the liberation struggle . . . the peoples of the young national states in solving tasks of the national liberation movement or of the working class, nor can they take the place of the working class, and working people of capitalist countries in the struggle to overthrow capitalism.

Rather,

> The socialist countries in building socialism and communism are making a most important and decisive contribution to the world liberation movement. This determines their vanguard role in the present-day revolutionary struggle,

that is, not, as Peking maintains, their armed aid to national liberation movements. The article continued, " some sort of international leveling " (that is, massive aid by Moscow to Peking, Hanoi, and other under-developed communist countries) would not bring " a fundamental improvement " in their position and therefore would " discredit socialism." Moreover,

> Aid to the developing countries is given not out of surpluses but by the allocation of funds and material that would be most useful to the socialist countries themselves; this is a manifestation of genuine inter-nationalism. And anyone who tries to discredit this aid insults the noblest feelings of the working people of the socialist countries.

Combined with the editorial's reiterated support for the March meeting, its contents strongly suggested that even if the Soviet leadership was being more delicate in its drive for an international conference, Moscow was not actually retreating. Rather, unlike Khrushchev, the Soviets were now convinced that time was on their side. As the *Pravda* editorial put it:

> Our party strictly upholds the appeal of the March, 1965, Con-sultative Meeting of Representatives of Communist and Workers' Parties on calling a halt to open polemics in the world Communist movement. The achievement of the unity of this movement on the basis of the principles of Marxism-Leninism is regarded by our party as one of its most important internationalist tasks. The C.P.S.U. and the other Marxist-Leninist parties strive to concentrate their attention not on what divides them but on what unites them.
> Calling for unity of action in the face of differences, our party proposes that time and practical life be permitted to decide the question of the justice and correctness of the various points of view. Only those who are not convinced of the correctness of their concepts are afraid

to submit them to the test of time and practice. This is all the more true in that the joint struggle against imperialism and for the building of socialism and communism must objectively further the overcoming of the differences and the elaboration of common points of view.

Given this pronouncement, it was not surprising that the November 7 celebrations concentrated on strengthening the Soviet military image and stressed Moscow's internal economic accomplishments.

Polyansky's major speech combined emphasis on the primacy of international communist construction with a pertinent reminder (in view of Indonesian developments) that revolution was not exportable. He reiterated Soviet support for peaceful coexistence, which had not become any more palatable to Peking in spite of recent setbacks, and said of Soviet-Chinese " differences ":

> We are trying to improve relations, to settle the differences and strengthen friendship with the Chinese People's Republic. Everything possible on our part has been done to this end. Now the question of developing relations between the Soviet Union and China, between the CPSU and the Communist Party of China, depends on the Chinese leaders.[440]

China's Total Defiance

> A few days ago when Chairman Mao received me, he said: " Our fatherland is truly a little more powerful than before, but it is not yet powerful enough. We must continue construction for at least 20 or 30 years before we gain real power." [441]

Peking's verbal reaction to its succession of setbacks, the *Pravda* October 27 editorial, and Moscow's November 7 celebration was to escalate its defiance of Washington and Moscow. In a long programmatic statement of November 11 entitled " Refutation of the New Leaders of the CPSU on ' United Action,' " [442] the Chinese leadership stepped up its fanaticism to hitherto unreached heights.

The article reiterated and sharpened all the most extreme Chinese theses, particularly those set forth concerning the Soviet Union in the ninth " Comment " [443]: alliance with all elements in the developed and

440 *Pravda*, November 7, 1965, quoted from *CDSP*, Vol. XVII, No. 44 (November 24, 1965), pp. 3–8, at p. 8. See also Fritz Ermarth, " A Roundup of the Moscow Celebrations," Radio Free Europe, Munich, November 8, 1965.

441 Li Tsung-jen (once Vice-President under Chiang Kai-shek), Radio Peking in Mandarin to Taiwan, August 8, 1965, 1100 GMT.

442 *Jen-min Jih-pao* and *Hung Ch'i*, November 11, 1965, quoted from *Peking Review*, Vol. VIII, No. 46 (November 12, 1965), pp. 10–21. See Wolfgang Leonhard, " ' Wir vertrauen euch nicht!' " *Die Zeit*, November 30, 1965. The preceding day *Jen-min Jih-pao* published three pages of " anti-Chinese " statements (see *Peking Review*, *ibid.*, pp. 22–23).

443 See pp. 43–45.

underdeveloped world who were both anti-American and anti-Soviet, as set forth notably in Mao's July 1964 interview with the Japanese socialists; and the perfidy of the new Soviet leadership, as set forth in " Why Khrushchev Fell." [444] It began with the last theme:

> The essence of the Khrushchev revisionist theory and line, which the new leaders of the CPSU are persisting in and developing further . . . but with double-faced tactics more cunning and hypocritical than those of Khrushchev . . . is to protect imperialist rule in the capitalist world and to restore capitalism in the socialist world.[445]

They can and will do nothing else, because

> It is inevitable that Khrushchev revisionism will exist as long as the social basis and the class roots which gave birth to it remain and as long as the privileged bourgeois stratum exists.[446]

Kosygin's economic decentralization proposals mean

> restoring capitalism, replacing socialist ownership by the whole people with ownership by the privileged bourgeois stratum, . . .

while Brezhnev's increased incentives to agriculture

> encourage and foster the growth of a new kulak economy, sabotaging and disintegrating all aspects of the socialist collective economy.[447]

In foreign policy Moscow's collaboration with Washington " for the domination of the world," the article went on, is demonstrated most conclusively by Soviet policy in the Vietnam crisis. The article then proceeded to reveal the series of hitherto secret Soviet moves in support of negotiation, which have been discussed earlier in the account of Vietnamese developments. The purpose of these revelations was to justify the thesis that the Soviet line of " joint action " against the imperialists in Vietnam was in fact intended

> to hoodwink the people at home and abroad, to keep the situation in Vietnam under their control, to gain a say on the Vietnam question and to strike a bargain with U.S. imperialism on it.[448]

To this end, Moscow's aid to Vietnam " is far from commensurate with the strength of the Soviet Union," and, moreover,

> the new leaders of the CPSU have disclosed the details of their so-called " aid " to Vietnam to the Americans

while falsely denouncing China for allegedly having obstructed it.

[444] See pp. 64–65.
[445] " Refutation of the New Leaders of the CPSU on ' United Action,' " *op. cit.*, pp. 12, 11, and 12.
[446] *Ibid.* pp. 19–20.
[447] *Ibid.* p. 19.
[448] *Ibid.* p. 16. For an important comment on Soviet aid to the North Vietnamese as well as the Chinese stand on " joint action," see Muhri's interview in *Volksstime* (Vienna), October 14, 1965, *op. cit.*, pp. 16 and 17.

In calling so vehemently for "united action" on the Vietnam question and trying by every means to bring about a summit conference of the Soviet Union, Vietnam and China and an international meeting of the socialist countries and the fraternal Parties, the new leaders of the CPSU have no other purpose in mind than to deceive the world, to tie the fraternal countries to the chariot of Soviet-U.S. collaboration for world domination, to use the question of Vietnam as an important counter in their bargaining with the United States, and to isolate and attack the Chinese Communist Party and all the other fraternal Parties which uphold Marxism-Leninism.[449]

The new Soviet leadership's attacks on China during the Indo-Pakistani conflict were described as making those of Khrushchev "pale into insignificance."[450] Finally, Moscow was accused of continuing Khrushchev's "anti-Albanian" policy, "subversion" of the Japanese, Indonesian, New Zealand and other communist parties, and attempting to wreck international communist organizations.[451]

What should Chinese policy be in the face of this challenge? The article minced no words in reply. It must arise out of the fact that

The antagonism between Marxism-Leninism and Khrushchev revisionism is a class antagonism between the proletariat and the bourgeoisie; it is the antagonism between the socialist and the capitalist roads and between the line of opposing imperialism and that of surrendering to it. It is an irreconcilable antagonism.[452]

It will therefore follow Mao's slogan of "establishing an international united front against U.S. imperialism," the logical adaptation to post-1945 events of Marx's and Engels' "Workers of the world, unite!" and Lenin's expanded "Workers and oppressed nations of the world, unite!"[453] (that is to say, Mao, not Khrushchev or Brezhnev, is the ideological leader of world communism). This means, the article went on, unity with "the upper strata in many nationalist countries" (that is, Sihanouk, Ayub Khan, and any bourgeois nationalist leaders who turn toward China, out of whatever motives) and also with those "monopoly capitalists . . . who desire in varying degrees to oppose the United States,"[454] that is, those in such countries as France and West Germany who agree with Peking that the Soviet-proposed nonproliferation treaty is

an effort to maintain the monopoly of the two nuclear overlords, the Soviet Union and the United States, against China and all other independent countries.[455]

[449] "Refutation of the New Leaders of the CPSU on ' United Action,' " *op. cit.*, p. 17.
[450] *Ibid.* p. 14.
[451] *Ibid.* pp. 17–18.
[452] *Ibid.* p. 13.
[453] *Ibid.* pp. 10–11.
[454] *Ibid.* pp. 14–15.
[455] *Ibid.* pp. 13–14.

Peking hardly could have been more explicit: China wanted to ally with all dissatisfied powers, notably West Germany and Japan, against the United States and the Soviet Union, just as Hitler did with Italy and Japan against the victors of the last war.

What does this mean in practice for Peking's policies? Unremitting polemics against Moscow and all its works, support for all anti-Soviet splinter groups, and " a clear line of demarcation " [456] against the Soviet Union and all its supporters.

Only at the end of the article was there an indirect reference to the Chinese defeats that had preceded it: " a certain unevenness in the degree of people's understanding of the struggle, . . . particularly conspicuous when the struggle becomes sharp. . . ." Thus the Chinese were apparently all ready to accept temporary losses:

> As the struggle against Khrushchev revisionism becomes sharper and deeper, a new process of division will inevitably occur in the revolutionary ranks, and some people will inevitably drop out.[457]

All the more reason, the article concluded, to " carry the struggle against Khrushchev revisionism through to the end!" [458]

The Soviet Reply

By November 1965, then, Chinese defiance of the Soviet Union was more violent than ever and it appeared that Peking at least as yet rejected any adjustment to its series of defeats. Nor did its near-admission to the United Nations later that month seem likely to change its course, even though the unexpectedly high vote it received, in spite of its extremist stand, reflected a desire in the underdeveloped world to contribute toward negotiations on the Vietnam crisis, just what Peking wanted to avoid.[459]

Five days after the November 11 Chinese *article fleuve* appeared, *Pravda* published a brief summary of it, ostensibly from its correspondent in Peking, and concluded with a sharp rebuke to the Chinese:

> The entire article from beginning to end is saturated with impermissible, utterly groundless, slanderous, and provocative fabrications and is pervaded with the spirit of hostility toward the Soviet people and the CPSU and its policy of rallying all anti-imperialist progressive forces throughout the world.[460]

456 *Ibid.* p. 21.
457 *Ibid.* p. 20.
458 *Ibid.* p. 21.
459 See Philippe Ben from New York in *Le Monde*, November 19, 1965, and " The Fundamental Question for the U.N. Is to Smash U.S. Domination," *Jen-min Jih-pao*, November 19, 1965, and *Peking Review*, Vol. VIII, No. 48 (November 26, 1965), pp. 15–18.
460 " Anti-Soviet Article in the Chinese Press," *Pravda*, November 16, 1965. It was also republished by *Jen-min Jih-pao* on November 20, with an editorial note taunting Moscow for not republishing Chinese articles. See " Pravda's Anti-Chinese Article," *Peking Review*, Vol. VIII, No. 48 (November 26, 1965), p. 23.

This article marked the first time since Khrushchev's fall that the Soviet public had been informed in any detail about Chinese attacks. Then, on November 28, *Pravda* published a full-length refutation of the November 11 Chinese attack.[461]

The article summarized, generalized, and made more explicit the Soviet rejection of Peking's opposition to the " joint action " line. The Chinese " policy of subverting unity of action, . . . of intensifying attacks on the Marxist-Leninist parties, . . . of splitting the communist movement," it declared, damages the international Communist movement, the national liberation struggle, and especially North Vietnam, thereby " encourages deliberately the enemies of peace, democracy, and socialism," and can only mean " disassociation from an overwhelming majority of Marxist-Leninist parties . . . the overwhelming majority of detachments of the liberation movement . . . hampering the struggle of the Vietnamese people . . . and helping the aggressor."

It was unclear from the article whether or not Moscow intended to resume polemics; the Soviet leadership itself may well have been uncertain. Nor was there any mention of an international conference, an omission that indicated continuing Soviet inability to summon one within a context Moscow would consider desirable.

* * * * * * *

The varying emphases in Soviet negotiations with other communist parties during the summer and autumn of 1965 have already been outlined. In sum, at least some elements in Moscow appeared to favor returning to a more organizational means of containing the Chinese, but the Italian, Cuban, Rumanian, North Vietnamese, and North Korean Communists opposed this, and improved Soviet relations with them, due to the abandonment of previous organizational methods, made it the more difficult for Moscow to resume its former tactics.

The Soviet Union had reluctantly, more by trial and error than by plan, readjusted somewhat, and with considerable success, to the changing communist and underdeveloped world of 1965. (Encouraged by Gaullist trends, fearful of rising West German power, and not yet forced to confront any decisive problems there, Moscow had not yet readjusted significantly to the changing scene in West Europe—but, then, neither had Washington.) Peking, on the other hand, whose defeats had been more recent, and followed a long period of rising influence, had not adjusted at all. Rather, it had reacted with rigidity and defiance.

Soviet policy toward the " third world " had adjusted to its increasingly less profitable influence therein—notably by cutting

461 " The International Duty of Communists of All Countries," *op. cit.*

economic and military aid. Moreover, the Chinese failures in sponsoring wars of national liberation, largely (like Moscow's) due to Peking's underestimation of Afro-Asian nationalism and intractibility, had not only lowered Soviet worries about Peking's influence there, and thus its own estimate of the necessity of Soviet engagement, but, notably in the two postponements of the Algiers Second Afro-Asian Conference, had demonstrated that there was no united underdeveloped world to capture.

Indeed, the world remained dominated during 1963–1965 by one overriding characteristic: the rise of nationalism. Pluralism ate away at the blocs in all three areas. NATO was threatened by French withdrawal; the Afro-Asian bloc as such seemed divided and increasingly powerless; the international Communist movement was not only cut in two by the Sino-Soviet split but was becoming increasingly pluralistic, diffentiated, and less clearly divided from the other two major world groupings.

In late 1965 both Moscow and Peking were faced with a series of ongoing crises that would probably influence their future relations with each other and with the rest of the world. The Vietnam crisis was the main one and here Washington would continue to play a major role and have a major effect on Sino-Soviet relations. The confused situation in West Europe was another which both Moscow and Peking hoped to use to their own advantage. Here Washington's inactivity, West Germany's rising power but political indecision, and de Gaulle's separatism would all affect Sino-Soviet relations.

Finally, most unpredictably, and perhaps most importantly, there remained the elements of time, personality, and accident. Certainly Khrushchev's fall significantly changed the character of Soviet policy; and Mao obviously feared that the passing of his own generation would criminally moderate Chinese policy as well. In any case, Sino-Soviet differences have become so great that any permanent reconciliation seems unlikely.

DOCUMENTS

DOCUMENT 1

Letter of the Central Committee of the CPSU of November 29, 1963 to the Central Committee of the CCP

Complete Text
[*Peking Review*, Vol. VII, No. 19 (May 8, 1964), pp. 18–21]
November 29, 1963

The Central Committee of the Communist Party of China

Comrade Mao Tse-tung

Dear Comrades,

The Communist press has recently published documents in which the Marxist-Leninist parties have publicly expounded their positions on fundamental questions of the international communist movement raised in the debate that has unfolded. These documents show that there are serious differences in the communist movement, differences in the understanding and interpretation of the fundamental theses of the Declaration and the Statement of the Moscow meetings. We will not conceal the fact that, like many other fraternal Parties, irrespective of the position they are taking, we are seriously concerned over the fact that the differences which have arisen are constantly becoming deeper and the scope of the questions under debate is constantly widening, while the sharp public polemics are assuming forms impermissible in relations among Marxist-Leninists.

Particularly disquieting is the fact that the differences on ideological questions are being transferred to inter state relations and are manifesting themselves in the field of concrete policies, thus shaking the friendship and unity of the peoples of the socialist community and weakening the anti-imperialist front. The strength and attention of the fraternal Parties are being deflected from the solution of urgent problems of socialist construction and from the struggle against imperialism.

This situation in the communist movement grieves us greatly. We have more than once declared, and now reiterate, that the abnormal relations between the CCP and CPSU are dividing the communist forces and benefiting only our enemies who on their part are seeking in every way to play on the contradictions and making use of the existing difficulties for their own anti-communist aims.

Of course Parties like the CPSU and the CCP, standing at the head of the world's two biggest states, can go on with their work even if the polemics continue. We agree that for our two Parties even in such circumstances, as you said to the Soviet Ambassador Comrade Chervonenko, the skies will not fall, and grass and trees will continue to grow, women to bear children and fish to swim in the water.

But we cannot fail to see that the differences and sharp polemics are doing great harm to the communist movement. We also have no right to fail to think of those detachments of the communist movement which are forced to carry on the struggle against imperialism in extremely difficult and

147

complex circumstances. Such Parties rightly consider that they require friendship with both the CPSU and the CCP. All Marxist-Leninist parties draw strength from the unity and solidarity of the communist movement for the overcoming of difficulties.

The Communists of all countries want unity of action. And they are right — without unity of action our struggle against class enemies will be many times harder.

In the present circumstances, the most important and urgent task of the Marxist-Leninists is to prevent an undesirable development of events, and to turn the events from the zone of danger towards normalization, towards the strengthening of co-operation and unity among all the fraternal Parties and socialist countries. Timelier than ever now are Lenin's injunctions that each Party must be conscious of its high responsibility for our common cause, and be ready to give first place to the fundamental interests of the communist movement.

The Communist Party of the Soviet Union, firmly following the Leninist course of the world communist movement as expressed in the Declaration and the Statement of the Moscow meetings, has considered, and still considers, itself duty bound to do all it can for the strengthening of unity.

We understand, of course, that the elimination of the difficulties that have arisen in the world communist movement requires great exertion by all the Marxist-Leninist parties. In this letter, we wish to give our views on the contribution which our two Parties could make towards the solution of this problem.

As before, we hold to the position that despite existing serious differences, there is an objective basis for the improvement of relations between the CPSU and the CCP and between our countries — the basis being the common fundamental interests of our two peoples and our common tasks in the struggle for socialism and communism, the support of the revolutionary workers' movement and national liberation movement, and the struggle for peace against the aggressive schemes of the imperialists.

One cannot fail to see that, besides the questions over which differences have arisen, there are also positions on which we are fully united, or at least very close in our views. We have, objectively, a common position on such basic questions as the class struggle, the struggle against imperialism for the victory of the working class and all the working people, and the dictatorship of the proletariat which is established, as is seen from the experience of the Soviet Union and other socialist countries, for the destruction of those forces which, after the victory of the proletarian revolution, offer resistance to the construction of socialism. Although our interpretations on these questions are not in all respects the same as yours, we are deeply convinced that a calm and unprejudiced understanding of our present discussion, and the elimination from it of everything that is non-essential and fortuitous, will reveal wide possibilities not only for the preservation of our co-operation along many lines but also for its growth and strengthening.

Now that the CPSU and the CCP, as well as other fraternal Parties, have stated their views on the questions in dispute, it would be correct not to concentrate attention on the problems on which there are differences between us but to let them wait until the heat of passion has cooled, to let time do its work. We are certain that life will demonstrate the correctness of the Marxist-Leninist line. At the same time, we could develop our co-operation in those spheres where favourable possibilities exist. Such co-operation is in the interest not only of the Soviet Union and China but also of all the peoples of the socialist community.

Concretely speaking, we propose that notwithstanding the differences we should place at the centre of our mutual relations the development of co-operation for the sake of strengthening friendship between the Soviet Union and China and among all the socialist countries and fraternal Marxist-Leninist parties, and of co-ordinating actions in the various international organizations for our common aim of defending peace and combating imperialism.

Particularly great possibilities exist for the strengthening of ties between the People's Republic of China and the USSR in the economic field and in the fields of scientific-technical co-operation and culture. In this letter, we would like to make a series of practical proposals, the realization of which could serve the cause of strengthening friendship between our countries.

The CC CPSU anticipates that the Central Committee of the Communist Party of China, on its part, will take concrete steps in this direction, particularly since the Premier of the State Council of the CPR, Comrade Chou En-lai, is reported in the press to have declared in recent talks with foreign personalities and journalists that China intends to develop contacts with the Soviet Union and other socialist states, that China is greatly interested in the development of trade and other economic contacts and that the CPR adheres to the Five Principles of peaceful coexistence. The Premier of the CPR said that China, on her part, will resist the efforts of the imperialists to use the existing differences for the aim of undermining the unity of the socialist community. Such a point of view coincides with the declarations which the CC CPSU and the Soviet government, on their part, have frequently made.

The interests of both sides permit one to conclude that it would already be possible today to talk of concrete steps for setting things right in Soviet-Chinese co-operation.

Specifically, it would be possible to start in the immediate future to draw up jointly agreed preliminary plans for the exchange of goods between the CPR and the Soviet Union. In the course of the next few years the USSR could increase its export to China of goods in which you are interested, and the import of goods from China into the USSR, which would be in the interest both of our economy and of yours.

As is known, the Protocol of May 13, 1962 concluded by the governments of our two countries provides for the renewal next year of negotiations concerning the delivery to the People's Republic of China of whole sets of equipment the manufacture of which was postponed for two years at the request of the Chinese side. If your side shows interest, it would be possible in our view to come to an understanding on the broadening of technical aid to the CPR in the building of industrial enterprises and specifically to discuss the possibility of aid in the development of the petroleum industry and the building of enterprises in the mining and other industries on terms beneficial to both our countries.

Once again we affirm our readiness to send Soviet specialists to the People's Republic of China should you consider it necessary.

The Soviet Union is now drawing up her Five-Year Plan for 1966–70. China too is drawing up her third Five-Year Plan. For this reason now

149

is a good time to discuss the possibilities of developing trade and other ties between our countries and to provide for corresponding measures in the plans for the national economies of both countries. Of course, it is never too late to start on the good work of strengthening co-operation between the USSR and the CPR, but it would be better to make a start now.

Both our countries would undoubtedly benefit from the broadening of scientific-technical co-operation and also from the development of cultural ties of many kinds. We consider that these questions could be the subject of mutual consultation and negotiation between the appropriate organs of the Soviet Union and the CPR. In making these proposals, we are naturally willing to consider attentively all your views as to the widening of the co-operation between the Soviet Union and the Chinese People's Republic in the economic, scientific-technical, cultural and other fields. We understand, of course, that such ties and co-operation can develop provided you consider this beneficial to China. We on our part are convinced that it would be mutually beneficial to both China and the Soviet Union.

It is well known that economic ties are the type of co-operation in which all nations are particularly interested. Economic ties have great significance even in the relations between countries with different social systems. They create favourable conditions for implementing the principle of peaceful coexistence and help the improvement of relations among states. Extensive economic ties are all the more necessary among socialist countries, which are bound together by a common social system and common aims. Such ties are an important factor in the construction of socialism and communism and in utilizing the advantages of international socialist division of labour, and they help in strengthening the friendship among fraternal peoples, achieving new successes in the economic competition with capitalism and uniting all anti-imperialist revolutionary forces. The development of such co-operation would be a gain for China and the Soviet Union, for the socialist camp and the cause of world socialism.

We understand, of course, that each nation builds socialism and communism by relying mainly on its own forces because no one except the people of a given country will build socialism there. But it is also evident that co-operation among socialist countries facilitates and accelerates the construction of socialism by each nation. The restoration and strengthening of the economic co-operation between our countries will help not only to accelerate the growth of the national economies of the USSR and China and the economy of the entire socialist system, but also to create favourable conditions for normalizing relations in other fields.

Highly favourable pre-conditions exist for the development of co-operation between the Soviet Union and China. Our countries possess a variety of natural riches and have accumulated considerable experience in economic and scientific-technical co-operation. How beneficial was the influence of Soviet-Chinese economic co-operation on the course of socialist construction in the People's Republic of China and also on the economic growth of the Soviet Union, is well known. It is all the more to be regretted that economic co-operation and trade between the Soviet Union and the Chinese People's Republic has not only failed to grow in recent years but on the contrary has constantly shrunk.

Experience shows that the development of trading, economic and other ties improves the atmosphere in mutual relations and helps to straighten out other problems on which the relations between our countries depend. And such problems unfortunately do exist and demand solution.

You will probably agree that the situation which has arisen in recent years along different sections of the Soviet-Chinese border cannot be regarded as normal. The Soviet government has already proposed that friendly consultations take place to define accurately the boundary in different sections, considering that this will result in removal of the causes of the present misunderstanding. Recently you, too, spoke in favour of solving this question on the basis of mutual consultation. In this connection, we are transmitting to you a relevant document.

Statements have recently been made in China concerning the aggressive policy of the Czarist government and the unjust treaties imposed upon China. Naturally, we will not defend the Russian Czars who permitted arbitrariness in laying down the state boundaries with neighbouring countries. We are convinced that you, too, do not intend to defend the Chinese emperors who by force of arms seized not a few territories belonging to others. But while condemning the reactionary actions of the top-strata exploiters who held power in Russia and in China at that time, we cannot disregard the fact that historically-formed boundaries between states now exist. Any attempt to ignore this can become the source of misunderstandings and conflicts; at the same time, they will not lead to the solution of the problem. It would be simply unreasonable to create territorial problems artificially at the present time, when the working class is in power and when our common aim is communism, under which state borders will gradually lose their former significance. We have all the possibilities for fully eliminating border frictions of any kind, and thus showing the peoples an example of truly friendly relations between two socialist states.

We should also create conditions favourable to the improvement of relations on the Party level and avoid anything that might aggravate the difficulties that have arisen in the communist movement. That the overcoming of the differences in the communist movement is a complex matter, demanding time and serious effort, is something we are fully aware of. But what is important is to go step by step in this direction, to show Leninist concern for the strengthening of the unity of the world communist movement on a principled Marxist basis, to bar any acts whatsoever that might undermine unity and to repulse factionalists and splitters.

We are of the opinion that even in the present complex situation there is a possibility of preventing the polemics that have spread from getting out of control, and of directing matters towards the strengthening of unity and solidarity between the CCP and the CPSU and among all the fraternal Parties. The CC CPSU has more than once advocated the cessation of public polemics. We again repeated this proposal on October 25 and November 7, 1963. The Soviet press has ceased to publish materials of a polemical character. In this letter we call once more on the Central Committee of the Chinese Communist Party to do everything necessary for the cessation of public polemics and of other activities that harm the unity of the international communist movement and the unity of the socialist countries. We do not propose a general cessation of the exchange of views on questions of principle concerning world developments, but desire only that it should take place in the forms provided for by the

Statement of the fraternal Parties in 1960 — through mutual consultation negotiations and exchanges of letters.

In making these proposals, the CC CPSU bases itself on the consideration that they will help strengthen confidence and create more favourable conditions for the preparation of a world meeting of the Communist and Workers' Parties. Recently, the CPSU and the CCP, like many other fraternal Parties, have more than once advocated the convening of such a meeting. We now reaffirm this position of ours. At the same time, we underline yet again that it is the duty of all Parties to help in the creation of a situation which will render such a meeting fruitful, so that it will lead not to a split in the world communist movement but to genuine unity and solidarity of all the fraternal Parties and all the forces of peace and socialism.

These are some of our views on concrete measures that could be taken with the aim of overcoming the difficulties that have arisen.

Please understand us correctly — our letter is dictated exclusively by concern for the strengthening of unity. We may differ in our understanding of this or that ideological problem, or in our estimates of specific phenomena of social development — life will correct those who are mistaken. But one must never even for a minute, under any circumstances, forget about the highest duty of Communists — to build the unity of the socialist community and of the entire front of the struggle against capital. The peoples trust the Communists. And we are called upon to justify their trust. Let us, by our common efforts, clear the way for the strengthening of co-operation, and take concrete measures to this end.

The CPSU and the Soviet people cherish friendly feelings for the Chinese people and the Communist Party of China and wish to strengthen the brotherhood built up in the struggle for socialism and communism. The CC CPSU is filled with determination to do all it can to achieve a turn of events for the better, and to strengthen the unity of the world communist movement and the friendship between the Chinese and Soviet peoples.

The CPSU guides itself unswervingly by the line of the world communist movement, and firmly defends the principles of the Declaration and the Statement of the Moscow meetings of 1957 and 1960. Our Leninist party is waging a historic struggle for the building of communism in the USSR, for peace, democracy, and the national independence of peoples, for the strengthening of the world socialist community and the entire anti-imperialist revolutionary front, for the proletarian revolution and the cause of international socialism, and this accords with the interests of all the peoples.

The CC CPSU calls on the CC CCP, on its part, to undertake practical steps for the strengthening of the unity of the fraternal Parties on the principles of Marxism-Leninism and proletarian internationalism in the struggle for the great cause of socialism.

First Secretary of the Central Committee of
the Communist Party of the Soviet Union
N. Khrushchev (*signed*)

DOCUMENT 2

The Fighting Task Confronting Workers
in Philosophy and the Social Sciences

(Speech at the Fourth Enlarged Session of the Committee of the Department of Philosophy and Social Science of the Chinese Academy of Sciences Held on October 26, 1963)

by Chou Yang

Excerpts

[*Peking Review*, Vol. VII, No. 1 (January 3, 1964), pp. 10–27, at pp. 12, 13–16, 20–22, and 27]

.　　.　　.　　.　　.　　.　　.　　.　　.

How can certain people who had previously been supporters of revolutionary scientific socialism degenerate into counter-revolutionary anti-scientific revisionists? Yet it is not at all strange. Everything tends to divide itself in two. Theories are no exception, and they also tend to divide. Wherever there is a revolutionary, scientific doctrine, its antithesis, a counter-revolutionary anti-scientific doctrine is bound to arise in the course of the development of that doctrine. As modern society is divided into classes and as the difference between progressive and backward groups will continue far into the future the emergence of antithesis is inevitable. This has long been borne out by the history of Marxist philosophy and the social sciences and also by the history of natural science. Science and the history of science themselves reflect the unity and struggle of opposites, and science develops through such unity and struggle.

.　　.　　.　　.　　.　　.　　.　　.　　.

Soon after Stalin's death, the leaders of the CPSU totally negated him. They followed in the wake of the Tito clique of Yugoslavia and sank deeper and deeper into the mire of revisionism. Modern revisionism is a repetition and a still more vicious outgrowth of old-line revisionism under new conditions and is the result of the attempt to cater to disintegrating imperialism. Because modern revisionism has arisen in a large socialist country which is moreover the birthplace of Lenin, it has far greater capacity to confuse people and is much more pernicious than the old revisionism. At the same time, the forces of revolutionary Marxism-Leninism are also stronger today than when they fought against old revisionism, and they are growing apace in the fight against modern revisionism. Revolutionary people and parties everywhere are increasingly placing their hopes on the genuine Marxist-Leninist parties, including the Communist Party of China, and the genuine Marxist-Leninist groups and individuals, whose thinking increasingly represents the banner of revolutionary Marxism-Leninism and the banner of world revolution.

In the current great debate between revolutionary Marxism-Leninism and modern revisionist, the modern revisionists have concentrated their unscrupulous and vicious attacks on the Chinese Communist Party and Comrade Mao Tse-tung. This is by no means accidental. It is because Comrade Mao Tse-tung has always firmly stood at the forefront in defence of Marxism-Leninism and against modern revisionism that they hate him so much.

For more than forty years Comrade Mao Tse-tung has led the Chinese Communist Party and the Chinese people in arduous and untiring struggles against imperialism and all kinds of counter-revolutionary forces at home. Applying Marxist-Leninist principles and methods, he has correctly solved the problems of the Chinese revolution, repeatedly defeated both Right and "Left" opportunism, and thus led the Chinese revolution to victory.

The Chinese people have come to understand Comrade Mao Tse-tung's greatness through their own experience, and the people of the world have also come to know him through the practical achievements of the Chinese revolution and his writings. All the calumnies poured on Comrade Mao Tse-tung by the modern revisionists are of no avail and cannot in the least hurt him.

In violation of the correct principles laid down in the Moscow Declaration and the Moscow Statement, the leaders of the CPSU arbitrarily denounced a fraternal Party, the Albanian Party of Labour, as "anti-Marxist-Leninist" at their own Party congress, thus bringing an inter-Party dispute into the open before the enemy for the first time. Since then they have committed a great many base acts against the Chinese Communists and against all Communists who do not approve of their wrong line. They consider this tactic clever, and have been arrogantly using it for quite a number of years. Actually it is not at all clever and will only ruin their prestige and make things more difficult for themselves. If they do not turn back and correct their errors, they are bound to fall on still harder times. If you doubt this, just wait and see!

There are three things the modern revisionists fear: first, imperialism; second, genuine Marxism-Leninism, or what they call dogmatism; and third, the revolutionary people. Cowardly as mice, they dare not let the people of their own countries read the replies of those whom they label "dogmatists" to their criticisms, and they try to quarantine these replies as though they were the plague. This single fact suffices to indicate the kind of future that is in store for the modern revisionists.

Lenin has said:

... I have seen too many sights in the history of the revolution to be disturbed by the hostile looks and shouts of people who abandon themselves to emotion and are unable to reason. ("Report on the Ratification of the Peace Treaty Delivered at the Fourth All-Russian Extraordinary Congress of Soviets," *Collected Works*, fourth Russian ed., Gospolitizdat, Moscow, 1950, Vol. 27, p. 158.)

He also said that his "fate" was "one battle after another against political stupidity, vulgarity, opportunism," etc. ("Letter to Inessa Armand, December 18, 1916," fourth Russian ed., Moscow, Vol. 35, p. 209.) Certainly, such was not the fate of Lenin alone. It was the fate of Marx and Engels, and of Stalin too. Indeed, it is the fate of all revolutionaries.

Looking back over the history of Marxism-Leninism, we can see that it gained ground and advanced step by step through "one battle after another." For more than a century, neither the enemy's attacks from without nor the enemy's "revisions" from within have been able to defeat it. On the contrary, it is precisely through repeated struggles against external and internal foes of all shades that the forces of Marxism-Leninism have grown strong.

In the beginning, Marxism was but one of many doctrines and schools in the socialist movement and this school consisted only of Marx and

Engels. But because it is right and because it truly and scientifically represents the revolutionary proletariat's interests and needs, Marxism has finally vanquished all antagonistic ideological systems in struggle and won the worldwide support of the revolutionary working class and the revolutionary people.

Lenin, too, was once in the minority in the struggle against revisionism. On the revisionist side at that time were the leaders of the Second International, the German Social-Democrat Party, which enjoyed great prestige, and such veteran leaders and authoritative theorists as Bernstein, Kautsky and Plekhanov. Lenin was beneath their notice. Nevertheless, as Lenin's thinking embodied the truth and reflected the needs of a new era, the era of imperialism and the proletarian revolution, it was not crushed by the then rampant revisionism; instead it eventually triumphed over revisionism and became the great banner of the whole international communist movement.

True revolutionaries, true proletarian revolutionary fighters and true Marxist-Leninists, who are militant materialists are dauntless. They fear neither isolation nor the abuse of the reactionaries and revisionists. For they know it is not these seemingly formidable giants but "nobodies" like themselves who represent the future. All great men were once nobodies. Provided they possess the truth, those who are seemingly isolated in the beginning are sure to be victorious in the end. So it was with Lenin and the Third International. On the contrary, the celebrities and big battalions are bound to decline and to dwindle and putrefy when they lose possession of the truth and therefore lose the support of the masses. So it was with Bernstein and the Second International. Under particular conditions, things are bound to change into their opposites.

There is inevitably a realignment in the forces of revolution in the course of the struggle between the proletariat and the revolutionary people on the one hand and the forces of reaction on the other and in the course of the struggle between Marxism on the one hand and opportunism and and revisionism on the other.

Marx and Engels once mentioned that the centre of gravity of the European working-class movement had temporarily shifted from France to Germany after the defeat of the Paris Commune. When history demanded that the German working class should stand at the forefront of the proletarian struggle, both Marx and Engels were proud of it. But Engels noted at the same time, "How long events will allow them to occupy this post of honour cannot be foretold." ("Preparatory Note to the *Peasant War In Germany*," *Selected Works of Marx and Engels*, F.L.P.H., Moscow, 1948, Vol. 1, p. 653.)

At the beginning of the twentieth century, Russia became the focal point of the various contradictions in the era of imperialism. When Kautsky was still a revolutionary, he said that the centre of revolution would shift from Germany to Russia. While Kautsky later became a renegade from the revolution, Lenin still quoted with approval this earlier revolutionary prediction of Kautsky's.

Then the storm of revolution reached the East. Marx, Engels and Lenin all spoke highly of the awakening of the peoples of the East and had the warmest sympathy for it. They consistently held that the revolutionary peoples of the East were the great ally of the proletariat of the Western capitalist countries and that their revolutionary movement would in turn influence and promote the proletarian revolution in these countries. At a time when the European working class was under the corrosive influence of revisionism, Lenin recognized the emerging power of the multi-million peoples of Asia who "have been drawn into the struggle for these same European ideals."

In their quest for truth from the West, progressive people in Asia finally discovered Marxism-Leninism and adopted the proletarian world outlook as the instrument for studying the destiny of their countries.

History has shown that whether the party or country is large or small, the proletarian party of a country can make its own specific contribution to the development of Marxism-Leninism, provided it is able to stand in the van of the people's revolutionary struggle, correctly lead it to victory and so enrich the experience of the proletarian revolutionary movement. If, on the other hand, a proletarian party fails to stand in the forefront of the people's revolutionary struggle, discards the banner of revolution, renounces the revolutionary tradition of its own country and adopts a passive or even negative attitude towards the cause of the proletarian revolution, then it is bound to become an opportunist, revisionist party and forfeit its place in the ranks of the vanguards of the international proletariat.

Certain persons who claim to have "creatively developed Marxism-Leninism" have actually thrown it overboard, and yet they are arrogantly trying to monopolize the right to interpret Marxism-Leninism. Like the French king who proclaimed "*L'Etat, c'est moi*" ("I am the State"), they talk as if "*Le Marxisme-Léninisme, c'est moi*" ("I am Marxism-Leninism"). Whoever refuses to endorse the resolutions of their Party congress and the programme of their Party is accused of departing from Marxism-Leninism and violating so-called international discipline. What does this abominable attitude reveal except their deep-seated great-power and great-Party chauvinism and their extremely backward feudal ideas on the line of succession and their out-and-out reactionary idealistic view of history?

The revolutionary storm is bound to rise and the sparks of Marxism-Leninism are bound to fly everywhere. No one can stop them.

What tremendous changes have taken place in the world revolutionary forces and revolutionary situation as compared with the times of Marx or Lenin! A number of new socialist countries have come into being since World War II. The people of the Asian, African and Latin American countries have awakened or are awakening; they are rising in heroic battles against imperialism and old and new colonialism. A widespread struggle is being waged by the people of all countries for world peace, national independence, people's democracy and socialism. For a long time in the past, the working-class movement and the struggle centring around it were mainly confined to the advanced capitalist countries in Europe and North America. Now, however, the people's struggle against imperialism headed by the United States and the struggle of the revolutionary Marxist-Leninists against modern revisionism are being waged on a much broader — indeed, on a worldwide — scale. In a number of countries the vanguard of the proletariat formerly standing at the forefront of the struggle is now corroded by modern revisionism, while the proletariat and revolutionary people of many countries in Asia, Africa and Latin America who have long been looked down upon now stand in the front line of battle.

In Europe, North America and Australasia, leaders of certain Communist Parties are increasingly singing the same tune as the social democrats in defence of the interests of imperialism and capitalism. As a result, there is hardly any substantial or even formal difference between them and the social democrats. Moreover, they are expelling true Marxists-Leninists from the Party and taking other measures to create splits. Under these circumstances, political parties genuinely representing the revolutionary proletariat are bound to appear on these continents. Such a process is also taking place among some of the Communists in Latin America and Asia. Some people who for a time fail to see things clearly and are misled by the revisionists will sooner or later learn from the facts, part ways with revisionism and return to the road of Marxism-Leninism.

In short, whatever the country or place may be, where there is oppression, there will be resistance; where there is revisionism, there will be Marxism-Leninism fighting against it; and where expulsion of Marxist-Leninists from the Party and other measures are taken to create splits, new outstanding Marxist-Leninists and strong revolutionary parties are bound to emerge. Changes are taking place which are contrary to what the modern revisionists and modern dogmatists expected. These persons are creating their own opposites and will be buried by them in the end. This is an inexorable law.

Reviewing the past and looking forward to the future, what else can we see but the magnificent spectacle of ceaseless growth for Marxism-Leninism and constant victories for the cause of proletarian revolution?

Lenin once said that the ideological struggle between revolutionary Marxism and revisionism at the end of the nineteenth century was the prelude to great revolutionary battles by the proletariat.

The present struggle between revolutionary Marxism-Leninism and modern revisionism is the prelude to new and still greater revolutionary battles by the world proletariat.

It can be anticipated that the next fifty to a hundred years will be the great epoch of the thorough transformation of society, an earth-shaking epoch without any parallel. In this great epoch, the revolutionary vanguard of the proletariat, leading the revolutionary people, who account for more than 90 per cent of the world's population, will overcome every difficulty on the road of revolution and march to the complete victory of the revolutionary cause of the people of the whole world.

.   .   .   .

The Yugoslav revisionists said that class struggle has already been abolished in their country, that no conditions whatsoever obtain for the " re-creation of the bourgeoisie as a class " [10] and that " the restoration of any system of exploitation of man by man has been precluded." [11] The leadership of the CPSU has also proclaimed that class struggle no longer exists in their country and that " the danger of capitalist restoration in the Soviet Union is ruled out." [12]

The Yugoslav revisionists said: if more people are enabled by democratic means to take part in the " socialist " regime, " there is no need whatsoever to keep on waving the red kerchief of the dictatorship of the proletariat." [13] The leaders of the CPSU followed suit by declaring that " the dictatorship

10 Programme of the League of Communists of Yugoslavia.
11 Constitution of the Socialist Federal Republic of Yugoslavia.
12 N. S. Khrushchev, " Control Figures for the Economic Development of the USSR for 1959–1965," report to the 21st Extraordinary Congress of the CPSU.
13 Edvard Kardelj's interview with the Italian Communist Party delegation, October 14, 1956.

of the proletariat . . . has ceased to be necessary in the USSR from the point of view of the tasks of internal development," [14] and that at the present stage the state of the dictatorship of the proletariat has become a " state of the whole people." They also allege that, in conformity with this situation, the party of the proletariat has become a " party of the entire people."

The leaders of the CPSU have energetically advertised their fallacies concerning the " state of the whole people " and the " party of the entire people," claiming them to be " new inventions by the Party."

" New inventions " forsooth!

The so-called state of the whole people is nothing but an old device used by reactionary classes to cover up their dictatorship and deceive the working people. The bourgeoisie used to call the state under its dictatorship a " state of the whole people." The classical Marxist writers exposed this fraud long ago and scientifically expounded the class nature of the state. The state is always an instrument of class dictatorship. There is no such thing as a " supra-class " state or a state " of the whole people." The task of the proletarian revolution is not to establish a " state of the whole people," but to replace the state of the dictatorship of the bourgeoisie by the state of the dictatorship of the proletariat. The state will disappear only with the ultimate elimination of classes through the dictatorship of the proletariat.

Lenin clearly pointed out, " The essence of Marx's teaching on the state has been mastered only by those who understand that the dictatorship of a *single* class [the proletariat] is necessary . . . for the entire *historical period* which separates capitalism from 'classless society,' from communism." (" The state and Revolution," *Selected Works*, F.L.P.H., Moscow, Vol. 2, Part 1, p. 234.) In socialist society, the dictatorship of the proletariat has not fulfilled its historical mission so long as there still exist remnants of the old exploiting classes and the possibility of the emergence of new bourgeois elements, and so long as there still exist the class difference between workers and peasants and the differentiation between manual and mental labour. The dictatorship of the proletariat will disappear only with the attainment of a communist society when classes and class differences will have been completely eliminated. The dictatorship of the proletariat will not disappear before this.

Similarly, political parties have always been instruments of class struggle. There is no political party that is " supra-class " or " of the entire people." The leadership of the proletarian party is the core of the dictatorship of the proletariat. The proletarian party cannot wither away before the dictatorship of the proletariat. The withering away of the dictatorship of the proletariat means the withering away of the state and of the Party.

It is a fact that all socialist countries without exception, including the Soviet Union, are still far, far removed from the fulfilment of the historical mission of the dictatorship of the proletariat and from classless, communist society. In all these countries without exception there are still classes and class struggle. And there is still the danger of capitalist restoration. Therefore, the struggle between the two roads of socialism and capitalism still exists in all socialist countries, and the question of who will win has not yet been completely and finally solved. Only by upholding the dictatorship of the proletariat and the leadership of the proletarian party and carrying

[14] Programme of the Communist Party of the Soviet Union, adopted at the 22nd Congress of the CPSU.

the socialist revolution through to the end, can the final victory of socialism and the transition to communist society be achieved. Conversely, if the dictatorship of the proletariat and the proletarian party are abolished, if the socialist revolution is left off unfinished half-way, it will lead to the loss of the fruits of the socialist revolution and the re-emergence of capitalism. The two different lines lead to different futures. This is an objective law independent of human will.

Both in theory and in practice, the fallacies of the state of the whole people and of the party of the entire people will inevitably result in the replacement of the state of the dictatorship of the proletariat by that of the dictatorship of another class, and the replacement of the party of the van-guard of the proletariat by a party of another character. There is no other possibility, Yugoslavia has already set an example. The Yugoslav modern revisionists are the political representatives of bourgeois forces. They usurped the leadership of the party and the state and brought about the degeneration of the dictatorship of the proletariat into that of the bourgeoisie and of the proletarian party into a bourgeois one. Undoubtedly, whoever takes the path of Yugoslavia will have no better future.

. . . .

In the field of the economic problems of socialism, Marxist-Leninists proceed from the collective interests of the working people and insist on the principle of " to each according to his work " on the basis of socialist ownership by the whole people and collective ownership. In other words, those who do not work shall not eat, those who work more shall receive more and those who work less shall receive less. In the interest of the high-income stratum, the modern revisionists have completely distorted the socialist principle of " to each according to his work " as set forth by Marxism-Leninism. They are actually using the slogan of individual " material incentive " and " material interest " surreptitiously to supersede the socialist principle of " to each according to his work " which Marxist-Leninists have always advocated. They describe their vaunted individual " material incentive " and " material interest " as " the motive force in the growth of socialist production," [16] as " the core and motive force of the socialist plan " [17] or, in Khrushchev's words, as " the foundation for the raising of production and the growth of labour productivity." [18]

The modern revisionists completely ignore the enthusiasm of the labouring masses for collective production in socialist society and are opposed to giving prime importance to political education which heightens the socialist consciousness of the masses. They are infatuated with the much vaunted idea of " individual material incentive," which can only lead people to the pursuit of purely personal interests, whet their desire for personal gain and profit, encourage the growth of bourgeois individualism and damage the socialist economy based on ownership by the whole people and on collective ownership or even cause it to disintegrate.

[16] *Political Economy* (in Russian), edited by the Institute of Economics of the Academy of Sciences of the USSR, Moscow, third revised edition, 1962, p. 499.
[17] " Planning, an Important Link in Running a Socialist Economy," *Pravda*, February 7, 1963.
[18] N. S. Khrushchev, Speech at a Meeting of Advanced Agricultural Workers of the States of the Central Black-Soil Zone of the Russian Federation in the City of Voronezh, February 11, 1961.

They also use the quest for profit to stimulate the management of enterprises and confuse socialist with capitalist profit in their attempt to replace the socialist economic principle of planning by the capitalist economic principle of profit, and so pave the way for the liberalization of the economy and the degeneration of socialist into capitalist economy. It is not surprising, therefore, that the modern revisionists are becoming more and more recipient to the fashions and vogues of bourgeois economic theory.

In the field of economic relations among socialist countries, under the guise of the international division of labour the leaders of the CPSU go to great lengths to slander the correct policy of building socialism by one's own efforts, which they term a "nationalist" policy. Their attack is wrong in theory and has an ulterior purpose in practice, namely to make some socialist countries dependent on them economically and hence subservient politically and obedient to their baton. Theirs is truly a policy of national egoism and great-power chauvinism. To this end, certain persons even demand that those socialist countries which are "backward in production" should confine themselves to developing agriculture and industries processing farm produce so as to provide agricultural products for other countries. This sounds like a variety of neo-colonialist theory under the signboard of "international socialist division of labour."

In short, the modern revisionists are savagely attacking the fundamental theories of Marxism-Leninism in every sphere of learning. Thus in every sphere they have set up concrete targets for our criticism. Revolutionary workers in philosophy and social science should come forward to smash the attacks of modern revisionism and in the course of this struggle further develop Marxist-Leninist theory in all spheres of learning.

DOCUMENT 3

The Leaders of the CPSU Are the Greatest Splitters of Our Times: Comment on the Open Letter of the Central Committee of the CPSU (7)

by the Editorial Departments of *Jen-min Jih-pao* and *Hung Ch'i*
(February 4, 1964)

Excerpts

[*Peking Review*, Vol. VII, No. 6 (February 7, 1964), pp. 5–21, at pp. 5, 9–11, 12, 13–16, 20–21 ; also in *The Polemic on the General Line of the International Communist Movement*, pp. 303–358]

Never before has the unity of the international communist movement been so gravely threatened as it is today when we are witnessing a deluge of modern revisionist ideology. Both internationally and inside individual Parties, fierce struggles are going on between Marxism-Leninism and revisionism. The international communist movement is confronted with an unprecedentedly serious danger of a split.

It is the urgent task of the Communists, the proletariat and the revolutionary people of the world to defend the unity of the socialist camp and of the international communist movement.

The Communist Party of China has made consistent and unremitting efforts to defend and strengthen the unity of the socialist camp and the international communist movement in accordance with Marxism-Leninism and the revolutionary principles of the 1957 Declaration and the 1960 Statement. It has been and remains the unswerving position of the Chinese Communist Party to uphold principle, uphold unity, eliminate differences and strengthen the struggle against our common enemy.

Ever since they embarked on the path of revisionism, the leaders of the CPSU have tirelessly professed their devotion to the unity of the international communist movement. Of late, they have been particularly active in crying for "unity." This calls to mind what Engels said ninety years ago. "One must not allow oneself to be misled by the cry for 'unity.' Those who have this word most often on their lips are the ones who sow the most dissension . . ." ". . . the biggest sectarians and the biggest brawlers and rogues at times shout loudest for unity." ("Engels to A. Bebel, June 20, 1873," *Selected Correspondence of Marx and Engels*, Foreign Languages Publishing House, Moscow, p. 345.)

While presenting themselves as champions of unity, the leaders of the CPSU are trying to pin the label of splittism on the Chinese Communist Party. In its open letter the Central Committee of the CPSU says:

> The Chinese leaders are undermining the unity not only of the socialist camp but of the entire world communist movement, trampling on the principles of proletarian internationalism and grossly violating accepted standards of relations between fraternal Parties.

And the subsequent articles published in the Soviet press have been condemning the Chinese Communists as "sectarians" and "splitters."

But what are the facts? Who is undermining the unity of the socialist camp? Who is undermining the unity of the international communist movement? Who is trampling on the principles of proletarian internationalism? And who is grossly violating the accepted standards of relations between fraternal Parties? In other words, who are the real, out-and-out splitters?

Only when these questions are properly answered can we find the way to defend and strengthen the unity of the socialist camp and the international communist movement and overcome the danger of a split.

.   .   .   .

The Greatest Splitters of Our Times

The events of recent years show that the leaders of the CPSU headed by Khrushchev have become the chief representatives of modern revisionism as well as the greatest splitters in the international communist movement.

Between the 20th and 22nd Congresses of the CPSU, the leaders of the CPSU developed a rounded system of revisionism. They put forward a revisionist line which contravenes the proletarian revolution and the dictatorship of the proletariat, a line which consists of "peaceful coexistence," "peaceful competition," "peaceful transition," "a state of the whole people" and "a party of the entire people." They have tried to impose this revisionist line on all fraternal Parties as a substitute for the common line of the international communist movement which was laid down at the meetings of fraternal Parties in 1957 and 1960. And they have attacked anyone who perseveres in the Marxist-Leninist line and resists their revisionist line.

The leaders of the CPSU have themselves undermined the basis of the unity of the international communist movement and created the present grave danger of a split by betraying Marxism-Leninism and proletarian internationalism and pushing their revisionist and divisive line.

Far from working to consolidate and expand the socialist camp, the leaders of the CPSU have endeavoured to split and disintegrate it. They have thus made a mess of the splendid socialist camp.

They have violated the principles guiding relations among fraternal countries as laid down in the Declaration and the Statement, pursued a policy of great-power chauvinism and national egoism towards fraternal socialist countries and thus disrupted the unity of the socialist camp.

They have arbitrarily infringed the sovereignty of fraternal countries, interfered in their internal affairs, carried on subversive activities and striven in every way to control fraternal countries.

In the name of the " international division of labour," the leaders of the CPSU oppose the adoption by fraternal countries of the policy of building socialism by their own efforts and developing their economies on an independent basis, and attempt to turn them into economic appendages. They have tried to force those fraternal countries which are comparatively backward economically to abandon industrialization and become their sources of raw materials and markets for surplus products.

The leaders of the CPSU are quite unscrupulous in their pursuit of the policy of great-power chauvinism. They have constantly brought political, economic and even military pressure to bear on fraternal countries.

The leaders of the CPSU have openly called for the overthrow of the Party and government leaders of Albania, brashly severed all economic and diplomatic relations with her and tyrannically deprived her of her legitimate rights as a member of the Warsaw Treaty Organization and the Council of Economic Mutual Assistance.

The leaders of the CPSU have violated the Sino-Soviet Treaty of Friendship, Alliance and Mutual Assistance, made a unilateral decision to withdraw 1,390 Soviet experts working in China, to tear up 343 contracts and supplementary contracts on the employment of experts and to cancel 257 projects of scientific and technical co-operation, and pursued a restrictive and discriminatory trade policy against China. They have provoked incidents on the Sino-Soviet border and carried on large-scale subversive activities in Sinkiang. On more than one occasion, Khrushchev went so far as to tell leading comrades of the Central Committee of the CCP that certain anti-Party elements in the Chinese Communist Party were his " good friends." He has praised Chinese anti-Party elements for attacking the Chinese Party's general line for socialist construction, the big leap forward and the people's communes, describing their action as a " manly act."

Such measures which gravely worsen state relations are rare even between capitalist countries. But again and again the leaders of the CPSU have adopted shocking and extreme measures of this kind against fraternal socialist countries. Yet they go on prating about being " faithful to proletarian internationalism." We would like to ask, is there a shred of internationalism in all these deeds of yours?

162

The great-power chauvinism and splittism of the leaders of the CPSU are equally glaring in their conduct vis-a-vis fraternal Parties.

Since the 20th Congress of the CPSU its leaders have tried, on the pretext of "combating the personality cult," to change the leadership of other fraternal Parties to conform to their will. Right up to the present they have insisted on "combating the personality cult" as a precondition for the restoration of unity and as a "principle" which is "obligatory on every Communist Party."[1]

Contrary to the principles guiding relations among fraternal Parties laid down in the Declaration and the Statement, the leaders of the CPSU ignore the independent and equal status of fraternal Parties, insist on establishing a kind of feudal patriarchial domination over the international communist movement and turn the relations between brother Parties into those between a patriarchal father and his sons. Khrushchev has more than once described a fraternal Party as a "silly boy" and called himself its "mother."[2] With his feudal psychology of self-exaltation, he has absolutely no sense of shame.

The leaders of the CPSU have completely ignored the principle of achieving unanimity through consultation among fraternal Parties and habitually make dictatorial decisions and order others about. They have recklessly torn up joint agreements with fraternal Parties, taken arbitrary decisions on important matters of common concern to fraternal Parties and forced *faits accomplis* on them.

The leaders of the CPSU have violated the principle that differences among fraternal Parties should be settled through inter-Party consultation : they first used their own Party congress and then the congresses of other fraternal Parties as rostrums for large-scale public attacks against those fraternal Parties which firmly uphold Marxism Leninism.

The leaders of the CPSU regard fraternal Parties as pawns on their diplomatic chessboard. Khrushchev plays fast and loose, he blows hot and cold, he talks one way one day and another the next, and yet he insists on the fraternal Parties dancing to his every tune without knowing whence or whither.

The leaders of the CPSU have stirred up trouble and created splits in many Communist Parties by encouraging the followers of their revisionist line in these Parties to attack the leadership, or usurp leading positions, persecute Marxist-Leninists and even expel them from the Party. It is this divisive policy of the leaders of the CPSU that has given rise to organizational splits in the fraternal Parties of many capitalist countries.

The leaders of the CPSU have turned the magazine *Problems of Peace and Socialism*, originally the common journal of fraternal Parties, into an instrument for spreading revisionism, sectarianism and splittism and for making unscrupulous attacks on Marxist-Leninist fraternal Parties in violation of the agreement reached at the meeting at which the magazine was founded.

---

[1] "For the Unity and Solidarity of the International Communist Movement," article by the editorial board, *Pravda*, Dec. 6, 1963.
[2] *Cf.* Khrushchev's interview with Gardner Cowles, Editor of the U.S. magazine *Look*, Apr. 20, 1962; report by Khrushchev to the Session of the Supreme Soviet of the USSR, Dec. 12, 1962.

163

In addition, they are imposing the revisionist line on the international democratic organizations, changing the correct line pursued by these organizations and trying to create splits in them.

The leaders of the CPSU have completely reversed enemies and comrades. They have directed the edge of struggle, which should be against U.S. imperialism and its lackeys, against the Marxist-Leninist fraternal Parties and countries.

The leaders of the CPSU are bent on seeking Soviet-U.S. co-operation for the domination of the world, they regard U.S. imperialism, the most ferocious enemy of the people of the world, as their most reliable friend, and they treat the fraternal Parties and countries adhering to Marxism-Leninism as their enemy. They collude with U.S. imperialism, the reactionaries of various countries, the renegade Tito clique and the Right-wing social democrats in a partnership against the socialist fraternal countries, the fraternal Parties, the Marxist-Leninists and the revolutionary people of all countries.

When they snatch at a straw from Eisenhower or Kennedy or others like them, or think that things are going smoothly for them, the leaders of the CPSU are beside themselves with joy, hit out wildly at the fraternal Parties and countries adhering to Marxism-Leninism, and endeavour to sacrifice fraternal Parties and countries on the altar of their political dealings with U.S. imperialism.

When their wrong policies come to grief and they find themselves in difficulties, the leaders of the CPSU become angrier and more red-faced than ever, again hit out wildly at the fraternal Parties and countries adhering to Marxism-Leninism, and try to make others their scapegoats.

These facts show that the leaders of the CPSU have taken the road of complete betrayal of proletarian internationalism, in contravention of the interests of the Soviet people, the socialist camp and the international communist movement and those of all revolutionary people.

These facts clearly demonstrate that the leaders of the CPSU counter-pose their revisionism to Marxsim-Leninism, their great-power chauvinism and national egoism to proletarian internationalism and their sectarianism and splittism to the international unity of the proletariat. Thus, like all the opportunists and revisionists of the past, the leaders of the CPSU have turned into creators of splits in many fraternal Parties, the socialist camp and the entire international communist movement.

The revisionism and splittism of the leaders of the CPSU constitute a greater danger than those of any other opportunists and splitters, whether past or present. As everyone knows, this revisionism is occurring in the CPSU, the Party which was created by Lenin and which has enjoyed the highest prestige among all Communist Parties; it is occurring in the great Soviet Union, the first socialist country. For many years, Marxist-Leninists and revolutionary people the world over have held the CPSU in high esteem and regarded the Soviet Union as the base of world revolution and the model of struggle. And the leaders of the CPSU have taken advantage of all this — of the prestige of the Party created by Lenin and of the first socialist country — to cover up the essence of their revisionism and splittism and deceive those who are still unaware of the truth. At the same time, these past masters in double-dealing are shouting "unity, unity," while actually engaged in splitting. To a certain extent, their tricks do temporarily confuse people. Traditional confidence in the

CPSU and ignorance of the facts have prevented quite a few people from recognizing the revisionism and splittism of the leaders of the CPSU sooner.

Because the leaders of the CPSU exercise state power in a large socialist country which exerts world-wide influence, their revisionist and divisive line has done far greater harm to the international communist movement and the proletarian cause of world revolution than that of any of the opportunists and splitters of the past.

It can be said that the leaders of the CPSU are the greatest of all revisionists as well as the greatest of all sectarians and splitters known to history.

.　　.　　.　　.　　.　　.　　.　　.

Refutation of the Charge of Being Anti-Soviet

The leaders of the CPSU accuse all who resist and criticize their revisionism and splittism of being anti-Soviet. This is a terrifying charge. To oppose the first socialist country in the world and the Party founded by the great Lenin — what insolence!

But we advise the leaders of the CPSU not to indulge in histrionics. The anti-Soviet charge can never apply to us.

We also advise the leaders of the CPSU not to become self-intoxicated. The anti-Soviet charge can never silence Marxist-Leninists.

Together with all other Communist and revolutionary people the world over, we Chinese Communists have always cherished sincere respect and love for the great Soviet people, the Soviet state and the Soviet Communist Party. For it was the people of the Soviet Union who, under the leadership of Lenin's Party, lit the triumphant torch of the October Revolution, opened up the new era of world proletarian revolution and marched in the van along the road to communism in the years that followed. It was the Communist Party of the Soviet Union and the Soviet state which, under the leadership of Lenin and Stalin, pursued a Marxist-Leninist domestic and foreign policy, scored unprecedented achievements in socialist construction, made the greatest contribution to victory in the war against fascism and gave internationalist support to the revolutionary struggles of the proletariat and working people of all other countries.

.　　.　　.　　.　　.　　.　　.　　.

The leaders of the CPSU have . . . disappointed the hopes of the fraternal Parties and pursued a revisionist and divisive line. This violates the interests not only of the international proletariat and working people but also of the CPSU, the Soviet state and the Soviet people themselves.

It is none other than the leaders of the CPSU headed by Khrushchev who are anti-Soviet.

The leaders of the CPSU have completely negated Stalin and painted the first dictatorship of the proletariat and socialist system as dark and dreadful. What is this if not anti-Soviet?

The leaders of the CPSU have proclaimed the abolition of the dictatorship of the proletariat, altered the proletarian character of the CPSU and opened the floodgates for capitalist forces in the Soviet Union. What is this if not anti-Soviet?

The leaders of the CPSU seek U.S.-Soviet co-operation and tirelessly fawn upon U.S. imperialism, and have thus disgraced the great Soviet Union. What is this if not anti-Soviet?

165

The leaders of the CPSU pursue the policy of great-power chauvinism and treat fraternal socialist countries as dependencies, and have thus damaged the prestige of the Soviet state. What is this if not anti-Soviet?

The leaders of the CPSU obstruct and oppose the revolutionary struggles of other peoples and act as apologists for imperialism and neo-colonialism, and have thus tarnished the glorious internationalist tradition of Lenin's Party. What is this if not anti-Soviet?

In short, the actions of the leaders of the CPSU have brought deep shame upon the great Soviet Union and the CPSU and seriously damaged the fundamental interests of the Soviet people. They are anti-Soviet action through and through.

Naturally, in these circumstances, the Chinese Communist Party and other Marxist-Leninist parties and Marxist-Leninists are bound to subject the revisionist and divisive line of the leaders of the CPSU to serious criticism for the purpose of defending the purity of Marxism-Leninism and the unity of the international communist movement and upholding the principle of proletarian internationalism. We oppose only the revisionist and divisive errors of the leaders of the CPSU. And we do so for the sake of defending the CPSU founded by Lenin and safeguarding the fundamental interests of the Soviet Union, the first socialist country, and of the Soviet people. How can this be described as anti-Soviet?

．　　．　　．　　．　　．　　．　　．　　．　　．

Refutation of the Charge of Seizing the Leadership

The leaders of the CPSU ascribe our criticisms and our opposition to their revisionist and divisive line to a desire to " seize the leadership."

First, we would like to ask the leaders of the CPSU: You say we want to seize the leadership. From whom? Who now holds the leadership? In the international communist movement, is there such a thing as a leadership which lords it over all fraternal Parties; And is this leadership in your hands?

Apparently, the leaders of the CPSU consider themselves the natural leaders who can lord it over all fraternal Parties. According to their logic, their programme, resolutions and statements are all infallible laws. Every remark and every word of Khrushchev's are imperial edicts, however wrong or absurd they may be. All fraternal Parties must submissively hear and obey and are absolutely forbidden to criticize or oppose them. This is outright tyranny. It is the ideology of feudal autocrats, pure and simple.

However, we must tell the leaders of the CPSU that the international communist movement is not some feudal clique. Whether large or small, whether new or old, and whether in or out of power, all fraternal Parties are independent and equal. No meeting of fraternal Parties and no agreement unanimously adopted by them has ever stipulated that there are superior and subordinate Parties, one Party which leads and other Parties which are led, a Party which is a father and Parties which are sons, or that the leaders of the CPSU are the supreme rulers over other fraternal Parties.

．　　．　　．　　．　　．　　．　　．　　．　　．

Even the vanguard position referred to by Engels and Lenin does not remain unchanged for a long time but shifts according to changing conditions. This shift is decided not by the subjective wishes of any individual or Party, but by the conditions shaped by history. If conditions change, other Parties may come to the van of the movement. When a Party which formerly held the position of vanguard takes the path of revisionism, it is bound to forfeit this position despite the fact that it has been the largest Party and has exerted the greatest influence. The German Social-Democratic Party was a case in point.

At one period in the history of the international communist movement, the Communist International gave centralized leadership to the Communist Parties of the world. It played a great historic role in promoting the establishment and growth of Communist Parties in many countries. But when the Communist Parties matured and the situation of the international communist movement grew more complicated, centralized leadership on the part of the Communist International ceased to be either feasible or necessary. In 1943 the Presidium of the Executive Committee of the Communist International stated in a resolution proposing to dissolve the Comintern:

> . . . to the extent that the internal as well as the international situation of individual countries became more complicated, the solution of the problems of the labour movement of each country through the medium of some international centre would meet with insuperable obstacles.

Events have shown that this resolution corresponded to reality and was correct.

In the present international communist movement, the question of who has the right to lead whom simply does not arise. Fraternal Parties should be independent and completely equal, and at the same time they should be united. On questions of common concern they should reach unanimity of views through consultation, and they should concert their actions in the struggle for the common goal. These principles guiding relations among fraternal Parties are clearly stipulated in the Declaration of 1957 and the Statement of 1960.

It is a flagrant violation of these principles, as laid down in the Declaration and the Statement, for the leaders of the CPSU to consider themselves the leaders of the international communist movement and to treat all fraternal Parties as their subordinates.

Because of their different historical backgrounds, the fraternal Parties naturally find themselves in different situations. Those Parties which have won victory in their revolutions differ from those which have not yet done so, and those which won victory earlier differ from those which did so later. But these differences only mean that the victorious Parties, and in particular the Parties which won victory earlier, have to bear a greater internationalist responsibility in supporting other fraternal Parties, and they have absolutely no right to dominate other fraternal Parties.

The Communist Party of the Soviet Union was built by Lenin and Stalin. It was the first Party to win the victory of the proletarian revolution, realize the dictatorship of the proletariat and engage in socialist construction. It was only logical that the CPSU should carry forward the revolutionary tradition of Lenin and Stalin, shoulder greater responsibility in supporting other fraternal Parties and countries and stand in the van of the international communist movement.

Taking these historical circumstances into account, the Chinese Communist Party expressed the sincere hope that the Communist Party of the Soviet Union would shoulder this glorious historic mission. At the 1957 Moscow Meeting of the fraternal Parties, our delegation emphasized that the socialist camp should have the Soviet Union at its head. The reason was that, although they had committed some mistakes, the leaders of the CPSU did finally accept the Moscow Declaration which was unanimously adopted by the fraternal Parties. Our proposal that the socialist camp should have the Soviet Union at its head was written into the Declaration.

We hold that the existence of the position of head does not contradict the principle of equality among fraternal Parties. It does not mean that the CPSU has any right to control other Parties; what it means is that the CPSU carries greater responsibility and duties on its shoulders.

However, the leaders of the CPSU have not been satisfied with this position of "head." Khrushchev complained of it on many occasions. He said, "What does 'at the head' give us materially? It gives us neither milk nor butter, neither potatoes nor vegetables nor flats. Perhaps it gives us something morally? Nothing at all!" [11] Later he said, "What is the use of 'at the head' for us? To hell with it!" [12]

The leaders of the CPSU say they have no desire for the position of "head," but in practice they demand the privilege of lording it over all fraternal Parties. They do not require themselves to stand in the van of the international communist movement in pursuing the Marxist-Leninist line and fulfilling their proletarian internationalist duty, but they do require all fraternal Parties to obey their baton and follow them along the path of revisionism and splittism.

By embarking on the path of revisionism and splittism, the leaders of the CPSU automatically forfeited the position of "head" in the international communist movement. If the word "head" is now to be applied to them, it can only mean that they are at the head of the revisionists and splitters.

The question confronting all Communists and the entire international communist movement today is not who is the leader over whom, but whether one should uphold Marxism-Leninism and proletarian internationalism or submit to the revisionism and splittism of the leaders of the CPSU. In spreading the slander that we want to seize the leadership, the leaders of the CPSU are in fact insisting that all fraternal Parties, including our own, must bow to their revisionist and divisive leadership.

Refutation of the Charge of Frustrating the Will of the Majority and Violating International Discipline

In their attacks on the Chinese Communist Party since 1960, the leaders of the CPSU have most frequently resorted to the charge that we "frustrate the will of the majority" and "violate international discipline." Let us review our debate with them on this question.

At the Bucharest meeting in June 1960 the leaders of the CPSU made a surprise assault on the Chinese Communist Party by distributing their

[11] Khrushchev's speech at the banquet given in honour of the delegations of the fraternal Parties of the socialist countries on Feb. 4, 1960.
[12] Khrushchev's speech at the meeting of the delegates of twelve fraternal Parties at Bucharest, June 24, 1960.

Letter of Information attacking it and tried to coerce it into submission by lining up a majority. Their attempt did not succeed. But after the meeting they advanced the argument that the minority must submit to the majority in relations among fraternal Parties, and demanded that the CCP should respect the " views and will unanimously expressed " at the Bucharest meeting on the pretext that the delegates of scores of Parties had opposed the views of the CCP.

This erroneous argument was refuted by the Central Committee of the CCP in its Letter of Reply, dated September 10, 1960, to the Letter of Information of the Central Committee of the CPSU. It pointed out:

> . . . where the fundamental principles of Marxism-Leninism are concerned, the problem of exactly who is right and who is wrong cannot in every case be judged by who has the majority. After all, truth is truth. Error cannot be turned into truth because of a temporary majority, nor will truth be turned into error because of a temporary minority.

Yet in its letter of November 5, 1960, the Central Committee of the CPSU repeated the fallacy about the minority's submitting to the majority in the international communist movement. Quoting a passage from Lenin's article " The Duma ' Seven,' " it accused the CCP, saying that " he who does not wish to respect the opinion of the majority of the fraternal Parties is in essence coming out against the unity and solidarity of the international communist movement."

At the Moscow Meeting of the fraternal Parties in 1960, the delegation of the CCP once more refuted this fallacy of the leaders of the CPSU. It declared that it is totally wrong to apply the principle of the minority's submitting to the majority to the relations among fraternal Parties in actual present day conditions in which centralized leadership such as that of the Comintern neither exists nor is desirable. Within a Party the principle that the minority should submit to the majority and the lower Party organization to the higher one should be observed. But it cannot be applied to relations among fraternal Parties. In their mutual relations, each fraternal Party maintains its independence and at the same time unites with all the others. Here, the relationship in which the minority should submit to the majority does not exist, and still less so the relationship in which a lower Party organization should submit to a higher one. The only way to deal with problems of common concern to fraternal Parties is to hold discussions and reach unanimous agreement in accordance with the principle of consultation.

The delegation of the CCP pointed out that by advancing the principle that the minority should submit to the majority in its letter, the Central Committee of the CPSU had obviously repudiated the principle of reaching unanimity through consultation. Our delegation asked, " On what supra-Party constitution does the Central Committee of the CPSU base itself in advancing such an organizational principle? When and where did the Communist and Workers' Parties of all countries ever adopt such a supra-Party constitution? "

The delegation of the CCP then proceeded to expose the ruse of the Central Committee of the CPSU in deliberately omitting the word " Russian " from its citation of a passage dealing with the situation within the Russian Social-Democratic Labour Party from Lenin's article " The

169

Duma 'Seven,'" in order to extend the principle of the minority's submitting to the majority, which is valid within a Party, to the relations among fraternal Parties.

The delegation of the CCP further stated:

. . . even within a Party, where the principle of the minority's submitting to the majority must be observed organizationally, it cannot be said that on questions of ideological understanding truth can always be told from error on the basis of which is the majority and which the minority opinion. It was in this very article, " The Duma 'Seven,' " that Lenin severely denounced the despicable action of the seven liquidationists in the Party fraction in the Duma who took advantage of a majority of one to suppress the Marxists who were in the minority. Lenin pointed out that although the seven liquidationists constituted the majority, they could not possibly represent the united will, united resolutions, united tactics of the majority of the advanced and conscious Russian workers who were organized in a Marxist way, and that therefore all shouts about unity were sheer hypocrisy. " The non-Party seven want to eat up the six Marxists and demand that this be called 'unity.' " (*Collected Works*, 4th Russian ed., Vol. 19, p. 407.) He continued that it was precisely these six Marxists in the Party fraction in the Duma who were acting in accordance with the will of the majority of the proletariat, and that unity could be preserved only if those seven delegates " renounce their policy of suppression." (*Ibid.*, p. 425.)

The delegation of the CCP continued that Lenin's words show:

. . . that even within a Party group the majority is not always correct, that on the contrary sometimes the majority have to " renounce the policy of suppression " if unity is to be preserved, and this is particularly the case where relations among fraternal Parties are concerned. The comrades of the Central Committee of the CPSU rashly quoted a passage from Lenin without having fully grasped its meaning. Moreover, they purposely deleted an important word. Even so, they failed in their aim.

We have quoted at length from a speech of the delegation of the CCP at the 1960 Moscow Meeting in order to show that the absurd charge of the leaders of the CPSU that we " frustrate the will of the majority " was completely refuted by us some time ago. It is precisely because the Chinese Communist Party and other fraternal Marxist-Leninist parties persistently opposed this fallacy that the principle of achieving unanimity through consultation among the fraternal Parties was written into the Statement of 1960.

Yet even now the leaders of the CPSU keep on clamouring that " the minority should submit to the majority." This can only mean that they wish to deny the independent and equal status of all fraternal Parties and to abolish the principle of achieving unanimity through consultation. They are trying to force some fraternal Parties to submit to their will on the pretext of a " majority," and to use the sham preponderance thus obtained to attack fraternal Marxist-Leninist parties. Their very actions are sectarian and divisive and violate the Declaration and the Statement.

Today, if one speaks of an international discipline binding on all Communist Parties, it can only mean observance of the principles guiding relations among fraternal Parties as laid down in the Declaration and the Statement. We have cited a great many facts to prove that these principles have been violated by the leaders of the CPSU themselves.

If the CPSU leaders insist on marking off the "majority" from the "minority," then we would like to tell them quite frankly that we do not recognize their majority. The majority you bank on is a false one. The genuine majority is not on your side. Is it true that the members of fraternal Parties which uphold Marxism-Leninism are a minority in the international communist movement? You and your followers are profoundly alienated from the masses, so how can the great mass of Party members and people who disapprove of your wrong line be counted as part of your majority?

The fundamental question is: Who stands with the broad masses of the people? Who represents their basic interests? And who reflects their revolutionary will?

.   .   .   .

Today, more than 90 per cent of the world's population desire revolution, including those who are not yet but will eventually become politically conscious. The real majority are the revolutionary Marxist-Leninist parties and Marxist-Leninists who represent the fundamental interests of the people, and not the handful of revisionists who have betrayed these interests.

The Way to Defend and Strengthen Unity

The revisionism and great-power chauvinism of the leaders of the CPSU are an unprecedented menace to the unity of the socialist camp and the international communist movement. By taking a revisionist and great-power chauvinist position, the leaders of the CPSU are standing for a split. So long as they maintain such a position, they are in fact working for sham unity and a real split no matter how volubly they may talk of "unity" and abuse others as "splitters" and "sectarians."

The Chinese Communist Party, other Marxist-Leninist parties and all Marxist-Leninists persevere in Marxism-Leninism and proletarian internationalism. This position is the only correct one for defending and strengthening the genuine unity of the socialist camp and the international communist movement.

Marxism-Leninism and proletarian internationalism constitute the basis of that unity. Only on this basis can the unity of fraternal Parties and countries be built. Such unity will be out of the question if one departs from this basis. To fight for Marxism-Leninism and proletarian internationalism is to work for the unity of the international communist movement. Persevering in principle and upholding unity are inextricably bound together.

If the leaders of the CPSU genuinely want unity and are not just pretending, they should loyally abide by the fundamental theories of Marxism-Leninism and by the Marxist-Leninist teachings concerning classes and class struggle, the state and revolution, and especially proletarian revolution and the dictatorship of the proletariat. It is absolutely impermissible for them to substitute class collaboration or class capitulation for class struggle, and social reformism or social pacifism for proletarian revolution, or abolish the dictatorship of the proletariat no matter under what pretext.

171

If the leaders of the CPSU genuinely want unity and are not just pretending, they should strictly abide by the revolutionary principles of the 1957 Declaration and the 1960 Statement. It is absolutely impermissible for them to substitute their own Party programme for the common programme which was unanimously agreed upon by the fraternal Parties.

If the leaders of the CPSU genuinely want unity and are not just pretending, they should draw a sharp line of demarcation between enemies and comrades and should unite with all socialist countries, all fraternal Marxist-Leninist parties, the proletariat of the whole world, all oppressed people and nations and all peace-loving countries and people in order to oppose U.S. imperialism, the arch-enemy of the people of the world, and its lackeys. It is absolutely impermissible for them to treat enemies as friends and friends as enemies, and to ally themselves with the U.S. imperialists, the reactionaries of various countries and the renegade Tito clique against fraternal countries and Parties and all revolutionary people in the vain pursuit of world domination through U.S.-Soviet collaboration.

If the leaders of the CPSU genuinely want unity and are not just pretending, they should be faithful to proletarian internationalism and strictly abide by the principles guiding relations among fraternal countries and Parties, as laid down in the Declaration and the Statement. It is absolutely impermissible for them to replace these principles with policies of great-power chauvinism and national egoism. In other words, they should

observe the principle of solidarity and never line up a number of fraternal Parties to attack other fraternal Parties and engage in sectarian and divisive activities ;

adhere to the principle of mutual support and mutual assistance and never try to control others in the name of assistance or, on the pretext of the " international division of labour," impair the sovereignty and interests of fraternal countries and oppose their building socialism through self-reliance ;

observe the principle of independence and equality and never place themselves above other fraternal Parties or impose their own Party's programme, line and resolutions on others ; never interfere in the internal affairs of fraternal Parties and carry out subversive activities under the pretext of " combating the personality cult " ; and never treat fraternal Parties as their property and fraternal countries as their dependencies ;

follow the principle of reaching unanimity through consultation and never force through their own Party's wrong line in the name of the so-called majority or use the congresses of their own Party or of other Parties and such forms as resolutions, statements and leaders' speeches for public and explicit attacks on other fraternal Parties, and certainly never extend ideological differences to state relations.

In short, if the leaders of the CPSU genuinely desire the unity of the socialist camp and the international communist movement, they must make a clean break with their line of revisionism, great-power chauvinism and splittism. The unity of the socialist camp and the international communist movement can be safeguarded and strengthened only by remaining loyal to Marxism-Leninism and proletarian internationalism and by opposing modern revisionism and modern dogmatism, great-power chauvinism and other forms of bourgeois nationalism, and sectarianism and splittism, and by doing so not merely in words but in deeds. This is the sole way to defend and strengthen unity.

Taken as a whole, the present world situation is most favourable. The international communist movement has already gained brilliant victories, bringing about a fundamental change in the international balance of class forces. At present the international communist movement is being assailed by an adverse current of revisionism and splittism; this phenomenon is not inconsistent with the law of historical development. Even though it creates temporary difficulties for the international communist movement and some fraternal Parties, it is a good thing that the revisionists have revealed their true features and that a struggle between Marxism-Leninism and revisionism has ensued.

Without any doubt, Marxism-Leninism will continue to demonstrate its youthful vitality and will sweep the whole world; the international communist movement will grow stronger and more united on the basis of Marxism-Leninism; and the cause of the international proletariat and the world people's revolution will win still more brilliant victories. Modern revisionism will undoubtedly go bankrupt.

We would like to advise the leaders of the CPSU to think matters over calmly: what will your clinging to revisionism and splittism lead to? Once again, we would like to make a sincere appeal to leaders of the CPSU: We hope you will be able to return to Marxism-Leninism and proletarian internationalism, to the revolutionary principles of the 1957 Declaration and the 1960 Statement and to the principles guiding relations among fraternal Parties and countries as laid down in these documents, so that the differences will be eliminated and the unity of the international communist movement and the socialist camp and unity between China and the Soviet Union will be strengthened on these principled bases.

Despite our serious differences with the leaders of the CPSU, we have full confidence in the vast membership of the CPSU and in the Soviet people, who grew up under the guidance of Lenin and Stalin. As always, the Communists and the people of China will unswervingly safeguard the unity between China and the Soviet Union, and consolidate and develop the deep-rooted friendship between our two peoples.

Communists of the world, unite on the basis of Marxism-Leninism!

DOCUMENT 4

Letter of the Central Committee of the CCP of February 20, 1964 to the Central Committee of the CPSU

Complete Text

[*Peking Review*, Vol. VII, No. 19 (May, 8, 1964), pp. 10–11]

February 20, 1964

The Central Committee of the Communist Party of the Soviet Union

Dear Comrades,

We have learnt from a number of quarters that the Central Committee of the CPSU recently sent to fraternal Parties a letter which is directed against the Communist Party of China. This letter distorts the facts of the current public polemics in the international communist movement, manufactures lies slandering the Chinese Communist Party and instigates a so-called "struggle against the great-power and Trotskyite views and the factional and disruptive activities of the Chinese leaders." This letter has not, however, been sent to the Chinese Communist Party, from which it has been kept a secret.

It must be noted in all seriousness that, while crying for a halt to public polemics under the pretence of desiring unity, the leaders of the CPSU are engineering a new campaign against the Chinese Communist Party and other Marxist-Leninist parties behind the back of the Chinese Communist Party and are unscrupulously engaging in sectarian, factional and divisive activities. Throughout the recent years the leaders of the CPSU have been wearing one face in public and another in private, and saying one thing and doing another. Your vicious two-faced tactics are a gross violation of the principles guiding relations among fraternal Parties laid down in the 1960 Statement as well as of proletarian internationalism.

You have launched the present campaign against the Chinese Communist Party on the new pretext that the CCP has not yet replied to your letter of November 29, 1962. But we would like to ask: Why were you free for a long time to act wilfully and refuse to accept the advice of fraternal Parties against bringing inter-Party differences into the open before the enemy and their proposal for a halt to public polemics, whereas the CCP must regard the letter from the leaders of the CPSU as God's will and give an immediate and affirmative reply or else be charged with the major crime of insubordination? Why are you privileged to publish thousands of lengthy articles and other items attacking us, whereas we may not make any reply to set the facts straight and distinguish truth from falsehood? A journey has to be made step by step, and problems have to be solved one by one. Your letter will be answered in due course. Your self-important and domineering attitude in maintaining that you can attack whenever you please and that we must stop as soon as you cry halt has fully exposed your inveterate habit of great-power chauvinism and posing as the "father Party."

The present grave act of the leaders of the CPSU to create a split has once again brought to light the intrigue you have been carrying on in behalf of a sham unity and a real split.

The Communist Party of China has been consistent in its stand of firmly defending the purity of Marxism-Leninism, upholding the revolutionary principles of the 1957 Declaration and the 1960 Statement, and on these foundations safeguarding the unity of the international communist movement, the unity of the Socialist camp and the unity of the Chinese and Soviet Parties and our two peoples. This stand of ours will never change. We obey the truth and the truth only and will never trade in principles.

The Central Committee of the Chinese Communist Party delegated Comrade P'eng Ch'en, Member of the Political Bureau and the Secretariat, to convey our views orally to Comrade Chervonenko, the Soviet Ambassador to China, on the afternoon of February 18.

We would like in all seriousness to repeat our request that the Central Committee of the CPSU send us a copy of the letter directed against the CCP, which it has recently addressed to fraternal Parties. We shall make our reply after studying this letter.

With fraternal greetings.

The Central Committee of the
Communist Party of China

DOCUMENT 5

Letter of the Central Committee of the CPSU of February 22, 1964 to the Central Committee of the CCP

Complete Text

[*Peking Review*, Vol. VII, No. 19 (May 8, 1964), pp. 22–24]

February 22, 1964

The Central Committee of the Communist Party of China

Dear Comrades,

The Central Committee of the CPSU has received your letter of February 20, 1964.

The rude tone and the unworthy and insulting methods in relation to the Communist Party of the Soviet Union to which you resort in this letter give us the moral right not to answer it at all. And if we have nevertheless considered it expedient to reply to you, we are doing so only in order to eliminate the possibility of any speculation or attempt to mislead the uninformed.

You express a simulated indignation at the fact that the letter of the CC CPSU dated February 12 this year, addressed to many fraternal Parties, was not sent to the Central Committee of the Communist Party of China, and represent this almost as an attempt to conceal the content of this letter from you and as " sectarian " and " factional activity by the CPSU."

How do matters stand in reality? It was no accident that we did not send you the letter of February 12 this year. In the past few months alone, the CC CPSU has repeatedly approached the leadership of the CCP both verbally and in writing with proposals that measures be taken jointly for strengthening the unity of the socialist community and the international communist movement. The Central Committee of the Communist Party of China has not considered it necessary even to reply to our proposals. You ignored the proposals for normalizing the situation in the communist movement which the CPSU delegation advanced during the Moscow talks in July 1963. You did not reply to the letter of the CC CPSU dated November 29, 1963, which contained a concrete programme of action for eliminating the existing differences. In exactly the same way no answer was given to the repeated verbal approaches of leaders of the CPSU to the leadership of the CCP made through Comrades Teng Hsiao-p'ing, P'eng Chen, Liu Hsiao and Pan Tze-li.

If you care to refer to the above-mentioned documents and material, it will be easy for you to convince yourselves that they discuss the very same problems about which the CC CPSU wrote briefly to the fraternal Parties in its letter of February 12 this year.

While not answering our letters, you at the same time unfolded a widespread campaign against the CPSU and other Marxist-Leninist parties and sharply intensified the schismatic factional activity in the international communist movement and the democratic organizations. In an article on February 4 this year, the newspaper *Jen-min Jih-pao* openly called for a split in the communist movement and demonstrated the unwillingness of the CCP leadership to reply to the positive proposals contained in the letter of the CC CPSU dated November 29, 1963.

In these circumstances the CC CPSU, in the interests of the unity of the communist movement and desirous of stating its Marxist-Leninist viewpoints which are being libellously assailed by the Chinese press, considered it necessary to discuss the question at the February Plenum of the Central Committee and thereafter to state its views openly. The CC CPSU decided to inform the fraternal Parties of this.

We had to tell them frankly that our proposals had not evoked any positive response from the leaders of the CCP and that the latter, broadening the schismatic activity, were continuing to intensify the attacks on the common course of the world communist movement. We declared that we shared the opinion of all the fraternal Parties standing genuinely on the positions of the Declaration and the Statement that it was necessary to give a rebuff to the schismatics and take collective measures for strengthening the unity of the communist movement on the principled basis of Marxism-Leninism. We asserted once more the desirability of calling a meeting of the Communist and Workers' Parties, concerning which you yourselves made repeated declarations at one time.

Our letter condemned the intention of the leadership of the CCP to create a factional bloc with a special programme under its own hegemony.

This is what was discussed in the February 12 letter of the CC CPSU.

Our principled position on all the questions contained in the February 12 letter was known to you long before we approached the fraternal Parties. Before approaching them in this letter, we tried more than once to discuss questions concerning the strengthening of the unity of the communist movement with the Central Committee of the Communist Party of China, and it is no fault of ours that all these efforts produced no results. Insofar as you persistently failed to reply to our repeated letters and approaches and, what is more, presented them as expressions of our weakness, it was unnecessary and indeed useless to send you our letter of February 12.

After all this, one can only be surprised at your allegations that the CPSU " is engineering a new campaign against the CCP " " behind the back of the CCP," adopting " two-faced tactics " and " engaging in divisive activities." It is not difficult to see that the intention of the leadership of the CCP in exaggerating the matter of the February 12 letter and distorting the real meaning of this step by the CC CPSU by every means represents yet another clumsy attempt to lay its own fault at somebody else's door and to shift to the CPSU the responsibility for the difficulties that have arisen in the communist movement exclusively through the fault of the CCP leadership.

As the saying goes among our people, this is using a well-known method, in which the real culprit cries, " Stop thief."

If one is to look for real double-dealers and schismatics acting " behind the backs of the fraternal Parties," one must speak of those who have carried on factional activity for many years, and must go to those who openly argue for the necessity of a split in the communist movement and even declare it to be " an inexorable law." How, for instance, is one to regard the following fact: as early as June 1960 Comrade Liu Shao-chi and other CCP leaders, in their talks with an Albanian delegation, slandered the CPSU, deliberately distorted the external and internal policies of our Party and tried to set the Albanian public leaders against the CPSU. These actions by the Chinese leadership evoked the just indignation of members of the Albanian delegation who openly said so to the Chinese comrades and informed the CC CPSU.

This is nothing but the most real behind-the-scenes factional activity against a fraternal Party.

One could cite innumerable facts, and if necessary publish documents, that expose the behind-the-scenes activity of the CCP leadership against the CPSU and other fraternal Parties, carried on over a number of years. Representatives of fraternal Parties already spoke about this to you directly at the Bucharest and Moscow meetings.

As for the CPSU, we do not conceal our views and activities from any fraternal Party, including the CCP to whose representatives we have repeatedly explained our views and standpoints on all the most important questions.

The CC CPSU has utilized its right, which every Communist Party has, the right to enter into consultation on whatever problems are of concern to it. Notwithstanding the fact that in your article of February 4 you permitted delirious invective against our Party and its leadership, the CC CPSU has not allowed itself to be provoked and has not taken the path of squabbling on the principle of "spearpoint against spearpoint." While considering it necessary to give a rebuff to your schismatic activity, we have decided, utilizing Party channels, to consult anew with the Central Committees of fraternal Parties and let them know the steps we plan for strengthening the unity of the communist movement. This is in full conformity with the principles and norms for relations between Marxist-Leninist parties stipulated in the Declaration and the Statement of the Moscow meetings.

The approach of the CC CPSU to the fraternal Parties in its letter of February 12 was dictated by our Party's profound concern that the abnormal situation which has now arisen in the communist movement should be liquidated. It reflects the basic interests of all the Marxist-Leninist parties, the interests of the defence of the purity of Marxism-Leninism.

As for your attempts to juggle with words like "great-power chauvinism," "self-important," "domineering," "inveterate habit of posing as the 'father party'," "God's will," etc., we have to tell you that the use of such expressions only testifies to the weakness of your position and to your wish to cover up by these means your own activities, which you try to ascribe to us.

For four years the fraternal Parties of the whole world have been appealing to the CC CCP to approach the matter from the point of view of common interests and to cease its attempts to impose its erroneous "general line" on the world communist movement. However, the leadership of the CCP has not only failed to heed the opinion of fraternal Parties but with growing ambition is posing as the sole heir of the founders of Marxism-Leninism and the supreme judge as regards the theory and practice of communism. After all it is none other than the leadership of the CCP that is attempting to dictate to the Communist Parties of the capitalist countries when they should begin the revolution and by what paths they should accomplish it. This leadership of the CCP pronounces sentence permitting no appeal on which country should be considered socialist and which not. It is that same leadership that affixes to whole Parties the labels of "correct" or "incorrect" and, depending upon whom it likes, declares some to be "outstanding Marxists" and others "modern revisionists."

Your great-power habits also appear in your last short letter when, addressing the CC CPSU, you demand that it send to you its letter of February 12. You do not request, but **demand.** One asks, by what right? Can it really be that you consider that anyone will take your tone seriously, become frightened and rush as fast as his legs can carry him to fulfil your every demand? This is not merely rude but simply ridiculous.

Your letter and its deliberately rude tone compels us to reflect once again: with what purpose was it sent? After all, nobody will believe that such an unseemly message was sent in the interests of the strengthening of friendship with the CPSU, of which you ceaselessly talk to your own people and the international communist movement, thus deceiving them. Anyone who acquaints himself with this letter will see that it is aimed at the aggravation of differences and the exacerbation of the situation in the communist movement.

If the leaders of the CCP genuinely cared for the solidarity and unity of the communist movement, they would have had to leave their erroneous path, cease schismatic activity and take their stand in the same ranks as all the world's fraternal Parties.

On its part, the CC CPSU is always ready to do everything in its power for the unity of the world communist movement on a principled Marxist-Leninist basis.

Our Party, which places the interests of the unity of the world communist movement above all else, expresses its willingness to continue to make exertions for normalizing relations with the CCP.

The CC CPSU expresses its firm conviction that the world communist movement will overcome the existing difficulties, unite its ranks even more closely under the banner of Marx-Engels-Lenin, and achieve new successes in the struggle for the great cause of the working class, for the victory of the national liberation movement, for the cause of peace and the security of the peoples, for the victory of communism.

With ardent fraternal greetings,

The Central Committee of the
Communist Party of the Soviet Union

DOCUMENT 6

Letter of the Central Committee of the CCP of February 27, 1964 to the Central Committee of the CPSU

Complete Text
[*Peking Review*, Vol. VII, No. 19 (May, 1964), pp. 11–12]
February 27, 1964

The Central Committee of the Communist
Party of the Soviet Union
Dear Comrades,

The Central Committee of the Communist Party of China has received your letter of February 22, 1964. The characteristic feature of this letter is the prodigality of the abuse — such as " unseemly," " a clumsy attempt to lay one's own fault at somebody else's door," " rude " and " ridiculous " — with which you try to evade the questions of substance which we raised in our letter of February 20, 1964. This is really a poor performance.

You accuse us of behaving like " the real culprit crying ' stop thief.' " In fact, it is you who are playing the trick of " the real culprit crying ' stop thief ' " to divert attention and steal away because you have been caught red-handed in sectarian, factional and divisive activities and confronted with irrefutable evidence. But however much you may quibble and sophisticate, you cannot deny the following facts. First, you have actually sent a letter behind our backs to fraternal Parties, a letter which is specifically directed against the Chinese Communist Party. Second, you are actually planning behind our backs to take " collective measures " from which the Chinese Communist Party will be excluded, and to go a step further in splitting the international communist movement.

In our letter of February 20, we point out that you " are unscrupulously engaging in sectarian, factional and divisive activities," that you adopt " vicious two-faced tactics," and that you have the " inveterate habit of great-power chauvinism and posing as the ' father Party.' " Your most recent letter proves that these criticisms completely fit the facts and are entirely correct.

Have you not repeatedly professed a desire to improve relations and uphold unity? If you really have such a desire, you ought to admit that right is right and wrong is wrong. One had better be honest. This is the only way to bring about a real settlement of problems. There is no other alternative.

You begin your letter with the assertion that you have the " right not to answer at all " the letter of the Central Committee of the CCP to the Central Committee of the CPSU, whereas we have repeatedly made it clear that we will answer your letter of November 29, 1963, in due course. We have advised you against impatience because we have not yet completed our reply to your numerous attacks. Whereupon you have flown into a rage as if we had committed a monstrous crime. Please think the matter over calmly: can this be described as treating fraternal Parties as equals?

Far from examining your own errors and publicly acknowledging and correcting them in all seriousness according to Lenin's teachings, you deny facts, call white black and turn on us by slanderously accusing us of factional activities. You even produced the Belishova case of June 1960 as an important piece of evidence against us. But you have lifted a rock only to crush your own toes. Our exchange of views with the responsible comrades of a fraternal Party on the international communist movement was above-board, entirely normal and beyond reproach. On the other hand, your intrigues on the question of Belishova cannot stand the light of day. You made Belishova your tool for subverting the leadership of a fraternal Party and country and for disrupting the unity of the socialist camp and the international communist movement. The Albanian comrades have exposed your intrigues and handled the Belishova case in the proper way.

It is the leaders of the CPSU themselves who have been conducting " the most real behind-the-scenes factional activity against a fraternal Party." As early as January 1960, that is, five months before the Belishova case, you delegated Comrade Mikoyan to meet the leading comrades of Albania in an effort to engineer activities against the Chinese Communist Party. Instances of such behind-the-scenes factional activity on your part were cited by Comrade Kapo, head of the Albanian delegation, in Comrade Khrushchev's presence on June 24, 1960, at the Bucharest meeting of representatives of the fraternal Parties of the socialist countries.

Yet acting like " knights for a day," you state in your letter that you will " publish documents " and " state our views openly." Moreover, you declared on September 21, 1963, that you would give us a " most resolute rebuff." Have you not played enough of such tricks? Have you not divulged enough information? Were these to be enumerated, we could cite a wealth of facts beginning from the 20th Congress of the CPSU. You are well aware of this and we do not need to waste our ink. Now you are again making an empty threat, and, to be blunt, this can only frighten people with weak nerves. In our opinion, all your bluster simply reminds one of a paper tiger. It is like a pewter-pointed spear. Please produce all the magic weapons in your treasure box for our enlightenment — the " most resolute rebuff," " open statement of our views," " collective measures " against the CCP, documents and materials, and what not.

If you do not fear the truth and the masses and if, instead of treating them as rabble, you have faith in the political consciousness and discernment of the members of the CPSU and the Soviet people, we propose that our two Parties reach an agreement, by which each side will, on an equal basis, publish in its own press the documents, articles and other material both sides have published or will publish in criticism of each other.

You accuse us of committing a blunder by " demanding " * instead of **" requesting "** that you send us a copy of your letter of February 12. In Chinese usage, these two words do not imply as big a difference as you describe. But since you take it so seriously and even make it an excuse for refusing to give us the letter of February 12, which is directed against the CCP, well then, we are now complying with your wish and **request** that you send us a copy of the letter which you gave the other fraternal Parties on February 12. It is our earnest hope that you will do so.

With fraternal greetings,

The Central Committee of the
Communist Party of China

* Following the Chinese usage this word was translated into "request" and not "demand" in the English version of the February 20 letter, of the Central Committee of the CCP to the Central Committee of the CPSU — *Translator*. [Original note. — Ed.]

DOCUMENT 7

Letter of the Central Committee of the CCP of February 29, 1964 to the Central Committee of the CPSU

Complete Text

[*Peking Review*, Vol. VII, No. 19 (May 8, 1964), pp. 12–18]

February 29, 1964

The Central Committee of the Communist
Party of the Soviet Union

Dear Comrades,

This letter from the Central Committee of the Communist Party of China is in reply to the letter of the Central Committee of the Communist Party of the Soviet Union, dated November 29, 1963.

The Chinese Communist Party has always regarded the safeguarding and cementing of the unity of the international communist movement as its sacred duty.

The unity of the Communists of all countries is not that of a club, it is the revolutionary unity of people guided by a common theory and fighting for a common ideal. The unity of the international communist movement can only be based on the revolutionary teachings of Marx and Lenin. Without this basis there can be no proletarian internationalist unity.

The differences between us and the leaders of the CPSU involve a number of major problems of principle concerning Marxist-Leninist theory and the whole international communist movement. These problems of principle must be solved if our differences are to be eliminated and the unity of the Chinese and Soviet Parties is to be strengthened.

The views we have expressed in our reply of June 14, 1963, to the letter of the Central Committee of the CPSU, that is, our proposal concerning the general line of the international communist movement, and in our articles about the international communist movement published both before and after that reply, are in full accord with Marxism-Leninism and the revolutionary principles of the 1947 Declaration and the 1960 Statement.

In this letter we would like to state our views on a number of questions raised in your letter.

1. The Question of the Sino-Soviet Boundary

The Government of the People's Republic of China has consistently held that the question of the boundary between China and the Soviet Union, which is a legacy from the past, can be settled through negotiation between the two Governments. It has also held that, pending such a settlement, the status quo on the border should be maintained. This is what we have done over the past ten years or more. Had the Soviet Government taken the same attitude, both sides could have lived in amity along the border and preserved tranquillity there.

With the stepping up of anti-Chinese activities by the leaders of the CPSU in recent years, the Soviet side has made frequent breaches of the status quo on the border, occupied Chinese territory and provoked border incidents. Still more serious, the Soviet side has flagrantly carried out large-scale subversive activities in Chinese frontier areas, trying to sow discord among China's nationalities by means of the press and wireless, inciting China's minority nationalities to break away from their motherland, and inveigling and coercing tens of thousands of Chinese citizens into going to the Soviet Union. Not only do all these acts violate the principles guiding relations between socialist countries, they are absolutely impermissible even in the relations between countries in general.

Among all our neighbours it is only the leaders of the CPSU and the reactionary nationalists of India who have deliberately created border disputes with China. The Chinese Government has satisfactorily settled complicated boundary questions, which were legacies from the past, both with all its fraternal socialist neighbours except the Soviet Union, and with its nationalist neighbours such as Burma, Nepal, Pakistan and Afghanistan, with the exception of India.

The delegations of our two Governments started boundary negotiations in Peking on February 24, 1964. Although the old treaties relating to the Sino-Russian boundary are unequal treaties, the Chinese Government is nevertheless willing to respect them and take them as the basis for a reasonable settlement of the Sino-Soviet boundary question. Guided by proletarian internationalism and the principles governing relations between socialist countries, the Chinese Government will conduct friendly negotiations with the Soviet Government in the spirit of consultation on an equal footing and mutual understanding and mutual accommodation. If the Soviet side takes the same attitude as the Chinese Government, the settlement of the Sino-Soviet boundary question, we believe, ought not to be difficult, and the Sino-Soviet boundary will truly become one of lasting friendship.

2. The Question of Aid

We have always had a proper appreciation of the friendly Soviet aid which began under Stalin's leadership. We have always considered that the Soviet people's friendly aid has played a beneficial role in helping China to lay the preliminary foundations for her socialist industrialization. For this the Chinese Communist Party and the Chinese people have expressed their gratitude on numerous occasions.

In recent years the leaders of the CPSU have habitually played the benefactor and frequently boasted of their " disinterested assistance." When commemorating the 14th anniversary of the signing of the Sino-Soviet Treaty of Friendship, Alliance and Mutual Assistance in February this year, *Pravda, Izvestiya* and other Soviet propaganda media again beat the drum to the same tune. We have not yet made a systematic reply in the press, but we must point out that, so far from being gratis, Soviet aid to China was rendered mainly in the form of trade and that it was certainly not a one-way affair. China has paid and is paying the Soviet Union in goods, gold or convertible foreign exchange for all Soviet-supplied complete sets of equipment and other goods, including those made available on credit plus interest. It is necessary to add that the prices of many of the goods we imported from the Soviet Union were much higher than those on the world market.

While China has received aid from the Soviet Union, the Soviet Union on its part has also received corresponding aid from China. No one can say that China's aid to the Soviet Union has been insignificant and not worthy of mention. Here are some examples:

Up to the end of 1962 China had furnished the Soviet Union with 2,100 million new rubles' worth of grain, edible oils and other foodstuffs. Among the most important items were 5,760,000 tons of soya beans, 2,940,000 tons of rice, 1,090,000 tons of edible oils and 900,000 tons of meat.

Over the same period, China furnished the Soviet Union with more than 1,400 million new rubles' worth of mineral products and metals. Among the most important items were: 100,000 tons of lithium concentrates, 34,000 tons of beryllium concentrates, 51,000 tons of borax, 270,000 tons of wolfram concentrates, 32.9 tons of piezoelectric quartz, 7,730 tons of mercury, 39 tons of tantalum-niobium concentrates, 37,000 tons of molybdenum concentrates and 180,000 tons of tin. Many of these mineral products are raw materials which are indispensable for the development of the most advanced branches of science and for the manufacture of rockets and nuclear weapons.

As for the Soviet loans to China, it must be pointed out that China used them mostly for the purchase of war materiel from the Soviet Union, the greater part of which was used up in the war to resist U.S. aggression and aid in Korea. In the war against U.S. aggression the Korean people carried by far the heaviest burden and sustained by far the greatest losses. The Chinese people, too, made great sacrifices and incurred vast military expenses. The Chinese Communist Party has always considered that this was the Chinese people's bounden internationalist duty and that it is nothing to boast of. For many years we have been paying the principal and interest on these Soviet loans, which account for a considerable part of our yearly exports to the Soviet Union. Thus even the war materiel supplied to China in the war to resist U.S. aggression and aid Korea has not been given gratis.

3. The Question of the Soviet Experts

The Soviet experts working in China were invariably made welcome, respected and trusted by the Chinese Government and people. The overwhelming majority of them were hard working and helpful to China's socialist construction. We have always highly appreciated their conscientious work, and still miss them to this day.

You will remember that when the leaders of the CPSU unilaterally decided to recall all the Soviet experts in China, we solemnly affirmed our desire to have them continue their work in China and expressed the hope that the leaders of the CPSU would reconsider and change their decision.

But in spite of our objections you turned your backs on the principles guiding international relations and unscrupulously withdrew the 1,390 Soviet experts working in China, tore up 343 contracts and supplementary contracts concerning experts, and scrapped 257 projects of scientific and technical co-operation, all within the short span of a month.

You were well aware that the Soviet experts were posted in over 250 enterprises and establishments in the economic field and the fields of national defence, culture, education and scientific research, and that they were undertaking important tasks involving technical design, the construction of projects, the installation of equipment, trial production and scientific research. As a result of your peremptory orders to the Soviet experts to discontinue their work and return to the Soviet Union, many of our country's important designing and scientific research projects had to stop halfway, some of the construction projects in progress had to be suspended, and some of the factories and mines which were conducting trial production could not go into production according to schedule. Your perfidious action disrupted China's original national economic plan and inflicted enormous losses upon China's socialist construction.

You were going completely against communist ethics when you took advantage of China's serious natural disasters to adopt these grave measures.

Your action fully demonstrates that you violate the principle of mutual assistance between socialist countries and use the sending of experts as an instrument for exerting political pressure on fraternal countries, butting into their internal affairs and impeding and sabotaging their socialist construction.

Now you have again suggested sending experts to China. To be frank, the Chinese people cannot trust you. They have just healed the wounds caused by your withdrawal of experts. These events are still fresh in their memory. With the leaders of the CPSU pursuing an anti-Chinese policy, the Chinese people are unwilling to be duped.

In our opinion, all the countries in the socialist camp should handle the question of sending experts in accordance with the principles of genuine equality, non-interference in each other's internal affairs, mutual assistance and internationalism. It is absolutely impermissible for any country unilaterally to annul or scrap any agreement or contract concerning the sending of experts. Any country which violates such an agreement or contract should, in accordance with international practice, compensate the other side for the losses thus inflicted. Only thus can there be an interchange of experts on a basis of equality and mutual benefit between China and the Soviet Union and among countries in the socialist camp.

We would like to say in passing that, basing ourselves on the internationalist principle of mutual assistance among countries in the socialist camp, we are very much concerned about the present economic situation in the Soviet Union. If you should feel the need for the help of Chinese experts in certain fields, we would be glad to send them.

4. The Question of Sino-Soviet Trade

Nobody is in a better position than you to know the real cause for the curtailment of Sino-Soviet trade over the last few years. This curtailment was precisely the result of your extending the differences from the field of ideology to that of state relations.

Your sudden withdrawal of all the Soviet experts working in China upset the schedules of construction and the production arrangements of many of our factories, mines and other enterprises and establishments, and had a direct impact on our need for the import of complete sets of equipment. Such being the case, did you expect us to keep on buying them just for display?

Moreover, in pursuance of your policy of further imposing restrictions on and discriminating against China in the economic and commercial fields, since 1960 you have deliberately placed obstacles in the way of economic and trade negotiations between our two countries and held up or refused supplies of important goods which China needs. You have insisted on providing large amounts of goods which we do not really need or which we do not need at all, while holding back or supplying very few of the goods which we need badly. For several years you have used the trade between our two countries as an instrument for bringing political pressure to bear on China. How could this avoid cutting down the volume of Sino-Soviet trade?

From 1959 to 1961, our country suffered extraordinary natural disasters for three years in succession and could not supply you with as large quantities of agricultural produce and processed products as before. This was the result of factors beyond human control. It is utterly unreasonable for you to attack China on this account and blame her for this reduction in trade.

Indeed, but for China's efforts the volume of Sino-Soviet trade would have decreased even more. Take this year for example. China has already put forward a list of 220 million new rubles' worth of imports from the Soviet Union and 420 million new rubles' worth of exports to the Soviet Union. But you have been procrastinating unreasonably, continuing to hold back goods we need while trying to force on us goods we do not need. You say in your letter, "In the course of the next few years the USSR could increase its export to China of goods in which you are interested . . ." But your deeds do not agree with your words.

You constantly accuse us of "going it alone" and claim that you stand for extensive economic ties and division of labour among the socialist countries. But what is your actual record in this respect?

You infringe the independence and sovereignty of fraternal countries and oppose their efforts to develop their economy on an independent basis in accordance with their own needs and potentialities.

You bully those fraternal countries whose economies are less advanced and oppose their policy of industrialization and try to force them to remain agricultural countries and serve as your sources of raw materials and as outlets for your goods.

You bully fraternal countries which are industrially more developed and insist that they stop manufacturing their traditional products and become accessory factories serving your industries.

Moreover, you have introduced the jungle law of the capitalist world into relations between socialist countries. You openly follow the example of the Common Market which was organized by monopoly capitalist groups.

All these actions of yours are wrong.

In the economic, scientific, technical and cultural spheres, we stand for relations of co-operation of a new type, based on genuine equality and mutual benefit, between China and the Soviet Union and among all the socialist countries.

We hold that it is necessary to transform the present Council of Mutual Economic Assistance of socialist countries to accord with the principle of proletarian internationalism and turn this organization, which is now solely controlled by the leaders of the CPSU, into one based on genuine equality and mutual benefit, which the fraternal countries of the socialist camp may join of their own free will. It is hoped that you will favourably respond to our suggestion.

5. The Question of Stopping Public Polemics

The public polemics were provoked by you. We maintained that differences in the international communist movement should be settled through inter-Party discussions. But you insisted on bringing them into the open. Beginning with the 22nd Congress of the CPSU, you imposed public polemics on the entire international communist movement in violation of the principles guiding relations among fraternal Parties as laid down in the 1960 Statement, and you asserted that to do so was to " act in Lenin's manner." What you did was a bad thing. You created difficulties for fraternal Parties and rendered a service to the imperialists and reactionaries. Now, with the extensive unfolding of the public debate, the truth is becoming clearer and clearer and Marxism-Leninism is making more and more progress. What was a bad thing is becoming a good thing.

In the course of this great debate, the Communists, proletarians, working people, revolutionary intellectuals, and other people who have an interest in opposing imperialism and reaction have become more discerning and increasingly awakened politically, and their revolutionary enthusiasm and theoretical level have been greatly enhanced. The effect of the public debate is the opposite of what you intended. It leads more and more people away from the bad influence of the baton and makes them think over the problems independently. Thus, as with the other debates in the history of the international communist movement, the present debate is undoubtedly the prelude to a new revolutionary upsurge.

When you wanted to start public polemics against the fraternal Marxist-Leninist parties, you said that such polemics represented " the only correct and genuinely Marxist-Leninist position of principle " and were " in the interests of the whole world communist movement." Yet now that the public polemics have more and more clearly exposed your revisionist features and placed you in an increasingly disadvantageous position, you declare that they " are doing great harm to the communist movement " and that it would be " most wise " and " in the interests of the solidarity of the world communist movement " to stop them. What truth or principle is to be found in you when you say one thing one day and another the next? Which of your statements do you expect others to believe? And which do you expect others to obey?

As to the proposal for stopping the public polemics, you seem to have forgotten that it was put forward by the Workers' Party of Viet Nam as early as January 1962. Similar proposals were put forward by the Communist Parties of Indonesia and of New Zealand. They all won our immediate approval. But you turned a deaf ear to them and, far from stopping the public polemics, you kept extending them. Why must others accept your proposal the instant it is made?

You also seem to have forgotten that in our letter to you of March 9, 1963, we said, " On the suspension of public polemics, it is necessary that our two Parties and the fraternal Parties concerned should have some discussion and reach an agreement that is fair and acceptable to all." You ignored our proposal. On July 20, 1963, when the talks between the Chinese and Soviet Parties were drawing to a close, we proposed to write into the communique: ". . . our two Parties and the fraternal Parties concerned should make joint efforts to seek a reasonable basis for achieving a fair agreement on the cessation of public polemics, which is acceptable to all." Once again you turned down our proposal.

In your letter you state that "it would be correct not to concentrate attention on the problems on which there are differences between us but to let them wait until the heat of passion has cooled, to let time do its work." Again, you seem to have forgotten that as far back as October 10, 1960, we pointed out in our written statement at the drafting committee of the 26 fraternal Parties that "as to the questions on which unanimity cannot be achieved for the time being, it would be better to leave them open than to reach a forced solution" and that "time will help us eliminate the differences." You then categorically rejected our proposal. In your letter of November 5, 1960, to the Central Committee of the Chinese Communist Party, which you circulated during the 1960 meeting of the fraternal Parties, you declared, "To wait for the 'verdict of history' would be a grave error fraught with serious consequences for the entire communist movement. . . ." But now you suddenly make a turn of 180 degrees on this question and say that we should let the differences wait. What are you up to? To put it plainly, you are merely resorting to this trick to deprive us of the right to reply, after you yourselves have heaped so much abuse on the Chinese Communist Party and other Marxist-Leninist parties.

While the talks between the Chinese and Soviet Parties were in progress in Moscow, despite our repeated sincere advice you published your Open Letter to Party organizations and all Communists in the Soviet Union on July 14, 1963, in order to curry favour with U.S. imperialism and to reach an agreement with it on the monopoly of nuclear weapons. You then launched an anti-Chinese campaign on an unprecedented scale. According to incomplete statistics, between July 15 and the end of October 1963 the Soviet press carried nearly 2,000 anti-Chinese articles and other items.

Meanwhile, under your influence the leaders of the fraternal Parties of socialist countries — the Communist Party of Czechoslovakia, the Bulgarian Communist Party, the Socialist Unity Party of Germany, the Hungarian Socialist Workers' Party and the Mongolian People's Revolutionary Party — have also published a great number of articles and other items against China.

You say in your letter that "the differences and sharp polemics are doing great harm to the communist movement." If you really think so, don't you find you ought to reproach yourselves, to ask yourselves why you again and again insisted on attacking and slandering the Chinese Communist Party and other Marxist-Leninist parties in a big way?

You also say in your letter that the difficulties of other fraternal Parties should be taken into account. We have always given full consideration to the difficulties of other fraternal Parties. It was for this very reason that we repeatedly advised the leaders of the CPSU against bringing the controversy into the open. But following the leaders of the CPSU, the leaders of the Communist and Workers' Parties of many capitalist countries, for example, the Parties of France, Italy, Belgium, Spain, the Netherlands, Switzerland, Denmark, Finland, Sweden, Austria, West Germany, Greece, Portugal, Britain, the United States of America, Canada, Chile, Brazil, Argentina, Mexico, Peru, Colombia, Paraguay, Uruguay, Australia, Ceylon, Syria, Lebanon, Iraq, Turkey, Iran, Jordan and Algeria — as well as the Dange clique, who are renegades from the Indian proletariat — published many articles attacking the Chinese Communist Party and other Marxist-Leninist parties, and some adopted resolutions, issued statements or open letters to Party members, or even unscrupulously attacked or expelled comrades adhering to the Marxist-Leninist stand. Did they ever take their own difficulties into account when they were doing all this? Did you ever take their difficulties into account when you were supporting them in all this?

These fraternal Parties have attacked us in numerous articles and other items, but we have all along exercised great restraint. We have replied to none of them except to a part of the attacks of the leaders of the Communist Parties of France, Italy and the U.S.A. We have merely reserved our right to reply. How was it possible for us to create difficulties for them when we have never disturbed them? If they have difficulties, these are of their own making.

Even after your letter of November 20, 1963, you and your followers did not stop your anti-Chinese propaganda. You attacked us by name in the *Pravda* articles, " Why Mislead? " and " The Soviet-Chinese Treaty — Fourteen Years," in the *Izvestiya* article " An Important Document," in " The World in a Week " in the magazine *Za Rubezhom*, and in many other articles and items. In addition, you have recently published books against China, such as *Talks on Political Subjects, Our Leninist Party, A Treaty That Purifies the Atmosphere . . ., The Leninist Teaching of the Party and the Contemporary Communist Movement* and *The General Crisis of Capitalism and Foreign Policy*, in which you make comprehensive and concentrated attacks on the Chinese Communist Party. You have also distributed pamphlets attacking China through your embassies abroad and your delegates to international mass organizations. As for the articles and other items your followers have published in the meantime, we shall not dwell on them here.

Moreover, since November 29, 1963, you have raised acute controversial questions and provoked debates at the Warsaw meeting of the World Peace Council, the Prague meeting of the Executive Bureau of the World Federation of Trade Unions, the Berlin meeting of the Bureau of the Women's International Democratic Federation, the Budapest meeting of the Executive Committee of the International Union of Students, and at a number of other international meetings. At these meetings, while we, together with the delegates from other countries, were actively promoting the struggle of the people of the world for peace, supporting the national-liberation movement and calling for a united front against U.S. imperialism, you on your part extolled U.S. imperialism and created splits by insisting on adopting resolutions in support of the tripartite treaty by which you allied yourselves with the United States against China.

All this provides ample proof that you say one thing and do another and that your cry for an end to public polemics is utterly false and demagogic.

While you have published so many articles and other items against China, we have so far printed only seven articles in reply to your Open Letter. We have not yet completed our reply to the important questions you raised in the Open Letter, and have not even started to reply to the questions you raised in your other anti-Chinese articles. In all our articles we have adduced facts and used reasoned arguments. How can it be said that they are " shaking the friendship and unity of the peoples of the socialist community and weakening the anti-imperialist front"? Do not these phrases neatly fit your own voluminous and unreasonable material and your countless lies and slanders?

You have used every conceivable term of abuse in attacking the Chinese Communist Party and called us a host of names such as "dogmatists," "Left adventurists," "pseudo-revolutionaries," "newly baked Trotskyites," "nationalists," "racists," "great-power chauvinists," "sectarians," "splitters," and people "falling into the company of the forces of imperialist reaction," "having an itch for war" and "playing the role of the Right wing in the rank of the American 'maniacs,' West German revanchists and French extremists." In short, according to you the Chinese Communists are undoubtedly 100 per cent arch-reactionaries. If so, we would like to ask: How can such fine fellows as you, who call yourselves 100 per cent Marxist-Leninists, talk of unity with those bad fellows whom you consider more hateful than the enemy? How are you going to wind up the whole affair? Do you propose to come forward with a public statement admitting that all your attacks on the Chinese Communist Party are lies and slanders and removing all the labels you have stuck on it? Or will you insist that we accept your verdict, give up the revolutionary banner of Marxism-Leninism and kowtow to your revisionist line?

It is now perfectly clear that our differences with you involve the questions of whether or not to adhere to the fundamental theories of Marxism-Leninism and whether or not to adhere to the revolutionary principles of the Declaration and the Statement, as well as a whole series of important questions of principle, such as the following:

Are the U.S. imperialists the sworn enemies of the people of the world, or are they sensible emissaries of peace? Are they overlords who determine the destiny of mankind?

What is the reliable way to prevent the imperialists from unleashing a world war and to safeguard world peace?

To defend world peace and serve the interests of revolution, should we unite the workers, peasants, revolutionary intellectuals, the anti-imperialist and anti-feudal revolutionaries among the national bourgeoisie, and all other forces of the world that can be united, and form the broadest possible united front in a common struggle against U.S. imperialism and its lackeys? Or should we pin all our hopes on U.S.-Soviet collaboration?

When the Indian reactionaries attack socialist China, should proletarian internationalism be observed and the Indian reactionaries' provocations be denounced, or should they be helped with arms to fight the brothers of the Soviet people?

Are the Titoites renegades or comrades? Are they a special detachment of U.S. imperialism or not? Is Yugoslavia a socialist country or not?

Is the socialist camp needed or not? On what principles is the unity of the socialist camp to be strengthened?

Should we actively support all the oppressed peoples and nations in their revolutionary and class struggles for emancipation, or should we forbid and oppose their revolutions?

Was Stalin a great Marxist-Leninist, or was he a murderer, a bandit and a gambler?

Should a socialist country maintain the dictatorship of the proletariat, or should it use the so-called state of the whole people and the so-called party of the entire people to pave the way for the restoration of capitalism?

These questions admit of no equivocation but must be thoroughly straightened out. How can issues of such magnitude be evaded? If they were, there would be no distinction between Marxism-Leninism and revisionism and dogmatism, between Marxism-Leninism and Trotskyism, between the Communist and the social democratic parties, or between communism and capitalism.

You frequently threaten others with a "most resolute rebuff." In fact, people have had plenty of experience of your tactics, whether hard or soft, bitter or sweet. It was you who exerted military, economic and political pressure on Albania, severed diplomatic relations, tore up agreements and broke off trade relations with her. It was you, too, who scrapped contracts with China, withdrew experts, discontinued aid and carried out subversive activities against her. The Chinese Communist Party and all other Parties adhering to Marxism-Leninism will never be misled by honeyed words or bow under pressure or barter away principles. If you are indeed ready to deliver a "most resolute rebuff" worthy of the term, "state our views openly," "publish documents and material," take "collective measures" or what not, well then, please do whatever you intend to do.

Despite the fact that the differences have grown to their present serious proportions, the Chinese Communist Party is willing to do its best for the restoration and strengthening of unity. In your letter of November 29 you merely cry for a halt to the public polemics without putting forward any concrete measures for solving the problem. We now propose to you the following concrete measures for the solution of the problem, and we hope you will consider them and give us an answer.

(1) For the cessation of the public polemics it is necessary for the Chinese and Soviet Parties and other fraternal Parties concerned to hold various bilateral and multilateral talks in order to find through consultation a fair and reasonable formula acceptable to all and to conclude a common agreement.

(2) The Chinese Communist Party consistently advocates and actively supports the convening of a meeting of representatives of all Communist and Workers' Parties. Prior to the meeting adequate preparations should be made, and difficulties and obstacles should be overcome. Together with the other fraternal Parties, we will do everything possible to ensure that this meeting will be a meeting of unity on the basis of the revolutionary principles of Marxism-Leninism.

(3) The resumption of talks between the Chinese and Soviet Parties is a necessary preparatory step for making the meeting of the fraternal Parties a success. We propose that the talks between the Chinese and Soviet Parties be resumed in Peking, from October 10 to 25, 1964.

(4) In order to make further preparations for the meeting of representatives of all fraternal Parties, we propose that the Sino-Soviet talks be followed by a meeting of representatives of seventeen fraternal Parties, namely, the Parties of Albania, Bulgaria, China, Cuba, Czechoslovakia, the German Democratic Republic, Hungary, Korea, Mongolia, Poland, Rumania, the Soviet Union and Viet Nam, and the Parties of Indonesia, Japan, Italy and France.

Unite under the banner of Marxism-Leninism!

The Central Committee of the Communist Party of China

DOCUMENT 8

Letter of the Central Committee of the CPSU of March 7, 1964 to the Central Committee of the CCP

Complete Text

[*Peking Review*, Vol. VII, No. 19 (May 8, 1964), pp. 24–27]

March 7, 1964

The Central Committee of the Communist Party of China

Dear Comrades,

The CC CPSU has received your letter of February 27, 1964. We have studied it carefully. We must tell you frankly that your letter has greatly astonished us. In this letter you again lavishly employ such words as " divisive," " factional " and " sectarian," with the help of which you attempt to accuse our Party of some sort of behind-the-scenes activity against the CCP.

Recently you have been trying more and more often to place the blame for the emergence of the differences and the exacerbation of the struggle on the shoulders of the CPSU. The meaning of all these attempts is perfectly clear to us — you wish to justify your own actions and inflame the differences by shifting the responsibility to others.

We can say with a clear conscience that we have no responsibility whatsoever for the situation that has been created. The CPSU and other Marxist-Leninist parties have made and are making every effort to settle the differences with the Communist Party of China on the basis of the principles in the Declaration and the Statement of the Moscow meetings. In its attitude toward your Party, the CC CPSU has at all times proceeded from the position of not allowing the intensification of differences. At first we thought that the divergencies that arose several years ago were fortuitous. We did not wish to believe the information we received that the Chinese comrades were acting behind our backs and taking a line of exacerbating the struggle. We have striven at all times for mutual relations of the greatest brotherhood and confidence.

The CC CPSU is well aware of the importance of friendship between the Communist Party of the Soviet Union and the Communist Party of China and between the Soviet Union and the People's Republic of China, whose relations must be built on the foundation of the teachings of Marxism-Leninism. We have more than once written and stated to you — as we did for instance when Comrade Liu Hsiao, Ambassador of the People's Republic of China to the USSR, was leaving Moscow in October 1962 — our sincere desire that the friendship between the CPSU and the CCP should remain as good as it was before 1958. This was what we most ardently hoped for. But now, unfortunately, we see that these hopes are not being realized.

The central point of the February 27 letter of the CC CCP is in fact a proposal for the intensification of public polemics. In proposing the conclusion of an agreement on mutual publication of critical materials directed against one another, what you desire is, in essence, that the polemics between the Parties should embrace the peoples of our countries.

191

You must understand, comrades, that were one to publish your articles which contain so many unjust assertions, and slanders against the internal and external policy of the Soviet Union, and which go so far as to assert that the " restoration of capitalism " is taking place in the USSR and it has entered into "collusion with American imperialism," it would only arouse a feeling of legitimate indignation among the Soviet people. Naturally, the Soviet press would not leave such attacks unanswered. And all this would mean not taking the line of strengthening the friendship between the great peoples of the Soviet Union and China but taking the line of inflaming hostility, mistrust and unfriendliness between them.

Indeed, the polemics you are conducting have long ago gone beyond the bounds of ideological dispute and been turned by you into a weapon for the struggle against the CPSU and the entire world communist movement. You pour torrents of dirt over our Party and our country, and are in essence employing the same tactics as that of the opponents of the Soviet state, who try to divide the people from the Party and the Party from the leadership. Such actions are impermissible, and calculations based on them are simply naive. Your attacks on the CPSU, which has rich experience of struggle against the Trotskyites, the Right opportunists and the nationalists, and against external enemies, are only promoting the even greater unity of Soviet Communists and the entire Soviet people around their militant communist vanguard.

In telling the Party the truth about your subversive activities, we have always retained and continue to adhere to self-restraint and a quiet tone of voice, and never permit any insults toward the fraternal Communist Party of China, its leaders and the Chinese people. Please consider what would happen if we too were to take your path and reply to you with the same abuse that you heap on us, and call upon the Chinese people to fight against their leadership. If we took this path, what sort of Communists or leaders of Communist Parties would we be and what sort of followers of the teachings of Marxism-Leninism who are confronted with the tasks of struggle to build a communist society? Communism is not the inflaming of enmity among nations; on the contrary it is their unification into a single fraternal family, regardless of nationality, colour of skin and language, for the irreconcilable struggle against exploiters and imperialism.

Guided by these very considerations, the CC CPSU in its letter of November 29, 1963 again proposed the cessation of public polemics and put forward a constructive programme for the improvement of Soviet-Chinese relations and normalisation of the situation in the communist movement. At the same time, the publication of polemical material in Soviet newspapers and periodicals was discontinued. All the fraternal Parties recognized these actions as expressions of the good will of the CPSU and hopefully expected that the leadership of the CCP would support our initiative.

Unfortunately the CC CCP did the opposite. While deliberately delaying an official answer to our appeal, you replied to it in fact by inflaming the polemics, by intensifying schismatic activities in the communist movement and by directing even more slanderous accusations at the CPSU and other Marxist-Leninist parties. This campaign culminated in the *Jen-min Jih-pao* and *Hung Ch'i* article of February 4, 1964 which proclaimed that the Soviet Union, together with American imperialism, was the " arch-enemy " of People's China and contained impermissible insinuations concerning our

Party and its Central Committee. The February 4 article represented an attempt to provide some kind of theoretical basis for the schismatic activities and to declare that a split in the communist movement was a phenomenon conforming to laws. This disgraceful document, like other similar material, was distributed in huge numbers and broadcast all over the world by radio in Russian and other languages.

In these circumstances, we could no longer remain silent, we had to tell the whole truth about the words and the real deeds of the Chinese leadership so that the Plenum of the CC CPSU could discuss and appraise the situation that had arisen and say its weighty word. After discussing the question of the struggle waged by the CPSU for the unity of the communist movement, the February Plenum of the CC CPSU, at which 6,000 Party activists were present, unanimously approved the line of the Presidium of the central Committee.

In full conformity with the accepted principles governing relations in the communist movement, the CC CPSU considered it its duty to inform fraternal Parties of our intention to publish in the press the relevant materials of the Plenum and to rebuff the schismatic activities of the CCP leadership.

It is quite understandable that there was no sense at all in sending you our letter addressed to other fraternal Parties. This would have been useless, if only because we had already repeatedly approached you with the same questions and received no answer. The February 12 letter of the CC CPSU contained no secrets, it contained nothing we had not talked about to the leadership of the CCP much earlier. Nonetheless, you decided to use this letter as a pretext for accusing the CPSU of "behind-the-scenes" "anti-Chinese" activity. It is appropriate first of all to ask: Has a Communist Party no right to address letters to whomever it considers necessary? Do we demand that the CC CCP give us an account of its correspondence?

But this is not the whole matter. We have already told you how absurd such accusations are, particularly when made by those who over several years have really carried on behind-the-scenes subversive activities against fraternal Parties. We can cite many examples of how the CC CCP, acting behind the backs of Marxist-Leninist parties and their leadership, is inspiring the creation of anti-Party schismatic groups and trying to unite them in opposition to the world communist movement.

Losing the sense of reality, the CC CCP attempted to present us with an ultimatum — it demanded that it be sent the CC CPSU letter of February 12. When we politely explained that no Communist Party should permit itself to talk with another in the language of ultimative demands, you alleged, obviously obscuring the issue, that there is no difference between the words "request" and "demand" in the Chinese language.

We hold a much higher opinion of the Chinese language. The Chinese are a great people with an ancient culture and understand perfectly well the shades of meaning between "request" and "demand." It may even happen that the words are the same but the music is quite different. Incidentally, the word "request" was found in the Chinese language, after all, when there was a desire to use it. We hope that from now on the language of ultimatums will be excluded forever from our relations.

Why, then, was it found necessary to permit oneself to address a fraternal Party in this way? Why was your entire letter of February 27, as were the

193

preceding ones, written in an exceptionally rude and impertinent tone, and studded with imprecations and insulting expressions? To irritate us, to force us to depart from principled ideological and communist positions and embark upon a " squabble at the well-mouth "? Apparently these were indeed your intentions.

Seeking political capital, you constantly deck yourselves out as " knights " of equality and at the same time try to convince people that the CPSU is clinging to the role of a " father party." We cannot avoid having the impression that all this is done solely to enable you yourselves to fill the role of a " father party." But our times are different now. Even in Stalin's lifetime this role had become obsolete, although he did take such a position. By permitting abuses of power within our Party and in relation to fraternal Parties and annihilating people who had opinions of their own, he forfeited people's confidence and destroyed his own prestige. During and after the war, it seems, Stalin himself felt that one should not order Parties about at one's own will. This, in particular, was one of the reasons for the dissolution of the Comintern.

After Stalin's death our Party, having analyzed all these things honestly and in a Marxist-Leninist way, took steps to correct the situation that had arisen. On its own initiative, the CC CPSU corrected Stalin's errors and restored the Leninist principle of equality in its relations with fraternal Parties and countries. We withdrew our troops from countries where they had previously been stationed, including the troops from Port Arthur. We liquidated the economic joint companies in China and in other countries and took a number of other measures. It is not superfluous to note that the CC CCP at one time fully approved and set a high value on these steps taken by our Party.

We still stand on the same positions. Today the situation is not what it was, for instance, in 1919: today Lenin is no longer alive, and no one living can take his place. It is only collectively that the Marxist-Leninist parties can work out a common line for the communist movement. There are no, and cannot be any, " father " or " son " parties, but there is and must be a family of fraternal Parties with equal rights and collective wisdom. Success will never attend efforts made in disregard of the opinions of others to impose one's own views on them and attach labels to all who disagree with such views. That is why, even today, we call on you yet to think over your viewpoints again, and to weigh up carefully where they can lead you. That is why, despite your incessant assaults on the CPSU and other Marxist-Leninist parties, we have exercised and are continuing to exercise patience and are ready to make every effort for normalizing the situation and strengthening the solidarity of the international communist movement.

The CC CPSU has repeatedly expressed the view that the best thing today for the interests of the working class and the revolutionary movement and the cause of world socialism would be the cessation of the public polemics between Communist Parties. Once again we propose — let us proceed in all matters from the principles of the Declaration and the Statement, and discuss disputed questions at meetings between fraternal Parties or at international conferences among them. The discussions should proceed with tact and self-respect, with an understanding of the full responsibility we bear in our actions, so that the dispute may not lead to a split and do damage to the holy of holies — the teachings of Marxism-Leninism and the cause of socialism.

We have no right to forget the behest of V. I. Lenin, who warned that dissensions among Communists serve to benefit the imperialists. " If discussions," said V. I. Lenin, " then arguments; if arguments, then dissensions; if dissensions, it means the Communists have become weaker; then press on, seize the moment, take advantage of their weakening. This has become the slogan of the world that is hostile to us. We must not forget this for an instant." (*Collected Works*, Fourth Russian ed., Vol. 32, pp. 144–145.)

If you were really interested in strengthening the unity of the international communist ranks, then you should have accepted our proposals long ago, listened to the voice of reason and taken account of the opinion of the overwhelming majority of the Marxist-Leninist parties. The more stubbornly you persist in your intention to inflame the polemics and in your schismatic activities, the more grounds will the Communists and all the progressive forces have to be convinced that the CC CCP is not guided by the interests of socialism at all, but by incorrectly understood national — in effect — nationalist, selfish interests.

We could refute point by point the slanderous accusations against the CPSU made off-handedly in the February 27 letter of the CC CCP, but we do not consider it necessary to do so now. What is the use of arguments, when you have no intention of seriously entering into the essence of the questions but instead simply pour yet another bucket of dirt over our Party?

We will not fall for any provocation but will proceed along Lenin's path together with the Communists of the whole world in one family. The CC CPSU again expresses confidence that the Communist Party of China will sooner or later find the correct path to unity with this family. The sooner this happens, the better. The Communist Party of the Soviet Union will continue to struggle for the unity of all fraternal Parties on Marxist-Leninist and proletarian-internationalist principles, and on the basis of the programmatic documents of the world communist movement — the Declaration and the Statement.

We have also received your letter of February 29. From this letter, which is a belated answer to ours of November 29, 1963, it is evident that you have rejected all the proposals we made for the sake of a radical improvement of Soviet-Chinese relations, of the strengthening of friendship and co-operation between the peoples of the USSR and the CPR and of the unity of the ranks of the world communist movement. The whole spirit of your letter demonstrates that the CC CCP is not concerned with improving relations between our Parties and countries but instead is inventing different accusations against the CPSU and the Soviet Union. We resolutely repudiate all your libellous attacks on the CPSU and the Soviet Union.

The CC CPSU will give its answer to this letter and will show the real meaning of your distortion of the ideological-political views of our Party and its practical activity; it will re-establish the truth.

But already in our present letter we deem it necessary to set forth our position on the question that worries the whole communist movement — that of ways to overcome the differences and attain unity and solidarity among the fraternal Parties.

We note that after many months of stalling and delay the CC CCP has agreed with our view concerning the necessity of continuing the bilateral meeting of representatives of the CPSU and the CCP and afterwards of preparing and calling a meeting of all the Communist and Workers' Parties.

The CC CPSU takes a positive view of this fact and considers it to be its internationalist duty to do its utmost, in the course of these projected meetings and discussions, to help strengthen the unity of the communist movement and the solidarity of the fraternal Parties on a Marxist-Leninist platform.

At the same time, we do not understand your motives for delaying for a long period the taking of these measures for which the time is fully ripe. By now it is perfectly clear what harm has been done to the communist movement as a result of your exacerbation of polemics and factional activity in its midst. The questions that demand discussion have emerged fully, and the aim of the meetings is perfectly clear. Moreover, one cannot ignore the fact that the majority of the Marxist-Leninist parties are stressing ever more urgently the necessity for an international meeting.

All the more inexplicable is the delaying of the bilateral meeting between representatives of the CPSU and the CCP. Eight months have already passed since the first meeting and you propose postponing the second for another period of similar length, at a time when the speediest possible settlement of existing differences is urgently required for the improvement of the relations between our two Parties and countries, and in the interests of the unity of the international communist movement and all democratic and revolutionary forces so that they can activize their joint struggle against imperialism. It is very important that our Parties should not be diverted into endless arguments but concentrate our main attention on the solution of the immense tasks confronting us in the building of socialism and communism and on the struggle against our common enemy — imperialism.

Your proposal that the meeting of representatives of the CCP and the CPSU be held as late as October 1964 means in fact that the meeting of fraternal Parties would be delayed by at least a year and that the settlement of the existing differences would thus be further postponed and these differences would be further exacerbated. In our opinion, this would only bring harm to the fraternal Parties and the whole world communist movement.

We also fail to understand the motives by which you were guided in making the proposal that a preparatory meeting be called composed of representatives of only seventeen fraternal Parties (Albania, Bulgaria, Hungary, Viet Nam, GDR, China, Korea, Cuba, Mongolia, Poland, Rumania, USSR, Czechoslovakia, Indonesia, Japan, Italy and France).

We consider it appropriate to hold the preparatory meeting with the participation of representatives of all the fraternal Parties that were on the drafting committee of the Moscow Meeting of 1960 and that jointly prepared the Statement (Albania, Bulgaria, Hungary, Viet Nam, GDR, China, Korea, Cuba, Mongolia, Poland, Rumania, USSR, Czechoslovakia, France, Italy, German Federal Republic, Great Britain, Finland, Argentina, Brazil, Syria, India, Indonesia, U.S.A., Japan and Australia).

This composition, covering the main areas of the revolutionary movement, was approved at that time by all the fraternal Parties, and experience showed it to be helpful to the successful conduct of the 1960 Meeting and the formulation of its documents. Naturally our Party, which is charged with the duty of calling the international conference, will approach all the Parties and consult with them.

Guided by all these considerations, the CC CPSU proposes:

1. That the meeting of representatives of the CPSU and the CCP be continued in Peking in May 1964.

2. That the preparatory meeting of representatives of 26 fraternal Parties be called in June–July 1964.

3. That the international meeting be held, with the agreement of the fraternal Parties, in the autumn of 1964.

The CC CPSU emphasizes that for the successful implementation of all these measures it is necessary that there be a cessation of public polemics and an abandonment of all types of subversive and schismatic activity in the socialist community and the communist movement.

We hope that the CC CCP will agree to these proposals and will make its constructive contribution to the preparation and implementation of the projected measures. Our proposal of these measures is prompted by deep concern for the settlement of the differences and for the unity of the international communist movement, and these measures are in accord with the fundamental interests of the peoples of the socialist countries, the working class and the working people of all countries, and with the interests of communism.

With comradely greetings,

The Central Committee of the
Communist Party of the Soviet Union

DOCUMENT 9

The Proletarian Revolution and Khrushchev's Revisionism: Comment on the Open Letter of the Central Committee of the CPSU (8)

by the Editorial Departments of *Jen-min Jih-pao* and *Hung Ch'i*
(March 31, 1964)

Excerpts

[*Peking Review,* Vol. VII, No. 14 (April 3, 1964), pp. 5–23, at pp. 7–9, 17 18, and 22–23; also in *The Polemic on the General Line of the International Communist Movement,* pp. 359–413]

.　　.　　.　　.　　.　　.　　.　　.　　.

Our Struggle Against Khrushchev's Revisionism

When Khrushchev first put forward the "parliamentary road" at the 20th Congress of the CPSU, the Chinese Communist Party considered it a gross error, a violation of the fundamental theories of Marxism-Leninism, and absolutely unacceptable.

As Khrushchev's revisionism was still in its incipient stage and the leaders of the CPSU had not as yet provoked open polemics, we refrained for a time from publicly exposing or criticizing Khrushchev's error of the " parliamentary road." But, as against his erroneous proposition, we stated the Marxist-Leninist view in a positive form in our documents and articles. At the same time we waged the appropriate and necessary struggle against it at inter-Party talks and meetings among the fraternal Parties.

Summing up the experience of the Chinese revolution, we clearly stated in the political report of our Central Committee to the Eighth National Congress of our Party in September 1956:

> While our Party was working for peaceful change, it did not allow itself to be put off its guard or to give up the people's arms. . . .
> Unlike the reactionaries, the people are not warlike. . . . But when the people were compelled to take up arms, they were completely justified in doing so. To have opposed the people's taking up arms and to have asked them to submit to the attacking enemy would have been to follow an opportunist line. Here, the question of following a revolutionary line or an opportunist line became the major issue of whether our six hundred million people should or should not capture political power when conditions were ripe. Our Party followed the revolutionary line and today we have the People's Republic of China.

On this question, the Marxist-Leninist view of the Eighth National Congress of the CCP is opposed to the revisionist view of the 20th Congress of the CPSU.

In December 1956 we explained the road of the October Revolution in a positive way in the article " More on the Historical Experience of the Dictatorship of the Proletariat," thus in fact criticizing the so-called parliamentary road which Khrushchev set against the road of the October Revolution.

In many private talks with the leaders of the CPSU, the leading comrades of the Central Committee of the CCP made serious criticisms of Khrushchev's erroneous views. We hoped in all sincerity that he would correct his mistakes.

At the time of the meeting of representatives of the Communist and Workers' Parties in 1957, the delegation of the CCP engaged in a sharp debate with the delegation of the CPSU on the question of the transition from capitalism to socialism.

In the first draft for the Declaration which it proposed during the preparations for the Moscow meeting, the Central Committee of the CPSU referred only to the possibility of peaceful transition and said nothing about the possibility of non-peaceful transition ; it referred only to the parliamentary road and said nothing about other means of struggle, and at the same time pinned hopes for the winning of state power through the parliamentary road on " the concerted actions of Communists and socialists." Naturally the Central Committee of the CCP could not agree to these wrong views, which depart from Marxism-Leninism, being written into the programmatic document of all the Communist and Workers' Parties.

After the delegation of the CCP made its criticisms, the Central Committee of the CPSU produced a second draft for the Declaration. Although phrases about the possibility of non-peaceful transition were added, the formulation of the question of peaceful transition in this draft still reflected the revisionist views put forward by Khrushchev at the 20th Congress of the CPSU.

The delegation of the CCP expressed its disagreement with these erroneous views in clear terms. On November 10, 1957, it systematically explained its own views on the question of the transition from capitalism to socialism to the Central Committee of the CPSU, to which it also presented a written outline.

The main points made in our written outline are summarized below.

> It is advantageous from the point of view of tactics to refer to the desire for peaceful transition, but it would be inappropriate to over-emphasize the possibility of peaceful transition. It is necessary to be prepared at all times to repulse counter-revolutionary attacks and, at the critical juncture of the revolution when the working class is seizing state power, to overthrow the bourgeoisie by armed force if it uses armed force to suppress the people's revolution (generally speaking, it is inevitable that the bourgeoisie will do so).
>
> The parliamentary form of struggle must be fully utilized, but its role is limited. What is most important is to proceed with the hard work of accumulating revolutionary strength; peaceful transition should not be interpreted in such a way as solely to mean transition through a parliamentary majority. The main question is that of the state machinery, namely, the smashing of the old state machinery (chiefly the armed forces) and the establishment of the new state machinery (chiefly the armed forces).
>
> The social democratic parties are not parties of socialism; with the exception of certain Left wings, they are a variant of bourgeois political parties. On the question of socialist revolution, our position is fundamentally different from that of the social democratic parties. This distinction must not be obscured.

These views of ours are in full accord with Marxism-Leninism.

The comrades of the delegation of the Central Committee of the CPSU were unable to argue against them, but they repeatedly asked us to make allowances for their internal needs, expressing the hope that the formulation of this question in the draft Declaration might show some connection with its formulation by the 20th Congress of the CPSU.

We had refuted the wrong views of the leadership of the CPSU and put forward a written outline of our own views. For this reason and for the sake of the common struggle against the enemy, the delegation of the CCP decided to meet the repeated wishes of the comrades of the CPSU and agreed to take the draft of the Central Committee of the CPSU on this question as the basis, while suggesting amendments in only a few places.

We hoped that through this debate the comrades of the CPSU would awaken to their errors and correct them. But contrary to our hopes, the leaders of the CPSU did not do so.

At the meeting of fraternal Parties in 1960, the delegation of the CCP again engaged in repeated sharp debates with the delegation of the CPSU on the question of the transition from capitalism to socialism, and thoroughly exposed and criticized Khrushchev's revisionist views. During the meeting, the Chinese and the Soviet sides each adhered to its own position, and no agreement could be reached. In view of the general wish of fraternal Parties that a common document should be hammered out at the meeting, the delegation of the CCP finally made a concession on this question again and agreed to the verbatim transcription of the relevant passages in the 1957 Declaration into the 1960 Statement, again out of consideration for the needs of the leaders of the CPSU. At the same time, during this meeting we distributed the Outline of Views on the Question of Peaceful Transition put forward by the Chinese Communist Party on November 10, 1957, and made it clear that we were giving consideration to the leadership of the CPSU on this issue for the last time, and would not do so again.

If comrades now make the criticism that we were wrong in giving this consideration to the leaders of the CPSU, we are quite ready to accept this criticism.

As the formulation of the question of peaceful transition in the Declaration and the Statement was based on the drafts of the CPSU and in some places retained the formulation by its 20th Congress, there are serious weaknesses and errors in the overall presentation, even though a certain amount of patching up was done. While indicating that the ruling classes never relinquish power voluntarily, the formulation in the two documents also asserts that state power can be won in a number of capitalist countries without civil war ; while stating that extra-parliamentary mass struggle should be waged to smash the resistance of the reactionary forces, it also asserts that a stable majority can be secured in parliament and that parliament can thus be transformed into an instrument serving the working people ; and while referring to non-peaceful transition, it fails to stress violent revolution as a universal law. The leadership of the CPSU has taken advantage of these weaknesses and errors in the Declaration and the Statement and used them as an excuse for peddling Khrushchev's revisionism.

It must be solemnly declared that the Chinese Communist Party has all along maintained its differing views on the formulation of the question of the transition from capitalism to socialism in the Declaration of 1957 and the Statement of 1960. We have never concealed our views. We hold that in the interest of the revolutionary cause of the international proletariat and in order to prevent the revisionists from misusing these programmatic documents of the fraternal Parties, it is necessary to amend the formulation of the question in the Declaration and the Statement through joint consultation of Communist and Workers' Parties so as to conform to the revolutionary principles of Marxism-Leninism.

In order to help readers acquaint themselves with the full views of the Chinese Communist Party on this question, we are republishing the complete text of the Outline of Views on the Question of Peaceful Transition put forward by the delegation of the CCP to the Central Committee of the CPSU on November 10, 1957, as an appendix to this article.

.   .   .   .

The whole history of the proletarian parties since the War has shown that those parties which have followed the line of revolution, adopted the correct strategy and tactics and actively led the masses in revolutionary struggle are able to lead the revolutionary cause forward step by step to victory and grow vigorously in strength. Conversely, all those parties which have adopted a non-revolutionary opportunist line and accepted Khrushchev's line of " peaceful transition " are doing serious damage to the revolutionary cause and turning themselves into lifeless and reformist parties, or becoming completely degenerate and serving as tools of the bourgeoisie against the proletariat. There is no lack of such instances.

The comrades of the Communist Party of Iraq were once full of revolutionary ardour. But acceptance of Khrushchev's revisionist line was forced on them by outside pressure, and they lost their vigilance against counter-revolution. In the armed counter-revolutionary coup d'etat, leading comrades heroically sacrificed their lives, thousands of Iraqi Communists and revolutionaries were massacred in cold blood, the powerful Iraqi Communist Party was dispersed, and the revolutionary cause of Iraq suffered a grave setback. This is a tragic lesson in the annals of proletarian revolution, a lesson written in blood.

The leaders of the Algerian Communist Party danced to the baton of Khrushchev and of the leadership of the French Communist Party and completely accepted the revisionist line against armed struggle. But the Algerian people refused to listen to this rubbish. They courageously fought for national independence against imperialism, waged a war of national liberation for over seven years and finally compelled the French Government to recognize Algeria's independence. But the Algerian Communist Party, which followed the revisionist line of the leadership of the CPSU, forfeited the confidence of the Algerian people and its position in Algerian political life.

During the Cuban revolution, some leaders of the Popular Socialist Party refused to pursue the revolutionary Marxist-Leninist line, the correct line of revolutionary armed struggle, but, following Khrushchev's revisionist line, advocated " peaceful transition " and opposed violent revolution. In these circumstances, Marxist-Leninists outside and inside the Cuban Party, represented by Comrade Fidel Castro, rightly bypassed those leaders who opposed violent revolution, joined hands and made revolution with the revolutionary Cuban people, and finally won a victory of great historic significance.

Certain leaders of the Communist Party of France of whom Thorez is representative have long been pursuing a revisionist line, have publicized the " parliamentary road " in response to Khrushchev's baton, and have actually reduced the Communist Party to the level of a social democratic party. They have ceased to give active support to the revolutionary aspirations of the people and rolled up the national banner of opposition to U.S. imperialism. The result of their pursuit of this revisionist line is that the Communist Party, which once had great influence among the people, has become increasingly isolated from the masses and has deteriorated more and more.

Certain leaders of the Indian Communist Party, typified by Dange, have long pursued a revisionist line, hauled down the banner of revolution and failed to lead the masses in national and democratic revolutionary struggles. The Dange clique has slid farther and farther down the path of revisionism and degenerated into national chauvinists, into tools of the reactionary policies of India's big landlords and big bourgeoisie, and into renegades from the proletariat.

The record shows that the two fundamentally different lines lead to two fundamentally different results. All these lessons merit close study.

· · · · · · · · ·

Appendix

Outline of Views on the Question of Peaceful Transition

A Written Outline Presented by the Delegation of the CCP to the Central Committee of the CPSU on November 10, 1957

I. On the question of the transition from capitalism to socialism, it would be more flexible to refer to the two possibilities, peaceful transition and non-peaceful transition, than to just one, and this would place us in a position where we can have the initiative politically at any time.

1. Referring to the possibility of peaceful transition indicates that for us the use of violence is primarily a matter of self-defence. It enables the Communist Parties in the capitalist countries to sidestep attacks on them on this issue, and it is politcally advantageous — advantageous for winning the masses and also for depriving the bourgeoisie of its pretexts for such attacks and isolating it.

2. If practical possibilities for peaceful transition were to arise in individual countries in the future when the international or domestic situation changes drastically, we could then make timely use of the opportunity to win the support of the masses and solve the problem of state power by peaceful means.

3. Nevertheless, we should not tie our own hands because of this desire. The bourgeoisie will not step down from the stage of history voluntarily. This is a universal law of class struggle. In no country should the proletariat and the Communist Party slacken their preparations for the revolution in any way. They must be prepared at all times to repulse counter-revolutionary attacks and, at the critical juncture of the revolution when the working class is seizing state power, to overthrow the bourgeoisie by armed force if it uses armed force to suppress the people's revolution (generally speaking, it is inevitable that the bourgeoisie will do so).

II. In the present situation of the international communist movement, it is advantageous from the point of view of tactics to refer to the desire for peaceful transition. But it would be inappropriate to over-emphasize the possibility of peaceful transition. The reasons are:

1. Possibility and reality, the desire and whether or not it can be fulfilled, are two different matters. We should refer to the desire for peaceful transition, but we should not place our hopes mainly on it and therefore should not over-emphasize this aspect.

2. If too much stress is laid on the possibility of peaceful transition, and especially on the possibility of seizing state power by winning a majority in parliament, it is liable to weaken the revolutionary will of the proletariat, the working people and the Communist Party and disarm them ideologically.

3. To the best of our knowledge, there is still not a single country where this possibility is of any practical significance. Even if it is slightly more apparent in a particular country, over-emphasizing this possibility is

inappropriate because it does not conform with the realities in the overwhelming majority of countries. Should such a possibility actually occur in some country, the Communist Party there must on the one hand strive to realize it, and on the other hand always be prepared to repulse the armed attacks of the bourgeoisie.

4. The result of emphasizing this possibility will neither weaken the reactionary nature of the bourgeoisie nor lull them.

5. Nor will such emphasis make the social democratic parties any more revolutionary.

6. Nor will such emphasis make Communist Parties grow any stronger. On the contrary, if some Communist Parties should as a result obscure their revolutionary features and thus become confused with the social democratic parties in the eyes of the people, they would only be weakened.

7. It is very hard to accumulate strength and prepare for the revolution, and after all parliamentary struggle is easy in comparison. We must fully utilize the parliamentary form of struggle, but its role is limited. What is most important is to proceed with the hard work of accumulating revolutionary strength.

III. To obtain a majority in parliament is not the same as smashing the old state machinery (chiefly the armed forces) and establishing new state machinery (chiefly the armed forces). Unless the military-bureaucratic state machinery of the bourgeoisie is smashed, a parliamentary majority for the proletariat and their reliable allies will either be impossible (because the bourgeoisie will amend the constitution whenever necessary in order to facilitate the consolidation of their dictatorship) or undependable (for instance, elections may be declared null and void, the Communist Party may be outlawed, parliament may be dissolved, etc.).

IV. Peaceful transition to socialism should not be interpreted in such a way as solely to mean transition through a parliamentary majority. The main question is that of the state machinery. In the 1870s Marx was of the opinion that there was a possibility of achieving socialism in Britain by peaceful means, because "at that time England was a country in which militarism and bureaucracy were less pronounced than in any other." For a period after the February Revolution, Lenin hoped that through "all power to the Soviets" the revolution would develop peacefully and triumph, because at that time "the arms were in the hands of the people." Neither Marx nor Lenin meant that peaceful transition could be realized by using the old state machinery. Lenin repeatedly elaborated on the famous saying of Marx and Engels, "The working class cannot simply lay hold of the ready-made state machinery and wield it for its own purposes."

V. The social democratic parties are not parties of socialism. With the exception of certain Left wings, they are parties serving the bourgeoisie and capitalism. They are a variant of bourgeois political parties. On the question of socialist revolution, our position is fundamentally different from that of the social democratic parties. This distinction must not be obscured. To obscure this distinction only helps the leaders of the social democratic parties to deceive the masses and hinders us from winning the masses away from the influence of the social democratic parties. However, it is unquestionably very important to strengthen our work with respect to the social democratic parties and strive to establish a united front with their Left and middle groups.

VI. Such is our understanding of this question. We do hold differing views on this question, but out of various considerations we did not state our views after the 20th Congress of the Communist Party of the Soviet Union. Since a joint declaration is to be issued, we must now explain our views. However, this need not prevent us from attaining common language in the draft declaration. In order to show a connection between the formulation of this question in the draft declaration and the formulation of the 20th Congress of the Communist Party of the Soviet Union, we agree to take the draft put forward today by the Central Committee of the Communist Party of the Soviet Union as a basis, while proposing amendments in certain places.

DOCUMENT 10

On the Struggle of the CPSU for the Solidarity of the International Communist Movement : Report by M. A. Suslov on February 14, 1964 at the Plenum of the CPSU Central Committee

Complete Text

[*Pravda*, April 3, 1964, pp. 1–8, quoted from *CDSP*, Vol. XVI, No. 13 (April 22, 1964), pp. 5–16, and No. 14 (April 29, 1964), pp. 3–17]

Comrades!

The plenary session of the CPSU Central Committee has discussed vital questions of the development of agriculture that have exceptional importance for our country and for the Soviet people. The plenary session is being held in an atmosphere of the complete unanimity of the Central Committee, the whole Party, the entire Soviet people. Its decisions will open broad horizons to the Soviet economy, great possibilities for the unswerving advance of socialist agriculture, for the burgeoning of the productive forces of our homeland, the creation of the material and technical base of communism and the fullest satisfaction of the material and spiritual needs of the Soviet people.

While displaying tireless concern for the development of the country's economy, our party is also fulfilling its internationalist duty to the working people of the whole world. The more substantial our economic successes and the better the life of the Soviet people, the higher will be the prestige of the first socialist state in the world and the more attractive will be the ideas of socialism and communism. Through their tireless labour the Soviet people are making a contribution to the strengthening of the world socialist system, are rendering ever-increasing aid and support to the struggle of the peoples of all countries for social and national liberation, against imperialism and colonialism.

The revolutionary process, which has embraced all the continents of the globe, continues to develop and deepen. New successes have been won in the development of the world socialist system. The workers' movement in the capitalist countries is growing stronger. The national-liberation struggle of the African, Asian and Latin American peoples is broadening. The superiority of the forces of socialism and peace over the forces of imperialism and war is becoming increasingly evident. Through the combined efforts of the world socialist system and all other peace-loving forces, it has been possible to bring about a certain relaxation of international tension, to take important new steps in the direction of strengthening peace, and to disrupt the attempts by the most aggressive imperialist circles to ignite a thermonuclear war. The whole course of world development confirms the correctness of the general line of the international Communist movement worked out at the 1957 and 1960 conferences of the fraternal parties, the vital force of the conclusions and tenets of the 20th and 22nd Congresses of our party and of the Leninist CPSU Program.

The achievements of the socialist countries, of the entire world Communist movement, are indisputable. However, our successes could have been even more significant were it not for the serious difficulties that have arisen in the socialist camp and the Communist movement in connection with the schismatic activity of the leaders of the Communist Party of China.

The members of the Central Committee have been repeatedly informed of the differences between the CCP leaders and the CPSU and other Marxist-Leninist parties. However, the Presidium of the Central Committee has considered it necessary to raise this question once again at this plenary session, inasmuch as the Chinese leaders have gone even further in their factional activities and have created the direct threat of a split in the world Communist movement.

If we analyze the evolution of the views and actions of the CCP leadership, beginning with the Moscow conference of 1960, we can see that during all these years the Chinese leaders have been working not toward eliminating but toward aggravating the differences that have arisen. Having begun with a revision of certain tactical postulates of the world Communist movement, they have widened step by step their divergence from the CPSU and the other fraternal parties on the most important problems of the present day and have in the end countered the general course of the world Communist movement with their own special course, which revises from positions of great-power chauvinism and petty-bourgeois adventurism the basic tenets of the Declaration and the Statement.

The new evaluations and conclusions worked out as a result of the collective efforts of the fraternal parties on the basis of the creative application of the principles of Marxism-Leninism to the conditions of our epoch — on the role of the world socialist system, on the paths of the construction of socialism and communism, on the possibility of averting a world war, on the peaceful coexistence of countries with different social systems, on the necessity for a struggle against the ideology and practice of the cult of the individual, on the forms of the transition to socialism in the developed capitalist countries and the countries that have liberated themselves from colonialism — all this is being distorted and in effect cast aside by the Chinese leadership.

Having virtually cast aside the Declaration and Statement collectively worked out by the Communist and Workers' Parties, the CCP leaders are proposing to the fraternal parties their own notorious " 25 points," the true sense of which in effect reduces to: denial of the increasingly decisive influence of the socialist system on the course of world development; a disdainful attitude toward the struggle of the working class in the capitalist countries; the counterposing of the national-liberation movement to the world system of socialism and the international workers' movement;

adventurism in foreign policy and the maintenance of the atmosphere of the " cold war "; sectarianism and putschism in questions of revolution; the defense and preservation of the methods and practises of the cult of the individual that have been condemned by the Communist movement; and justification of the factional struggle within the Communist movement.

Thus the Chinese leaders have brought their divergencies from the Communist movement to such a stage that they have actually grown into differences on all vital questions.

The participants in the plenary session know that the CPSU Central Committee has more than once displayed initiative and striven to create conditions for overcoming the differences, for normalizing the relations of the CCP with the CPSU and other parties.

We and other Marxist-Leninist parties have repeatedly proposed to the CCP leadership that public polemics be halted. To be specific, this proposal was made in Comrade N. S. Khrushchev's speeches on Oct. 25 and Nov. 7, 1963. At the end of November, 1963, the CPSU Central Committee sent the Central Committee of the Communist Party of China a letter in which it proposed a number of concrete steps toward eliminating the differences and strengthening economic, scientific, technical and cultural cooperation between the USSR and the CPR. In this letter the CPSU Central Committee again proposed the cessation of open polemics. You know, comrades, that in conformity with this proposal the Soviet press in recent months has refrained from publishing any polemical materials.

But how did the Chinese leaders regard these steps? Blinded by nationalistic arrogance, the Chinese leadership did not heed the opinion and appeal of the fraternal parties. It rejected our initiative and embarked on the path of open political struggle against the collectively worked-out course of the Marxist-Leninist parties.

The CPR press has been uninterruptedly publishing materials containing the grossest attacks on the CPSU and other Marxist-Leninist parties. More than 200 articles of this nature have been printed in the newspaper *Jen-min Jih-pao*, an organ of the CCP Central Committee, in the period since Oct. 25, 1963, alone. Slanderous articles are being distributed throughout the world by Chinese organizations and broadcast in foreign languages on the radio; many of the anti-Soviet articles have been broadcast scores of times. Strange as it may seem, the inculcation in the Chinese population of a spirit of hostility to the USSR and the CPSU has today become all but the chief aspect in the activity of the Central Committee of the Communist Party of China. An enormous propaganda apparatus is now engaged chiefly in preparing materials aimed at smearing the CPSU and the Soviet Union.

In its general direction and in the brazenness of its attacks on the CPSU and other Marxist-Leninist parties, Chinese propaganda is increasingly entering the same ranks as the anti-Soviet, anticommunist agencies of the reactionary imperialist circles.

Let us take, for example, an article published in the newspaper *Jen-min Jih-pao* and the magazine *Hung Ch'i* on Feb. 4, from a series of so-called " answers " to the July 14, 1963, open letter of the CPSU Central Committee. This entire article, starting with its headline, " The CPSU Leaders Are the Greatest Splitters of Our Time," consists of filthy anti-Soviet attacks and slander against the CPSU Central Committee and its leadership. It has nothing in common with the elementary norms of relations between Communists and is an insult to our whole party, to the entire Soviet people.

The article contains such wild allegations as that our party, " in collusion with American imperialism, world reaction, Tito's clique of renegades and right-wing social-democrats, is waging a struggle against the fraternal socialist countries, against the fraternal parties, against all Marxist-Leninists and revolutionary peoples of the world."

Whereas a short time ago Chinese propaganda aimed its attacks largely at the foreign-policy course of the CPSU, our internal policy is now being subjected to open attacks. The CCP leadership is endeavouring in every way to discredit the line of the 20th CPSU Congress on all questions, to declare the struggle against the Stalin cult a mistake and to cast aspersions on the Program of the CPSU.

Reviving practices and methods already applied by the Trotskyites, the Chinese leaders are attempting to place the Soviet people, Soviet Communists in opposition to the leadership of the Party, the leadership of the country. Matters have come to such a pass that the Chinese press and radio are appealing to Soviet people to fight against the Central Committee of our party and the Soviet government.

What is this? A struggle for the " purity " of Marxism-Leninism? No, it is the most outright rejection of the elementary norms of mutual relations between Communist Parties, rejection of Marxist-Leninist principles of relations between socialist countries, a transition to a position of open anti-Sovietism.

The CCP leaders no longer limit their actions to the sphere of ideology. They have carried over ideological differences to interstate relations, to the realm of the practical policies of the socialist countries and the Communist Parties. Striving to weaken the unity and solidarity of the socialist commonwealth, the CCP leadership is permitting itself every kind of maneuver and contrivance to undermine the economic and political relations between the socialist countries, to introduce discord into their actions in the international arena. The undermining, schismatic activity of the Chinese leaders in the world Communist movement has recently been sharply stepped up. There is no longer any doubt that Peking has plotted a course toward a split in the Communist Parties, toward the creation of factions and groups hostile to Marxism-Leninism.

Such, comrades, is the actual state of affairs that has taken shape in the Communist movement as a result of the schismatic activities of the CCP leadership.

Attempting to conceal their departure from the positions of Marxism-Leninism, the Chinese leaders have recently been maneuvering intensively, masking their objectives and schemes and talking at length about their " revolutionism," " boldness," resoluteness " and so on. But the further events develop and the more hysterical becomes the tone of Chinese propaganda, the more obvious it is that the true plans of the Chinese leadership have nothing in common with Marxism-Leninism, with the interests of world socialism. It is becoming increasingly clear that under the cloak of ultrarevolutionary phrases and slogans, the CCP leadership is now waging a furious attack upon the gains of world socialism, concentrating its main fire not against the imperialists but predominantly against the CPSU and other Marxist-Leninist parties.

True, the Chinese leaders still have a lot to say about their desire for the unity and solidarity of the socialist commonwealth. But their deeds are completely divorced from these words.

They trumpet about unity, but all their actions pursue another purpose: To disorganize and split the socialist camp, to undermine the ideological foundations and the organizational and political principles that rally and unite the peoples of the socialist commonwealth. They are striving to impose on the socialist countries a " Sinicized " socialism, an adventurist course in foreign and domestic policy, and the ideology and practice of the cult of the individual.

The Chinese leaders intrusively reiterate their desire to " strengthen " the international Communist movement, to " cleanse " it of " modern revisionism " and to unite it on a " new basis." However, the true purpose of the CCP leadership consists in employing every kind of political turn-coat — renegades from Communism, anarchists, Trotskyites and so on — to split the united front of the Communists, to knock together a bloc of pro-Chinese factions and groupings counterposed to the Communist movement, and to subordinate the Communist Parties to their influence.

The Chinese leaders run on and on about how it is they who are the most reliable and tested friends of the national-liberation movement. However, anyone who believes this will be profoundly deceived. The scheme of the CCP leadership reduces to imposing its adventurist concepts and methods on the peoples of Asia, Africa and Latin America, opposing the peoples to one another on racial principles and disrupting the alliance between the national-liberation and the workers' movements, which can in fact only disorganize and weaken the national-liberation movement.

The Chinese leaders have recently been asserting that they are sincere advocates of peace and persistent fighters for the peaceful coexistence of states with different social and economic systems. But who will believe this? By its provocational position in the days of the Caribbean crisis, by its refusal to sign the Moscow treaty banning nuclear weapons tests in three environments, by its constant eagerness to smear the peace-loving foreign policy of the Soviet Union, the CCP leadership has demonstrated to the whole world its reluctance to fight for the relaxation of international tension, its eagerness to preserve the atmosphere of the " cold war " as a suitable background for an adventurist policy.

All the arguments about the interests of the world revolution and the liberation struggle of the peoples to which the leaders of the CCP Central Committee so eagerly devote themselves are in effect called upon to conceal from general public opinion, from Communists, the chief strategic postulate of the Chinese leadership — the subordination at all costs of the Communist and national-liberation movements to their own great-power, narrowly egoistic interests. It is precisely for this reason that they crudely trample on the principles of proletarian internationalism. It is for this reason that they reshape and distort Marxist-Leninist teaching. It is for this reason that they are taking up as weapons the worst traditions of petty-bourgeois nationalism, the most unconscionable demagoguery and slander.

In view of the schismatic position taken by the CCP leaders and the intensification of their attempts to disorganize the international Communist and workers' movement, the urgent need has arisen to look more deeply into where the Chinese theoreticians have gone astray and into the consequences that can ensue from the schismatic activity of the CCP leaders.

I. Two Approaches to the Question of the Role of the World System of Socialism. — The radical changes that have taken place in the world since World War II are linked primarily with the rise and development of the world system of socialism. The countries of the socialist commonwealth are the main bulwark of all the revolutionary forces of modern times, a sturdy support for the cause of peace throughout the world. The struggle between world socialism and world imperialism is the chief content of our epoch, the pivot of the class struggle on a world scale.

There was a time when the Chinese leaders shared this highly important proposition of Marxism-Leninism. Recently, however, the CCP leadership has been counterposing the national-liberation movement to the socialist system and the workers' movement in the capitalist countries, proclaiming it the chief force in the struggle against imperialism and undermining the revolutionary forces of modern times. In the June 14, 1963, letter from the CCP Central Committee it is bluntly asserted that the center of the contradictions of the modern world, " the chief zone of storms, of the world revolution is the vast areas of Asia, Africa and Latin America." [In the Chinese letter the passage reads: " The various types of contradictions in the contemporary world are concentrated in the vast areas of Asia, Africa and Latin America ; these are the most vulnerable areas under imperialist rule and the storm centers of world revolution dealing direct blows at imperialism." — Trans.]

An editorial in *Jen-min Jih-pao* and *Hung Ch'i* on Oct. 22, 1963, says: " The national-liberation revolution in Asia, Africa and Latin America is today operating as the most important force dealing direct blows at imperialism."

The Marxist teaching about the historical role of the working class is obviously being revised here and the workers' movement in the developed capitalist countries is being belittled. As for the world socialist system, the Chinese theoreticians assign to it the role of a mere " support base " for bolstering and developing the revolution of the oppressed nations and peoples of the whole world. It goes without saying that such a position can bring nothing but harm to both the socialist system and the national-liberation movement, the great cause of the struggle of the international proletariat.

According to the view of the Chinese theoreticians, it seems that the world socialist system is not only failing to render increasingly decisive influence on the entire course of world development but is not even playing an independent role in the revolutionary struggle of the masses against imperialism.

Such a treatment of the role and importance of the world system of socialism does not conform to the actual correlation of forces in the world and directly contradicts the conclusions drawn in the 1960 Statement of the fraternal parties.

The idea that the contradiction between socialism and capitalism lies at the basis of modern world development belong to V. I. Lenin. He said: " . . . The relations between peoples, the entire world system of states are determined by the struggle of small groups of imperialist nations against the Soviet movement and the Soviet states, headed by Soviet Russia. If we lose sight of this we will be unable to formulate correctly a single national or colonial question, even though it concern the remotest corner of the world. Only by proceeding from this point of view can the Communist Parties in both the civilized and backward countries correctly formulate and resolve political questions " (" Works," Vol. XXXI, p. 216).

This was said in the first years of Soviet rule. In our time, when there exists not one socialist state but a mighty camp of socialism, its influence on the "relations between peoples," on the "entire world system of states" and, in the final analysis, on the world revolutionary process has grown enormously.

While attaching great significance to the national-liberation movement, Marxist-Leninists hold at the same time that the chief content, the chief direction and the chief features of the historical development of human society in the modern epoch are determined by the world socialist system, the forces fighting against imperialism and for the socialist reorganization of society. It is precisely on this beachhead that the most highly organized class forces are concentrated, and primarily the basic masses of the working class — the most advanced class of modern society, the one that, as our teachers Marx, Lenin and Engels pointed out, is the gravedigger of capitalism.

The prime role in the world revolutionary process belongs to the socialist countries. This is demonstrated first in the fact that the working class, the working people of these countries are successfully solving social problems and are creating a new society without oppression and exploitation, for the sake of which the peoples are working toward revolution. In creating the material and technical base of socialism and communism, the socialist countries are delivering imperialism blow after blow in the decisive sphere of social activity — the sphere of material production. When the workers and peasants of the capitalist countries see the successes of the socialist states in the area of economic construction, in raising the living standard of the working people, in developing democracy and drawing the masses into the management of the state, they are convinced in practice that satisfaction of the vital needs of the laboring people is possible only on the paths of socialism. All this revolutionizes the masses, helps accustom them to the active struggle against the capitalist system and for social and national liberation.

In the second place, the farther we progress the greater becomes the role of the socialist states as a force directly opposing the aggressive counterrevolutionary schemes of imperialism. Under conditions in which the might of the Soviet Union and the entire socialist commonwealth is fettering the main forces of international reaction and aggression, the working masses and peoples of the colonial countries have the most favourable opportunities for the struggle against imperialism and internal reaction. Everyone who has followed the development of international events in the postwar years cannot but see that the most intimate bond exists between the successes of the revolutionary struggle in the countries of capital, the victories of national-liberation movement and the growth of the might of the world socialist system.

Victory over capitalism on a global scale can be achieved only through the joint efforts of the world socialist system, the workers' movement and the national-liberation struggle of the peoples. Each of these forces makes its own contribution to the anti-imperialist struggle. However, one cannot fail to see that the central point of world policy, of the whole of social development, is the struggle of the world socialist system against imperialism.

Marxist-Leninists can have no doubts about the paramount, increasingly decisive role that the world socialist system plays and must play in the great cause of the victory of the new social system throughout the earth.

The historical mission of the socialist countries is determined by the objective laws of social development, by the immutable fact that the countries in which socialism has been victorious are actually today leading not only all the socialist forces but also all the progressive forces in the world. They are not only a beacon for all mankind to the paths of social development but a powerful material force that embodies Marxist-Leninist ideas, a force that is waging a struggle against and bringing defeat to capitalism in a decisive sphere of human activity — the sphere of material production.

All the facts indicate that the socialist countries have the possibilities for surpassing the capitalist countries in the area of the economy in the shortest historical periods. We will remind you that by 1962 the volume of industrial production in the socialist countries had grown approximately 700% in comparison with production on their territory in 1937, while production in the capitalist countries has grown only 160%. The world socialist system has now emerged on a new frontier of the economic competition with capitalism. Whereas the socialist countries' share of world industrial output amounted to about one-fifth in 1950, it now exceeds one-third.

It is the internationalist duty of the Communists of the socialist countries to build the new society well and successfully, to develop the economy, to strengthen defense capability, to consolidate the socialist camp and to strive to ensure that through the practical implementation of the ideas of socialism they become increasingly attractive to all working people. In our time the merits of socialism are being judged not only by theoretical works but primarily by how Communists solve in practice the tasks of building the new society. If we solve this task well, it will enormously promote the struggle for socialism in other countries. But if we solve it poorly, it will be a blow to this struggle.

What is the attitude of the CCP leadership toward the Leninist conclusion that the socialist countries exert their chief influence on the development of the world revolution through their economic successes? Is it in favour of peaceful economic competition?

Distorting the essence of the matter, the CCP leadership is attempting to prove that economic competition allegedly means that " the oppressed peoples and nations in general no need to wage a struggle, to rise up in revolution . . ." and that " it remains for them only to wait quietly, to wait until the Soviet Union overtakes the most developed capitalist country in the level of production and material well-being. . . ."

It would not occur to a single Marxist-Leninist to assert that peaceful economic competition " can replace the struggle for liberation on the part of the peoples of different countries," that the victory of socialism in economic competition will " automatically " lead to the downfall of capitalism and will save the peoples the need to wage a class and national-liberation struggle. Such myths are being circulated from Peking expressly to discredit the idea of economic competition between the two systems. In fact, Marxist-Leninists see the revolutionary importance of the victories of socialism in economic competition precisely in that they stimulate the class struggle of the working people and make them conscious fighters for socialism. Peaceful economic competition not only does not doom the masses to passive waiting but, on the contrary, kindles their revolutionary activeness. The imperialists are well aware of this; they are afraid of successes in the development of the socialist countries and strive to restrain their progress.

As you see, comrades, in essence the question of peaceful economic competition is far from being an economic one alone. It contains a profound political idea: To win out over capitalism economically means seriously to facilitate the struggle against imperialism by all revolutionary forces. And it now becomes a political question.

Our party sees its chief task to lie in strengthening the economic and defensive might of the USSR and the world socialist system as a whole, in intensifying its influence on the entire revolutionary process. We shall continue to pursue unswervingly and persistently a line aimed at fulfilling the CPSU Program for the construction of communism — the most just social system — in our country. Communist construction is the greatest contribution to the fulfillment of the internationalist duty of the Soviet people. This path was outlined by the great Lenin. Nothing and no one will ever turn us from this Leninist path. (*Applause.*)

In order to win the economic competition with capitalism, the socialist countries must make good use of socialism's advantages, both within each country and in the framework of the world socialist system as a whole. In practice, this means the broad development of both political and mutually profitable economic ties among all the socialist countries, as well as the consolidation of cultural, scientific and technical cooperation among them. The activities of the CPSU and the other fraternal parties have developed and are developing in precisely this direction.

In contrast to this, the Chinese leadership has for the past few years been demonstrating its lack of interest in consolidating the unity of the world socialist system. The CPR has not only ceased coordinating its actions with the other countries in the socialist commonwealth but is now waging an open struggle against the agreed-upon line of the socialist countries in the international arena. The Chinese leadership has openly set a course toward shaking the foundations of the socialist commonwealth and has embarked on the path of curtailing economic ties with the socialist countries, particularly with the countries of the Council for Mutual Economic Aid and above all the Soviet Union. In 1962 the CPR's trade turnover with the Council's member-countries was 2.8 times less than in 1959, and in 1963 it went down almost 20% more.

In their propaganda, the Chinese leaders are openly attempting to discredit economic ties among the socialist countries that are members of the Council for Mutual Economic Aid, which evidently corresponds to their schismatic goals. In their attempts to set the peoples of the socialist countries at odds, the Chinese leaders do not hesitate to use the lies and slander of imperialist propaganda. No sooner does some kind of fabrication about the Soviet Union or another socialist country appear in the pages of the bourgeois press than this slander is seized upon by Chinese propaganda.

In liquidating the consequences of the cult of the individual, the Communist Parties of the socialist countries cleared the ground for the consolidation of relations among the fraternal countries on the basis of the Leninist principles of proletarian internationalism. It is well known that the strengthening of the independence and sovereignty of each socialist country is a mandatory condition for the development of the socialist system as a whole. Without this there can be no voluntary and durable union of nations. The course of the 20th Congress of the CPSU was taken up by the fraternal parties as the sole correct Leninist orientation for the further development of relations among the countries of socialism.

But this course is not to the taste of the Chinese leaders. There is every indication that they would like to give orders in the socialist common-wealth as they do in their private domain, to impose their will upon other countries, to dictate the terms on which they will either admit parties and peoples to socialism or " excommunicate " them from it, according to their whim.

Take, say, the CCP leadership's attitude toward Yugoslavia. As recently as 1955–1956, the Chinese leadership gave a high appraisal to the successes of socialist construction in the Federal People's Republic of Yugoslavia. In the autumn of 1957 the newspaper *Jen-min Jih-pao* said in an article devoted to Sino-Yugoslav friendship: " The peoples of our countries are advancing on the road of socialism." The same newspaper declared: ". . . Yugoslavia has achieved great successes in building socialism." This is how China appraised the nature of the social-political system in Yugoslavia only five or six years ago. Now they are saying and writing something altogether different about Yugoslavia. The same newspaper, *Jen-min Jih-pao*, today asserts that in Yugoslavia " there exists a dictator-ship of the bourgeoisie, and, moreover, it not only exists but is a most barbarous, fascist dictatorship," and that Yugoslavia is a "counter-revolutionary special-purpose detachment of American imperialism. . . ."

It may be asked, what has happened in Yugoslavia. What facts, what real processes in the socio-economic and political life of this country have given the Chinese theoreticians the right to change their evaluations so sharply? There have not been and are not any such changes. If one proceeds not from subjective views but from objective laws, from the teachings of Marxism-Leninism, one cannot deny that Yugoslavia is a socialist country, and that, moreover, the positions of socialism in Yugoslavia are growing stronger. Indeed, whereas in 1958 the socialist sector amounted to 100% in industry, to 6% in agriculture and to 97% in trade, now, a few years after the Chinese press was praising the successes of socialist construction in Yugoslavia, the socialist sector in Yugoslav industry amounts, as before, to 100%, in agriculture no longer to 6% but to 15%, and in trade not to 97% but to a full 100%. All these facts indicate that the economy of Yugoslavia is developing like the economy of a socialist state.

If one does not mistake black for white but looks at things objectively, he cannot fail to see that in the international arena, too, Yugoslavia is coming forward together with the other socialist states for peace and peaceful coexistence, general and complete disarmament, the banning of nuclear weapons, the restoration of the CPR's legitimate rights in the United Nations, and other questions.

Why have the Chinese leaders closed their eyes to all these phenomena? Why are they now insulting the heroic Yugoslav people, calling their country fascist? We have more than once put this question to the Chinese leaders, but we have yet to hear any intelligible explanations from them.

The Chinese leaders allude to the fact that the 1960 Statement of the fraternal parties said that the revolutionary gains of Yugoslavia were jeopardized as a result of the mistakes of the League of Communists of Yugoslavia. In the first place, however, as is clear from the text of the Statement, it did not then deny but on the contrary confirmed the existence

213

in Yugoslavia of revolutionary, socialist gains, and in the second place, as the ensuing years have shown, the positions of socialism in Yugoslavia have been substantially strengthened, which of course cannot but be welcomed.

While striving to improve relations with Yugoslavia and being firmly convinced that this conforms to the interests of the cause of socialism, we Soviet Communists are at the same time not in the least concealing the ideological differences that exist between the Communist movement and the League of Communists of Yugoslavia. We have talked frankly about them with the Yugoslav comrades. But we maintain that the existence of differences is by no means a basis for " excommunicating " Yugoslavia from socialism. One cannot on the basis of whim, on the basis of subjective motives and especially by garbling and distorting the facts, permit or forbid this or that people to build socialism, yet this is exactly what the Chinese leaders are trying to do.

The example of Yugoslavia shows particularly clearly the Chinese leaders' pretensions to being the " supreme arbiters " in relations among the socialist states, their appropriation of the right to judge which country is socialist and which is not. Today, without taking the facts into account, they save " excommunicated " Yugoslavia from socialism. Tomorrow the CCP leadership may hit upon the idea of doing the same with respect to other socialist countries. Can such subjectivism and caprice have anything in common with Marxism-Leninism? Only those who have absolutely no regard for the interests of the unity and solidarity of the socialist countries can act in such a way.

Or let us take, for example, the so-called Albanian question, about which the members of the Central Committee and our entire party have been repeatedly informed. It is known that, beginning in 1960, the leadership of the Albanian Party of Labor, without any provocation from our side, radically changed its political course and embarked on a path of hostile acts against the CPSU and other fraternal parties. The government of the Albanian People's Republic has to all intents and purposes broken off its political, economic and military cooperation with the Soviet Union and a majority of the other socialist countries.

At first it was difficult to understand what motives guided the anti-Soviet actions of Hoxha and Shehu. However, as events progressed it became obvious that the Albanian leaders were singing with someone else's voice, were repeating word for word what was being said and written in Peking.

The Chinese-Albanian alliance is not accidental. It arose on the soil of opposition to the Leninist course of the 20th Congress of the CPSU, on the soil of a hostile attitude toward the liquidation of the consequences of the Stalin cult. As in China, the Albanian leaders' defense of the cult of the individual is linked with the fact that for many years they themselves have been implanting a cult of the individual and resorting to the most vicious methods of guiding the party and the country.

At the Third Congress of the Albanian Party of Labor in 1956, under pressure from party members who, in the wake of the 20th CPSU Congress, were demanding the liquidation of the stifling atmosphere of the cult of the individual and the restoration in the APL of Leninist norms of party life, the Albanian leaders were compelled to admit publicly that a cult of the individual " had made a strongly marked appearance " in the APL. But these " admissions," as well as the promise to put an end to the cult of the individual, were only a maneuver. In fact, the Albanian leaders had no intention of forsaking their vicious practice. At precisely the same time as Hoxha was coming forward with " self-criticism " at the Third Congress, the Albanian authorities were imprisoning and exiling Communists from the Tirana party organization who had spoken out at the city party conference in criticism of the Albanian leaders for violating Leninist norms of party life, for arbitrariness and repressions against honest Communists.

Hoxha and Shehu fought against the course of the 20th Congress because they were afraid for their own situation, because the establishment of Leninist norms of party life in the APL would mean the end of their arbitrary rule. By setting out on an anti-Soviet path, the Albanian leaders have placed their people in a trying position, have created difficulties in Albania that would have been quite out of the question given conditions of normal cooperation with the Soviet Union and other socialist countries.

The Soviet people are confident that despite the present difficulties in Soviet-Albanian relations evoked by the policy of the Albanian top leadership, the peoples of our countries will advance together toward our common goal — the triumph of socialism and communism. As far as the CPSU is concerned, we are ready, as before, to take all the necessary steps in this direction.

The CPSU considers as one of its chief tasks to struggle for the comprehensive strengthening of the world socialist system, for the development of fraternal relations with all the socialist countries on the basis of complete equality and voluntary cooperation, for intensifying the solidarity of all the socialist countries in the joint struggle against the imperialist aggressors, for universal peace, for the complete triumph of socialism. (*Applause*.)

II. Questions of War, Peace and Revolution. — Comrades! The destinies of our great cause, the destinies of the peoples depend to a decisive degree on the correct strategic and tactical postulates on the part of the Communist movement when it comes to questions of war, peace and revolution. It is especially important to take into account the interconnection and interdependence of these questions in the contemporary epoch, for never before in the history of mankind have the successes of revolutionary struggle in each country been so directly linked with the development of the international situation as a whole, with the world revolutionary process.

The Marxist-Leninist parties consider the persistent struggle for peace not only as the fulfillment of their historic mission to mankind — to prevent the annihilation of the peoples in the holocaust of a thermonuclear war — but as the most important condition for the successful building of socialism and communism, the unfolding of the revolutionary struggle of the proletariat in the capitalist countries and the liberation movement of the peoples oppressed by imperialism.

A comprehensive analysis of the correlation of forces in the international arena has enabled the Communist and Workers' Parties to draw the highly important conclusion that it is possible to avert a world war even before the complete victory of socialism on earth and to emphasize once again that the Leninist principle of peaceful coexistence of states with different social systems is the unshakable foundation of the foreign policy of the socialist countries.

These postulates, as is known, were set forth in the Declaration and Statement of the 1957 and 1960 Moscow conferences. The experience of recent years not only has failed to shake but, on the contrary, has confirmed the vital need for a policy of peaceful coexistence. It is thanks to the persistent implementation of this policy by the socialist countries, supported by hundreds of millions of people throughout the world, that it has been possible to disrupt the schemes aimed against peace by imperialist reaction. The fact that mankind today enjoys the blessings of peace is not a gift from the gods. It is the real result of the persistent struggle of all peace-loving forces against attempts to unleash a thermonuclear war, the result of the growth in the might of the Soviet Union and the other socialist countries, as well as of the correct policy of the Communist Parties, which have raised aloft the banner of the struggle for peace and have united all progressive mankind under this banner.

Having embarked on the path of polemics and then of political struggle against the CPSU and the other Marxist-Leninist parties, the CCP leaders have attacked with particular zeal the conclusions of the 20th CPSU Congress and the postulates of the Moscow conferences of fraternal parties on questions of war, peace and revolution. They have supposed that it is precisely here that they will be able to pile up political capital for themselves, and to this end they have flooded the entire Communist movement with accusations of " a loss of revolutionary perspectives," of " capitulation to imperialism."

In order to give some semblance of plausibility to these infamous accusations, the Chinese theoreticians have been resorting to a clumsy and timeworn method: Artificially separating two aspects of a single social process, they counterpose the struggle for peace to the revolutionary movement, representing matters as though these highly important tasks were mutually exclusive. According to the scheme of the Chinese theoreticians, it follows that he who fights for peace and for the prevention of a world war is against revolution, is hindering the revolutionary struggle.

No special Marxist education is required to understand that the CCP leaders, pretending to the role of great masters of dialectics, have in fact simply killed this " living soul " of Marxism, to use Lenin's excellent term. The Communist Parties, bearing aloft the banner of the struggle for peace, are with increasing energy developing the class struggle of the proletariat and the working people and the national-liberation movement against imperialism.

In waging their struggle against the Leninist course of peaceful coexistence and counterposing to it the path of " prodding " revolution through war, the CCP leaders have gone so far as to assert that war is an acceptable and even, in essence, the only means for resolving the contradictions between capitalism and socialism. Ignoring the experience of the whole world Communist movement, they are setting forth the path of the victory of revolution in China as an absolute, trying to elevate it to an immutable truth for all countries and peoples. Chinese propaganda, relevantly and irrelevantly, quotes Mao Tse-tung's statements on questions of war and peace made as long ago as the 1930s, during the period of the civil war in China.

They are widely popularizing, for example, such statements by Mao Tse-tung as: " The war that the overwhelming majority of mankind will have to wage . . . will become a bridge over which mankind can cross to a new historical epoch "; " The world can be rebuilt only with the help

216

of rifles"; "We are for the abolition of war, we do not need war, but war can be abolished only by war. If you would like rifles to disappear — pick up a rifle."

Almost three decades have passed since these statements were made. Radical changes have taken place in the world: The world socialist system has evolved and grown into a mighty force, the revolutionary movement of the working class has acquired a mass character and the national-liberation movement has achieved historic victories. The alliance of peace-loving forces, as has been pointed out in the documents of the Communist Parties, is now in a position to overpower the forces of imperialism and to prevent them from unleashing a new world war. The task of preventing war has become especially urgent by virtue of the fact that the most destructive weapons in the history of mankind have been created and reserves of them that could bring incalculable calamities upon all peoples have been stockpiled.

The Chinese leaders do not want to take all this into consideration. Openly flaunting their foolhardiness, they affirm that the nuclear bomb is a "paper tiger" and that it allegedly introduces nothing new into the question of war and peace. In keeping with this logic, which contradicts elementary common sense, Mao Tse-tung tried to prove at the 1957 Moscow conference that the cause of the struggle for socialism would even benefit as a result of a world thermonuclear war. "Can one foretell," he said, "the number of human lives that might be lost as a result of a future war? Possibly it will be one-third of the world's total population of 2,700,000,000, that is, only 900,000,000 people. . . . I argued with Nehru on this question. He was more pessimistic about it. I told him that even if half of mankind was annihilated, the other half would still remain, while imperialism would be completely destroyed and only socialism would exist throughout the world, and in half a century or a whole century the population would again grow, by even more than half."

Such a concept is even more plainly expressed in the anthology "Long Live Leninism! ", approved and distributed by the CCP Central Committee. "The victorious peoples," it says, "will create rapidly on the ruins of dead imperialism a future that is a thousand times more beautiful." This is an example of ultrarevolutionary phrasemongering and complete political irresponsibility that is especially dangerous because it is being displayed by people who stand at the helm of a great socialist state.

It is known that as far back as 1918, V. I. Lenin pointed out that a world war in which mighty technological achievements are used with such energy for the mass destruction of millions of human lives not only would be a crime of the greatest magnitude but could lead "to the undermining of the very conditions for the existence of human society " ("Works," Vol. XXVII, p. 386). In our time, with the creation and development of nuclear missiles, this danger has grown even greater. How can people, especially those who adhere to communist teaching, ignore this fact?

A world war is not needed by the socialist countries, is not needed by the working people, it cannot serve the cause of the triumph of socialism. Specialists have drawn completely unambiguous conclusions about the possible consequences of a new world war. Thus Linus Pauling, the progressive American scientist, has cited calculations showing that within 60 days after the outbreak of a nuclear war, 170,000,000 of the 190,000,000 Americans would have perished, 15,000,000 would have suffered gravely

217

and only 5,000,000 would remain relatively unharmed. A similar situation would apparently take shape in other regions drawn directly into the sphere of military actions. In addition, we must take into account such delayed consequences of a nuclear war as the disorganization of society stemming from the destruction of the most important industrial centers and of the means of transportation and communications and the build-up of radioactive contamination. It can be said bluntly that should a thermonuclear world conflict arise, it would be the greatest tragedy for mankind and would, of course, bring grave losses to the cause of communism.

Not one party that truly cherishes the interests of the people can fail to be aware of its responsibility in the struggle to avert a new world war. Yet the Chinese leaders, as we have seen, are even bragging that they are ready, allegedly " for the sake of the revolution," to consent to the annihilation of one-half of mankind. They are not in the least troubled by the fact that, should this destruction occur, the losses in densely populated countries located in the center of military operations would be so great that the question of the victory of socialism would no longer arise for entire peoples, inasmuch as they would have disappeared from the face of the earth.

This is an appropriate moment to recall certain facts. When a Czechoslovak journalist mentioned in a conversation with T'ao Chu, a member of the CCP Central Committee, that in the event of a thermonuclear war the whole nation of Czechoslovakia, with its population of 14,000,000, might perish, he was answered: " In the event of a devastating war, the small countries in the socialist camp will have to subordinate their interests to the general interests of the camp as a whole." Another high official of the CPR asserted in a conversation with Soviet representatives that Comrade Togliatti, General Secretary of the Italian Communist Party, was in error when he said, expressing alarm over the fate of his people, that in the event of a thermonuclear war all Italy would be destroyed. " After all, other peoples will remain," this official declared, " and imperialism will be wiped out. . . ."

In order to disprove the conclusions of the international Communist movement on the possibility of averting war, Peking has been claiming that the CPSU and the other fraternal parties, in conducting a policy of peaceful coexistence, are allegedly assuming that the nature of imperialism has changed, are pinning all their hopes on " the love for peace and the humaneness of the imperialists " and " are begging and imploring " them for peace, but the CCP leaders say they themselves are waging a resolute and implacable struggle against imperialism and are exposing its aggressive essence.

However, no one will be deceived by such crude falsifications and distortions. Attempts to depict Marxist-Leninists in the role of pacifists of some kind look simply ridiculous. The 1957 Declaration noted that as long as imperialism exists, the soil for aggressive wars is preserved. However, the Communist Parties have not drawn from this the conclusion that a world war is fatally inevitable. They have shown that although the nature of imperialism, its predatory essence, remains unchanged, the correlation of forces in the world arena *has* changed, the place and role of imperialism in world economics and world politics has altered and the opportunities for its influence on the course of world events is diminishing. All this compels the imperialists to accede to peaceful coexistence.

The point, consequently, is not that the imperialists have become more " peace-loving " and more " complaisant " but that they cannot refuse to take the growing strength of socialism into account. The imperialists know that the Soviet Union and the socialist countries possess formidable weapons and are capable of giving a devastating rebuff to any aggressor. The imperialists cannot but reckon with the strength of the mighty workers' and democratic movements in the capitalist countries, with the enormous scale of the peoples' national-liberation struggle. The truth that should the imperialist madmen unleash a world war capitalism would be swept away and buried is becoming increasingly clear in the camp of our class enemies. (*Applause.*)

The possibility of averting war, the threat of which remains as long as imperialism exists, does not, of course, arise of itself. It demands that the peace-loving forces exert the greatest energy in the struggle for peace, the greatest vigilance against the intrigues of its enemies. It depends to an enormous degree on the policy of the socialist countries, on their defensive might, on the constant implementation of Leninist principles of peaceful coexistence. It is precisely this policy that the Soviet Union and the other socialist countries are pursuing, standing firmly on the positions of the Declaration and the Statement of the fraternal parties.

It is precisely against this, the sole rational policy, however, that the Chinese leaders have declared a struggle. Proceeding from their own special motives, they are attempting to discredit the principle of peaceful coexistence, assuring the peoples of the futility of their efforts to preserve peace. And, strange as it may seem, the Chinese leaders have declared such a point of view to be an optimistic one.

The anthology " Long Live Leninism! " asserts: " Until an end is put to the imperialist system and the exploiter classes, wars of one kind or another may always arise " ; " Of course, whether or not the imperialists do in the end unleash a war does not depend on us, we are not the heads of the imperialists' general staffs." At the Peking session of the World Federation of Trade Unions in June, 1960, Liu Ning-yi, a member of the CCP Central Committee, said: " Assertions about the possibility of peaceful coexistence only gladden the imperialists." At the session of the World Peace Council in Stockholm in December, 1961, this same Liu Ning-yi spoke out even more plainly: " Those who think that agreement can be reached with the imperialists and that peaceful coexistence can be ensured are only deluding themselves." It is not difficult to observe that all these declarations are notable for one and the same obtrusive and gloomy refrain — " War cannot be averted."

Closely linked with the Chinese leaders' statements against the policy of peaceful coexistence is their position on questions of disarmament, on questions of international negotiations between the socialist countries and the Western powers. They regard disarmament as " an illusion, an unrealizable slogan " allegedly capable only of confusing people. For example, Liu Chang-sheng, a member of the CCP Central Committee, declared at the 1960 session of the General Council of the World Federation of Trade Unions in Peking: " Certain people feel that disarmament proposals can be effected in the conditions of the existence of imperialism. This is an illusion that does not conform to reality. . . . A world without wars and without weapons can come only in an epoch when socialism has gained victory throughout the globe."

Behind these declarations it is not hard to see the Chinese leaders' eagerness to distort the clear position of the CPSU and all the Marxist-Leninist parties, and at the same time to undermine the policy of disarmament, which is an important condition in the struggle to prevent a new world war and bring about a relaxation in international tension.

It is absurd to assert that our party nurtures any illusions with respect to the military policies of the imperialist powers, with respect to their preparedness to accede to general and complete disarmament. As long as imperialism exists, the reactionary forces will cling to weapons as the ultimate means of preserving their supremacy and will use them in wars if they are able to unleash them. All this is perfectly obvious.

But does this mean that Communists must abandon the struggle for disarmament and admit the inevitability of the arms race and a new world war? No, such a passive position would contradict the entire revolutionary spirit of our teaching and the vital interests of the peoples.

We are convinced that the revolutionary struggle of the working people, the general democratic upsurge, the growing might of socialism and the resolute actions of all peace-loving forces can and must constrain the imperialists to reckon, contrary to their desires, with the people's demands for disarmament. We are not fatalists, we believe in the enormous potentials of the popular masses. It is no accident that as much as 70 years ago Friedrich Engels called on Communists to fight for disarmament, and this at a time when capitalism completely dominated the world.

"For 25 years now all Europe has been arming itself on an unprecedented scale. Each great power is striving to overtake another with respect to military might and preparedness for war. Germany, France and Russia are straining all their forces to surpass one another." Thus Engels wrote in the articles "Can Europe Disarm?" "Is it not foolish to speak of disarmament under such conditions?" he asked. And he answered: "I maintain: *Disarmament, and thereby the guarantee of peace, is possible*" ("Works," second edition, Vol. XXII, p. 387).

This is how Engels posed the question! Even at that time he saw the vast social forces that were rising against war. How, then, can one speak of disarmament as an "unrealizable illusion" today, when all progressive mankind is coming forward in favor of disarmament, when the forces of peace have a mighty support in the socialist countries?

The slogan "A world without weapons, a world without war" is in the hands of the Communist Parties a mighty weapon for the consolidation and mobilization of the popular masses for an active struggle against the shameless militarist imperialist circles. Every person, regardless of his political convictions, understands this slogan. Disarmament means an end to the arms race and, consequently, a reduction in the tax burden. It conforms to the vital interests of the broadest sections of the population. Not only Communists but many other social forces are actively supporting and propagandizing this slogan. Why, then, should we Communists forsake it? Isn't it clear that the rejection of this slogan could only weaken the Communists' influence on the popular masses, which would play into the hands of reaction?

Can it be that the Chinese leaders are so naive they do not understand whither their strange logic is leading them and what a great responsibility they bear to the peoples of the world for their reckless postulates, fraught with the gravest consequences?

Not only do the Chinese leaders hold negative positions on such vitally important questions of international politics as disarmament, the cessation of thermonuclear weapons tests and the relaxation of international tension; they are also attempting to paralyze the efforts of the Soviet Union and the other socialist countries that are struggling against the threat of a world war.

The facts show that the CPR government has more than once come forward in the international arena as a force opposing the peace-loving foreign policy of the socialist countries and disorganizing the general antiwar front. It has happened more than once that when an acute situation has formed in the world, one in which unity of action on the part of the socialist countries and all peace-loving forces has been especially imperative, the Chinese leaders have stirred themselves to action. But against whom? Against the Soviet Union and the other socialist countries that were striving to ease tension. It has been observed, too, that each time that it has proved possible to normalize the situation and avoid a military conflict, Peking has been unable to conceal its irritation and annoyance. It was thus during the Caribbean crisis, for example. The CCP leadership did nothing to contribute to the prevention of a worldwide military conflict or to give active help to revolutionary Cuba. In no way did it support the defensive measures the Warsaw Treaty member-states undertook against the event of imperialist aggression, and not a word was uttered to the effect that China would stand together with all the socialist countries in the event of a U.S. attack on Cuba. It was apparent from everything that at that time, when the Soviet Union was prepared to defend the Cuban revolution with all its forces, the Chinese leaders were trying to extract some advantage for themselves from the crisis that had formed in the Caribbean.

It is a fact that precisely at the height of the Caribbean crisis, the CPR government extended the armed conflict on the Chinese-Indian border. No matter how the Chinese leaders have tried since then to justify their conduct at that time, they cannot escape responsibility for the fact that through their actions they in effect aided the extreme reactionary circles of imperialism, aggravating an already complex and difficult situation in the world.

The Chinese-Indian conflict arose over the question of the possession of border territories in the Himalayas over which no clashes had arisen between China and India during the course of many centuries. However, inasmuch as this question did arise, everything possible should have been done to settle it by peaceful means, through negotiations. The USSR government has repeatedly supported just such a solution to this border dispute. However, military operations were unloosed in the Himalaya region. The baneful consequences of this conflict have by now become fully clear. It rendered a great service to the forces of imperialism and did grave harm to the national-liberation movement, the progressive circles of India and the entire front of the anti-imperialist struggle. The imperialists and their supporters, taking advantage of the Chinese-Indian conflict for their own purposes, are striving to undermine the trust in the socialist countries on the part of the peoples of the young national states, to drag India into military blocs and to strengthen the positions of extreme reaction in that country.

221

While permitting a sharp deterioration in relations with India, which, as is known, is not a member of the military groupings, the leadership of China at the same time actually entered into a bloc with Pakistan — a member of the SEATO and CENTO military alliances, which threaten the peace and security of the peoples of Asia. It is a fact that the Chinese leaders, having cast aside all their " revolutionary phrases," in reality have taken up a line with regard to the imperialist blocs that is difficult to reconcile with the principled positions of the socialist commonwealth countries.

It cannot be denied that the Chinese leaders' approach to the selection of friends and allies is rather strange. It may be asked: How is it possible to pour filth on the socialist countries and the Communist Parties and at the same time, and in the eyes of the whole world, shower compliments on the reactionary regime of Pakistan? This is simply incomprehensible.

Can anyone believe that the rapprochement with Pakistan was prompted by the interests of the development of the revolutionary struggle of the Asian peoples against imperialism, about which the Chinese leaders make so much noise?

It is perfectly understandable that the dangerous, adventurist views and postulates on questions of war and peace that the CCP leaders would like to impose upon the fraternal parties have met with a decisive rebuff on the part of the international Communist movement and the broad circles of the progressive world public.

Not only Marxist-Leninists but all the friends of socialism and peace have noted with alarm that the " bellicose " sermons emanating from Peking border on outright justification and even glorification of world war as a means for solving social conflicts.

By coming out on July 31, 1963, with hysterical attacks on the Moscow treaty banning nuclear weapons tests in three environments and thus turning up in the company of the most aggressive circles of imperialism, the Chinese leaders have even further exposed themselves as adversaries of the policy of the struggle for peace and the peaceful coexistence of states with different social systems. The enemies were heartened by this, and friends could not but condemn it.

The Chinese leaders sensed that they had gone too far, and in order to extricate themselves from this situation they began to turn their propaganda around, as they say, 180 degrees. A flood of " peace-loving " declarations has recently begun to gush forth from Peking, and the representatives of the Chinese government are hastening to sign documents having to do with the struggle for peace and fidelity to the policy of peaceful coexistence. This is precisely the nature of many of the statements made by Chou En-lai during his tour of the countries of Africa and Asia.

" A world war cannot be averted," they were saying unequivocally in Peking yesterday. Today they are declaring that to none other than the CCP leaders belongs the credit for advancing the thesis on the averting of war. Yesterday they were reviling peaceful coexistence; today they are passing themselves off as its most zealous and all but sole advocates. Yesterday they were asserting that disarmament is a deception of the peoples; today they sign communiques in which they pledge to fight for disarmament.

This turnabout could only be welcomed if there were any signs that the CCP leadership had actually recognised its mistakes and was taking a correct position. Unfortunately, everything indicates that the goals and intentions of the Chinese leaders have not changed. Their " love of peace " is no more than a pretence masking their true views, which have received the rebuff and censure of the world public. One cannot fail to see that the " love of peace " that is showering down from Peking today is in glaring contradiction to the actual deeds, the concrete policy of the CPR government.

The manifestly adventurist position of the CCP leadership has shown itself with respect to the question of nuclear weapons. It is known that the CPR leaders have stubbornly sought to get the Soviet Union to hand over atomic bombs to them. They took extreme offense that our country did not offer them samples of atomic weapons.

The CPSU Central Committee and the Soviet government have already explained why we consider it inadvisable to help China to produce nuclear weapons. This would inevitably evoke a retaliatory reaction in the form of the atomic arming of the powers of the imperialist camp, particularly West Germany and Japan. As countries that are more highly developed economically, scientifically and technically, they could undoubtedly produce more bombs than China and could create a nuclear potential sooner. And after all, these countries have especially strong revanchist aspirations. It is they that in the past have been the major centers of military threats and militarism.

The Soviet Union's atomic weapons are a reliable guarantee of the defense not only of our country but of the entire socialist camp, including China. The CPR leaders are well aware of this. Nevertheless, they are striving to obtain nuclear weapons at any cost. Very characteristic in this light is an interview that Ch'en Yi, a member of the Politburo of the CCP Central Committee and Deputy Premier of the Chinese People's Republic, gave to Japanese journalists in October, 1963. Saying that China would create nuclear weapons whatever the price, Ch'en Yi declared, according to Japanese press reports, that it might take China several years, or even more, to begin the mass production of bombs. But China, he said, would produce the most modern weapons even if it had to go without pants. And a few days later, a statement by a representative of the Chinese government, published in *Jen-min Jih-pao*, said that China would cling to this course " even if the Chinese people are unable to create an atom bomb in 100 years. . . ."

Thus it turns out that the possession of atomic weapons, which the Chinese leaders call a " paper tiger," is the goal they are lusting after.

In a paroxysm of irritation, the CCP leaders have even gone so far as to say that the threat of an atomic war stems not from imperialism but from " modern revisionists," transparently hinting at the Soviet Union and other socialist countries. In a speech at Pyongyang on Sept. 18, 1963, Liu Shao-chi, Chairman of the CPR, said: " Imperialism has not employed nuclear weapons everywhere and arbitrarily, and wouldn't dare to do so." He followed this with the wild assertion that the Soviet Union, " in collusion with the imperialists," " has monopolized nuclear weapons " and is " organizing nuclear blackmail with respect to the peoples of the socialist countries and the revolutionary peoples of the whole world." If the " modern revisionists," he cried with fervor, " go so far as to use nuclear weapons first and thereby provoke a nuclear world war, they will meet with the sternest censure on the part of the peoples of the whole world."

How touching is Liu Shao-chi's concern lest, God save us, it occur to someone to suspect the imperialists of intending to unleash a nuclear war. And after this, what is the value of the CCP leadership's hypocritical appeals to "adhere to the class approach," to "differentiate between friends and enemies," to fight against the imperialism of the U.S.A. as the chief enemy of peace? Here one cannot fail to recall the crafty rule of bourgeois diplomacy, as expressed by Palmerston: "We have no eternal allies or eternal enemies; only our interests are eternal." It is apparent from all this how little importance the Chinese leaders attach to their own declarations about the aggressive nature of imperialism and about their irreconcilability toward class enemies.

One cannot fail to point out the following example of the discrepancy between the words and the deeds of the Chinese leaders. The question concerns the relations between the socialist countries and the countries of the capitalist world. Here the Chinese leaders have a double standard: one to evaluate the policy of the USSR and other countries of socialism, and the other to evaluate the foreign policy of China itself. Everyone knows the sharply negative reaction of the Chinese leaders to the efforts the Soviet Union and the other socialist countries have been making to normalize and improve economic and other relations with the capitalist countries, including the United States of America. The question arises involuntarily: Why should the normalization of relations between the two great nuclear powers — the USSR and the U.S.A., on whom the relaxation of international tension largely depends — evoke such opposition on the part of the Chinese government? With an obstinacy worthy of better application, the Chinese leaders are striving to prevent the improvement of Soviet-American relations, representing it as "collusion with the imperialists." At the same time, the CPR government is exerting feverish efforts to establish relations with Britain, France, Japan, West Germany and Italy. It is obvious from all this that they would not reject an improvement in relations with the U.S.A. as well but cannot so far see suitable conditions for this.

Never before have so many businessmen, political leaders and statesmen from the capitalist countries come to Peking. CPR representatives have been conducting negotiations with them and concluding agreements on trade, credits, scientific and technical aid, and even political problems.

Do we want to reproach the CCP leaders for such activity? Of course not. This is a normal procedure, constituting an organic element of the policy of peaceful coexistence. All socialist countries will inevitably have to do business with people from the bourgeois states, including not only friends but representatives of the ruling imperialist circles. But the whole trouble is that the Chinese leaders feel that when they themselves develop such activity, it is the policy of true "revolutionaries," while when other socialist countries do the same thing, it is allegedly "revisionism" and "betrayal."

But the attempts to slander our peace-loving foreign policy will inevitably go bankrupt. And our party will continue to fight for the prevention of a thermonuclear world war and for a lasting peace among peoples, will persistently implement the Leninist policy of the peaceful coexistence of states with different social systems. Our peaceful policy, V. I. Lenin said, is approved by the overwhelming majority of the earth's population. Peace serves the cause of strengthening socialism. The working people of all countries and all continents thirst for peace. The Communist Party of the Soviet Union has earned itself deserved glory as the standard-bearer of peace, and it will always remain true to this banner. (*Applause.*)

Life itself has confirmed that the program of the struggle for peace, democracy, national independence and socialism worked out by the Moscow conferences is a program that, by closely linking the struggles for the immediate and the final goals of the working class, ensures the progress of the cause of world revolution.

At the same time, the theoretical platform and, most important, the practical activity of the CCP leaders not only fail to promote the development of the world revolutionary process but, on the contrary, create additional difficulties for the realization of the age-old aspirations of the peoples, who are thirsting for peace and social progress.

It is absurd to counterpose the struggle for peace, for the peaceful coexistence of states with different social systems, to the revolutionary class struggle of the working class of the capitalist countries and the national-liberation struggle of the peoples. For Marxist-Leninists the dilemma " Either a struggle for peace or a struggle for revolution " does not and cannot exist. The former and the latter struggle are intertwined, and in the last analysis are aimed against imperialism. The struggle for peace is one of the most important forms of the people's struggle against imperialism, against the new wars it is preparing, against the imperialists' aggressive actions in the colonial countries, against the imperialists' military bases on the territory of other countries, against the arms race, and so on. Can it be that this struggle does not express the vital interests of the working class and all working people?

We know that peace is the loyal ally of socialism. The atmosphere of peaceful coexistence also favorably influences the development of the national-liberation movement and the revolutionary struggle of the working class in the capitalist countries.

The workers' movement has acquired especially broad scope in recent years. Experience shows that in many countries the struggle of the working class for democratic and social rights is closely interwoven with the struggle for peace and against militarist forces. The struggle against militarism lends political coloration even to the economic actions of the working class. The efforts of the working class and all working people aimed at averting the threat of a new world war contribute to fostering a spirit of international solidarity in the peoples, for under present-day conditions the struggle for peace is as never before international in essence.

What does it mean to fight for peace in a country such as the Federal Republic of Germany, for example? It means first of all to actively oppose the large monopolies, which are nurturing ideas of revanche, to oppose their attacks on the vital rights and political freedoms of the working people. In participating in such a struggle the revolutionary working class not only does not " become dissolved " in the mass democratic movement, as the Chinese leaders assert, but undergoes a unique schooling in revolutionary organization and discipline, consolidates its ranks and intensifies its influence on the masses.

It goes without saying that the struggle for peace is a general democratic movement and does not and cannot set itself the task of socialist transformations. Incidentally, the CCP leaders, who are attempting to thrust upon the movement of peace partisans tasks that are not germane to it, do not understand this at all. But the struggle for peace works for socialism, inasmuch as it is waged against militarism — the source of the threat of war — and brings to the broadest popular masses a clearer understanding of their vital interests.

The repudiation of the extremely close tie between the struggle for peace and the struggle for socialism exposes the essence of the CCP leaders' profound lack of faith in the strength of the popular masses, in their capability for organized action in the class struggle. The essence of the present concepts of the CCP leadership on the question of revolution consists in the rejection of Lenin's teaching on the socialist revolution as the result of a struggle by the popular massses, in their orientation exclusively toward armed uprising everywhere and in all cases, without taking into account the mood of the masses, their readiness for revolution, without taking into account the internal and external conditions.

The extraordinary harm of such a course lies in the fact that laborious and patient work with the masses and reliance on the ripening of objective and subjective conditions for a socialist revolution are replaced by revolutionary phrases or, even worse, by adventurist acts on the part of a handful of men who have been cut off from the people. Can this kind of action have anything in common with Marxism-Leninism, or is it not rather the propaganda of Blanquist and Trotskyite ideas that were refuted long ago?

No matter how the CCP leaders try to prove the contrary, one of the sharpest points of the polemic that has flared up in the Communist movement lies not in the dilemma of "whether or not to carry out the revolution" but in the problem of "the paths for carrying out the revolution." If the Communist Parties pin all their hopes solely and exclusively on armed struggle, without always taking into consideration whether the popular masses are ready to support such a struggle, it will inevitably lead only to bitter defeats.

In other words, the Chinese leaders have forgotten one of the most important tenets of Marxist-Leninist teaching, namely: A revolution cannot be hastened or made to order, it cannot be prodded from without. V. I. Lenin said that "there are people who think that a revolution can be brought about in a foreign country by command, by agreement. These people are either madmen or provocateurs" (Vol. XXVII, p. 441). Revolution is a task for the hands of the popular masses, guided by the proletariat and its revolutionary vanguard. Needless to say, this does not in the least mean that Marxist-Leninists are obliged to wait passively until a favorable situation takes shape. The experience of the CPSU shows that even a party that is comparatively small in numbers but that has been tempered and that enjoys the support of the proletarians and the progressive part of the peasantry is capable of heading a revolution and leading the people. But in order to do this, as V. I. Lenin never grew tired of emphasizing, it is necessary that a revolutionry situation evolve in each country, a situation in which the "upper strata" can no longer govern and the "lower strata" no longer want to live in the old way.

Realistically evaluating the present-day situation, the fraternal parties admit of the possibility of a transition from capitalism to socialism by either peaceful or nonpeaceful means.

However, regardless of the form in which the transition from capitalism is carried out, it is possible only through a socialist revolution, the dictatorship of the proletariat in its various forms. In each separate country the real possibility of the peaceful or nonpeaceful transition to socialism is determined by concrete historical conditions. The fraternal parties in the capitalist countries are invariably guided by Lenin's instruction that the working class must master all the forms and means of revolutionary struggle without exception, must be ready for the swiftest and most unexpected substitution of one form of struggle for another, employing them in conformity with the concrete situation. The Chinese leaders, however, are coming out against this creative approach to questions of the tactics of the fraternal parties and are trying to decree from Peking how and when they should effect the revolution in their countries. It is completely understandable that such " decrees " evoke a unanimous rebuff from Marxist-Leninists.

Our party has always stood immovably on the positions of proletarian internationalism. No slander and no filthy fabrications can smear the banner of proletarian internationalism that we hold sacred. Our party will continue tirelessly to strengthen its solidarity with the working class, the toiling masses of the capitalist countries, who are fighting for the downfall of the capitalist system and the transformation of society on socialist foundations. This is the path bequeathed to us by Lenin, and we shall follow this path unswervingly. (*Applause.*)

III. The Course of the CCP Leaders Toward Isolating the National-Liberation Movement From the International Working Class. — The Chinese leaders are pinning special hopes on using the national-liberation movement for their own ends.

The downfall of the colonial system of imperialism and the tasks and prospects of the countries that have liberated themselves represent one of the cardinal problems of the social progress of all mankind. Imperialism and internal reaction are attempting to halt the development of national-liberation revolutions and to push the liberated countries into the snare of neocolonialism. The progressive democratic forces are fighting for complete national liberation, for the transition to the noncapitalist path of development. The historical destinies of hundreds and hundreds of millions of people depend on the outcome of this struggle.

The Communist Parties of the world, having generalized the vast experience of the anti-imperialist movement at their international conferences, have advanced a clear-cut program of action aimed at further developing the struggle of the Asian, African and Latin American peoples for final national and social liberation.

The Chinese leaders have countered this Marxist-Leninist program with their special course and are attempting to impose upon the national-liberation movement tenets that could push it off onto a dangerous path and that jeopardize the gains of the peoples of Asia, Africa and Latin America.

The Chinese leaders are characterized first and foremost by their complete disregard for the whole vast diversity of conditions in which the Asian, African and Latin American countries find themselves. As is known, these countries are at different stages of socio-economic and political development. There is a group of countries that have already embarked on the path of socialism. There is a group of countries that have won political independence and have set about making radical social transformations. There is a group of countries where power has been seized by the national bourgeoisie, which by and large stands on anti-imperialist positions. There are countries that, although they have formally receive independence, have actually not become independent because of the rise to power of puppet regimes or because of their participation in imperialist blocs. Finally, there are still countries where the colonial regimes remain and where the peoples are waging a heroic struggle for their freedom.

It is clear to Marxist-Leninists that the peoples of each of these groups of countries are faced with different tasks. The Chinese leaders, however, are attempting to impose uniform, stereotyped patterns and methods of struggle on the Communist Parties and all progressive forces. This is expressed especially graphically in what they are passing off as the chief tasks of the national-liberation movement at the present stage.

Marxist-Leninists consider that for the former colonies where the political sway of the imperialists has been ended — and such is the case for the overwhelming majority — the chief task consists in strengthening the independence that has been won, extirpating the roots of colonialism in their economy, developing the national economy at rapid rates, bringing about economic independence and pursuing the path of social and economic progress. Moving into the foreground are such general national problems as the squeezing out of foreign monopolies; agrarian reforms in the interests of the peasantry; the development of national industry, primarily along the path of creating a state sector; and the democratization of public and political life. In the course of the solution of these tasks the prerequisites are already being laid down in a number of countries for development along the noncapitalist path, along the path of socialism.

In conversations with delegations from the Communist Parties of the liberated countries and in speeches at international conferences, the Chinese representatives talk about nothing except the need to unloose an armed struggle in these countries. Thus, for example, Liu Ning-yi, a member of the CCP Central Committee, asserted at the Stockholm session of the World Peace Council that " the path of armed struggle is the path toward achieving the final liberation of the oppressed nations."

Marxist-Leninists have always supported and still support armed uprisings against the colonialists, against tyrannical regimes, the liberation wars of oppressed peoples. But they have always opposed stereotyped tactics based on the dogmatic use of any single form of struggle irrespective of the concrete conditions. Such tactics are all the more fallacious in today's situation, when national governments that pursue an anti-imperialist policy have come to power in a large number of the countries of Asia, Africa and Latin America. In this situation, to advance the slogan of armed struggle as something universal means to do twofold harm — to disorient the forces of national liberation and to distract them from the struggle against imperialism.

It is after all absurd to say that the working people of Algeria, Ghana, Mali and certain other countries are faced with the task of an armed uprising. Such a stand in effect signifies an appeal to support the reactionaries who are striving to overthrow these governments. And what except harm could result from an attempt to implement this stand in such countries as, say, Indonesia and Ceylon?

The " leftist " stand of the Chinese leaders for an armed struggle everywhere is nothing but an attempt to push Communists and all democratic forces in the liberated countries onto the path of adventurism.

Experience shows that those who blindly adhere to such a stand do not take actual conditions into account, doom themselves to isolation, cause senseless sacrifices and, far from contributing to the social progress of their countries, actually begin to hinder it.

On the question of the prospects of the historical development of the liberated countries, the Chinese leaders are coming out against such highly important tenets of the Communist movement as Lenin's thesis on the possibility of a noncapitalist path of development for the liberated countries.

Teng Hsiao-ping, General Secretary of the Central Committee of the Communist Party of China, bluntly declared at the bilateral meeting in Moscow in July 1963, that the thesis of the noncapitalist path is "idle chatter," although every Communist knows that this thesis was advanced by V. I. Lenin and has been confirmed by the experience of a number of formerly colonial peoples.

The idea of the noncapitalist path is gaining ever-increasing ground among the peoples of Asia, Africa and Latin America, and for the peoples of a number of countries it has become the slogan for practical action. And this is a tremendous victory for socialism! Capitalism has discredited itself in the eyes of the peoples, and such is the attraction of the ideas of socialism for the liberated countries that the progressive forces, the national leaders of many countries are supporting a transition to the path of socialism and are taking practical measures in this direction, justifiably counting on the support of the socialist countries and the Marxist-Leninist parties.

Except for "leftist" phrases about armed struggle, the Chinese leaders have nothing to say to the peoples of the liberated countries about the paths of the struggle for a better future; in point of fact, they have no positive ideas that could help the progressive forces in the former colonies to fight for socialism.

The Chinese leaders represent matters as though the interests of the peoples of Asia, Africa and Latin America were especially close and understandable to them, as though they were concerned most of all for the further development of the national-liberation movement. The facts, however, decisively refute these declarations. It is becoming increasingly evident that they are in fact guided by other motives. The CCP leadership is obviously striving to seize control of the forces of the national-liberation struggle in order to turn them into a tool for the realization of their hegemonic plans. The arguments of the newspaper *Jen-min Jih-pao* contained in the Oct. 22, 1963, editorial are characteristic in this respect. Straining to prove that "true" Marxist-Leninists exist only in Peking, the newspaper unequivocally lets it be understood that the national-liberation movement should be guided by them. The Chinese leaders call on the peoples of Asia, Africa and Latin America to follow Peking in everything. The article clearly expresses the CCP leaders' pretensions to hegemony in the national-liberation movement and their desire to subordinate it to their own special purposes.

And this perhaps more than anything else sheds light on the true aims of the course of the Chinese leaders are pursuing toward divorcing the national-liberation movement from the world socialist system and the international working class.

It is to these ends that the CCP leaders have circulated their infamous myth that the CPSU "underestimates" the historical role of the national-liberation movement, that the Soviet Union, under the pretext of the struggle for peaceful coexistence, is "refusing to help" the national-liberation movement. There is no need for us to refute this malicious slander. No matter what "strong words" the Chinese leaders use against the CPSU, they are unable to cite a single fact to confirm their fabrications.

But the CCP leadership does not confine itself to slander. In the actions it has undertaken both on the state level and in various international democratic organizations, it is concentrating its efforts not on strengthening the unity of the anti-imperialist forces but on a struggle against the CPSU and other countries of socialism. In particular, this is the way the CPR delegates to the Afro-Asian Solidarity Conference in Moshi behaved.

At this conference Liu Ning-yi, head of the Chinese delegation, said in a conversation with our representatives: "The countries of Eastern Europe should not interfere in the affairs of Asia and Africa. . . . We regret your having come here at all; why are you needed here? It is an insult to the movement for the solidarity of the African and Asian countries. . . . Do as you like, but we will oppose you." The Chinese delegates at this conference suggested to the representatives of the African and Asian countries that inasmuch as the Russians, Czechs and Poles are white "you can't rely on them," that they will allegedly "always be in collusion with the Americans — with whites," that the peoples of Asia and Africa have their own special interests and must create their own separate associations.

The Chinese leaders have recently set about the creation of separate organizations for the countries of Asia, Africa and Latin America (organizations of trade unions, journalists, writers, students, sportsmen and so on), which they intend to counterpose to the World Federation of Trade Unions and other international associations.

In the light of the Chinese leaders' practical activities in recent years, the true political meaning of the slogan they have advanced — " The wind from the East is prevailing over the wind from the West " — has become especially clear. As long ago as the 1960 conference, this slogan was subjected to resolute criticism as being nationalistic, one that substitutes for the class approach a geographical and even a racist one. It plainly bespeaks a belittling on their part of the role of the world socialist system, the working class and popular masses of Western Europe and America.

For Lenin's idea of uniting the anti-imperialist forces of all countries and continents — expressed in the slogan " Proletarians of all countries and oppressed peoples, unite! " — the Chinese theoreticians would like to substitute an appeal for setting the peoples of the East apart on a nationalist and even racial basis. Their slogan about some magic power in wind from the East is clearly calculated to inflame nationalist and even racial moods among the peoples fighting against colonialism.

The long years of enslavement and exploitation by the imperialists and their scoffing at the honor and national dignity of the oppressed peoples have engendered and are nurturing among part of the population of the former colonies and semicolonies a mistrust of people of the white race. The Chinese leaders are trying to fan these feelings, in the hopes of setting the peoples of the former colonies and semicolonies against the socialist countries, against the working people in the developed capitalist countries, and of presenting themselves as the sole defenders of the interests of these peoples. For if one is to expose the secret scheme that stands behind the Chinese slogan, if one is to reveal the long-range goal of the CCP leaders, it consists in the following: China, they reason, is the largest country of the East and embodies its interests; here are born the "winds of history" that are to prevail over the "winds of the West."

Thus this slogan is nothing but an ideological and political expression of the hegemonic aspirations of the Chinese leadership.

It is understandable that, in nurturing this kind of plan, the Chinese leaders consider close ties of the national-liberation movement with the world system of socialism and the international workers' movement to be a serious barrier on the path toward the realization of their schemes. Hence the CCP leaders' course toward alienating the countries of Asia, Africa and Latin America from the USSR and the other socialist states and from the working class of the capitalist countries. It goes without saying that such a course is in radical contradiction to the vital interests of the peoples of Asia, Africa and Latin America, and, as the facts show, it is meeting with growing opposition on their part.

And this is understandable, since the line of the CCP leaders, aimed at undermining the alliance of the liberated states and the countries of socialism, can bring enormous harm to the peoples of Asia, Africa and Latin America first of all. In point of fact, it condemns the peoples of these countries to isolation, separation and the preservation of national narrowness, it shuts them off from the international experience of the revolutionary movement and the construction of the new society and thereby facilitates the imperialists' struggle against the national-liberation movement.

The enormous successes the national-liberation movement has achieved in our time were made possible thanks to its close ties with the people of the Soviet Union and other socialist countries, with the revolutionary movement of the international working class. The Communist Party of the Soviet Union and all Marxist-Leninist parties consider the national-liberation movement to be one of the major revolutionary forces of today, one that is making a contribution of historic importance to the struggle against imperialism and for peace and socialism.

The Great October Socialist Revolution showed all enslaved peoples for the first time in history the real paths of liberation from national oppression. It laid the foundation for that great revolutionary process that has today been crowned with an event of world-historic importance — the downfall of the colonial system.

The national-liberation revolutions have triumphed in new historical conditions. In the first place, the world system of socialism, which is becoming the decisive factor in the development of human society, has arisen and is developing and gaining strength. In the second place, the rout of the striking forces of imperialism — Hitlerite Germany, fascist Italy and militarist Japan — in the second world war has weakened world reaction to a substantial degree. In the third place, the working class and all working people of the mother countries have intensified the struggle against the colonial policy of the imperialists.

All this has created an exceptionally favorable situation for the victory of the national-liberation movement and has enabled it to embrace the colonial and semicolonial peripheries of imperialism on three continents —

Asia, Africa and Latin America. We highly appreciate the help that the national-liberation movement is giving to the socialist countries and all revolutionary forces through its struggle.

The earnest of the victory of all revolutionary forces in their struggle against imperialism lies in their unity. The vital national interests of the peoples of Asia, Africa and Latin America fully coincide with the interests of the socialist commonwealth countries, the working class and the working people of all countries. In this is the objective foundation for the growing solidarity of the revolutionary forces that are fighting against imperialism.

Even in the days when our country was the only socialist state, Lenin wrote that "the revolutionary movement of the peoples of the East can now receive successful development, it can receive solution only through a direct link with the revolutionary struggle of our Soviet republic against international imperialism" ("Works," Vol. XXX, p. 130). Lenin's words resound with especial force now that there exists a world socialist system.

What is the specific meaning today of support for the national-liberation movement on the part of the socialist countries?

The internationalist duty of the socialist states is to thwart the attempts of the imperialists, who are striving to restore colonial systems in the liberated countries and to hamper the realization of the national aspirations of the peoples who have cast off the colonial yoke. In all such instances, the direct duty of the socialist states is to render these countries political and diplomatic support and, when necessary, to restrain the imperialist aggressors, relying on the entire might of the world system of socialism.

Our policy, aimed at helping those peoples that are fighting for their liberation, is based on the loftly principles of proletarian internationalism, on the behests of the great Lenin.

Our party and our government have many times expounded clearly and in detail their views on questions of the national-liberation struggle. In Comrade N. S. Khruschev's recently published answers to questions from the editors of a number of African and Asian newspapers, he said with the utmost clarity: "Every people that has fought against the colonialists has felt the firm support of the Soviet Union and other socialist states. Today we declare once again for all to hear that peoples fighting for their liberation can continue to count firmly on such support." (Applause.)

The peoples of Asia, Africa and Latin America are well aware that the Soviet Union actively supports the just national-liberation wars of the peoples against their enslavers. The Soviet Union, like the other socialist countries, is rendering comprehensive aid to the national-liberation movement — economic, political and, if necessary, military as well — and is doing everything possible to prevent the imperialists from unleashing local wars and exporting counterrevolution by force of arms.

It is sufficient to refer to such instances as the support for Egypt during the Suez adventure of the Anglo-French-Israeli aggressors, the aid to Indonesia in its struggle to strengthen its independence and to bring about reunion with West Irian, and many others. There is not a single people that, having turned to us for support, has not received it. (Applause.) The fighters of the heroic national-liberation army of Algeria, the armed forces of Indonesia, Yemen and other countries well know whose weapons it was that helped them in the struggle against the colonialists for freedom and independence. (Applause.)

In the recent period alone the Soviet goverment has resolutely come forth many times in defense of peoples fighting for national independence. It has given support to the anti-imperialist struggle of the peoples of Panama and Cyprus, has identified itself with the Vietnamese people's courageous opposition to American aggression, warned the imperialists of Britain and the U.S.A. against interfering in the internal affairs of the People's Republic of Zanzibar and exposed colonialist schemes in East Africa.

Now that the winning of economic independence and forward movement on the path of social progress have become the chief direction of the anti-imperialist struggle of the liberated countries, particular importance attaches to the expansion of economic cooperation between them and the socialist states and the extension of economic assistance to them.

The Soviet Union is unswervingly fulfilling its obligation. The sum of Soviet credits on favourable terms to the liberated countries has exceeded 3,000,000,000 rubles. The USSR is aiding in the construction of about 500 industrial and other installations in scores of liberated countries. The Soviet Union is unselfishly aiding in the creation in the liberated countries of a state industry — the bulwark of their economic independence. The Bhilai Metallurgical Combine and the Aswan Dam will forever remain in the memories of the peoples as symbols of fraternal cooperation between the socialist states and the countries that have liberated themselves from the colonial yoke.

Thousands of students from the young sovereign states are being educated in our country. The growth of economic ties between countries of Asia, Africa and Latin America and the USSR and other socialist states has led to the elimination of the monopoly held by the imperialist powers on deliveries of equipment and the extension of credits. These powers have been compelled time and again to accede to concessions to the underdeveloped countries with respect to conditions for loans, in the area of trade, and so on. The weapon of the economic blockade, which had previously operated so smoothly, has been knocked from the hands of the imperialists.

The peoples of the liberated countries know that by relying on the economic might of socialism they can achieve victory in the struggle against the coercion of the international monopolies. They have a vital interest in the economic potential of the socialist countries. In today's conditions, the successes of the socialist countries in the economic competition with capitalism and the expansion of their economic ties with the young sovereign states constitute one of the most important forms of socialism's active support for the peoples of the liberated countries.

The Chinese leaders, however, are attempting to suggest to the peoples of the Asian, African and Latin American countries that the socialist countries' course toward peaceful coexistence allegedly contradicts their interests; they are doing their best to smear the economic aid the USSR and other socialist states render to the underdeveloped countries and are attempting to sow doubts as to the purposes of this aid. But the peoples of the liberated countries, having amassed no small amount of political experience, are able to perceive what the Chinese leaders are driving at and what they really want and will reject a policy aimed at subordinating them to the selfish plans of the Chinese leaders.

The Soviet people are confident that the peoples of Asia, Africa and Latin America, who are well acquainted with the real facts about Soviet aid, will draw their own conclusions as to the value of the Chinese leaders' slanderous falsifications. This will be all the easier for them since they can compare the real deeds of the Soviet Union with the actions of the Chinese leaders in recent years.

We are profoundly convinced that the national-liberation movement, which in our time has become one of the greatest progressive forces of the modern world, will, despite all difficulties and in close alliance with the world system of socialism and all anti-imperialist forces, pursue its own road toward final victory over the forces of imperialism, will deliver the peoples of Asia, Africa and Latin America from their age-old backwardness and will lead them to national and social prosperity.

The Soviet Union has been and still is invariably in favor of the obliteration of all forms of colonial oppression and considers fraternal alliance with the peoples who have cast off the colonial and semicolonial yoke one of the cornerstones of its international policy.

The Communist Party of the Soviet Union has always given and will continue to give comprehensive help to the peoples fighting against imperialism for their freedom and national independence. No slander and no fabrications will prevent the strengthening of friendship between the peoples of the Soviet Union and other countries of socialism and the peoples of the countries that have liberated themselves from colonial dependence. (*Applause*.)

IV. Concerning Soviet-Chinese Relations. — Comrades! The CPSU Central Committee and the Soviet government have always attached great importance to the development of friendship and cooperation with the Chinese People's Republic. Our party's attitude toward the Communist Party of China and the Chinese people is in the fullest sense disinterested and internationalist.

Through the course of many years we have rendered support to the working people of China and their Communist vanguard in the struggle for independence and the victory of the socialist revolution. We considered it our duty to help the Chinese people in a fraternal way in the construction of socialism, in strengthening the international positions of the CPR and in defending its socialist gains.

Our party and the Soviet people know the scope and nature of the economic aid the Soviet Union has given China. The USSR helped the Chinese People's Republic construct in a short time more than 200 major industrial enterprises, shops and other projects, furnished with the most modern equipment. With the Soviet Union's help, entire branches of industry that did not previously exist in China have been created in the CPR: aircraft, motor vehicle and tractor building; power, heavy and precision machine building; instrument making; radiotechnology; and various branches of the chemical industry.

Enterprises built or reconstructed with the aid of the Soviet Union provide China with 8,700,000 tons of iron, 8,400,000 tons of steel and 32,200,000 tons of coal and shale a year. Enterprises created with our country's assistance account for 70% of the total output of tin, 100% of the synthetic rubber, 25%–30% of the electric power and 80% of the trucks and tractors. Defense enterprises built with the technical assistance of the Soviet Union were the basis for the creation of China's defense industry.

During the period 1950–1960 more than 10,000 Soviet specialists were sent on missions to China for various periods. In the years 1951–1962 some 10,000 Chinese engineers, technicians and skilled workers and about 1,000 scientists underwent instruction, scientific training and practice in the USSR. During this time more than 11,000 students and higher-degree candidates graduated from Soviet higher educational institutions.

Soviet-Chinese cooperation achieved its greatest development after 1953, when, on the initiative of the CPSU and Comrade N. S. Khrushchev personally, the elements of inequality in the mutual relations between our countries that had been one of the phenomena of the Stalin cult were eliminated. In 1957 Mao Tse-tung said, " The credit for eliminating all the unpleasantness and accretions in the Chinese question belongs to N. S. Khrushchev."

In 1959 the extent of Soviet-Chinese economic ties was almost double the 1953 figure, and the volume of deliveries for construction projects grew eightfold during this same time. In the period 1954–1963 the Soviet Union gave China more than 24,000 complete sets of scientific-technical documents, including designs for 1,400 major enterprises. This documentation embodied the enormous experience of the Soviet people and its scientific and technical intelligentsia. All this scientific and technical documentation was, in essence, given to China free.

The Soviet Union granted the Chinese People's Republic 1,816,000,000 rubles in long term credits on favorable terms.

The CPSU Central Committee and the Soviet government exerted strenuous efforts in order that China might firmly occupy the position of a great socialist power in the international arena, and they unswervingly strove for the restoration of the CPR's rights in the United Nations. We kept the CPR leadership constantly informed of all the Soviet Union's most important foreign-policy actions and strove to coordinate the foreign policies of our countries.

It should be said that the CPSU Central Committee, while rendering aid to People's China, for its part highly appreciated the support of the CPR. We have in mind not only the deliveries to the USSR of a number of valuable Chinese export goods or the sharing of the experience accumulated by the Chinese people, but the joint struggle for the strengthening of peace and against imperialism and colonialism.

In 1950 a treaty of friendship, alliance and mutual aid was signed between the Soviet Union and the Chinese People's Republic, and it became an important factor not only in the development of multifaceted relations between our countries but in the strengthening of peace in the Far East.

The Soviet Union has observed as sacred all its pledges under this treaty. Every time a threat to the security of the CPR arose, the Soviet Union displayed its readiness to fulfill to the end its duty as an ally. Thus, for example, in the autumn of 1958 Comrade N. S. Khrushchev, the head of the Soviet government, declared in a message to U.S. President Eisenhower that " an attack on the Chinese People's Republic, which is the great friend, ally and neighbor of our country, would be an attack on the Soviet Union." This declaration was decisively reaffirmed in June,

1962. It is apparent from all this how seriously the Soviet government has regarded the cause of strengthening Soviet-Chinese friendship.

Unfortunately, however, starting in 1958 the CPR government began with increasing frequency to take various steps toward undermining Soviet-Chinese friendship, and through its uncoordinated actions in the international arena to create difficulties not only for the Soviet Union but for other socialist countries as well.

Soviet-Chinese relations became especially bad after the CCP leaders went over from individual unfriendly acts to the sharp curtailment of economic and cultural ties with the Soviet Union and other socialist countries. Even on the eve of the 1960 Moscow conference of fraternal parties, the Chinese government demanded from the USSR a revision of all the previously concluded agreements and protocols on economic and scientific-technical cooperation, refused a considerable part of the planned deliveries of Soviet equipment and reduced the volume of Soviet-Chinese trade to a minimum.

Although the Soviet government knew that by such a course the Chinese leaders would bring harm to the friendship and cooperation between the USSR and the CPR, it had no choice but to consent to this. As a result, by 1962 the total volume of economic cooperation between the Soviet Union and the CPR (including trade and technical assistance) had fallen to 36.5% of the 1959 level, while deliveries of sets of equipment and materials stood at only one-fortieth the 1959 figure. The volume of economic cooperation and trade declined even further in 1963.

It goes without saying that we could not be indifferent to the sharp reduction in Soviet-Chinese cooperation. The CPSU Central Committee repeatedly appealed to the CCP Central Committee to avert this process. We proposed a number of concrete steps in this direction. But these proposals found no response among the Chinese leaders. Step by step they worsened China's relations with the Soviet Union for their own special purposes and began to extend the ideological differences to the area of interstate relations.

In setting their course toward the curtailment of economic ties with the USSR and other socialist countries, the CCP leaders initially explained this as follows:

"First, thanks to the aid of the Soviet Union preliminary foundations for modern industry and technology have been created in China; therefore in the future the construction and design of the majority of projects will be carried out with our own forces. We want to lighten the efforts of the USSR with respect to aid to China. However, in the future we shall have to turn to the Soviet Union for aid on those projects that we cannot design, build and equip on our own.

"Second, the CCP Central Committee and the Chinese government have deemed it necessary to concentrate forces on the construction of the most important projects, reducing the total number of capital construction projects and nonurgent projects in order to implement more fully the principle of socialist construction in the CPR: 'Better, more, faster and cheaper.' The scale of construction in the country will continue to be big and the tempos fast.

"Third, as a result of the calamaties in agriculture resulting from the weather in the past two years, certain difficulties have arisen with respect to the balance of payments. Therefore, by reducing the number of projects being built with the aid of the Soviet Union, we hope to create conditions for more favorable cooperation between our countries." (From a declaration on Feb. 10, 1961, by Ku Cho-hsin, leader of the CPR government delegation at the Soviet-Chinese negotiations.)

Now, having apparently "forgotten" its earlier explanations, the CPR government is asserting that the Soviet-Chinese ties were curtailed on the initiative of the Soviet Union and that precisely this is the reason for the grave situation in which the Chinese national economy has found itself in recent years.

Now the Chinese leaders are bending over backwards to prove that, in general, Soviet aid to China never existed, that there were only ordinary trade operations. Striving to erase Soviet aid from the memory of the people, the Chinese are not even shrinking from knocking the plant trade-marks from Soviet machine tools and machines and from concocting the slander that the Soviet Union allegedly delivered obsolete equipment to China. And this is said despite the fact that not only the Chinese themselves but even the foreign press has asserted that such enterprises as the Changchun Motor Vehicle Plant, the Harbin Electrical Equipment Plant, the Loyang Tractor Plant and many others that were built with the aid of the Soviet Union are excellent examples of modern industry.

Such actions have little in common with the concept of elementary decency. While leaving them to the conscience of the Chinese leadership, one cannot help noticing the glaring contradictions in their accusations against the Soviet Union. On the one hand, they are attempting to accuse the Soviet Union of reducing its aid and causing serious difficulties for China's economy; on the other, they are spreading rumors that the Soviet Union's aid was ineffective and insignificant. But if you assume that our aid was "ineffective and insignificant," how could its cessation have harmed the Chinese economy?

To use a favorite expression of the Chinese leaders, where is the truth here and where is the falsehood? The facts show that in all cases there is only falsehood.

Despite the openly hostile actions of the CCP leadership, our country, conscientiously fulfilling its earlier commitments, even now continues to assist China in the construction of 80 industrial enterprises, and engineering and technical workers, scientists and students from the CPR are under-going production practice and instruction in the USSR as before. The Soviet Union responded in a fraternal way to the economic difficulties that arose in China in 1960 and 1961. During the period when the CPR was experiencing an especially acute food shortage, the CPSU Central Committee and the Soviet government offered the CCP leadership a loan of 1,000,000 tons of grain and 500,000 tons of sugar. At that time the Soviet Union granted the CCP five years to liquidate 288,000,000 rubles of its indebtedness in commercial accounts.

If, as the Chinese leadership asserts, the Soviet Union strove to curtail its economic ties with China, why did it have to take all these steps, to continue to render aid in the construction of industrial enterprises and to make proposals again and again on expanding mutually profitable trade and economic cooperation? The CCP leadership offers no answer to this question. And it cannot offer one, since it is the Chinese leadership itself that brought about the reduction in cooperation between our countries.

In order to provide at least some justification for the failures in the development of the CPR's economy that arose as a result of the policy of "the great leap," the CCP leaders quite often advance the question of the Soviet specialists. And although this question has already been repeatedly explained in official documents of our party, we shall have to dwell on it again.

In sending specialists to China, the USSR government assumed that they were needed to assist the development of the national economy of the CPR, which did not have an adequate number of the appropriate cadres. This was in no way a commercial deal but a real manifestation of fraternal aid to the Chinese people.

Aware that the need for foreign specialists is only temporary, that the fraternal socialist countries are quickly preparing their own skilled cadres, the Soviet government in 1956 and again in 1958 raised the question of the recall of our workers. Similar proposals were made at the time to other people's democracies in which Soviet specialists were still working during those years. Inasmuch as the need for specialists had declined, these proposals were accepted by all the countries except the CPR, whose government requested that the Soviet specialists remain for a certain time.

While insisting that the Soviet specialists remain, the Chinese authorities at the same time deliberately treated them worse and created intolerable conditions for their work.

The last years of our specialists' stay in the CPR coincided with the policy of "the great leap," which resulted in violation of proportions in the development of the economy and deviation from technical norms. The Soviet people could not fail to see the dangerous consequences of such a policy. They warned the Chinese organizations about the violation of technical requirements. But their advice went unheeded. As a result of this ignoring of the recommendations of the Soviet specialists and the gross violations of technical norms by the Chinese officials, many major mishaps occurred, from time to time accompanied by the loss of human life. This, for example, is what happened at the construction site of the Sinan River Hydroelectric Station, where thousands of tons of rock came crashing down because of the disregard of technical conditions and the work was delayed for a long period. At the Sinfeng River Hydroelectric Station the coffer-dams burst and the foundation pit was flooded for the same reason. In both cases the destruction was accompanied by loss of life. It is understandable that the Soviet engineers and technicians could not remain indifferent to all this. They protested, but since they were not heeded our specialists began to request that they be returned to their homeland.

Furthermore, beginning in the spring of 1960 the Chinese authorities began to "work on" the Soviet specialists, trying to turn them against the CPSU Central Committee and the USSR government; this evoked the legitimate indignation of our people.

The USSR government repeatedly called the attention of the Chinese authorities to all these disturbing instances and insistently requested that they create normal conditions for the work of the Soviet specialists. But in answer the Chinese authorities only adopted an even more hostile and insulting attitude toward our workers, looking down on them as "conservatives," and began to defame Soviet experience and technology in every way. Surveillance of Soviet people increased, and searches of their personal

238

belongings and so on became more frequent. Under such conditions, the recall of our specialists was the only solution.

Now, when many additional facts have become known, there is every basis for believing that after 1959, when it began to exacerbate its relations with the USSR, the Chinese leadership did not need the specialists themselves as much as it needed an issue about them that it could use in the struggle against the CPSU.

After the recall of the specialists, the Soviet government strove to settle this question in the interests of strengthening Soviet-Chinese friendship. In November, 1960, during official talks with the Chinese leaders at the Moscow conference of fraternal parties, Comrade A. I. Mikoyan declared to them at the request of the CPSU Central Committee that if the Soviet specialists were really needed in China and if normal work conditions were created for them, we were ready to send them back to the CPR. Comrade N. S. Khrushchev said the same thing in a conversation with Chou En-lai and other members of the CCP delegation to the 22nd Party Congress. At the bilateral meeting of delegations from the CPSU and the CCP in July, 1963, and in the CPSU Central Committee's letter of Nov. 29, 1963, the Chinese leadership was again officially informed that if it needed the technical aid of our specialists, the Soviet government was ready to consider the question of sending them to the CPR. The Chinese leaders gave no answer at all to any of these proposals and at the same time continued to use the question of the Soviet specialists for their unseemly purposes. They even attempted to use the recall of our specialists to explain the revision of economic plans and the reduction in the volume of capital construction, as well as difficulties that arose in various branches of the national economy.

But in the first place, everyone knows that economic hardship arose in the CPR long before the recall of the Soviet specialists, as a result of the dangerous experiments of "the great leap." And in the second place, the biggest difficulties arose precisely in those branches in which no Soviet specialists at all, or at most very few, were working.

How, for example, could the recall of the Soviet specialists have affected the work of the coal, petroleum, lumber and light industries and other branches of industry and agriculture if in 1960 just two specialists were working in the coal industry, three in the Ministry of State Farms and Virgin Lands and one each in the systems of the Ministries of Agriculture and Forestry? Meanwhile, the greatest failures occurred in precisely those branches of industry and particularly in agriculture.

Isn't it time for the Chinese leaders to stop misleading their party, their people and the world public and to speak the truth about the real reasons for the difficult situation of the Chinese people?

And the real reasons consist in the ignoring by the CCP leaders of the objective natural laws in the area of economic policy.

What explains the fact that in recent times not only economic cooperation between the USSR and China but cultural relations and exchanges between public organizations as well have been dropping year by year as a result of the efforts of the CCP leadership, while at the same time insinuations and slander against the Soviet people are being intensified? Only one thing: The Chinese leaders are striving to isolate their people from the Soviet Union; they fear that their people will find out the truth about the unselfish, fraternal proposals of the Soviet Union on the development of relations between the USSR and the CPR, and then all their infamous slander, with which they are attempting to smear our party and the Soviet people, will collapse. The CCP leadership is apprehensive lest cooperation with our country bring to China the cleansing breeze of the ideas of the 20th Congress, which blew away the intolerable atmosphere that had been created by the Stalin cult. (*Applause.*)

We also feel it necessary to tell the plenary session about the violations of the Soviet-Chinese border that have been perpetrated through the fault of the Chinese side. Documents of the CPSU and the Soviet government have already mentioned this. Violations of the Soviet border became a constant occurrence in 1962 and 1963, sometimes assuming the form of gross provocations.

The Soviet government has taken the initiative on the holding of consultations relating to defining the frontier between the USSR and the CPR on certain of its sections. In doing so, we proceed from the fact that no territorial disputes exist between the USSR and the CPR, that the Soviet-Chinese border evolved historically and that there can be a question only of a certain clarification of the border where this may be necessary.

Undermining the foundations of Soviet-Chinese friendship, the CCP leaders have organized unbridled anti-Soviet propaganda both in their own country and abroad. The Chinese newspapers are filled with slanderous articles that denigrate Soviet reality and contain filthy slander about the Soviet people. The Soviet Union's foreign policy is described in one CPR government statement as " a policy of associating with the forces of war in order to struggle against the forces of peace, associating with imperialism in order to struggle against socialism."

All these assertions are slanderous mumbo-jumbo from beginning to end, completely obvious not only to our friends but even to our enemies. Soviet Communists and all Soviet people indignantly reject these brazen lies. Let the slanderers go about their dirty business. The Soviet Union will still pursue its Leninist course.

V. Attacks by the CCP Leaders on the CPSU Program. — Comrades! The CCP leaders have recently been extending their polemic to questions of the internal development of the Soviet Union and other socialist countries.

They have chosen the CPSU Program as the center of their attacks.

It is generally recognized that the Program of our party is one of the most outstanding documents of modern times and that it reflects with exceptional depth and force the practice of the building of a new society in the USSR and the fraternal countries on the basis of the implementation of the theory of scientific communism. In defiance of good sense, Chinese propaganda has gone so far in its attacks on the CPSU Program as to make the absurd, monstrous and slanderous assertions that the Program of our party " is aimed against the revolution of the peoples who are still under the sway of imperialism and capitalism," that it is " aimed against bringing to completion the revolution by peoples who have already embarked on the path of socialism " and even " at preserving and restoring capitalism " (articles in *Jen-min Jih-pao* and *Hung Ch'i* on Sept. 6, 1963).

In coming out against the CPSU Program, the Chinese leaders are trying to discredit the theory and practice of proletarian socialism, which gained victory in the workers' movement after long struggle against petty-bourgeois socialism, anarchism and other antiscientific tendencies. The CCP leaders — whether they recognize it or not — are resurrecting the idea of petty-bourgeois socialism and from these positions are attempting to criticize the international experience of the building of the new soceity.

The Chinese leaders attack the CPSU because it is pursuing a line toward raising the people's well-being. They call the improvement of the life of the Soviet people " bourgeoisification " ; the principle of material incentive, in their opinion, " leads to people's pursuit of personal profit, money-grubbing, desire for gain, the growth of bourgeois individualism, harm to the socialist economy . . . and even its corruption " (*Jen-min Jih-pao*, Dec. 26, 1963).

Is there not concealed beneath these strident words a profound contempt for man's vital needs, for the principles and ideals of a socialist society?

We know what great importance V. I. Lenin attached to the principle of socialist distribution according to labor, to the material interest of workers in developing social production. He taught that the building of the new society must be carried out not by enthusiasm alone but, with the aid of the enthusiasm born of the great revolution, by personal interest, personal incentives and cost accounting.

The Chinese leaders are savagely attacking the CPSU Program's con clusions on questions of the political organization of a socialist society on the way to communism. They assert that the tenets of the Party Program about the state of the entire people and the party of the entire people are all but the substitution of bourgeois theories for Marxist-Leninist teaching about the state, that they amount to the disarming of the working class.

The Chinese leaders do not even try to analyze the actual processes in the socialist countries; they capriciously juggle with out-of-context and falsely interpreted quotations from the classics of Marxism-Leninism. They are attempting to lead the international Communist movement onto the path of pseudo-theoretical discussions of questions that were resolved long ago in the classics of Marxism-Leninism.

One of these questions is their dogmatic assertions with respect to the dictatorship of the proletariat. The Chinese leaders stubbornly reiterate that the dictatorship of the proletariat must be preserved " right up to the entry into the highest phase of communist society." In saying this, they allude to a quotation from K. Marx to the effect that " between the capitalist and the communist societies lies the period of the revolutionary transformation of the former into the latter. To this period there corresponds a period of political transition, and the state during this period can be nothing other than *a revolutionary dictatorship of the proletariat*" (K. Marx and F. Engels, " Works," second [Russian] edition, Vol, XIX, p. 27).

They are trying to utilize this quotation, taken out of the context of the entire course of Marx's arguments, as a theoretical basis for " criticism " of the CPSU Program.

However, plucking out this thought of Marx's, the Chinese leaders make no mention of the next two lines from the same work by Marx, in which he says, with respect to the Gotha Program: " But the program does not concern itself either with this last " — i.e., the dictatorship of the proletariat — " or with the future state system of the communist society." If one is to follow the logic of the Chinese theoreticians, Marx should be declared an anti-Marxist for such a thought. In fact, the Chinese leaders, purportedly basing themselves on Marx's ideas, say: " The withering away of the dictatorship of the proletariat is also the withering away of the

241

state." Marx, however, speaks of "the state system of the communist society," which is no longer a dictatorship of the proletariat.

There is the key. In speaking about the period of transition from capitalism to communism, Marx has in mind the first phase of communism — socialism.

The Chinese leaders are aware, of course, of the repeated statements of Marx and Engels about the two phases of communism, that the dictatorship of the proletariat is the state of the transitional period, the goal of which — the building of socialism — is the first phase of communism. V. I. Lenin, pointing out the inevitability of a long and stubborn struggle for the socialist reorganization of society, wrote about "the whole period of the dictatorship of the proletariat as the period of the transition from capitalism to socialism" ("Works," Vol. XXIX, p. 358).

The Peking theoreticians are doing all they can to hush up this tenet, which Lenin empasized. He said that the dictatorship of the proletariat is needed "for purposes of the final creation and consolidation of socialism" (Vol. XXIX, p. 351), that the disappearance of the danger of the restoration of capitalist relations signifies "the end of the dictatorship of the proletariat" (Vol. XXXIII, p. 75).

This is how Vladimir Ilyich Lenin stated the question.

Life has completely confirmed the correctness of Lenin's tenets. Were the Chinese leaders actually interested in the truth, they might turn to the practice of our daily life to see how the economic basis and the social structure of Soviet society have changed. Lenin considered the most important task of the dictatorship of the proletariat to be the suppression of the overthrown exploiter classes. The socialist society in the USSR, as is known, has long consisted of friendly classes — workers and peasants and the social group of the people's intelligentsia. They are united by a community of vital interests, Marxist-Leninist ideology and unity of purpose — the building of communism.

Against whom do the Chinese theoreticians propose that we implement this dictatorship? What are they getting at, how can one understand their demand that the CPSU pursue a "policy of class struggle" within the country?

We know the result of the theory advanced by Stalin about the inevitability of a sharpening of the class struggle as successes are achieved in the building of socialism. This theory, as is known, served as justification for the grossest violations of socialist legality. The CPSU has put an end to it and will never again permit anything like it. It has pursued and will continue to pursue a policy of consolidating the alliance of the working class and the peasantry, of uniting all the working people in a single collective of builders of communism. (*Applause.*)

The ideas of the state of the entire people and the party of the entire people are not the fruit of armchair meditation; they were engendered by life and reflect the lofty maturity that socialist social relations have achieved in the USSR. In view of the fact that exploiter classes in the Soviet Union were liquidated long ago, the Soviet state, having lost the character of an agency for suppressing the overthrown exploiters, today expresses the interests and the will of all the people, and the party of the working class has become the party of the entire people.

After the complete and final victory of socialism, the working class no longer implements its guiding role through the dictatorship of the proletariat.

The working class remains the most advanced class of society under conditions of full-scale communist construction as well. Its leading role is determined, like its economic position, by its being directly linked with the highest form of socialist ownership and by the fact that it possesses the greatest tempering, acquired through decades of class struggle and revolutionary experience.

All these provisions of the CPSU Program do not in the least have merely theoretical importance. They express the practical line of our party, its policy aimed at enlisting the entire people in managing the affairs of society, at raising the people's activeness in the building of communism, at extending socialist democracy. Yet the Chinese leaders are ignoring V. I. Lenin's precept that "socialism is impossible without democracy" ("Works," Vol. XXIII, p. 62). It is indicative that in the CCP Central Committee's letter of June 14, 1963, and in other statements the Chinese leadership does not even mention socialist democracy or the need for its development in step with the advance to communism.

Can the CCP leaders' idealization of methods of violence, methods of oppression on the entire path from capitalism to communism have anything in common with the Marxist-Leninist statement of the question?

While pointing out that the proletariat could not be victorious without revolutionary violence against the landlords and the capitalists, V. I. Lenin wrote at the same time that " revolutionary violence is a necessary and legitimate method of revolution only at certain moments of its development, only in the presence of definite and special conditions, while the organization of the proletarian masses, the organization of the working people, has been and remains a much more profound and constant property of this revolution and the prerequisite for its victory" ("Works," Vol. XXIX, p. 70).

The Chinese theoreticians assert: "Everyone who has an elementary knowledge of Marxism-Leninism knows that the so-called 'state of the entire people' is nothing new. The representatives of the bourgeoisie always call a bourgeois state a 'state of the entire people' or a 'state of popular sovereignty.'"

This is really a strong argument! By following such logic, Communists would have to abandon the implementation of such slogans as freedom, equality, fraternity and democracy, on the basis that these slogans were advanced by a bourgeois revolution and were then distorted and debased by the bourgeoisie that came to power. We think, on the contrary, that the true meaning of these slogans must be returned to them, they must be embodied in life, and this can be done only on the paths of socialism and communism.

That is how matters stand with respect to the state of the entire people.

When Lassalle spoke about such a state or when the imperialist ideologists talk about it today, Marxists rightly declare that their theory is a deception of the people. After all, in this case reference is being made to a state of the entire people in the conditions of a class society, but such a state cannot exist in a society that is broken up into hostile classes. A state that has outgrown the dictatorship of the proletariat and completed its historical mission of building communism within the country is something else again. Such a state can be nothing other than an agency for expressing the interests and the will of the entire people.

The Soviet state of the entire people, in which the guiding role of the working class is preserved, is continuing the task begun by the state of the dictatorship of the proletariat. It is sacredly fulfilling its internationalist duty to the international working class and to all the peoples of the world. The state of the entire people is constantly waging a struggle against imperialism, reliably ensuring the country's security, making its contribution to the cause of defending the whole socialist camp, and developing fraternal cooperation with the socialist countries.

It is characteristic of the methods the Chinese leaders use in their polemic that they falsely represent the CPSU Program's conclusion about the development of the dictatorship of the proletariat into a state of the entire people under certain historical conditions as a rejection of the dictatorship of the proletariat during the period of socialist construction. The Chinese theoreticians have even gone so far as to allege that the CPSU has " completely jettisoned the quintessence of Marxism-Leninism — the teaching of the dictatorship of the proletariat."

A filthy, unpardonable lie! The CPSU Program says in black and white: " The experience of the USSR has shown that peoples can achieve socialism only as a result of *socialist revolution and the dictatorship of the proletariat.*"

Not troubling themselves to examine the essence of the question, the Chinese leaders are even attempting to smear the CPSU Program's conclusion about *the transformation of the Communist Party of the working class in our country into a party of the entire people.* This conclusion is described as the " organizational and moral disarming of the proletariat " and even as doing " a service to the restoration of capitalism."

Have the Chinese leaders perhaps attempted in any way to validate their monstrous accusations against our party, which is heading the building of communism? They have not! The Chinese theoreticians, without any logic or argumentation, have simply pinned this question to the question of the state. They say that if the state cannot be of the entire people before the complete victory of communism, there can be no party of the entire people. This is the whole of their argument!

The party of the working class, without which the dictatorship of the class is unrealizable, preserves both the form and the substance of its proletarian class nature right up to the complete victory of socialism. This is an irrefutable truth.

But it is also irrefutable that the party, as a political organization, reflects in itself the changes that take place in the class structure of society. The CPSU emphasized in its Program that until the complete victory of communism, the working class will remain the guiding force of Soviet society. And during the period of the full-scale building of communism, the Party will remain the spokesman of communist ideals, the goals of the working class and its vital interests. At the same time, it becomes a party of the entire people. This occurs not because of someone's subjective desires but because the goals and ideals of the working class have become the goals and ideals of all the classes and strata of the people that have built socialism.

In attacking the CPSU Program's conclusions about the historical destinies of the dictatorship of the proletariat, about the nature of the state and the party of the working class in the Soviet Union, the Chinese theoreticians are ignoring the new phenomena of social life, they stubbornly refuse to see that the new conclusions and tenets of the CPSU Program were not arrived at arbitrarily but express what has come into life. In attacking the line of the 20th and 22nd CPSU Congresses, they have gone so far as to cast doubts on the right of our party and our people to build communism.

The transition of a society that has built socialism to the full-scale building of communism is a historically natural and objectively necessary process. For the Soviet people this is an urgent task that has been advanced by life itself. We have all the necessary economic, political and other prerequisites, created as a result of the victory of the socialist system, to resolve it. To impede this process means to attempt to stop social progress. Life has repeatedly confirmed the truth that both attempts to bypass historically inevitable stages of the development of a society and attempts to delay and impede social development are equally unsound and harmful.

The people in Peking have apparently been so blinded by the factional struggle that in the heat of their fever they have not noticed where they have fallen into contradiction with themselves. Indeed, only a few years ago, proclaiming the course of the "great leap" and the "people's communes," the CCP Central Committee asserted: "It appears that the implementation of communism in our country is no longer remote" (Aug. 29, 1958, decision of the CCP Central Committee). Consequently, the Chinese leaders at that time felt it completely possible to make a transition to the building of communism in their own country even though the building of socialism had only started in China. Now, however, they are questioning the building of communism in the USSR, where socialism has completely and finally conquered.

How can one fail to see that the building of communism in countries that have built socialism conforms to the interests of the peoples of all the socialist countries, all the revolutionary forces of modern times? Is it not clear that it increases to an enormous degree the attractive force of the example of socialism, raises the economic and defensive might of the socialist camp and in fact creates increasingly favorable opportunities for expanding real economic, technical, cultural and other aid and support to all the peoples fighting for the construction of socialism, for national independence and peace and against imperialism?

The Chinese leaders are attacking our party for having worked out a scientifically based plan for building communism, for having placed the task of creating the material and technical base for communism at the center of the creative activity of the whole Soviet people and for displaying constant concern for raising the material and cultural living standard of all the working people in the country. This is truly monstrous and strange. It appears that the Chinese leaders' idea of socialism and communism and their practice of building a new society have an extremely remote relation to the Marxist-Leninist theory of scientific communism. Neither in Marx nor in Lenin can one find even a hint that the vital tasks of socialist construction can be solved by the method of "leaps" and cavalry charges, leaving out of account the degree of maturity of the socio-economic and spiritual prerequisites for the movement forward and ignoring the task of raising the material well-being of the people.

And if the Chinese leaders endeavour to impose their practice on us as a "universal truth," if they want to offer us as a "model" a society in which violence is idealized, democracy is curtailed, the cult of the individual

245

flourishes and concern for the working people is ignored, we shall tell them bluntly: Such a "universal truth" and such a "model" do not suit the Soviet people and, we are sure, will not suit other peoples either.

Socialism, communism, which brings the peoples peace, labor, freedom, equality, brotherhood and the happiness of all peoples, has been and remains the goal of the Communist movement. We are following the theory and practice of scientific communism, we are proceeding and will continue to proceed along the path pointed out by Marx, Engels and Lenin. (*Applause.*)

The Chinese leaders have embarked on the dangerous path of undermining Soviet-Chinese friendship, and we, naturally, decisively condemn their incorrect actions. The positions the Chinese leaders are taking today have an unfavorable effect on the entire socialist camp and the Communist movement. They are also doing enormous harm to China itself.

As for the CPSU and the Soviet Union, we shall remain true to the principles of Marxism-Leninism, we shall unswervingly fulfill our internationalist duty, we have taken and will continue to take all the necessary steps toward normalizing Soviet-Chinese relations and strengthening the friendship of our peoples.

The Communist Party of the Soviet Union will continue to strive for a normalization of the situation, for a strengthening of the friendship between the CPSU and the Communist Party of China. Our party is profoundly convinced that this friendship will continue to exist, will grow and gain strength. (*Applause.*)

VI. The Schismatic Activities of the Chinese Leaders in the World Communist Movement. — The Chinese leaders recently have sharply intensified their undermining activities aimed at bringing about a split both within the world Communist movement and in a number of Marxist-Leninist parties. These schismatic activities have acquired an open nature, are unfolding along a broad front and have become especially insidious and unprecedented in their methods. The CCP leaders have turned the polemic they unleashed in the ranks of the world Communist movement into a tool of open political struggle against the fraternal parties.

The Chinese leaders have apparently decided to pursue to the end their undermining activity against the Leninist unity of the world Communist movement. In recent days they have openly announced that a split has become "inevitable." In other words, they have now fully revealed the real aims they have nurtured for a number of years with respect to the international Communist movement.

The Chinese leaders have gone so far in their factional struggle as to break off relations with certain Marxist-Leninist parties, arbitrarily declaring them "nonexistent" and proclaiming the schismatic groups they have knocked together to be the "parties." They have announced for all to hear that they support the factional, schismatic groups they themselves have set up in a number of countries to struggle against the Marxist-Leninist parties. Thus the CCP leadership has openly assumed the responsibility for the infamous activities of all these groups and for their struggle against the fraternal parties.

The CCP leadership is obviously working toward forming under its aegis something in the nature of a special international bloc and counterposing it to the world Communist movement as a weapon for intensifying the struggle against it.

The Chinese representatives in international democratic associations have sharply intensified their schismatic activities and have openly set a course toward creating separate organizations, undermining the ties between the progressive, democratic forces of the various countries and regions of the world.

Thus, although the Chinese leaders still hide from time to time behind phrases about solidarity and unity, all their practical activities are in fact aimed at shaking the international Communist movement, at splitting it. The policy and activities of the Chinese leaders today constitute the chief danger to the unity of the world Communist movement.

The appearance in the CCP Central Committee's organs *Jen-min Jih-pao* and *Hung Ch'i* on Feb. 4, 1964, of a factional article that was directed against the CPSU and the entire world Communist movement and was a kind of platform for the splitting of the revolutionary movement of the working class must be evaluated in this light.

In the article the Chinese leaders assert that the development of the Communist movement is proceeding according to the formula: " Solidarity — a struggle, or even a split — a new solidarity on a new basis." They refer in this to the laws of the dialectic. But it is clear to every Marxist-Leninist that this so-called " dialectic " is only a new attempt to conceal the pseudo-theoretical arguments of their schismatic policy.

Who can talk today about the " inevitability " of a split? Only one who himself breaks with Marxism-Leninism, from the principles of proletarian internationalism. On the other hand, no one who cherishes the interests of the great cause of the international working class can see any objective reasons for a split in the present-day Communist movement. It has a political line that has been tested in the long experience of struggle, a line that has brought so many outstanding victories to the working class and the cause of socialism and that enjoys enormous authority among the popular masses.

What would a split in the world Communist movement lead to under today's conditions? It is clear that it would lead to the undermining of the unity of the main forces of the world anti-imperialist front — the socialist camp, the international workers' movement, the national-liberation movement and the general democratic movement of the popular masses. And this would only play into the hands of the aggressive forces of imperialism and facilitate their attack on the positions of the world liberation movement. It is clear that one who works toward a split is assuming an incomparably big historical responsibility.

As long as the international Communist movement has existed, the reactionaries of the whole world have been exerting frantic efforts toward bringing about a split in its ranks. Now the Chinese leaders want to achieve what imperialist reaction has been unable to do.

In the light of the present schismatic activities of the Chinese leaders, it has become clearer why the CCP representatives at the 1960 conference strove so zealously to get the point about the impermissibility of factional activity in the ranks of the international Communist movement dropped from the Statement. At that time the fraternal parties unanimously rejected the Chinese delegation's overtures. The 1960 conference noted in its Statement that one of the mandatory conditions for the victory of the Communists in the struggle for their goals is the impermissibility of any actions that could undermine the unity of the international Communist movement.

Soon after the conference the Chinese leaders broke this pledge, which they had made together with all the fraternal parties. They even attempted — specifically in the article "Proletarians of All Countries, Unite, Fight Against Our Common Enemy" (December, 1962) — to supply a "theoretical" basis for their refusal to fulfill this general decision. The CCP leaders advanced a certain concept of "the majority and the minority," according to which the minority should have the right to disregard jointly-adopted decisions and to wage a struggle against an approved general line. This is nothing but revision of the fundamental organizational principle of Leninism, for V. I. Lenin taught that "only the subordination of the minority to the majority can be the principle of the workers' movement" ("Works," Vol, XX, p. 354).

The majority against whom the Peking leaders are coming forth is a majority that includes Communist Parties that have led the working class of the countries to the winning of power and that are securing world-historic victories of socialism. It is a majority that includes Communist Parties on all continents without exception, marching in the vanguard of the revolutionary struggle.

In their factional blindness the Chinese leaders have not even hesitated to call the Marxist-Leninist parties no more or less than a "fictitious" majority.

This is far from a new method. Splitters even used it against Lenin boastfully declaring that one day the majority would follow them and they would then recognize its will. Lenin wrote about such people that they "recognize the will of the majority of politically conscious workers *not* in the present but in the future, namely in, and only in, that future when the workers agree with them, with the liquidators, with Plekhanov, with Trotsky!!" ("Works," Vol. XX, p. 451).

It seems that throughout all time splitters have resorted to one and the same device in opposing the will of the majority.

Recently, in its struggle against the principle of the subordination of the minority to the majority, the CCP leadership has been the first of all the opportunists and splitters with whom the international Communist movement has ever come into conflict to advance the thesis of the "legitimacy" of the existence of several Communist Parties in one and the same country. From its arguments it follows that such parties must fight not so much against the enemies of the working class as among themselves. There is no need to give a detailed rebuttal here to this fundamentally vicious concept, for it is clear to every politically conscious worker that the unity of the class interests and will of the proletariat, its ideology and its class organization find their embodiment in a single and monolithic Marxist-Leninist party. But one should once again point out what vagaries the modern splitters are resorting to in order to introduce confusion into the ranks of the workers' movement and to undermine the unity of the Communists' ranks. To this end they do not even hesitate to distort the statements of V. I. Lenin. Here is one characteristic example.

In the well-known work "On Violation of Unity Concealed by Cries About Unity," V. I. Lenin stigmatizes Trotsky's splitting activities and exposes his slander against the Bolshevist Party and his attempts to disorganize the workers' movement through the propagation of the nonsubordination of the minority to the will of the majority of workers. V. I. Lenin wrote: "Where the *majority* of politically conscious workers have rallied around precise and definite decisions, there is *unity* of opinions and actions, there is party spirit and a party. . . . Now, by trying to convince the workers *not to implement the decisions* of this 'whole' that the Marxists-Pravdists recognize, Trotsky *is attempting* to disorganize the movement and cause a split." Lenin appraised Trotsky's activities as "splitting, in the sense that they are the most shameless violation of the will of the majority of workers" (Vol. XX, pp. 310, 312).

The authors of the Feb. 4, 1964, article in *Jen-min Jih-pao* and *Hung Ch'i* quote V. I. Lenin's article in such a way as to distort the position of Lenin, who always emphasized the compulsoriness of general proletarian discipline and demanded the subordination of the minority to the will of the majority of workers. The Chinese splitters have resorted to outright forgery in trying to disorganize the Communist Parties.

Furthermore, the Chinese leaders are confusing even such a clear question as the need for definite international discipline in the ranks of the Communist movement. They assert that there cannot even be a question of such discipline, since there is no longer a centralized organization like the Comintern.

But, apparently without noticing it, the CCP leaders are betraying themselves by such arguments. They do not understand that in present-day conditions the international discipline of Communists does not consist in the execution of orders of some kind dictated by someone higher up but in the voluntary assumption by the Communist Parties of certain commitments to the international Communist movement and to one another, based on a lofty understanding of their internationalist duty, as well as the consistent implementation of their commitments in practice. This is what prompted the fraternal parties when in the 1960 Statement they pledged to observe strictly the following principles: To cherish party unity as the apple of their eye; to maintain solidarity in the observance of the jointly worked out evaluations and conclusions concerning the general tasks of struggle against imperialism and for peace, democracy and socialism; to prevent any actions that could undermine the unity of the international Communist movement; to give one another mutual support and to respect the independence and equality of rights of all the Marxist-Leninist parties.

The consistent observance of the collectively expressed will of the international Communist movement is an index of the Marxist maturity of each party and of its internationalism, since Marxism-Leninism and internationalism are indivisible.

The Chinese leaders' arguments on this question are apparently affected by their general view of discipline, which they regard not as the conscientious fulfilment of an obligation to all the detachments of the great alliance of like-minded Communists but as enforced subordination and command. Manifested here, evidently, is the influence of the practice that is so characteristic of the methods of the leaders of the Chinese Communist Party themselves.

But how alien this is to the entire spirit of Marxism-Leninism! V. I. Lenin, speaking about the Russian Bolsheviks, wrote: "We are proud that in solving the great questions of the workers' struggle for their liberation we subordinate ourselves to the international discipline of the revolutionary proletariat, taking into account the experience of workers of various countries, reckoning with their knowledge and their will, in this way implementing in deeds (and not in words, like the Renners, Fritz Adlers and Otto Bauers) the unity of the class struggle of the workers for communism throughout the world " (" Works," Vol. XXXI, p. 244).

Now, however, the Chinese leaders take special pride in their complete disdain for the international discipline of Communists and in their truly anarchistic conduct both in polemics and in their dealings with fraternal parties.

At present the true state of affairs with respect not only to the " theories " the Chinese leaders are publicizing to justify their schismatic activities but the basic directions along which these activities, their methods and devices, are developing in practice is becoming conclusively clear.

The CCP leaders are concentrating their chief blows against the most powerful and authoritative detachments of the international Communist movement — the Communist Party of the Soviet Union and the Communist Parties of other socialist countries, and the French, Italian and other Communist Parties. They have set as their goal the discrediting at any cost of all the truly Marxist-Leninist parties that enjoy deserved respect in the world Communist movement and in the eyes of the popular masses.

Special indignation is evoked by the position of the CCP Central Committee with respect to the Communist Parties that are waging their struggles in the capitalist countries. The Chinese leaders are now creating no little additional hardship for these parties, which are already operating under difficult conditions. They smear the Marxist-Leninist leadership of these parties in every way and strive to undermine its authority. Such insults as " mouselike cowards," " parrots," " double-dealers " and so on are being hurled at these experienced leaders of the working class.

This is being said about the leaders of parties that have set an example of heroic struggle against fascism and that are now marching in the vanguard of the antimonopoly struggle and represent a major national force. It is being said about militant and esteemed comrades who are fighting under difficult conditions and are being subjected to persecution. What but dismay can be evoked by declarations that the leaders of the U.S. Communist Party " are operating hand in hand with the most adventurist American imperialists," that the positions of the Chilean Communists " answer the purposes of American imperialism aimed at maintaining its supremacy in Latin America," that the leadership of the Communist Party of India is no more than a " clique," and the like?

How Peking understands proletarian solidarity can be judged by the CCP Central Committee's attitude toward the Baathist nationalists' repression of Salam Adil and other leaders of the Communist Party of Iraq. In conversations with foreign delegations, the Chinese leaders rejoiced openly and maliciously at the brutal murder of the Iraqi comrades. Immediately after the Baath takeover they began to seek contacts with the assassins. As has now become clear, the Chinese representatives in Iraq wanted to take advantage of the fact that the Iraqi Communist Party had become leaderless to create their own schismatic group there.

The entire Chinese propaganda machine — the Hsinhua news agency, information centers, various kinds of bulletins, the radio — has now been turned to the struggle against the Marxist-Leninist parties. In effect, the Chinese leaders have opened a new ideological front against the fraternal parties. In doing so, they have not shrunk from methods borrowed directly from the arsenal of anticommunism. What is the value, for example, of the fabrication circulated by Chinese propaganda about the "baton of Moscow," at a wave of which the Communist Parties allegedly turn first one way and then the other? This fabrication is equally insulting to the fraternal parties that constantly champion the national interests of their peoples and to the CPSU, to which any interference in the internal affairs of other parties is alien. This is nothing but a new variation of the old fable about the "hand of Moscow," invented by imperialist propaganda. It was used as far back as the struggle against Lenin and the Comintern by the right-wing Social-Democratic leaders. It has now been taken up as a weapon by Peking.

The height of the schismatic activity of the Chinese leaders in recent times has been the recruiting of adherents from the ranks of the fraternal parties and the creation of factional groups from them. Even in the letter of June 14, 1963, the CCP leadership threatened the fraternal parties that if they rejected Peking's postulates, they would be replaced by new people from "inside and outside party." Recent facts show that the Chinese leaders are now translating this threat into reality, are trying to implant all kinds of renegades, degenerates and adventurists at the head of the workers' movement of certain countries. The CCP leaders are striving to turn the schismatic groups that they have knocked together out of these renegades into the basic tool for their own struggle against the Marxist-Leninist parties.

At present anti-Party schismatic groups of renegades have been set up with Peking's help and support in Belgium, Brazil, Australia, Ceylon, Great Britain and certain other countries. The size of these groups is still numbered in single figures in some places and in the tens in others. But this does not bother the Chinese leaders, since the groups shout loudly and in unison at Peking's command, disgorging a flood of lies and slander on the world Communist movement and on the Marxist-Leninist parties. Large sums of money have suddenly appeared in the hands of the leaders of these groupings. They are starting up newspapers and magazines and beginning to publish all kinds of slanderous literature, and often they open their own shops to sell Chinese propaganda products.

The political physiognomy of the participants in these groupings once again illustrates the Chinese leadership's complete lack of principle. They are as a rule opportunistic, unstable elements who have been expelled from the Communist Parties for propagating anti-Marxist views, for factional activity or for immoral behaviour. There are also glory-loving careerists, political "weathervanes" and the like. The members of the anti-Party groupings in certain countries have displayed right-opportunist tendencies. Adventurists and people with shady pasts are working in the ranks of the schismatic groups in Austria, Chile and the U.S.A.

It is understandable that the fraternal parties cannot tolerate factional groups and are hurling them from their ranks. Each time this happens there follows from Peking a "threatening" cry against the fraternal parties, which are accused of no more or less than "using illegal methods." The Chinese leaders declare the expelled splitters to be "genuine revolutionaries" and "courageous fighters," even though their "struggle" reduces to the concoction of noisy "manifestos" directed against the Communist Parties. They make frequent trips to Peking, where they are received with much pomp and their verbose, slanderous articles are printed.

The meaning of the racket Peking has raised around the factional groups has become perfectly obvious in recent months. The Chinese leaders have revealed it themselves. Quite recently they widely publicized an assemblage of renegades in Belgium, which declared itself to be no less than " a national conference " and adopted a ludicrous decision " to re-create (!) the Communist Party of Belgium " and " to condemn the anti-Party acts of the former (!) Central Committee of the Belgian Communist Party." And on the basis of this fiction, the Chinese leaders are referring to the Central Committee of the Communist Party of Belgium elected by its congress as " former," as though it were Peking and not the working class of this or that country that creates its own Communist Party. The CCP leaders used the same maneuver to " close down " the Central Committees of certain other Communist Parties — the Communist Party of Ceylon, for example.

It must be said bluntly that nothing like this has ever been encountered in the history of the Communist movement. Never has it occurred to a single Communist Party to declare a sorry group of splitters who have been expelled from the Communist Party of another country to be the real " party " and to refer to that country's actual Communist Party as " former." The Chinese leaders, who make so much noise about equality and the noninterference by parties in one another's internal affairs, are now pretending to the role of a kind of " supreme court " within the Communist movement that would decide for these parties questions of their internal life.

The schismatic groupings created by Peking do not and cannot have any roots in either the workers' movement or the general democratic struggle of the popular masses. They stand outside the ranks of the world Communist movement, and not a single politically conscious worker ever wants to have anything to do with them. They have sprung up and exist completely artificially, born of the schismatic activities of Peking. One cannot fail to note that their rise has been warmly welcomed by the ruling circles of the capitalist countries, which rightly perceive in them a gift " fifth column " in the workers' movement.

The CCP Central Committee's leadership is now carrying matters even further — it has obviously plotted a course of knocking together, as a counterbalance to the world Communist movement, a bloc of its sympathizers with its own special platform and group discipline and with its center in Peking. Mehmet Shehu blurted out these plans as long ago as the end of 1962, when he declared that a bloc of parties, true to Marxism-Leninism, headed by the Chinese, was then being formed.

Why is such a bloc being created? It is clear to everyone that it is not for the purpose of fighting for the goals of the workers' movement and against world imperialism, since the very idea of the bloc bears within itself the seeds of schism, and thus of a weakening of the forces of the working class. No, this bloc is being created to struggle against the Marxist-Leninist parties, against the world Communist movement on behalf of the special purposes of the leadership of the CCP Central Committee.

The Chinese leaders have extended the line of splitting the world Communist movement to the ranks of the international front of democratic forces. For several years now the Chinese representatives have been taking advantage of congresses and conferences of fighters for peace and of women's, young people's and other international associations for schismatic sallies. This is how it was at the conference of the Organization of Afro-Asian Solidarity, at the Moscow Women's Congress, at the Warsaw session of the World Peace Council and at other international forums. Juggling with "revolutionary phrases," the Chinese leaders are thrusting upon all these organizations tasks and functions that are irrelevant to them and are trying to discredit and declare unnecessary the basic slogans and demands under the banner of which these decomratic movements were born. It is clear that the sectarian position of the Chinese representatives is aimed at alienating from these movements extremely broad sections of the population that adhere to different convictions, at narrowing the mass base of the general democratic struggle.

Comrades! The world Communist movement has become the most infiuential political force of our times. In the savage struggle against imperialist reaction and for the interests of the working class and all working people, for peace, democracy, national independence and socialism, it has moved far ahead, substantially expanded its ranks and won outstanding victories. Dozens of new Communist Parties have arisen during the postwar period, and there is no longer a single corner of the earth where there are no Communists bringing to the masses the great ideas of Marxism-Leninism. Special significance for the life of the international Communist movement belongs to the past decade, when, in overcoming the harmful consequences of the cult of the individual, it has considerably stepped up its theoretical thought and practical activities, has linked them even more firmly to the demands of life and to the needs and aspirations of the broad popular masses.

Against this historical background, not only the harm of the Chinese leaders' schismatic activities but the hopelessness of their attempts to drive world Communism from its Leninist path and to subordinate it to their schemes are especially apparent.

But it would be incorrect to underestimate the danger of the factional activities of the CCP Central Committee. The Chinese leaders are pinning their hopes on all kinds of immature and unstable elements, as well as on those who, untouched by the new spirit that has swept over the Communist movement in the past ten years, are grasping at the practices of the cult of the individual and who have been captivated by the dogmatism and doctrinaire schemes implanted by it.

The factional methods of the Chinese leadership are also being taken up by all kinds of renegades and turncoats, who are ready to fight communism under any flag.

At the same time, the Chinese leaders obviously want to exploit the real resentment of the masses at the antipopular reactionary policy of the ruling classes of the capitalist states. In our day, when hundreds upon hundreds of millions of people, including those who are politically unsophisticated and inadequately experienced, are being drawn into active political struggle, the "ultra-left" revolutionary phraseology in which the Chinese leaders couch their adventurist concepts may find a certain response. This applies in particular to countries that have either no industrial proletariat at all or only a small one, where the influence of petty-bourgeois ideology is great and the level of theoretical maturity of the revolutionary cadres is not yet sufficiently high.

The Chinese leaders are coming forward under the flag of a struggle against "modern revisionism" in order to conceal their anti-Leninist line and schismatic activities. They are pasting the label of "revisionists" on Marxist-Leninist parties and are assuming for themselves the mantle of "true" revolutionaries. They calculate that they will thereby be able to mislead people who are unacquainted with the true history of the struggle of the international Communist movement against right and "left" opportunism and who tend to grasp only the superficial patterns of the revolutionary struggle rather than the substance of our great teaching.

It is well known from the history of the Communist movement that irresponsible accusations of revisionism have more than once been hurled at representatives of creative Marxism by every kind of dogmatic and petty-bourgeois revolutionary. Thus, for example, in the autumn of 1920 G. Gorter, a "left-wing" Communist who had been expelled from the Dutch Communist Party, wrote V. I. Lenin an open letter in answer to his book "'Left-Wing' Communism, an Infantile Disorder": "You and the Third International are now acting as the Social Democrats did in the past. . . . Two trends exist in conformity with the development of the workers' movement in Western Europe: the radical and the opportunist. And you, Comrade Lenin, are supporting the opportunist. . . . From a leader of the Marxists you are turning into a leader of the opportunists."

Do many people still recall these pitiful sallies against the greatest revolutionary in world history?

The methods of the Chinese schismatics cannot deceive the Marxist-Leninists of the world. The anti-Leninist, adventurist course of the leaders of the CCP Central Committee has been openly condemned by the absolute majority of the world's Marxist-Leninist parties. The fallacious postulates and the factional, schismatic actions of the Chinese leaders have been subjected to profound criticism in numerous documents and speeches by the most outstanding figures of the world Communist movement and in the party press. All this means that, on the whole, the world Communist movement is standing on the only correct Marxist-Leninist positions.

Fostered by Lenin, our party, together with the other fraternal parties, will continue persistently to fight against all opportunist actions from both the right and the "left," for the solidarity of the ranks of all the fraternal parties, for the unity of all detachments of the world revolutionary movement, for the purity of the all-conquering Marxist-Leninist teaching. (*Applause.*)

VII. Concerning the Danger of Petty-Bourgeois, Nationalistic, Neo-Trotskyite Deviation. — Soviet Communists, like Marxist-Leninists the world over, cannot confine themselves merely to criticizing and politically assessing the wrong, anti-Leninist views of the leadership of the Communist Party of China. Inevitably, each of us asks how it could have happened that the leaders of a party such as the Communist Party of China, which has had much experience in revolutionary struggle and in building the new society, took the path of struggle against the world Communist movement. With whom are we dealing in the person of the leaders of the CCP?

The experience of our party and of the whole international workers' movement shows that Leninism has more than once encountered views and postulates similar to those the Chinese leadership is now promoting. Of course, the present bearers of these views are not simply repeating their predecessors. They are adapting old ideas to today's conditions and to their own needs.

As is known, V. I. Lenin pointed out that Bolshevism grew, gained strength and was tempered chiefly in the struggle against right opportunism. " This was, naturally, the chief enemy of Bolshevism within the workers' movement," he wrote. At the same time, Lenin stressed the importance of another aspect of the experience of Bolshevism about which, he noted, too little was as yet known abroad. In " 'Left-Wing' Communism, an Infantile Disorder," he wrote that " Bolshevism grew, took shape and was tempered in long years of struggle against *petty-bourgeois revolutionism*, which smacks of anarchism or borrows something from it and which, in anything essential, falls short of the conditions and requirements of a consistent proletarian class struggle " (Vol. XXXI, p. 15).

It is characteristic that the Chinese leaders, who love to cite examples of past ideological disagreements and to draw historical parallels, whether the examples and parallels are relevant or not, maintain complete silence about this aspect of the Bolshevist experience. This is understandable ; each of Lenin's words directed against the representatives of petty-bourgeois revolutionism — or, as Lenin ironically called it, petty-bourgeois "revolutionary-ism " — hits squarely at the present ideological-political conceptions and postulates of the CCP leadership.

A comprehensive characterization of petty-bourgeois revolutionism is presented in numerous works by V. I. Lenin, in the decisions of our party and in the documents of the Communist International. Lenin saw its sources in the special situation of the petty proprietor, the small owner, who turns easily to " extreme revolutionism " but is incapable of displaying restraint, organization, discipline or staunchness, and is inclined to go from one extreme to another.

Everyone knows, for example, about Bolshevism's struggle against the Socialist-Revolutionaries, a party that, Lenin noted, " expressed more than any other the tendencies of petty-bourgeois revolutionism " (Vol. XXXI, p. 16). One cannot help but recall now that the Socialist-Revolutionaries denied the leading role of the working class and tried to show that the peasant movement is the truly socialist movement.

From time to time, particularly at history's sharp turns, petty-bourgeois vacillation made itself felt in the ranks of proletarian parties also. Lenin pointed out more than once that the proletariat is not insured against penetration of its ranks by petty-bourgeois ideology and prejudices. The best of the petty-bourgeois revolutionaries, entering the ranks of proletarian parties, re-educate themselves, study Marxism seriously, and finally become genuine revolutionaries. Others fail to learn or are incapable of learning anything from the proletarian party " except a few memorized words, ' striking ' slogans learned by rote. . . ." (Vol. XVI, p. 44–45).

Our party had to wage a struggle against " leftist " petty-bourgeois vacillations most of all after taking power, in the early years of building the Soviet state. We know what an implacable struggle V. I. Lenin waged against the " Left Communists," the " workers' opposition," Trotskyism and " ultra-leftists " in the then young Communist movement.

Let me remind you of the struggle against the " Left Communists " in the period of the conclusion of the Brest peace, when they tried to impose the adventurist tactic of " revolutionary war," a tactic that would have been disastrous for the Soviet Republic. Lenin held that the views of the " Left Communists," despite loud revolutionary phraseology, were based on attitudes of hopeless pessimism and utmost desperation (Vol. XXVII,

255

p. 51). (*Applause.*) As for the objective role played by the "Left Communists" at that time, Lenin, addressing them, said bluntly: "You are a tool of imperialist provocation, by your objective role. And subjectively your 'psychology' is the psychology of an infuriated petty bourgeois who swaggers and boasts, but realizes perfectly well that the proletariat is *right* . . ." (Vol. XXVII, p. 297). (*Applause.*)

In the situation that has now taken shape in the international Communist movement, special mention must be made of the sharp struggle that our party has conducted against Trotskyism. Trotskyism constituted a clearly expressed petty-bourgeois deviation. It operated under the false banner of a trend more "left," more "revolutionary" than Bolshevism. Trotsky and his adherents, while proclaiming themselves the "true" fighters for world revolution, in actuality fought against Leninism. Trotskyism likewise represented a rejection of Bolshevist partisanship, rejection of solidarity of the Party ranks. Factionalism was the "heart" of Trotskyism. The Trotskyites joined not only with the factional groupings that existed within the Comintern but also with organizations, groups and individuals that had never belonged to Communist Parties, as well as with enemies and traitors expelled from their ranks.

Need all these facts be recalled? Yes, comrades, they must be recalled, in order that the lessons of the struggle against Leninism in the past may be taken into account.

Do not the present concepts of the Chinese theoreticians remind us of the many ideas of the petty-bourgeois trends that were smashed by Leninism long ago? Only a petty-bourgeois "ultra"-revolutionary could see in the policy of the peaceful coexistence of states with different social systems a "repudiation" of the struggle against imperialism and a "denial" of the revolution. Only he could welcome the thesis of "revolutionary war" as the "ultimate, decisive" weapon with which to put an end to the contradictions between the two social systems. Only a petty-bourgeois "super"-revolutionary could demand that the revolution be begun "at once" and "everywhere," without taking into account the concrete conditions and the correlation of forces that have taken shape. Only he could oppose the employment of the peaceful path of revolution, since for him the sole criterion of "revolutionism" is the use of armed violence whether or not this is dictated by the circumstances.

It is therefore completely understandable that, having taken this path, the Chinese leaders have naturally descended to borrowing many of their ideas and concepts from the ideological store of Trotskyism, just as they have inherited from it the factional, schismatic methods of struggle against the Marxist-Leninist parties.

Yes, comrades, it must be said openly: The entire conglomeration of the theoretical and political views of the leaders of the Communist Party of China is largely a rehash of Trotskyism, which was discarded long ago by the international revolutionary movement.

What in fact are the Chinese leaders' views on problems of war and peace? They are nothing but a restatement in new conditions of the Trotskyite slogan "Neither peace nor war."

Or take the active opposition of the leadership of the CCP Central Committee to economic competition with capitalism. Is this a new statement of the question? No, it is a reiteration of the old Trotskyite postulate about rejecting peaceful economic construction and going over to the tactic of " revolutionary war," of " prodding " a world revolution with weapons in hand.

Everyone knows that the true sense of Trotsky's theory of " permanent revolution " lay precisely here. The struggle against Trotskyism on this question was of historic importance. The destinies of the world's first socialist country, the destinies of the entire world revolutionary movement depended on its outcome. What would have happened if our party had adopted such a course? It would have proved defenseless in the face of world imperialism, it would have been easy prey for it in the event of an armed attack.

As a matter of fact, the Chinese leaders are now forcing a dispute on the same question — whether to follow the path of " revolutionary " adventures or to adhere to the Leninist course of strengthening the economic and political might of the world socialist system, of developing the revolutionary movement in the capitalist countries and the national-liberation struggle of the peoples, taking fully into account Lenin's teaching that revolution is the result of the exacerbation of internal class contradictions in each country.

This kinship with Trotskyism stands out no less graphically in the Chinese theses about the danger of " bourgeois degeneration " in the socialist countries. We can say in answer to such fabrications — this is not new, our party has heard it before. It is a restatement in new conditions of the Trotskyite slander about the " degeneration " of the USSR into a " Thermidorean " state.

Can it be that we do not recognize the characteristic features of Trotsky-ism in the Chinese concepts, which exaggerate the role of violence and coercion in revolution and in socialist construction?

Also, compare the CCP leaders' views with the " ideas " of present-day Trotskyism. Can anyone think that the Chinese theory that the regions of Asia, Africa and Latin America are the " chief zone of storms of the world revolution " is an original formulation? No, this is almost a verbatim repetition of one of the fundamental theses of present-day Trotskyism. In the decisions of the so-called Fourth (Trotskyite) International one can read: " . . . As a result of the successive defeats of the two major revolutionary waves of 1919–1923 and 1943–1948, as well as the weaker wave of 1934–1937, the chief center of the world revolution has temporarily shifted to the colonial world."

There is the source of the Chinese leadership's political wisdom for you!

In the writings of today's Trotskyites one can find other " ultra "-revolutionary phrases that are reproduced almost word for word in the Chinese press and are passed off as so-called " revolutionary principles." The peaceful coexistence of states with different social systems, the Trotskyite bawlers prophesy, " is not only impossible but even harmful for the working class of all countries," since it leads to " the strengthening of the positions of capitalism and the weakening of the positions of socialism." They boastfully declare that " only those . . . who are unflinch-ingly ready to meet the consequences of the atomic war that capitalism is preparing " should be considered true revolutionaries, and so on and so forth.

After this, it is no surprise that the leaders of present-day Trotskyism tell the CCP leaders (as Posadas, one of the leaders of Trotskyism in Latin America, did in July, 1963): " Comrade Chinese, you cannot assert that all

257

the questions you are raising as revolutionary conclusions are the result of your theoretical and political work alone. They are the conclusions of the Fourth International."

It is no accident that the Trotskyites are pinning their hopes for a revival of their own long-moribund movement on the present political course of the Chinese leadership. "The political positions of the Communist Party of China," the "Manifesto" of the Sixth Congress of their "International" states, "indicate enormous possibilities, which are opening up a field of activity that Trotskyism never had in the past."

The Chinese leaders are pretending they don't notice all this. Apparently they reason thus: "Present-day Trotskyism is a little-known trend; we can utilize its ideas and give them a 'Sinified' appearance." But the truth will out! No matter how much the Chinese leadership wants to keep silent about the true source of its ideas, it cannot conceal the coincidence of its views with the views of the old and modern Trotskyites.

Like the Trotskyites, the Chinese leaders demand freedom for factions and groupings within the Communist movement and are conducting undermining activity within it using the same methods. Can we not recognize in the malicious personal attacks of Chinese propaganda on the leaders of the CPSU and the Communist Parties of France, Italy, the U.S.A., India and other countries the same familiar "handwriting" of the Trotskyites, who even in their sleep dream of how they can slander still more viciously the popular leaders of the working class?

The present-day Trotskyites do not conceal their delight at these actions of the CCP leaders. In a statement published in Paris at the end of July, 1963, the joint secretariat of the Trotskyite "International" assured the Chinese leaders that it "would support them" in the struggle against the CPSU as well as against the Indian, American, French, Italian and other Communist Parties. In a special resolution, the "International's" executive committee, meeting in the summer of 1963, approved "the historical task of joining with the Chinese and fighting for the creation of a united front between the Fourth International and the Chinese comrades."

These facts speak for themselves. The logic of the struggle with the CPSU and the world Communist movement has led the CCP leaders even closer to Trotskyism, the most vicious enemy of Marxism-Leninism.

It must be said that at one time the Chinese leaders themselves saw the danger of petty-bourgeois pressure on the Communist Party of China. "Our party," Mao Tse-tung said, for example, "not only is externally surrounded by this broad social stratum, but even within it the offspring of the petty bourgeoisie constitute an enormous majority. . . . Petty-bourgeois ideology of all shades often finds reflection in our party" (Mao Tse-tung, Vol. IV, pp. 386–387). Elsewhere he said that petty-bourgeois ideology finds expression in the CCP in " dashes to the left and to the right, in a weakness for leftist revolutionary phrases and slogans, in sectarian isolationism and adventurism."

The Chinese leaders wrote correctly at one time! But they have now stopped talking about the danger of petty-bourgeois degeneration. Is this not because petty-bourgeois ideology has gained ascendancy in their own views, in their political line, in the methods of their activity?

But at the same time, in a country such as China, just as in tsarist Russia, with an enormous preponderance of nonproletarian strata of the population, Communists must be especially vigilant against the penetration of the ranks of the working class by petty-bourgeois views and traditions. Under the guidance of Lenin, our party was able to cope with this task. From its first steps it was a party of the militant working class, linked with major industry, undergoing the excellent school of proletarian class struggle. At this time fundamental importance attached to the fact that Lenin and the Bolsheviks relied on the experience of the entire international proletarian movement and were firmly guided by the principles and ideals of the scientific socialism of Marx and Engels.

Apparently the leaders of the Communist Party of China lack the Marxist-Leninist tempering to oppose firmly the pressure of the petty-bourgeois elements, to uphold the line of proletarian socialism. Only this can explain the fact that petty-bourgeois ideology has left its imprint on both their domestic and their foreign policy.

We would have preferred not to touch on questions of the domestic policy of the CCP leadership. But inasmuch as the Chinese leaders' adventurist course in the international arena is linked with their mistakes in domestic policy, we shall have to speak about it.

Marxist-Leninists of all countries now know the results of the so-called policy of the " great leap " and the people's communes. In this policy one cannot fail to see " leftist " attempts to " skip over " necessary stages of social development.

Our party has always given due credit to the experience of the Chinese Communists in carrying out democratic and social reforms after the victory of the revolution. During the period 1949–1957 the Communist Party of China, pursuing a realistic course, making use of the experience of the other socialist countries and relying on their support, achieved great successes in the economic, social and political development of the country. The Soviet people sincerely rejoiced at these successes.

In 1958, however, this course was suddenly revised and replaced by the so-called course of " the three red banners — the general line, the great leap and the people's communes." The Chinese leaders decided to carry out in only a few years tasks to whose solution three five-year plans and more had been allotted as recently as 1956. It was decided to increase the gross output of industry by 550% (with an average annual growth of 45%!) and the gross output of agriculture by 150% (with an average annual growth rate of 20%!) in five years (1958–1962).

These plans were drawn up without any kind of economic foundation, without taking the country's real possibilities into account. The people's communes that were set up in the countryside were supposed to ensure the " leap to communism " in three or four, or perhaps five or six, years.

The results of these experiments are generally known. The economy of the CPR was thrown back several years. The course of " the three red banners " led to serious disorganization of the entire national economy and a sharp slowdown in the rates of industrialization and was reflected in the material situation of the people.

Of course, we are not mentioning this in order to rejoice over the failures of the Chinese Communists. Like them, we are dismayed at the hardships that have fallen to the lot of the fraternal Chinese people. And if we speak about these facts, it is solely in order to show what a departure from the tested Leninist principles of socialist construction can lead to.

In analyzing the sources of the present positions of the Chinese leadership, one cannot fail to see them also in the ever-intensifying, openly nationalistic great-power aspirations that have so powerfully manifested themselves in the foreign policy activity of the CCP leaders. It has happened more than once in history that vociferous "revolutionism" has walked hand in hand with the most frantic nationalism. Lenin pointed out several times that the same social and economic conditions that engender the small owner give special stability to one of the "deepest of the petty-bourgeois prejudices, namely: the prejudice of national egotism, national narrow-mindedness." (Vol. XXXI, p. 128).

The facts indicate that nationalism is gaining increasing ascendancy in the entire policy of the Chinese leadership and is becoming the mainspring of their actions. This was manifested back during the period of the "great leap," which was obviously conceived as an attempt to catch up to all the socialist countries "in one jump," to seize a dominant position in the world socialist system.

More recently these tendencies have become even more intense. This has found reflection in such acts of the Chinese government as the artificial stirring up of nationalist passions over border questions, the behavior of the CCP leaders during the Caribbean crisis, and the Chinese government's position on the nuclear question.

These and other facts reveal the complete discrepancy between the words and the deeds of the Chinese leaders. It is becoming increasingly clear that the "leftist" phrases and recipes were primarily meant for "export," to be thrust upon the Communist Parties of other countries. When the question comes down to their own practical steps in the international arena, the Chinese leaders prefer not to operate from positions of the revolutionary struggle against imperialism at all. It is extremely bewildering what reasons Chinese propaganda could have at the present time for reducing the entire struggle against imperialism merely to a struggle against the U.S.A., ignoring its allies — the Japanese, West German and French imperialists. Can it be that they are seeking partners for themselves among the monopolist circles of these countries in the struggle against what they call "modern revisionism"?

Great suspicion has been evoked by the so-called theory the Chinese leaders have advanced about an "intermediate zone," which regards West Germany, Britain, France and Japan as countries that are in servitude to American imperialism, thereby "prettifying" the imperialists of Britain, France, Japan and particularly West Germany and glossing over their aggressive essence and the danger they represent for the peoples of the socialist countries, the national-liberation movement and the general peace. The 1960 Statement emphasized the special threat to the cause of peace represented by West German imperialism and set the Communist Parties the task of intensifying the struggle against its aggressive desires. The Soviet people know from experience how dangerous this imperialist predator is. The imperialism of the Federal Republic of Germany is now far from a simple satellite of U.S. imperialism. Relying on a mighty economic potential, which considerably exceeds the potential of the whole of Hitler's Germany, West German imperialism has created a major military force and is increasingly setting the tone in NATO.

No small danger is represented by the imperialism of Britain, France and Japan. This can be seen in the example of the recent events in Cyprus, in East Africa, in Gabon and in Southeast Asia, where the British and French imperialists have been resorting to the use of armed force to suppress the national-liberation movement.

The CPSU assumes that all the anti-imperialist forces must set themselves the task of struggling against the aggressive, reactionary forces of British, French, West German and Japanese imperialism, in addition to struggling resolutely against American imperialism, as the greatest international exploiter and gendarme. The Chinese theory of an "intermediate zone" objectively whitewashes the imperialists of Britain, France, West Germany and Japan and is to their advantage.

It must be said that the ruling circles of the imperialist powers have "seen through" the secret of the Chinese policy. They have understood that the "revolutionary phrases" of the Chinese leaders are not aimed against imperialism at all. These phrases have in fact been called on to conceal a savage struggle against the CPSU and the world Communist movement, and in no way threaten imperialism. Hence the turnabout that is now being observed with respect to China in the policy of the leading imperialist states.

We shall not conceal it. Watching all these maneuvers by the Chinese leadership, we, like all the Marxist-Leninists of the world, are justifiably alarmed at the dangerous path along which the Chinese leaders are dragging their great country. It is very likely that by following their incorrect, anti-Leninist path, the Chinese leaders will to all intents and purposes close ranks with the reactionary, bellicose elements of imperialism, as has already occurred in connection with the CPR government's refusal to sign the Moscow treaty on the banning of nuclear weapons tests.

The nationalist course of the CCP leaders has nothing in common with the genuinely national interests of the fraternal Chinese people. It is the peoples of the socialist countries most of all who can be sincere allies of the Chinese people. The people of China have a vital stake in strengthening the world socialist system and in a firm alliance with all anti-imperialist forces. In this lies the earnest of the rapid progress of People's China along the path of socialism.

The present positions of the CCP Central Committee both domestically and in the international arena cannot be understood without examining the situation that has taken shape within the Communist Party of China and in the country itself as a result of the implanting of the cult of the individual. It is impossible to pass over in silence the fact that the Mao Tse-tung cult is having an increasingly unfavorable effect on the activities of the Communist Party of China.

For many years now Chinese propaganda has been persistently suggesting to everyone that the ideas of Mao Tse-tung are the "supreme incarnation of Marxism-Leninism" and that our epoch is "the epoch of Mao Tse-tung." Asserting that the generalization of the historical tasks of modern times has fallen wholly on the shoulders of Mao Tse-tung alone, Chinese propaganda is representing matters as though the ideas of Mao Tse-tung are the Marxism-Leninism of our epoch, "the scientific theory of socialist revolution and the building of socialism and communism."

It is now perfectly clear that the CCP leadership is striving to spread the Mao Tse-tung cult to the entire world Communist movement, so that the CCP leader, like Stalin in his time, might be elevated like a god above all the Marxist-Leninist parties and might decide all questions of their policy and activities according to his whims. The ideology and practice of the cult

261

of the individual largely explain the appearance of the Chinese leaders' hegemonic schemes.

However, history does not repeat itself. And what was once a tragedy can seem a mere farce the second time. The CCP leaders should know that the Communist movement will never permit a repetition of the practices of the cult of the individual, which are alien to Marxism-Leninism and for which it paid such a high price in the past. The Communist movement and the cult of the individual are incompatible. (*Applause.*)

The 20th Congress of the CPSU put an end forever to this manifestation, alien to Marxism-Leninism, in our party, creating all the conditions so that practices similar to those that existed during the period of the cult of the individual can never be repeated. (*Applause.*)

The Party has fully restored Leninist principles in Party and state life, has restored and developed the principles of socialist democracy. The course of the 20th Party Congress received full support in the declaration and Statement of the Moscow conferences. It is therefore clear that to condemn the struggle against the ideology of the cult of the individual means to diverge from the agreed-upon line of the Communist movement, means to push it deliberately onto an incorrect path that is alien to Marxism-Leninism and to the nature of the socialist system.

But this is precisely how the Chinese leaders are acting. They have openly assumed the role of defenders of the Stalin cult and have declared that to fight against it means "to subvert Marxism-Leninism," "to smear the dictatorship of the proletariat."

However, it is precisely the cult of the individual that leads to the distortion of important aspects of the dictatorship of the proletariat, which is the highest form of democracy — democracy for the working people. Under Lenin, the strictest observance of democratic principles of Party and state life and socialist legality was ensured. He fought against anti-Party groups and trends, using Party methods and relying on the Party masses. During the period of the Stalin cult another method held sway — the method of the physical repression of those Party figures whom Stalin suspected of disagreeing with his views; moreover, repressions and arbitrariness with respect to tried and true Party and state cadres descended with special force just when the struggle against the opposition was over and the victory of socialism had been achieved. Stalin turned the cutting edge of the dictatorship of the proletariat, which had been created to deal blows at enemies, against the cadres of the Communist Party and the socialist state.

But it can be seen that it is precisely this aspect of Stalin's activity that has captivated the Chinese leaders; therefore they identify his incorrect methods of leadership with the dictatorship of the proletariat. Despite the fact that many instances of Stalin's abuses of power during the period of the cult of the individual have become generally known and despite Stalin's deviation from Leninist principles on a number of important questions, the Chinese leaders have put Stalin on a pedestal, representing him as the "great continuer" of Lenin's cause. The Chinese leaders write and speak about the mass repressions during the cult of the individual as though they were merely a question of petty "excesses."

This line of the Chinese leaders bodes no good for the people. In it are displayed the ideology and morality not of Marxists and Leninists but of people who are placing their stake on methods of violence and suppression.

Let the Chinese leaders ask the Soviet Communists, the workers, peasants and intelligentsia who have experienced the grave consequences of the cult of the individual how they feel about attempts to revive the distortions and mistakes that Stalin made, attempts to restore the practices of the cult of the individual. They would receive only one answer: This shall not be! (*Prolonged applause!*)

Our party routed the anti-Party group of Molotov, Kaganovich and Malenkov. This group resisted the elimination of the cult of the individual for several reasons, not the least of which was the fact that certain of its members also bore responsibility for the mass repressions against innocent people during the period when they stood together with Stalin at the head of the country.

The facts of the repressions committed by Stalin and the later-exposed members of the anti-Party group against prominent figures in the Communist Party and the Soviet state are already known. But, as became clear, not only did Molotov, together with Stalin, sanction the sentencing of the wives of these figures as well to the supreme penalty, under the so-called "List No. 4 of Wives of Enemies of the People," which included V. A. Dybenko-Sedyakina, Ye. S. Kosior, A. I. Chubar, Ye. Ye. Eikhe-Rubtsova and others; in many cases Molotov also tried to be "more Catholic than the Pope," as they say. In one document sanctioning long-term prison confinement for a large group of wives of officials who had been repressed, Molotov wrote opposite one name in the list: "SP" — that is, supreme penalty.

Is it the restoration of such inhuman practices that the Chinese leaders are concerned about? Is this why they manifest sympathy for people who have been expelled from the ranks of our party?

In the question of the cult of the individual, the Chinese leaders have rejected not only the conclusions and postulates of the international Communist movement but their own previous declarations as well.

Everyone knows that in 1956 and 1957 — in speeches by Mao Tse-tung and Liu Shao-chi and in articles about the historical experience of the dictatorship of the proletariat, all of which were approved by the Politburo of the CCP Central Committee — the activities of the CPSU in eliminating the consequences of the cult of the individual were highly appraised. At the 1957 conference of Communist and Workers' Parties, Mao Tse-tung said: "In the past four or five years, since the death of Stalin, the situation in the Soviet Union has improved considerably in both the area of domestic policy and the area of foreign policy. This testifies to the fact that the line that Comrade Khrushchev is presenting is more correct, and that opposition to this line is mistaken." At that time the Chinese leaders rightly said that only "the reactionaries throughout the world" could oppose the line of the 20th CPSU Congress.

Now the Chinese leaders, proceeding from their own political calculations, have taken up the defense of the cult of the individual. They have taken Stalin's distortions and mistakes under their protection primarily because they themselves are implanting the Mao Tse-tung cult.

The world Communist movement and politically conscious workers the world over are once again becoming convinced by the example of the present political course of the CCP leaders that the practice of the cult of the individual was and still is vicious, that it inflicts enormous harm on the interests of the peoples and on the great cause of the struggle against imperialism and for socialism. The assertion of the ideology of the cult of the individual in the Communist movement would lead it into a blind alley and would do serious harm to the cause of socialism and communism.

Thus an examination of the sources of the present anti-Leninist, schismatic course of the CCP leadership forces one to the conclusions: The world Communist movement faces the real danger of petty-bourgeois, nationalist deviation concealed under " leftist " phrases. The danger of this deviation is the greater since we are dealing with the leaders of a party that is in power and that possesses a large state apparatus and the weapons of mass ideological influence.

It is clear that the CPSU, like all the Marxist-Leninist parties, cannot fail to take steps toward weakening as much as possible the harm that the activity of this petty-bourgeois deviation can bring to the world Communist movement.

VIII. For the Unity of the World Communist Movement on the Principles of Marxism-Leninism! — Comrades! Our party has every right to say: We have done and are now doing everything we can to overcome the differences, to restore cooperation between the CCP and the CPSU, to strengthen friendship between the CPR and the Soviet Union and to strengthen the unity of the world Communist movement. Despite the intolerable methods of polemic used by the CCP leaders and despite their open struggle against the CPSU and the other fraternal parties, our party has displayed maximum restraint, maximum responsibility and maximum concern for the solidarity of the Communist ranks.

In recent years, on the initiative of Comrade N. S. Khrushchev, the CPSU Central Committee and the Soviet government have undertaken many practical steps aimed at solidifying our party and at preserving and expanding cooperation with the CPR in the political, economic, scientific-technical and cultural fields. And if these steps have yielded no results, this is wholly the fault of the Chinese leaders.

When the Chinese leaders began to come out openly against our party, the CPSU Central Committee several times sent the CCP Central Committee letters in which it pointed out that the vital interests of the course of socialism and communism demand that our parties, despite the existing differences, implement as before a coordinated line on all questions of principle. We proposed the cessation of unnecessary disputes about questions on which we have a different understanding and the abandonment of public statements, which lead only to a deepening of the rift. The letters contained specific proposals envisaging coordination of actions in the foreign-policy arena, expanded exchange of foreign-policy information, harmony of actions in international democratic organizations, etc.

In October, 1962, in a conversation with the Chinese Ambassador to the USSR, who was then returning home, Comrade N. S. Khrushchev asked him to tell the Chinese leaders that we proposed to " lay aside all disputes and differences, not to argue over who is right and who is in error, nor to stir up the past but to begin our relations with a clean page."

Even after the Chinese press had published a whole series of articles containing crude attacks on the CPSU and the other fraternal parties, Comrade N. S. Khrushchev declared in January, 1963, in a conversation with the new Chinese Ambassador, that " we want to return to our former fraternal relations and are prepared to do anything for the sake of this."

But every time, in answer to the display of good will on the part of the Central Committee of our party, the CCP leaders deliberately did everything to exacerbate the differences further and launched more and more attacks against the CPSU, against the Soviet government and against the general line of the world Communist movement.

In their struggle against the CPSU and its Leninist course, the Chinese leaders are concentrating their fire primarily against Nikita Sergeyevich Khrushchev. Of course, they cannot fail to see that it is Nikita Sergeyevich himself who stands at the head of those remarkable processes that arose in our party and country after the 20th Congress and that are ensuring the Soviet people's successful progress toward Communism. (*Prolonged applause.*) This is why, for their subversive purposes, they would like to isolate Comrade Khrushchev from the Central Committee and place our Central Committee in opposition to the Party and the Soviet people.

But this filthy scheme is adventurist and hopeless, it is doomed to complete and shameful failure. (*Stormy, prolonged applause. All rise.*)

Our Central Committee, headed by that true Leninist Nikita Sergeyevich Khrushchev, is united and monolithic as never before, and the Chinese leaders — and not they alone — should make up their minds to that. (*Prolonged applause.*)

Comrade N. S. Khrushchev, with his inexhaustible energy, his truly Bolshevist ardor and adherence to principle, is the recognized leader of our party and people. He expresses the most cherished thoughts and aspirations of the Soviet people. The Leninist line pursued by our party cannot be divorced from the Central Committee, from Nikita Sergeyevich Khrushchev. This line has raised our country's prestige in the international arena to an unprecedented height, has lifted its authority in the eyes of working people throughout the world. All the Communists and all the people of our country adhere firmly to this Leninist line. (*Stormy applause. All rise.*)

Our party has never shrunk from ideological struggle and does not shrink from it now. But it believes that ideological differences should be resolved on the basis of Leninist principles, that the development of the polemic must be subordinated to the interests of the workers' movement.

The CPSU Central Committee clearly foresaw the danger in the Chinese leaders' striving to turn the open polemic from a means for clarifying controversial issues into a pretext for piling up absurd and slanderous accusations, into a weapon of ideological and political struggle against the Communist movement.

Together with the other Marxist-Leninist parties, our party has exerted great efforts to halt the open polemic forced by the CCP leaders. As is known, the CPSU Central Committee has repeatedly come forward with this kind of initiative, including the January, 1963, speech by First Secretary of the CPSU Central Committee N. S. Khrushchev to the Sixth Congress of the Socialist Unity Party of Germany. This initiative was supported by the overwhelming majority of Marxist-Leninist parties. But the Chinese government refused to discuss this proposal, widened the circle of controversial questions and sharpened and provoked the polemic.

An agreement was reached last spring on a bilateral meeting of representatives of the CPSU and the CCP. We went to it in the hope that the Chinese representatives would display a readiness to concentrate their efforts not on what divides us but on what unites the CCP with the CPSU and the other fraternal parties. The CPSU proposed that all controversial questions be discussed earnestly and in a businesslike way and that the path be cleared for a normalization of relations, for strengthening the unity of our parties and the entire international Communist movement. Our side proposed a concrete program for the development of relations between the USSR and the CPR.

However, the CCP delegation took advantage of the meeting to further exacerbate the differences and to make crude and unfounded attacks on the CPSU and other Marxist-Leninist parties. After reading prepared speeches that completely ignored our arguments and proposals, the Chinese delegates called for a recess in the bilateral meeting.

All the steps of the CPSU Central Committee have been prompted by a sincere concern for strengthening the unity of the Marxist-Leninist parties and the solidarity of the socialist countries. We were obliged not to yield to the heat of the struggle but to take full advantage of the existing possibilities for quelling the differences and averting a split.

Apparently the Chinese leadership appraised these steps on our part in a different light. It became clear that it regarded our restraint, our desire for unity as a manifestation of weakness. It has recently begun to say that it would work toward an improvement in relations with the CPSU only under conditions of the " unconditional surrender " of our side. What do the Chinese leaders want?

What it comes down to is that they want the Communist movement to yield its positions on all the vital problems that have been advanced by modern times.

The international Communist movement considers it vitally necessary to use the situation that has taken shape for bringing about the closer solidarity of all the revolutionary forces of the present day and for the further development of the world-wide revolutionary process.

As opposed to this, the Chinese leaders are working toward dividing the main revolutionary forces of modern times — the world socialist system, the international working class and the national-liberation movement ; this can only hold back the development of the world revolutionary process.

Marxist-Leninists believe that a paramount task of the Communist Parties is to consolidate all peace-loving forces for the defense of peace and to save mankind from a nuclear catastrophe ; they consider peaceful coexistence to be the general principle in relations between the socialist countries and the capitalist countries.

The Chinese leaders disregard this task. They are actually whipping up the nuclear arms race, fighting for the inclusion of more and more powers in it, pursuing a line that could lead to an atomic war, considering the struggle for peace a secondary task and opposing it to the struggle for socialism.

Marxist-Leninists see it as their duty to strengthen in every way the unity and solidarity of the socialist commonwealth on the principles of Marxism-Leninism and to focus the special attention of the socialist countries on the tasks of economic construction in order that socialism may win the victory in peaceful economic competition with capitalism.

The actions of the Chinese leaders are undermining and shaking the unity of the socialist camp and are increasingly isolating China from the other socialist countries. The CCP Central Committee underestimates economic construction and ignores the tasks of the socialist countries in their economic competition with the countries of capitalism. Such a course leads to a weakening of the might of the socialist countries and complicates their practical struggle against imperialism.

Marxist-Leninists and the working class of the capitalist countries see it as their task to develop the struggle against monopoly capital, to defend the vital interests of the popular masses, to take maximum advantage of the now existing possibilities for a peaceful path of socialist revolution that does not involve civil war, while at the same time being prepared for a nonpeaceful path, for armed suppression of resistance by the bourgeoisie.

In contrast to this, the CCP leaders are smearing in every way the struggle of the working class and its Communist vanguard for the vital interests of the working people, for peace and democracy, are rejecting the line toward the creation of broad antimonopoly alliances and the possibility of affecting the socialist revolution peacefully and are fighting for adventurist actions with weapons in hand, regardless of the concrete circumstances.

Marxist-Leninists and the peoples fighting for national independence consider it their task to bring the anti-imperialists, democratic revolution to completion, to create and consolidate the national front, and to struggle for the formation of national democratic states, for the noncapitalist path of development.

The Chinese leaders are sidestepping the essence of the present stage of the national-liberation revolution, do not see the differences in the situations of individual countries and are offering the peoples of all countries the same recipe — armed struggle and the establishment of the dictatorship of the proletariat. Such postulates can lead in practice to the undermining of the national front and a strengthening of the positions of the colonialists and neocolonialists.

Marxist Leninists are striving to strengthen the unity and solidarity both of each individual Communist Party and of the entire world army of Communists on the principles of the Declaration and the Statement.

The Chinese leaders are undermining the unity of the Communist movement and the democratic organizations, are creating factions and are striving to split our movement and its national detachments.

Thus the CCP leaders are coming out against the Communist movement on all the basic questions of its strategy and tactics. Their course is one in which petty-bourgeois revolutionism merges with nationalist, great-power aspirations.

In the malicious, completely slanderous anti-Soviet article printed in the press organs of the CCP Central Committee on Feb. 4, 1964, the Chinese leaders declare for all to hear that they will intensify their subversive activity against the international Communist movement. In their nationalist self-love they are boasting that they will continue their attacks on the CPSU in order to disorganize the activity of the Party created by the great Lenin.

The Soviet Communists — the sons and daughters of the October Revolution, the pioneers of the new Communist world to whose lot so many heavy tribulations have fallen — find it simply ridiculous to hear such threats.

The Soviet Communists will not keep silent when the Chinese leaders wage an unbridled attack on our great cause of communist construction, on the Leninist course of our party and on the positions of the international Communist movement. We shall be forced to explain for all to hear

267

the essence of the anti-Marxist, neo-Trotskyite positions of the Chinese leaders.

The task of defending Marxism-Leninism from the distortions of the Chinese leaders is now rising in all its sharpness. The interests of preserving the purity of the Marxist-Leninist teaching, the interests of the world Communist movement and, in the final analysis, the interests of the Chinese people themselves demand that we come out openly and resolutely against the incorrect views and dangerous actions of the CCP leadership. (*Prolonged applause.*)

We are in favour of strengthening friendship with the Chinese people and are prepared to develop cooperation with the CPR along all lines. The Soviet Communists regard the great Chinese people with sincere sympathy and have deep respect for the revolutionary traditions of the Communist Party of China. We are sure that no one will ever be able to undermine the foundations of the friendship of the great peoples of the Soviet Union and China, and that the present positions of the CCP leadership do not reflect the genuine national interests of the Chinese people. We will do everything in our power to return the relations between the Soviet Union and the Chinese People's Republic to a path that answers the vital interests of the working class and all the working people of our countries. (*Applause.*)

We are fully aware of the danger represented by the present position of the Chinese leaders. The facts show that we are in for a serious and from every indication a prolonged struggle for the strengthening of the unity of all socialist forces, for friendship and cooperation between the Soviet and Chineses peoples. It is now perfectly clear that the CCP leaders intend to continue stubbornly defending their mistaken line, intend to develop further their factional activity within the world Communist movement. Our party, together with the other fraternal parties, will resolutely defend Marxism-Leninism, will defend the unity and solidarity of the Communist movement on the principles of the Declaration and Statement of the 1957 and 1960 Moscow conferences of Communist and Workers' Parties and the unity and solidarity of all forces that support peace, democracy, national independence and socialism. (*Applause.*)

Our party is in favour of convening a new conference of fraternal parties to discuss the vital problems of the present day, of conducting at this conference the broadest exchange of opinions in the interests of overcoming difficulties within the Communist movement. These difficulties have been evoked by the CCP leadership's differences with the international Communist movement. It is therefore completely logical that the collective efforts of all the fraternal parties be exerted in order to determine the necessary ways and means for preserving and strengthening the Marxist-Leninist unity of the Communist ranks. It is perfectly clear to the CPSU that the conference should serve precisely these ends.

The CPSU Central Committee is confident that no matter how serious the difficulties in the world Communist movement may be, it will find within itself the strength to overcome them and to rally its ranks in the struggle for the great cause of communism.

The Communist Party of the Soviet Union will continue to pursue a line toward solidarity with all the fraternal parties on the principles of Marxism-Leninism and proletarian internationalism, on the basis of the program documents of the world Communist movement — the 1957 Declaration and the 1960 Statement.

The road our party and the international Communist movement are following is the Leninist, and therefore the only correct, road. We have adopted a new Program outlining the paths of our development for the next 20 years. Our party and the entire Soviet people regard the fulfilment of the Program, persistent and purposeful progress toward the heights of communism, as their supreme internationalist duty to the international workers' and Communist movement. And, as always, our party has been fulfilling and will continue to fulfill its internationalist duty with honour!

Under the invincible banner of the great Lenin, the Communist Party of the Soviet Union will continue unswervingly and persistently to pursue a line aimed at fulfilling the CPSU Program for the construction in our country of the most just of all social systems — communism. (*Stormy, prolonged applause. All rise.*)

DOCUMENT 11

Statement on the Stand of the Rumanian Workers' Party Concerning the Problems of the International Communist and Working-Class Movement

Adopted by the Enlarged Plenum of the Central Committee of the RWP Held in April 1964

Complete Text

[Translation based on the English-language version published by the Rumanian Workers' Party (Bucharest: Meridiane Publishing House, 1964) but revised from the original Rumanian text by Stephen Fischer-Galati, December 1965]

COMMUNIQUÉ[1]

The enlarged plenum of the Central Committee of the Rumanian Workers' Party was held between April 15 and 22, 1964. Attending the plenum were, in addition to the members and alternate members of the CC of the RWP, ministers, heads of central institutions, of mass and public organizations, of local party and state bodies, as well as other people holding responsible jobs in the central party and state apparatus.

The plenum heard the report on the activity of the delegation of the Rumanian Workers' Party that had conducted talks with the delegations of the Chinese Communist Party, the Korean Party of Labor, and the Communist Party of the Soviet Union.

The plenum of the Central Committee of the Rumanian Workers' Party unanimously approved the actions undertaken by the Politburo of the CC of the RWP in connection with the public controversy in the world Communist and working-class movement and the activity of the delegation of the Rumanian Workers' Party.

---

[1] *Scînteia*, April 23, 1964.

During the discussions that were held in a spirit of complete unity, the enlarged plenum unanimously adopted the relevant documents, which are going to be published.

STATEMENT

The enlarged plenum of the Central Committee of the Rumanian Workers' Party held in April 1964 has heard and discussed the report on the talks held by the delegation of the Rumanian Workers' Party with the leadership of the Chinese Communist Party, of the Korean Party of Labor, and of the Communist Party of the Soviet Union on the problem of the unity of the Communist and working-class movement. The plenum has unanimously adopted the actions undertaken by the Politburo of the Central Committee concerning the public controversy in the international Communist and working-class movement as well as the activity of the delegation of the Rumanian Workers' Party.

I. The Action of Our Party for the Cessation of the Public Controversy

As is known, differences of views and interpretation have arisen in recent years in the world Communist and working-class movement on the problems of the general line of the Communist movement — the assessment of the character of the contemporary era and its moving forces, the problem of peace and war, the paths of transition from capitalism to socialism, the norms of relations between Communist and workers' parties, among the socialist states, as well as other problems.

In discussing these problems a particularly sharp public controversy has ensued. The world Communist movement and the socialist camp are at present faced with the danger of a split.

Since the public controversy started, the Rumanian Workers' Party has given its full support to the proposals aimed at putting an end to it, has repeatedly appealed and insisted that it cease without delay, and spoken out for the settlement of controversial issues in conformity with the norms jointly established at the 1957 and 1960 conferences concerning relations among Communist parties.

On February 4, 1964 the newspaper *Jen-min Jih-pao* and the review *Hung Ch'i* published a polemic article in which, affirming that history demonstrates that "the international working-class movement is tending to split into two," the conclusion is drawn that this thesis is valid for the contemporary Communist movement as well. Stating that revisionism and opportunism have spread in the latter movement, the article declares that "wherever opportunism and revisionism play havoc, on the international plane and in each and every country, a split in the ranks of the proletariat becomes inevitable," and that "unity, struggle, and even splits, as well as a new unity, on a new basis — such is the dialectics of the development of the international working-class movement."

On February 13, 1964 the CC of the CPSU informed us that it had decided to publish the materials of its plenary meeting related to differences with the Chinese Communist Party; having decided on "a collective rebuff by the Marxist-Leninist parties" to the concepts and actions of the leaders of the Chinese Communist Party, the CC of the CPSU expressed the opinion that the convening of a conference of representatives of Communist and workers' parties was becoming increasingly timely.

All this has caused us great anxiety, since it aggravated the danger of a split that is threatening the international Communist movement.

Considering it the duty of every party to do its utmost to avert this danger, the Central Committee of the Rumanian Workers' Party decided to send the Central Committee of the CPSU and the Central Committee of the Chinese Communist Party a proposal for the immediate cessation of the public controversy. Thus on February 14, 1964, during the proceedings of the plenum of the CC of the CPSU, the Politburo of the CC of the RWP addressed to it a comradely and insistent appeal not to publish the materials of the plenum concerning the divergences with the Chinese Communist Party. Concomitantly the Politburo of the CC of the Rumanian Workers' Party addressed to the Central Committee of the Chinese Communist Party the same insistent appeal for a prompt end to the public controversy, at the same time suggesting to the Chinese comrades a meeting of the representatives of the top echelons of the two parties in order to discuss the problem of the unity of the socialist camp and of the international Communist movement.

The Central Committee of the CPSU gave us a reply on the same day to the effect that, heeding the intervention of the RWP, it had decided to delay the publication of the materials of the plenum and to refrain from publishing polemic material if the Chinese comrades would also cease the public controversy.

On February 17, 1964 the Central Committee of our party received a letter from Comrade Mao Tse-tung indicating that the CC of the Chinese Communist Party agreed to a meeting of the representatives of the leadership of the Chinese Communist Party and the Rumanian Workers' Party, and he invited a delegation of our party to China with this end in view. We were also informed that if the Rumanian Workers' Party decided to send its delegation to China soon, the Central Committee of the Chinese Communist Party could temporarily suspend the publication of polemic materials.

The Central Committee of the Rumanian Workers' Party informed the other fraternal parties too about the approach it had made and expressed the view that it was necessary for all Communist and workers' parties to discontinue the public controversy in the interest of finding ways and means to ensure unity ; at the same time we voiced our hope that our party's proposals and position would meet with understanding and support.

In the replies transmitted to us numerous fraternal parties welcomed the initiative of the Rumanian Workers' Party and considered it particularly useful, declaring that it met with their approval.

In the Chinese People's Republic the delegation of our party had talks with the delegation of the Chinese Communist Party and with Comrade Mao Tse-tung. The situation created in the international Communist and working-class movement as well as problems of joint interest to the two parties and countries were discussed in full sincerity and in a comradely spirit. The exchange of views enabled the two sides to become better acquainted with their respective points of view.

The fundamental aim of the Rumanian party delegation was to obtain an agreement on the immediate cessation of the open polemics. The Chinese comrades declared that the open polemics could be stopped only after an agreement was reached through bilateral and multilateral discussions on the conditions of its cessation. In their opinion the polemics were to continue till then, while in the meantime bilateral talks could take place between the Chinese Communist Party and the Communist Party of the Soviet Union and other fraternal parties.

As a result of the action undertaken by the Rumanian Workers' Party, the open polemics were interrupted for almost one month by both the CPSU and the CCP. Encouraged by this fact, as well as by its positive response in the Communist movement, the delegation of our party proposed to the CC of the CCP that, at least while discussing the conditions for its cessation, the two sides should continue to abstain from publishing polemic materials. However, this proposal was not accepted; the Chinese comrades restated their opinion that the discussions could take place also while the public controversy was going on.

In response to the invitation of the Korean Party of Labor, our party delegation paid a short visit to the Korean People's Democratic Republic. During the exchange of views with Comrade Kim Il-sŏng and with other leaders of the Korean Party of Labor, our delegation gave an account of the talks held in Peking and presented the stand of the Rumanian Workers' Party on problems of common interest affecting our two parties and countries, on the solidarity of the socialist camp, and on the unity of the world Communist movement.

After the visit to China and Korea, on its way home, our delegation, following the proposal of the Central Committee of the Rumanian Workers' Party, had talks with Comrade Khrushchev and with other CPSU leaders in the Soviet Union regarding the problem of the unity of the socialist countries and of the world Communist movement. During the meetings, held in an atmosphere of friendship and mutual understanding, our delegation informed the Soviet comrades about the talks held in China and Korea and again stated our party's point of view concerning the question of the total cessation of the public controversy.

The Soviet comrades declared that since the Chinese side had reopened the controversy, they were compelled to publish the report related to the question of divergences that was presented at the plenum. As a consequence of the talks, the Soviet comrades agreed to postpone the publication of the report, stating that if, after a renewed approach of ours, the Chinese comrades agreed to stop the controversy the Soviet side would be ready to act likewise and not resume publication of polemic materials.

In the period in which the action of our party was under way, we were informed that letters between the Central Committee of the Chinese Communist Party and the Central Committee of the Communist Party of the Soviet Union had been exchanged, whereby — despite the differences of views on the manner of approaching the question of the cessation of the controversy, on the dates proposed, and on other measures — both parties pronounced themselves in favor of the continuation of their talks and the setting up of a commission with a view to preparing for the conference of the representatives of all Communist and workers' parties. In our opinion these common elements can constitute a starting point for an action aimed at normalizing relations within the Communist movement.

Having heard the report presented by our party delegation, the Politburo of the Central Committee decided to undertake a new action to safeguard the unity of the Communist movement by proposing to the Central

Committee of the Communist Party of the Soviet Union and to the Central Committee of the Chinese Communist Party that those two parties, together with the Rumanian Workers' Party, jointly address an appeal to all the Communist and workers' parties.

On March 25, 1964 the Central Committee of the Rumanian Workers' Party sent the draft appeal to the Central Committees of the CPSU and the CCP; we mentioned that in the event of both parties agreeing in principle to this action, the draft appeal could be discussed and finalized at a meeting of the representatives of the three parties while, until its finalizing, both sides should refrain from engaging in any form of public controversy.

An answer to this proposal has been given only by the Central Committee of the Communist Party of the Soviet Union, which, in its letter of March 28, 1964, informed us that " in general the Central Committee of the Communist Party of the Soviet Union agrees to the draft appeal to the fraternal parties prepared by the Central Committee of the Rumanian Workers' Party. If the Central Committee of the Chinese Communist Party also manifests a positive stand on your proposal concerning the immediate cessation of controversy in any form and agrees to the proposal concerning the joint appeal of the Communist Party of the Soviet Union, the Chinese Communist Party and the Rumanian Workers' Party to all the Communist workers' parties, we agree to proceed immediately to the examination of the draft appeal in order to work out jointly its final form."

On March 31, 1964 the Chinese press published a new leading article in the newspaper *Jen-min Jih-pao* and the review *Hung Ch'i*.

On April 3, 1964 the Soviet press published the materials of the plenum of the Central Committee of the Communist Party of the Soviet Union held in February 1964.

The public controversy, joined by numerous fraternal parties, is proceeding with growing intensity. A particularly serious situation has been created in the international Communist movement. The question arises as to what the prospects of this situation are in case the public controversy is not terminated and in case it goes on aggravating the relations among the Communist workers' parties, among the socialist states and their peoples, thus aggravating the danger of splitting the world Communist movement and the camp of the socialist countries.

Analyzing this state of affairs, the Central Committee of the Rumanian Workers' Party deems it necessary to expound in greater detail its viewpoint on the main problems of contemporary social life and the development of the international Communist and working-class movement, as well as on ways of safeguarding its unity.

II. Our Epoch — the Epoch of Transition from Capitalism to Socialism

An analysis of contemporary reality spotlights the huge social-economic transformations that have taken place in the world, the change in the balance of forces in favor of socialism, in the first place as a result of the formation of the world socialist system.

The victory of the new social order in a number of states, comprising one third of the world's population, has made a huge breach in the imperialist front, has created new, incomparably more favorable conditions for the struggle of the peoples in fulfilment of their aspirations for freedom and progress, has carried the entire world revolutionary process of mankind's transition from capitalism to socialism into a new stage. Nowadays there is no field in the evolution of society, in political, economic, and social life, no problem pertaining to class relations in the capitalist countries, in the national liberation movement, in international relations, and in the ideological struggle that is not profoundly influenced by the existence of the world socialist system.

At present, more strongly than ever before, the historic role of the working class as the most advanced force in society is asserting itself, and so is the role of the Communist and workers' parties as the vanguard of the broad masses of the people in the battle for socialism and peace.

The renewing changes in today's world find a mighty expression in the upsurge of the national liberation movement and in the collapse of the colonial system, in the struggle of the new independent states for consolidating their sovereignty, for peace and economic and social development.

An unprecedented scope has been assumed by the struggle for averting the danger of thermonuclear war and to ensure peace.

The narrowing down of the sphere of action of imperialism, as a result of the development of all these forces, has caused a sharpening of the economic, political, and social contradictions in the capitalist world. Although even in the conditions of the deepening of its general crisis capitalism still has possibilities for achieving progress in the field of science and technology and for obtaining output increases in certain countries or in certain economic branches, important production capacities remain idle ; there is a permanent worsening of the phenomena of instability of the capitalist economy. The concentration of capital on both the internal and international planes, the setting up of big monopoly unions, and the growth of their omnipotence in state life sharpen class antagonisms and the contradiction between the interests of the monopolies and those of the nation as a whole.

There is a striking gap between the group of capitalist countries advanced from the economic point of view and the numerous underdeveloped countries. If there is a current problem of the underdeveloped countries it is due to imperialism, to the colonial policy that has created this situation by exploiting the resources of the weak countries, preventing the creation in those countries of a developed national industry, arresting their progress. The struggle waged by these countries in various forms with a view to removing the consequences of colonial domination creates new contradictions within the capitalist world.

There is a sharpening of contradictions between the big monopoly unions, between the chief imperialist powers, in their struggle for raw materials, for markets, and areas of investment, for dominating positions in the imperialist military alliances.

The setting up of interstate economic organizations or of superstate bodies, such as the Common Market, the Coal and Steel Community, and others, leads to intensified interimperialist contradictions, encroaching on the sovereignty of smaller or weaker member countries. In the Common Market, contradictions, particularly among its principal member nations, between the countries in that category and other capitalist states, between the West European countries and the United States, are becoming more pronounced. In this knot of contradictions the United States strives to maintain its position as the leading force of the capitalist world, whereas the tendencies of other imperialist states endeavoring to rid themselves of U.S. tutelage run in the opposite direction.

Characteristic of the deepening of the general crisis in capitalism is the growing tendency to impose limitations on bourgeois democracy. The crisis in capitalist ideology is also manifest; despite its powerful means to exert pressure, it is unable to arrest the ever-growing power of attraction of the ideas of socialism.

To the question of which is the essential problem of our era and which are its determining factors, the principal moving forces of world development, life provides but one answer: **the quintessence of our epoch is the transition from capitalism to socialism; at present the character, direction, and particularities in the historical evolution of human society are determined by the world socialist system, by the forces fighting against imperialism, for the socialist transformation of society.**

The clarification of problems linked to the assessment of the contemporary epoch and its principal features is of particular significance, from the viewpoint of both principle and practice. Based on the correct understanding of the social and historical framework in which they carry on their activity, of the stage of social evolution, on the accurate assessment of the class forces in every country, and the balance of forces in the world arena, the Communist parties work out a correct strategy and tactics, set themselves realistic battle objectives.

Marx, Engels, and Lenin assigned the greatest significance to the thorough study of concrete historical conditions and demanded of Communists that they analyze the changes that appear in the course of social evolution in order to draw the appropriate theoretical and practical conclusions.

Today the prevailing international conditions are more favorable than ever for waging the struggle for the social and national liberation of the peoples, for peace, and for socialism. The sharp public controversy in the Communist movement hampers the full utilization of these conditions, diminishes the role and influence of the world socialist system, diverts the Communist and workers' parties from their major tasks, adversely affects the fighting unity of the international working class and the national liberation movement, and disorients the masses.

As the Statement of the 1960 conference points out, in our days the union into a single torrent, into a single stream, of all the revolutionary forces and progressive currents of contemporaneity imposes itself as an objective necessity. Their close cohesion and their united action are the decisive factors in the victory over imperialism, in the triumph of socialism, national liberation and peace throughout the world.

III. The Defense of Peace, the Vital Cause of All Mankind

Peace is the burning aspiration of all mankind. Given the serious peril that a new world war would represent to all peoples, a war that would cause calamities and sufferings incomparable to those of the past, the largest masses of people, political and social forces all over the world have taken up the struggle for safeguarding and strengthening peace.

The most important results obtained in recent years in this struggle are that peace has been maintained and that the beginnings of a détente in international life are noticeable. The actions of aggressive military circles are meeting with growing opposition; world public opinion increasingly isolates the supporters of war and those eager to keep tensions and the arms race alive. Reappraisals are occurring also in capitalist countries, which manifest tendencies toward the normalization of international relations to prevent events from drifting toward a world conflagration.

To Communists it is absolutely obvious that the aggressive and reactionary nature of imperialism has not changed, that as long as there is imperialism there remains a breeding ground for aggressive wars. The extremist, militarist circles have not renounced the idea of changing history's course, which is unfavorable to them, of quelling the people's liberation struggle, and to this end are resorting to all means, including arms.

However, a scientific analysis aimed at mapping out a correct policy cannot be limited to noting the characteristic features of imperialism but must take into account the decisive fact that, although the essence of imperialism has not changed, the balance of forces has undergone a radical change in favor of peace.

Gigantic, ever-growing forces are opposing imperialism: the community of socialist countries, with its huge material strength, the working class in the capitalist countries, the national liberation movement, the states that have recently achieved independence, the extensive movement for the defense of peace. The rallying of all these forces, their joining into the broadest of fronts, their resolute struggle prevent imperialism from calling its own shots in the international arena any longer, make it possible to foil the attempts of the imperialist circles to hurl mankind into a new world war, make it possible to enforce and consolidate peace. The Communists consider their historical mission not only to abolish exploitation on a world scale but, already in our era, to save mankind from the nightmare of a new world war and are devoting their capacity and energy to the implementation of this lofty task.

Undoubtedly the existence of nuclear missiles does not and cannot change the nature of the relations between antagonistic classes, the laws of class struggle and of the evolution of society along the road of progress. The fact cannot be ignored, however, that the appearance, development, and stockpiling of nuclear weapons have brought about essential changes in the mode of warfare as well as in the scope of the destructive effects war would entail for all mankind. A world conflagration, in which nuclear weapons would inevitably be used, would lead to the destruction of whole countries and peoples, be they belligerent or nonbelligerent, to the leveling of the chief centers of production and culture, to the extermination of hundreds of millions of people and would create a serious biological danger for the human species, for life on earth.

The steady increase in the destructive power of armaments fully bears out Engels' and Lenin's forecast regarding the consequences of improvements in the field of military techniques. Thus Engels pointed out that, according to the inner laws of the dialectical movement, " militarism, like any other historical phenomenon, perishes as a result of its own development." [2] And Lenin pointed out as far back as 1918 that the rapid development of military techniques increasingly contributes to the aggravation of the destructive nature of war, and he expressed his conviction that war would eventually become so destructive as to be generally impossible.

[2] F. Engels, *Anti-Duhring*, Rumanian ed., 1955, p. 192.

Aware of the great responsibility devolving on them as regards mankind's future, the Communist parties consider it their duty to make known the actual extent of the danger of thermonuclear war so as to mobilize and rally to resolute struggle the international working class, the revolutionary forces, the peoples throughout the world with a view to barring the path of war.

While militating for the safeguarding of peace, the socialist countries show unflinching vigilance and strengthen their defense capacity so as to be able to cope with any aggressor. In this respect, the huge force created by the Soviet Union in terms of missiles and nuclear weapons, placed in the service of the security of the socialist countries and of peace, is of paramount importance.

Realizing the risks a nuclear conflict would entail for their own countries, influential political circles in the West come out in favor of forsaking war as a means of setting international issues, in favor of a rational policy.

The great powers, especially those possessing nuclear weapons, bear particular responsibility for preserving and consolidating peace. But no state, big or small, can escape the responsibility of ensuring peace. Every state has the sacred duty of militating actively and tirelessly, of making its own contribution to the lessening of international tension and the settlement of interstate issues through negotiation.

The principle of peaceful coexistence among countries with different social systems underlies the foreign policy of the socialist states. This principle implies the settlement of international controversial issues by negotiation, without resorting to war, on the basis of acknowledging the right of every people to decide its own fate, of observing the sovereignty and territorial integrity of states, of full equality, and of mutual noninterference in internal affairs.

Peaceful coexistence among states with different social systems does not mean abandoning class policy; it does not apply to relations between antagonistic classes, between exploiters and exploited, between oppressed peoples and their oppressors; it does not mean cessation of the struggle between bourgeois and socialist ideology. Under conditions of peaceful coexistence the forces of the world socialist system have continued to strengthen themselves, the struggle of the working class in capitalist countries, the national liberation movement have developed further.

The policy of peaceful coexistence pursued by the socialist countries is one of the main sources of the prestige and esteem enjoyed by socialism throughout the world and stands as the bedrock of the successes that have so far been obtained with regard to preserving and consolidating peace. The Rumanian Workers' Party, our people, highly appreciate the persevering activity of the Soviet Union, its initiatives and proposals aimed at easing international tension, at settling outstanding international issues by means of negotiation, at ensuring lasting peace.

As experience has shown, the statesmen who abandon the language of threats, who give proof of realism, wisdom, patience, and perseverance, are able to find through negotiation mutually acceptable solutions to the most complex and thorny issues of interstate relations. Negotiation on this basis with any capitalist country to seek solutions to outstanding issues and improve interstate relations in no way means abandonment of principles: rather, it means serving the interests of peace.

The method of negotiation in international relations demands that persevering efforts be made, that proof be given of flexibility, that there be taken into account the contradictions prevailing in the capitalist world, the existence of those circles that assess in a lucid manner the present-day balance of forces in the international arena, that use be made of this situation in order to isolate the ultrareactionary circles promoting international tension. Highly relevant in this respect are Lenin's indications: " It is not indifferent to us," he said in 1922, " whether we have to deal with those representatives of the bourgeois camp who tend to settle the issue by means of war or with those of its representatives who incline towards pacifism, no matter how deficient this pacifism may be or how little it could withstand, from the viewpoint of communism, even the feeblest of criticisms." [3] In its relations with capitalist countries, our country is guided by these judicious recommendations of Lenin's and consistently speaks out in favor of the settlement of outstanding issues between states by means of negotiation.

The development of trade, of economic relations based on mutual advantage, as well as the extension of technical and scientific ties, of cultural exchanges, are an extremely important means of advancing peaceful coexistence among states with different social systems, of improving the international climate, of bringing about a lessening of tension, and of strengthening peace throughout the world.

As is known, the supporters of the " cold war," intending to hamstring the development of the socialist countries, have been pursuing for quite a long time a policy of embargo and discrimination in trade relations with these countries. This policy of narrowing down economic relations, however, not only failed to hinder the forward march of the socialist countries but boomeranged against its initiators through the negative effects produced by the violation of the objective necessities of the development of world economic relations. Western businessmen and even certain economic circles in the United States of America show growing interest in developing trade with the socialist countries.

General and complete disarmament is an important objective of the fight for peace. An idea with broad popular appeal, the problem of disarmament, has long since been raised by the leaders of the proletariat as a fighting slogan of the working-class party. As early as the eighties of the last century Engels stated: " In all countries, the broad strata of the population, who are almost exclusively carrying the burden of providing the rank and file of soldiers and of paying the bulk of taxes, call for disarmament." [4] Proposals concerning the general reduction of armaments and general disarmament were first submitted, on Lenin's recommendation, by the Soviet state to the Genoa conference of 1922. They were continued and developed in the proposals for general and complete disarmament advocated by the Soviet delegation at the League of Nations in 1927–1932.

Today the problem of disarmament is much more acute because of the danger posed by modern weapons, as well as the enormous waste of resources inherent in the process of arming. According to estimates of the United Nations, 120 billion dollars are spent annually on stockpiling weapons of destruction and on the upkeep of immense armed forces ; this

[3] V. I. Lenin, *Works*, Vol. 33, Rumanian ed., 1957, p. 256.
[4] K. Marx and F. Engels, *Works*, Vol. 22.

sum could be used for doing away with the economic backwardness of a large number of countries, illiteracy, and disease as well as for improving the life of all peoples.

Of historical importance for mankind would be the adoption of the program of general and complete disarmament put forward by the Soviet Union and backed by the other socialist countries as well as by other peace-loving states ; this program provides for the prohibition of and the putting an end to the production of all kinds of weapons, including atomic, hydrogen, chemical, and bacteriological weapons, the destruction of all stocks of weapons and of all means of carrying nuclear missiles to their targets, the dismantling of military bases on foreign territory, and the abolition of all armed forces.

The most aggressive monopolistic circles, which profit from the arms drive, stubbornly oppose any measure aimed at disarmament and at a relaxation of tension. The fight for peace, for disarmament, has a profoundly anti-imperialist nature ; it mobilizes and unites the broad masses of the people and the nations of the world precisely against the aggressive circles of imperialism, against the most reactionary forces of contemporary society.

As was pointed out in the Statement of the 1960 conference, " it is necessary to wage this struggle on an increasing scale and to strive perseveringly to achieve tangible results — the banning of the testing and manufacture of nuclear weapons, the abolition of military blocs and war bases on foreign soil, and a substantial reduction of armed forces and armaments, all of which should pave the way to general disarmament." It is along this road that one must advance steadfastly, adopting any measure favoring a détente, bringing nearer a settlement of the problem of disarmament.

It is in this sense that we appraise the importance of the Moscow treaty on the banning of nuclear weapons tests in the atmosphere, outer space, and underwater, of which the Rumanian People's Republic was one of the first signatory states. The conclusion of this treaty represents an achievement for the forces of peace that have sought to put an end to the pollution of air and water by radiation, which has already jeopardized the health and life of people ; the conclusion of the treaty strengthens the people's resolution to pursue even more energetically the struggle for cessation of all nuclear tests, for the banning of atomic weapons, for the implementation of disarmament. Although it does not solve the major problems of averting war, the importance of the treaty lies in the fact that it has contributed to a certain improvement in the international atmosphere ; its conclusion has shown that disputed international issues can be settled through negotiations. That is why we hold it unjust to term this treaty an act of betrayal of the interests of the peoples in the countries of the socialist camp, a great piece of humbug, or an expression of allying with the forces of war against the forces of peace, of allying with imperialism against socialism.

The Rumanian People's Republic is promoting a policy of developing relations of friendship and fraternal cooperation with all socialist countries, of constantly strengthening the unity of the socialist camp, of solidarity and of resolute support for the people's liberation movement, and of developing relations of cooperation with countries that have a different social-political system, on the basis of the principles of peaceful coexistence. Joining efforts with the other socialist countries, with all forces of peace and progress, our country staunchly militates for international détente, for frustrating the actions of aggressive circles, for attaining disarmament, for strengthening peace and friendship among nations.

We stand for the abolition of all military blocs and, as a transitional measure in this direction, we declare ourselves in favor of the conclusion of a nonaggression pact between the Warsaw Treaty Organization and the North Atlantic Treaty Organization.

Our country stands for the setting up of denuclearized zones as a means of reducing the danger of war. We support the plans for the creation of such zones in Central and Northern Europe, in Latin America, in Africa, in the Pacific area, and in other regions of the world, and we make persevering efforts for the transformation of the Balkans into a zone without nuclear weapons, into a zone of peace and international cooperation.

We consider that **doing away with the remnants of the Second World War,** through conclusion of the German peace treaty, would be most important for the elimination of the danger created to peace in Europe by the revenge-seeking circles.

Appreciating the role incumbent on the United Nations in ensuring peace and developing international cooperation, Rumania emphasizes that the United Nations should become a genuinely universal organization, and therefore Rumania consistently upholds that the legitimate rights of the Chinese People's Republic in the United Nations be restored without further delay.

The guarantee for the victory of the cause of peace rests in the unity of the socialist countries — the fundamental force of the struggle for peace, in the unity of the Communist and workers' parties — the vanguard of this struggle. It is a pressing task of the socialist countries, of the fraternal parties not to agree to anything that might lead to a weakening of the peace forces, to militate for closely rallying all these forces into a huge fighting front, to mobilize them for new, resolute actions aimed at ensuring peace.

IV. The World Socialist System — a Decisive Factor of Historical Development

The decisive influence exerted by the world socialist system upon historical development is indissolubly related to its force in all fields — economic, political, and social.

In the economic field, thanks to the rapid rates of industrial development, which are higher than those in the capitalist world, the share of the world socialist system in the world's industrial production rose from 20 per cent in 1950 to 38 per cent in 1963.

In the Soviet Union the all-round construction of communism is successfully being achieved; the upsurge of the productive forces finds expression in the fulfillment and overfulfillment of assignments under the seven-year plan; the Soviet Union holds first place in the world as to volume of output in a number of industrial products; a vast program of agricultural development is being carried out. Remarkable results have been obtained in the technical-scientific and cultural fields, in improving the people's well-being.

In the Chinese People's Republic, following the efforts made during the first two five-year plans, the basis for the country's socialist industrialization has been built. In 1963 significant successes were achieved in raising industrial and farm output, in developing the national economy, and in the continuous improvement in the working people's living standard.

Substantial achievements have also been recorded by other socialist countries in their economy and culture, science and technology; several socialist countries, including Rumania, have entered the phase of completing socialist construction.

The achievement of so vast a task as the building of a new society calls for the solution of a large number of complex problems; in this connection difficulties may occur and mistakes may be made, but characteristic in the evolution of socialist countries are exactly the great successes obtained in making the economy and culture flourish, in continuously developing the social order and the state system.

In accordance with the changes in the economic foundation, deep-going transformations have taken place in the social structure of these countries, a new society has taken shape, the alliance of the working class and the peasant masses under the leadership of the former has strengthened and so has the moral and political unity of the people. The Communist and workers' parties, accumulating rich experience, are the leading political force of society. Socialist democracy develops; people's power has proved its durability.

Through the results they obtain, the socialist countries show that socialism does away with the evils, inequalities, and contradictions inherent in capitalism, creates an equitable, superior social system, provides the prerequisites for a high and permanently rising labor productivity, ensures the continuous extension and full utilization of the technical and scientific means devised by man's genius, and that the fundamental goal of socialism is the maximum satisfaction of the ever-growing material and spiritual requirements of those who work.

Of course, an objective analysis cannot ignore the fact that most of the countries in which socialism has triumphed started from a low economic level. The distance they have covered within an historically short period, the important successes they have achieved in industrialization, the steady narrowing down of the gap separating them from the advanced capitalist countries go to show that only socialism opens up vistas of rapid progress to all peoples. These results are in striking contrast with the uneven development and the instability characteristic of the economy of capitalist countries, with the inability of the capitalist system to wrest the underdeveloped countries, which account for the overwhelming majority of the capitalist world, from their state of economic and cultural backwardness.

The socialist countries' achievements and perspectives arouse a mighty international response, inspire the masses of working people in the capitalist countries to revolutionary struggle under the guidance of the Communist and workers' parties for the overthrow of the rule of capital and the setting up of the power of the working people, and are a stimulus for the socialist transformation of society. This confirms Lenin's foresight when, at the time of the emergence of the very first socialist state, he already stressed the importance of the historic competition between capitalism and socialism.

The construction of a new society is the historical achievement of the people of that country, the fruit of their creative activities, of their efforts and labors.

The successes obtained by the Rumanian People's Republic and by the other socialist countries show that the successful solution of the tasks of developing the economy depends first and foremost on the utilization of each country's internal possibilities, through an intense mustering of its own forces and the maximum use of its natural resources. Decisive for the development of the countries that inherited economic backwardness from capitalism is socialist industrialization, the only road that ensures the harmonious, balanced, and ever ascending as well as rapid growth of the whole national economy, the continuous rise of the productivity of social labor, the intensive and complex development of agriculture, the systematic improvement in the people's living standards. The results obtained by our country in all fields of socialist construction are indissolubly linked to this policy, which is consistently pursued by the Rumanian Workers' Party.

At the same time the economic and technical-scientific progress of the socialist countries relies on the relations of cooperation and mutual assistance established among them. These fruitful relations have seen a steady development; they have proved their efficiency, making a particularly important contribution to the successes scored by the socialist countries.

With a view to the complete utilization of the advantages of these relations, the Council for Mutual Economic Aid was set up. According to its statutes it aims to contribute, through the uniting and coordination of efforts, to the development of the national economy, to speeding up economic and technological progress, to raising the level of industrialization of the less developed countries, to the steady increase in labor productivity, and to the ceaseless improvement in the welfare of the peoples in the member countries.

Cooperation within CMEA is achieved on the basis of the principles of fully equal rights, of observance of national sovereignty and interests, of mutual advantage and comradely assistance.

As concerns the method of economic cooperation, the socialist countries that are members of CMEA have established that the main means of achieving the international socialist division of labor, the main form of cooperation among their national economies, is to coordinate plans on the basis of bilateral and multilateral agreements.

During the development of the relations of cooperation among the socialist countries that are members of CMEA, forms and measures have been projected, such as a joint plan and a single planning body for all member countries, interstate technical-productive branch unions, enterprises jointly owned by several countries, interstate economic complexes, etc.

Our party has very clearly expressed its point of view, declaring that, since the essence of the projected measures lies in shifting some functions of economic management from the competence of the respective state to that of superstate bodies or organisms, these measures are not in keeping with the principles that underlie the relations among the socialist countries.

The idea of a single planning body for all CMEA countries has the most serious economic and political implications. The planned management of the national economy is one of the fundamental, essential, and inalienable attributes of the sovereignty of the socialist state — the state plan being the chief means through which the socialist state achieves its political and socioeconomic objectives, establishes the directions and rates of development of the national economy, its fundamental proportions, the accumulations, the measures for raising the people's living standard and cultural level. The sovereignty of the socialist state requires that it effectively and fully avail itself of the means for the practical implementation of these functions, holding in its hands all the levers of managing economic and social life. Transmitting such levers to the competence of superstate or extrastate bodies would turn sovereignty into a meaningless notion.

All these are also fully valid as concerns interstate technical-productive branch unions as well as enterprises commonly owned by two or several states. The state plan is one and indivisible; no parts or sections can be separated from it in order to be transferred outside the state. The management of the national economy as a whole is not possible if the questions of managing some branches or enterprises are taken away from the competence of the party and government of the respective country and transferred to extrastate bodies.

Sometimes such forms of superstate economic management are presented as deriving from Lenin's words on " the tendency of creating a single world economy, regulated by the proletariat of all nations according to a general plan, a tendency that appears quite evidently already in capitalism and which undoubtedly will be developed and fully accomplished in socialism." [5]

This presentation, however, ignores the fact that Lenin referred to a problem of the time when socialism would be victorious throughout the world, when " **the general plan** " of a " **single world economy** " would be carried out by the proletariat " **of all nations.**"

Even when socialism has triumphed on a world scale or at least in most countries, the diversity of the peculiarities of these countries, of the distinctive national and state features, which, as Lenin pointed out, will prevail for a long time even after the victory of the proletariat on a world scale, will make it an extremely complex task to find the organizational forms of economic cooperation. Life, experience, will shape these forms, the concrete methods of cooperation. To establish now these forms linked to the setting up of a single world economy, a problem of a future historical stage, lacks any real basis.

The trend toward the creation of a single world economy as indicated by Lenin is an objective factor in the development of society, one manifest in present-day conditions as well, but this factor cannot operate by violating the objective laws characteristic of the present stage of the socialist world economic system, which comprises the national economies of sovereign and independent countries.

Such is the viewpoint of the Rumanian Workers' Party on the nature of the relations of economic cooperation among the socialist countries in the present stage of history.

Undoubtedly if some socialist countries deem it fit to adopt in the direct relations between them forms of cooperation different from those unanimously agreed upon within CMEA, that is a question that exclusively concerns those countries, and can be decided by them alone in a sovereign way.

In the present conditions, when there are 14 socialist countries in the world, and only some of them are CMEA members, so that the latter's

[5] V. I. Lenin, *Works*, Vol. 31, Rumanian ed., 1956, p. 129.

structure only partially reflects the configuration of the world socialist system, an aim that would contribute to the development of economic cooperation among all socialist countries would be that, together with those not belonging to CMEA at present, the best ways be found for the participation in CMEA of all socialist countries, that the broadest and most flexible forms and methods of cooperation be secured that should attract more and more states and facilitate their inclusion, in step with the progress of the world revolutionary process. In this way CMEA would meet to the highest degree the interests of enhancing the economic might of the socialist community, fully using the advantages of the transformation of socialism into a world system, and securing a firm material base for the unity of the socialist countries. Moreover, we consider that forms and methods of participation in CMEA activity have to be found even for those countries that proceed along the path of noncapitalist development in the areas that would be of interest to them.

As for the Rumanian Workers' Party, it steadfastly stands for the strengthening and extension of cooperation with all the socialist countries, for the implementation of the socialist international division of labor within the whole socialist economic system as an objective necessity for developing this system.

At the same time the socialist international division of labor cannot mean isolation of the socialist countries from the general framework of world economic relations. Standing consistently for normal, mutually advantageous economic relations, without political strings and without restrictions or discriminations, the Rumanian People's Republic, like the other socialist states, develops its economic links with all states irrespective of their social system. Highly topical and fully corroborated are Lenin's words to the effect that "there is a force more powerful than the wish, will or determination of any of the governments or classes hostile to us; this force consists in the general economic world relations that compel them to take this path of establishing links with us." [6]

The transformation of socialism into a world system, the winning of power by the working people in a number of states, has faced the Communist and workers' parties with the task of radically changing not only social relations on a national level in their own country but also of organizing mutual relations among these countries, of working out the norms of cooperation within the framework of a great world community of states. This has arisen as an entirely new problem, one for which there was no previous practical experience — and which was all the more complex as it concerned countries differing in size, might, degree of economic, political, and social development, in addition to their national distinctions and historic peculiarities.

By promoting in the international arena a qualitatively new system of relations, unprecedented in history, the Communist and workers' parties in the socialist countries have placed at the foundation of these relations the principles of **national independence and sovereignty, equal rights, mutual advantage, comradely assistance, noninterference in internal affairs, observance of territorial integrity, the principles of socialist internationalism.**

As underlined in the Statement of the 1960 conference, and fully confirmed by historical experience, these principles form the immutable law and the

---

[6] *Ibid.*, Vol. 33, Rumanian ed., 1957, p. 142.

guarantee of the development of the entire world socialist system. They have imposed themselves as an objective necessity for the development of relations of cooperation, for securing the unity of action and cohesion of a community of independent states, with equal rights. Any curtailment or violation of these principles can be only a source of misunderstanding and discord.

It is a matter of great concern that the present divergences and the ever-sharper public controversy within the international Communist and working-class movement have repercussions in the field of relations among the countries of the socialist camp. Economic relations are affected, trade exchanges are diminished, mutual political relations deteriorate, and an atmosphere of distrust and tension is created among the respective countries, and this weakens the unity and force of the entire world socialist system.

The fundamental interests of all peoples and of all socialist countries without exception, the interests of the world Communist and working-class movement, the supreme interests of the international working class and of the working people everywhere call for the speedy normalization of relations among the socialist countries. Our party believes that even if the divergences are not solved now and, to the deep regret of the Communists, the public controversy is continued, the interstate relations among the socialist countries must resume their normal course. Our party regards this as an immediate and pressing obligation of the Communist and workers' parties in all the socialist countries, big or small, and of the governments of these countries, as an imperative duty toward their own as well as all peoples.

In their historical development the socialist countries have become stronger economically, politically, and socially; the Communist and workers' parties of these countries have matured; and their capacity to solve various problems pertaining to construction at home and the international relations of their countries has grown. In the evolution of the world socialist system, alongside the growth of its force and influence, the all-round development of every socialist country, a diversity of concrete tasks appear, varying from one country to another, as part of the common fundamental aims. Acting in a spirit of unity and solidarity, giving each other mutual assistance, it is natural for the socialist states to display initiative, to manifest themselves actively in the international arena, to undertake various actions in line with the specific problems and interests of each of them as well as with the general interests of the socialist community as a whole.

Fully valid are the words of Lenin who pointed out that "as long as there are national and state distinctions among peoples and countries — and such distinctions will continue to exist for a very long time even after the establishment of the proletarian dictatorship on a world scale — the unity of the international tactics of the Communist and working-class movement of all countries does not require the elimination of diversities or the abolition of national distinctions (which would be an absurd dream at present), but on the contrary the implementation of the *fundamental* principles of communism . . . which should modify these principles in a correct way in their details, to adapt them properly and apply them according to the national distinctions of each national state." [7]

[7] *Ibid.*, Vol. 31, Rumanian ed., 1956, p. 75.

Starting from this Leninist truth, according to which the states and the national distinctions will be maintained until the world-wide victory of socialism, and even a long time after it, the socialist countries achieve their unity of action in all domains, economic as well as political, by reciprocal consultations, the joint elaboration of certain common stands as regards the major problems of principle, and not by establishing unique solutions by some superstate authority. This is the only correct and possible way of developing cooperation among sovereign and equal states; it guarantees the adoption of realistic and efficient solutions and secures a lasting basis for the common efforts aiming at the implementation of the decisions or general line that have been adopted.

It is possible for differences of view to appear among the socialist countries in relation to certain problems, but whenever such is the case they should be analyzed and tackled in a comradely way, in a spirit of mutual understanding, without resorting to epithets and labels, without pressure, and without resorting to measures of a discriminatory character.

In the nature of the socialist system there are no objective causes for contradictions between the national and international tasks of the socialist countries, between the interests of each country and the interests of the socialist community as a whole. On the other hand, specific and individual interests cannot be presented as general interests, as objective requirements of the development of the socialist system.

The consolidation of the socialist states and the maturity acquired by the Communist and workers' parties of these countries should be regarded as a mark of their strength, as an expression of the growing force of each socialist country and of the world socialist system as a whole, as positive and heartening factors in the development of the entire Communist movement.

The experience gained by the countries of the world socialist system has verified the need for the Communist and workers' parties to take into account the action of the general laws of socialist construction, which are universally valid in substance. These laws are of an objective nature, and evidently it is impossible for anybody to arbitrarily " create " new general laws or to proclaim specific individual phenomena as having a universal value, or to try to impose them upon other countries and in different historical conditions.

The requirements of these laws are applied to concrete conditions of a great diversity, in keeping with the level or stage of development of each socialist country and its historic peculiarities. Infringement of the general laws of socialist construction, departure from their basic principles, just as the ignoring of national peculiarities, cannot but harm socialist construction in each country.

In establishing the most adequate forms and methods of building socialism the Communist and workers' parties take into account both the require ments of the objective laws and the concrete historic conditions prevailing in their own countries and carry on an intensive creative activity, grasping the requirements of social development, synthesizing their own experience, and studying the experience won by other fraternal parties.

Bearing in mind the diversity of the conditions of socialist construction, there are not nor can there be any unique patterns and recipes; no one can decide what is and what is not correct for other countries or parties. It is up to every Marxist-Leninist party, it is a sovereign right of each socialist state, to elaborate, choose, or change the forms and methods of socialist construction.

The strict observance of the basic principles of the new-type relations among the socialist countries is the primary prerequisite of the unity and cohesion of these countries and of the world socialist system performing its decisive role in the development of mankind.

The consistent implementation of the basic principles of the relations among socialist states is an obligation of paramount significance, both nationally and internationally, bearing in mind that these relations exert a strong appeal in the world arena, are watched with the utmost attention by all peoples, and represent a mobilizing factor in the struggle waged by the working people in the capitalist countries and in the newly independent states. Lenin's words about the power of example set by the victorious proletariat prove their validity in respect to both the successes scored by the socialist countries and the influence of the international relations promoted by these countries.

The ties of internationalist solidarity among the countries of the socialist system rely on a solid foundation: identity of the state system, in which the working class performs the role of the leading social force, common fundamental interests of defending and developing the revolutionary achievements of the peoples, unity of aims of building socialism and communism, and the common Marxist-Leninist ideology.

The experience of all these years of existence of the world socialist system has shown that the force and invincibility of each socialist country spring from the unity and cohesion of the world socialist system. It is not what now divides but, on the contrary, what unites the socialist countries that is more powerful and must prevail and be victorious.

V. The National Liberation Movement—Integrating Part of the World Revolutionary Process

The analysis of the role of the national liberation movement as part of the world revolutionary process occupies an important place in the debate within the international Communist and working-class movement. The collapse of the system of colonial slavery under the blows dealt by the national liberation revolutions is the second phenomenon in historical importance next to the setting up of the world socialist system. In the last twenty years more than 1.5 billion people have shaken off the fetters of colonial oppression, more than 50 new states have appeared on the ruins of the former colonial empires. The Communist and workers' parties are unanimous in appreciating the tremendous importance of the national liberation movement as one of the great revolutionary forces of our times, which contributes to the deepening of the contradictions of the world capitalist system, to the steady strengthening of the superiority of the forces of socialism, democracy, and peace over the force of imperialism, reaction, and war, and to a change in the world's configuration.

In the battle for the fulfillment of the aspirations toward freedom and a better life, huge masses of people on vast expanses of the globe have become an active anti-imperialist force, the revolutionary energies of the peoples have been released tempestuously. The independence won by hundreds of millions of people in Asia, Africa, and other parts of the world is the fruit of the staunch battles they have waged against imperialism.

The victories scored by the liberation struggle are indissolubly linked to the balance of forces in the international arena changed in favor of socialism, to the chief contradiction of the contemporary world — that between socialism and capitalism — undermining and weakening the forces of imperialism. The growth of the forces of socialism and, above all, the emergence of the world socialist system have decisively contributed to the qualitative change that has come about in the unfolding of the national liberation movement. Today it is no longer a question of one country or another casting off the chains of colonial dependence but of the breakdown of the entire colonial system. The continuous strengthening of the world socialist system and the growth of the working-class movement in metropolitan areas and in capitalist countries in general create increasingly favorable conditions for the anticolonialist struggle of the oppressed peoples and the final abolition of colonial rule in all its forms.

To emphasize the decisive role played by the forces of world socialism in the struggle against imperialism, in carrying through the revolutionary transformation of the world, does not in the least diminish the huge contribution that the national liberation movement, as an integral part of the world revolutionary process and as the natural ally of socialism, makes in the struggle against imperialism, in the struggle for peace and social progress.

Declaring themselves the firmest advocates of peaceful coexistence among states with different social systems, of the struggle for general disarmament, the socialist countries and the Communist parties consider it the sacred right of the oppressed peoples to achieve and defend freedom and independence weapon in hand. The socialist countries and the Communist parties have granted and continue to grant full support to the national liberation movement, to the just wars against colonial bondage, against foreign occupation. It is a grave error to present the struggle for general and complete disarmament as paving the way to the disarming of the national liberation movement, of the oppressed peoples confronting their oppressors.

The advance of the young states along the road of progress produces numerous specific, original forms and elements. Drawing on the example and experience of the socialist countries, the peoples that have shed the colonial yoke are becoming more and more convinced that the safest road to elimination of the age-old backwardness and improvement of living conditions is the road of noncapitalist development — as shown in the 1960 Statement.

Concentrating on the consolidation of their gains and on achieving economic independence, the peoples of the liberated countries develop the productive forces of their countries and carry out changes in the economic, political, and social life. In some Asian and African states measures are taken to curb the positions and influence of foreign monopolies in the economy, to build up and develop the national industry, to expand the state sector, and to restrict the ownership of latifundia ; economic development programs are being carried out and new forms of social organization are being introduced. The democratic forces and the Communist parties in the newly sovereign states, which have to play an essential role in effecting the progressive transformations, fight for the carrying out of the anti-imperialist, antifeudal, democratic revolution.

The independent development of the newly liberated states is greatly assisted by their economic cooperation with the socialist countries, a cooperation based on strict observance of national sovereignty, equal rights, noninterference in domestic affairs, and mutual advantage.

The socialist countries, the international working class headed by Communist parties and the peoples who struggle for winning and consolidating national independence, all the revolutionary forces of the contemporary world, form a united anti-imperialist front. To separate the countries of Asia, Africa, and Latin America from the socialist countries, to separate the national liberation and Afro-Asian solidarity movement from the international working class and from the forces of world socialism means greatly to harm the interests both of the national liberation movement and of socialism.

Lenin's ardent call is more topical than ever. Tirelessly militating for the close union of the national liberation movement and the forces of socialism as the main prerequisite for the successful unfolding of the world revolutionary process, he said: "We have stood, stand, and will always stand for the closest link and unity between the class-conscious workers in the advanced countries and the workers, peasants, the slaves in all the oppressed countries. We have always advised and will always advise all the oppressed masses in all the oppressed countries, including the colonies, not to separate themselves from us, but to come closer and unite with us as closely as possible." [8]

VI. The International Communist Movement—the Most Influential Political Force of Our Time

Having the ideas of Marxism-Leninism as their beacon, the Communist and workers' parties — the most important political force of our time, the most influential factor of social progress — are in the vanguard of the struggle for peace and socialism; they number at present over 42 million members and increasingly rally around them the democratic and progressive forces.

The political and ideological maturity of the Communist movement has found powerful expression in the Statements adopted by the Conferences of Representatives of Communist and Workers' Parties held in Moscow in 1957 and 1960. These Statements contain the common assessments and conclusions of the Communist movement on the most important issues of our time.

In the socialist countries the Marxist-Leninist parties guide the destinies of hundreds of millions of people. The Communist parties in the capitalist countries are at the head of intense social struggles. The scope and militancy of workers' demonstrations and strikes are growing — some 57 million men and women took part in strikes in 1963 alone. In these actions, economic claims are ever more frequently interwoven with political ones.

In the capitalist countries numerous Communist parties have developed and been tempered in the heat of the class struggle; they have gained rich experience in leading the working people and have enhanced their influence in political life. Significant are the important successes scored by a number

[8] *Ibid.*, Vol. 23, Rumanian ed., 1957, p. 59.

of Communist parties in parliamentary and municipal elections, in trade-union elections.

In a series of capitalist countries the Communist parties work underground ; heroically defying police terror and persecution, they give proof of boundless selflessness and deep devotion to the working class and to their peoples, holding aloft the banner of liberty and social progress, of national independence and peace.

The Communist and workers' parties regard the unity of action of the working class, of the Communist and socialist parties, to be of decisive significance and militate for its implementation. In the struggle to defend economic rights and democratic freedoms, national independence, and sovereignty, the working class headed by the Communists is joined by large segments of the peasantry, by new strata and groups of the population ; this struggle is joined by Communists and socialists, trade-union organizations of diverse orientations, youth, women's, and other civic organizations, broad democratic movements. The idea of forming a broad front against monopoly rule, on behalf of the vital interests of the masses, is gaining ground.

The struggle for socialism in capitalist countries is taking place under extremely complex conditions, varying from one country to another. The whole course of history points to the correctness of Lenin's idea concerning the abundance and tremendous diversity of forms, methods, and ways of applying the general laws of socialist revolution. Lenin's forecast that this diversity will inevitably increase with the spreading of the revolutionary process to other countries and peoples is borne out.

The highly responsible task of elaborating the political line most appropriate to the concrete conditions, to the peculiarities of individual countries, of establishing the stages of the revolutionary process, the most suitable ways and means to carry out the socialist revolution, belongs to the working class, to the internal revolutionary forces, to the Marxist-Leninist party of each country. Socialist revolution is the result of an objective historical process, of the sharpening of contradictions, and of the struggle waged by the masses of people in each country.

In our times of great social changes, when the influence of the working class, of the world socialist system, and of all anti-imperialist forces has grown considerably, ever more favourable conditions arise for the conquest of political power by its allies.

One of the most controversial problems in the contemporary Communist movement is that of peaceful or nonpeaceful transition from capitalism to socialism, which has occasioned the expression of dogmatic views proclaiming the correctness of only the road chosen by one side or the other.

The possibility of transition from capitalism to socialism in a peaceful or nonpeaceful way is determined in each country by concrete historical conditions. The working class is interested in winning power without a civil war. The exploiting classes, however, do not yield power of their own accord, and the degree of sharpening of the class struggle does not depend so much on the proletariat as on the utilization of violence by the exploiting classes, on the strength of their opposition.

In order to ensure the success of the proletarian revolution, it is essential for the working class and its party to master **all** forms of struggle, **without exception,** to be able to use them all, to be fully prepared **for any contingency,** so as to be in a position **to rapidly replace one form of struggle by**

another, in keeping with the changes taking place in the concrete conditions in which the revolution unfolds.

"History in general and the history of revolutions in particular," Lenin teaches us, "is always richer in contents, more varied, more multilateral, more vivid, more 'cunning' than is imagined by the best of parties, by the most conscious vanguards of the most advanced classes. . . . Hence two very important practical conclusions: first — to implement its task, the revolutionary class must know how to master **all** forms or facets of social activity, without any exception whatever (realizing, upon conquest of political power and sometimes at great risk and immense danger, what it had been unable to achieve before victory); second — the revolutionary class must be prepared for the most rapid and the most unexpected substitution of one form for another.

"Everybody will agree that it is devoid of sense and even criminal for an army not to acquire proficiency in handling all kinds of weapons, in mastering all means and methods of struggle that the enemy possesses or may possess. This observation regarding the art of war is even more valid in politics. In politics it is even less possible to foresee which means of struggle will prove applicable and advantageous for us at one or another time in the future. Not to master all means of struggle is to risk a big defeat — sometimes even a decisive defeat — should changes over which we have no control, determined by other classes, impose a form of activity for which we are very poorly prepared. If we will master all means of struggle, we will surely win, because we do represent the interests of the truly advanced, truly revolutionary class. This will happen even if circumstances may prevent our using the weapon most dangerous to the enemy, the weapon inflicting mortal blows most readily." [9]

History confirms that the transition from capitalism to socialism is possible only by carrying out the proletarian revolution, through setting up, in one form or another, the proletarian dictatorship destined to defend the revolutionary gains, to render possible the socialist transformation of society. The proletarian revolution presupposes the involvement of mighty social forces, the alliance between the working class and the working peasantry, the union in a broad front of all forces and mass movements directed against the exploiting classes and their attempts to restore their domination; it is directly bound up with the intense organizational, political, and ideological activity carried on by the Communists among the ranks of the working class, among the other masses of people, with a view to rallying them to struggle, with a view to their revolutionary education and tempering.

The party's force and strength, its capacity to fulfill its historic mission are ensured by the unflagging attention paid to the continuous strengthening of its ranks to the enhancing of its political and ideological influence by uncompromising struggle against all alien conceptions and in defense of the purity of Marxism-Leninism.

VII. For Safeguarding the Unity and Cohesion of the International Communist Movement

Of late the divergences in the international Communist and working-class movement have deepened, and the public controversy has assumed particular

[9] *Ibid.*, Vol. 31, Rumanian ed., 1956, pp. 78–79.

sharpness. Instead of a debate imbued with the endeavour to bring stand-points closer to each other and to find solutions based on Marxist-Leninist ideology, forms and methods have been adopted in the course of the public controversy that considerably envenom relations among parties, and offensive judgements, as well as accusations and imputing of nefarious intentions, are being resorted to.

Particularly serious is the fact that almost all fraternal parties are drawn into the controversy and that the keynote is set by parties that owing to their merits and revolutionary experience have a great influence in the Communist movement.

The elaboration of a common general line and of the norms to ensure the unity of action of the Communist and workers' parties can only be the fruit of their collective wisdom. Considering the great variety of conditions in which the Marxist-Leninist parties carry on their activity, the cohesion of the Communist movement has to be conceived in the light of the historic necessities to ensure, while paying heed to this variety, unity on the issues of common interest, on the fundamental problems of social development. This unity does not, of course, preclude different opinions on one problem or another of internal or international life.

When differences of opinion appear with regard to the general problems of the Communist and working-class movement, it is essential that they should not lead to tension in the relations between parties, to irreconcilable contradictions, to reciprocal accusations and excommunications from the family of Marxist-Leninist parties.

At the 1960 conference the representatives of the fraternal parties from all over the world established by common agreement the norms and methods to be used in discussing the problems of the world Communist movement to ensure its unity of action.

If between two or several Communist parties differences of opinion arise on problems of common or general interest, the discussion of such problems should be prepared and organized in such a way as to lead to the parties' genuine unity of action, to enrich and creatively develop Marxist-Leninist teaching in keeping with the conditions of our time and of each country. In case the comradely, constructive debates fail to lead to a unitary point of view on certain problems, we may allow life and social practice to prove the correctness of one position or another, while the parties should act in a spirit of mutual understanding and respect with a view to achieving the common goals.

The long history of the Communist movement reveals the kind of negative results to which nonobservance of the correct norms governing relations among parties leads, norms based on the collective working out of decisions, on each party's independence and equal right, on noninterference in the internal affairs of other parties.

As far back as the last stage of existence of the Comintern, it had become obvious that the solution of the problems of the working-class movement, in one country or another, by an international centre was no longer adequate at that stage of development of the world Communist and working-class movement. Wrong methods, interference in the domestic affairs of Communist parties went as far as the removal and replacement of leading party cadres and even of entire Central Committees, as far as the imposing from without of leaders, the suppression of distinguished leading cadres of various parties, as far as the censure and even dissolving of Communist parties.

In that period our party also underwent hard trials. Interference in its internal affairs was most detrimental to the party line, to its cadres' policy and organizational work, to the party's ties with the masses.

The practices engendered by the cult of the individual within the Comintern also found a reflection in the Information Bureau. After the emergence of the world socialist system those practices were also extended to interstate relations, which further aggravated their consequences. In 1948 the Communist Party of Yugoslavia was condemned and excluded from the Information Bureau, and Yugoslavia — a country that builds socialism — was expelled from the community of socialist states. In some socialist countries there were numerous cases of expulsion from the party, arrests, trials, and suppressions of many leading party and state cadres. Their rehabilitation was possible only after the Twentieth Congress of the CPSU had exposed and criticized the cult of the individual and the practices engendered thereby.

Our party regarded as correct and greatly appreciated the critical analysis of the cult of the individual by the Twentieth CPSU Congress, as well as the underlining, by the same congress, of the need for vigorous application of Leninist standards in party life and in the world Communist movement.

Our party considers these conclusions highly relevant under present circumstances, when sharp divergencies prevail in the Communist movement, when the danger of reoccurrence of the methods and practices generated by the cult of the individual seems possible.

The entire experience of the Communist movement points to the decisive role played by the application of Leninist standards in the activity of Communist parties and in intraparty relations, as well as in relations among the socialist countries themselves.

Strict observance of the principle according to which all Marxist-Leninist parties enjoy equal rights, of the principle of noninterference in other parties' domestic affairs, of each party's exclusive right to solve its own political and organizational problems, to appoint its leaders, to orient its members in problems of internal and international politics — is an essential condition for the correct settlement of issues in which there are divergences, as well as of all problems raised by their common struggle.

The ratio and deployment of the forces of classes in one country or another, the shifts in forces and evolution of the frame of mind of the masses, the peculiarities of the internal and international political conditions of a country cannot be better and more thoroughly known by anybody than by the Communist party of the respective country. It is the exclusive right of each party to work out independently its political line, its concrete objectives, the ways and means of attaining them by creatively applying the general truths of Marxism-Leninism and the conclusions it reaches from an attentive analysis of the experience of the other Communist and workers' parties.

There does not and cannot exist a " parent " party and a " son party," or " superior " parties and " subordinate " parties, but there exists the great family of Communist and workers' parties, which have equal rights. No party has or can have a privileged place, or can impose its line and opinions on other parties. Each party makes its own contribution to the development of the common treasure store of Marxist-Leninist teaching, to enriching the forms and practical methods of the revolutionary struggle for winning power and building a socialist society.

In discussing and confronting different points of view on problems concerning the revolutionary struggle or socialist construction, no party should attach the label of anti-Marxist or anti-Leninist to the fraternal party whose opinions it does not share.

We consider as unjust the practice in party documents, in the press, and over the radio, at meetings of international organizations, and so forth of using offensive assessments, accusations, and epithets against fraternal parties and their leadership, of expounding in an unfriendly and distorted manner within the ranks of the party or among the mass of the people and stand of other parties, of condemning at congresses or in the resolutions of a party the point of view or positions adopted by other Communist parties.

No party is allowed to go over the heads of the party leaders of one country or another, and even less to launch appeals for the removal or the change of the leadership of a party. Remarks and manifestations disrespectful to a Communist party and its leadership may justly be interpreted as a lack of respect for the working class, for the people who trust the party and the leadership of the Communist party of their country; and this further worsens relations among parties, among socialist states, and it affects the friendship of the respective peoples.

Unfortunately, in the heat of the controversy reciprocal accusations have been substituted for scientific analysis of the differences of opinion; they are obscuring the fundamental issues and overstepping all bounds.

It is inconceivable that in relations among Communist parties reciprocal and deeply offensive accusations should be levelled against the leaders of a fraternal party such as being "the biggest revisionists of our time," who are in "collusion with U.S. imperialism," and "throw wide open the gates for the restoration of capitalism," or that they are "Trotskyites" who "furiously attack world socialism," "partners on the right-flank of the American 'wild men,'" and so forth.

Such grave invectives cannot but lead to tension in interparty relations, render difficult contacts between the leaderships of the respective parties, and drive things toward a break, toward a split in the Communist movement.

At a time when decisive tasks for the destinies of mankind are incumbent upon the Communist and workers' parties, when their unity is needed more than ever, the public controversy and its manifestations have created confusion in a number of Communist parties and among the ranks of the working people in several countries. On numerous occasions leaders of the peoples of the recently liberated countries and of the national liberation movement have shown their bitterness and anxiety over dissensions among the socialist countries and expressed their hope that these dissensions will be ended without delay.

Particularly serious is the fact that under the circumstances the central press organs of one of the largest fraternal parties, the Chinese Communist Party, assert that in the conditions now prevailing in the Communist movement a split, both on the international plane and within various parties, becomes necessary and unavoidable and that the dialectic of the development of the international working-class movement is "unity, struggle, and even splits, as well as unity on a new basis."

In our opinion this represents a theoretical justification for a split, a call for a split.

Taking advantage of the present state of affairs in the Communist movement, all kinds of dissatisfied, antiparty, and dissolving elements of a series of parties are rising against the party leaderships, setting up splittist groups, calling themselves "true Marxist-Leninist parties," and actively seeking to split the working-class movement of the respective country.

It is regrettable that these groups meet with the approval and support of the Chinese comrades.

The conferences, sessions, and congresses held in the last years by various international democratic organizations, and particularly the most recent ones, show that open controversy leads to undermining the influence and prestige enjoyed by the Communists, by the socialist countries in these organizations, leads to weakening the unity and the fighting power of the international working-class and democratic organizations.

We note with regret that in materials released by some Communist and workers' parties, fraternal parties are advised to sharpen the public controversy; this strains relations, aggravates the danger of a split.

The Communist Party of the Soviet Union and the Chinese Communist Party have, owing to their prestige, a particular responsibility and role in re-establishing the unity of the Communist movement. **We address an appeal to all the fraternal parties and above all to the two big parties, the Communist Party of the Soviet Union and the Chinese Communist Party : Let all of us unite to bar the road to a split, to safeguard the unity and cohesion of the countries of the socialist camp, of the world Communist and working class movement !**

The first and most important step at the present moment is the immediate termination, under all forms, of the public controversy among Communist and workers' parties.

We address a heartfelt call to all parties for the immediate cessation of the public controversy and for preparing a conference of the representatives of the Communist and workers' parties with a view to defending and strengthening the unity of the camp of the socialist countries, of the world Communist and working-class movement.

The immediate cessation of the public controversy would be looked upon by all mankind as proof of the strength and vitality of Marxism-Leninism, of the ability of the Communist parties to resolve their differences in a comradely, principled manner. This would considerably enhance the prestige and influence of socialism and give strong impetus to the forces of the anti-imperialist revolutionary movement, with particularly favorable consequences for the entire world revolutionary process.

If a complete cessation of the open controversy cannot be achieved, differences of opinion should be discussed in a principled, objective manner. Invectives and offensive appraisals, reciprocal charges, ascribing nefarious intentions, distorting and maligning the stands taken by other parties, are not convincing arguments capable of contributing to a solution of outstanding problems.

The Rumanian Workers' Party deems it necessary that immediate consultations begin between the Communist Party of the Soviet Union, the Chinese Communist Party, and the other fraternal parties with a view to setting up a commission consisting of representatives of a number of parties,

295

which commission should initiate preparations for a conference of representatives of the Communist and workers' parties.

Such a conference should be organized only on the basis of the participation of all Communist and workers' parties and should be convened only after thorough preparation.

The Central Committee of the Rumanian Workers' Party considers that a conference attended by only part of the Communist and workers' parties would run counter to the cause of unity, exacerbate the situation, bring about the isolation of certain fraternal parties, make definitive the split in the world Communist and working-class movement.

We are convinced that unity on the main problems of social development can and must be achieved if the fraternal parties perseveringly and patiently search for ways and means for mutual understanding and bridging of their positions.

The Central Committee of the Rumanian Workers' Party reiterates its conviction that what is common to all the Communist and workers' parties transcends all differences; that the *essential* unites them and is infinitely stronger than any difference of opinion. We are united in the common goals of bringing about the conquest of power by the working class, the victory of socialism and communism throughout the world. We are united in the common struggle against imperialism, for the vital interests and democratic rights of the people at large, against colonialism in all its forms, for the peoples' national liberation ; we are united by the common goal of establishing a lasting world peace, a vital task for all mankind. We are united by proletarian internationalism and internationalist class solidarity, by our historic responsibility before the international proletariat and the working people everywhere ; we are united by our common ideology, the Marxist-Leninist teaching.

These bonds unite the Communist and workers' parties in a great family of fraternal parties, they form the unshakable foundation of the cohesion of the world Communist and working-class movement and represent the objective factors for solving any issues affecting our parties in a comradely manner.

Today the conclusions of the 1960 Moscow Statement are more relevant than ever : **" The interests of the struggle for the cause of the working class demand the ever tighter closing of the ranks of each Communist party and of the great army of Communists of all countries."**

April 22, 1964

The Central Committee
of the Rumanian Workers' Party

DOCUMENT 12

Letter of the Central Committee of the CCP
of May 7, 1964 to the Central Committee
of the CPSU

Complete Text

[*Peking Review*, Vol. VII, No. 19 (May 8, 1964), pp. 7–10]

May 7, 1964

The Central Committee of the Communist
    Party of the Soviet Union

Dear Comrades,

The Central Committee of the Communist Party of China has received the letter of the Central Committee of the Communist Party of the Soviet Union dated March 7, 1964.

In your letter you talk glibly about your desire for " the speediest possible settlement of existing differences " and " the cessation of the public polemics between Communist Parties " and about your willingness to do your utmost " to help strengthen the unity of the communist movement." But the facts show the complete falsity of your fine words. Both before and since the delivery of your letter, you have never ceased your attacks on the Chinese Communist Party and other fraternal Marxist-Leninist parties. At every single meeting of the international democratic organizations in the past few months, you have energetically preached and pushed your wrong line and conducted activities against China. Already in the middle of February this year, that is, three weeks before your letter of March 7, you made an anti-Chinese report and adopted an anti-Chinese decision at the Plenum of your Central Committee, at which 6,000 people were present, declaring that you would " publicly explain " the " mistakes " of the CCP and " come out openly and strongly " against it.

All this clearly reveals that in writing the letter of March 7 you were simply playing a two-faced game. Under the guise of " deep concern for the settlement of the differences and for the unity of the international communist movement," you were diligently preparing a new onslaught against the Chinese Communist Party and other fraternal Marxist-Leninist parties and hatching a big plot for openly splitting the socialist camp and the international communist movement.

We have given you repeated explanations of our consistent stand on public polemics. Since you have ignored our repeated advice, obdurately provoked and extended the public polemics and made massive public attacks upon us and other fraternal Parties, we and the other fraternal Parties are of course entitled to make public replies according to the principle of equality among fraternal Parties. It is our right to reply as much as you attack us.

Our press has not yet finished replying to your Open Letter of July 14, 1963. We have not yet started — to say nothing of completing — our reply to the more than 2,000 anti-Chinese articles and other items which you published after your Open Letter and to the great number of resolutions, statements and articles in which scores of fraternal Parties have attacked us. How can we be asked to give up our right of public reply when you

297

have issued such a mass of resolutions, statements, articles, books and pamphlets attacking the Chinese Communist Party without ever publicly revoking them?

On many public occasions, including international meetings, you have violated the fundamental theories of Marxism-Leninism and the revolutionary principles of the 1957 Declaration and the 1960 Statement by spreading and pushing your general line of "peaceful transition," "peaceful competition" and "peaceful coexistence," and have set your minds on uniting with U.S. imperialism, the common enemy of the people of the whole world, to oppose the national-liberation movement, proletarian revolution and the dictatorship of the proletariat, and to undermine the unity of the socialist camp and the international communist movement. You have tried to impose your erroneous line on fraternal Parties and on the international democratic organizations. How can you expect us and all other Marxist-Leninists to keep silent about these foul deeds of yours and about such important questions of principle affecting the future of the world revolution and the destiny of mankind? And how can you expect us to refrain from exposing and publicly opposing your revisionist and divisive errors and from publicly stating our position and views?

You said earlier that in starting the public polemics at the 22nd Congress of the CPSU you were "acting in Lenin's manner," yet you say now in your letter that to refrain from public polemics is "the behest of V. I. Lenin." Which of your two statements is correct? If you really want a cessation of the public polemics, does that not mean your 22nd Congress was wrong? And are you ready to admit your mistake?

The anti-Chinese report and decision of the February Plenum of the Central Committee of the CPSU published on April 3, 1964, and the ensuing events make it all the more clear that your call for a cessation of the public polemics was intended solely to gag us so that you could have a free rein to push ahead with your revisionist and divisive line.

Regarding the question of talks between the Chinese and Soviet Parties and a meeting of representatives of all fraternal Parties, the proposal we made in our letter of February 29, 1964, was as follows: The talks between the Chinese and Soviet Parties should be resumed in October so as to make preparations for a meeting of representatives of all fraternal Parties; in order to make further preparations for the meeting of representatives of all fraternal Parties, the two-Party talks should be followed by a meeting of representatives of seventeen fraternal Parties; the meeting of representatives of all fraternal Parties should be convened after the completion of preparations, so that it will be a meeting of unity on the basis of the revolutionary principles of Marxism-Leninism.

In your letter of March 7, 1964, you disagree with this reasonable proposal of ours and charge us with deliberate stalling. You want the talks between the Chinese and Soviet Parties to be held in May, the preparatory meeting of representatives of fraternal Parties in June-July and the international meeting of all fraternal Parties in autumn this year.

At first glance you are most eager and enthusiastic. But it is not for the purpose of eliminating differences and strengthening unity that you have put forward this pressing timetable. On the contrary, more and more facts testify that it is a step in your plot to accelerate an open split in the international communist movement.

On February 12 this year you sent a letter directed against the Communist Party of China to fraternal Parties and behind our backs. Your letter of February 22, 1964, to us divulged that in that anti-Chinese letter you had called for a " rebuff " to us and threatened to " take collective measures." At the Plenum of the Central Committee of the CPSU on February 14–15 this year you decided to "come out openly and strongly against the incorrect views and dangerous actions of the leadership of the CCP." This means that you have pushed the cartridge into the chamber and are ready to press the trigger. In such circumstances, is it not utterly hypocritical of you to suggest that Sino-Soviet talks be held in May this year for " the speediest possible settlement of existing differences "?

We would like to ask the comrades of the CPSU: Why were you in such a great hurry? Was it not your intention, upon our rejection of your proposal for holding the talks between the Chinese and Soviet Parties in May 1964, to use it as a pretext for brazenly and unilaterally calling an international meeting and effecting an open split?

The consistent stand of the Chinese Communist Party is to uphold unity and oppose a split. We have worked unswervingly for the elimination of differences and the restoration of unity. At the same time, we are fully aware that our difference with you is a grave one involving a whole series of fundamental principles of Marxism-Leninism. It began with the 20th Congress of the CPSU and was aggravated at the 22nd Congress and later. It is obviously impossible for such long-accumulated differences of principle to be solved overnight. Time and patience are needed.

When in our letter of February 29, 1964, we proposed that the talks between the Chinese and Soviet Parties should be resumed in October this year, our chief consideration was to have seven months for doing a number of things by way of preparation. For instance, we would have to receive a copy of the letter of February 12, 1964, which you sent to fraternal Parties and acquaint ourselves with its contents; we would like to see the magic weapons you threatened to use, such as " stating our views openly," " publishing documents and material," giving " the most resolute rebuff " and applying " collective measures "; and we would have to answer your attacks and react to your new magic weapons. All this would take time.

It is regrettable that to date you have still groundlessly refused to give us a copy of your letter of February 12, 1964, to fraternal Parties in spite of our repeated requests. It must be understood that this is a letter attacking us, and since you have given it to many fraternal Parties, why do you particularly deny it to us? We have the right to ask you to send us a copy. Now we again request you to send us the letter. If you go on refusing, our request will stand for ten thousand years.

As for your magic weapons, at least you have produced a few beginning with April 3 this year. It seems that you have now warmed up and have a lot more to say. But we still do not know what other magic weapons you have and what your " most resolute rebuff " and " collective measures " really are.

In these circumstances, how can the talks between the Chinese and Soviet Parties and the international meeting of fraternal Parties be successful? What will there be to say except for quarrels ending up in a fruitless adjournment, or a final open split with each side going its own way? Can it be that you are resolved to have an open split?

Comrades! we are against a split. Before all your vaunted magic weapons are produced, before each side's case and intentions are made clear, and before full preparations are completed, the holding of talks between the Chinese and Soviet Parties and of an international meeting of fraternal Parties can only lead to a split, and to this we cannot agree.

Judging by present circumstances, not only is it impossible to hold the two-Party talks in May, but it will also be too early to hold them in October. We consider it more appropriate to postpone them till some time in the first half of next year, say May. And if either the Chinese or the Soviet Party then considers that the time is still not ripe, they can be further postponed.

The timing of the preparatory meeting for the meeting of representatives of all Communist and Workers' Parties will depend on the results of the talks between the Chinese and Soviet Parties. The composition of the preparatory meeting can be decided through consultation among fraternal Parties, but we still consider it appropriate for the preparatory meeting to consist of the seventeen fraternal Parties proposed in our letter of February 29, 1964, namely, the Parties of Albania, Bulgaria, China, Cuba, Czechoslovakia, the German Democratic Republic, Hungary, Korea, Mongolia, Poland, Rumania, the Soviet Union and Viet Nam, and the Parties of Indonesia, Japan, Italy and France.

In principle we are not against increasing the number of participants in the preparatory meeting. But we cannot agree with the proposal, put forward in your letter, that it should be increased from seventeen to twenty-six fraternal Parties. For the situation now is vastly different from that in 1960. There are two Parties in some of the countries mentioned in your list. In Australia, for instance, there is a Party represented by E. F. Hill and another by L. L. Sharkey. The former is a Marxist-Leninist and the latter a revisionist Party. A similar situation obtains in Brazil. Obviously you and we differ as to which of these Parties should attend the meeting. In another case, that of India, the Dange clique have degenerated into pawns of the Indian big bourgeoisie and big landlords and into renegades from communism. How can the Dange clique of renegades be allowed to participate in a meeting of fraternal Parties? In our opinion, if the membership of the preparatory meeting is to be increased, the first consideration should be given to those fraternal Parties which uphold Marxism-Leninism and which are waging heroic revolutionary struggles.

As for the meeting of representatives of all Communist and Workers' Parties, we hold that it must be a meeting of unity on the basis of Marxism-Leninism and that it should definitely not become a meeting for a split. Therefore, ample preparations have to be made and it should not be called in a hurry. This is our consistent attitude and it is also the attitude of many other fraternal Parties, including some which have ideological differences with us. In the past you too, approved of this attitude. In your letter to us of November 29, 1963, you agreed that conditions should be created so that the meeting "will lead not to a split in the world communist movement but to genuine unity and solidarity of all the fraternal Parties and all the forces of peace and socialism." If you do not want an immediate open split, you should not be in too much of a hurry to call the international meeting in the coming autumn. We advise you to think this over calmly: it would be better to hold the international meeting of fraternal Parties later rather than earlier, or even not to hold it, in these circumstances.

There is now no international organization like the Third International nor any body like the permanent bodies of the Third International which were entitled to call international meetings. In these circumstances, it would be wrong and impermissible for one or more Parties to make a unilateral decision to call a meeting of representatives of all Communist and Workers' Parties in violation of the principles of consultation and the attainment of unity among the fraternal Parties. To do so would be illegitimate and entirely wrong and would lead to grave consequences. This is clear to you, to us and to all the other Communist and Workers' Parties. If, in arrogant disregard of the advice of our Party and of many other fraternal Parties, the Central Committee of the CPSU should cling to its own course, insist on hurriedly convening such a meeting by calling together those Parties that support its wrong, revisionist and divisive line, and treat it as a meeting of all the Communist and Workers' Parties of the world, you would then be strongly condemned by the working class, the revolutionary people and all genuine Marxist-Leninist parties throughout the world, you would cast to the four winds the banner of unity which you profess to uphold, and would have to bear the responsibility for a split. Do you want to do this? Do you want to put yourselves in such an inextricable predicament? We are saying this in all sincerity and clearly pointing to where interests or dangers lie, so do not say that you have not been forewarned.

We maintain that a series of preparatory steps are necessary in order to make the international meeting of fraternal Parties a success, and that these should include the holding of talks between the Chinese and Soviet Parties and of bilateral or multilateral talks among fraternal Parties, the convening of a preparatory meeting by fraternal Parties and the reaching of unanimous agreement at this meeting. Judging by present circumstances, it may require perhaps four or five years, or even longer, to complete these preparations.

Our views are based on deep concern for the unity of the socialist camp and the international communist movement. We hope that they will receive your serious and earnest consideration.

Furthermore, we would like to ask you to reconsider the proposal we made in our letter of February 27 this year, namely, that our two Parties reach an agreement, by which each side will, on an equal basis, publish in its own press the documents, articles and other material which both sides have published or will publish in criticism of each other. Although you rejected this proposal in your letter of March 7, 1964, you failed to give any really tenable reason. You have one-sidedly published many statements vilifying the Chinese Communist Party, and yet you prevent the members of the CPSU and the Soviet People from reading our replies and becoming acquainted with our actual position and views; this is indeed a deliberate attempt to inflame hostility between the Chinese and Soviet peoples. If you have real faith in the members of the CPSU and the Soviet people as well as in yourselves, you will find no reason whatever not to reach an agreement with us on this question.

The documents of the February Plenum of your Central Committee and the *Pravda* editorial of April 3, 1964, divulged information from the letters exchanged between the Central Committees of the Chinese and Soviet Parties since November 1963 and distorted the facts, in an attempt to delude the members of the CPSU, the Soviet people, and people everywhere else unfamiliar with the true state of affairs. In order to clarify matters and give the true picture, the Central Committee of the CPSU deems it necessary to publish in full all the letters exchanged between the Chinese and Soviet Parties since November 1963. Those comprise: the letters of the Central Committee of the CPSU dated November 29, 1963, February 22 and March 7, 1964, and the letters of the Central Committee of the CCP dated February 20, 27 and 29 and May 7, 1964. We hope that you will be able to do likewise and will publish the full text of this exchange of letters between our two Parties in your own press.

With fraternal greetings,

The Central Committee of the
Communist Party of China

DOCUMENT 13

CPSU Central Committee's Letter of June 15, 1964 to the Central Committee of the Communist Party of China

Complete Text

[*Kommunist*, No. 10, July 1964, pp. 9–20, quoted from *CDSP*, Vol XVI, No. 30 (August 19, 1964), pp. 5–10]

June 15, 1964

To the Central Committee of the Communist Party of China

Dear Comrades!

The Central Committee of the Communist Party of the Soviet Union has received your letter of May 7 replying to our letter of March 7, 1964. In your letter you not only reject all the proposals of the CPSU and other Marxist-Leninist parties on overcoming the difficulties in the Communist movement but you actually refuse to meet with representatives of the parties, to hold negotiations, to discuss with them the common problems that are troubling Communists throughout the world. Never before has the CCP Central Committee so openly expressed its scorn of the opinion of fraternal parties, its unwillingness to listen to their voice, to participate in a joint search for ways to overcome differences. The entire content of your letter, as well as its rude tone, speaks for the fact that, despite the CCP Central Committee's numerous declarations about its efforts to prevent a split, to uphold solidarity, you do not want the differences to be overcome, that you are in fact opposed to unity of the international Communist movement. You do not even attempt to hide the fact that your goal is to free your hands for carrying out factionalist,- splitting activity. This is the only way your letter can be evaluated by the Marxist-Leninist parties that are concerned about the difficulties that have arisen in our movement.

In sending you its letter of March 7, the CPSU Central Committee was proceeding from the premise that the situation that had formed in the world Communist movement required collective review, joint elaboration of feasible ways of overcoming the difficulties, of achieving the solidarity of all fraternal parties. To these ends, we proposed the speedy convening of a meeting of CPSU and CCP delegations and of a preparatory meeting of representatives of 26 parties, and the holding of an international conference, by agreement of the fraternal parties, as early as this year. The necessary conditions for successfully implementing these measures we considered to be a cessation of open polemics and repudiation of all kinds of disruptive, splitting activities in the socialist commonwealth and the Communist movement, which have already done our cause no little damage. We took into consideration the will of the majority of fraternal parties, which have insistently advocated that a meeting of CPSU and CCP representatives be held and that an international Communist forum be summoned, which would make it possible to discuss in a comradely atmosphere, within the fraternal family of Communists, the problems that have arisen and to eliminate the divergences caused by the splitting activities of the CCP leadership.

The proposals advanced by the CPSU Central Committee in its March 7 letter have found active support in the world Communist movement. As of the present time, an overwhelming majority of the fraternal parties have already spoken out for calling a conference without delay. Some parties, while favoring a conference in principle, at the same time have reservations regarding the specific time for holding it, in view of your opposition to a conference. However, we know that there is not a single party besides the Communist Party of China and the Albanian Party of Labor whose leadership would come out against the need for collective measures directed toward overcoming the difficulties in the Communist movement and strengthening its unity.

In its May 7 letter the CCP Central Committee proposes postponing the conference "four or five years, or even longer," and furthermore states that "it might be better even not to convene it." A bilateral meeting, which quite recently the CCP Central Committee was still proposing for October of this year, you once again put off for a long time, accompanying your consent to it with reservations that raise doubts as to whether the Chinese side is interested in its being held at all.

We assert, therefore, that the CCP Central Committee is repudiating its own proposals. The CCP leaders have long depicted themselves as the initiators of the idea of holding a conference as early as possible, presenting the matter as though the CPSU were opposing it. When in the winter of 1962 the Communist Parties of Indonesia, Vietnam and New Zealand proposed that a conference be called, you supported their proposal. You wrote on April 7, 1962, that calling a conference was of "urgent, positive importance for overcoming the differences now existing among fraternal parties." At the end of 1962 this stand of the CCP Central Committee was publicly confirmed in your delegations' speeches at the congresses of the fraternal parties of Hungary and Czechoslovakia. Subsequently, you advocated calling a conference in the letters to the CPSU Central Committee of March 9, 1963, and June 14, 1963. Finally, your letter of February 29, 1964, stated in black and white: "The Chinese Communist Party consistently advocates and actively supports the convening of a conference of representatives of all Communist and Workers' Parties."

However, the CPSU Central Committee and other fraternal parties had but to put the question of a conference on a concrete footing for you to make an about-face. The extreme contradictoriness and illogic of the CCP Central Committee's stand is apparent to everyone. Only recently you were warmly advocating a conference, even priding yourselves on having been the first to raise the proposal to convene it, regarding it as useful. Now the CCP leadership has started to talk quite differently — it turns out that, in its opinion, a conference is inopportune and even threatens the Communist movement with all sorts of disasters. Such vacillation can obviously be explained solely by the fact that you have not, either earlier or now, seriously thought of calling a conference because you could not count on support for your ideological-political platform from an international forum of Communists. The legitimate supposition arises that the CCP Central Committee is little concerned about the problems of preserving and strengthening the unity of the Communist movement, and that it has turned the question of a conference into the object of an unseemly political game with the aim of creating additional difficulties.

Although you flaunt in every way your indifference to the opinions of other parties and declare that you are not afraid of their "resolute rebuff," you are in fact afraid to come to an international Communist conference, are trying to avoid honest and direct discussion, to avoid confrontation of your erroneous platform with the line of the international Communist movement.

The objections you have advanced to convening a conference are completely groundless. You assert that an international conference, and also a meeting of CCP and CPSU representatives, will only "lead to the result that quarrels will flare up and all will disperse without having achieved any results" and that "an open split will take place and each will go his own road."

To put the issue this way, to predict ahead of time that a conference will lead to a split, is possible only for someone who has himself decided to carry matters to a split. Indeed, if at the conference one pursues the line of aggravating the differences, sees its purpose as being to censure someone, to attach abusive labels, to make irresponsible accusations, it is possible that further estrangement, rather than consolidation of unity, will be the outcome.

But the CPSU and the fraternal parties that have at all stages of the disagreement consistently advocated a new international meeting resolutely reject this line, this very approach to a conference. For us the question of a conference is indivisibly linked with the problem of preserving and strengthening the unity of our movement. We proceed from the premise that, in the face of the differences that the Communist movement has encountered, it is necessary first of all to concentrate efforts on discovering the common ground that unites all the fraternal parties, on seeking ways to overcome the difficulties that have arisen. The fraternal parties have no better method for overcoming differences and working out common positions than the collective exchange of views at an international forum, which allows each party fully to preserve its independence and at the same time to participate actively in the formulation of a single line for the world Communist movement.

The differences and disputes that have flared up in the Communist movement and done it no small damage affect the interests of all parties without exception, and therefore each of them has a right and a duty to make its contribution to the discussion and solution of the urgent problems, to the common cause of strengthening unity. It is precisely a conference that would offer each party an opportunity to hear the opinion of all sides and to present its own point of view frankly and in businesslike fashion, so that it will be taken into consideration in the future when a joint line and common decisions are being worked out.

As for the CPSU, in proposing that a conference be convened, it intends — in full accordance with the principles affirmed in the Communist movement since the 20th CPSU Congress and the Moscow conferences of 1957 and 1960— to pursue at it a line for consolidation, for normalizing the situation in our movement, for the businesslike discussion of disputed questions, which would promote not a deepening of the differences but a strengthening of unity on the basis of principle. It is our profound conviction that there are no insurmountable obstacles on this path. All that is needed is for all the participants in the international meeting to show at least a minimum of good will, to be ready to listen conscientiously to and understand the opinions of others, to seek ways toward unity, not toward estrangement. If the representatives of all parties show an interest in overcoming the difficulties, if the delegation of the Communist Party of China comes to the conference with a desire to seek mutual understanding with all the other participants, with a constructive program, as the CPSU and other parties think necessary, then the conference could become a turning point toward the strengthening of solidarity.

The CPSU Central Committee is fully aware that the divergences between the CCP Central Committee and other fraternal parties are serious and far-reaching. In the course of the public polemics, quite a lot that is superficial and artificial and that hinders mutual understanding has accumulated in the relations among parties. A whole series of differences in principle on very important problems of the present day and world communist policy have emerged and become quite acute. As a result it is possible that, no matter how the Marxist-Leninist parties strive for it, they will not immediately manage in the course of a conference to arrive at a common opinion on all questions. However, the CPSU Central Committee is convinced that such an outcome of the conference would not mean the split that the CCP leaders persistently predict. Even in this event, we see an opportunity for the conference to achieve an agreement that the Communist parties will undertake to consider the opinions of all the conference participants, of all the Marxist-Leninist parties, to cooperate conscientiously in the areas where common positions and interests are revealed and to refrain in the future from any action that would aggravate the difficulties and give joy only to class enemies. It may be asked: Why, given such an approach, should a conference lead to a split or somehow worsen the situation in the Communist movement?

We think that the procedure we have proposed for the work of the conference fully corresponds to the norms and principles of relations among Communist Parties and is fully realistic. It is simply a question of displaying the elementary concern for unity, the patience and good will that the Communist movement has a right to expect of all in its ranks. If all the fraternal parties and their leaders are imbued with a sense of historic responsibility for the destinies of our movement, with an understanding of the seriousness of the matter and the possible consequences of a split, there can be no doubt of the success of the conference.

In advocating the idea of a new international meeting, the CPSU Central Committee proceeds from the premise that the need for it is determined not only by the interests of overcoming differences, no matter how important this task may be in itself. Communists cannot for one moment forget their obligations in the struggle against imperialism, for peace, democracy and national independence, for a successful advance along the road of socialism and communism.

About four years have passed since the last international conference. During these years quite a few important changes have taken place in the world which require study, generalization and conclusions. In the intervening years considerable successes have been achieved by the world system of socialism, its economic power has grown, its political and ideological influence on world development has intensified. The majority of socialist countries are completing an important phase of their development and are approaching new frontiers in the building of a new society. The tasks of their further advance along the path of socialism and communism more and more insistently require improvement in the forms of cooperation and mutual aid, of exchanges of opinion, of the coordination of political and economic action.

In the international situation two opposing courses are becoming more and more clearly marked out: One, pursued by the socialist states and supported by the overwhelming majority of mankind, is directed at preserving peace, at peaceful coexistence; the other course, which is pursued by the imperialist reaction headed by the " madmen " of the U.S.A. and other imperialist powers, is the course of increasing international tension, pressing military threats. The past years have shown how right have been the conclusions of the Communist Parties with regard to the possibilities of averting war, of isolating and defeating the forces that oppose peace.

Recently there has been increasingly clear evidence that the general crisis of capitalism is deepening, that the social and political contradictions rending the capitalist system both within bourgeois society and in the international arena are growing. Much that is new has appeared in the forms of organization and the methods used by the working class in the capitalist countries in its fight for its immediate and ultimate interests. The disintegration of the colonial system of imperialism is in its final stages. The liberated peoples' irresistible inclination toward socialism, their desire to embark on the noncapitalist path of development, has become particularly obvious in recent years.

Great new opportunities are opening up for the revolutionary movement, for the champions of the cause of peace and socialism, and we Communists must consider how best to make use of these opportunities in the interests of the working class and of all peoples.

We are deeply convinced that a conference would be the exactly appropriate place to analyze collectively the new economic and socio-political phenomena and processes, agree on evaluations and positions and enrich and make concrete the common political line in accordance with them. It can be stated with satisfaction that the correctness of the general line of the world Communist movement as defined in the 1957 and 1960 documents has been fully confirmed by developments and has brought new successes to the fraternal parties. However, it is high time to gather together in order to sum up the results of the past stage, exchange opinions, review the whole complex of problems facing world communism and, in accordance with the shifts that have taken place in the international situation, to augment and develop the ideas of the Declaration and the Statement, creatively examine and solve the new problems.

In the light of these tasks, the CCP Central Committee's proposal to postpone for a long time the convening of a new international conference is especially unacceptable. Everything indicates that a conference remains necessary and that the question of convening it should not be shelved.

But the chief thing, in the opinion of the CPSU Central Committee, is for each Marxist-Leninist party, regardless of the specific date for a new international meeting, to make its contribution to the cause that the conference is called upon to serve, the cause of strengthening the unity of the ranks of Communists throughout the world, of joining efforts to achieve common goals. What is important now is that all the fraternal parties fight even more actively for these goals. Every fraternal party faces urgent tasks of profoundly studying the situation that has formed in the Communist movement, participating constructively in discussing the difficulties and seeking ways to overcome them, basing all its everyday actions on the interests of strengthening the international solidarity of our ranks. This is a practical way of showing one's fidelity to the principles and requirements of proletarian internationalism, to the entire spirit of Marxism-Leninism. At the same time, it is also the best way toward convening and successfully conducting an international Communist forum. We are resolutely opposed to letting the question of the date of the conference become a pretext for new quarrels, a stumbling block on the path to solving the chief tasks facing the Communist movement. However, we are resolutely opposed to postponing the conference " four or five years, or even longer," as the CCP Central Committee proposes.

Such is our stand on the basic question raised in the letters recently exchanged by the CPSU Central Committee and the CCP Central Committee — the question of the aims and prospects of a new international conference.

The CCP Central Committee's May 7 letter touches on a number of other problems, some linked with the holding of an international meeting and some having no direct relation to it. Among them there is, for instance, the question of the procedure for convening a conference.

The CCP Central Committee asserts that under present conditions no one has the right to call international conferences, since there is no permanent agency of the Comintern type. If one proceeds from the democratic principles on which the Communist movement is constructed, it is impossible not to recognize that such an initiative may be taken by any party or group of parties. In this event, it is the duty of the other detachments of the Communist movement to examine this initiative carefully and to support it if it is directed toward the good of our common cause. As for the CPSU, the fraternal parties have, as is known, given it special responsibility on the question of calling international conferences. A decision adopted by the 1957 conference says: " The Communist Party of the Soviet Union is charged with taking upon itself the function of calling conferences of Communist and Workers' Parties in consultation with the fraternal parties." This decision was adopted unanimously, with the Chinese Communist Party delegation participating. Moreover, at the evening session on Nov. 14, 1957, Mao Tse-tung declared that " it is necessary to recognize the CPSU as the initiator in convening conferences."

We cite these facts in the interests of establishing the truth, so that the question of the initiative in convening a conference cannot become a new subject of dispute, a pretext for delaying the urgently needed international meeting of representatives of fraternal parties.

In advancing new obstacles to the conference one after another, the CCP Central Committee writes of the need for " carrying out a great deal of preparatory work." Our party has always believed and continues to believe that to have a successful conference it is necessary to prepare for it thoroughly. It is precisely to this end that we have again and again proposed cessation of open polemics and renunciation of the methods of factionalist activity in the ranks of the international Communist movement.

Everything makes it evident that what the CCP Central Committee means by " preparatory work " is actually its direct opposite, namely, an intensification of factionalist splitting activity, and a sharpening of polemics in every way. To speak frankly, it is here, essentially, that the real reasons of the Chinese leadership for procrastinating on calling a conference lie. In a situation of aggravated conflict, to judge by all the evidence, it expects to rally a bloc of parties and groups subservient to Peking. This is also indicated by the fact that you are now openly seeking invitations to the conference table for like-minded persons you have recruited in different countries.

Since the CCP Central Committee has now turned the question of the composition of the conference into a subject of disagreement, we consider it necessary to express our own attitude on this. In our opinion, those who may take part in the conference are the parties that participated in the 1957 and 1960 conferences and signed their documents. This is all the more right since the differences in the Communist movement concern the interpretation of the Declaration and the Statement. Obviously, a correct interpretation can be given only by a forum of the parties that worked out and signed these documents. Only the conference itself has the right to make a decision to invite new participants. In the years since the last international meeting, parties have arisen in several countries (particularly in Africa) that recognize the general line of the Communist movement expressed in the Declaration and the Statement, are implementing it in practice and are the recognized representatives of the workers' movement in their countries. Naturally, such parties have a right to expect an invitation to participate in a new international meeting.

But when the CCP Central Committee raises the question of inviting new participants to the conference, it is by no means this kind of party it has in mind but rather the anti-party factionalist groups it has itself set up and bombastically refers to as " parties." However, these groups in the first place do not represent the workers' movements of their countries but have been artificially planted from outside. The fact that the anti-party groups in Australia, Brazil, Belgium, Ceylon and several other countries appeared just when the CCP Central Committee was developing factionalist activity in the ranks of the international Communist movement cannot be regarded as a chance coincidence. In the second place, these groups do not support either in theory or in practice the general line of the world Communist movement defined by the Declaration and the Statement. On the contrary, the views they are propagating completely betray them as opponents of this line. In the third place, they are composed of anti-party opposition elements that have been expelled from the Marxist-Leninist parties and are waging a struggle against the legitimately elected central committees, the experienced and authoritative leaders of these parties. It is indicative of the political physiognomy and composition of these groups that they have been joined by Trotskyites, anarchists and all kinds of renegades. It must be stated frankly that such adherents to the Chinese leadership's line are no ornament for it. No matter how you try to depict these imposters as "genuine revolutionaries," they are outside the Communist movement and will not manage to insinuate themselves into its ranks by any means.

The CPSU Central Committee cannot overlook the attempt made in the CCP Central Committee's May 7 letter to defame the experienced Marxist-Leninist parties of Australia, Brazil and India. We resolutely reject the unworthy method whereby the leaders of one party — the Communist Party of China — advance claims to a special position in the Communist movement, to the right to pass judgment on entire parties and their leaders, to decide according to their own arbitrary rules questions that can be judged only by the working class of the country concerned.

If you are going to continue to carry out this kind of "preparatory work" for the conference, that is, to strive for a further expansion of factionalist activity, you will only confirm once again the opinion that has already formed that the CCP leadership is directly pursuing a split.

The CCP Central Committee's desire to aggravate the open polemics in the Communist movement has long been obvious. The propaganda campaign it has unfolded has exceeded all bounds of ideological polemics and turned into an open political struggle against the Marxist-Leninist parties. It has nothing in common with elucidation of the truth, with working out vital problems of the theory and policy of our movement. The entire content, method and tone of your statements indicate a deliberate effort to extend the range of disputed issues even further, to distort the true stand of the Marxist-Leninist parties, to slander their leaderships and set the masses against them. It is clear to everyone that this is not polemics but incitement to differences and hostility. It shakes the friendship of the peoples of socialist countries, sows confusion and mistrust in the ranks of the revolutionary workers' and national-liberation movement and compromises world socialism. The CCP leaders are thereby supplying grist for the mills of the aggressive imperialist groups, who, as is known, are eagerly assisting in the dissemination of Chinese propaganda materials.

We understand preparation for the conference differently. The CPSU Central Committee has advocated and continues to advocate that in the course of the preparations there be creative discussion of the important problems of the Communist movement, using the methods of comradely exchange of opinions envisaged in the 1960 Statement. We regard discussion of one or another current problem of Marxism-Leninism, of questions of the strategy and tactics of our movement, as normal and useful. Such discussion helps to advance Marxist thought, to link the activities of the Communist Parties more closely with the requirements of life and to work out a common policy in the course of preparing for meetings and conferences. However, the propaganda campaign, hostile to the Communist movement, that has been unleashed by the CCP Central Committee can in no way serve these purposes.

You threaten that you intend to reply "to the more than 2,000 anti-Chinese articles and materials" that allegedly have been published in the

Soviet press, and also "to the many resolutions, declarations and articles of scores of fraternal parties." In other words, you intend to carry on the public polemics endlessly. Obviously, this constitutes one of your purposes; you started the polemic, forced fraternal parties to rebuff your erroneous views, and now, in the guise of "replies," you intend to extend still further the political struggle against the Marxist-Leninist parties.

The proposal advanced in the CCP Central Committee's May 7 letter that the two parties agree to publish each other's materials in their press has unmasked your plans as nothing else could. It is aimed at further inflaming the polemics.

We would like to note in this connection that as long as it was possible to hope that the discussions would not exceed the bounds of a principled debate on theoretical and political questions, we reprinted some Chinese materials in our press. But when it became evident that it was not a question of principled debate but of hostile propaganda, we were obliged to adopt a different approach. No Communist Party has ever taken upon itself the obligation to reprint, disseminate and propagandize slanderous materials alien to the cause of socialism. No matter from whom these materials come, they help only the reactionary imperialist circles in their struggle against world socialism.

Reprinting articles that ascribe to our Party and our country "collusion with American imperialism," "betrayal of the revolution" and "restoration" of capitalist procedures would lead to nothing but the undermining of our people's feelings of friendship and fraternity toward the Communist Party of China and the Chinese people, who, of course, cannot bear responsibility for the present actions of their leaders. In printing such articles one after another, the Soviet press would be forced to reply to each of them. The polemic with the Chinese leadership would thereby become the basic content of the entire ideological life of our country. And this would mean diverting the attention of the Party and the people from the chief tasks — the tasks of building communism, combating imperialism, aiding the revolutionary workers' and national-liberation movement. It is clear that our Party will not do this.

It must be stated once more that all your designs are aimed at further exacerbating the polemics, intensifying factionalist activity, repudiating the collective method of discussing the problems that confront the Communist movement. On all the questions that are disturbing the Communist world, the CCP Central Committee has taken a stand directly at odds with the common interests of our movement, the interests of strengthening the unity of its ranks.

In this light, words to the effect that the CCP Central Committee "consistently takes the stand of defending solidarity and opposing a split" and that it has made "unremitting efforts to overcome differences" are in direct contradiction to the facts. The struggle for unity under present conditions requires practical constructive actions as never before. However, your activities have been directed toward applying all efforts and means toward making it more difficult to overcome the differences, toward exacerbating the situation. The negative approach that permeates the entire May 7 letter of the CCP Central Committee, the total unwillingness to meet the initiative of the fraternal parties halfway, can have only one explanation: The Chinese leaders do not wish to consider the opinions and interests of the overwhelming majority of Communist Parties and are waging a bitter struggle against them, deliberately seeking a split in the Communist movement.

It is clear to all the participants in the Communist movement that in postponing an international conference for a long time, the CCP Central Committee is reckoning on increasing the number of its supporters during this time, turning them into an obedient instrument of its policy and attempting in this way to set up favorable conditions for itself at a future conference. One need not be a prophet to predict the complete failure of these calculations. We have not the slightest doubt that the more time passes, the better will life demonstrate the unsoundness of the ideological-political platform and the tactical line the CCP leaders are thrusting upon the international Communist movement. The unseemly goals pursued by the Chinese leadership will become more and more apparent, and those who have been temporarily deluded will see the light. It goes without saying that the splitting activities of the CCP Central Committee can harm and are harming the international Communist movement, and especially those of its detachments that are fighting for the cause of the working class and against imperialist reaction in the difficult conditions of the capitalist countries. But every stride forward in the struggle of the working class, every new success in the development of the world socialist system will deal a blow at the mistaken and unrealistic aims of the Chinese leadership and will demonstrate the correctness and vitality of the Leninist course of the Communist movement.

The CCP Central Committee's letter touches on a number of its ideological-political differences with the CPSU and other Marxist-Leninist parties. Our party has already set forth more than once its stand on these problems. Therefore we think it unnecessary to dwell on them again in this letter, the more so since your attacks contain nothing new. You have long been subsisting on coarse language and label-pasting as a substitute for honest discussion of the questions on which the CCP Central Committee has its own special opinion. The CPSU Central Committee emphatically rejects as obvious slander your irresponsible allegations that the CPSU is "striving with every fibre of its being for an alliance with American imperialism," is "opposing the national-liberation movement, opposing proletarian revolution" and is "plotting a major conspiracy — an open split in the socialist camp and the international Communist movement." Such statements only discredit their authors, those who permit themselves to make such malicious attacks on the first country to win socialism, which bears the main burden of the struggle against imperialism. For whom are these absurd inventions intended? Do you seriously hope to find simpletons who will believe such slander? The real purport of your assertions is that you wish to lead the popular masses of China into error, set them against the Soviet people, the friend and brother of the Chinese workers and peasants. All this only plays into the hands of the imperialist reaction, which dreams of somehow disuniting the peoples of the socialist countries, sowing enmity among them, setting them against one another.

By such methods you strive to obscure the real nature of the differences you actually have with the present political line of the international Communist movement. Marxist-Leninists throughout the world have long since grasped that the Chinese leaders have diverged from the Communist movement on such fundamental, vitally important problems as questions of war and peace, of the peaceful coexistence of states with different social

311

systems, of forms for carrying out the socialist revolution, of the role of the national-liberation movement and paths for developing it, of combating the ideology and practices of the cult of the individual and of methods of building socialism and communism.

You proclaim from the housetops that you are irreconcilably opposed to the ideas of the 20th CPSU Congress. You brag of this in vain, comrades! After all, this more than anything else gives you away as people who today still hold to obsolete positions that have been rejected by life, by the practice of the entire world liberation movement. The 20th Congress of the CPSU, by the acknowledgement of the entire international Communist movement — and this was affirmed in the Declaration and the Statement — initiated a new stage in the development of our movement. It has become the symbol of the creative spirit of Leninism, the new line of the entire world Communist movement, the symbol of the turn away from the ideology and practices of the Stalin cult toward Leninist principles and norms.

It was precisely this turn that provided the prerequisites for new successes in the struggle against imperialism and for peace and socialism, for the rise in the authority and influence of the world Communist movement, its transition to a new offensive against the forces of reaction and war. The bitter attacks on the decisions of the 20th and 22nd CPSU Congresses, on the propositions and stands confirmed in the Declaration and the Statement are nothing but the reaction of conservative forces in the Communist movement to the creative Marxism-Leninism of the modern epoch.

You evidently do not notice how much the CCP Central Committee's May 7 letter itself is permeated with the ideology of the cult of the individual. Your demonstrative scorn for the will of fraternal parties, your unconcealed attempt to avoid collective discussion of the problems that have arisen, your methods of conducting polemics by piling up all sorts of political insinuations and the most fantastic accusations, your intolerance and animosity toward comrades in the common struggle — all this bears the indelible imprint of the practices of the cult of the individual.

The CCP Central Committee attempts to conceal its deviation from the general line of the Communist movement behind the banner of revolution and struggle against imperialism, which is sacred to all Communists. But the practical activity of the CCP leadership indicates the true price of this " revolutionariness "; it is directed toward disuniting the revolutionary forces of the present day. For example, it has recently become particularly obvious what meaning the CCP leaders attach to their notorious theory of a so-called " intermediate zone," which embraces, along with China, the imperialists of Japan, the Federal Republic of Germany, France and Britain. How greatly the imperialists rejoice in the appearance of a split in the Communist movement and the socialist camp may be gathered from their attempts to find some means for rapprochement with those who are causing such a split. Have the CCP leaders given attention to the fact that it is precisely now, when Chinese propaganda is more than ever shouting about " revolution " and " struggle against imperialism," that the right-wing circles of these powers are showing particular readiness to form closer ties with Peking? Yes, even the American imperialists, as is evidenced in many statements by U.S. officials, are declaring that, despite the belligerent tone of Chinese propaganda, China is behaving " moderately," and therefore the United States should " hold the door open " for a possible change in relations with China.

It is becoming increasingly clear to Marxist-Leninists throughout the world that " leftist " phrases in the mouths of the leaders of the CCP are nothing but a screen for the great-power schemes and hegemonism that are becoming more and more apparent in their practical activities in the international arena and in the Communist movement. We would like to warn you, comrades, that the path you are taking is an extremely dangerous one, that it is gambling with the fate of the people of China, with their revolutionary gains.

You try to depict criticism of your anti-Leninist views and stands as an " anti-Chinese campaign." You know perfectly well that all our Party documents lay special emphasis on the Soviet Communists' extremely friendly feelings toward the Chinese people, to whom we have rendered and are prepared to render in the future the utmost assistance in building socialism. The CPSU Central Committee is not engaged in kindling among its people mistrust and hostile feelings toward China, toward its great people, nor toward the peoples of any other countries.

It is precisely because we value the friendship of the Soviet and Chinese peoples, the unity of the Communist Party of the Soviet Union and the Communist Party of China and the interests of the solidarity of the entire world liberation movement that we are not slackening our efforts to normalize relations with the CCP, despite the fact that the Chinese leadership is more and more openly demonstrating its unwillingness to improve these relations. Our patience and self-restraint are due to the fact that we are true to the Leninist principles of internationalism, we look to the future and have faith in the ultimate triumph of these principles in the socialist commonwealth and the Communist movement.

We again affirm our position with regard to the necessity for convening an international conference of Communist and Workers' Parties as a reliable and tested method for achieving the unity of Marxist-Leninist parties. We propose that in the very near future there be an agreement in principle that a conference should be called and that it should not be long postponed, while the question of its specific date, as well as of its agenda and composition, should be discussed in the course of further consultations with the fraternal parties.

The CPSU Central Committee thinks that at the present stage the major effort should be concentrated on holding a preparatory meeting. We reiterate our proposal that a preparatory meeting be convened composed of representatives of the 26 parties that were supported by the international conference of Communist Parties as members of the Editorial Commission in 1960 and that represent the interests of Communists of all major parts of the world. We think it necessary to reach an agreement on the specific date of this meeting as soon as possible.

The CPSU Central Committee, as before, expresses its readiness to hold bilateral meetings of representatives of the CPSU and the CCP at any date that might be agreed upon. This question can be resolved at any time by agreement between the CPSU and the CCP.

The collective method of reviewing problems of the international Communist movement is at present the only proper method recognized by all Communist Parties. Therefore no party can, without breaking with internationalism, block the convening of a conference or unilaterally dictate

313

the conditions for holding it. All parties have equal rights and, according to the democratic principles entailed in the Declaration and the Statement, they decide questions affecting our movement jointly.

In conclusion, the CPSU Central Committee considers it necessary to stress that the Communist Party of the Soviet Union will firmly travel the Leninist course defined by its 20th and 22nd Congresses and will consistently pursue the general line of the world Communist movement expressed in the 1957 Declaration and the 1960 Statement. Our party and the entire Soviet people are confronted with the world-historic tasks of building a communist society. Together with all peace-loving forces, we bear responsibility for preventing world nuclear war, for the victory of the cause of peace, democracy, national independence and socialism. We will spare no effort in the struggle to solve these great tasks of the present day.

It is from this position, too, that we approach the matter of overcoming the difficulties in the world Communist movement, strengthening the unity of its ranks. The interests of world communism are paramount for us; we are guided by them in our relations with the Communist Party of China, as with any other party.

The CPSU Central Committee would like to hope that the CCP Central Committee will consider with all seriousness the proposals advanced in this letter, will once again weigh all the possible consequences of the stand it has taken and for its part will undertake steps directed not toward a split but toward solidarity with all Marxist-Leninist parties.

With fraternal greetings,

Central Committee of the
Communist Party of the Soviet Union

June 15, 1964

DOCUMENT 14

On Khrushchev's Phoney Communism and Its Historical Lessons for the World: Comment on the Open Letter of the Central Committee of the CPSU (9)

by the Editorial Departments of *Jen-min Jih-pao* and *Hung Ch'i*
(July 14, 1964)

Complete Text

[*Peking Review*, Vol. VII, No. 29 (July 17, 1964), pp. 7–24; also in *The Polemic on the General Line of the International Communist Movement*, pp. 415–480]

The theories of the proletarian revolution and the dictatorship of the proletariat are the quintessence of Marxism-Leninism. The questions of whether revolution should be upheld or opposed and whether the dictatorship of the proletariat should be upheld or opposed have always been the focus of struggle between Marxism-Leninism and all brands of revisionism and are now the focus of struggle between Marxist-Leninists the world over and the revisionist Khrushchev clique.

At the 22nd Congress of the CPSU, the revisionist Khrushchev clique developed their revisionism into a complete system not only by rounding off their anti-revolutionary theories of "peaceful coexistence," "peaceful competition" and "peaceful transition" but also by declaring that the dictatorship of the proletariat is no longer necessary in the Soviet Union and advancing the absurd theories of the "state of the whole people" and the "party of the entire people."

The Programme put forward by the revisionist Khrushchev clique at the 22nd Congress of the CPSU is a programme of phoney communism, a revisionist programme against proletarian revolution and for the abolition of the dictatorship of the proletariat and the proletarian party.

The revisionist Khrushchev clique abolish the dictatorship of the proletariat behind the camouflage of the "state of the whole people," change the proletarian character of the Communist Party of the Soviet Union behind the camouflage of the "party of the entire people" and pave the way for the restoration of capitalism behind that of "full-scale construction."

In its Proposal Concerning the General Line of the International Communist Movement dated June 14, 1963, the Central Committee of the Communist Party of China pointed out that it is most absurd in theory and extremely harmful in practice to substitute the "state of the whole people" for the state of the dictatorship of the proletariat and the "party of the entire people" for the vanguard party of the proletariat. This substitution is a great historical retrogression which makes any transition to communism impossible and helps only to restore capitalism.

The open letter of the Central Committee of the CPSU and the press of the Soviet Union resort to sophistry in self-justification and charge that our criticisms of the "state of the whole people" and the "party of the entire people" are allegations "far removed from Marxism," betray "isolation from the life of the Soviet people" and are a demand that they "return to the past."

Well, let us ascertain who is actually far removed from Marxism-Leninism, what Soviet life is actually like and who actually wants the Soviet Union to return to the past.

Socialist Society and the Dictatorship of the Proletariat

What is the correct conception of socialist society? Do classes and class struggle exist throughout the stage of socialism? Should the dictatorship of the proletariat be maintained and the socialist revolution be carried through to the end? Or should the dictatorship of the proletariat be abolished so as to pave the way for capitalist restoration? These questions must be answered correctly according to the basic theory of Marxism-Leninism and the historical experience of the dictatorship of the proletariat.

The replacement of capitalist society by socialist society is a great leap in the historical development of human society. Socialist society covers the important historical period of transition from class to classless society. It is by going through socialist society that mankind will enter communist society.

The socialist system is incomparably superior to the capitalist system. In socialist society, the dictatorship of the proletariat replaces bourgeois dictatorship and the public ownership of the means of production replaces private ownership. The proletariat, from being an oppressed and exploited class, turns into the ruling class and a fundamental change takes place in social position of the working people. Exercising dictatorship over a few exploiters only, the state of the dictatorship of the proletariat practices the broadest democracy among the masses of the working people, a democracy which is impossible in capitalist society. The nationalization of industry and collectivization of agriculture open wide vistas for the vigorous development of the social productive forces, ensuring a rate of growth incomparably greater than that in any older society.

However, one cannot but see that socialist society is a society born out of capitalist society and is only the first phase of communist society. It is not yet a fully mature communist society in the economic and other fields. It is inevitably stamped with the birth marks of capitalist society. When defining socialist society Marx said:

> What we have to deal with here is a communist society, not as it has *developed* on its own foundations, but, on the contrary, just as it *emerges* from capitalist society; which is thus in every respect, economically, morally and intellectually, still stamped with the birth marks of the old society from whose womb it emerges.[1]

Lenin also pointed out that in socialist society, which is the first phase of communism, "Communism *cannot* as yet be fully ripe economically and entirely free from traditions or traces of capitalism." [2]

In socialist society, the differences between workers and peasants, between town and country, and between manual and mental labourers still remain, bourgeois rights are not yet completely abolished, it is not possible " at once to eliminate the other injustice, which consists in the distribution of articles of consumption 'according to the amount of labour performed' (and not according to needs)," [3] and therefore differences in wealth still exist. The disappearance of these differences, phenomena and bourgeois rights can only be gradual and long drawn-out. As Marx said, only after these differences have vanished and bourgeois rights have completely disappeared, will it be possible to realize full communism with its principle, " from each according to his ability, to each according to his needs."

Marxism-Leninism and the practice of the Soviet Union, China and other socialist countries all teach us that socialist society covers a very, very long historical stage. Throughout this stage, the class struggle between the bourgeoisie and the proletariat goes on and the question of " who will win " between the roads of capitalism and socialism remains, as does the danger of the restoration of capitalism.

In its Proposal Concerning the General Line of the International Communist Movement dated June 14, 1963, the Central Committee of the Chinese Communist Party states:

> For a very long historical period after the proletariat takes power, class struggle continues as an objective law independent of man's will, differing only in form from what it was before the taking of power.

---

[1] Marx, " Critique of the Gotha Programme," *Selected Works of Marx and Engels*, Foreign Languages Publishing House, Moscow, 1958, Vol. 2, p. 23.
[2] Lenin, " The State and Revolution," *Selected Works*, F.L.P.H., Moscow, 1952, Vol. 2, Part 1, p. 302.
[3] *Ibid.*, p. 296.

After the October Revolution, Lenin pointed out a number of times that:

a) The overthrown exploiters always try in a thousand and one ways to recover the " paradise " they have been deprived of.

b) New elements of capitalism are constantly and spontaneously generated in the petty-bourgeois atmosphere.

c) Political degenerates and new bourgeois elements may emerge in the ranks of the working class and among government functionaries as a result of bourgeois influence and the pervasive, corrupting atmosphere of the petty bourgeoisie.

d) The external conditions for the continuance of class struggle within a socialist country are encirclement by international capitalism, the imperialists' threat of armed intervention and their subversive activities to accomplish peaceful disintegration.

Life has confirmed these conclusions of Lenin's.

In socialist society, the overthrown bourgeoisie and other reactionary classes remain strong for quite a long time, and indeed in certain respects are quite powerful. They have a thousand and one links with the international bourgeoisie. They are not reconciled to their defeat and stubbornly continue to engage in trials of strength with the proletariat. They conduct open and hidden struggles against the proletariat in every field. Constantly parading such signboards as support for socialism, the Soviet system, the Communist Party and Marxism-Leninism, they work to undermine socialism and restore capitalism. Politically, they persist for a long time as a force antagonistic to the proletariat and constantly attempt to overthrow the dictatorship of the proletariat. They sneak into the government organs, public organizations, economic departments and cultural and educational institutions so as to resist or usurp the leadership of the proletariat. Economically, they employ every means to damage socialist ownership by the whole people and socialist collective ownership and to develop the forces of capitalism. In the ideological, cultural and educational fields, they counterpose the bourgeois world outlook to the proletarian world outlook and try to corrupt the proletariat and other working people with bourgeois ideology.

The collectivization of agriculture turns individual into collective farmers and provides favourable conditions for the thorough remoulding of the peasants. However, until collective ownership advances to ownership by the whole people and until the remnants of private economy disappear completely, the peasants inevitably retain some of the inherent characteristics of small producers. In these circumstances spontaneous capitalist tendencies are inevitable, the soil for the growth of new rich peasants still exists and polarization among the peasants may still occur.

The activities of the bourgeoisie as described above, its corrupting effects in the political, economic, ideological and cultural and educational fields, the existence of spontaneous capitalist tendencies among urban and rural small producers, and the influence of the remaining bourgeois rights and the force of habit of the old society all constantly breed political degenerates in the ranks of the working class and Party and government organizations, new bourgeois elements and embezzlers and grafters in state enterprises owned by the whole people and new bourgeois intellectuals in the cultural and educational institutions and intellectual circles. These new bourgeois elements and these political degenerates attack socialism in collusion with the old bourgeois elements and elements of other exploiting classes which

317

have been overthrown but not eradicated. The political degenerates entrenched in the leading organs are particularly dangerous, for they support and shield the bourgeois elements in organs at lower levels.

As long as imperialism exists, the proletariat in the socialist countries will have to struggle both against the bourgeoisie at home and against international imperialism. Imperialism will seize every opportunity and try to undertake armed intervention against the socialist countries or to bring about their peaceful disintegration. It will do its utmost to destroy the socialist countries or to make them degenerate into capitalist countries. The international class struggle will inevitably find its reflection within the socialist countries.

Lenin said:

The transition from capitalism to communism represents an entire historical epoch. Until this epoch has terminated, the exploiters inevitably cherish the hope of restoration, and this *hope* is converted into *attempts* at restoration.[4]

He also pointed out:

The abolition of classes requires a long, difficult and stubborn *class struggle*, which *after* the overthrow of the power of capital, *after* the destruction of the bourgeois state, *after* the establishment of the dictatorship of the proletariat, *does not disappear* (as the vulgar representatives of the old Socialism and the old Social-Democracy imagine), but merely changes its forms and in many respects becomes more fierce.[5]

Throughout the stage of socialism the class struggle between the proletariat and the bourgeoisie in the political, economic, ideological and cultural and educational fields cannot be stopped. It is a protracted, repeated, tortuous and complex struggle. Like the waves of the sea it sometimes rises high and sometimes subsides, is now fairly calm and now very turbulent. It is a struggle that decides the fate of a socialist society. Whether a socialist society will advance to communism or revert to capitalism depends upon the outcome of this protracted struggle.

The class struggle in socialist society is inevitably reflected in the Communist Party. The bourgeoisie and international imperialism both understand that in order to make a socialist country degenerate into a capitalist country, it is first necessary to make the Communist Party degenerate into a revisionist party. The old and new bourgeois elements, the old and new rich peasants and the degenerate elements of all sorts constitute the social basis of revisionism, and they use every possible means to find agents within the Communist Party. The existence of bourgeois influence is the internal source of revisionism and surrender to imperialist pressure the external source. Throughout the stage of socialism, there is inevitable struggle between Marxism-Leninism and various kinds of opportunism — mainly revisionism — in the Communist Parties of socialist countries. The characteristic of this revisionism is that, denying the existence of classes and class struggle, it sides with the bourgeoisie in attacking the proletariat and turns the dictatorship of the proletariat into the dictatorship of the bourgeoisie.

[4] Lenin, " The Proletarian Revolution and the Renegade Kautsky," *Selected Works*, F.L.P.H., Moscow, Vol. 2, Part 2, p. 61.
[5] Lenin, " Greetings to the Hungarian Workers," *Selected Works*, F.L.P.H., Moscow, Vol. 2, Part 2, pp. 210–11.

In the light of the experience of the international working-class movement and in accordance with the objective law of class struggle, the founders of Marxism pointed out that the transition from capitalism to communism, from class to classless society, must depend on the dictatorship of the proletariat and that there is no other road.

Marx said that " the class struggle necessarily leads to the *dictatorship of the proletariat*." [6] He also said:

> Between capitalist and communist society lies the period of the revolutionary transformation of the one into the other. There corresponds to this also a political transition period in which the state can be nothing but *the revolutionary dictatorship of the proletariat*.[7]

The development of socialist society is a process of uninterrupted revolution. In explaining revolutionary socialism Marx said:

> This socialism is the *declaration of the permanence of the revolution*, the *class dictatorship* of the proletariat as the necessary transit point to the *abolition of class distinctions generally*, to the abolition of all the relations of production on which they rest, to the abolition of all the social relations that correspond to these relations of production, to the revolutionizing of all the ideas that result from these social relations.[8]

In his struggle against the opportunism of the Second International, Lenin creatively expounded and developed Marx's theory of the dictatorship of the proletariat. He pointed out:

> The dictatorship of the proletariat is not the end of class struggle but its continuation in new forms. The dictatorship of the proletariat is class struggle waged by a proletariat which has been victorious and has taken political power in its hands against a bourgeoisie that has been defeated but not destroyed, a bourgeoisie that has not vanished, not ceased to offer resistance, but that has intensified its resistance.[9]

He also said:

> The dictatorship of the proletariat is a persistent struggle — bloody and bloodless, violent and peaceful, military and economic, educational and administrative — against the forces and traditions of the old society.[10]

In his celebrated work *On the Correct Handling of Contradictions Among the People* and in other works, Comrade Mao Tse-tung, basing himself on the fundamental principles of Marxism-Leninism and the historical experience of the dictatorship of the proletariat, gives a comprehensive and systematic analysis of classes and class struggle in socialist society, and creatively develops the Marxist-Leninist theory of the dictatorship of the proletariat.

[6] " Marx to J. Weydemeyer, March 5, 1852," *Selected Works of Marx and Engels*, F.L.P.H., Moscow, Vol. 2, p. 452.
[7] Marx, " Critique of the Gotha Programme," *Selected Works of Marx and Engels*, F.L.P.H., Moscow, Vol. 2, pp. 32–33.
[8] Marx, " The Class Struggles in France, 1848 to 1850," *Selected Works of Marx and Engels*, F.L.P.H., Moscow, Vol. 1, p. 223.
[9] Lenin, " Foreword to the Speech ' On Deception of the People with Slogans of Freedom and Equality,' " *Alliance of the Working Class and the Peasantry*, F.L.P.H., Moscow, 1959, p. 302.
[10] Lenin, " ' Left-Wing ' Communism, an Infantile Disorder," *Selected Works*, F.L.P.H., Moscow, Vol. 2, Part 2, p. 367.

Comrade Mao Tse-tung examines the objective laws of socialist society from the viewpoint of materialist dialectics. He points out that the universal law of the unity and struggle of opposites operating both in the natural world and in human society is applicable to socialist society, too. In socialist society, class contradictions still remain and class struggle does not die out after the socialist transformation of the ownership of the means of production. The struggle between the two roads of socialism and capitalism runs through the entire stage of socialism. To ensure the success of socialist construction and to prevent the restoration of capitalism, it is necessary to carry the socialist revolution through to the end on the political, economic, ideological and cultural fronts. The complete victory of socialism cannot be brought about in one or two generations; to resolve this question thoroughly requires five or ten generations or even longer.

Comrade Mao Tse-tung stresses the fact that two types of social contradictions exist in socialist society, namely, contradictions among the people and contradictions between ourselves and the enemy, and that the former are very numerous. Only by distinguishing between the two types of contradictions, which are different in nature, and by adopting different measures to handle them correctly is it possible to unite the people, who constitute more than 90 per cent of the population, defeat their enemies, who constitute only a few per cent, and consolidate the dictatorship of the proletariat.

The dictatorship of the proletariat is the basic guarantee for the consolidation and development of socialism, for the victory of the proletariat over the bourgeoisie and of socialism in the struggle between the two roads.

Only by emancipating all mankind can the proletariat ultimately emancipate itself. The historical task of the dictatorship of the proletariat has two aspects, one internal and the other international. The internal task consists mainly of completely abolishing all the exploiting classes, developing socialist economy to the maximum, enhancing the communist consciousness of the masses, abolishing the differences between ownership by the whole people and collective ownership, between workers and peasants, between town and country and between mental and manual labourers, eliminating any possibility of the re-emergence of classes and the restoration of capitalism and providing conditions for the realization of a communist society with its principle, "from each according to his ability, to each according to his needs." The international task consists mainly of preventing attacks by international imperialism (including armed intervention and disintegration by peaceful means) and of giving support to the world revolution until the people of all countries finally abolish imperialism, capitalism and the system of exploitation. Before the fulfilment of both tasks and before the advent of a full communist society, the dictatorship of the proletariat is absolutely necessary.

Judging from the actual situation today, the tasks of the dictatorship of the proletariat are still far from accomplished in any of the socialist countries. In all socialist countries without exception, there are classes and class struggle, the struggle between the socialist and the capitalist roads, the question of carrying the socialist revolution through to the end and the question of preventing the restoration of capitalism. All the socialist countries still have a very long way to go before the differences between ownership by the whole people and collective ownership, between workers and peasants, between town and country and between mental and manual labourers are eliminated, before all classes and class differences are abolished and a communist society with its principle, " from each according to his ability, to each according to his needs " is realized. Therefore, it is necessary for all the socialist countries to uphold the dictatorship of the proletariat.

In these circumstances, the abolition of the dictatorship of the proletariat by the revisionist Khrushchev clique is nothing but the betrayal of socialism and communism.

Antagonistic Classes and Class Struggle Exist in the Soviet Union

In announcing the abolition of the dictatorship of the proletariat in the Soviet Union, the revisionist Khrushchev clique base themselves mainly on the argument that antagonistic classes have been eliminated and that class struggle no longer exists.

But what is the actual situation in the Soviet Union? Are there really no antagonistic classes and no class struggle there?

Following the victory of the Great October Socialist Revolution, the dictatorship of the proletariat was established in the Soviet Union, capitalist private ownership was destroyed and socialist ownership by the whole people and socialist collective ownership were established through the nationalization of industry and the collectivization of agriculture, and great achievements in socialist construction were scored during several decades. All this constituted an indelible victory of tremendous historic significance won by the Communist Party of the Soviet Union and the Soviet people under the leadership of Lenin and Stalin.

However, the old bourgeoisie and other exploiting classes which had been overthrown in the Soviet Union were not eradicated and survived after industry was nationalized and agriculture collectivized. The political and ideological influence of the bourgeoisie remained. Spontaneous capitalist tendencies continued to exist both in the city and in the countryside. New bourgeois elements and kulaks were still incessantly generated. Throughout the long intervening period, the class struggle between the proletariat and the bourgeoisie and the struggle between the socialist and capitalist roads have continued in the political, economic and ideological spheres.

As the Soviet Union was the first, and at the time the only, country to build socialism and had no foreign experience to go by, and as Stalin departed from Marxist-Leninist dialectics in his understanding of the laws of class struggle in socialist society, he prematurely declared after agriculture was basically collectivized that there were "no longer antagonistic classes" [11] in the Soviet Union and that it was "free of class conflicts," [12] one-sidedly stressed the internal homogeneity of socialist society and overlooked its contradictions, failed to rely upon the working class and the masses in the struggle against the forces of capitalism and regarded the possibility of the restoration of capitalism as associated only with armed attack by international imperialism. This was wrong both in theory and in practice. Nevertheless, Stalin remained a great Marxist-Leninist. As long as he led the Soviet Party and state, he held fast to the

[11] Stalin, " On the Draft Constitution of the USSR," *Problems of Leninism*, F.L.P.H., Moscow, 1954, p. 690.
[12] Stalin, " Report to the Eighteenth Congress of the CPSU (B.) on the Work of the Central Committee," *Problems of Leninism*, F.L.P.H., Moscow, p. 777.

dictatorship of the proletariat and the socialist course, pursued a Marxist-Leninist line and ensured the Soviet Union's victorious advance along the road of socialism.

Ever since Khrushchev seized the leadership of the Soviet Party and state, he has pushed through a whole series of revisionist policies which have greatly hastened the growth of the forces of capitalism and again sharpened the class struggle between the proletariat and the bourgeoisie and the struggle between the roads of socialism and capitalism in the Soviet Union.

Scanning the reports in Soviet newspapers over the last few years, one finds numerous examples demonstrating not only the presence of many elements of the old exploiting classes in Soviet society, but also the generation of new bourgeois elements on a large scale and the acceleration of class polarization.

Let us first look at the activities of the various bourgeois elements in the Soviet enterprises owned by the whole people.

Leading functionaries of some state-owned factories and their gangs abuse their positions and amass large fortunes by using the equipment and materials of the factories to set up " underground workshops " for private production, selling the products illicitly and dividing the spoils. Here are same examples.

In a Leningrad plant producing military items, the leading functionaries placed their own men in " all key posts " and " turned the state enterprise into a private one." They illicitly engaged in the production of non-military goods and from the sale of fountain pens alone embezzled 1,200,000 old rubles in three years. Among these people was a man who " was a Nepman . . . in the 1920's " and had been a " lifelong thief." [13]

In a silk-weaving mill in Uzbekistan, the manager ganged up with the chief engineer, the chief accountant, the chief of the supply and marketing section, heads of workshops and others, and they all became " newborn entrepreneurs." They purchased more than ten tons of artificial and pure silk through various illegal channels in order to manufacture goods which " did not pass through the accounts." They employed workers without going through the proper procedures and enforced " a twelve-hour working day." [14]

The manager of a furniture factory in Kharkov set up an " illegal knitwear workshop " and carried on secret operations inside the factory. This man " had several wives, several cars, several houses, 176 neckties, about a hundred shirts and dozens of suits." He was also a big gambler at the horse-races.[15]

Such people do not operate all by themselves. They invariably work hand in glove with functionaries in the state departments in charge of supplies and in the commercial and other departments. They have their own men in the police and judicial departments who protect them and act as their agents. Even high-ranking officials in the state organs support and shield them. Here are a few examples.

The chief of the workshops affiliated to a Moscow psychoneurological dispensary and his gang set up an " underground enterprise," and by bribery " obtained 58 knitting machines " and a large amount of raw material. They entered into business relations with " 52 factories, handicraft co-

---

[13] *Krasnaya Zvezda*, May 19, 1962.
[14] *Pravda Vostoka*, Oct. 8, 1963.
[15] *Pravda Ukrainy*, May 18, 1962.

operatives and collective farms " and made 3 million rubles in a few years. They bribed functionaries of the Department for Combating Theft of Socialist Property and Speculation, controllers, inspectors, instructors and others.[16]

The manager of a machinery plant in the Russian Federation, together with the deputy manager of a second machinery plant and other functionaries, or 43 persons in all, stole more than 900 looms and sold them to factories in Central Asia, Kazakhstan, the Caucasus and other places, whose leading functionaries used them for illicit production.[17]

In the Kirghiz SSR, a gang of over forty embezzlers and grafters, having gained control of two factories, organized underground production and plundered more than 30 million rubles' worth of state property. This gang included the chairman of the planning commission of the republic, a vice-minister of commerce, seven bureau chiefs and division chiefs of the republic's council of ministers, national economic council and state control commission, as well as " a big kulak who had fled from exile." [18]

These examples show that the factories which have fallen into the clutches of such degenerates are socialist enterprises only in name, that in fact they have become capitalist enterprises by which these persons enrich themselves. The relationship of such persons to the workers has turned into one between exploiters and exploited, between oppressors and oppressed. Are not such degenerates who possess and make use of means of production to exploit the labour of others out-and-out bourgeois elements? Are not their accomplices in government organizations, who work hand in glove with them, participate in many types of exploitation, engage in embezzlement, accept bribes, and share the spoils, also out-and-out bourgeois elements?

Obviously all these people belong to a class that is antagonistic to the proletariat — they belong to the bourgeoisie. Their activities against socialism are definitely class struggle with the bourgeoisie attacking the proletariat.

Now let us look at the activities of various kulak elements on the collective farms.

Some leading collective-farm functionaries and their gangs steal and speculate at will, freely squander public money and fleece the collective farmers. Here are some examples.

The chairman of a collective farm in Uzbekistan " held the whole village in terror." All the important posts on this farm " were occupied by his in-laws and other relatives and friends." He squandered " over 132,000 rubles of the collective farm for his personal ' needs '." He had a car, two motor-cycles and three wives, each with " a house of her own." [19]

The chairman of a collective farm in the Kursk Region regarded the farm as his " hereditary estate." He conspired with its accountant, cashier, chief warehouse-keeper, agronomist, general-store manager and others. Shielding each other, they " fleeced the collective farmers " and pocketed more than a hundred thousand rubles in a few years.[20]

The chairman of a collective farm in the Ukraine made over 50,000 rubles at its expense by forging purchase certificates and cash-account

16 *Izvestiya*, Oct. 20, 1963, and *Izvestiya Sunday Supplement*, No. 12, 1964.
17 *Komsomolskaya Pravda*, Aug. 9, 1963.
18 *Sovietskaya Kirghizia*, Jan. 9, 1962.
19 *Selskaya Zhizn*, June 26, 1962.
20 *Ekonomicheskaya Gazeta*, No. 35, 1963.

orders in collusion with its woman accountant, who had been praised for keeping "model accounts" and whose deeds had been displayed at the Moscow Exhibition of Achievements of the National Economy.[21]

The chairman of a collective farm in the Alma-Ata Region specialized in commercial speculation. He bought "fruit juice in the Ukraine or Uzbekistan, and sugar and alcohol from Djambul," processed them and then sold the wine at very high prices in many localities. In this farm a winery was created with a capacity of over a million litres a year, its speculative commercial network spread throughout the Kazakhstan S.S.R., and commercial speculation became one of the farm's main sources of income.[22]

The chairman of a collective farm in Byelorussia considered himself " a feudal princeling on the farm" and acted "personally" in all matters. He lived not on the farm but in the city or in his own splendid villa, and was always busy with "various commercial machinations" and "illegal deals." He bought cattle from the outside, represented them as the products of his collective farm and falsified output figures. And yet "not a few commendatory newspaper reports" had been published about him and he had been called a "model leader."[23]

These examples show that collective farms under the control of such functionaries virtually become their private property. Such men turn socialist collective economic enterprises into economic enterprises of new kulaks. There are often people in their superior organizations who protect them. Their relationship to the collective farmers has likewise become that of oppressors to oppressed, of exploiters to exploited. Are not such neo-exploiters who ride on the backs of the collective farmers one-hundred-per-cent neo-kulaks?

Obviously, they all belong to a class that is antagonistic to the proletariat and the labouring farmers, belong to the kulak or rural bourgeois class. Their anti-socialist activities are precisely class struggle with the bourgeoisie attacking the proletariat and the labouring farmers.

Apart from the bourgeois elements in the state enterprises and collective farms, there are many others in both town and country in the Soviet Union.

Some of them set up private enterprises for private production and sale; others organize contractor teams and openly undertake construction jobs for state or co-operative enterprises; still others open private hotels. A "Soviet woman capitalist" in Leningrad hired workers to make nylon blouses for sale, and her "daily income amounted to 700 new rubles."[24] The owner of a workshop in the Kursk Region made felt boots for sale at speculative prices. He had in his possession 540 pairs of felt boots, 8 kilogrammes of gold coins, 3,000 metres of high-grade textiles, 20 carpets, 1,200 kilogrammes of wool and many other valuables.[25] A private enterpreneur in the Gomel Region "hired workers and artisans" and in the course of two years secured contracts for the construction and overhauling of furnaces in 12 factories at a high price.[26] In the Orenburg Region there are "hundreds of private hotels and trans-shipment points,"

[21] *Selskaya Zhizn*, Aug. 14, 1963.
[22] *Pravda*, Jan. 14, 1962.
[23] *Pravda*, Feb. 6, 1961.
[24] *Izvestiya*, April 9, 1963.
[25] *Sovietskaya Rossiya*, Oct. 9, 1960.
[26] *Izvestiya*, Oct. 18, 1960.

and "the money of the collective farms and the state is continuously streaming into the pockets of the hostelry owners." [27]

Some engage in commercial speculation, making tremendous profits through buying cheap and selling dear or bringing goods from far away. In Moscow there are a great many speculators engaged in the resale of agricultural produce. They " bring to Moscow tons of citrus fruit, apples and vegetables and resell them at speculative prices." " These profit-grabbers are provided with every facility, with market inns, store-rooms and other services at their disposal." [28] In the Krasnodar Territory, a speculator set up her own agency and "employed 12 salesmen and two stevedores." She transported "thousands of hogs, hundreds of quintals of grain and hundreds of tons of fruit " from the rural areas to the Don Basin and moved " great quantities of stolen slag bricks, whole wagons of glass " and other building materials from the city to the villages. She reaped huge profits out of such resale.[29]

Others specialize as brokers and middlemen. They have wide contacts and through them one can get anything in return for a bribe. There was a broker in Leningrad who "though he is not the Minister of Trade, controls all the stocks," and " though he holds no post on the railway, disposes of wagons." He could obtain " things the stocks of which are strictly controlled, from outside the stocks." " All the store-houses in Leningrad are at his service." For delivering goods, he received huge " bonuses " — 700,000 rubles from one timber combine in 1960 alone. In Leningrad, there is " a whole group " of such brokers. [30]

These private entrepreneurs and speculators are engaged in the most naked capitalist exploitation. Isn't it clear that they belong to the bourgeoisie, the class antagonistic to the proletariat?

Actually the Soviet press itself calls these people " Soviet capitalists," "newborn entrepreneurs," " private entrepreneurs," " newly emerged kulaks," " speculators," " exploiters," etc. Aren't the revisionist Khrushchev clique contradicting themselves when they assert that antagonistic classes do not exist in the Soviet Union?

The facts cited above are only a part of those published in the Soviet press. They are enough to shock people, but there are many more which have not been published, many bigger and more serious cases which are covered up and shielded. We have quoted the above data in order to answer the question whether there are antagonistic classes and class struggle in the Soviet Union. These data are readily available and even the revisionist Khrushchev clique are unable to deny them.

These data suffice to show that the unbridled activities of the bourgeoisie against the proletariat are widespread in the Soviet Union, in the city as well as the countryside, in industry as well as agriculture, in the sphere of production as well as the sphere of circulation, all the way from the economic departments to Party and government organizations, and from the grass-roots to the higher leading bodies. These anti-socialist activities are nothing if not the sharp class struggle of the bourgeoisie against the proletariat.

[27] *Selskaya Zhizn*, July 17, 1963.
[28] *Ekonomicheskaya Gazeta*, No. 27, 1963.
[29] *Literaturnaya Gazeta*, July 27 and Aug. 17, 1963.
[30] *Sovietskaya Rossiya*, Jan. 27, 1961.

It is not strange that attacks on socialism should be made in a socialist country by old and new bourgeois elements. There is nothing terrifying about this so long as the leadership of the Party and state remains a Marxist-Leninist one. But in the Soviet Union today, the gravity of the situation lies in the fact that the revisionist Khrushchev clique have usurped the leadership of the Soviet Party and state and that a privileged bourgeois stratum has emerged in Soviet society.

We shall deal with this problem in the following section.

The Soviet Privileged Stratum and the Revisionist Khrushchev Clique

The privileged stratum in contemporary Soviet society is composed of degenerate elements from among the leading cadres of Party and government organizations, enterprises and farms as well as bourgeois intellectuals ; it stands in opposition to the workers, the peasants and the overwhelming majority of the intellectuals and cadres of the Soviet Union.

Lenin pointed out soon after the October Revolution that bourgeois and petty-bourgeois ideologies and force of habit were encircling and influencing the proletariat from all directions and were corrupting certain of its sections. This circumstance led to the emergence from among the Soviet officials and functionaries both of bureaucrats alienated from the masses and of new bourgeois elements. Lenin also pointed out that although the high salaries paid to the bourgeois technical specialists staying on to work for the Soviet regime were necessary, they were having a corrupting influence on it.

Therefore, Lenin laid great stress on waging persistent struggles against the influence of bourgeois and petty-bourgeois ideologies, on arousing the broad masses to take part in government work, on ceaselessly exposing and purging bureaucrats and new bourgeois elements in the Soviet organs, and on creating conditions that would bar the existence and reproduction of the bourgeoisie. Lenin pointed out sharply that " without a systematic and determined struggle to improve the apparatus, we shall perish before the basis of socialism is created." [31]

At the same time, he laid great stress on adherence to the principle of the Paris Commune in wage policy, that is, all public servants were to be paid wages corresponding to those of the workers and only bourgeois specialists were to be paid high salaries. From the October Revolution to the period of Soviet economic rehabilitation, Lenin's directives were in the main observed: the leading personnel of the Party and government organizations and enterprises and Party members among the specialists received salaries roughly equivalent to the wages of the workers.

At that time, the Communist Party and the Government of the Soviet Union adopted a number of measures in the sphere of politics and ideology and in the system of distribution to prevent leading cadres in any department from abusing their powers or degenerating morally or politically.

The Communist Party of the Soviet Union headed by Stalin adhered to the dictatorship of the proletariat and the road of socialism and waged a staunch struggle against the forces of capitalism. Stalin's struggles against the Trotskyites, Zinovievites and Bukharinites were in essence a reflection within the Party of the class struggle between the proletariat and the

---

[31] Lenin, " Plan of the Pamphlet ' On the Food Tax,' " *Collected Works*, 4th Russian ed., Moscow, Vol. 32, p. 301.

bourgeoisie and of the struggle between the two roads of socialism and capitalism. Victory in these struggles smashed the vain plot of the bourgeoisie to restore capitalism in the Soviet Union.

It cannot be denied that before Stalin's death high salaries were already being paid to certain groups and that some cadres had already degenerated and become bourgeois elements. The Central Committee of the CPSU pointed out in its report to the 19th Party Congress in October 1952 that degeneration and corruption had appeared in certain Party organizations. The leaders of these organizations had turned them into small communities composed exclusively of their own people, " setting their group interests higher than the interests of the Party and the state." Some executives of industrial enterprises " forget that the enterprises entrusted to their charge are state enterprises, and try to turn them into their own private domain." " Instead of safeguarding the common husbandry of the collective farms," some Party and Soviet functionaries and some cadres in agricultural departments " engage in filching collective-farm property." In the cultural, artistic and scientific fields, too, works attacking and smearing the socialist system had appeared and a monopolistic " Arakcheyev regime " had emerged among the scientists.

Since Khrushchev usurped the leadership of the Soviet Party and state, there has been a fundamental change in the state of the class struggle in the Soviet Union.

Khrushchev has carried out a series of revisionist policies serving the interests of the bourgeoisie and rapidly swelling the forces of capitalism in the Soviet Union.

On the pretext of "combating the personality cult," Khrushchev has defamed the dictatorship of the proletariat and the socialist system and thus in fact paved the way for the restoration of capitalism in the Soviet Union. In completely negating Stalin, he has in fact negated Marxism-Leninism which was upheld by Stalin and opened the floodgates for the revisionist deluge.

Khrushchev has substituted " material incentive " for the socialist principle, " from each according to his ability, to each according to his work." He has widened, and not narrowed, the gap between the incomes of a small minority and those of the workers, peasants and ordinary intellectuals. He has supported the degenerates in leading positions, encouraging them to become even more unscrupulous in abusing their powers and to appropriate the fruits of labour of the Soviet people. Thus he has accelerated the polarization of classes in Soviet society.

Khrushchev sabotages the socialist planned economy, applies the capitalist principle of profit, develops capitalist free competition and undermines socialist ownership by the whole people.

Khrushchev attacks the system of socialist agricultural planning, describing it as " bureaucratic " and " unnecessary." Eager to learn from the big proprietors of American farms, he is encouraging capitalist management, fostering a kulak economy and undermining the socialist collective economy.

Khrushchev is peddling bourgeois ideology, bourgeois liberty, equality, fraternity and humanity, inculcating bourgeois idealism and metaphysics and the reactionary ideas of bourgeois individualism, humanism and pacifism among the Soviet people, and debasing socialist morality. The rotten bourgeois culture of the West is now fashionable in the Soviet Union, and socialist culture is ostracized and attacked.

Under the signboard of "peaceful coexistence," Khrushchev has been colluding with U.S. imperialism, wrecking the socialist camp and the international communist movement, opposing the revolutionary struggles of the oppressed peoples and nations, practising great-power chauvinism and national egoism and betraying proletarian internationalism. All this is being done for the protection of the vested interests of a handful of people, which he places above the fundamental interests of the peoples of the Soviet Union, the socialist camp and the whole world.

The line Khrushchev pursues is a revisionist line through and through. Guided by this line, not only have the old bourgeois elements run wild but new bourgeois elements have appeared in large numbers among the leading cadres of the Soviet Party and Government, the chiefs of state enterprises and collective farms, and the higher intellectuals in the fields of culture, art, science and technology.

In the Soviet Union at present, not only have the new bourgeois elements increased in number as never before, but their social status has fundamentally changed. Before Khrushchev came to power, they did not occupy the ruling position in Soviet society. Their activities were restricted in many ways and they were subject to attack. But since Khrushchev took over, usurping the leadership of the Party and the state step by step, the new bourgeois elements have gradually risen to the ruling position in the Party and Government and in the economic, cultural and other departments, and formed a privileged stratum in Soviet society.

This privileged stratum is the principal component of the bourgeoisie in the Soviet Union today and the main social basis of the revisionist Khrushchev clique. The revisionist Khrushchev clique are the political representatives of the Soviet bourgeoisie, and particularly of its privileged stratum.

The revisionist Khrushchev clique have carried out one purge after another and replaced one group of cadres after another throughout the country, from the central to the local bodies, from leading Party and government organizations to economic and cultural and educational departments, dismissing those they do not trust and planting their proteges in leading posts.

Take the Central Committee of the CPSU as an example. The statistics show that nearly 70 per cent of the Members of the Central Committee of the CPSU who were elected at its 19th Congress in 1952 were purged in the course of the 20th and 22nd Congresses held respectively in 1956 and 1961. And nearly 50 per cent of the Members of the Central Committee who were elected at the 20th Congress were purged at the time of the 22nd Congress.

Or take the local organizations. On the eve of the 22nd Congress, on the pretext of "renewing the cadres," the revisionist Khrushchev clique, according to incomplete statistics, removed from office 45 per cent of the members of the Party Central Committees of the Union Republics and of the Party committees of the territories and regions, and 40 per cent of the members of the municipal and district Party committees. In 1963, on the pretext of dividing the Party into "industrial" and "agricultural" Party committees, they further replaced more than half the members of the

Central Committees of the Union Republics and of the Regional Party Committees.

Through this series of changes the Soviet privileged stratum has gained control of the Party, the government and other important organizations.

The members of this privileged stratum have converted the function of serving the masses into the privilege of dominating them. They are abusing their powers over the means of production and of livelihood for the private benefit of their small clique.

The members of this privileged stratum appropriate the fruits of the Soviet people's labour and pocket incomes that are dozens or even a hundred times those of the average Soviet worker and peasant. They not only secure high incomes in the form of high salaries, high awards, high royalties and a great variety of personal subsidies, but also use their privileged position to appropriate public property by graft and bribery. Completely divorced from the working people of the Soviet Union, they live the parasitical and decadent life of the bourgeoisie.

The members of this privileged stratum have become utterly degenerate ideologically, have completely departed from the revolutionary traditions of the Bolshevik Party and discarded the lofty ideals of the Soviet working class. They are opposed to Marxism-Leninism and socialism. They betray the revolution and forbid others to make revolution. Their sole concern is to consolidate their economic position and political rule. All their activities revolve around the private interests of their own privileged stratum.

Having usurped the leadership of the Soviet Party and state, the Khrushchev clique are turning the Marxist-Leninist Communist Party of the Soviet Union with its glorious revolutionary history into a revisionist party; they are turning the Soviet state under the dictatorship of the proletariat into a state under the dictatorship of the revisionist Khrushchev clique; and, step by step, they are turning socialist ownership by the whole people and socialist collective ownership into ownership by the privileged stratum.

People have seen how in Yugoslavia, although the Tito clique still displays the banner of " socialism," a bureaucrat bourgeoisie opposed to the Yugoslav people has gradually come into being since the Tito clique took the road of revisionism, transforming the Yugoslav state from a dictatorship of the proletariat into the dictatorship of the bureaucrat bourgeoisie and its socialist public economy into state capitalism. Now people see the Khrushchev clique taking the road already travelled by the Tito clique. Khrushchev looks to Belgrade as his Mecca, saying again and again that he will learn from the Tito clique's experience and declaring that he and the Tito clique " belong to one and the same idea and are guided by the same theory." [32] This is not at all surprising.

As a result of Khrushchev's revisionism, the first socialist country in the world built by the great Soviet people with their blood and sweat is now facing an unprecedented danger of capitalist restoration.

The Khrushchev clique are spreading the tale that " there are no longer antagonistic classes and class struggle in the Soviet Union " in order to cover up the facts about their own ruthless class struggle against the Soviet people.

[32] N. S. Khrushchev, Interview with Foreign Correspondents at Brioni in Yugoslavia, Aug. 28, 1963.

The Soviet privileged stratum represented by the revisionist Khrushchev clique constitutes only a few per cent of the Soviet population. Among the Soviet cadres its numbers are also small. It stands diametrically opposed to the Soviet people, who constitute more than 90 per cent of the total population, and to the great majority of the Soviet cadres and Communists. The contradiction between the Soviet people and this privileged stratum is now the principal contradiction inside the Soviet Union, and it is an irreconcilable and antagonistic class contradiction.

The glorious Communist Party of the Soviet Union, which was built by Lenin, and the great Soviet people displayed epoch-making revolutionary initiative in the October Socialist Revolution, they showed their heroism and stamina in defeating the White Guards and the armed intervention by more than a dozen imperialist countries, they scored unprecedentedly brilliant achievements in the struggle for industrialization and agricultural collectivization, and they won a tremendous victory in the Patriotic War against the German Fascists and saved all mankind. Even under the rule of the Khrushchev clique, the mass of the members of the CPSU and the Soviet people are carrying on the glorious revolutionary traditions nurtured by Lenin and Stalin, and they still uphold socialism and aspire to communism.

The broad masses of the Soviet workers, collective farmers and intellectuals are seething with discontent against the oppression and exploitation practised by the privileged stratum. They have come to see ever more clearly the revisionist features of the Khrushchev clique which is betraying socialism and restoring capitalism. Among the ranks of the Soviet cadres, there are many who still persist in the revolutionary stand of the proletariat, adhere to the road of socialism and firmly oppose Khrushchev's revisionism. The broad masses of the Soviet people, of Communists and cadres are using various means to resist and oppose the revisionist line of the Khrushchev clique, so that the revisionist Khrushchev clique cannot so easily bring about the restoration of capitalism. The great Soviet people are fighting to defend the glorious traditions of the Great October Revolution, to preserve the great gains of socialism and to smash the plot for the restoration of capitalism.

Refutation of the So-Called State of the Whole People

At the 22nd Congress of the CPSU Khrushchev openly raised the banner of opposition to the dictatorship of the proletariat, announcing the replacement of the state of the dictatorship of the proletariat by the " state of the whole people." It is written in the Programme of the CPSU that the dictatorship of the proletariat " has ceased to be indispensable in the USSR " and that " the state, which arose as a state of the dictatorship of the proletariat, has, in the new, contemporary stage, become a state of the entire people."

Anyone with a little knowledge of Marxism-Leninism knows that the concept of the state is a class concept. Lenin pointed out that " the distinguishing feature of the state is the existence of a separate class of people in whose hands *power* is concentrated." [33] The state is a weapon

[33] Lenin, " The Economic Content of Narodism and the Criticism of It in Mr. Struve's Book," *Collected Works*, F.L.P.H., Moscow, 1960, Vol. 1, p. 419.

of class struggle, a machine by means of which one class represses another. Every state is the dictatorship of a definite class. So long as the state exists, it cannot possibly stand above class or belong to the whole people.

The proletariat and its political party have never concealed their views; they say explicitly that the very aim of the proletarian socialist revolution is to overthrow bourgeois rule and establish the dictatorship of the proletariat. After the victory of the socialist revolution, the proletariat and its party must strive unremittingly to fulfil the historical tasks of the dictatorship of the proletariat and eliminate classes and class differences, so that the state will wither away. It is only the bourgeoisie and its parties which in their attempt to hoodwink the masses try by every means to cover up the class nature of state power and describe the state machinery under their control as being " of the whole people " and " above class."

The fact that Khrushchev has announced the abolition of the dictatorship of the proletariat in the Soviet Union and advanced the thesis of the " state of the whole people " demonstrates that he has replaced the Marxist-Leninist teachings on the state by bourgeois falsehoods.

When Marxist-Leninists criticized their fallacies, the revisionist Khrushchev clique hastily defended themselves and tried hard to invent a so-called theoretical basis for the " state of the whole people." They now assert that the historical period of the dictatorship of the proletariat mentioned by Marx and Lenin refers only to the transition from capitalism to the first stage of communism and not to its higher stage. They further assert that " the dictatorship of the proletariat will cease to be necessary before the state withers away " [34] and that after the end of the dictatorship of the proletariat, there is yet another stage, the " state of the whole people."

These are out-and-out sophistries.

In his *Critique of the Gotha Programme*, Marx advanced the well-known axiom that the dictatorship of the proletariat is the state of the period of transition from capitalism to communism. Lenin gave a clear explanation of this Marxist axiom.

He said:

> In his *Critique of the Gotha Programme* Marx wrote:
>
> " Between capitalist and communist society lies the period of the revolutionary transformation of the one into the other. There corresponds to this also a political transition period in which the state can be nothing but *the revolutionary dictatorship of the proletariat*."
>
> Up to now this axiom has never been disputed by Socialists, and yet it implies the recognition of the existence of the *state* right up to the time when victorious socialism has grown into complete communism.[35]

Lenin further said:

> The essence of Marx's teaching on the state has been mastered only by those who understand that the dictatorship of a *single* class is necessary not only for every class society in general, not only for the *proletariat* which has overthrown the bourgeoisie, but also for the entire *historical period* which separates capitalism from " classless society," from Communism.[36]

[34] *Pravda* editorial board's article, " Programme for the Building of Communism," Aug. 18, 1961.

[35] Lenin, " The Discussion on Self-Determination Summed Up," *Collected Works*, International Publishers, New York, 1942, Vol. 19, pp. 269–70.

[36] Lenin, " The State and Revolution," *Selected Works*, F.L.P.H., Moscow, Vol. 2, Part 1, p. 234.

It is perfectly clear that according to Marx and Lenin, the historical period throughout which the state of the dictatorship of the proletariat exists, is not merely the period of transition from capitalism to the first stage of communism, as alleged by the revisionist Khrushchev clique, but the entire period of transition from capitalism to "complete communism," to the time when all class differences will have been eliminated and "classless society" realized, that is to say, to the higher stage of communism.

It is equally clear that the state in the transition period referred to by Marx and Lenin is the dictatorship of the proletariat and not anything else. The dictatorship of the proletariat is the form of the state in the entire period of transition from capitalism to the higher stage of communism, and also the last form of the state in human history. The withering away of the dictatorship of the proletariat will mean the withering away of the state. Lenin said:

> Marx deduced from the whole history of Socialism and of the political struggle that the state was bound to disappear, and that the transitional form of its disappearance (the transition from state to nonstate) would be the "proletariat organized as the ruling class." [37]

Historically the dictatorship of the proletariat may take different forms from one country to another and from one period to another, but in essence it will remain the same. Lenin said.

> The transition from capitalism to Communism certainly cannot but yield a tremendous abundance and variety of political forms, but the essence will inevitably be the same: *the dictatorship of the proletariat*.[38]

It can thus be seen that it is absolutely not the view of Marx and Lenin but an invention of the revisionist Khrushchev that the end of the dictatorship of the proletariat will precede the withering away of the state and will be followed by yet another stage, "the state of the whole people."

In arguing for their anti-Marxist-Leninist views, the revisionist Khrushchev clique have taken great pains to find a sentence from Marx and distorted it by quoting it out of context. They have arbitrarily described the future *nature of the state* [*Staatswesen* in German] of communist society referred to by Marx in his *Critique of the Gotha Programme* as "'the state of communist society.' [государственность коммунисти-ческого общества in Russian] which is no longer a dictatorship of the proletariat." [39] They gleefully announced that the Chinese would not dare to quote this from Marx. Apparently the revisionist Khrushchev clique think it is very helpful to them.

As it happens, Lenin seems to have foreseen that revisionists would make use of this phrase to distort Marxism. In his *Marxism on the State*, Lenin gave an excellent explanation of it. He said, ". . . the dictatorship of the proletariat is a 'political transition period.' . . . But Marx goes on to speak of 'the future *nature of the state* [государственность in Russian, *Staatswesen* in German] of communist society'!! Thus, there will be a state even in 'communist society'!! Is there not a contradiction in this?"

[37] *Ibid.*, pp. 256–57.
[38] *Ibid.*, p. 234.
[39] M. A. Suslov, Report at the Plenary Meeting of the Central Committee of the CPSU, February 1964. (*New Times*, English ed., No. 15, 1964, p. 62.)

Lenin answered, " No." He then tabulated the three stages in the process of development from the bourgeois state to the withering away of the state:

The first stage — in capitalist society, the state is needed by the bourgeoisie — the bourgeois state.

The second stage — in the period of transition from capitalism to communism, the state is needed by the proletariat — the state of the dictatorship of the proletariat.

The third stage — in communist society, the state is not necessary, it withers away.

He concluded: "Complete consistency and clarity! ! "

In Lenin's tabulation, only the bourgeois state, the state of the dictatorship of the proletariat and the withering away of the state are to be found. By precisely this tabulation Lenin made it clear that when communism is reached the state withers away and becomes non-existent.

Ironically enough, the revisionist Khrushchev clique also quoted this very passage from Lenin's *Marxism on the State* in the course of defending their error. And then they proceeded to make the following idiotic statement:

In our country the first two periods referred to by Lenin in the opinion quoted already belong to history. In the Soviet Union a state of the whole people — *a communist state system*, and the state of the *first phase of communism*, has arisen and is developing.[40]

If the first two periods referred to by Lenin have already become a thing of the past in the Soviet Union, then the state should be withering away, and where could a " state of the whole people " come from? If the state is not yet withering away, then it ought to be the dictatorship of the proletariat and under absolutely no circumstances a " state of the whole people."

In arguing for their " state of the whole people," the revisionist Khrushchev clique exert themselves to vilify the dictatorship of the proletariat as undemocratic. They assert that only by replacing the state of the dictatorship of the proletariat by the " state of the whole people " can democracy be further developed and turned into " genuine democracy for the whole people." Khrushchev has pretentiously said that the abolition of the dictatorship of the proletariat exemplifies " a line of energetically developing democracy " and that " proletarian democracy is becoming socialist democracy of the whole people." [41]

These utterances can only show that their authors either are completely ignorant of the Marxist-Leninist teachings on the state or are maliciously distorting them.

Anyone with a little knowledge of Marxism-Leninism knows that the concept of democracy as a form of the state, like that of dictatorship, is a class one. There can only be class democracy, there cannot be " democracy for the whole people."

[40] " From the Party of the Working Class to the Party of the Whole Soviet People," editorial board's article of *Partyinaya Zhizn*, Moscow, No. 8, 1964.

[41] N. S. Krushchev, " Report of the Central Committee of the CPSU," and " On the Programme of the CPSU," delivered at the 22nd Congress of the CPSU, October 1961.

Lenin said:

Democracy for the vast majority of the people, and suppression by force, i.e., exclusion from democracy, of the exploiters and oppressors of the people — this is the change democracy undergoes during the *transition* from capitalism to Communism.[42]

Dictatorship over the exploiting classes and democracy among the working people — these are the two aspects of the dictatorship of the proletariat. It is only under the dictatorship of the proletariat that democracy for the masses of the working people can be developed and expanded to an unprecedented extent. Without the dictatorship of the proletariat there can be no genuine democracy for the working people.

Where there is bourgeois democracy there is no proletarian democracy, and where there is proletarian democracy there is no bourgeois democracy. The one excludes the other. This is inevitable and admits of no compromise. The more thoroughly bourgeois democracy is eliminated, the more will proletarian democracy flourish. In the eyes of the bourgeoisie, any country where this occurs is lacking in democracy. But actually this is the promotion of proletarian democracy and the elimination of bourgeois democracy. As proletarian democracy develops, bourgeois democracy is eliminated.

This fundamental Marxist-Leninist thesis is opposed by the revisionist Khrushchev clique. In fact, they hold that so long as enemies are subjected to dictatorship there is no democracy and that the only way to develop democracy is to abolish the dictatorship over enemies, stop suppressing them and institute " democracy for the whole people."

Their view is cast from the same mould as the renegade Kautsky's concept of " pure democracy."

In criticizing Kautsky Lenin said:

. . . " pure democracy " is not only an *ignorant* phrase, revealing a lack of understanding both of the class struggle and of the nature of the state, but also a thrice-empty phrase, since in communist society democracy will *wither away* in the process of changing and becoming a habit, but will never be " pure " democracy.[43]

He also pointed out:

The dialectics (course) of the development is as follows: from absolutism to bourgeois democracy; from bourgeois to proletarian democracy; from proletarian democracy to none.[44]

That is to say, in the higher stage of communism proletarian democracy will wither away along with the elimination of classes and the withering away of the dictatorship of the proletariat.

To speak plainly, as with the " state of the whole people," the " democracy for the whole people " proclaimed by Khrushchev is a hoax. In thus retrieving the tattered garments of the bourgeoisie and the old-line revisionists, patching them up and adding a label of his own, Khrushchev's sole purpose is to deceive the Soviet people and the revolutionary people of the world and cover up his betrayal of the dictatorship of the proletariat and his opposition to socialism.

[42] Lenin, " The State and Revolution," *Selected Works*, F.L.P.H., Moscow, Vol. 2, Part 1, p. 291.
[43] Lenin, " The Proletarian Revolution and the Renegade Kautsky," *Selected Works*, F.L.P.H., Moscow, Vol. 2, Part 2, p. 48.
[44] Lenin, *Marxism on the State*, Russian ed., Moscow, 1958, p. 42.

What is the essence of Khrushchev's " state of the whole people "?

Khrushchev has abolished the dictatorship of the proletariat in the Soviet Union and established a dictatorship of the revisionist clique headed by himself, that is, a dictatorship of a privileged stratum of the Soviet bourgeoisie. Actually his " state of the whole people " is not a state of the dictatorship of the proletariat but a state in which his small revisionist clique wield their dictatorship over the masses of the workers, the peasants and the revolutionary intellectuals. Under the rule of the Khrushchev clique, there is no democracy for the Soviet working people, there is democracy only for the handful of people belonging to the revisionist Khrushchev clique, for the privileged stratum and for the bourgeois elements, old and new. Khrushchev's " democracy for the whole people " is nothing but out-and-out bourgeois democracy, i.e., a despotic dictatorship of the Khrushchev clique over the Soviet people.

In the Soviet Union today, anyone who persists in the proletarian stand, upholds Marxism-Leninism and has the courage to speak out, to resist or to fight is watched, followed, summoned, and even arrested, imprisoned or diagnosed as " mentally Ill " and sent to " mental hospitals." Recently the Soviet press has declared that it is necessary to " fight " against those who show even the slightest dissatisfaction, and called for " relentless battle " against the " rotten jokers " [45] who are so bold as to make sarcastic remarks about Khrushchev's agricultural policy. It is particularly astonishing that the revisionist Khrushchev clique should have on more than one occasion bloodily suppressed striking workers and the masses who put up resistance.

The formula of abolishing the dictatorship of the proletariat while keeping a state of the whole people reveals the secret of the revisionist Khrushchev clique; that is, they are firmly opposed to the dictatorship of the proletariat but will not give up state power till their doom. The revisionist Khrushchev clique know the paramount importance of controlling state power. They need the state machinery for repressing the Soviet working people and the Marxist-Leninists. They need it for clearing the way for the restoration of capitalism in the Soviet Union. These are Khrushchev's real aims in raising the banners of the " state of the whole people " and " democracy for the whole people."

Refutation of the So-Called Party of the Entire People

At the 22nd Congress of the CPSU Khrushchev openly raised another banner, the alteration of the proletarian character of the Communist Party of the Soviet Union. He announced the replacement of the party of the proletariat by a " party of the entire people." The Programme of the CPSU states, " As a result of the victory of socialism in the U.S.S.R. and the consolidation of the unity of Soviet society, the Communist Party of the working class has become the vanguard of the Soviet people, a party of the entire people." The open letter of the Central Committee of the CPSU says that the CPSU " has become a political organization of the entire people."

How absurd!

Elementary knowledge of Marxism-Leninism tells us that, like the state, a political party is an instrument of class struggle. Every political party

[45] *Izvestiya*, Mar. 10, 1964.

has a class character. Party spirit is the concentrated expression of class character. There is no such thing as a non-class or supra-class political party and there never has been, nor is there such a thing as a "party of the entire people" that does not represent the interests of a particular class.

The party of the proletariat is built in accordance with the revolutionary theory and revolutionary style of Marxism-Leninism; it is the party formed by the advanced elements who are boundlessly faithful to the historical mission of the proletariat, it is the organized vanguard of the proletariat and the highest form of its organization. The party of the proletariat represents the interests of the proletariat and the concentration of its will.

Moreover, the party of the proletariat is the only party able to represent the interests of the people, who constitute over 90 per cent of the total population. The reason is that the interests of the proletariat are identical with those of the working masses, that the proletarian party can approach problems in the light of the historical role of the proletariat and in terms of the present and future interests of the proletariat and the working masses and of the best interests of the overwhelming majority of the people, and that it can give correct leadership in accordance with Marxism-Leninism.

In addition to its members of working-class origin, the party of the proletariat has members of other class origins. But the latter do not join the Party as representatives of other classes. From the very day they join the Party they must abandon their former class stand and take the stand of the proletariat. Marx and Engels said:

> If people of this kind from other classes join the proletarian movement, the first condition must be that they should not bring any remnants of bourgeois, petty-bourgeois, etc., prejudices with them but should wholeheartedly adopt the proletarian outlook.[46]

The basic principles concerning the character of the proletarian party were long ago elucidated by Marxism-Leninism. But in the opinion of the revisionist Khrushchev clique these principles are "stereotyped formulas," while their "party of the entire people" conforms to the "actual dialectics of the development of the Communist Party."[47]

The revisionist Khrushchev clique have cudgelled their brains to think up arguments justifying their "party of the entire people." They have argued during the talks between the Chinese and Soviet Parties in July 1963 and in the Soviet press that they have changed the Communist Party of the Soviet Union into a "party of the entire people" because:

1. The CPSU expresses the interests of the whole people.
2. The entire people have accepted the Marxist-Leninist world outlook of the working class, and the aim of the working class — the building of communism — has become the aim of the entire people.
3. The ranks of the CPSU consist of the best representatives of the workers, collective farmers and intellectuals. The CPSU unites in its own ranks representatives of over a hundred nationalities and peoples.
4. The democratic method used in the Party's activities is also in accord with its character as the party of the entire people.

---

[46] "Marx and Engels to A. Bebel, W. Liebknecht, W. Bracke and Others ("Circular Letter"), Sept. 17–18, 1879," *Selected Works of Marx and Engels*, F.L.P.H., Moscow, Vol. 2, pp. 484–85.
[47] "From the Party of the Working Class to the Party of the Whole Soviet People," editorial board article of *Partyinaya Zhizn*, Moscow, No. 8, 1964.

It is obvious even at a glance that none of these arguments adduced by the revisionist Khrushchev clique shows a serious approach to a serious problem.

When Lenin was fighting the opportunist muddle-heads, he remarked:

> Can people obviously incapable of taking serious problems seriously, themselves be taken seriously? It is difficult to do so, comrades, very difficult! But the question which certain people cannot treat seriously is in itself so serious that it will do no harm to examine even patently frivolous replies to it.[48]

Today, too, it will do no harm to examine the patently frivolous replies given by the revisionist Khrushchev clique to so serious a question as that of the party of the proletariat.

According to the revisionist Khrushchev clique, the Communist Party should become a " party of the entire people " because it expresses the interests of the entire people. Does it not then follow that from the very beginning it should have been a " party of the entire people " instead of a party of the proletariat?

According to the revisionist Khrushchev clique, the Communist Party should become a " party of the entire people " because " the entire people have accepted the Marxist-Leninist world outlook of the working class." But how can it be said that everyone has accepted the Marxist-Leninist world outlook in Soviet society where sharp class polarization and class struggle are taking place? Can it be said that the tens of thousands of old and new bourgeois elements in your country are all Marxist-Leninists? If Marxism-Leninism has really become the world outlook of the entire people, as you allege, does it not then follow that there is no difference in your society between Party and non-Party and no need whatsoever for the Party to exist? What difference does it make if there is a " party of the entire people " or not?

According to the revisionist Khrushchev clique, the Communist Party should become a " party of the entire people " because its membership consists of workers, peasants and intellectuals and all nationalities and peoples. Does this mean then that before the idea of the " party of the entire people " was put forward at its 22nd Congress none of the members of the CPSU came from classes other than the working class? Does it mean that formerly the members of the Party all came from just one nationality, to the exclusion of other nationalities and peoples? If the character of a party is determined by the social background of its membership, does it not then follow that the numerous political parties in the world whose members also come from various classes, nationalities and peoples are all " parties of the entire people "?

According to the revisionist Khrushchev clique, the Party should be a " party of the entire people " because the methods it uses in its activities are democratic. But from its outset, a Communist Party is built on the basis of the principle of democratic centralism and should always adopt the mass line and the democratic method of persuasion and education in working among the people. Does it not then follow that a Communist Party is a " party of the entire people " from the first day of its founding?

Briefly, none of the arguments listed by the revisionist Khrushchev clique holds water.

[48] Lenin, " Clarity First and Foremost!", *Collected Works*, F.L.P.H., Moscow, 1964, Vol. 20, p. 544.

Besides making a great fuss about a "party of the entire people," Khrushchev has also divided the Party into an "industrial party" and an "agricultural party" on the pretext of "building the Party organs on the production principle." [49]

The revisionist Khrushchev clique say that they have done so because of "the primacy of economics over politics under socialism" [50] and because they want to place "the economic and production problems, which have been pushed to the forefront by the entire course of the communist construction, at the centre of the activities of the Party organizations" and make them "the cornerstone of all their work." [51] Khrushchev said, "We say bluntly that the main thing in the work of the Party organs is production." [52] And what is more, they have foisted these views on Lenin, claiming that they are acting in accordance with his principles.

However, anyone at all acquainted with the history of the CPSU knows that, far from being Lenin's views, they are anti-Leninist views and that they were views held by Trotsky. On this question, too, Khrushchev is a worthy disciple of Trotsky.

In criticizing Trotsky and Bukharin, Lenin said:

> Politics are the concentrated expression of economics. . . . Politics cannot but have precedence over economics. To argue differently means forgetting the A B C of Marxism.

He continued:

> . . . without a proper political approach to the subject the given class cannot maintain its rule, and *consequently* cannot solve *its own production problems.*[53]

The facts are crystal clear: the real purpose of the revisionist Khrushchev clique in proposing a "party of the entire people" was completely to alter the proletarian character of the CPSU and transform the Marxist-Leninist party into a revisionist party.

The great Communist Party of the Soviet Union is confronted with the grave danger of degenerating from a party of the proletariat into a party of the bourgeoisie and from a Marxist-Leninist into a revisionist party.

Lenin said:

> A party that wants to exist cannot allow the slightest wavering on the question of its existence or any agreement with those who may bury it.[54]

At present, the revisionist Khrushchev clique is again confronting the broad membership of the great Communist Party of the Soviet Union with precisely this serious question.

[49] N. S. Khrushchev, Report at the Plenary Meeting of the Central Committee of the CPSU, November 1962.

[50] "Study, Know, Act," editorial of *Economicheskaya Gazeta*, No. 50, 1962.

[51] "The Communist and Production," editorial of *Kommunist*, No. 2, 1963.

[52] N. S. Khrushchev, Speech at the Election Meeting of the Kalinin Constituency of Moscow, Feb. 27, 1963.

[53] Lenin, "Once Again on the Trade Unions, the Present Situation and the Mistakes of Trotsky and Bukharin," *Selected Works*, International Publishers, New York, 1943, Vol. 9, pp. 54 and 55.

[54] Lenin, "How Vera Zasulich Demolishes Liquidationism," *Collected Works*, F.L.P.H., Moscow, 1963, Vol. 19, p. 414

Khrushchev's Phoney Communism

At the 22nd Congress of the CPSU, Khrushchev announced that the Soviet Union had already entered the period of the extensive building of communist society. He also declared that "we shall, in the main, have built a communist society within twenty years." [55] This is pure fraud.

How can there be talk of building communism when the revisionist Khrushchev clique are leading the Soviet Union on to the path of the restoration of capitalism and when the Soviet people are in grave danger of losing the fruits of socialism?

In putting up the signboard of "building communism" Khrushchev's real aim is to conceal the true face of his revisionism. But it is not hard to expose this trick. Just as the eyeball of a fish cannot be allowed to pass as a pearl, so revisionism cannot be allowed to pass itself off as communism.

Scientific communism has a precise and definite meaning. According to Marxism-Leninism, communist society is a society in which classes and class differences are completely eliminated, the entire people have a high level of communist consciousness and morality as well as boundless enthusiasm for and initiative in labour, there is a great abundance of social products and the principle of "from each according to his ability, to each according to his needs" is applied, and in which the state has withered away.

Marx declared:

> In the higher phase of communist society, after the enslaving subordination of the individual to the division of labour, and therewith also the antithesis between mental and physical labour, has vanished; after labour has become not only a means of life but life's prime want; after the productive forces have also increased with the all-round development of the individual, and all the springs of co-operative wealth flow more abundantly — only then can the narrow horizon of bourgeois right be crossed in its entirety and society inscribe on its banners: From each according to his ability, to each according to his needs! [56]

According to Marxist-Leninist theory, the purpose of upholding the dictatorship of the proletariat in the period of socialism is precisely to ensure that society develops in the direction of communism. Lenin said that "forward development, i.e., towards Communism, proceeds through the dictatorship of the proletariat, and cannot do otherwise." [57] Since the revisionist Khrushchev clique have abandoned the dictatorship of the proletariat in the Soviet Union, it is going backward and not forward, going backward to capitalism and not forward to communism.

Going forward to communism means moving towards the abolition of all classes and class differences. A communist society which preserves any classes at all, let alone exploiting classes, is inconceivable. Yet Khrushchev is fostering a new bourgeoisie, restoring and extending the system of exploitation and accelerating class polarization in the Soviet Union. A privileged bourgeois stratum opposed to the Soviet people now occupies

[55] N. S. Khrushchev, "On the Programme of the Communist Party of the Soviet Union," at the 22nd Congress of the CPSU in October 1961.
[56] Marx, "Critique of the Gotha Programme," *Selected Works of Marx and Engels*, F.L.P.H., Moscow, Vol. 2, p. 24.
[57] Lenin, "The State and Revolution," *Selected Works*, F.L.P.H., Moscow, Vol. 2, Part 1, p. 291.

the ruling position in the Party and Government and in the economic, cultural and other departments. Can one find an iota of communism in all this?

Going forward to communism means moving towards a unitary system of the ownership of the means of production by the whole people. A communist society in which several kinds of ownership of the means of production coexist is inconceivable. Yet Khrushchev is creating a situation in which enterprises owned by the whole people are gradually degenerating into capitalist enterprises and farms under the system of collective ownership are gradually degenerating into units of a kulak economy. Again, can one find an iota of communism in all this?

Going forward to communism means moving towards a great abundance of social products and the realization of the principle of "from each according to his ability, to each according to his needs." A communist society built on the enrichment of a handful of persons and the impoverishment of the masses is inconceivable. Under the socialist system the great Soviet people developed the social productive forces at unprecedented speed. But the evils of Khrushchev's revisionism are creating havoc in the Soviet socialist economy. Constantly beset with innumerable contradictions, Khrushchev makes frequent changes in his economic policies and often goes back on his own words, thus throwing the Soviet national economy into a state of chaos. Khrushchev is truly an incorrigible wastrel. He has squandered the grain reserves built up under Stalin and brought great difficulties into the lives of the Soviet people. He has distorted and violated the socialist principle of distribution of "from each according to his ability, to each according to his work," and enabled a handful of persons to appropriate the fruits of the labour of the broad masses of the Soviet people. These points alone are sufficient to prove that the road taken by Khrushchev leads away from communism.

Going forward to communism means moving towards enhancing the communist consciousness of the masses. A communist society with bourgeois ideas running rampant is inconceivable. Yet Khrushchev is zealously reviving bourgeois ideology in the Soviet Union and serving as a missionary for the decadent American culture. By propagating material incentive, he is turning all human relations into money relations and encouraging individualism and selfishness. Because of him, manual labour is again considered sordid and love of pleasure at the expense of other people's labour is again considered honourable. Certainly, the social ethics and atmosphere promoted by Khrushchev are far removed from communism, as far as far can be.

Going forward to communism means moving towards the withering away of the state. A communist society with a state apparatus for oppressing the people is inconceivable. The state of the dictatorship of the proletariat is actually no longer a state in its original sense, because it is no longer a machine used by the exploiting few to oppress the overwhelming majority of people but a machine for exercising dictatorship over a very small number of exploiters, while democracy is practised among the overwhelming majority of the people. Khrushchev is altering the character of Soviet state power and changing the dictatorship of the proletariat back into an instrument whereby a handful of privileged bourgeois elements exercise dictatorship over the mass of the Soviet workers, peasants and intellectuals. He is continuously strengthening his dictatorial state apparatus and intensifying his repression of the Soviet people. It is indeed a great mockery to talk about communism in these circumstances.

A comparison of all this with the principles of scientific communism readily reveals that in every respect the revisionist Khrushchev clique are leading the Soviet Union away from the path of socialism and on to the path of capitalism and, as a consequence, further and further away from, instead of closer to, the communist goal of " from each according to his ability, to each according to his needs."

Khrushchev has ulterior motives when he puts up the signboard of communism. He is using it to fool the Soviet people and cover up his effort to restore capitalism. He is using it to deceive the international proletariat and the revolutionary people the world over and betray proletarian internationalism. Under this signboard, the Khrushchev clique has itself abandoned proletarian internationalism and is seeking a partnership with U.S. imperialism for the partition of the world; moreover, it wants the fraternal socialist countries to serve its own private interests and not to oppose imperialism or to support the revolutions of the oppressed peoples and nations, and it wants them to accept its political, economic and military control and be its virtual dependencies and colonies. Furthermore, the Khrushchev clique wants all the oppressed peoples and nations to serve its private interests and abandon their revolutionary struggles, so as not to disturb its sweet dream of partnership with imperialism for the division of the world, and instead submit to enslavement and oppression by imperialism and its lackeys.

In short, Khrushchev's slogan of basically " building a communist society within 20 years " in the Soviet Union is not only false but also reactionary.

The revisionist Khrushchev clique say that the Chinese " go to the length of questioning the very right of our Party and our people to build communism." [58] This is a despicable attempt to fool the Soviet people and poison the friendship of the Chinese and Soviet people. We have never had any doubt that the great Soviet people will eventually enter into communist society. But right now the revisionist Khrushchev clique are damaging the socialist fruits of the Soviet people and taking away their right to go forward to communism. In the circumstances, the issue confronting the Soviet people is not how to build communism but rather how to resist and oppose Khrushchev's effort to restore capitalism.

The revisionist Khrushchev clique also say that " the CCP leaders hint that, since our Party has made its aim a better life for the people, Soviet society is being ' bourgeoisified,' is ' degenerating.' " [59] This trick of deflecting the Soviet people's dissatisfaction with the Khrushchev clique is deplorable as well as stupid. We sincerely wish the Soviet people an increasingly better life. But Khrushchev's boasts of " concern for the well-being of the people " and of " a better life for every man " are utterly false and demagogic. For the masses of the Soviet people life is already bad enough at Khrushchev's hands. The Khrushchev clique seek a " better life " only for the members of the privileged stratum and the

[58] M. A. Suslov, Report at the Plenary Meeting of the Central Committee of the CPSU, February 1964.
[59] " Open Letter of the Central Committee of the Communist Party of the Soviet Union to Party Organizations and All Communists in the Soviet Union," July 14, 1963.

bourgeois elements, old and new, in the Soviet Union. These people are appropriating the fruits of the Soviet people's labour and living the life of bourgeois lords. They have indeed become thoroughly bourgeoisified.

Khrushchev's "communism" is in essence a variant of bourgeois socialism. He does not regard communism as completely abolishing classes and class differences but describes it as "a bowl accessible to all and brimming with the products of physical and mental labour." [60] He does not regard the struggle of the working class for communism as a struggle for the thorough emancipation of all mankind as well as itself but describes it as a struggle for "a good dish of goulash." There is not an iota of scientific communism in his head but only the image of a society of bourgeois philistines.

Khrushchev's "communism" takes the United States for its model. Imitation of the methods of management of U.S. capitalism and the bourgeois way of life has been raised by Khrushchev to the level of state policy. He says that he "always thinks highly" of the achievements of the United States. He "rejoices in these achievements, is a little envious at times." [61] He extols to the sky a letter by Roswell Garst, a big U.S. farmer, which propagates the capitalist system [62]; actually he has taken it as his agricultural programme. He wants to copy the United States in the sphere of industry as well as that of agriculture and, in particular, to imitate the profit motive of U.S. capitalist enterprises. He shows great admiration for the American way of life, asserting that the American people "do not live badly" [63] under the rule and enslavement of monopoly capital. Going further, Khrushchev is hopeful of building communism with loans from U.S. imperialism. During his visits to the United States and Hungary, he expressed on more than one occasion his readiness "to take credits from the devil himself."

Thus it can be seen that Khrushchev's "communism" is indeed "goulash communism," the "communism of the American way of life" and "communism seeking credits from the devil." No wonder he often tells representatives of Western monopoly capital that once such "communism" is realized in the Soviet Union, "you will go forward to communism without any call from me." [64]

There is nothing new about such "communism." It is simply another name for capitalism. It is only a bourgeois label, sign or advertisement. In ridiculing the old-line revisionist parties which set up the signboard of Marxism, Lenin said:

> Wherever Marxism is popular among the workers, this political tendency, this "bourgeois labour party," will swear by the name of Marx. It cannot be prohibited from doing this, just as a trading firm cannot be prohibited from using any particular label, sign, or advertisement.[65]

[60] N. S. Khrushchev, Speech for the Austrian Radio and Television, July 7, 1960.
[61] N. S. Khrushchev, Interview with Leaders of U.S. Congress and Members of the Senate Foreign Relations Committee, Sept. 16, 1959.
[62] N. S. Khrushchev, Speech at the Plenary Meeting of the Central Committee of the CPSU, February 1964.
[63] N. S. Khrushchev, Talk at a Meeting with Businessmen and Public Leaders in Pittsburg, U.S.A., Sept. 24, 1959.
[64] N. S. Khrushchev, Talk at a Meeting with French Parliamentarians, Mar. 25, 1960.
[65] Lenin, "Imperialism and the Split in Socialism," *Selected Works*, International Publishers, New York, Vol. 11, p. 761.

It is thus easily understandable why Khrushchev's "communism" is appreciated by imperialism and monopoly capital. The U.S. Secretary of State Dean Rusk has said:

> . . . to the extent that goulash and the second pair of trousers and questions of that sort become more important in the Soviet Union, I think to that extent a moderating influence has come into the present scene.[66]

And the British Prime Minister Douglas-Home has said:

> Mr. Khrushchev said that the Russian brand of communism puts education and goulash first. That is good; goulash-communism is better than war-communism, and I am glad to have this confirmation of our view that fat and comfortable Communists are better than lean and hungry Communists.[67]

Khrushchev's revisionism entirely caters to the policy of "peaceful evolution" which U.S. imperialism is pursuing with regard to the Soviet Union and other socialist countries. John Foster Dulles said:

> . . . there was evidence within the Soviet Union of forces toward greater liberalism which, if they persisted, could bring about a basic change within the Soviet Union.[68]

The liberal forces Dulles talked about are capitalist forces. The basic change Dulles hoped for is the degeneration of socialism into capitalism. Khrushchev is effecting exactly the "basic change" Dulles dreamed of.

How the imperialists are hoping for the restoration of capitalism in the Soviet Union! How they are rejoicing!

We would advise the imperialist lords not to be happy too soon. Notwithstanding all the services of the revisionist Khrushchev clique, nothing can save imperialism from its doom. The revisionist ruling clique suffer from the same kind of disease as the imperialist ruling clique; they are extremely antagonistic to the masses of the people who comprise over 90 per cent of the world's population, and therefore they, too, are weak and powerless and are paper tigers. Like the clay Buddha that tried to wade across the river, the revisionist Khrushchev clique cannot even save themselves, so how can they endow imperialism with long life?

Historical Lessons of the Dictatorship of the Proletariat

Khrushchev's revisionism has inflicted heavy damage on the international communist movement, but at the same time it has educated the Marxist-Leninists and revolutionary people throughout the world by negative example.

If it may be said that the Great October Revolution provided Marxist-Leninists in all countries with the most important positive experience and opened up the road for the proletarian seizure of political power, then on its part Khrushchev's revisionism may be said to have provided them with the most important negative experience, enabling Marxist-Leninists in all countries to draw the appropriate lessons for preventing the degeneration of the proletarian party and the socialist state.

[66] Dean Rusk, Interview on British Broadcasting Corporation Television, May 10, 1964.
[67] A. Douglas-Home, Speech at Norwich, England, Apr. 6, 1964.
[68] J. F. Dulles, press conference, May 15, 1956.

Historically all revolutions have had their reverses and their twists and turns. Lenin once asked:

> . . . if we take the matter in its essence, has it ever happened in history that a new mode of production took root immediately, without a long succession of setbacks, blunders and relapses? [69]

The international proletarian revolution has a history of less than a century counting from 1871 when the proletariat of the Paris Commune made the first heroic attempt at the seizure of political power, or barely half a century counting from the October Revolution. The proletarian revolution, the greatest revolution in human history, replaces capitalism by socialism and private ownership by public ownership and uproots all the systems of exploitation and all the exploiting classes. It is all the more natural that so earth-shaking a revolution should have to go through serious and fierce class struggles, inevitably traverse a long and tortuous course beset with reverses.

History furnishes a number of examples in which proletarian rule suffered defeat as a result of armed suppression by the bourgeoisie, for instance, the Paris Commune and the Hungarian Soviet Republic of 1919. In contemporary times, too, there was a counter-revolutionary rebellion in Hungary in 1956, when the rule of the proletariat was almost overthrown. People can easily perceive this form of capitalist restoration and are more alert and watchful against it.

However, they cannot easily perceive and are often off their guard or not vigilant against another form of capitalist restoration, which therefore presents a greater danger. The state of the dictatorship of the proletariat takes the road of revisionism or the road of " peaceful evolution " as a result of the degeneration of the leadership of the Party and the state. A lesson of this kind was provided some years ago by the revisionist Tito clique who brought about the degeneration of socialist Yugoslavia into a capitalist country. But the Yugoslav lesson alone has not sufficed to arose people's attention fully. Some may say that perhaps it was an accident.

But now the revisionist Khrushchev clique have usurped the leadership of the Party and the state, and there is grave danger of a restoration of capitalism in the Soviet Union, the land of the Great October Revolution with its history of several decades in building socialism. And this sounds the alarm for all socialist countries, including China, and for all the Communist and Workers' Parties, including the Communist Party of China. Inevitably it arouses very great attention and forces Marxist-Leninists and revolutionary people the world over to ponder deeply and sharpen their vigilance.

The emergence of Khrushchev's revisionism is a bad thing, and it is also a good thing. So long as the countries where socialism has been achieved and also those that will later embark on the socialist road seriously study the lessons of the " peaceful evolution " promoted by the revisionist Khrushchev clique and take the appropriate measures, they will be able to prevent this kind of " peaceful evolution " as well as crush the enemy's armed attacks. Thus, the victory of the world proletarian revolution will be more certain.

[69] Lenin, " A Great Beginning," *Selected Works*, F.L.P.H., Moscow, Vol. 2, Part 2, p. 229.

The Communist Party of China has a history of 43 years. During its protracted revolutionary struggle, our Party combated both Right and "Left" opportunist errors and the Marxist-Leninist leadership of the Central Committee headed by Comrade Mao Tse-tung was established. Closely integrating the universal truth of Marxism-Leninism with the concrete practice of revolution and construction in China, Comrade Mao Tse-tung has led the Chinese people from victory to victory. The Central Committee of the Chinese Communist Party and Comrade Mao Tse-tung have taught us to wage unremitting struggle in the theoretical, political and organizational fields, as well as in practical work, so as to combat revisionism and prevent a restoration of capitalism. The Chinese people have gone through protracted revolutionary armed struggles and possess a glorious revolutionary tradition. The Chinese People's Liberation Army is armed with Mao Tse-tung's thinking and inseparably linked to the masses. The numerous cadres of the Chinese Communist Party have been educated and tempered in rectification movements and sharp class struggles. All these factors make it very difficult to restore capitalism in our country.

But let us look at the facts. Is our society today thoroughly clean? No, it is not. Classes and class struggle still remain, the activities of the overthrown reactionary classes plotting a comeback still continue, and we still have speculative activities by old and new bourgeois elements and desperate forays by embezzlers, grafters and degenerates. There are also cases of degeneration in a few primary organizations; what is more, these degenerates do their utmost to find protectors and agents in the higher leading bodies. We should not in the least slacken our vigilance against such phenomena but must keep fully alert.

The struggle in the socialist countries between the road of socialism and the road of capitalism — between the forces of capitalism attempting a comeback and the forces opposing it — is unavoidable. But the restoration of capitalism in the socialist countries and their degeneration into capitalist countries are certainly not unavoidable. We can prevent the restoration of capitalism so long as there is a correct leadership and a correct understanding of the problem, so long as we adhere to the revolutionary Marxist-Leninist line, take the appropriate measures and wage a prolonged, unremitting struggle. The struggle between the socialist and capitalist roads can become a driving force for social advance.

How can the restoration of capitalism be prevented? On this question Comrade Mao Tse-tung has formulated a set of theories and policies, after summing up the practical experience of the dictatorship of the proletariat in China and studying the positive and negative experience of other countries, mainly of the Soviet Union, in accordance with the basic principles of Marxism-Leninism, and has thus enriched and developed the Marxist-Leninist theory of the dictatorship of the proletariat.

The main contents of the theories and policies advanced by Comrade Mao Tse-tung in this connection are as follows:

FIRST, it is necessary to apply the Marxist-Leninist law of the unity of opposites to the study of socialist society. The law of contradiction in all things, i.e., the law of the unity of opposites, is the fundamental law of materialist dialectics. It operates everywhere, whether in the natural world, in human society, or in human thought. The opposites in a contradiction both unite and struggle with each other, and it is this that forces things to move and change. Socialist society is no exception. In socialist society there are two kinds of social contradictions, namely, the contradictions among the people and those between ourselves and the enemy. These two kinds of social contradictions are entirely different in their essence, and the methods for handling them should be different, too. Their correct handling will result in the increasing consolidation of the dictatorship of the proletariat and the further strengthening and development of socialist society. Many people acknowledge the law of the unity of opposites but are unable to apply it in studying and handling questions in socialist society. They refuse to admit that there are contradictions in socialist society — that there are not only contradictions between ourselves and the enemy but also contradictions among the people — and they do not know how to distinguish between these two kinds of social contradictions and how to handle them correctly, and are therefore unable to deal correctly with the question of the dictatorship of the proletariat.

SECOND, socialist society covers a very long historical period. Classes and class struggle continue to exist in this society, and the struggle still goes on between the road of socialism and the road of capitalism. The socialist revolution on the economic front (in the ownership of the means of production) is insufficient by itself and cannot be consolidated. There must also be a thorough socialist revolution on the political and ideological fronts. Here a very long period of time is needed to decide "who will win" in the struggle between socialism and capitalism. Several decades won't do it; success requires anywhere from one to several centuries. On the question of duration, it is better to prepare for a longer rather than a shorter period of time. On the question of effort, it is better to regard the task as difficult rather than easy. It will be more advantageous and less harmful to think and act in this way. Anyone who fails to see this or to appreciate it fully will make tremendous mistakes. During the historical period of socialism it is necessary to maintain the dictatorship of the proletariat and carry the socialist revolution through to the end if the restoration of capitalism is to be prevented, socialist construction carried forward and the conditions created for the transition to communism.

THIRD, the dictatorship of the proletariat is led by the working class, with the worker-peasant alliance as its basis. This means the exercise of dictatorship by the working class and by the people under its leadership over the reactionary classes and individuals and those elements who oppose socialist transformation and socialist construction. Within the ranks of the people democratic centralism is practised. Ours is the broadest democracy beyond the bounds of possibility for any bourgeois state.

FOURTH, in both socialist revolution and socialist construction it is necessary to adhere to the mass line, boldly to arouse the masses and to unfold mass movements on a large scale. The mass line of "from the masses, to the masses" is the basic line in all the work of our Party. It is necessary to have firm confidence in the majority of the worker-peasant masses. We must be good at consulting the masses in our work and under no circumstances alienate ourselves from them. Both commandism and the attitude of one dispensing favours have to be fought. The full and frank expression of views and great debates are important forms of revolutionary struggle which have been created by the people of our country in the course of their long revolutionary fight, forms of struggle which rely on the masses for resolving contradictions among the people and contradictions between ourselves and the enemy.

346

FIFTH, whether in socialist revolution or in socialist construction, it is necessary to solve the question of whom to rely on, whom to win over and whom to oppose. The proletariat and its vanguard must make a class analysis of socialist society, rely on the truly dependable forces that firmly take the socialist road, win over all allies that can be won over, and unite with the masses of the people, who constitute more than 95 per cent of the population, in a common struggle against the enemies of socialism. In the rural areas, after the collectivization of agriculture it is necessary to rely on the poor and lower-middle peasants in order to consolidate the dictatorship of the proletariat and the worker-peasant alliance, defeat the spontaneous capitalist tendencies and constantly strengthen and extend the positions of socialism.

SIXTH, it is necessary to conduct extensive socialist education movements repeatedly in the cities and the countryside. In these continuous movements for educating the people we must be good at organizing the revolutionary class forces, enhancing their class consciousness, correctly handling contradictions among the people and uniting all those who can be united. In these movements it is necessary to wage a sharp, tit-for-tat struggle against the anti-socialist, capitalist and feudal forces — the landlords, rich peasants, counter-revolutionaries and bourgeois Rightists, and the embezzlers, grafters and degenerates — in order to smash the attacks they unleash against socialism and to remould the majority of them into new men.

SEVENTH, one of the basic tasks of the dictatorship of the proletariat is actively to expand the socialist economy. It is necessary to achieve the modernization of industry, agriculture, science and technology, and national defence step by step under the guidance of the general policy of developing the national economy with agriculture as the foundation and industry as the leading factor. On the basis of the growth of production, it is necessary to raise the living standards of the people gradually and on a broad scale.

EIGHTH, ownership by the whole people and collective ownership are the two forms of socialist economy. The transition from collective ownership to ownership by the whole people, from two kinds of ownership to a unitary ownership by the whole people, is a rather long process. Collective ownership itself develops from lower to higher levels and from smaller to larger scale. The people's commune which the Chinese people have created is a suitable form of organization for the solution of the question of this transition.

NINTH, " Let a hundred flowers blossom and a hundred schools of thought contend " is a policy for stimulating the growth of the arts and the progress of science and for promoting a flourishing socialist culture. Education must serve proletarian politics and must be combined with productive labour. The working people should master knowledge and the intellectuals should become habituated to manual labour. Among those engaged in science, culture, the arts and education, the struggle to promote proletarian ideology and destroy bourgeois ideology is a protracted and fierce class struggle. It is necessary to build up a large detachment of working-class intellectuals who serve socialism and who are both " red and expert," i.e., who are both politically conscious and professionally competent, by means of the cultural revolution, and revolutionary practice in class struggle, the struggle for production and scientific experiment.

TENTH, it is necessary to maintain the system of cadre participation in collective productive labour. The cadres of our Party and state are ordinary workers and not overlords sitting on the backs of the people. By taking part in collective productive labour, the cadres maintain extensive, constant and close ties with the working people. This is a major measure of fundamental importance for a socialist system; it helps to overcome bureaucracy and to prevent revisionism and dogmatism.

ELEVENTH, the system of high salaries for a small number of people should never be applied. The gap between the incomes of the working personnel of the Party, the Government, the enterprises and the people's communes, on the one hand, and the incomes of the mass of the people, on the other, should be rationally and gradually narrowed and not widened. All working personnel must be prevented from abusing their power and enjoying special privileges.

TWELFTH, it is always necessary for the people's armed forces of a socialist country to be under the leadership of the party of the proletariat and under the supervision of the masses, and they must always maintain the glorious tradition of a people's army, with unity between the army and the people and between officers and men. It is necessary to keep the system under which officers serve as common soldiers at regular intervals. It is necessary to practise military democracy, political democracy and economic democracy. Moreover, militia units should be organized and trained all over the country, so as to make everybody a soldier. The guns must for ever be in the hands of the Party and the people and must never be allowed to become the instruments of careerists.

THIRTEENTH, the people's public security organs must always be under the leadership of the party of the proletariat and under the supervision of the mass of the people. In the struggle to defend the fruits of socialism and the people's interests, the policy must be applied of relying on the combined efforts of the broad masses and the security organs, so that not a single bad person escapes or a single good person is wronged. Counterrevolutionaries must be suppressed whenever found, and mistakes must be corrected whenever discovered.

FOURTEENTH, in foreign policy, it is necessary to uphold proletarian internationalism and oppose great-power chauvinism and national egoism. The socialist camp is the product of the struggle of the international proletariat and working people. It belongs to the proletariat and working people of the whole world as well as to the people of the socialist countries. We must truly put into effect the fighting slogans, "Workers of all countries, unite!" and "Workers and oppressed nations of the world, unite!", resolutely combat the anti-communist, anti-popular and counter-revolutionary policies of imperialism and reaction and support the revolutionary struggles of all the oppressed classes and oppressed nations. Relations among socialist countries should be based on the principles of independence, complete equality and the proletarian internationalist principle of mutual support and mutual assistance. Every socialist country should rely mainly on itself for its construction. If any socialist country practises national egoism in its foreign policy, or, worse yet, eagerly works in partnership with imperialism for the partition of the world, such conduct is degenerate and a betrayal of proletarian internationalism.

FIFTEENTH, as the vanguard of the proletariat, the Communist Party must exist as long as the dictatorship of the proletariat exists. The Communist Party is the highest form of organization of the proletariat. The leading role of the proletariat is realized through the leadership of the

Communist Party. The system of Party committees exercising leadership must be put into effect in all departments. During the period of the dictatorship of the proletariat, the proletarian party must maintain and strengthen its close ties with the proletariat and the broad masses of the working people, maintain and develop its vigorous revolutionary style, uphold the principle of integrating the universal truth of Marxism-Leninism with the concrete practice of its own country, and persist in the struggle against revisionism, dogmatism and opportunism of every kind.

In the light of the historical lessons of the dictatorship of the proletariat Comrade Mao Tse-tung has stated:

> Class struggle, the struggle for production and scientific experiment are the three great revolutionary movements for building a mighty socialist country. These movements are a sure guarantee that Communists will be free from bureaucracy and immune against revisionism and dogmatism, and will forever remain invincible. They are a reliable guarantee that the proletariat will be able to unite with the broad working masses and realize a democratic dictatorship. If, in the absence of these movements, the landlords, rich peasants, counter-revolutionaries, bad elements and ogres of all kinds were allowed to crawl out, while our cadres were to shut their eyes to all this and in many cases fail even to differentiate between the enemy and ourselves but were to collaborate with the enemy and become corrupted and demoralized, if our cadres were thus dragged into the enemy camp or the enemy were able to sneak into our ranks, and if many of our workers, peasants, and intellectuals were left defenceless against both the soft and the hard tactics of the enemy, then it would not take long, perhaps only several years or a decade, or several decades at most, before a counter-revolutionary restoration on a national scale inevitably occurred, the Marxist-Leninist party would undoubtedly become a revisionist party or a fascist party, and the whole of China would change its colour.[70]

Comrade Mao Tse-tung has pointed out that, in order to guarantee that our Party and country do not change their colour, we must not only have a correct line and correct policies but must train and bring up millions of successors who will carry on the cause of proletarian revolution.

In the final analysis, the question of training successors for the revolutionary cause of the proletariat is one of whether or not there will be people who can carry on the Marxist-Leninist revolutionary cause started by the older generation of proletarian revolutionaries, whether or not the leadership of our Party and state will remain in the hands of proletarian revolutionaries, whether or not our descendants will continue to march along the correct road laid down by Marxism-Leninism, or, in other words, whether or not we can successfully prevent the emergence of Khrushchevite revisionism in China. In short, it is an extremely important question, a matter of life and death for our Party and our country. It is a question of fundamental importance to the proletarian revolutionary cause for a hundred, a thousand, nay ten thousand years. Basing themselves on the changes in the Soviet Union, the imperialist prophets are pinning their hopes of " peaceful evolution " on the third or fourth generation of the Chinese Party. We must shatter these imperialist prophecies. From our highest organizations down to the grass-roots, we must everywhere give constant

---

[70] Mao Tse-tung, Note on " The Seven Well-Written Documents of the Chekiang Province Concerning Cadres' Participation in Physical Labour," May 9, 1963.

attention to the training and upbringing of successors to the revolutionary cause.

What are the requirements for worthy successors to the revolutionary cause of the proletariat?

They must be genuine Marxist-Leninists and not revisionists like Khrushchev wearing the cloak of Marxism-Leninism.

They must be revolutionaries who wholeheartedly serve the majority of the people of China and the whole world, and must not be like Khrushchev who serves both the interests of the handful of members of the privileged bourgeois stratum in his own country and those of foreign imperialism and reaction.

They must be proletarian statesmen capable of uniting and working together with the overwhelming majority. Not only must they unite with those who agree with them, they must also be good at uniting with those who disagree and even with those who formerly opposed them and have since been proved wrong. But they must especially watch out for careerists and conspirators like Khrushchev and prevent such bad elements from usurping the leadership of the Party and Government at any level.

They must be models in applying the Party's democratic centralism, must master the method of leadership based on the principle of "from the masses, to the masses," and must cultivate a democratic style and be good at listening to the masses. They must not be despotic like Khrushchev and violate the Party's democratic centralism, make surprise attacks on comrades or act arbitrarily and dictatorially.

They must be modest and prudent and guard against arrogance and impetuosity; they must be imbued with the spirit of self-criticism and have the courage to correct mistakes and shortcomings in their work. They must not cover up their errors like Khrushchev, and claim all the credit for themselves and shift all the blame on others.

Successors to the revolutionary cause of the proletariat come forward in mass struggles and are tempered in the great storms of revolution. It is essential to test and know cadres and choose and train successors in the long course of mass struggle.

The above series of principles advanced by Comrade Mao Tse-tung are creative developments of Marxism-Leninism, to the theoretical arsenal of which they add new weapons of decisive importance for us in preventing the restoration of capitalism. So long as we follow these principles, we can consolidate the dictatorship of the proletariat, ensure that our Party and state will never change colour, successfully conduct the socialist revolution and socialist construction, help all peoples' revolutionary movements for the overthrow of imperialism and its lackeys, and guarantee the future transition from socialism to communism.

*   *   *

Regarding the emergence of the revisionist Khrushchev clique in the Soviet Union, our attitude as Marxist-Leninists is the same as our attitude towards any "disturbance"—first, we are against it; second, we are not afraid of it.

We did not wish it and are opposed to it, but since the revisionist Khrushchev clique have already emerged, there is nothing terrifying about them, and there is no need for alarm. The earth will continue to revolve, history will continue to move forward, the people of the world will, as always, make revolutions and the imperialists and their lackeys will inevitably meet their doom.

The historic contributions of the great Soviet people will remain for ever glorious; they can never be tarnished by the revisionist Khrushchev clique's betrayal. The broad masses of the workers, peasants, revolutionary intellectuals and Communists of the Soviet Union will eventually surmount all the obstacles in their path and march towards communism.

The Soviet people, the people of all the socialist countries and the revolutionary people the world over will certainly learn lessons from the revisionist Khrushchev clique's betrayal. In the struggle against Khrushchev's revisionism, the international communist movement has grown and will continue to grow mightier than ever before.

Marxist-Leninists have always had an attitude of revolutionary optimism towards the future of the cause of the proletarian revolution. We are profoundly convinced that the brilliant light of the dictatorship of the proletariat, of socialism and of Marxism-Leninism will shine forth over the Soviet land. The proletariat is sure to win the whole world and communism is sure to achieve complete and final victory on earth.

DOCUMENT 15

Revolutionary Science and Our Age : * Against the Anti-Leninist Course of the Chinese Leaders

by Leonid Ilyichev
(June 1964) †

Excerpts

[*Kommunist*, No. 11, 1964, pp. 12–35, quoted from *Information Bulletin*, No. 21 (October 1, 1964), pp. 21–52, at pp. 21–34 and 34–39]

.   .   .   .

At the present time the ideological and theoretical life of the Communist parties is centred around the struggle against the aggressive nationalism, the "Left" opportunism and the anti-Leninist line of the leaders of the Chinese Communist Party. This has now become the main issue in today's ideological battles.

Politically this is a struggle for the further development of the world revolutionary movement, for strengthening the socialist system; it is a struggle for utilizing the new opportunities opened up in our days for the transition of the peoples to socialism, for the final abolition of colonialism, for ensuring a lasting peace and general security; it is a struggle for the cohesion of all the anti-imperialist forces, with the socialist world system

---

* Report delivered in June 1964 at a scientific session on the " Struggle of the CPSU for the Purity of Marxism-Leninism," sponsored by the Academy of Social Sciences and the Institute of Marxism-Leninism of the CPSU Central Committee and social sciences institutes of the USSR Academy of Sciences. The report, reprinted from *Kommunist*, No. 11, 1964, is given here with some additions. [Note in *Information Bulletin*, No. 21.]

† *Kommunist*, No. 11, 1964 was signed to the press on July 31, 1964.— Ed.

and the international working class playing the leading role; it is a struggle for the fulfilment by the working class of its great historical mission in the socialist revolution, in the liberation movement of the peoples.

Ideologically and theoretically this is a struggle for proletarian, communist ideology against petty-bourgeois ideology; socialist internationalism against nationalism; revolutionary science against revisionism and paralyzing dogmatism.

To fight in our days for the purity of revolutionary science, for its creative development means to fight for the future of the revolutionary movement.

Our Party's assessment of the anti-Marxist, great-power, neo-Trotskyite position of the Chinese leaders is given in the decision of the February Plenary Meeting of the CPSU Central Committee and in M. A. Suslov's report "Struggle of the CPSU for Unity of the World Communist Movement." Discussion of the materials of the plenary meeting has demonstrated the complete unity of our Party, solidly rallied behind the Central Committee. Our Party and the entire Soviet people have unanimously approved the decision of the plenary meeting, the policy and practical activity of the CPSU Central Committee and its Presidium, headed by the outstanding Leninist N. S. Khrushchev, activity aimed at building communist society in the USSR and ensuring the victory of the cause of peace, democracy, national independence and socialism, at strengthening the unity of the world Communist movement.

The position of our Party has been approved by the absolute majority of fraternal Marxist-Leninist parties.

The documents of the CPSU and other fraternal parties have already demonstrated the danger of the present stand of the Chinese leaders. Their anti-Leninist course has created serious difficulties in the socialist camp and the Communist movement. But the Chinese leaders, ignoring the calls of the Marxist-Leninist parties to take the road of eliminating the differences, are intensifying their splitting, factional, subversive activity in the ideological and political spheres. Our Party, together with the other fraternal parties, will therefore continue unswervingly to defend Marxism-Leninism, to uphold and strengthen the unity of the socialist camp and the world Communist movement on the principles of the 1957 Declaration and the 1960 Statement, the unity and solidarity of all the forces for peace, democracy, national independence and socialism.

I. Struggle for Hegemony — Strategic Aim of Present-Day Splitters

The assessment of revisionism and dogmatism given in the documents jointly adopted by the fraternal parties in 1957 and 1960 is generally known.

Together with the other fraternal parties, the CPSU held that in the interests of the further development of the Communist and working-class movement a vigorous struggle must be waged against revisionism, which at certain stages becomes the chief danger in the world Communist movement, and against dogmatism and sectarianism.

But the 1960 Statement contains the following highly important proposition:

"Dogmatism and sectarianism in theory and practice can also become the main danger at some stage of development of individual parties, unless combated unrelentingly." It did not take much time for all to see how correct this conclusion was. "The events that have occurred in the Communist movement since that Statement was adopted by the fraternal parties have fully demonstrated the foresight of this conclusion," N. S. Khrushchev remarked in 1962.

What happened at the meeting of the fraternal parties in 1960 and what position the delegates of the Communist Party of China took at that time is common knowledge. Soon after the adoption of the Statement they sharply stepped up their factional, subversive activity, acting at first from positions of dogmatism and sectarianism, and subsequently revealing themselves as bellicose nationalists harboring far-reaching great-power, hegemonistic designs. Now there is every reason to say that while the struggle against revisionism remains and will continue to remain on the order of the day so long as bourgeois pressure on the proletariat exists, "*Left*" *opportunism is becoming the chief danger in the international Communist movement.*

It is not the first time the CPSU and the other Marxist-Leninist parties have been faced with attempts to revise the revolutionary teaching both from the Right and from the "Left".

Struggle against "Left-wing communism" passes through the entire history of the development of Marxism. Let us recall the struggle Marx and Engels waged against the "Lefts" in the First International and later on, in the course of decades. Lenin's scathing criticism of "Left" opportunism on questions of the theory and practice of socialist construction is well known. The experience of this struggle against "Left" opportunism is of international significance; it is especially important in our days since contemporary "Left" opportunism has borrowed a great deal from its predecessors.

But no "Left" deviation in the past represented such a danger to the Communist movement as present-day "Left" opportunism.

Why? First of all, because it is being practised by the leadership of a ruling party. There is no need to prove how much more dangerous "Left" opportunism becomes when it is accepted as the basis of political line not by a faction in one or another party, but by the leadership of the ruling party in a socialist country. All ideological media in China are now concentrated on conditioning the minds of the people in the nationalistic, chauvinist spirit, while the party and government machinery of the country, instead of fighting against imperialism, is engaged in a struggle against the Communist parties, in organizing subversive activities within those parties, in struggle against the strategy and tactics of the international Communist movement jointly elaborated by them.

It is nationalism and great-power aspirations that underlie the present-day policy of the Chinese leaders. They are camouflaged by revolutionary phraseology, and to carry them out, the principles of Marxism-Leninism are distorted in the spirit of "Left" opportunism. The social base for nationalism and Leftism has been greatly extended in our days. Huge masses, peasants in the majority, are taking part in the national liberation movement. Millions of people, including those not versed in politics, have been drawn into the vortex of the struggle. The Chinese leaders are trying to capitalize both on the legitimate dissatisfaction of the masses with the exploiting system and on the political backwardness of some sections, especially on nationalist and even racist prejudices engendered by colonial rapine and imperialist oppression.

353

The line adopted by the Chinese leaders is not confined to separate, specific questions; it constitutes the essence of their current theoretical and practical activities. It is counterposed to the general line of the world Communist movement and is being intensively foisted by Peking on the Communist parties of the other countries. What we are faced with is an attempt to divert the international Communist movement from the Leninist path, to subordinate it to the narrow nationalistic ends of one party. The methods they use are well known: to shout as loudly as possible about " class struggle," " revolution," " dictatorship of the proletariat," to create the impression that they are the sole guardians of revolutionary science, and to accuse of apostasy, " revisionism," " betrayal," etc., all who oppose their splitting activity and expose them as anti-Leninists. But does it necessarily follow that he who shouts the loudest is in the right?

We have to deal here with subversive work on an international scale.

Splitting activity by individual leaders or groups in the Communist movement has always been condemned by the Leninists as a grave crime against the working class. This is all the more applicable to the splitting activity of the Chinese leaders, since it is being conducted at a time when a sharp struggle is being fought between socialism and imperialism, a time when the cohesion of the world Communist movement, the unity of all the revolutionary contingents is especially vital.

Objectively, the position of the latter-day splitters plays into the hands of the forces hostile to socialism; it is doing grave harm to the revolutionary struggle of the peoples for social and national emancipation, for peace, democracy and socialism.

It is sometimes asked: what is the reason for the deviation of the Chinese leadership from the general line of the world Communist movement, their desire to break away from it? How did it come about that the leadership of a party which led its people to victory in the revolution, which in the past did much to strengthen the friendship of the Chinese people with the peoples of the USSR and the other socialist countries, has altered its line, launched a campaign of lies and slander against the Soviet Union and the Communist Party of the Soviet Union, begun to treat the CPSU and the other Marxist-Leninist parties as political enemies, come out against the strategy and tactics of the world Communist movement on all the main questions of our time, and is trying to break up the unity of that movement?

The reasons for the shift on the part of the Chinese leaders to nationalist, Leftist opportunist positions are rooted both in subjective and objective factors, both in the external and internal situation.

Let us consider the level of China's economic development. Economically, pre-revolutionary China was one of the most backward countries in the world. Her economy had a strongly pronounced agrarian character. It is indicative that even tsarist Russia, the most backward of the great powers, in 1913 produced 3.3 times more steel and 3 times more pig iron per capita than People's China produced in 1957. On the eve of the revolution locomotives of more than 200 models were running on the railways of China, but not one of them had been built in China. The textile industry had four million spindles, none of them of Chinese make. A world supplier of tungsten, China was importing filaments for electric bulbs.

The social structure of China's society is bound up with her economic backwardness.

China is the biggest peasant country in the world. Today too the peasantry comprises more than 80 per cent of her population. The urban petty bourgeoisie — small tradesmen and artisans — make up a considerable section of the population. The industrial proletariat, which is the leading force of socialist revolution, did not comprise even one per cent of the population at the moment when the revolution won in China. It now numbers about 20 million, that is less than three per cent of the population. Moreover, it is a young working class consisting to a large extent of yesterday's peasants.

The Communist Party of China has undergone considerable revolutionary schooling, but the proletarian stratum in it is extremely small. The Party grew numerically and replenished its ranks most from among the working class but chiefly from the peasantry, intellectuals, and other sections. The present leaders of the Party and the state, too, have come from their midst. Many non-proletarians joined the Party not because of their Marxist convictions, but only because they saw in it an effective force fighting against the Japanese imperialists, for the country's liberation. Some of them joined the Party prompted not by class proletarian interests, which most fully express also the basic national interests, but solely by the national sentiments. In an interview given to the American author Edgar Snow, Mao Tse-tung said that books by Chinese bourgeois nationalists and also anarchists, had greatly influenced his political awakening. As he himself noted, he had also been under the strong influence of Chen Tu-siu, who subsequently went over to Trotskyite positions and turned renegade.

Prior to the victory of the revolution, the CCP worked chiefly in remote rural localities, isolated from the main centers of the working class, the big cities and industrial areas.

For more than ten years after 1935 the Chinese revolution had its center in the border area located at the junction of three peasant provinces (Shensi, Kansu and Ningsia) with headquarters in the small district town of Yenan. Here were the Central Committee of the CCP, all the central offices of the Party and most of its members. Mao Tse-tung wrote at one time " China is a country with an extremely numerous petty bourgeoisie and our Party is surrounded by this huge social stratum. Very many members of our Party themselves came out of a petty-bourgeois environment and each one of them has inevitably dragged along with him in to the Party a more or less long petty-bourgeois tail." (*Selected Works*, Russ. ed., Vol. 4, p. 96.)

Is not this petty-bourgeois tail dragging the Chinese leaders to subjectivism and nationalism?

It was Mao Tse-tung himself who wrote that the Communist Party of China is inclined to be strongly influenced by petty-bourgeois ideology which, as he put it, is expressed in " dashing " now to the left, now to the right, in a weakness for " Left " revolutionary phraseology and slogans, in sectarian exclusiveness and adventurism.

Naturally, economic backwardness and pressure from petty-bourgeois elements do not in themselves inevitably lead to Leftist opportunist views. After all, our Party, at one time also labored under the effects of economic backwardness and no small pressure from the petty-bourgeoisie. More than that, having won power, it carried on its activities for a long time in a country which was surrounded by capitalist states and was subjected to considerable bourgeois influence from without. Nevertheless, our Party has always firmly relied on the revolutionary working class, on the alliance of the working class with the working peasantry, upheld the immutable principles of Marxism-Leninism, and resolutely defeated all opportunist deviations.

Consequently, it is not only the objective factors that matter. However strong the pressure of the petty-bourgeois element, it can be overcome if the party leadership applies a correct, sustained proletarian policy, if it is loyal to Leninism. But it is loyalty to Leninism that the Chinese leaders lack. Far from launching a struggle against the pressure of the petty-bourgeois element they have themselves succumbed to it. As far back as 1956 the Eighth All-China Congress of the CCP pointed to big shortcomings in the ideological sphere and to the need for Marxist-Leninist schooling, especially of the higher party functionaries, and the importance of ever-coming subjectivism. We see that the warning of the congress has not done any good.

The sources of the Left opportunist, nationalist views of the Chinese leaders are rooted in subjective factors, too. The Communist Party of China is known to be functioning and working today not on the basis of the principles of democratic centralism, but in an atmosphere of the personality cult. The ideology of the personality cult runs counter to the very spirit of Leninism, to the nature of the evolutionary working-class movement and of the socialist system. The practice of concentrating all power in the hands of a single individual is alien to the nature of the proletarian state, to the principles of socialist democracy. It is especially baneful in a country still weighted down by the unpleasant " burden " of such survivals of the feudal past as worship of the monarch, domination of a hierarchy and omnipotence of bureaucracy.

The cult of Mao Tse-tung's personality could not but lead in China to distortions of the socialist principles of state and Party development and of the democratic forms and methods of administration.

Materials on the gross violations of inner-party democracy in China have already been published in our press. Incidentally, the Chinese press, far from reprinting the article entitled " Certain Aspects of Party Life in the Communist Party of China " published in *Pravda*, has not uttered a single word in refutation of the facts cited in it. For 20 years prior to the victory of the revolution, all ideological and organizational work in the Communist Party of China was conducted along military lines, subordinated to wartime needs. For that period this procedure evidently was justified. But 15 years have already passed since the end of hostilities. With the switchover to peaceful work, have the Chinese leaders taken any measures to change the Party's style of work, to promote democratic centralism? No, they have not. The army style, based on one-man command, on unquestioning obedience to orders from above, has remained the basis of Party activity. Moreover, militarization of all aspects of social life has been intensified in recent years. As before, criticism and other elementary standards of inner-party democracy are lacking.

True, at one time after the 20th Congress of the CPSU, the Chinese leadership began to speak about developing democracy. But that is as far as it went.

An extensive campaign is now being conducted in China under the slogan: " Learn to work like the People's Liberation Army." Political bodies patterned after the army political departments are being set up in the entire system of the Party, state and economic apparatus of China, from the Central Committee of the CCP down to enterprises and communes. Mao Tse-tung has declared: "All our economic branches, branches of industry, agriculture and trade must study the methods of the People's Liberation Army, must organize and intensify political work. Only in this way will it be possible to arouse the revolutionary spirit of millions and tens of millions of personnel and the masses on the entire economic front." (*Hung Ch'i*, No. 6, 1964.)

Note, it is not the army that has to learn from the Party, but the Party from the army. In other words, the accent is on the army and the principles of army discipline, while the Leninist teaching on the Party is discarded.

What should be learned from the army? Party organizations of China are given the following directive: Communists must learn from the army "to carry out orders resolutely, swiftly and strictly, without entering into arguments and without haggling — do what you are ordered " (*Jen-min Jih-pao*, February 1, 1964). How can one speak of Party democracy when all that is demanded of a Party member is blind obedience. The demand that you unquestioningly carry out orders and, moreover, pretend that this is inner-party democracy, is sheer blasphemy. This is how the elementary standards of Party life are violated, criticism from below and the creative activity of Communists crushed, how informing and servility are encouraged. The Political Bureau of the Central Committee of the Communist Party of China and Mao Tse-tung who judging from his directive, only issue orders, consider themselves to be exempt from Party control, from control of the Party members.

The atmosphere created by the personality cult cannot but lead to a situation when *subjectivism and the personal whims of one man become an official policy, create fertile soil for unjustified experiments, absence of control, inordinate ambition, make for extremes, instability, adventurism and nationalism*. It is in this atmosphere that the nationalist, Left opportunist, neo-Trotskyite deviation has made its nest.

The question arises: what brings together the neo-Trotskyism of the Chinese leaders with the old, " classical " Trotskyism, defeated in the past by our Party?

First of all, they have one and the same anti-Leninist ideological platform, follow the same petty-bourgeois adventurism in foreign and home policy, factional methods and splitting activity in the Communist movement, they both reject democratic principles and adhere to military, compulsory forms in state and party development. Both deviations are marked by disbelief in the forces of the working people, their ability to build socialist society, although they have been holding forth at length about loyalty to the people and faith in their revolutionary forces. Both are characterized by a desire to cover up their capitulatory essence by Leftist principles.

It would of course be historically wrong to equate the " old " Trotskyism with the " new " Trotskyism, neo-Trotskyism.

To begin with, the historical situation has radically changed. Moreover, the former reflected primarily the ideology of the urban petty bourgeosie, while the latter reflect primarily the ideology of the peasantry, although it experiences the pressure of urban bourgeois elements too. The former was under the strong influence of anarcho-syndicalism; the latter is influenced by various forms of Utopian, chiefly peasant socialism. Speculating on the slogan of world revolution, the old Trotskyism absolutized a falsely-interpreted internationalism, counterposing it to national interests. Neo-

Trotskyism is marked by strongly pronounced nationalism, and great-power chauvinism. The old Trotskyism advocated its sectarian concept of the "ultra-revolutionism" of the working class, and ignored the revolutionary potentialities of the peasantry as an ally of the proletariat. Neo-Trotskyism advocates the "ultra-revolutionism" of the peasantry and does not believe in the forces of the working class.

However specific the views of the Chinese leaders may be, their kinship with Trotskyism is obvious, especially if account is taken of the historical evolution of Trotskyism itself. The views of the Chinese leaders on many basic questions coincide with the views of the leaders of the so-called Fourth (Trotskyite) International.

Now let us put the following question: why have the views of the Chinese leadership taken such a pronounced hegemonistic turn?

There are enough facts to give the right answer. The political evolution of China, for example, calls for profound study. Let us take the first years after the victory of the revolution. The Chinese people were successfully laying the foundations of socialism with the generous and unselfish fraternal assistance of the socialist countries. Although already then, as the Chinese leaders say, they did not subscribe in every respect to the positions of the international Communist movement, still they concealed their divergencies for the time being, declaring their full agreement with the line of the world Communist movement.

But in the spring of 1958, the Chinese leadership began to veer round sharply. Instead of approximately 15 years, in the course of which it was planned to lay the foundation of socialism in China, a period of only three years was proclaimed to be sufficient for the transition to communism. The so-called "big leap" was announced, a political and economic gamble unprecedented in conception and scale. It was a policy divorced from the actual, objective possibilities, and was based on the desire to accomplish as swiftly as possible the immense tasks and "to teach" others the newly-invented methods of building socialism and communism. The slogan of the "people's communes" was likewise proclaimed then. It was based on an attempt to skip the natural stages of socialist construction in the countryside, tested by the experience of the socialist countries, and to be "ahead of progress" in this sphere too. In a word, the economy of China, which had not gained strength as yet, was subjected to an avalanche of unjustified experiments, beyond the strength of the country's economy and running counter to the laws of economic development.

What prompted the Chinese leaders to take these steps? Evidently the successes — undoubted successes — scored by China in 1958 with the help of the fraternal socialist countries. But these successes had a dual effect on the minds of the Chinese leaders.

On the one hand, achievements in economic development made them dizzy with success, intoxicated them. "China can accomplish anything " — such was the official conclusion. On the other hand, a comparison of what had been achieved with the tasks still to be accomplished demonstrated to the Chinese leaders, perhaps for the first time, the colossal complexity and difficulty of the process of building socialism in economically backward China. "The successes are great, but all this is a mere drop in the ocean, much more work lies ahead " — such approximately was the unofficial conclusion. "We have to make haste,' the Chinese leaders concluded. Since "China can accomplish anything," is there any sense in dragging out socialist construction for decades? Would it not be simpler to try skipping the socialist stage and leap directly into communism in three years? Petty-bourgeois impatience and scorn for objective laws gained the upper hand over common sense. It may be assumed that foreign-policy, or to be more precise, great-power aspirations too played their part here.

Towards the end of 1959 it had become absolutely clear for the Chinese leadership that the " big leap " had led the economy and policy of China into a blind alley and confronted the country with grave economic difficulties.

In this situation they swung to another extreme in economic policy — agriculture was declared the basis of the economy. The calls to outstrip the most developed countries in a short time quietly died down and then disappeared completely from the Chinese press. More than that, even the victory of socialism was declared to be a matter of the remote future. The Chinese leaders shifted their claims to the role of teacher, to hegemony chiefly to the political sphere.

It is no longer a secret that the verbal acrobatics around theoretical questions, the ultra-revolutionary phrasemongering and flirting with unstable elements in other parties, the forming of blocs with all kinds of renegades and traitors to the cause of the working class, the noisy campaign called a struggle against " contemporary revisionism," and many other things have served and are serving the Chinese leaders merely as a means in their attempts to assert their special position in the socialist world, in the international Communist and national-liberation movement.

Nationalism and its poisoned fruits can be discerned lately in many of the political actions of the CCP Central Committee and the Chinese government. The biased evaluation of China's historical past, for example, cannot but attract attention.

It will be recalled that since ancient times the ideologists of China have built up an image of their country as the " Middle Empire," the oldest civilization, the custodian of world order and spiritual harmony, as the " Celestial Empire " which wields power on earth. The imperial ideology of China's special role in the history of mankind is to a certain extent influencing the minds of the present Chinese leaders.

It would be unjust, of course, to deny the tremendous contribution made by the Chinese people to the development of world civilization, to under-estimate their spiritual influence on the culture of other peoples. But it would be absolutely wrong, while paying due tribute to China's role in history, not to notice the great-power aspirations which thrived in China, to ignore or belittle the role of other countries and peoples in the history of mankind. But it is this chauvinistic and even outright racialist appraisal of China's role that can be frequently found in the writings of Chinese ideologists. According to some Chinese historians, the history of mankind is concentrated in the part of Asia where China is situated. The country's historical past is idealized, the history of other peoples is referred to slightingly and " Sino-centric " concepts are made the basis of everything. Philosophy and history, literature and art in present-day China are subordinated to substantiating such ideas.

The Chinese historians go to all lengths to extol, to demonstrate China's special role in the destinies of mankind.

If Europe had classical forms of slavery, in China, it turns out, they were " highly classical." And the feudal system in China, in contrast to

359

Europe, was also a "model" one. True, the capitalist system developed earlier in Europe, but because the "leading position of people of the yellow race from Asia was firmly captured by people of the white race from Europe." America was discovered by the Chinese. China had Confucius, Europe did not. Europe experienced the fall of the Roman Empire, but in China this did not happen. And so on and so forth. Everyone understands the national pride of the scholar if his people performed an exploit or made a great discovery. National prides is not alien to the peoples. There is nothing wrong in this, but why belittle other peoples, other countries. In China arrogant nationalism comes to the surface not only when hoary antiquity is assessed. It is openly said in China that without reference to Chinese history it is impossible "to explain the general laws governing the development of human society."

To achieve their hegemony-seeking schemes, the Chinese leaders are pursuing a thoroughly planned and coordinated policy. Its main trends are clear already now.

First, a struggle against the CPSU and the Soviet Union, because the Chinese leaders see in the high prestige enjoyed by our Leninist Party and the USSR — the first socialist country which is successfully building communism — the main stumbling block to realizing their nationalistic, great-power plans.

Second, a struggle against the unity of the socialist camp, the Communist movement, the working people of all countries and continents, because this unity and proletarian internationalism are a major obstacle to the hegemonistic aspirations of the Peking leaders. That is why they have taken the line of forming factions in the Communist movement as a whole and in individual Communist parties, factions which would obediently carry out directives from Peking; the line of forming a grouping of some socialist countries, of setting the peoples of Asia, Africa and Latin America against the peoples who are building socialism and communism and against the working class of the capitalist countries.

It can be considered an accomplished fact that of the two diametrically opposed slogans, political lines and world outlooks — proletarian internationalism and bourgeois nationalism — the Chinese leaders have chosen nationalism. They scorned the warning made by Lenin: ". . . One who has adopted the standpoint of nationalism naturally arrives at the desire to erect a Chinese Wall around his nationality, his national working-class movement . . . is unembarrassed even by the fact that by his tactics of division and dismemberment *he is reducing to nil* the great calls for rallying and unity of the proletarians of all nations, all races and all languages." (Lenin, *Complete Works*, Russ. ed., Vol. 7, p. 325.)

Third, a struggle against the policy of peaceful coexistence of states with different social systems and of easing international tensions; this is tantamount to spurring on nuclear armaments and pursuing a line which can lead to atomic war. As time goes on it is becoming increasingly clear that the mainspring of many foreign-policy actions of the Chinese splitters is hidden in the wish for a big military conflict, while they themselves stand aloof, "watching from the mountain top the battle of tigers" and profiting by it.

Fourth, the persistent attempts of the Chinese leaders to dominate the national-liberation movement. To this end they flatter and play up to nationalist circles and declare the national-liberation movement to be the leading element in the world revolutionary process. Hence the theory of the " storm-center of the revolution " in the " three-A " zone (Asia, Africa, Latin America), hence the political actions aimed at dividing the world revolutionary forces according to national and even racial features.

Fifth, one of the trends of the Chinese leaders' battle for hegemony is to flirt with the imperialist powers behind the cover of talk about the " intermediate zone." The political meaning of this strategic " innovation " is to substantiate the need for separate political cooperation between China and imperialist states — West Germany, Britain, France, Japan — while loudly accusing others of a " compact with imperialism."

This is the first time in its history that the world Communist movement is faced with such far-reaching efforts by a group of splitters to capture leadership of the revolutionary struggle at all costs and subordinate it to its great-power ambitions.

.   .   .   .

The truth must be squarely faced: Peking is casting doubts on the successes of the socialist states also because it hopes with the help of such disgraceful methods to justify its own gross miscalculations and failures in socialist construction.

Both the " go-it-alone " theory of building socialism and the " philosophy " of inevitable split of the revolutionary forces are of a similarly utilitarian character. Never before in the history of the Communist movement have the leaders of a Communist Party frankly and cynically proclaimed the philosophy of split to be their credo. Yet this is precisely what the Chinese leaders with their formula: " unity — struggle and even a split — a new unity on a new basis " have done. What is this: a meaningless phrase or a thoroughly considered policy? Of course, the latter. Now it is already possible to speak about a peculiar " unity " of word and deed of the Chinese neo-Trotskyites and nationalists: they have not only formulated their " philosophy of split " but are applying it in practice, are trying to realize their nefarious factionalist, disruptive schemes.

The chest where the Chinese leaders keep their " ideas " obviously has two bottoms.

From one of them for a time they extracted ideas adapted to the jointly-charted course of the world Communist movement, and from the other they are intensively drawing ideas for anti-Soviet slander, for substantiating their nationalistic line. On many questions of development of the world revolutionary process — whether major fundamental problems or concrete political actions — the present-day splitters have two positions, each of which is utilized depending on the circumstances.

Let us see how the position of the Chinese leadership has changed, for example, on the question of peaceful coexistence of states with different social systems and the economic competition of socialism with capitalism.

Liu Shao-chi stated in the political report of the CCP Central Committee to the Eighth All-China Congress of the CCP (1956): " In foreign relations we undeviatingly pursue a consistent policy of peace and champion peaceful coexistence and friendly cooperation between all states. We are convinced of the advantages of the socialist system and are not afraid to engage in peaceful competition with the capitalist countries . . ."

This was said at the highest forum of the Party seven years ago.

Have any big changes occurred in the world since then, have the imperialists succeeded in undermining to any extent the policy of peaceful coexistence pursued by the countries of the socialist community? No, they have not. On the contrary, the forces of socialism, peace and the national-liberation movement have grown still stronger during these years; the correctness of the Leninist policy of peaceful coexistence has been corroborated by the entire course of international development. But what does this matter to the Chinese leaders, gripped by their hegemonistic ambitions! Behind the back of their Party they renounced the foreign-policy line laid down in the decisions of the Eighth CCP Congress and began to oppose the Leninist principle of relations between states with different social systems. " . . . Peaceful coexistence," *Jen-min Jih-pao* and *Hung Ch'i*, organs of the CCP Central Committee, wrote in December 1963, "meets the needs of imperialism and aids the imperialist policy of aggression and war . . . It means replacement of the class struggle by class collaboration on a world scale."

Such an about-face of the Peking leaders on the question of peaceful coexistence reflects their present policy directed against the Soviet Union and the other countries of the socialist community, against the general foreign-policy line of the socialist countries elaborated by the world Communist movement.

The Chinese leaders are veering from one position to another also on such a major question as the methods and peace of building socialism and communism. Here too the main thing for them is not to find a constructive and real solution of the problem, not to theoretically comprehend the real processes in socialist society, but again to discredit the Soviet Union and communist construction at all costs, to denigrate the experience of the CPSU. Having proclaimed in 1958 the " big leap " and " people's communes " slogans, the Chinese leaders declared at that time that the Soviet Union had got stuck at the stage of socialism and was marking time, while China was advancing to communism with seven-league strides.

Posing as clairvoyants who had discovered a short cut to communism, they put forward a slogan: " Three years of hard work — ten thousand years of happy life."

But when their policy of the " big leap " to communism failed, the Peking leaders at once began to attack the CPSU from diametrically opposite positions. This time they accused our Party of drawing up Utopian plans of building communism in the USSR in the lifetime of the present generation. They " forgot " everything they had said earlier, and are now asserting that to build socialism, communism, the efforts of many generations — five and perhaps ten generations are needed in any case " not tens of years but a hundred and even hundreds of years." (Article in *Jen-min Jih-pao* and *Hung Ch'i* of July 14, 1964.)

But to tell the working class, the entire people that socialism, communism can be built only centuries later means ideologically to disarm the working people, to revise Lenin's well-known propositions on the building of communism. This is nothing but surrender on the part of the Chinese leaders in the face of the difficulties of building a new society, betrayal of revolutionary science.

As recently as a few years ago the Chinese leaders still recognized the inseverable bond between the international and national tasks of the revolutionary movement, the need "closely to co-ordinate the national democratic revolution of the oppressed peoples with the socialist revolution of the proletariat." Today, however, the Chinese leaders state the very opposite: to suit their purposes they are trying to sever the national-liberation movement from the socialist community, from the entire international working-class movement and thereby weaken and undermine the forces of the national-liberation movement. At the Afro-Asian Solidarity Conference, held in Moshi in February 1963, Liu Ning-yi, one of the Chinese leaders, told the Soviet delegates: "East European countries should not interfere in Asian and African affairs. . . . We are sorry you came here at all. You have no business here, your presence is an insult to the solidarity movement of the Afro-Asian countries. . . . Do as you wish, but we shall be against you."

Reducing theory to the role of an auxiliary instrument, the Chinese leaders are willing to make use of anything that can in some degree help realize their plans.

The political complexion and ideological sympathies of those who subscribe to the views of the Peking splitters are quite variegated. The Chinese leaders have dragged into their ideological lumber-room "Left" phrases, Trotskyite slogans, nationalistic calls and apologia of the personality cult. All this is calculated to "catch" people, to win supporters whatever their views might be.

The "Left" phrases and the parading of a revolutionary spirit are intended for unstable, politically immature elements who are easily intoxicated by calls for the immediate armed overthrow of capitalism, without pausing to consider whether there are objective conditions for the victory of the socialist revolution or not.

The Trotskyite slogans are designed to attract all sorts of renegades ejected from the Communist parties, to draw them into a common factional bloc and to step up their subversive activity.

The nationalist calls are addressed to the young anti-imperialist forces of Asia, Africa and Latin America. Juggling with such calls, speculating on the community of historical destinies of the "three A's" the Chinese leaders expect to rally round themselves nationalistic-minded people.

The apology for the personality cult should, in the Chinese leaders' view, rally round them men in the Communist parties who adhere to doctrinaire conservative views and who abhor the revolutionary, creative spirit of the decisions of the 20th and 22nd congresses of the CPSU, the Declaration and Statement adopted by the meetings of the Communist and Workers' parties.

In view of this, there is nothing surprising in the eclectic nature of the ideological and theoretical platform of the Chinese splitters. It is a con-glomeration of "Left" opportunism, dogmatism and frankly revisionist ideas, fragments of revolutionary theory, Trotskyite theses, idealist opinions and sophistry of ancient Chinese philosophers, nationalistic and at times racialist ideas.

The lack of principle on theoretical questions displayed by the Chinese leaders is amazing. Today they can put forward one slogan, proclaim it the last word in Marxist science, and tomorrow replace it by another, directly the opposite and again announce that another great theoretical discovery has been made. But the logic of the splitter clearly stands out behind this "theoretical" shuffling and manipulation of theses and slogans.

The Chinese leadership is prepared to uphold any position as long as it is opposed to the views of the CPSU and the other Marxist-Leninist parties, the single general line of the world Communist movement, as long as it benefits the present-day splitters and helps them gain their ends.

The Chinese leaders cannot conceal the utilitarian nature of their ideological and theoretical platform however hard they try. Nor can anyone be deceived by their assurances that they are "defending" revolutionary theory from distortions of "contemporary revisionism."

The present-day splitters are trying to play the role of ideological pontiffs, "custodians" of revolutionary science; they lay claim to a monopoly of theory by stressing the universal significance of "Mao Tse-tung's ideas." They proclaim as illegitimate any new theoretical proposition not fathered by Mao Tse-tung. Small wonder that they are so vexed by the fact that the Communist parties are enriching the revolutionary teaching with new theoretical conclusions and propositions born in the struggle for socialism, the national independence of the peoples, and peace.

It is not accidental that the Chinese leaders are trying to discredit the conclusions and assessments made by the CPSU and the other Marxist-Leninist parties on the basis of an analysis of the changed historical conditions and generalization of rich revolutionary experience. Quotation juggling is a favorite method of the Chinese theorists: passages are torn out, literally plucked out of the classics of Marxism-Leninism and quoted frequently without any relation to their context.

They do not care in the least at what period, in what concrete situation the proposition quoted was put forward and in what conditions it was applied. Moreover, one and the same quotations migrate from one article to another, from one statement to another. It is not in this way, not by citing quotations that loyalty to the revolutionary teaching is demonstrated! We all know how scathingly Lenin ridiculed such a method of utilizing quotations.

Revolutionary reality, revolutionary action that is the proving-ground where the theoretical weapon of Marxism-Leninism is tested and perfected!

The Chinese leaders do not stop at outright distortion of statements by the founders of scientific communism when this suits their purpose. Many such instances have been exposed by the press of the CPSU and the fraternal parties. The dogmatism of the Chinese theorists is closely intertwined with an open revision of important tenets of Marxism-Leninism. In general, a rather peculiar situation has arisen: those who at every step are revising the revolutionary teaching are screaming loudest about "contemporary revisionism." A combination of Leftist doctrinairism and revisionist tendencies is not in the least original and has been long familiar to the Communist movement. The point is that both dogmatism and revisionism are fed by a more or less homogeneous social source. Dogmatism is merely the reverse side of revisionism.

Constant rejection of the fundamental gains of Marxist thought in our time, just as frank revision of basic propositions of revolutionary theory, is ultimately crowned by attempts to replace Marxism by "Sinified Marxism," by the "ideas of Mao Tse-tung."

It is here that the political and ideological efforts of the Chinese leaders link up. It is characteristic that while in their articles addressed to the outside world the Chinese leaders appear to speak in the name of Marxism-Leninism, the articles addressed to the Chinese Communists talk only of the ideas of Mao Tse-tung and urge the Chinese Communists and all the working people to study only these ideas. So far the Chinese leaders still say formally that the ideas of Mao Tse-tung are connected with Marxism-Leninism, although they have already declared them to be the "most advanced stage in the development of Marxism-Leninism today." But judging by the Chinese press, the relation of Mao Tse-tung's ideas to Marxism-Leninism is mentioned in China more for tactical considerations, for the time being. Actually the indications are that the founding of a "new teaching" is about to be proclaimed.

DOCUMENT 16

Interview with Chairman Mao Tse-tung by a Delegation of the Japanese Socialist Party
(July 10, 1964)

Excerpts

[*Sekai Shūhō* (Tokyo), August 11, 1964,* quoted from Dennis J. Doolin, *Territorial Claims in the Sino-Soviet Conflict: Documents & Analysis* (Stanford, Cal.: The Hoover Institution, 1965), pp. 42–44]

On July 10, a five-man group of parliamentary deputies, headed by Kozo Sasaki, from . . . the Japanese Socialist Party had a lengthy talk in Peking with Mao Tse-tung, Chairman of the Chinese Communist Party. In the course of this talk, Mao Tse-tung declared that he "supported the position of Japan on the question of the return of the Kuriles." After arriving in Hong Kong on July 12, the group told this to a group of Japanese correspondents accredited there. The contents of the talk deserve special attention.

.   .   .   .

Chairman Mao Tse-tung bitterly criticized the Soviet Union for its territorial ambitions. In appraising this statement, however, we must keep in mind that it was made amid circumstances that have brought diplomatic relations between the two countries to the point of rupture.

.   .   .   .

The Sino-Soviet dispute: Touching upon the so-called Sino-Soviet dispute, Mao spoke about the question of Soviet military assistance to India, the recall of Soviet specialists and technicians from China [in July of 1960], etc. Having pointed out that "relations between us and the Soviet Union have become worse and worse since the Twentieth Congress of the CPSU in 1956," he then declared:

* The abridged Russian translation published in *Pravda* (September 2, 1964) shows only stylistic differences; see the complete *Pravda* translation in *CDSP*, Vol. XVI, No. 34 (September 16, 1964), pp. 6–7.— Ed.

" We have been challenged and we are resisting. It has been proposed to us that we stop the open discussion, if even for three months. We have told them we will not stop even for so many days. We have waged war for twenty-five years. Of these twenty-five years, twenty-two years were taken up by the Civil War and the war against Japan, three years by the Korean War. In the past, [although] I was a teacher, I did not know what war was. Three teachers taught me what war was. The first was Chiang Kai-shek, the second was Japanese imperialism, and the third was American imperialism. War is a well-known phenomenon ; when it is waged, people die. During these twenty-five years of war, the Chinese people lost several tens of millions of dead and wounded. As regards war on paper, there are no dead in such a war. We have been waging such a war for several years now, and not a single person has died. We are prepared to wage this war for another twenty-five years. The Rumanian delegation [that recently visited China] proposed that we end the dispute. However, as soon as the delegation returned home, Rumania started fighting with the Soviet Union. What is the crux of the matter? The crux lies in the fact that a certain large country is trying to control a number of smaller countries. When one country tries to control another, the latter will resist without fail. Now two large powers — i.e., the United States and the Soviet Union — are trying to become friends and take over control of the whole world. How can we approve of such a development? "

The territorial question : The head of the delegation of the staff of the Socialist Party on the island of Hokkaido, Tetsuo Ara, asked, " At a time when we were kept in ignorance, the Kuriles were taken away from us in accordance with the Yalta Agreement and the Potsdam Declaration. We demand their return [by the Soviet Union] and, in this connection, would like to hear Chairman Mao's opinion."

The following was said in reply: " There are too many places occupied by the Soviet Union. In accordance with the Yalta Agreement, the Soviet Union, under the pretext of assuring the independence of Mongolia, actually placed the country under its domination. Mongolia takes up an area which is considerably greater than the Kuriles. In 1954, when Khrushchev and Bulganin came to China, we took up this question but they refused to talk to us. They [i.e., the Soviet Union] also appropriated part of Rumania Having cut off a portion of East Germany, they chased the local inhabitants into West Germany. They detached a part of Poland, annexed it to the Soviet Union, and gave a part of East Germany to Poland as compensation. The same thing took place in Finland. The Russians took everything they could. Some people have declared that the Sinkiang area and the territories north of the Amur River must be included in the Soviet Union. The Soviet Union is concentrating troops along its border.

" The Soviet Union has an area of 22 million square kilometers and its population is only 220 million. It is about time to put an end to this allotment. Japan occupies an area of 370,000 square kilometers and its population is 100 million. About a hundred years ago, the area to the east of [Lake] Baikal became Russian territory, and since then Vladivostok, Khabarovsk, Kamchatka, and other areas have been Soviet territory. We have not yet presented our account for this list. In regard to the Kurile Islands, the question is clear as far as we are concerned — they must be returned to Japan."

DOCUMENT 17

Letter of the Central Committee of the CPSU
of July 30, 1964 to the Central Committee
of the CCP

Complete Text

[*Peking Review*, Vol. VII, No. 36 (September 4, 1964), pp. 8–9]

July 30, 1964

To the Central Committee of the Communist Party of China

Dear Comrades!

The Central Committee of the CPSU has sent to all the fraternal Parties its letter of June 15 addressed to the Central Committee of the Communist Party of China. The letter sets our positions on the basic questions connected with the existing differences in the international communist movement, and also advances concrete proposals on measures for strengthening its unity.

Up to the present, an absolute majority of the fraternal Parties have spoken out in favour of the necessity for collective action to overcome the difficulties which have sprung up in our ranks. They advocate the holding of a new international meeting of representatives of the Communist and Workers' Parties, and, moreover, many Parties insist that the convening of the meeting must not be postponed for a long time.

The Central Committee of the CPSU sees in this position taken by the fraternal Parties new evidence of their great concern for the fate of the communist movement and of their awareness of the high responsibility which the current situation imposes on Communists.

Marxist-Leninists cannot shut their eyes to the fact that the differences which sprang up in our ranks four years ago not only have not lost their acuteness but are becoming more and more serious. Ideological differences have grown into open conflict which can lead to a split in the international communist movement if measures are not taken. All this is rather adversely affecting the activities of the Communist Parties, especially those in the capitalist countries, doing harm to the entire world communist movement and undermining the unity of the world socialist system, and it may weaken the attractive force of the ideas of socialism.

More and more facts show that our class enemy is reckoning on making every possible use of the discord in the ranks of the Communists. Imperialist reaction, especially in the U.S.A., is stepping up its activities, striving to strengthen its positions and launch an offensive against the workers' movement, the national liberation movement and the democratic movement, trying to undermine the unity of the socialist countries and intensifying the threat of war.

No genuinely Marxist-Leninist Party can remain indifferent in the face of such developments. No one else can solve the problems confronting the communist movement on behalf of us Communists. No one Party alone is able to undertake the solution of the problems affecting the interests and the fate of the whole movement. Here common collective efforts are essential, by all the fraternal Parties and all Marxist-Leninists. The fraternal Parties have come precisely to these conclusions, in persistently advocating

367

the organization of a new international meeting as the tested method for overcoming differences and working out common positions.

As is known, at the 1957 meeting the fraternal Parties unanimously adopted the following decision: "Entrust the Communist Party of the Soviet Union with the function of convening meetings of the Communist and Workers' Parties in consultation with the fraternal Parties."

Up to the present, necessary consultations have been held, the question of convening an international meeting of the Communist Parties has been discussed in a sufficiently detailed and thorough way, and the positions of all the Communist Parties have become manifest. The job now is to shift the solution of the problem to a practical basis. Taking into consideration the clearly expressed will of the absolute majority of the fraternal Parties, the CC of the CPSU considers that the time is ripe to begin preparatory work for the convening of an international meeting. We hold that, already this year, a drafting committee should be convened. In so far as it has already become clear in the process of preliminary exchange of views that the question of the composition of the drafting committee could become a new obstacle to its convening, we regard as the only reasonable way out the convening of the drafting committee with the same composition with which it worked during the preparations for the 1960 meeting, that is, comprising of the representatives of the Communist and Workers' Parties of the following 26 countries: Australia, Albania, Argentina, Bulgaria, Brazil, Great Britain, Hungary, Viet Nam, the German Democratic Republic, West Germany, India, Indonesia, Italy, the CPR, Korea, Cuba, Mongolia, Poland, Rumania, the USA, Syria, the USSR, Finland, France, Czechoslovakia and Japan.

The CC of the CPSU invites the representatives of the fraternal Parties listed above to come to Moscow by December 15, 1964, so as to start on the practical work of preparation for an international meeting.

Undoubtedly, it would conform to the common wish if the committee could start working with its full membership from the beginning. However, in our opinion, the committee should also begin its work in the case that any of the 26 Communist Parties fails to send its representatives by the appointed time.

In accordance with the experience of past meetings, the drafting committee will prepare drafts of the principal documents to be submitted to the international meeting for discussion. The committee could discuss the whole range of questions concerning the holding of the international meeting and put forward its proposals on them. The drafting committee should send its proposals and recommendations on all these questions to all the fraternal Parties.

The CC of the CPSU expresses the conviction that, despite the complicated situation in the communist movement, there is every ground for the drafting committee to cope with its task successfully. After the committee has accomplished the necessary preparatory work, the international meeting should be convened at the time set by the committee.

On the aims and perspectives of the meeting, the CC of the CPSU has stated its views in its letter of June 15. We want to stress once again that for us the question of the meeting is inseparably linked up with the problem of preserving and strengthening the unity of the world communist movement. The meeting will be called not to condemn anybody, to " excommunicate " anybody from the communist movement and the socialist camp, to attach insulting labels, or to throw irresponsible charges at each other — this would lead only to further divisions, and not to the strengthening of unity. We consider that the meeting should concentrate its efforts on finding out the things in common which unite all the fraternal Parties, and on seeking ways to overcome the existing differences.

In the opinion of the CC of the CPSU, each fraternal Party could state its viewpoint at the meeting in a frank and matter-of-fact way, so that its viewpoint can be considered in working out the common line and joint decisions, and it should also listen to the opinions of other Parties.

Apparently, the starting point of the work of the new meeting will be the decisions of the previous meetings — the Declaration of 1957 and the Statement of 1960 in which the general line of the world communist movement was laid down. At the same time, reaffirming the principles of the Declaration and the Statement, the new meeting might sum up the past stage, exchange experiences, go over the whole complex of problems confronting world communism, and, in accordance with the shifts that have taken place in the international situation, enrich and develop the ideas of the Declaration and the Statement and creatively consider and solve new problems. Collectively to analyse the new economic and socio-political phenomena and processes which have occurred in the past four years since the last international meeting, to co-ordinate appraisals and positions and to enrich and concretize the common political line accordingly — this, in our opinion, is the most important task of the new international meeting.

Like other fraternal Parties, the CPSU fully realizes that the holding of the meeting in a situation in which there are acute differences is a difficult and complicated matter. It is possible that in the course of the meeting unanimity may not be reached on all questions at once, however hard all the consistent supporters of unity may strive to do so. Nevertheless, we are deeply convinced that this, too, would not mean the "formalization" of the split or the creation of obstacles to the further seeking of ways to unity. In that case, it should be possible to try to reach agreement that the participants of the meeting should undertake the obligation to take account of the opinions of all the fraternal Parties, conscientiously co-operate in those fields in which common positions and interests are found, and refrain in the future from any actions which aggravate the difficulties and only gladden the class enemies.

We hope that all the fraternal Parties will consider these proposals with due attention, make use of the time before the convening of the meeting to make a profound study of the situation that has arisen in the communist movement and make constructive contributions to the discussion and the search for ways to overcome the difficulties.

It is our deep conviction that there are no insurmountable obstacles to the international meeting starting its work as soon as drafts of documents are prepared by the drafting committee — about the middle of 1965. The representatives of all the 81 Parties which participated in the meeting of 1960 may take part in the international meeting. The refusal of this or that Party to join in this collective work cannot serve as a ground for further delays in carrying out measures for which the time has matured with the aim of working out ways and means of strengthening the international unity of the Marxist-Leninists of the whole world.

Being convinced that the above proposals conform to the highest interests of world communism and to the interests of strengthening the solidarity of all the progressive and revolutionary forces of our times, and that these proposals express the will of the absolute majority of the Marxist-Leninist parties, the CC of the CPSU expects that the proposed measures will be carried out in good time and be crowned with success.

In order to enable us to keep all the fraternal Parties informed of the preparatory work for the meeting, we request you to communicate to us the composition of your delegation to take part in the work of the drafting committee.

With communist greetings,

The Central Committee of
the Communist Party of the Soviet Union

DOCUMENT 18

CCP Central Committee's Reply to the CPSU
Central Committee's Letter of July 30th, 1964
(August 30, 1964)

Complete Text

[*Peking Review*, Vol. VII, No. 36 (September 4, 1964), pp. 6–7]
August 30, 1964

The Central Committee of the Communist
Party of the Soviet Union

Dear Comrades,

The Central Committee of the Communist Party of China has received the letter of the Central Committee of the Communist Party of the Soviet Union dated July 30, 1964. Completely ignoring the desire of many fraternal Parties for unity and their opposition to a split, your letter slams the door tight against consultations on the question of convening an international meeting of the fraternal Parties and issues the order for an open split in the international communist movement.

We pointed out in our letter to you of July 28 this year that " you are determined to prepare and call a meeting arbitrarily, unilaterally and illegally with the aim of effecting an open split in the international communist movement " and that " you have laid down a revisionist political programme and a divisive organizational line for an international meeting of the fraternal Parties." We stated, " You have premeditated everything: what kind of meeting it is to be, who should prepare it, who should take part in it and who should convene it — on all these questions you claim the last word. To you, all the fraternal Parties are mere puppets qualified only to move at your command." We also explained the consequences to you, pointing out that in calling a small schismatic gathering which is against communism, against the people and against the revolution you would wilfully take the road to your doom, and we sincerely advised you to rein in on the brink of the precipice.

In your letter of July 30, you pay no heed whatsoever to our letter of July 28. You also turn a deaf ear to the recent appeals of many fraternal Parties opposing the calling of a hasty schismatic meeting.

370

In your letter you arbitrarily lay it down that a drafting committee shall be convened without the prior attainment of unanimous agreement through bilateral and multilateral talks by the Chinese and Soviet Parties and all the other fraternal Parties concerned. The members of the drafting committee must be the 26 Parties you have designated, no more and no less, and there is no room for any discussion on this question. Every member Party of the drafting committee must immediately submit to you a list of its delegates who must report in Moscow before December 15 without fail.

You even decide before the convening of your appointed drafting committee that an international meeting shall be held in the middle of next year.

Furthermore, you have the effrontery to declare in your letter that, whether or not the fraternal Parties participate, the drafting committee you have designated shall open shop as scheduled and the international meeting unilaterally called by you shall begin on the date prescribed.

Thus the day in December 1964 on which you convene your drafting committee will go down in history as the day of the great split in the international communist movement.

You have used many fine words in your letter in order to deceive public opinion. You say that your purpose in calling an international meeting is to " preserve " and " strengthen " unity and not to effect a split. If that were so, then at least the procedures and steps for preparing and convening an international meeting of the fraternal Parties should be decided by unanimous agreement among all the fraternal Parties of the world through bilateral or multilateral talks in accordance with the principle of consultation on an equal footing. But completely violating the principle of achieving unanimity through consultation among the fraternal Parties, ignoring the views of fraternal Parties opposed to a hurried meeting, and not caring whether or not the fraternal Parties participate, you are determined to call a meeting. Is there the least desire for unity in all this? Is it not clear that you are working for a split?

You say that in calling the international meeting you want to seek " things in common which unite all the fraternal Parties." This is a whopping lie. The fraternal Parties do indeed have things in common — they are the revolutionary principles of the Declaration of 1957 and the Statement of 1960. But you have long since thrown these things in common overboard and are proceeding further and further down the road of revisionism. So far from showing any desire to renounce your revisionist line, you now insist on forcing it on the international meeting. In these circumstances, what is there in common between yourselves and the world's Marxist-Leninists?

Today, the most urgent common task before the Communists and revolutionary people of the world is to oppose U.S. imperialism and its lackeys. But you are bent on colluding with the U.S. imperialists and on seeking common ground uniting you with them. You have repeatedly indicated to U.S. imperialism that you want to disengage from all fronts of struggle against it. When U.S. imperialism recently launched its armed aggression against a fraternal socialist country, the Democratic Republic of Viet Nam, not only did you fail to declare explicit support for Viet Nam in its struggle against U.S. aggression, but you even aided and abetted the aggressor by actively supporting the U.S. attempt to intervene in Viet Nam through the United Nations. While you pursue this anti-communist, anti-popular and anti-revolutionary line, how can the Marxist-Leninists reach any agreement to take any common action with you?

Moreover, you are using every kind of threat to intimidate other fraternal Parties as well as us. In fact, you are banking on your subversion and disruption of fraternal Parties through your collusion with the imperialists and reactionaries and through your employment of Right-wing social democrats, Trotskyites, defectors and renegades. These activities of yours are nothing to be afraid of; you have already done more than enough in this line. The more you act in this way, the more things will develop contrary to your wish. It is beyond your power to subvert or disrupt the fraternal Parties upholding Marxism-Leninism. On the contrary, in the struggle against you they will grow in staunchness and in numbers. Your contemptible activities will only further reveal your true features as betrayers of the revolution. "How can ants topple the giant tree?" Taken together, the imperialists, the reactionaries and the revisionists are a mere handful whom history will discard.

Concerning the preparation and convening of an international meeting and its composition, we have repeatedly said that it is necessary to achieve unanimity of views through consultation among all the fraternal Parties, including the old ones and those rebuilt or newly founded. Otherwise, no matter what drafting committee or international meeting you convene, it will be illegal.

We will never be taken in by your fine words, never submit to your threats, never be accomplices in your divisive activities and never share with you the responsibility for splitting the international communist movement. If we were to take part in your schismatic meeting, it would be tantamount to legalizing your illegal activities, to recognizing your right to destroy the principles guiding relations among fraternal Parties as laid down in the Declaration and the Statement, and to accepting the CPSU as a patriarchal father Party. Naturally we will never act in this way, for we hold ourselves bound by principles and responsible to history.

Here we reiterate the stand of the Central Committee of the Communist Party of China as stated in our letter to the Central Committee of the CPSU dated July 28, 1964:

" The Communist Party of China persists in its stand for an international meeting of the fraternal Parties for unity on the basis of Marxism-Leninism, to be held after ample preparations, and we are firmly opposed to your schismatic meeting.

" The Central Committee of the CCP solemnly declares : We will never take part in any international meeting or any preparatory meeting for it, which you call for the purpose of splitting the international communist movement."

In unilaterally deciding to convene a drafting committee in December this year and an international meeting in the middle of next year, you must be held responsible for all the consequences of openly splitting the international communist movement.

Together with all the fraternal Marxist-Leninist Parties and all the Marxist-Leninists of the world, the Communist Party of China is determined to raise still higher the revolutionary banner of Marxism-Leninism, the banner of unity based on proletarian internationalism and the militant banner of anti-imperialism, and is determined to carry to the end the struggle against your revisionism, your splittism and your capitulationism.

We have already warned you that the day you call a schismatic meeting will be the day you step into your grave. Your letter of July 30 shows that, disregarding all consequences, you have taken another long step towards this grave of your own digging. At this critical juncture, we hope you will weigh the pros and cons and choose carefully between continuing on the road to doom and turning back to safety.

With fraternal greetings,

The Central Committee of the
Communist Party of China

DOCUMENT 19

Togliatti Memorandum
(September 4, 1964)

Complete Text

[*L'Unità*, September 4, 1964, quoted from *The New York Times*, September 5, 1965]

ROME, Sept. 4 — Following is the text of a memorandum on world Communist problems prepared in Yalta before his death last month by Palmiro Togliatti, secretary general of the Italian Communist party, as translated from the Italian, with an introduction by Luigi Longo, his successor:

Introduction

The memorandum that we publish on the problems of the international workers and Communist movement and its unity was concluded by Comrade Togliatti a few hours before he was struck down by the fatal illness that ended his life.

The text was to be typed while Comrade Togliatti went to Artek to visit the International Pioneers Camp. On his return he had intended to revise the typewritten manuscript.

It is known that Comrade Togliatti composed his writings with great security of expression and in a clear and precise language, without, or with very few corrections, at the most additions made in the margin. Also in his last document one is struck by this quality.

It is a testimony that, up to the very last moment, Comrade Togliatti was working in a vigorous and lucid manner. Nothing presages the coming of the atrocious illness that prevented Comrade Togliatti from looking through once again, as he had intended, his memorandum.

But we believe, also without this final revision, that we can regard the text left to us as the precise expression of his thoughts on the problems it deals with. The direction Political Committee of our party took cognizance with deep emotion of the document prepared by Comrade Togliatti.

It recognised that " in it are repeated with great clarity the views of our party regarding the present situation of the international Communist movement " and adopted it as its own.

We are therefore publishing the memorandum of Comrade Togliatti as a precise expression of the position of the party on the problems of the international workers and Communist movement and its unity.

Memorandum

The letter from the Soviet Communist party, with the invitation to the [December] preparatory meeting for the international [Communist] conference, reached Rome a few days before my departure. We have therefore not had the possibility of examining it at a joint meeting of the Direction (Political Committee), also because of the absence of many comrades.

We could only have a rapid exchange of ideas between some comrades of the Secretariat. The letter will be submitted to the Central Committee of the party, which is to meet in mid-September. Nevertheless, it remains clear we shall take part, and take part actively, in the preparatory meeting.

However, we retain our doubts and reservations on the opportuneness of the international conference, above all because it is now clear that a not to be ignored number of parties will not be present, apart from the Chinese party.

In this preparatory meeting, there will undoubtedly be offered the possibility for us to expound and motivate our views, also because they affect a whole series of problems of the international workers and Communist movement.

I shall make a short reference to these problems in this memorandum, also with the aim of facilitating further exchanges of ideas with you whenever this will be possible.

On the Best Way to Combat the Chinese Positions

The plan we had proposed for an effective struggle against the erroneous political lines and against the splitting activity of the Chinese Communists was different from that effectively followed. In substance, our plan was based on these points:

Never to interrupt the polemic against the positions of principle and the the political views of the Chinese.

To conduct the polemic, contrary to what the Chinese do, without verbal exacerbations and without generic condemnations, on concrete themes, in an objective and persuasive manner and always with a certain respect for the adversary.

At the same time to proceed by groups of parties to a series of meetings for a profound examination and a better definition of the tasks presenting themselves today in the different sectors of our movement (western Europe, the countries of Latin America, the countries of the third world and their contacts with the Communist movement of the capitalist countries, the countries of popular democracy, etc.).

This work should have taken place taking into account that, since 1957 and since 1960, the situation in all these sectors has seriously altered and that, without a careful collective elaboration, it is not possible to arrive at a correct definition of the common tasks of our movement.

Only after this preparation, which could take a year or more of work, could one have examined the question of an international conference that could truly be a new stage for our movement, its effective strengthening on new and correct lines. In this way we would also have been able better to isolate the Chinese Communists, to face them with a more compact front, united not only through the use of common general definitions of the Chinese line, but also because of a more profound knowledge of the common tasks of the entire movement and those concretely facing each one of its sectors.

Furthermore, once the tasks and our political line had been well-defined, sector by sector, one could also have renounced the international conference, if this were to appear necessary, in order to avoid a formal split.

Policy Questioned

A different line was pursued and I do not consider the results as altogether beneficial. Some (possibly also many) parties were expecting a conference to be convened within a short period in order to pronounce an explicit and solemn condemnation, valid for the entire movement. Their expectation may also have disorientated them.

In the meantime, the Chinese attack has been widely developed and thus their action to establish small splinter groups and to win some parties for their viewpoint. One has replied to their general attack through an ideological and propagandist polemic, not through a development of our policy linked to the struggle against the Chinese views.

Some actions have been taken in this latter direction by the Soviet Union (the signing of the Moscow agreement on nuclear tests, the visit of Comrade Khrushchev in Egypt, etc.) and they have been real and important victories obtained over the Chinese.

The Communist movement in other countries has not succeeded, however, in doing anything of this nature. To explain myself better, I am thinking, for instance, of how important would have been an international meeting, convened by some Western Communist parties, with widespread representation from the democratic countries of the "third world" and their progressive movements, in order to elaborate a concrete line of cooperation and of help to these movements. It was a way to combat the Chinese with deeds, not just with words.

In this connection, I consider to be of interest our experience as a party. In the party and on its periphery we have some small groups of comrades and sympathizers tending toward and defending the Chinese views. Some party members have had to be thrown out of our ranks because they were responsible for activity of building factions and of indiscipline.

Concrete Discussions

However, in general we conduct a broad discussion on all theses of the polemic with the Chinese within cell and section meetings and in town groups. One has the most success when one passes from examining general themes (the nature of imperialism and the state, the driving force of the revolution, etc.) to concrete questions of our current policy (struggle against the Government, criticism of the Socialist party, trade-union unity, strikes, etc.). On these themes, the Chinese polemic is completely disarmed and impotent.

From these observations, I draw the conclusion that (even if today one is already working for the international conferences) one must not abandon political initiatives helping to defeat the Chinese positions, that the terrain on which it is most easy to defeat them is that of the judgment of the concrete situation facing us today and the action to solve the problems arising in the individual sectors of our movement, in the individual parties and in the movement in general.

On the Perspectives of the Present Situation

We regard with a certain pessimism the perspectives of the present situation internationally and within our country. The situation is worse than that facing us two or three years ago.

Today there comes a more serious danger from the United States. That country is passing through a profound social crisis. The racial conflict between white and colored people is only one aspect of this crisis. The assassination of Kennedy disclosed what point the attack of the groups could reach.

On cannot under any circumstances exclude the possibility that the Presidential elections may be won by the Republican candidate (Goldwater), who includes war in his program and speaks like a Fascist. The worst is that the offensive he conducts moves increasingly to the right the entire American political front, strengthens the tendency to seek in greater international aggressivity a way out of internal contradictions and to seek the basis for an agreement with the reactionary groups of Western Europe. This makes the general situation somewhat dangerous.

In Western Europe the situation is very differentiated. What prevails, however, as a common factor, is the process of further monopolist concentration with the Common Market as the place and the means.

American economic competition, which is becoming more intense and aggressive, helps to accelerate the process of concentration. Thus are strengthened the objective conditions for a reactionary policy tending to liquidate or limit democratic liberties, to keep alive Fascist regimes, to create authoritarian regimes, to prevent any advance of the working class and sizably to reduce its living standard.

Rivalry and contradictions about international policy are deep. The old organization of NATO is going through an obvious and grave crisis, due specially to [President] de Gaulle's policy. However, one must not have any illusions. There are certain contradictions we can exploit to the full.

Up to now, however, there does not appear within the leading groups of the Continental countries any tendency to develop in an autonomous and coherent fashion an action to lessen tension in international relations.

All these groups then move in one way or another, and to a less or greater degree, on the terrain of neocolonialism in order to prevent the economic and political progress of the newly liberated African states.

'Acute Crises' Possible

Events in Vietnam, events in Cyprus, show how, above all, if the move to the right of the entire situation were to continue, we could suddenly be faced with very acute crises and dangers in which the entire Communist movement and all the working class and Socialist forces of Europe and the entire world would have to be involved.

It is this situation, we believe, that one must take into account in all our conduct toward the Chinese Communists. The unity of all Socialist forces in a common action, going also beyond ideological differences, against the most reactionary imperialist groups, is an indispensable necessity.

One cannot imagine that China or the Chinese Communists could be excluded from this unity. Therefore, from now onward we must behave in such a manner as not to create obstacles to attaining this objective, indeed to facilitating it.

We must not interrupt in any way the polemic, but always have as its point of departure the demonstration, on the basis of the facts of today, that the unity of the entire Socialist world and all the workers and Communist parties is necessary and can be achieved.

As regards the meeting of the preparatory committee on Dec. 15, one could already be thinking about some special initiatives. For example, the sending of a delegation, composed of representatives from several parties, to expound to the Chinese comrades our intention of being united and of collaborating in the struggle against the common enemy, to present to them the problem of finding a way and concrete form for this collaboration.

In addition, one should be considering that if, as we think is necessary, our entire struggle against the Chinese positions must be conducted as a struggle for unity, the resolutions one might adopt must take account of this fact leaving aside the general negative qualifications and having, on the contrary, a strong and prevailing positive and united political content.

On the Development of Our Movement

We have always considered it to be incorrect to give a prevalently optimistic judgement of the workers and Communist movement of the Western countries.

In this part of the world, even if here and there some progress has been achieved, our development and our forces are still today inadequate for the tasks facing them, with the exception of some parties (in France, Italy, Spain, etc.) we have not yet emerged from the situation where the Communists do not succeed in pursuing a real and efficacious political action linking them with the large mass of the workers.

They confine themselves to propaganda work and do not have an effective influence on the political life in their countries. One must try with every means to overcome this phase urging the Communists to overcome their relative isolation, to play an active and continuous role in political and social reality and to take political initiatives, to become an effective mass movement.

Also for this reason, though having always regarded the Chinese views as erroneous and ruinous, we have always had (and retain them) strong reservations on the utility of an international conference dedicated solely, or mainly, to denunciations and to the struggle against these views.

This because we feared (and we fear) that in this manner the Communist parties of the capitalist countries would be pushed into the opposite direction to that necessary, that is, to enclose themselves in internal polemics of a purely ideological nature, far removed from reality.

The danger would become particularly serious if one were to arrive at a declared break within the movement, with the formation of an international Chinese Center which would create its " sections " in all countries. All the parties, and especially the weakest, would be placed in the position of devoting a large part of their activity to the polemic and to the battle against these so-called " sections " of a new " International."

This would create discouragement among the masses and the development of our movement would be gravely impaired. It is true that already today the fractionist efforts of the Chinese are in full swing and in almost all countries. One must prevent the quantity of these efforts becoming quality, that is, a real, general and consolidated split.

Objectively, there exists very favourable conditions for our advance in the working class, among the working masses and in social life in general. But it is necessary to know how to take advantage of, and exploit, these conditions. For this the Communists must have much political courage ; they must overcome every form of dogmatism, face and resolve new problems in a new manner. They must use working methods suitable for a political and social ambient continually and rapidly changing.

New Policies Advocated

Very briefly I shall give some examples.

The crisis in the economic bourgeois world is very profound. Within the system of state monopoly capitalism quite new problems are emerging that the dominant classes no longer succeed in resolving with traditional methods.

In particular, there arises today in the largest countries the question of a centralization of economic direction, which one tries to bring about through planning from above in the interests of the large monopolies and through state intervention. This problem is on the order of the day in the entire West, and already there is talk of international planning on which the leading Common Market bodies are working.

It is clear that the workers and Democratic movement cannot be indifferent to this question. One must also fight on this terrain. This demands a development and coordination of the workers' immediate demands and of the proposals for economic structural reforms (nationalization, land reform, etc.) within a general plan of economic development to counterpose to capitalist planning. Certainly this will not yet be a Socialist plan because conditions for this are lacking, but it is a new form and a new means of struggle for advancing towards Socialism.

The possibility of a peaceful way of this advance is today closely linked to the way this problem is presented and solved. A political initiative in this direction can help us to acquire a new, large degree of influence over all strata of the population not yet won over for Socialism, but who are seeking a new path.

Realities Emphasized

Within this framework the struggle for democracy must assume a different content from that it has hitherto had. It must be more concrete, more linked to the reality of economic and social life. In fact, capitalist planning is always linked with antidemocratic and authoritarian tendencies, which it is necessary to counter through the adoption of a democratic method, also in the direction of economic life.

As the attempts at capitalist planning mature, so the trade unions' position becomes more difficult. An essential part of planning, in fact, is the so-called income policy, consisting of a series of measures designed to prevent the free development of the wage struggle with a system of control from above of the wage levels and the ban on their increase beyond a certain limit.

It is a policy designed to fail (of interest is the example of Holland), but it can fail only if the unions know how to comport themselves with decision and intelligence, linking also their immediate demands with the demands for economic reforms and with a plan of economic development corresponding to the interests of the workers and the middle class.

Isolation Deplored

In present-day conditions in the West the unions' struggle, however, can no longer be conducted in an isolated fashion, country by country. It must also be developed at the international level, with common demands and actions. And here is one of the most serious Lacunae of our movement.

Our international trade-union movement (WFTU) only conducts general propaganda. Up to now it has not taken any effective initiative for united action against the policy of the large monopolies. What has hitherto been lacking is our initiative toward the other international trade-union organizations, and this is a serious error because in these organizations there are already those who criticize and try to oppose the proposals and policies of the large monopolies.

But there are, beyond these, many other areas where we can and must act with greater courage, eradicating outmoded formulas no longer corresponding to present-day reality.

In the organized Catholic world and among the mass of the Catholics there was a clear move to the left during the time of Pope John. At the base, however, there persists the conditions and the pressure for a move to the left which we must understand and assist. For this purpose the old atheist propaganda is of no use.

"Hypocrisy" on Religion

The very problem of religious conscience, its content and its roots among the masses, how to overcome it, must be presented in a different manner from the past if we wish to reach the Catholic masses and to be understood by them. Otherwise our " stretched-out hand " to the Catholics would be regarded as pure expediency and almost as hypocrisy.

Also today in the world of culture (literature, art, scientific research, etc.) the doors are wide open for Communist penetration. In the capitalist world, in fact, such conditions are being created as to tend to destroy the liberty of intellectual life. We must become the champions of liberty of intellectual life, of free artistic creation and of scientific progress.

This requires that we do not counterpose in an abstract manner our conceptions to trends and currents of a different nature. But let us initiate a discussion with these currents and thus make effort to deepen the discussion on the cultural themes as they exist today.

Not all those who, in the various sections of culture, in philosophy, in historical and social science, are today far from us, are our enemies or agents of our enemy. It is reciprocal understanding, attained through a continual discussion, that gives us authority and prestige and, at the same

379

time, enables us to reveal the true enemies, the false thinkers, the charlatans of artistic expression and so on.

Communist Inaction Noted

In this area, much assistance could come to us, but it has not always arrived from the countries where we already direct the entire social life.

For reasons of brevity I shall not touch on many other subjects that could be mentioned.

On the whole we take as a starting point — and we are still convinced that one must depart from this — for the elaboration of our policy the lines of the 20th [Soviet party] congress. However, these lines must today be more elaborated and developed.

For instance, there must be deeper reflection on the theme of the possibility of a peaceful road of access to Socialism. This leads us to make clear what we understand by democracy in a bourgeois state, how one can extend the limits of liberty and of democratic institutions, and what are the most effective forms of participation for the working masses and the workers in economic and political life.

Thus arises the question of the possibility of the conquest of positions of power by the working class within a state that has not changed its character as a bourgeois state, and, therefore, whether the struggle for a progressive transformation of this nature, from within, is possible.

Sharpening of Struggle

In countries where the Communist movement is becoming strong, such as in our country (and in France), this is the basic question that today arises in the political struggle. This leads, naturally, to a sharpening of this struggle and on it depends the further perspectives.

Undoubtedly, an international conference can help toward a better solution of these problems, but essentially the task of going deeper into them and resolving them is up to the individual parties. One might even be apprehensive that the adoption of rigid, general formulas could be a hindrance.

It is my opinion that, on the line of the present historical development and its general perspectives (the advance and victory of Socialism in the whole world), the concrete forms and conditions for the advance and victory of Socialism will today and in the immediate future be very different from those of the past.

At the same time, the diversities between one country and the other are rather great. That is why every party must know how to act in an autonomous manner. The autonomy of parties, of which we are decisive champions, is not just an internal necessity for our movement but an essential condition for our development under present conditions.

Therefore, we would be against any proposal to create once again a centralized international organization. We are firm supporters of the unity of our movement and of the international workers movement, but this unity must be achieved in the diversity of our concrete political positions, conforming to the situation and degree of development in each country.

Danger of Isolation

There is naturally the danger of the isolation of the parties, one from another, and, therefore, of a certain confusion. One must fight against these dangers and, for this reason, we believe the following methods should be adopted: rather frequent contacts and exchange of experiences among the parties on a broad scale, convocation of collective meetings dedicated to studying common problems by a certain group of parties, international study meetings on general problems of economy, philosophy, history, etc.

In addition to this, we are in favor of there being discussions, also of a public nature and on themes of common interest, between single parties in a way to interest entire public opinion. This naturally requires that the debate be conducted in a correct manner, with objective argumentation, and not with the vulgarity and violence adopted by the Albanians and the Chinese.

Relations With the Movements in Colonial and Former Colonial Nations

We attribute a decisive importance for the development of our movement to the establishment of broad relations of reciprocal knowledge and collaboration between the Communist parties of the capitalist countries and the liberation movements of colonial and ex-colonial countries. However, these relations must not be created only with the Communist parties of these countries, but with all the forces struggling for independence and against imperialism, and also, as far as is possible, with governmental circles of newly liberated countries having a progressive government.

The aim should be to arrive at the elaboration of a common, concrete program against imperialism and colonialism. Contemporaneously, we must deepen further our research into the problem of the paths of development of formerly colonial countries, what the objective of Socialism means for them, and so on.

It is a question of new subjects, hitherto not faced. For this, as I have already stated, we would have welcomed with pleasure an international meeting completely dedicated to these problems. And, in any case, one will have to dedicate ever-increasing attention to them in all our work.

Problems of the Socialist World

I believe one can declare, without fearing to err, that the unbridled and shameful campaign of the Chinese and Albanians against the Soviet Union, against the CPSU [Communist Party of the Soviet Union], its leaders and, in particular, against Comrade Khrushchev, has not had among the masses results worthy of great note, despite its being exploited to the full by bourgeois and governmental propaganda, the authority and prestige of the Soviet Union, its leaders and, masses remain enormous. The crude Chinese calumnies (that the Soviet Union was becoming bourgeois, etc.) have not taken hold. On the other hand, there is some perplexity on the question of the recall of the Soviet technicians from China.

What preoccupies the masses and also (at least in our country) a by no means small proportion of Communists is the fact in itself of such an acute clash between two countries that have become Socialist through the victory of two great revolutions. That fact brings under discussion the very principles of Socialism, and we must make a great effort to explain what are the historical and political conditions of the parties and personalities that have contributed to creating the present-day difference and conflict.

To this one must add that in Italy there exist large areas inhabited by poor peasants among whom the Chinese revolution became rather popular as a peasants' revolution. This forces the party to discuss the Chinese views, to criticize and reject them, also in public meeting. On the contrary, nobody pays any attention to the Albanians, even if we have in the south some ethnic groups whose language is Albanian.

Problems of Socialism

Beyond the conflict with the Chinese there are, however, other problems of the Socialist world to which we ask that attention be paid.

It is not correct to refer to the Socialist countries (including the Soviet Union) as if everything were always going well in them. This is the mistake, for instance, in that section of the 1960 declaration dealing with these countries. In fact, there continually arise in all the Socialist countries difficulties, contradictions and new problems that must be presented in their effective reality.

The worst is to give the impression that everything is always going well, while suddenly we find ourselves faced with the necessity of referring to difficult situations and explaining them.

But it is not merely a matter of single events. It is the entire problem of the Socialist economic structure and policy which, in the West, is known in a far too summary manner and often also in an elementary fashion. There is a lack of knowledge about the differences in the situation between the different countries, the various methods of planning and their progressive transformation, of the methods adopted and the difficulties, arising about economic integration among the various countries, and so on.

Open Debates Suggested

Some situations appear hard to understand. In many cases one has the impression there are differences of opinion among the leading groups, but one does not understand if this is really so and what the differences are. Perhaps it could be useful in some cases for the Socialist countries also to conduct open debates on current problems, the leaders also taking part. Certainly, this would contribute to a growth in the authority and prestige of the Socialist regime itself.

The criticism of Stalin, there is no need to hide this, has left rather deep traces. The most serious thing is a certain degree of scepticism with which also some of those close to us greet reports of new economic and political successes.

Beyond this must be considered in general as unresolved the problem of the origin of the cult of Stalin and how this became possible. To explain this solely through Stalin's serious personal defects is not completely accepted.

There is an attempt to investigate what could have been the political errors that contributed to giving rise to the cult. This debate is taking place among historians and qualified cadres of the party.

We do not discourage it because it helps toward a more profound awareness of the history of the revolution and its difficulties. However, we advise prudence in coming to conclusions and the taking into account of publication and research in the Soviet Union.

Restraints Denounced

The problem that claims greater attention, one affecting as much the Soviet Union as the other Socialist countries, however, is today, especially that of overcoming the regime of restrictions and suppression of democratic and personal freedom introduced by Stalin.

Not all the Socialist countries present the same picture. The general impression is that of a slowness and resistance in returning to the Leninist norms that insured, within the party and outside it, a wide liberty of expression and debate on culture, art and also on politics.

This slowness and resistance is for us difficult to explain, above all in consideration of the present conditions when there is no longer capitalist encirclement and economic construction has had tremendous successes.

We always start from the idea that Socialism is the regime in which there is the widest freedom for the workers, that they in fact participate in an organized manner in the direction of the entire social life. Therefore, we greet all positions of principle and all facts showing us that this is the reality in all the Socialist countries and not only in the Soviet Union. On the other hand, events that sometimes disclose the contrary to us damage the entire movement.

Revival of Nationalism

A fact worrying us and one we do not succeed in explaining fully is the manifestation among the Socialist countries of a centrifical tendency. In this lies an evident and serious danger with which the Soviet comrades should concern themselves.

Without doubt there is a revival of nationalism. However, we know that the national sentiment remains a permanent factor in the working class and Socialist movement for a long period, also after the conquest of power.

Economic progress does not dispel this, it nurtures it. Also in the Socialist camp perhaps (I underline this perhaps because many concrete facts are unknown to us) one needs to be on one's guard against the forced exterior uniformity and one must consider that the unity one ought to establish and maintain lies in the diversity and full autonomy of the individual countries.

In conclusion, we consider that also as regards the Socialist countries one needs the courage to face with a critical spirit many situations and many problems if one wishes to create the basis for a better comprehension and a closer unity of our entire movement.

On the Italian Situation

I ought to add many things to give exact information on the situation in our country. But these notes are already too long and I ask to be excused for this. It is better to deal with matters exclusively Italian through verbal explanations and information.

383

DOCUMENT 20

47th Anniversary of the Great October Socialist Revolution : Report by Comrade L. I. Brezhnev at Formal Meeting in Kremlin Palace of Congresses, November 6, 1964

Excerpts

[*Pravda and Izvestiya*, November 7, 1964, pp. 1–3, quoted from *CDSP*, Vol. XVI, No. 43 (November 18, 1964), pp. 3–9, at pp. 6–7 and 9]

The Banner of October Is the Banner of Struggle for Peace and Socialism

Comrades!

The birth of the first socialist state in the world signified the birth of a new policy in international affairs. Socialism, peace, freedom for peoples — such were the slogans that October inscribed on its banners. The Communist Party and the entire Soviet people are faithful to the cause and ideas of the October Revolution.

The foreign policy of the Soviet state stems from its socialist nature, from the noble goals and tasks set by our party and people. This policy was founded by the great Lenin.

Today the frontiers of the struggle for peace, democracy, national independence and socialism pass through all the continents ; imperialism is losing one position after another. The chief achievement in this struggle has been the creation of the world system of socialism. And in this lies one of the most important results of the revolutionary transformation of the world begun by Great October. (*Prolonged applause.*)

The Communist Party of the Soviet Union and the entire Soviet people are guided in relations with the socialist countries by the principles of socialist internationalism, the desire to strengthen fraternal friendship, cooperation and mutual understanding on the basis of complete equality, independence and the correct combination of the interests of each country with the interests of the whole commonwealth. (*Applause.*)

Our country is celebrating its 47th year. This year other socialist countries celebrated their 20th or 15th anniversary. Heroic Cuba took the socialist path quite recently. (*Applause.*) We are deeply convinced that new and memorable dates, marking the entry of other countries and peoples into our common socialist family, will appear on the calendar of history. (*Applause.*) But no matter what length of experience one or another country may possess in socialist construction, the world socialist system is a social, economic and political commonwealth of free and equal peoples. (*Prolonged applause.*)

As far back as 1920 Lenin, outlining the path for ensuring the fraternal alliance of the working people of different nations that had cast off the imperialist yoke, pointed to the need for basing the relations among them on the fullest trust, on clear awareness of fraternal unity, on entirely voluntary assent. " Such an alliance," wrote V. I. Lenin, " cannot be brought about immediately ; it must be attained with the greatest patience and care, so as not to spoil matters, so as not to arouse distrust, so as to allow the distrust left by centuries of oppression by landowners and capitalists to be outlived." *

In the relations among the sovereign states constituting the world system of socialism, the application of this Leninist behest acquires even greater importance.

All the objective conditions exist for the cooperation of socialist countries to become increasingly stronger. Our peoples are united by a community of fundamental interests; we have the same type of economic foundation — public ownership of the means of production. We have the same type of state system — rule by the people, headed by the working class. We have a single ideology — Marxism-Leninism. We have common interests in ensuring security, in safeguarding the peace and security of peoples, in defending revolutionary gains from the imperialists' encroachments. We have a single great goal — communism. (*Stormy, prolonged applause.*)

The attention given by each socialist country to the experience of building the new society in other countries is understandable. At the same time, we consider that it would be wrong to force the experience of any one party and country on other parties and countries. The choice of various methods, forms and means of socialist construction is the sovereign right of each people.

We proceed from the fact that individuality in ways of building socialism should by no means hinder the development of friendly relations among the fraternal socialist countries. The correctness of this or that point of view on specific questions of socialist construction should, it seems to us, be tested in deed, by the effectiveness of the results achieved in building the new society.

The family of socialist states, which have forever taken leave of capitalism and are building a new, happy life for people of labor, is great and mighty. The world of socialism has spread for many thousands of kilometers across the boundless expanses of Europe and Asia. A center of socialism has arisen on the American continent also. Socialism serves as an inspiring example for the peoples of many countries of Africa. The influence that the socialist world exerts on the entire course of man's history is becoming stronger and more tangible with each passing day.

Allow me, comrades, from this festive platform, on the eve of a day of celebration dear to the heart of every Soviet person, to declare: The Communist Party of the Soviet Union and our government consider it their sacred duty to do everything necessary to strengthen the solidarity of the socialist countries on the reliable foundation of Marxism-Leninism and proletarian internationalism. (*Stormy, prolonged applause.*) This is called for by the interests of the most successful building of socialism and communism in each of our countries. This is called for by the interests of the victory of our great common cause throughout the globe.

May the friendship and solidarity of the countries of socialism grow stronger! (*Stormy, prolonged applause.*)

.   .   .   .

The general course of the foreign policy of the Soviet Union, determined by the decisions of the latest Congresses of our party, by its Program, is consistent and unchanging. This is the course of ensuring peaceful

* *Complete Collected Works*, Vol. XL, p. 43.

conditions for the construction of socialism and communism, of ensuring the unity and solidarity of the socialist countries, their friendship and brotherhood, a course of supporting liberating revolutionary movements, of comprehensive development of solidarity and cooperation with the independent states of Asia, Africa and Latin America, of affirming the principles of peaceful coexistence with capitalist states, of ridding mankind of world wars. Such a course is the only true one. Our people and the overwhelming majority of the population of our planet approve it completely. (*Prolonged applause.*)

Comrades! Our Leninist party has always held high this banner of proletarian internationalism. We see the unity of the international Communist and workers' movement, the solidarity of the national-liberation and democratic forces, as the guarantee of new successes of the cause of peace and socialism.

The Communist movement is tempered in fierce battles with imperialist reaction, in the struggle for peace, national independence, democracy, for the triumph of the ideas of socialism. In the countries of capital, the Communist Parties have been and are being hounded and persecuted. But despite all difficulties, they hold high the revolutionary banner of Marxism-Leninism. By their deeds they show the working people the vital force of their ideas. The glorious names of Communist heroes who have given their lives in the struggle for freedom live in the memory of the peoples, summoning them to new feats. (*Applause.*)

On the day of the great October holiday our party and the entire Soviet people send ardent greetings to and express solidarity with and support for all the fraternal Communist Parties. (*Stormy applause.*)

Our enemies are trying to weaken the Communist movement. They would like to take advantage of the differences that have arisen in it in order to harm the revolutionary forces. In these circumstances, the task of rallying and strengthening the unity of the world Communist movement takes on particular significance. To accomplish it, concrete, effective measures are needed, it is necessary to go step by step along the path of cohesion. It cannot be permitted that the differences of views that have manifested themselves should undermine the chief thing in which the Communists are strong — unity in the struggle with the common enemy, imperialism. (*Applause.*) To settle the problems that concern the whole movement is the cause of all the fraternal parties.

The world army of Communists has a precise and clear general line, worked out jointly at the Moscow conferences of 1957 and 1960. (*Prolonged applause.*)

The Communists have an effective method of overcoming differences of opinion that arise among the parties and strengthening solidarity. The Statement of 81 parties, adopted in 1960, states this clearly. It says: " The Communist and Workers' Parties hold conferences whenever necessary to discuss urgent problems, to exchange experience, to acquaint themselves with one another's views and positions, to work out common views through consultations, and to coordinate joint actions in the struggle for common goals." *

It seems to us that a better method of strengthening the solidarity of the world Communist movement cannot be found. (*Prolonged applause.*)

* *Current Digest of the Soviet Press*, Vol. XII, No. 49, p. 7.

The need for a new international conference of fraternal parties has obviously matured. And the purpose of such a conference, its chief motto, should be — solidarity on the basis of the principles of Marxism-Leninism and proletarian internationalism, unity of fellow Communists in the struggle for our common great goals. (*Stormy applause.*)

The Communist Party of the Soviet Union will do everything that depends upon it to achieve such solidarity. (*Stormy, prolonged applause.*)

May the great movement of the Communists of the whole world broaden and grow stronger with each day, drawing new forces from strengthening its unity, winning new successes in the struggle with imperialism, for a happy future for all people of labor! (*Prolonged applause.*)

.   .   .   .

DOCUMENT 21

Why Khrushchev Fell

(November 21, 1964)

Complete Text

[Editorial, *Hung Ch'i*, Nos. 21–22, November 21, 1964, *Peking Review*, Vol. VII, No. 48 (November 27, 1964), pp. 6–9 ; also in *The Polemic on the General Line of the International Communist Movement*, pp. 481–492]

Khrushchev has fallen.

This arch-schemer who usurped the leadership of the Soviet Party and state, this Number One representative of modern revisionism, has finally been driven off the stage of history.

This is a very good thing and is advantageous to the revolutionary cause of the people of the world.

The collapse of Khrushchev is a great victory for the Marxist-Leninists of the world in their persistent struggle against revisionism. It marks the bankruptcy, the fiasco, of modern revisionism.

How was it that Khrushchev fell? Why couldn't he muddle on any longer?

This question has aroused different comments from different political groups all over the world.

The imperialists, the reactionaries, and the opportunists and revisionists of all shades, whether they sympathize with Khrushchev or have had conflicts of interest with him, have expressed varied views on the sudden collapse of this seemingly " strong man," Khrushchev.

Many Communist and Workers' Parties have also published articles or documents expressing their opinion on Khrushchev's downfall.

In the present article we too would like to discuss the question of Khrushchev's downfall.

For Marxist-Leninists, this downfall is not something which is hard to understand. Indeed, it may be said to have been fully expected. Marxist-Leninists had long forseen that Khrushchev would come to such an end.

People may list hundreds or even thousands of charges against Khrushchev to account for his collapse. But the most important one of all is that he has vainly tried to obstruct the advance of history, flying in the face of the law of historical development as discovered by Marxism-Leninism and of the revolutionary will of the people of the Soviet Union and the whole world. Any obstacle on the people's road of advance must be removed. The people were sure to reject Khrushchev, whether he and his kind liked it or not. Khrushchev's downfall is the inevitable result of the anti-revisionist struggle waged staunchly by the people of the Soviet Union and revolutionary people throughout the world.

Ours is an epoch in which world capitalism and imperialism are moving to their doom and socialism and communism are marching towards victory. The historic mission this epoch has placed on the people is to bring the proletarian world revolution step by step to complete victory and establish a new world without imperialism, without capitalism and without the exploitation of man by man through their own efforts and in the light of the concrete conditions of their respective countries. This is the inexorable trend of historical development and the common demand of the revolutionary people of the world. This historical trend is an objective law which operates independently of man's will, and it is irresistible. But Khrushchev, this buffoon on the contemporary political stage, chose to go against this trend in the vain hope of turning the wheel of history back on to the old capitalist road and of thus prolonging the life of the moribund exploiting classes and their moribund system of exploitation.

Khrushchev collected all the anti-Marxist views of history's opportunists and revisionists and out of them knocked together a full-fledged revisionist line consisting of "peaceful coexistence," "peaceful competition," "peaceful transition," "the state of the whole people" and "the party of the entire people." He pursued a capitulationist line towards imperialism and used the theory of class conciliation to oppose and liquidate the people's revolutionary struggles. In the international communist movement, he enforced a divisive line, replacing proletarian internationalism with great-power chauvinism. In the Soviet Union he worked hard to disintegrate the dictatorship of the proletariat, attempting to replace the socialist system with the ideology, politics, economy and culture of the bourgeoisie, and to restore capitalism.

In the last eleven years, exploiting the prestige of the Communist Party of the Soviet Union and of the first socialist country that had been built up under the leadership of Lenin and Stalin, Khrushchev committed all the bad things he possibly could in contravention of the genuine will of the Soviet people. These bad things may be summed up as follows:

1. On the pretext of "combating the personality cult" and using the most scurrilous language, he railed at Stalin, the leader of the Communist Party of the Soviet Union and the Soviet people. In opposing Stalin, he opposed Marxism-Leninism. He tried at one stroke to write off all the great achievements of the Soviet people in the entire period under Stalin's leadership in order to defame the dictatorship of the proletariat, the socialist system, the great Soviet Communist Party, the great Soviet Union and the international communist movement. In so doing, Khrushchev provided the imperialists and the reactionaries of all countries with the dirtiest of weapons for their anti-Soviet and anti-Communist activities.

2. In open violation of the Declaration of 1957 and the Statement of 1960, he sought "all-round co-operation" with U.S. imperialism and fallaciously maintained that the heads of the Soviet Union and the United

States would "decide the fate of humanity," constantly praising the chieftains of U.S. imperialism as "having a sincere desire for peace." Pursuing an adventurist policy at one moment, he transported guided missiles to Cuba, and pursuing a capitulationist policy at another, he docilely withdrew the missiles and bombers from Cuba on the order of the U.S. pirates. He accepted inspection by the U.S. fleet and even tried to sell out Cuba's sovereignty by agreeing, behind the Cuban Government's back, to the " inspection " of Cuba by the United Nations, which is under U.S. control. In so doing, Khrushchev brought a humiliating disgrace upon the great Soviet people unheard of in the forty years and more since the October Revolution.

3. To cater to the U.S. imperialist policy of nuclear blackmail and prevent socialist China from building up her own nuclear strength for self-defence, he did not hesitate to damage the defence capabilities of the Soviet Union itself and concluded the so-called partial nuclear test ban treaty in collusion with the two imperialist powers of the United States and Britain. Facts have shown that this treaty is a pure swindle. In signing this treaty Khrushchev perversely tried to sell out the interests of the Soviet people, the people of all the socialist countries and all the peace-loving people of the world.

4. In the name of " peaceful transition " he tried by every means to obstruct the revolutionary movements of the people in the capitalist countries, demanding that they take the so-called legal, parliamentary road. This erroneous line paralyses the revolutionary will of the proletariat and disarms the revolutionary people ideologically, causing serious setbacks to the cause of revolution in certain countries. It has made the Communist Parties in a number of capitalist countries lifeless social-democratic parties of a new type and caused them to degenerate into servile tools of the bourgeoisie.

5. Under the signboard of " peaceful coexistence " he did his utmost to oppose and sabotage the national-liberation movement and went so far as to work hand in glove with U.S. imperialism in suppressing the revolutionary struggles of the oppressed nations. He instructed the Soviet delegate at the United Nations to vote for the dispatch of forces of aggression to the Congo, which helped the U.S. imperialists to suppress the Congolese people, and he used Soviet transport facilities to move these so-called United Nations troops to the Congo. He actually opposed the revolutionary struggles of the Algerian people, describing the Algerian national-liberation struggle as an " internal affair " of France. He had the audacity to " stand aloof " over the events in the Gulf of Bac Bo engineered by U.S. imperialism against Viet Nam and cudgelled his brains for ways to help the U.S. provocateurs get out of their predicament and to whitewash the criminal aggression of the U.S. pirates.

6. In brazen violation of the Statement of 1960, he spared no effort to reverse its verdict on the renegade Tito clique, describing Tito who had degenerated into a lackey of U.S. imperialism as a " Marxist-Leninist " and Yugoslavia which had degenerated into a capitalist country as a " socialist country." Time and again he declared that he and the Tito clique had " the same ideology " and were " guided by the same theory " and expressed his desire to learn modestly from this renegade who had betrayed the interests of the Yugoslav people and sabotaged the international communist movement.

7. He regarded Albania, a fraternal socialist country, as his sworn enemy, devising every possible means to injure and undermine it, and only wishing he could devour it in one gulp. He brazenly broke off all economic and diplomatic relations with Albania, arbitrarily deprived it of its legitimate rights as a member state in the Warsaw Treaty Organization and in the Council of Mutual Economic Assistance, and publicly called for the overthrow of its Party and state leadership.

8. He nourished an inveterate hatred for the Communist Party of China which upholds Marxism-Leninism and a revolutionary line, because the Chinese Communist Party was a great obstacle to his effort to press on with revisionism and capitulationism. He spread innumerable rumours and slanders against the Chinese Communist Party and Comrade Mao Tse-tung and resorted to every kind of baseness in his futile attempt to subvert socialist China. He perfidiously tore up several hundred agreements and contracts and arbitrarily withdrew more than one thousand Soviet experts working in China. He engineered border disputes between China and the Soviet Union and even conducted large-scale subversive activities in Sinkiang. He backed the reactionaries of India in their armed attacks on socialist China and, together with the United States, incited and helped them to perpetrate armed provocations against China by giving them military aid.

9. In flagrant violation of the principles guiding relations among the fraternal countries, he encroached upon their independence and sovereignty and wilfully interfered in their internal affairs. In the name of " mutual economic assistance," he opposed the independent development of the economies of fraternal countries and forced them to become a source of raw materials and an outlet for finished goods, thus reducing their industries to appendages. He bragged that these were all new theories and doctrines of his own invention, but in fact they were the jungle law of the capitalist world which he applied to relations among socialist countries, taking the Common Market of the monopoly capitalist blocs as his model.

10. In complete violation of the principles guiding relations among fraternal Parties, he resorted to all sorts of schemes to carry out subversive and disruptive activities against them. Not only did he use the sessions of the Central Committee and congress of his own Party as well as the congresses of some fraternal Parties to launch overt large-scale unbridled attacks on the fraternal Parties which uphold Marxism-Leninism, but in the case of many fraternal Parties he shamelessly bought over political degenerates, renegades and turncoats to support his revisionist line, and to attack and even illegally expel Marxist-Leninists from these Parties, thus creating splits without considering the consequences.

11. He wantonly violated the principle of reaching unanimity through consultation among fraternal Parties and, playing the " patriarchal father Party " role, he wilfully decided to convene an illegal international meeting of the fraternal Parties. In the notice dated July 30, 1964, he ordered that a meeting of the so-called drafting committee of the twenty-six fraternal Parties be held on December 15 this year, so as to create an open split in the international communist movement.

12. To cater to the needs of the imperialists and the domestic forces of capitalism, he pursued a series of revisionist policies leading back to capitalism. Under the signboard of the " state of the whole people," he abolished the dictatorship of the proletariat ; under the signboard of the

" party of the entire people," he altered the proletarian character of the Communist Party of the Soviet Union and divided the Party into an " industrial " and an " agricultural " party in contravention of the Marxist-Leninist principle of Party organization. Under the signboard of " full-scale communist construction " he tried in a thousand and one ways to switch back to the old path of capitalism the world's first socialist state which the Soviet people under the leadership of Lenin and Stalin had created by their sweat and blood. His blind direction of Soviet agriculture and industry wrought great havoc with the Soviet national economy and brought great difficulties to the life of the Soviet people.

Everything Khrushchev did over the last eleven years proves that the policy he pursued was one of alliance with imperialism against socialism, alliance with the United States against China, alliance with the reactionaries everywhere against the national-liberation movements and the people's revolutions, and alliance with the Tito clique and renegades of all description against all Marxist-Leninist fraternal Parties and all revolutionaries fighting imperialism. This policy of Khrushchev's has jeopardized the basic interests of the Soviet people, the people of the countries of the socialist camp and the revolutionary people all over the world.

Such are the so-called meritorious deeds of Khrushchev.

The downfall of a fellow like Khrushchev is certainly not due to old age or ill health, nor is it merely due to mistakes in his methods of work and style of leadership. Khrushchev's downfall is the result of the revisionist general line and the many erroneous policies he pursued at home and abroad.

Khrushchev considered the masses of the people as simply beneath his notice, thinking that he could manipulate the destiny of the Soviet people at his own sweet ill and that the " heads " of the two great powers, the Soviet Union and the United States, could settle the destiny of the people of all countries. To him, the people were nothing but fools and he alone was the " hero " making history. He vainly tried to force the Soviet people and the people of other countries to prostrate themselves under his revisionist baton. Thus he placed himself in direct opposition to the Soviet people, to the people of the countries of the socialist camp and to the proletariat and revolutionary people of the whole world, and got himself into an impasse — he was deserted by his own followers and could not extricate himself from internal and external difficulties. He put the noose around his own neck — dug his own grave.

History has witnessed many buffoons who cherished the idle hope of turning back the tide of history, but they all came to an ignominious end. Countless instances have demonstrated that the evil-doer who goes counter to the needs of social development and the will of the people can only end up as a ridiculous good-for-nothing, no matter what kind of " hero " he may have been, and no matter how arrogant. To start with the aim of doing harm to others only to end up by ruining oneself — such is the general law governing these people.

" Personages " such as Bakunin in the period of the First International were arrogant anti-Marxist " heroes " in their day, but they were soon relegated to the garbage-heap of history. Anti-Marxist " heroes " like Bernstein and Kautsky in the period of the Second International were once " formidable giants " entrenched in leading positions, but in the end history wrote them down as notorious renegades. Trotsky, the ringleader of the opposition faction, decked himself out as a "hero" after Lenin's death, but facts confirmed the correctness of Stalin's remark: ". . . he resembles an actor rather than a hero; and an actor should not be confused with a hero under any circumstances."

"But progress is the eternal law of man's world." History has taught us that whoever wants to stop the wheel of history will be ground to dust. As Comrade Mao Tse-tung has repeatedly pointed out, imperialism and all reactionaries are paper tigers, and the revisionists are too. However rampant and overbearing they may be, "heroes" representing reactionary classes and reactionary forces are actually paper tigers, powerful only in appearance; they are only fleeting transients soon to be overwhelmed by the surging waves of history. Khrushchev is no exception. Just think of his inordinate arrogance in the days when he viciously attacked Stalin and Marxism-Leninism at the 20th and 22nd Congresses, and when at the Bucharest meeting he launched his surprise attack on the Chinese Communist Party which upholds Marxism-Leninism. But it did not take long for this anti-Soviet, anti-Communist and anti-Chinese "hero" to meet the same fate as his revisionist predecessors. However much people reasoned with him and asked him to return to the fold, he paid not the slightest heed and finally plunged to his doom.

Khrushchev has fallen and the revisionist line he enthusiastically pursued is discredited, but Marxism-Leninism will continue to overcome the revisionist trend and forge ahead, and the revolutionary movement of the people of all countries will continue to sweep away the obstacles in its path and surge forward.

Nevertheless, the course of history will continue to be tortuous. Although Khrushchev has fallen, his supporters — the U.S. imperialists, the reactionaries and the modern revisionists — will not resign themselves to this failure. These hobgoblins are continuing to pray for Khrushchev and are trying to "resurrect" him with their incantations, vociferously proclaiming his "contributions" and "meritorious deeds" in the hope that events will develop along the lines prescribed by Khrushchev, so that "Khrushchevism without Khrushchev" may prevail. It can be asserted categorically that theirs is a blind alley.

Different ideological trends and their representatives invariably strive to take the stage and perform. It is entirely up to them to decide which direction they will take. But there is one point on which we have not the slightest doubt. History will develop in accordance with the laws discovered by Marxism-Leninism; it will march forward along the road of the October Revolution. Beyond all doubt, the great Communist Party of the Soviet Union and the great Soviet people, with their revolutionary traditions, are fully capable of making new contributions in safeguarding the great socialist achievements, the lofty prestige of the first socialist power founded by Lenin, the purity of Marxism-Leninism and the victorious advance of the revolutionary cause of the proletariat,

Let the international communist movement unite on the basis of Marxism-Leninism and proletarian internationalism!

DOCUMENT 22

Communiqué on the Consultative Meeting of Representatives of Communist and Workers' Parties in Moscow
(March 10, 1965)

Complete Text

[*Pravda* and *Izvestiya*, March 10, 1965, p. 1, quoted from *CDSP*, Vol. XVII, No. 9 (March 24, 1965), pp. 7–8]

A consultative meeting was held in Moscow March 1–5 of representatives of the Communist Party of Australia, the Communist Party of Argentina, the Bulgarian Communist Party, the Brazilian Communist Party, the Communist Party of Great Britain, the Hungarian Socialist Workers' Party, the Socialist Unity Party of Germany, the Communist Party of Germany, the Communist Party of India, the Italian Communist Party, the United Party of the Socialist Revolution of Cuba, the Mongolian People's Revolutionary Party, the Polish United Workers' Party, the Syrian Communist Party, the Communist Party of the Soviet Union, the Communist Party of Finland, the French Communist Party and the Communist Party of Czechoslovakia. Representatives of the Communist Party of the United States of America attended the meeting as observers.

The participants in the meeting held consultations on questions of mutual interest and exchanged opinions on ways for overcoming disagreements and strengthening the solidarity of the world Communist movement.

The meeting proceeded in an atmosphere of fraternity and friendship and was permeated with a spirit of active struggle for the solidarity of the Communist movement for the sake of fulfilling its great historical tasks. The participants in the meeting expressed the firm determination of their parties to do everything in their power to consolidate the international Communist movement, to strengthen its unity on the basis of Marxism-Leninism and proletarian internationalism, on the basis of the line defined by the 1957 Declaration and the 1960 Statement.

The representatives of the parties stated that the basic tendency of world development in today's conditions is the strengthening of the positions of socialism, the upsurge of the national-liberation and international workers' movement and the growth of the forces favoring the preservation and strengthening of peace. At the same time, it was noted that world reaction, first of all American imperialism, is becoming more active in various regions of the world, is striving to aggravate the situation, and is undertaking aggressive actions aimed against the socialist countries and the states that have freed themselves from colonial domination, against the revolutionary movement of the peoples.

In this situation, all Communist Parties are required more than ever before to display an understanding of their international responsibility, to rally together for the common struggle against imperialism, colonialism and neocolonialism and against the rule of monopoly capital, to rally for the active support of the liberation movement and the defense of peoples subjected to imperialist aggression, for the struggle for a general peace founded on respect for the sovereignty and integrity of all states.

In their statement the participants in the meeting expressed solidarity with the heroic Vietnamese people and the Vietnamese Workers' Party and called for international solidarity in the struggle against the aggressive actions of the American military.

The solidarity of all the revolutionary forces of modern times — the socialist commonwealth, the national-liberation movement and the international working class — has decisive importance for the successful struggle against imperialism. The interests of the solidarity of these forces insistently demand the strengthening of the unity of the world Communist movement.

The differences in the Communist movement, which weaken its solidarity, harm the cause of the world liberation movement and the cause of communism.

The participants in the meeting stated the conviction that what unites the Communist Parties is much stronger than what disunites them at a given moment. Even given the existence of disagreements concerning the political line and many important problems in theory and tactics, it is fully possible and necessary to strive for unity of action in the struggle against imperialism, in the cause of comprehensive support for the liberation movement of the peoples, in the struggle for universal peace and the peaceful coexistence of states with different social systems — regardless of whether the countries involved are large or small — in the struggle for the vital interests and historical tasks of the working class. Joint action in the struggle for these common goals is the most correct path for overcoming the existing differences.

The participants in the meeting emphasized the need for the Communist Parties to dedicate collective efforts to improving mutual relations among the parties, to strengthening the solidarity of the international Communist movement, while observing democratic principles of independence and the equality of all the fraternal parties.

In the struggle for the resolution of the tasks common to the whole Communist movement, it is expedient to use all possibilities and paths, bilateral and multilateral meetings of representatives of the fraternal parties and other forms of party communication and exchanges of opinion.

The participants in the meeting held unanimously that in today's conditions, as the 1960 Statement points out, international conferences of Communist and Workers' Parties are an effective form for the mutual exchange of opinions and experience, for enriching Marxist-Leninist theory through collective efforts and working out single positions in the struggle for common goals. Such conferences, carried out with the observance of the principles of full equality and the independence of each party, can well serve the cause of overcoming disagreements and consolidating the Communist movement on the basis of Marxism-Leninism and proletarian internationalism. Therefore the active and thorough preparation of a new international conference and its convocation at a suitable time, in the opinion of the participants in the meeting, fully answer the interests of the world Communist movement.

In order to convene and successfully carry out the new conference, it should be thoroughly prepared both from the standpoint of content and with respect to organization; joint efforts should be actively exerted to create favorable conditions for participation in its preparation by all the fraternal parties, and it is necessary to strive tirelessly to improve the atmosphere in the international Communist movement. The conference is called upon to serve the common cause of all Communists. The focusing of attention and the concentration of efforts on the urgent tasks now facing the Communist movement will best of all serve the rapprochement of our positions on the vital questions of the day.

The participants in the meeting expressed the opinion that it would be desirable to hold a preliminary consultative meeting of representatives of the 81 parties that participated in the 1960 conference to discuss the question of a new international conference. It is necessary to carry out consultations with all these parties to solve the question of calling such a preliminary meeting.

The parties represented at the present meeting favored the cessation of open polemics, which have been of a nature that is unfriendly and offensive to fraternal parties. At the same time, they deem it useful to continue the exchange of opinions on important contemporary questions of common interest in a comradely form, without mutual attacks. The participants in the meeting favor strict observance of the norms for relations between parties established by the 1957 and 1960 conferences and oppose the interference of some parties in the internal affairs of others.

In stating their opinion on ways for overcoming the difficulties in the international Communist movement and for its further development, the representatives of the parties were guided by concern for strengthening the Marxist-Leninist unity of the Communist ranks in the struggle against imperialism and colonialism, for national liberation, for peace, democracy, socialism and communism.

The representatives of the parties express the conviction that the meeting that has been held will receive a favourable response from the fraternal parties.

DOCUMENT 23

Position of the PCI at the Moscow Meeting :
Interview with Enrico Berlinguer
(March 13, 1965)

Complete Text

[*Rinascita*, March 13, 1965, pp. 3–5 ; translation based on that in JPRS 39,236, May 25, 1965 (TICD 714), and revised by William E. Griffith]

We reprint here, from the text of Comrade Berlinguer's interview, in the general discussion at the Moscow consultative meeting held between the 1st and the 5th of March, the exposition of the line and political positions of the Italian Communist Party. Subsequent discussion concerned the problems of editing the communiqué and an exchange of opinions on labor and employment of the Communist and workers' parties for an effective internationalist unity and for the pursuit of the debate and its political elaboration.

Dear Comrades,

We have listened with great interest and attention to the speeches of those comrades who have already made their contributions to this discussion of ours. From these speeches, as well as from conversations we have had during these few days with many of the delegations present, we have decided that on certain questions our viewpoint is different from those of other comrades.

We wish to stress, at the same time, that we also find ourselves in agreement on questions of fundamental importance, especially on the necessity of and the common desire to do everything possible to defend and reinforce the unity of our movement on the basis of Marxism-Leninism.

The international situation that we are facing presents profoundly contradictory aspects. From all parts of the world and in all fields, a positive movement toward profound changes in the structure of international relations is appearing, in the relations among nations, continents, and classes. From the working classes, from the peoples, from the socialist countries comes a powerful impulse toward social and national liberation and toward peace. Tendencies toward a peace policy are also making themselves felt, moreover, in governing circles in various capitalist states as well. But at the same time we must consider with concern — and this is the fundamental point on which to concentrate attention — the fact that in the last few months signs of serious worsening in the area of international relations have appeared, and there are newly significant threats to peace, to the independence of peoples, to the advancement of democratic forces in individual countries and on the global scale.

The principal cause of this worsening lies in the increased aggressiveness with which the great imperialist powers, and particularly the United States, are opposing the struggle for the liberation of the peoples, the successes that this struggle has achieved in the last few years, and the perspective that this struggle has opened up of a new restriction of the area of imperialist domination, of a further weakening of the imperialist camp before its fundamental antagonist, before the socialist countries.

It is important certainly that in many areas of economics and politics there has been in recent times a sharpening of the contrasts among the imperialist countries and that in international politics as well there are present today tendencies that compel a more realistic evaluation of the current condition of the world. Nor certainly can the uncertainties and the contrasts that are showing themselves within the governing circles of the United States itself be underestimated. But it is a fact that in the complex of imperialist policy, and in particular in American policy, those tendencies seeking to push the whole situation toward a new crisis have gained ground. These aggressive tendencies are being manifested today in the most barbaric and threatening way against the heroic people of South Vietnam, which is struggling gloriously with arms for its own liberation, and against the Democratic Republic of Vietnam, which has been made the object of pirate-like military actions and has been threatened by aggression. More generally, the whole situation in Southeast Asia is loaded with danger because of the aggressive policy of American and British imperialism. Nor can it be forgotten that in the heart of the African continent, and in order to push back the whole liberation movement in this great continent, the people of the Congo are being subjected to bloody aggression.

On the American continent, U.S. imperialism has certainly not given up aggressive movements toward Cuba and is subjecting the island to continuous acts of provocation, while in the other countries of Latin America the policy of intervention in support of military and reactionary cliques does not cease.

In Europe the problem, decisive for world peace, of NATO's multilateral atomic rearmament — which would open up the route to the atomic rearmament of West Germany — is still open. Despite the rebuffs experienced on the international level, the German militarists have not given up their plans for revenge and are rather seeking to chain all the Atlantic powers to their warmongering policy.

Finally, even beyond these critical points, it is a fact that the disarmament negotiations are completely washed up and that a serious crisis and a paralysis of the U.N. are beginning.

In our opinion it is necessary to recognize that the divisions that have manifested themselves so much in this last year within the socialist camp as well as in the third world and in the ranks of the nonaligned countries have objectively encouraged this aggressiveness on the part of the imperialists and made the necessary response more difficult. The global struggle for peace has been weakened as a result.

We are all in agreement, therefore, on the necessity of overcoming these divisions. The whole framework of the international situation shows the unavoidable necessity of unity. But this framework also shows that the ground on which we can and must seek and build unity today is first of all precisely that of action and common struggle against the common enemy, for concrete objectives of peace, of liberation, and of democracy.

The comrades will permit me to recall the words that Comrade Togliatti wrote in this regard a few days prior to his decease:

> The unity of all Socialist forces in a common action, going also beyond ideological differences, against the most reactionary imperialist groups, is an indispensable necessity.
> One cannot imagine that China or the Chinese Communists could be excluded from this unity. Therefore, from now onward we must behave in such a manner as not to create obstacles to attaining this objective, indeed to facilitating it.
> We must not interrupt in any way the polemic, but always have as its point of departure the demonstration, on the basis of the facts of today, that the unity of the entire Socialist world and all the workers and Communist parties is necessary and can be achieved.

And the comrades will also permit me to recall that these words came and come from the leadership of a party whose ideological positions and policies have always been, on fundamental questions, at the diametrical opposite of the Chinese positions.

In the first place, it is a question today of supporting, as yesterday's last serious news stressed, against all forces and in all necessary forms, the struggle of the Vietnamese people against American aggression. In this regard we salute the firm position and the concrete solidarity of the USSR and the other socialist countries, and the trip to Asia of the Soviet delegation led by Comrade Kosygin, and we maintain that to push back the threat of aggression it is necessary to have that full and vigorous action of the Communist parties and the forces of peace throughout the world, which our appeal calls for. In Italy there have already taken place hundreds of demonstrations and manifestations of solidarity with the heroic Vietnamese people, and it is our commitment to develop to the maximum this movement, in full awareness of the ineradicable bonds of interests and ideals that unite the working class of the capitalist countries with the peoples that are fighting for their own liberation. More generally we hold the support that has come and can come to the liberation movements and the newly independent countries from the socialist states to be fundamental, but we must not forget the role that belongs, in this direction, to the working classes of the capitalist West.

Another fundamental area of immediate united commitment is that of the struggle against the multilateral atomic force, against German atomic rearmament, and for European security. In this regard, the position recently taken by the Warsaw Pact nations is very important, but at the same time let us not forget the necessity of raising again these problems that are vital to the conscience of all peoples and of developing in Europe and in the world coordinated initiatives on the part of all workers', democratic, and antifascist forces.

Many other fields of immediate action could also be pointed out, upon which common activity on the part of all Communist parties could be developed, helping to advance their unity and achieving at the same time a broader contact with other labor and popular forces.

Parallel with the development of these common actions we think that for the reinforcement of unity it is indispensable to carry forward decisively the analysis of the modifications that have arisen in these years in the global situation, in the structures of any socioeconomic countries, in political life, and in the field of culture and thought.

The XX Congress of the CPSU opened up a great road in this direction, but in our opinion it is necessary to take cognizance of the serious delays and areas of backwardness that we still have in so many fields, and to free ourselves from dogmatic incrustations that have accumulated during long years and hold up the development of thought and political initiative. To this end, the road to follow certainly does not seem to us to be the one that pretends to attain some ordering of all questions in one fell swoop but rather that of a deepened examination of the principal problems and tasks that arise in various fields and in the different sectors of our movement. We wish to stress particularly the need for deepening our own analyses and for debating in depth with other fraternal parties the problems that have arisen in the working class of the capitalist countries, in their immediate struggles and also in their battle strategy for the advancement toward democracy and socialism in the current, altered historical conditions. But we feel that analogous needs for deepening the debate exist today in other fundamental fields. We are referring, for example, to the original experiences and the entirely new problems that have arisen in those ex-colonial countries that are oriented in a socialist direction, and we are referring to the questions arising in the socialist countries about their economic development, their democratic life, and their mutual relations.

To face these problems, what is necessary first of all is the autonomous and creative effort of each party in the actual course of its political activity. Many of these problems, however, call for a collaboration of more parties or of all the parties. For this reason we are decidedly in favor of the intensification not only of bilateral contacts but also of meetings, conventions, congresses, and all forms of multilateral consultation. A highly positive example in this regard seems to us to be the recent conference of the Communist and workers' parties of Latin America. We continue to attribute great actuality and importance to the projected meeting of the Communist and workers' parties of Western Europe.

It is our profound conviction, dear comrades, that this road is the best, the most effective, the most realistic to promote the advancement of the line and the struggle of the whole movement and also first to attenuate and then to overcome the divisions that are now weakening the workers' and Communist movement. The international road of common initiatives in the struggle, of intervention on the most serious questions before us, the road of bilateral and multilateral meetings and work pledges, is in fact the one that will make our activity immediately effective, and will influence the great masses of the people and the great currents of world public opinion ; it is the road that, with the overcoming of our weaknesses and the development of positive initiatives, permits us to attenuate the contrasts in facts and to cut down the influence and capacity for influence of the mistaken and factional positions of the Chinese comrades. We all know that the overcoming of divergences will not be easy and cannot be accomplished in a short time because it is a question of divergences that have deep roots and objective causes, related, moreover, in large measure, to the global dimensions that the revolutionary process has assumed, to the victories it has won, and to the entrance of new peoples into the world political arena. But precisely for this reason we are convinced that it is necessary to proceed with wisdom and prudence, to avoid precipitous acts and consequences, to move always on the ground of concrete and constructive action. Things cannot be left as they are, we cannot remain in a position of passive waiting ; but it would be illusory and dangerous also to aim at the myth of an immediate and world-wide solution. The master road of unity cannot for this reason, in our opinion, be anything but the road of a gradual construction through common initiative and action.

We also wish to add that the unitary process must take on a breadth that goes well beyond the Communist movement. Such a process must in fact tend to embrace the entire revolutionary movement in the world, as it has been developing and articulating itself in this last decade. There are in the world today, for example, imposing revolutionary forces, already in power in certain countries, which, although not themselves Communist, oppose decisively imperialism and are moving toward transformations in the direction of socialism. But this breadth and originality assumed by the world revolutionary process makes it even more urgent that the Communist movement itself liquidate schema and methods that are now outdated and that the autonomy of each party be affirmed as the indispensable condition for its development and for the vitality of the whole movement. At the same time it is necessary for the Communist movement not to be conceived as something that is closed within itself but rather as something that multiplies its contacts with all the revolutionary and progressive forces to create the bases for a world-wide unity of the whole revolutionary movement. Within the limits of our possibilities and taking inspiration from this orientation, we have sought to develop informal contacts, especially in the direction of certain African revolutionary movements ; we have established, as the French comrades have also, a relationship of genuine and reciprocal understanding with the Algerian party of the FLN, and just in the last weeks a delegation of our party had fruitful official meetings with the leaders of the Arab Socialist Union.

From what we have hitherto affirmed, and from all our political activity, we are certain that you will understand, dear comrades, that our conception of the autonomy of each party, if it excludes any form whatsoever, even new ones, of centralized organization of the movement, is clearly opposed to and rejects any isolationist tendency or movement of national closing-in or of regional subdivisions and derives its inspiration from the fullest and most operative internationalism and an international conception of the class struggle.

From all this is also derived the way in which we consider the problem of meetings and international conferences of all Communist and workers' parties. We have no objection whatsoever in principle to this form of consultation and collaboration on an international level.

Rather, we maintain that meetings and international conferences can be useful and fruitful. We are for this reason not opposed to the eventuality of a conference of this nature taking place, and we will work to make the necessary conditions for it mature. What is essential, from this point of view, is that it be a unitary conference, in which all the parties really participate, which proposes well-defined goals, which proceeds from an appropriate analysis of today's new problems, and which, for this reason, signals a real step forward with respect to the 1957 and 1960 conferences.

We repeat that we are not against the eventuality of such a conference and that we have made and are making efforts to take into consideration the pre-eminent importance that other fraternal parties assign to it. We shall permit ourselves, however, to call to the attention of the comrades the fact that, in our opinion, the experience of these last two years cannot be judged entirely positive in this regard. The fact that at a given moment the problem of a new international conference was at the center of our internal and public debate has not always been useful. Rather, it has produced serious difficulties at times.

In certain cases, for example, we have the impression that waiting for a conference that was considered to be close at hand and of such a quality as to solve problems has created illusions in certain sectors of the movement and has retarded for a certain time the development of other initiatives that could have helped us to make progress that would have been real and concrete even if it would not have solved everything.

Moreover, on the question of the conference there have arisen reciprocal diffidences and incomprehension, which have been added to the deeper ones that derive from the real contrasts with certain parties. Our own criticism of the erroneous political positions of the Chinese comrades, rather than being aimed, as was and is indispensable, at the ideological and political substance of those positions, rather than being made concrete in a position of struggle on our part capable of progressively weakening the influence that such positions could exercise in certain sectors of the popular movement and of making verbal revolutionarism increasingly evident, has at times been translated into a dispute that has given the impression of abstractly dividing our parties into the supporters and the adversaries of a conference, with the practical result, moreover, that the conference, long considered imminent, did not take place. And it did not take place precisely because the necessary conditions had not been established, because we were aware of the risk that its results could have had, that of the schism of the movement into two organized centers, one against the other, rather than unity.

In recent times, it is true, there have appeared signs and possibilities of improving relations with the parties that have positions close to those of the Chinese party, and relations with the Chinese party itself have not been as bitter in the last few months as in the past. We are deeply gratified by all this and we appreciate the steps that the CPSU comrades and those of other countries have taken in this direction. But it is precisely the appearance of these possibilities for improvement of the political climate among the parties that must, in our opinion, make inadvisable any act that threatens to compromise such possibilities, to lead us back to a situation similar to the serious and threatening one our movement went through between the end of 1963 and the first part of 1964.

We are quite happy to be able to meet here with the representatives of fraternal parties to whom we feel united by bonds of profound and lasting solidarity and with whom we wish to develop increasingly great reciprocal understanding and collaboration. We cannot, however, underestimate the fact that other important fraternal parties are absent from this meeting, parties with which we all have profound and serious divergences but who still represent the fundamental part of the revolutionary forces of a whole continent like Asia.

These absences can be lamented, we may grieve that these parties did not wish to take part in an amicable exchange of views, but no one can ignore or underestimate the political significance and the lack of a positive impression that this fact creates in a part of the popular masses.

Despite these reservations, manifested on many occasions, we have come to this meeting in a constructive spirit and animated by the will to unity to expound our point of view frankly and to hear and judge with full consideration the different opinions of other fraternal parties. Our point of view may be summed up in the conviction that it is right to recognize that the conditions for a new and fruitful international conference of all parties are not yet mature. It is not enough for a thing to be right and reasonable, it also has to be possible. It is not enough to declare that the idea of the conference is in itself a profoundly unifying idea. It is necessary for the conditions to exist for it to become a true step forward toward unity and not to crystallize the present divisions.

In our opinion it is not a matter of giving up the idea, the possibility, or the proposal of a new international conference that would be prepared for by all the fraternal parties and in which all the fraternal parties would take part. We want to make it quite clear that this is not our position, and that our view is precisely the opposite of passive waiting. And it is not a question of submitting to blackmail or someone's veto. But it is necessary actively to make mature increasingly more favorable conditions for the realization of the conference, cutting off in this way any eventual persistence of vetoes, and we maintain that the most effective road to this end is that of common action in struggle, of overcoming delays and lacunae that divert our planning and initiative, by developing a debate that would avoid bitter and violent forms, and by multiplying the opportunities for contact among all the parties. The central objective that must inspire all our work is that of unity in the struggle of the movement and thus of the reconquest of its political and ideological unity. For this it is well, in our opinion, that the question of the conference be maintained as a prospect but that it not become in itself the pivot of everything.

We are rather in favor of the question of the conference being still debated in a constructive manner so that new ways may be sought to promote the active participation of all parties in its preparation. We are opposed, however, to an organizational mechanism being put in motion before the necessary political conditions are achieved, which would in any event be entirely contrary to the purely consultative character of our meeting. We are thus absolutely in agreement with those comrades who have excluded any possibility of there being adopted at this conference decisions or proposals relative to the date of the conference or to the date of the meetings that could prepare for it, to the definition of the issues for discussion, and so forth. We are not, on the other hand, in agreement with the allusions that have been made by certain comrades to the possibility of considering dates and time limits for the next meeting. Rather, let us add as explicitly as possible that we would be completely opposed to any and all proposals that would tend to give organizational continuity in any form whatsoever to this assembly of ours. We can in no way give the impression of constituting ourselves an organizing committee of the conference or even of an eventual preparatory conference of the 81 parties — a meeting that could also represent, as soon as results from it seemed possible, a reasonable solution.

We maintain, moreover, in the light of the conversations we have had in these few days, that it is possible to reach a unanimous agreement at this meeting, through a common communiqué that would express a firm wish for unity centered about common anti-imperialist objectives and peace objectives, and that would also contain some of the ideas that have been proposed here: for example, that new and broader consultations among all the parties that participated in the 1960 conference be promoted to arrive at an eventual consultative meeting of all these parties. An agreement on these bases, which would coherently maintain the consultative nature that has justly been conferred on our conference, would in our opinion represent a positive and unitary conclusion for our work. Such an agreement could have a beneficial unifying influence on all workers and popular public opinion, and it is our strong desire to do everything in our power to promote it.

Our common goal is the unity of the whole revolutionary movement. Imperialism is ready to exploit every new division on our part, and even hopes that this meeting of ours produces decisions that would sharpen and crystallize our internal polemics and the division of our movement into two around a new bone of contention. Our goal is to disappoint this hope and to arrive at decisions that would rather give new force to action and struggle against imperialism at the very moment in which it is accentuating its aggression still further, a new force to action and struggle for the inseparable cause of peace and the advancement of socialism, for the cause of the unity of all the forces of communism.

DOCUMENT 24

Soviet Note of March 12, 1965 Concerning
Injuries to Chinese Students during
March 4, 1965 Demonstrations in Moscow

Complete Text

[*Pravda*, March 13, 1965, p. 3, and *Izvestiya*, March 14, 1965, quoted from *CDSP*, Vol. XVII, No. 10 (March 31, 1965), pp. 4–5]

In the USSR Ministry of Foreign Affairs

On March 12 the USSR Ministry of Foreign Affairs handed the CPR Embassy in Moscow the following note:

" The Ministry of Foreign Affairs of the Union of Soviet Socialist Republics considers it necessary to declare the following to the Embassy of the Chinese People's Republic:

" In the past few days a loud propaganda campaign has been unleashed in China in the course of which facts relating to the demonstration by foreign students in front of the U.S. Embassy in Moscow have been presented in a distorted light. Matters went so far that on March 6 a ' demonstration ' was organized outside the USSR Embassy in Peking, which is unprecedented in relations between socialist countries. The CPR Embassy in Moscow has handed the USSR Ministry of Foreign Affairs a note that represents a conglomeration of fabrications.

" It is known that, in accordance with a treaty with the government of the Democratic Republic of Vietnam, the Soviet government is undertaking practical measures to give assistance in safeguarding the security and strengthening the defense capacity of the DRV. The government and people of the Soviet Union resolutely condemn the U.S. aggression in Vietnam and the savage bombing of the territory of the DRV by American aircraft. The Soviet people have expressed their feelings of deep indignation over the aggressive actions of the American military and their fraternal solidarity with the Vietnamese people at numerous demonstrations, gatherings and protest meetings that have been held throughout the country. The statements by the Soviet government and the political demonstrations by the working people of the Soviet Union are exposing to all the world the criminal policy of the U.S.A. in Vietnam and mobilizing the public in the struggle against American aggression.

" The Soviet people share and understand the feelings of indignation over the acts of American aggression against the Vietnamese people expressed by the participants in the March 4 demonstration by foreign students.

" But decisive practical steps to suppress aggression, political statements and demonstrations of a political nature against the misdeeds of American imperialism are one thing, and provocational actions and outrages against a foreign embassy and Soviet officials charged with maintaining public order are something else again. Undoubtedly, the Chinese side is well aware of the existence of norms of international law according to which states that accept foreign diplomatic representatives bear a responsibility to ensure their inviolability and security. By the way, during all the years of the existence of the CPR, the Chinese authorities have never permitted demonstrations in Peking against the representatives of imperialist states in which these representatives might be subjected to outrages and material and other damage might be inflicted.

" And yet what the Chinese citizens perpetrated during the March 4 demonstration was nothing less than a previously prepared attempt at violence directed against both a foreign embassy and the representatives of Soviet agencies of authority.

" Soviet militiamen who were entrusted with safeguarding the embassy properly called for restraint within the framework of a political demonstration and for the abjuring of violence. However, the Chinese citizens who participated in the demonstration chose the path of direct attack on the Soviet militia. They struck the militiamen, shouted crude insults and committed other acts subject to criminal prosecution under Soviet legislation. Against the unarmed militiamen the provocateur elements used sticks, iron rods, stones and sharp instruments they had gathered beforehand and brought with them.

" More than 30 militiamen and military personnel who were safeguarding public order and, in accordance with the generally accepted international norms and Soviet laws, ensuring the security of a foreign embassy suffered seriously, and a fourth of them received grave injuries.

" In order to lend a semblance of truth to its version of the ‘ suppression of the demonstration,’ the CPR Embassy in Moscow organized a new escapade after the demonstration, this time in the Botkin Hospital. A group of Chinese citizens, organized by the embassy, appeared there and demanded, without any foundation, hospitalization on the issuance of affidavits stating that they had received serious injuries. After careful medical examination, Soviet doctors established that these persons did not require hospital treatment. But the Chinese citizens began to create an uproar in the hospital and crudely insulted the doctors and medical personnel.

" It is around all these actions by Chinese citizens in Moscow, which the Chinese authorities would never permit at home, that a broad and slanderous campaign is now being unfolded in Peking. Such actions on the part of the Chinese can only gratify the forces that are hostile to the socialist states and are counting on disunity among our countries.

" Let the provocational campaign against the USSR that has been artificially inflated in China in recent days rest on the consciences of those who organized it. Placing the interests of our common cause above everything and unswervingly striving for the development and improvement of Soviet-Chinese relations, the Soviet side has no intention of embarking on such a path.

" The USSR Ministry of Foreign Affairs categorically denies the statements in the CPR Embassy’s note of protest as completely unfounded. It considers it necessary to point out the fact that in its note the embassy permits itself intolerable attacks against the Soviet Union and even attempts to give instructions on how to combat imperialism. We have no intention of taking lessons on this subject from anyone. The Soviet Union has always waged and still is waging this struggle consistently — not in words but in deeds — in the common interests of all the socialist countries and in the interests of the peoples of the whole world.

" The USSR Ministry of Foreign Affairs demands that the CPR Embassy take steps that would fully rule out the possibility of the repetition by

Chinese citizens in the USSR of actions such as those that took place during the demonstration by foreign students on March 4, 1965, and that they conduct themselves as they should in a country that has shown them hospitality. All persons living in the USSR, including Chinese citizens, are obliged to respect and strictly observe Soviet laws. The Soviet authorities will continue to demand of foreign citizens the same absolute observance of the laws and procedures that have been established in the USSR as they demand of Soviet citizens.

"The USSR Ministry of Foreign Affairs warns that any violations of public order or outrages, no matter by what foreign citizens they may be committed, will be resolutely suppressed, and persons guilty of such actions will be prosecuted with all the strictness of the Soviet laws."

DOCUMENT 25

Chinese Protest Against Suppression of Demonstrations and Persecution of Chinese Students

(March 16, 1965 Note of the Chinese Ministry of Foreign Affairs to the Soviet Embassy in Peking)

Complete Text

[*Peking Review*, Vol. VIII, No. 12 (March 19, 1965), pp. 7–8]

The Ministry of Foreign Affairs of the People's Republic of China has received the note dated March 12 of the Ministry of Foreign Affairs of the Soviet Union addressed to the Chinese Embassy in the Soviet Union. In its note, the Soviet Ministry of Foreign Affairs tried hard to prove that the Soviet Government did not suppress the March 4 anti-U.S. demonstration in Moscow, and that it was rather the students, particularly Chinese students, who had assaulted Soviet policemen, as if the entire bloody incident and the public indignation against the Soviet authorities which it inevitably aroused were provoked by China. This is an utter distortion of the facts, making black white and white black. The Chinese Government categorically rejects the note of the Soviet Ministry of Foreign Affairs.

What after all was the unusual thing that took place in Moscow on March 4? The students' anti-U.S. demonstration that day was similar to those one very often witnesses on other occasions. All they did was to march to the U.S. Embassy, shout slogans, paste up posters and deliver letters of protest. This was nothing unusual even though the students, impelled by their righteous indignation, threw stones and broke some windows of the U.S. Embassy. In Asia, Africa or Latin America, wherever there is a U.S. Embassy or an office of the U.S. Information Agency, such incidents are quite common; they occur almost every month, if not every day. Why was it in Moscow, of all places, that a bloody incident in which police and troops injured more than 130 students from Viet Nam, China, Indonesia, Cuba, Somalia and other countries should have taken place?

The facts are crystal clear. The students did not do anything "wild." It was the Soviet Government that behaved most strangely on this occasion.

Earlier, on February 9, students in Moscow staged an anti-U.S. demonstration in which they smashed several hundred windows of the U.S. Embassy. This enraged Lyndon B. Johnson, chieftain of U.S. imperialism,

405

who insisted that the Soviet Government give "adequate protection" to the U.S. Embassy. You were thus put in an awkward position. Were you to ban such demonstrations outright, you would not be able to justify your action before the public. Were you to permit such demonstrations, you would run the risk of offending the United States. So this time, you permitted the students to hold the anti-U.S. demonstration on the one hand, while adopting various extraordinary measures on the other. More than seven hundred soldiers, police and mounted guards and a large number of snow ploughs and fire-engines were rushed to the scene to throw a tight cordon around the U.S. Embassy. They formed four barriers as if they were facing a formidable enemy, and desperate attempts were made to prevent the demonstrating students from getting near the U.S. Embassy. When the demonstrators pressed on, you ordered the police and soldiers to crack down on them. That was how the bloody incident was brought about.

After the incident, the Soviet Ministry of Foreign Affairs lost no time in making apologies to the U.S. Ambassador, and on the very next day hastened to send workers to clean the walls and glaze the windows of the U.S. Embassy. How ruthless you were to the demonstrators against U.S. imperialism, and how abjectly subservient you were to the U.S. imperialists!

It is groundless to allege that such demonstrations against the missions of imperialist powers would not be permitted in Peking either. When the people of Peking were holding gigantic demonstrations against Anglo-French aggression in Egypt at the time of the Suez events, their representatives entered the compound of the Office of the British Charge d'Affaires in Peking to deliver innumerable letters of protest and plastered the walls of the compound with posters denouncing British imperialism. The Chinese Foreign Ministry did not send anyone to the Office of the British Charge d'Affairs to help clean the walls, and there was no question at all of the Chinese Government apologizing to it.

Greatly indignant upon learning of the Soviet Government's suppression of their comrades, students in Peking held a demonstration and went to the Soviet Embassy to lodge protests. We have not the slightest doubt that the Soviet people who have the glorious tradition of the Great October Revolution behind them would also protest if only they knew the facts.

However, it was after all something disgraceful to have beaten up and injured so many foreign students. So you tried hard to deny it, asserting that no such thing had happened or that in any event the students had not been so badly beaten up as to need hospitalization. The Soviet Government has stopped at nothing to achieve its aim.

Nine seriously injured Chinese students needed hospitalization as proved by the doctors of the Botkin Hospital who examined them. They were hospitalized, but on the following day, seven of them were expelled from the hospital by the Soviet authorities who asserted that they needed no medical treatment and that they should not have been in the hospital at all. And Huang Chao-keng, one of the Chinese students who remained in the Botkin Hospital, was ruthlessly beaten up by Soviet plainclothes men and was tied up hand and foot for as long as seven or eight hours. They beat up and injured people, but flatly denied it. They would not allow the seriously injured to be hospitalized. Those who refused to leave were tortured. This would be something unthinkable in all revolutionary anti-imperialist countries in Asia, Africa, Latin America and elsewhere, but it did happen in the Soviet Union.

The Chinese Government hereby lodges a resolute protest with the Soviet Government against the shameless suppression of the anti-U.S. demonstration and the persecution of Chinese students. The Chinese Government once again demands that the Soviet Government admit its mistakes and make an apology to the students of the various countries who took part in the demonstration.

DOCUMENT 26

A Comment on the March Moscow Meeting

by the Editorial Departments of *Jen-min Jih-pao* and *Hung Ch'i* (March 22, 1965)

Complete Text

[*Peking Review*, Vol. VIII, No. 13 (March 26, 1965), pp. 7–13]

1. What Kind of Meeting Was It?

The schismatic meeting contrived by the new leadership of the CPSU which inherited the mantle of Khrushchev was finally held from March 1 to 5, 1965. On March 10 a statement entitled " Communique of the Consultative Meeting of Representatives of Communist and Workers' Parties in Moscow " was issued.

After making herculean efforts and combining hard tactics with soft to knock something together, the leaders of the Communist Party of the Soviet Union finally managed to convene a fragmented meeting. The divisive meeting was quite small and most unseemly. It was a gloomy and forlorn affair.

Attending this meeting, besides the Soviet Party, were representatives and observers of 15 Parties, plus the two splinter revisionist factions of Australia and Brazil and the notorious clique of the renegade Dange, which was also dragged in to swell the total, adding up to 19 units in all.

Of the 26 Parties whose attendance was ordered by the leaders of the CPSU, the seven fraternal Parties of Albania, China, Indonesia, Japan, Korea, Rumania and Viet Nam firmly refused to take part in the divisive meeting. The fraternal Marxist-Leninist Parties of Australia, Brazil and India likewise condemned and opposed the meeting.

The 19 units in attendance were rent by contradictions and disunity. Some of them wholeheartedly supported Khrushchev's revisionism and splittism ; some did so half-heartedly ; others, for reasons they might find it awkward to divulge, had to attend under orders to serve as a claque at the show ; and still others may have temporarily fallen into the trap from naivete.

No one can deny that this meeting was the self-same illegal and schismatic meeting which Khrushchev had ordered to be held on December 15, 1964, in the CPSU's letter of July 30, 1964.

People may ask, what grounds are there for saying so? Didn't the new leaders of the CPSU postpone the meeting? Didn't they change its name from a drafting committee meeting to a consultative meeting? Didn't they speak of unity against the enemy and other good things in the communique?

By playing tricks, in appearance the new leaders of the CPSU made some changes and a number of Khrushchev's original aims which were based on wishful thinking have not been fulfilled. But in essence, the new leaders of the CPSU have taken over Khrushchev's revisionism and splittism lock, stock and barrel, and they carried out his behest for a divisive meeting very faithfully. Please consider the following facts:

The new leaders of the CPSU repeatedly declared to us that the international meeting of fraternal Parties and the meeting preparatory to it must be linked with the illegal and schismatic meetings for which Khrushchev issued the order on July 30, 1964.

The new leaders of the CPSU reiterated Khrushchev's order in the letter of the Central Committee of the CPSU to the Central Committee of the Chinese Communist Party dated November 24, 1964, in the letters addressed to other fraternal Parties around that time, as well as in the " Announcement on the Convocation of the Drafting Committee for the Preparation of the International Conference of the Communist and Workers' Parties " carried in *Pravda* on December 12, 1964. They insisted that the preparatory meeting for the international meeting of fraternal Parties be held on the basis of the drafting committee which the leadership of the CPSU had decided on. They also said that they had reached the conclusion that " the fraternal Parties which have declared themselves for the convening of the drafting committee have the right to embark on practical preparations for its meeting."

They adhered to and carried out Khrushchev's order by telling only the 26 Parties — no more and no less — which had been members of the long defunct drafting committee of 1960 to attend the meeting.

They adhered to and carried out Khrushchev's order by insisting on convening the meeting no matter how many Parties refused to attend. And so they held the meeting despite the firm opposition of a number of fraternal Parties and their flat refusal to participate.

They only postponed the meeting because under the circumstances they could not do anything else. Nevertheless, in the manner of a patriarchal party they still issued orders that it be held on March 1, 1965. And so the meeting began on that date.

On the eve of the meeting they changed its name, giving it the cloak of a " consultative meeting." In fact, this change of name did not change the nature of the divisive meeting which had been ordered by Khrushchev.

It thus became clear that despite their many tricks and conjuring feats the new leaders of the CPSU were still peddling Khrushchev's old wares. Their purpose was simply to put up a false front and inveigle people into attending the meeting, into acknowledging their status as the patriarchal party, into recognizing their right to do one thing today and another tomorrow and to wave their baton, and into following them down the blind alley of Khrushchev's revisionism and splittism.

Things could not be plainer. If the new leaders of the CPSU really wanted unity and not a continuation of Khrushchev's old practice of plotting sham unity and a genuine split, why did they not discard the order issued by Khrushchev on July 30, 1964? Why did they come out with another letter on November 24, 1964? And why could they not accept the advice of fraternal Parties, abandon this illegal schismatic meeting, change their direction and make a fresh start?

Indeed, if the new leaders of the CPSU had not been determined to carry out Khrushchev revisionism after Khrushchev's fall, they could have very well used that fine opportunity and made a start by abandoning the divisive meeting and thus shown a desire to eliminate the differences and strengthen unity on a new basis. We sincerely hoped that the new leaders of the CPSU would make use of that fine opportunity and seek new ways to eliminate the differences and strengthen unity in conjunction with us as well as the other Marxist-Leninist parties.

But what did we get instead? When the Chinese Party and Government Delegation made contact with the new leaders of the CPSU in Moscow in 1964 during the anniversary of the October Revolution, the latter explicitly stated that there was not a shade of difference between themselves and Khrushchev on the question of the international communist movement and in their attitude towards China. They obdurately held to their stand on an illegal schismatic meeting. What is more, the plan for the divisive meeting which Khrushchev had not had time to fulfil was carried through by his successors.

It is now possible for people to see more clearly that these new leaders of the CPSU had to oust Khrushchev, not because they had any difference of principle with him, but because Khrushchev had become too odious and had been too stupid in some of his practices and because Khrushchev himself had become a serious obstacle to the carrying out of Khrushchev revisionism. In replacing Khrushchev they simply changed the signboard and employed more cunning methods and subterfuges in order the better to push through and develop Khrushchevism and to carry out the general line of revisionism, great-power chauvinism and splittism which Khrushchev had put forward at the 20th Congress of the CPSU, systematized at its 22nd Congress and embodied in the Programme of the CPSU.

II. What Are the Deeds of the New Leaders of the CPSU

Of late the new leaders of the CPSU have uttered quite a few fine words, and the communique of this divisive meeting is also larded with many high-sounding hypocritical phrases, such as "oppose imperialism," "support Viet Nam against U.S. imperialism," "support the national-liberation movement," "support the people's revolutions in various countries," "unity against the enemy" and "concerted action." The new leaders of the CPSU have taken over certain slogans advanced by the Marxist-Leninists in an attempt to create the illusion that they have changed somewhat and taken a stand differing from Khrushchev's revisionism and splittism.

What a striking similarity there is here to the adoption by U.S. imperialism of some of the main slogans of the leaders of the CPSU! Peaceful coexistence, peaceful competition, peaceful transition, relaxation of tension, general and complete disarmament, the two-power domination of the world, joint assistance to India, joint support to the reactionaries of all countries, joint efforts to undermine the world revolutionary movements through the United Nations, joint efforts to oppose China, and so on — these slogans and schemes of Khrushchev's have all been taken over by U.S.

imperialism! The leaders of the CPSU and the U.S. imperialism have joined in a love feast, exchanging information and working in common against communism, against the people, against revolution and against the national-liberation movement for the purpose of maintaining imperialism, revisionism and reaction everywhere against all revolutionaries. But we are not the United States, we are Marxist-Leninists. We shall expose the intrigues and plots of the new leaders of the CPSU.

Marxism-Leninism teaches us that just as an individual must as a matter of course be judged " not by his professions, but by his actions; not by what he pretends to be, but by what he does, and what he really is," [1] so must a political party. " In historical struggles one must distinguish still more the phrases and fancies of parties from their real organism and their real interests, their conception of themselves from their reality." [2]

If in the light of this principle we examine what the new leaders of the CPSU have done since Khrushchev's fall, we shall be able to understand that all their fine words only amount to selling horse meat as beefsteak and that they are saying one thing and doing another. We shall likewise be able to understand the real meaning of certain slogans contained in the communique.

The communique says, " Divergences in the communist movement weaken its unity and thereby do damage to the world liberation movement, to the communist cause." We would like to ask: Whence the divergences? What is actually weakening the unity of the international communist movement and doing damage to the cause of the people's revolutions in different countries? Quite plainly, it is Khrushchev revisionism, as expressed in concentrated form in the 20th and 22nd Congresses of the CPSU and the Programme of the CPSU. The divergence between Marxism-Leninism and Khrushchev revisionism is a divergence between two roads, between defending Marxism-Leninism and opposing Marxism-Leninism; it is a divergence between two antagonistic classes, the proletariat and the bourgeoisie. Since the new leaders of the CPSU are now following Khrushchev's whole revisionist general line of " peaceful coexistence," " peaceful competition," " peaceful transition," " the state of the whole people " and " the party of the entire people," this only goes to prove that they are still bent on deepening the differences, wrecking unity and doing fresh damage to the international communist movement.

The communique reads, " The participants voiced their conviction that what unites the Communist Parties greatly outweighs that which at the present time disunites them." This assertion is sheer hypocrisy; it is an attempt to whitewash the actions of the new leaders of the CPSU in openly splitting the international communist movement.

In the incipient stages of Khrushchev revisionism and in the course of its development, we invariably proceeded from the desire for unity and offered our advice and criticism, in the hope that Khrushchev might turn back. We indicated on many occasions that the points the fraternal Marxist-Leninist Parties had in common were basic while the differences among them were partial in character, and that they should seek common ground while reserving their differences. But Khrushchev and his like turned a deaf ear to

[1] Frederick Engels, *Germany: Revolution and Counter-Revolution*, Eng. ed., International Publishers, New York, 1933, p. 93.
[2] Karl Marx, " The Eighteenth Brumaire of Louis Bonaparte," *Selected Works of Marx and Engels*, Eng. ed., F.L.P.H., Moscow, Vol. 1, p. 272.

these words. They kept widening the differences and going farther down the revisionist road. They formulated a revisionist general line and a whole set of revisionist internal and external policies and worked out a revisionist programme. Hence, the nature of the differences clearly became one of fundamental opposition between the Marxist-Leninist general line and the revisionist general line. In addition, Khrushchev issued his order for the convening of the divisive meetings and went a step further in setting the revisionists against the Marxist-Leninists in the organizational sphere and in splitting the international communist movement.

After Khrushchev's downfall, we hoped that the new leaders of the CPSU would proceed from the common interests of the international communist movement, abandon Khrushchev revisionism and return to a Marxist-Leninist and proletarian internationalist stand. But the new leaders of the CPSU have obstinately clung to the whole of Khrushchev's revisionist theories, general line and policies and have declared that there is not a shade of difference between Khrushchev and themselves on the question of the international communist movement and in their attitude towards China. And they have taken the serious step of convening the divisive meeting regardless of the consequences. Quite obviously, the new leaders of the CPSU have gone a step further in destroying the basis for the unity of the Communist Parties. In these circumstances we would like to ask: When they exclaim, "what unites the Communist Parties greatly outweighs that which at the present time disunites them," what is this if not an effort to conceal their revisionist and schismatic essence?

The new leaders of the CPSU claim that we can take "concerted action against the enemy" and adopt "united action"! This is likewise a swindle. One of the important characteristics of Khrushchev revisionism is its complete reversal of enemies and friends. The new leaders of the CPSU are continuing to practise Khrushchev revisionism, and they regard U.S. imperialism, the common enemy of the people of the world, as their friend and all Marxist-Leninists and revolutionaries as their enemies. This being the case, what concerted action against the enemy or what united action can one speak of?

Let us now examine the actual policy the new leaders of the CPSU have pursued towards U.S. imperialism since they came into power.

In a nutshell, they are continuing to adhere to Khrushchev's reactionary policy of Soviet-U.S. co-operation for the domination of the world. They are proclaiming that there are "sufficiently broad areas for co-operation" between the Soviet Union and the United States and extolling the U.S. chieftain Johnson as being "sensible" in their efforts to prettify U.S. imperialism.

In their dealings with U.S. imperialism, the new leaders of the CPSU do not make as much noise as did Khrushchev; but they are "men of action." After taking office, they hurriedly struck several bargains with the U.S. imperialists, on some of which no agreement had been reached for a long time during Khrushchev's leadership. What deserves special attention is the fact that the new leaders of the CPSU should have agreed to contribute, in the guise of a donation, to the expenses incurred by the United States in its armed intervention in the Congo in the name of the United Nations. Moreover, for the purpose of helping U.S. imperialism to suppress and stamp out the people's revolutions in various countries they have given active support to the United States in its scheme to utilize the

U.N. "Special Committee for Peace-Keeping Operations" to establish a standing U.N. armed force. They have taken over Khrushchev's policy of fraternizing with, currying favour with and capitulating to U.S. imperialism.

The leaders of the CPSU have been trying in every possible way to bring within the orbit of Soviet-U.S. talks for the "settlement of problems" all revolutionary struggles in the front line of the battle against U.S. imperialism in Asia, Africa and Latin America, the storm-centres of world revolution. The new leaders of the CPSU are now loudly proclaiming their support for the revolutionary struggle of the people of southern Viet Nam, but in reality they are trying to gain political capital for their dealings with the U.S. imperialists and to carry out plots for "peace talks," in a futile attempt to extinguish the revolutionary struggle of the south Vietnamese people against U.S. imperialism and its lackeys.

At a time when the Democratic Republic of Viet Nam is being wantonly bombed by the U.S. gangsters, all the countries of the socialist camp and the revolutionary people throughout the world should, as a matter of course, unite and wage a tit-for-tat struggle against the U.S. aggressors. Instead, in order to serve U.S. imperialism the new leaders of the CPSU insisted on holding the schismatic meeting and took this grave divisive step. The statement against U.S. imperialist aggression in Viet Nam which they issued in the name of this divisive meeting was itself an irony of the first magnitude. Within twenty-four hours after the statement had been issued, they dispatched troops as well as ordinary and mounted police brutally to suppress the demonstration of students in Moscow against U.S. imperialism, an action which resulted in bloodshed, and they have persecuted foreign students who took part in this struggle. At the same time, the Soviet Government made prompt and obsequious apologies to U.S. imperialism.

The new leaders of the CPSU have exposed their fraudulence by their deeds. They have revealed themselves in their true colours to the whole world. They are directing the spearhead of their struggle not against U.S. imperialism and its lackeys but against the revolutionary people of all countries who are fighting imperialism and its lackeys.

It seems that "what unites" the new leaders of the CPSU and U.S. imperialism is becoming stronger and stronger and is making them well-nigh inseparable. Naturally, what separates them from the Marxist-Leninists will become greater and greater and "what unites" them with the Marxist-Leninists smaller and smaller the longer this goes on.

Next, let us consider the policies the new leaders of the CPSU have adopted towards fraternal countries and fraternal Parties.

In a nutshell, the new leaders of the CPSU have persisted in Khrushchev's policies against China, Albania, the Japanese Communist Party, the Indonesian Communist Party, the New Zealand Communist Party and all the fraternal countries and Parties which uphold Marxism-Leninism.

The new leaders of the CPSU still cling to the views expressed in the Open Letter of the Central Committee of the CPSU of July 14, 1963, in Suslov's anti-Chinese report at the February 1964 plenum of the Central Committee of the CPSU and in the resolution adopted on this report. They are still energetically mobilizing the whole Soviet Party and the entire Soviet people to read these anti-Chinese documents. In other words, they have taken over all the worn-out weapons from Khrushchev's anti-Chinese and anti-Communist arsenal. Moreover, they continue to give all kinds of support to the Indian reactionaries in the latter's opposition to China.

The new leaders of the CPSU have persisted in the entire set of erroneous policies against Albania which Khrushchev adopted at and around the period of the 22nd Congress of the CPSU.

The new leaders of the CPSU continue to practise Khrushchev's great-power chauvinisim towards fraternal socialist countries and to carry out a policy of exerting control over them.

The new leaders of the CPSU continue to follow Khrushchev's policy of unscrupulous interference in the internal affairs of the fraternal Parties and engage in disruptive and subversive activities against them. They have been colluding with Japanese Trotskyites, Right-wing Social-Democrats and renegades from the Japanese Communist Party, and have perpetrated every kind of disruption and subversion against the Japanese Communist Party which upholds Marxism-Leninism. Moreover, they publish articles in their press attacking it and giving open support to a handful of renegades such as Yoshio Shiga, Ichizo Suzuki and Shigeo Kamiyama. They have been supporting Indonesian Trotskyites and other counter-revolutionary forces in opposing the Indonesian Communist Party which opholds Marxism-Leninism and in disrupting the anti-imperialist national united front of Indonesia. They have been attacking the New Zealand Communist Party which upholds Marxism-Leninism and trying to subvert its leadership. And they have been carrying on all kinds of disruption and subversion against the Communist Party of Burma and other fraternal Parties upholding Marxism-Leninism.

The new leaders of the CPSU continue to pursue Khrushchev's policy of strenuous support for the clique headed by Dange, that renegade from the Indian working class and running dog of the Indian big bourgeoisie, in its anti-communist, anti-popular and counter-revolutionary activities.

From all this people can see at whom the new leaders of the CPSU are aiming when they speak of "concerted action against the enemy," and what they are actually about when they speak of "united action." People can also see that the new leaders of the CPSU do not want to strengthen what unites the fraternal Parties but ceaselessly aggravate what disunites them.

Numerous facts show that the clamour of the new leaders of the CPSU against U.S. imperialism is a sham while their capitulation to U.S. imperialism is the essence, that their issuing of the statement against U.S. imperialism is a sham while their suppression of the masses struggling against U.S. imperialism is the essence, that their support for revolution is a sham while their disruption of revolution is the essence, that their statements such as "unity against the enemy" and "concerted action" are a sham while their actions to undermine unity and create splits everywhere, even to the point of convening a meeting to create an open split in the international communist movement, are the essence.

To sum up, what the new leaders of the CPSU have been doing can be described as "three shams and three realities"; sham anti-imperialism but real capitulation, sham revolution but real betrayal, sham unity but a real split. They are still doing what Khrushchev did, which can be described as "four alignments with and four alignments against": alignment *with* imperialism *against* socialism, alignment *with* the United States *against* China and the other revolutionary countries, alignment *with*

413

the reactionaries everywhere *against* the national-liberation movements and the people's revolutions, and alignment *with* the Tito clique and renegades of all descriptions *against* all the fraternal Marxist-Leninist Parties and all revolutionaries fighting imperialism.

III. Answers to Some Questions

The communique of the schismatic Moscow meeting once again strikes up the old tune about the cessation of public polemics, saying that " the Parties represented at this meeting have declared themselves in favour of discontinuing open polemics, which are in character unfriendly and degrading to the fraternal Parties." It adds that " they consider it useful to continue, in a comradely form and without mutual attacks, an exchange of opinions on the important contemporary issues of mutual interest."

The communique dare not face this basic fact: it is the leaders of the CPSU themselves who started the public polemics in complete violation of the principles guiding relations among fraternal Parties and who have taken an " unfriendly " attitude towards fraternal Parties and launched " degrading " attacks on them. Nor dare it touch on the crucial matter of whether the numerous resolutions, statements and articles attacking the Chinese Communist Party and other Marxist-Leninist parties, which the leaders of the CPSU and their followers published, still stand or not.

We understand full well what is really meant when the leaders of the CPSU and their followers call for the ending of the public polemics; it means drawing no distinction between right and wrong, showing no respect for the truth, and allowing the revisionists to slander and attack the Marxist-Leninists while forbidding the Marxist-Leninists to answer and refute the revisionists.

So far, we have published only a small number of articles in reply to the attacks and slanders levelled at us by the leaders of the CPSU and their followers and are a long way from having completed our replies, while in many cases we have not yet made any reply at all. Unless they openly announce the withdrawal of these anti-Chinese resolutions, statements and articles and publicly admit their mistakes, it will be absolutely impossible to silence us. Can the whole affair be reckoned as ended when Your Lordships go off, shrugging your shoulders, after abusing others? Can it be that you may abuse people whenever you please and then call a halt whenever you want to, while forbidding us to make a fair answer? Is there any such unequal and wholly unreasonable principle governing relations among fraternal Parties?

The Chinese Communist Party has on many occasions made clear its stand on the question of the public polemics, and we now once again announce it to the world: Since there are differences of principle between Marxism-Leninism and modern revisionism and since the modern revisionists have maligned us so much and refused to acknowledge their mistakes, it goes without saying that we have the right to refute them publicly. In these circumstances, it will not do to call for an end to the public polemics, it will not do to stop for a single day, for a month, a year, a hundred years, a thousand years, or ten thousand years. If nine thousand years are not enough to complete the refutation, then we shall take ten thousand.

The communique also declares itself "against the interference by any Party in the internal affairs of other Parties." As everyone knows, what is meant here is but another version of the "denunciation of the factional activities of the Chinese Communist Party."

For years we have heard this kind of talk about opposing "factional activities" from Khrushchev, the greatest splitter in the international communist movement. There are indeed quite a few persons who have engaged in factional activities, namely, Khrushchev and his disciples, and since his downfall, those who cling to Khrushchev revisionism without Khrushchev and those who want to make Communist Parties degenerate into social-democratic parties. They direct their factional activities against Marxism-Leninism, against revolution and against the proletariat and the masses of the people who constitute the overwhelming majority of the population of the world. To oppose revolution and undermine the revolutionary unity of the proletariat they have carried out subversive activities in all the Communist and Workers' Parties by every conceivable means. Acting thus, they will inevitably be deserted by their followers and eventually become a miserable and negligible faction. And the "faction" which these gentlemen are attacking consists precisely of the Marxist-Leninists and revolutionaries who stand with the masses of the people. It should be stressed that the small schismatic Moscow meeting was itself grave factional activity.

The Communist Party of China never conceals its views. We approve of and support all the world forces, including all the political parties, groups and individuals, that persevere in revolution and in opposition to imperialism and reaction. As Lenin taught, the only correct policy is one based on principle. We shall never barter away principle. The more the revisionists abuse us, the stronger the proof that we are right, and the more firmly shall we maintain our principled stand. In this connection, if we need to make self-criticism, we should say that, in comparison with the support given by the leaders of the CPSU to the revisionist groups in many countries, we have not given enough support to the revolutionary Left in some countries and henceforth must greatly intensify our endeavours in this respect.

To put it bluntly, it will never work in the future any more than it did in the past to allow the adherents of Khrushchev revisionism to conspire with each other in opposing the Marxist-Leninists of all countries, while forbidding the Marxist-Leninists to support each other and unite in their struggle against Khrushchev revisionism and its adherents.

The communique says not a single word about whether the so-called new international meeting, which was to have been held in the middle of 1965 according to Khrushchev's order last year, has been cancelled or postponed. It equivocates by talking of "active and all-sided preparations" and of the meeting "to be held at a suitable date." At the same time, the communique advocates the holding of a so-called "Preliminary Consultative Conference of representatives of the 81 Parties that gathered at the 1960 Meeting." What does this mean? Doesn't it mean that they are desperately hanging on to the so-called drafting committee in Khrushchev's order of July 30, 1964? Or does it mean that they are insisting on the 81-Party meeting ordered by Khrushchev? Or are they up to some new trick?

We must solemnly tell the new leaders of the CPSU: In convening the illegal schismatic meeting you took a most serious step to effect an open split in the international communist movement. You must be held responsible for all the grave consequences.

In calling the divisive meeting, you have placed new and serious obstacles in the way of convening an international meeting for the unity of the fraternal Parties. We said before that in order to hold a successful meeting for unity, some four or five years of preparatory work might be required to remove the obstacles, but now it seems that a period twice as long, or even longer, will be needed.

IV. Unite on the Basis of Marxism-Leninism and Revolution

The new leaders of the CPSU have now held their schismatic meeting. They probably think that they can thereby curry favour with imperialism and somehow maintain their revisionist " legitimacy," and that they can use it for some political sleight of hand. But their action can neither intimidate nor deceive the Marxist-Leninists and the revolutionary people of the world. They were unable to block the advance of the people's revolutionary struggles in the past, and they will be still less able to do so in the future.

Comrade Mao Tse-tung has taught us time and again that the people — including those of the Soviet Union — who constitute the overwhelming majority of the population of the world want to make revolution. The overwhelming majority of Communists and cadres in the international communist movement, including those in the Communist. Party of the Soviet Union, want to make revolution. Persons like Khrushchev, whose thinking is ossified and who obtusely pursue the revisionist road and are bent on opposing communism, the people and revolution, are a mere handful, a tiny minority. For a while some people may not see things clearly or may be hoodwinked or may commit mistakes, but so long as they want to make revolution, having once understood the true situation and seen revisionism in its true colours, they will eventually break with revisionism and come over to the side of Marxism-Leninism in the course of their revolutionary practice. The masses of the people and the revolutionary cadres, who constitute over 90 per cent of the population of the world, will certainly unite.

The number of those believing in Khrushchev revisionism was already dwindling in any case. Now, of course it is even harder to make others believe in Khrushchevism without Khrushchev. Similarly, the number of those obeying Khrushchev's baton was already decreasing. Now, of course it is even harder to make others obey the baton taken over from Khrushchev. The small divisive meeting so painstakingly contrived by the new leaders of the CPSU turned out to be neither fish nor fowl; this not only shows that Khrushchev revisionism without Khrushchev is wrong and bankrupt, it also shows the great importance of the persistent struggle of the Marxist-Leninist parties and the Marxist-Leninists against modern revisionism and against this divisive meeting.

All the same, we have to thank the new leaders of the CPSU for insisting on calling the divisive meeting. This bad thing can be turned into a good thing. It has helped people quickly to strip the new leaders of the CPSU of their veil of Marxism-Leninism and to expose their true revisionist features. It is helping people to see through their fine words to the essence behind the appearance. It is helping all Communists and revolutionary people the world over to realize that the emergence and development of Khrushchev revisionism is by no means a matter of a few individuals or an accidental phenomenon. It has profound social and historical causes. So long as imperialists and reactionaries exist and so long as there are classes and class struggle in the world, Khrushchev revisionism will inevitably recur in one form or another and the struggle against it will not come to an end.

The communique of the schismatic Moscow meeting states that the Communists of all countries should concentrate on what it calls " the urgent tasks." What are the urgent tasks? In our view, the most urgent task facing the international communist movement is to unite with all the forces that can be united in order to oppose U.S. imperialism and its lackeys, to oppose the reactionaries of all countries, and to win victories in the struggle for world peace, national liberation, people's democracy and socialism. The Declaration of 1957 and the Statement of 1960 have explicitly pointed out that modern revisionism is the main danger in the international communist movement at the present time. In order to wage the struggle against imperialism and reaction successfully and further strengthen the unity of the international proletariat, it is imperative to continue to expose the true features of the modern revisionists, help those who lack an understanding of the true situation to acquire it, and help those who hesitate on the road of revolution to march ahead with the revolutionary people. It is likewise imperative to isolate to the maximum the modern revisionists, who are the accomplices of imperialism and reaction, and to carry the struggle against Khrushchev revisionism through to the very end.

The grave action of the new leaders of the CPSU in calling the divisive meeting has given the Marxist-Leninist parties and the Marxist-Leninists of the world the right to take the initiative. There is all the more reason now why we should openly criticize and thoroughly expose the revisionist line of the new leaders of the CPSU, give more vigorous support to the people's revolutionary movements and the revolutionary Left in different countries, and promote the speedier development of the Marxist-Leninist forces and the unity of the international communist movement on the basis of Marxism-Leninism and revolution.

The struggle between the two lines in the international communist movement has now entered a new stage. At this crucial juncture, we would like once again to give the new leaders of the CPSU a piece of sincere advice. Why should you put your neck into the noose left by Krushchev? Why can't you start afresh?

In our view, it is at once difficult and not difficult for you really to take the side of the fraternal Marxist-Leninist Parties and the revolutionary people in concerted action against the enemy and in unity against imperialism. The question hinges on whether or not you will do the following:

Publicly declare that all orders for convening divisive meetings are wrong and illegal. Openly admit the error of illegally convening the schismatic meeting.

Publicly and solemnly admit before the Communists and the people of the world that Khrushchev's revisionism, great-power chauvinism and splittism are wrong.

Publicly admit that the revisionist line and programme adopted at the 20th and 22nd Congresses of the CPSU presided over by Khrushchev are wrong.

Publicly admit that all the words and deeds of the leaders of the CPSU against China, Albania, the Japanese Communist Party and the other Marxist-Leninist parties are wrong.

Publicly pledge yourselves to desist from the error of Khrushchev revisionism and return to the road of Marxism-Leninism and proletarian internationalism, and to the revolutionary principles of the 1957 Declaration and the 1960 Statement.

It is imperative to solve these questions of principle if the genuine elimination of the differences and genuine unity against the enemy are to be achieved. Unless these questions of principle are solved and the serious obstacles placed in the way of unity of the international communist movement are removed, then all words about eliminating differences, strengthening unity, ending public polemics and calling an international meeting of the fraternal Parties are empty talk.

The show put on by Khrushchev was but a brief interlude in the history of the international communist movement, much briefer than the performances of the old-line revisionists, Bernstein and Kautsky. The subsequent performance of those who want Khrushchevism without Khrushchev can only be a brief interlude too, and no better than the show put on by Khrushchev himself.

The victorious advance of the revolutionary struggle of the people of the world represents the trend of history, and this trend is independent of the will of the imperialists, the reactionaries of all countries and the modern revisionists. As always, they keep on exposing their reactionary features by their deeds and will thus serve as teachers by negative example for the proletariat and revolutionary people of the world. We are convinced that over 90 per cent of the people of the world will join the revolutionary front against imperialism and that over 90 per cent of the people in the ranks of the international communist movement will advance along the road of Marxism-Leninism. We are also convinced that the revolutionary people of the world, the great international communist movement, the great socialist camp and the great Chinese and Soviet peoples will finally sweep away all obstacles and unite on the basis of Marxism-Leninism and proletarian internationalism. The future is infinitely bright for the cause of world revolution. In the end monsters of every description will be completely destroyed.

Let all the parties upholding Marxism-Leninism and all the revolutionary people of the world unite in the great struggle against imperialism, against the reactionaries of all countries and against modern revisionism! The Marxist-Leninists and the revolutionary people of the world will undoubtedly win even greater victories in their struggle for world peace, national liberation, people's democracy and socialism!

DOCUMENT 27

On Results of the March 1 — 5, 1965 Consultative
Meeting of Representatives of Communist and
Workers' Parties : Resolution of the Plenary
Session of the CPSU Central Committee
Adopted March 26, 1965

Complete Text

[*Pravda* and *Izvestiya*, March 27, p. 1, quoted from *CDSP*, Vol. XVII, No. 11 (April 7, 1965), pp. 5 and 13]

The plenary session of the CPSU Central Committee, having heard the report by Comrade M. A. Suslov on the results of the consultative meeting of representatives of Communist and Workers' Parties held in Moscow March 1–5, 1965, fully approves the documents adopted at the meeting — the communiqué and the statement on the events in Vietnam — as well as the activity of the CPSU delegation.

The plenary session believes that the meeting was an important step on the path toward the consolidation of the world Communist movement for the struggle against imperialism and colonialism, for national liberation, peace, democracy and socialism.

The results of the meeting show that the Communist Parties participating in it were firmly determined to do everything in their power to strengthen the unity of the international Communist movement on the basis of Marxism-Leninism and proletarian internationalism, on the basis of the line defined by the 1957 Declaration and the 1960 Statement.

The plenary session of the CPSU Central Committee expresses its full accord with the opinion of the participants in the meeting that the chief path toward the strengthening of unity is the raising by each Communist Party of its international responsibility, its active participation in joint actions in the common struggle against imperialism, colonialism and neocolonialism, in support of the liberation struggle of the peoples, against the domination of monopoly capital, for universal peace and the establishment of the principles of the peaceful coexistence of states with different social systems, for the cause of socialism and communism. Special attention attaches today to joint actions by the Communist Parties of all countries of the world and all peace-loving and democratic forces to repel the aggression of the American imperialists against South Vietnam, in defense of the Democratic Republic of Vietnam, in defense of the peoples who are being subjected to imperialist aggression. The highly important statement on the events in Vietnam adopted by the participants in the meeting is an appeal for such actions.

The plenary session of the Central Committee considers correct and fully approves the measures carried out by the Presidium of the CPSU Central Committee in reaching an agreement with the leadership of the Vietnamese Workers' Party to give further assistance and support to the heroic struggle of the Vietnamese people, to strengthen the defense capacity of the DRV in order to repel the aggression by American imperialism.

The plenary session of the Central Committee expresses its full agreement with the opinions and considerations contained in the communique. For its part, our party will undertake everything necessary so that they may find their practical embodiment and lead to the strengthening of the unity of the international Communist movement on the principles of Marxism-Leninism.

The CPSU shares the conclusion of the participants in the meeting that the disagreements in the Communist movement, by weakening its solidarity, harm the cause of the world liberation movement, the cause of communism. Our party, like the other fraternal parties that participated in the meeting, believes that in the present situation it is especially necessary to take effective steps toward overcoming the difficulties in the Communist movement, toward restoring the unity of its ranks.

The plenary session of the Central Committee supports the proposals worked out by the participants in the meeting in conditions of full equality and mutual respect for the opinions of all parties — proposals on ways for strengthening the solidarity of the Communist movement that envisage: joint actions in the struggle for common goals, collective efforts to improve the mutual relations among the parties, the use of bilateral and multilateral meetings and other forms of party intercourse, the cessation of open polemics that contain attacks and that bear an uncomradely form. At the same time, an exchange of opinions should be developed on important contemporary questions in a comradely form, and the norms for relations between parties established by the 1957 and 1960 conferences should be strictly observed.

The strengthening of the solidarity of the fraternal parties would be served by the holding in the near future of a preliminary consultative meeting of representatives of the 81 parties that participated in the 1960 conference. Such a meeting would make it possible to employ more democratic methods in defining the paths and forms for preparing a new international conference of representatives of the Communist Parties. The active and thorough preparation of a new international conference and its convocation at a suitable time answer the interests of the world Communist movement — this conclusion of the participants in the consultative meeting is fully supported by the CPSU.

The plenary session of the CPSU Central Committee approves the measures for strengthening fraternal friendship with the socialist countries and the solidarity of the international Communist movement, including the steps taken for the further development of ties and cooperation with all Communist and Workers' Parties, that have been implemented by the Presidium of the Central Committee since the October, 1964, plenary session.

The CPSU will continue unswervingly to pursue the Leninist line expressed in the CPSU Program and in the Declaration and Statement of the Moscow conferences, to defend firmly the principles of Marxism-Leninism and proletarian internationalism, and, together with the other Communist Parties, to strive for the consolidation of all the socialist countries, all the Marxist-Leninist parties and all the revolutionary forces of the present day in the struggle against imperialism and colonialism and for national liberation, peace, democracy and socialism.

DOCUMENT 28

Americans, Get Out of Vietnam: That Is the Condition for Peace

Statement Made by Giancarlo Pajetta at a Press Conference in Rome
upon the PCI Delegation's Return from North Vietnam
(May 20, 1965)

Excerpt

[*L'Unitá*, May 20, 1965, quoted, with revisions, from abridged translation
in *Information Bulletin*, No. 48 (July 16, 1965), pp. 38–44, at pp. 42–44]

.   .   .   .

Lastly, I would like to say something about our meeting with representatives of the Vietnamese Workers' Party [Dang Lao Dong Viet Nam]. We think they understand our policy, and have made theirs clearer to us, above all as regards the problems I have already indicated. We agreed that it is necessary to work jointly as well as separately in order to achieve broader and more effective international unity, to overcome the divergences existing between many Communist parties. The Vietnamese Workers' Party is a party enjoying great authority and prestige. To anyone who felt like speaking of it as a party manipulated from without, a party whose strings are allegedly being pulled by Peking or could tomorrow be pulled by Moscow, I would suggest studying its record over many years before 1945 and afterwards, from 1945 to 1949, when it fought in the van of the Resistance and when Chiang Kai-shek's reactionaries stood at the border. I would suggest studying the life story of a man like Ho Chi Minh, who took part in the constituent congress of the French Communist Party and who during his long imprisonment demonstrated his faith in the Resistance.

As for the consistency and strength of that movement, it might be a good idea to re-read the French press between 1945 and 1954, when it treated the Vietnamese fighters as visionaries and their Resistance as bluff, and never mentioned their government except in inverted commas. That government " shed " the inverted commas after an extraordinary event which took place at the time of the Geneva conference — the Dien Bien Phu battle.

We made a long trip that took us to other places besides Hanoi. I read in a paper that our Party was trying, and hence we are alleged to have been instructed, to " patch up " the international working-class movement still being rent by conflicting views. Understandably, the phrase used by a hostile paper is not the same as we would have used in a document. But if they feel like saying " patch up," let them. We did make an effort toward unity, and we made it because we think this unity today, that the progress in this matter registered to date, is inadequate. Our watchword is unity in diversity, but it has to be real unity clearly expressed. We made the effort on the basis of the recommendations of our Party and those of the Yalta Memorandum. We spoke in that sense with everyone — the comrades of the Secretariat of the CC CP of Czechoslovakia in Prague, the comrades of the Secretariat and the Presidium of the CC CPSU in

Moscow, the Chinese comrades, the General Secretary of the Chinese Party, the comrades in Hanoi, and lastly the leaders of the CP of Indonesia in Djakarta.

It was no accident that we visited, in addition to Hanoi, two of the countries that had declined to attend the Moscow meeting. I say "no accident" because we said before the Moscow meeting and during it, and say now that we Italian Communists do not divide the world Communist movement into two parties: the parties which attended the Moscow meeting and those that didn't. A debate is going on today, a debate in which we are taking part and which occasionally becomes sharp and is even marked by deep contradictions. But we do not think the Communist movement should be regarded as split in two, and think an effort should be made to restore unity.

In any case, our task was not to discuss every problem with those comrades, but to see, in keeping with the principles of our Party and the recommendations of the Yalta Memorandum, whether it was possible even in the face of divergences to achieve effective unity on specific points and on this basis to ensure that unity manifested itself as political action.

We stated our policy and our position. What we can say now and what you are interested in, you who have come to find out the Communist position on the Vietnamese question — is that the Communists of all the countries we visited, of all the parties we established contact with, were agreed on the need for concrete aid to Vietnam, for resistance to the imperialist aggression, and for the ridding of Vietnam of all of the aggressors' troops. We fully subscribe to this policy.

In Vietnam, we did not speak on behalf of our Party alone. We spoke — I think nobody can hold it against us — on behalf of all the Italians who consider that an aggression is taking place in Vietnam and who want the people of that country to live in freedom and peace, That is why the expression of friendly solidarity and of faith conveyed to us was meant not only for the Communists but for the Italians generally.

DOCUMENT 29

On the Situation in the World Communist Movement: Resolution of the CC, Portuguese Communist Party

Excerpt

[Portuguese statement of May 1965, published in *Pravda* on June 13, 1965; quoted from *Information Bulletin*, No. 50 (August 6, 1965), pp. 18–21, at pp. 19–21]

.   .   .   .

III

Besides these general conclusions, the 19 parties that took part in the Consultative Meeting put forward a *new* proposal aimed at finding a way out of the difficulties, namely, that representatives of the 81 parties that attended the 1960 Conference assemble at a preliminary Consultative

Conference to discuss all the problems pertaining to the new international Conference.

The PCP considers that such a preliminary Consultative Conference would constitute a good form of joint discussion of all the problems connected with the holding of the new international Conference of the Communist and Workers' parties. Each party would have an opportunity of stating before the other parties its view on this problem; it would be possible to compare views, try to bridge the positions, and reach agreed conclusions regarding the expediency or inexpediency of convening the Conference, the most suitable bodies for preparing it, the most suitable date for convening it, the agenda, and so on.

The PCP sees no special reasons for any party to reject *in principle* the idea of a preliminary Consultative Conference of the 81 parties for a collective discussion of these problems.

The PCP considers that reaching agreement *in principle* on holding such a Conference would be the first major step in developing this initiative. The thing is that the particular questions of the date, place and powers of the Conference can and must be discussed at length at bilateral and multi-lateral meetings. If all the parties agree *in principle* to hold the preliminary Consultative Conference, this will facilitate agreement on these particular questions.

The PCP, for its part, expresses its agreement in principle with the proposal, contained in the Communique of the Moscow Consultative Meeting, on convening a preliminary Consultative Conference of the 81 parties that took part in the 1960 Conference, to discuss the question of a new international Conference.

Communist and Workers' parties are known to differ in their views on the forms and methods of overcoming the existing disagreements. In most cases this divergence reflects the different ways in which each party strives to contribute to the restoration and consolidation of unity. However, whereas differences in opinion facilitate rather than hamper the search for joint decisions, this cannot be said about the harmful actions and manifestly unfriendly attitudes of some parties toward other parties.

As far as the Moscow Consultative Meeting of 19 parties is concerned, no party which views the facts objectively has any doubt that this Meeting was a positive constructive attempt to find ways of bringing the Communist and Workers' parties together, of pooling their efforts against the common enemy.

The insults, the charge levelled at some fraternal parties that they are subservient to the bourgeoisie and imperialism, the abusive attacks on the Communist Party of the Soviet Union and other fraternal parties cannot promote the cause of restoring world Communist unity and unity of action of the world forces fighting against imperialism, colonialism, national oppression, reaction and war.

The need to serve, in deeds not in words, the cause of proletarian internationalism, the cause of the exploited classes and oppressed peoples, the cause of socialism and peace, is greater today than ever before.

The differences in the world Communist movement encourage imperialism to new acts of aggression against the socialist camp, against the national-liberation movement and the working-class and democratic movements in the capitalist countries. The criminal U.S. aggression against Vietnam demands unity of action of the socialist camp, the Communist parties, all the revolutionary and peace-loving forces. In the struggle against the common enemy, nothing can justify the lack of unity in the Communist movement.

The Portuguese Communist Party considers, as before, that it is the imperative duty of all the Marxist-Leninist parties to promote actively and constructively the unity of the world Communist movement.

The Portuguese Communist Party will, for its part, work consistently for this unity based on the principles of Marxism-Leninism, continue to strengthen the bonds of friendship and cooperation with the fraternal parties, and actively cooperate with them in the fight against the common enemy, for the common cause.

DOCUMENT 30

Long Live the Victory of People's War !

In Commemoration of the 20th Anniversary of Victory in the
Chinese People's War of Resistance Against Japan

by Lin Piao

Excerpt

[*Jen-min Jih-pao*, September 2, 1965, quoted from *Peking Review*, Vol. VIII, No. 36 (September 3, 1965), pp. 9–30, at pp. 17–30]

.   .   .   .

Carry Out the Strategy and Tactics of People's War

Engels said, " The emancipation of the proletariat, in its turn, will have its specific expression in military affairs and create its specific, new military method." [8] Engels' profound prediction has been fulfilled in the revolutionary wars waged by the Chinese people under the leadership of the Chinese Communist Party. In the course of protracted armed struggle, we have created a whole range of strategy and tactics of people's war by which we have been able to utilize our strong points to attack the enemy at his weak points.

During the War of Resistance Against Japan, on the basis of his comprehensive analysis of the enemy and ourselves, Comrade Mao Tse-tung laid down the following strategic principle for the Communist-led Eighth Route and New Fourth Armies: " Guerrilla warfare is basic, but lose no chance for mobile warfare under favourable conditions." [9] He raised guerrilla warfare to the level of strategy, because, if they are to defeat a formidable enemy, revolutionary armed forces should not fight with a reckless disregard for the consequences when there is a great disparity between their own strength and the enemy's. If they do, they will suffer serious losses and bring heavy setbacks to the revolution. Guerrilla warfare

---

[8] Frederick Engels, " Possibilities and Perspectives of the War of the Holy Alliance Against France in 1852," *Collected Works of Marx and Engels*, Russ. ed., Moscow, 1956, Vol. VII, p. 509.

[9] Mao Tse-tung, " On Protracted War," *Selected Works*, Vol. II.

is the only way to mobilize and apply the whole strength of the people against the enemy, the only way to expand our forces in the course of the war, deplete and weaken the enemy, gradually change the balance of forces between the enemy and ourselves, switch from guerrilla to mobile warfare, and finally defeat the enemy.

In the initial period of the Second Revolutionary Civil War, Comrade Mao Tse-tung enumerated the basic tactics of guerrilla warfare as follows: " The enemy advances, we retreat; the enemy camps, we harass; the enemy tires, we attack; the enemy retreats, we pursue." [10] Guerrilla war tactics were further developed during the War of Resistance Against Japan. In the base areas behind the enemy lines, everybody joined in the fighting — the troops and the civilian population, men and women, old and young; every single village fought. Various ingenious methods of fighting were devised, including " sparrow warfare," [11] land-mine warfare, tunnel warfare, sabotage warfare, and guerrilla warfare on lakes and rivers.

In the later period of the War of Resistance Against Japan and during the Third Revolutionary Civil War, we switched our strategy from that of guerrilla warfare as the primary form of fighting to that of mobile warfare in the light of the changes in the balance of forces between the enemy and ourselves. By the middle, and especially the later, period of the Third Revolutionary Civil War, our operations had developed into large-scale mobile warfare, including the storming of big cities.

War of annihilation is the fundamental guiding principle of our military operations. This guiding principle should be put into effect regardless of whether mobile or guerrilla warfare is the primary form of fighting. It is true that in guerrilla warfare much should be done to disrupt and harass the enemy, but it is still necessary actively to advocate and fight battles of annihilation whenever conditions are favourable. In mobile warfare superior forces must be concentrated in every battle so that the enemy forces can be wiped out one by one. Comrade Mao Tse-tung has pointed out:

> A battle in which the enemy is routed is not basically decisive in a contest with a foe of great strength. A battle of annihilation, on the other hand, produces a great and immediate impact on any enemy. Injuring all of a man's ten fingers is not as effective as chopping off one, and routing ten enemy divisions is not as effective as annihilating one of them. [12]

Battles of annihilation are the most effective way of hitting the enemy; each time one of his brigades or regiments is wiped out, he will have one brigade or one regiment less, and the enemy forces will be demoralized and will disintegrate. By fighting battles of annihilation, our army is able

[10] Mao Tse-tung, " A Single Spark Can Start a Prairie Fire," *Selected Works*, Eng. ed., FLP, Peking, 1965, Vol. I, p. 124.

[11] Sparrow warfare is a popular method of fighting created by the Communist-led anti-Japanese guerrilla units and militia behind the enemy lines. It was called sparrow warfare because, first, it was used diffusely, like the flight of sparrows in the sky; and because, second, it was used flexibly by guerrillas or militiamen, operating in threes or fives, appearing and disappearing unexpectedly and wounding, killing, depleting and wearing out the enemy forces.

[12] Mao Tse-tung, " Problems of Strategy in China's Revolutionary War," *Selected Works*, Eng. ed., FLP, Peking, 1965, Vol. I, p. 248.

to take prisoners of war or capture weapons from the enemy in every battle, and the morale of our army rises, our army units get bigger, our weapons become better, and our combat effectiveness continually increases.

In his celebrated ten cardinal military principles Comrade Mao Tse-tung pointed out:

> In every battle, concentrate an absolutely superior force (two, three, four and sometimes even five or six times the enemy's strength), encircle the enemy forces completely, strive to wipe them out thoroughly and do not let any escape from the net. In special circumstances, use the method of dealing crushing blows to the enemy, that is, concentrate all our strength to make a frontal attack and also to attack one or both of his flanks, with the aim of wiping out one part and routing another so that our army can swiftly move its troops to smash other enemy forces. Strive to avoid battles of attrition in which we lose more than we gain or only break even. In this way, although we are inferior as a whole (in terms of numbers), we are absolutely superior in every part and every specific campaign, and this ensures victory in the campaign. As time goes on, we shall become superior as a whole and eventually wipe out all the enemy.[13]

At the same time, he said that we should first attack dispersed or isolated enemy forces and only attack concentrated and strong enemy forces later; that we should strive to wipe out the enemy through mobile warfare; that we should fight no battle unprepared and fight no battle we are not sure of winning; and that in any battle we fight we should develop our army's strong points and its excellent style of fighting. These are the major principles of fighting a war of annihilation.

In order to annihilate the enemy, we must adopt the policy of luring him in deep and abandon some cities and districts of our own accord in a planned way, so as to let him in. It is only after letting the enemy in that the people can take part in the war in various ways and that the power of a people's war can be fully exerted. It is only after letting the enemy in that he can be compelled to divide up his forces, take on heavy burdens and commit mistakes. In other words, we must let the enemy become elated, stretch out all his ten fingers and become hopelessly bogged down. Thus, we can concentrate superior forces to destroy the enemy forces one by one, to eat them up mouthful by mouthful. Only by wiping out the enemy's effective strength can cities and localities be finally held or seized. We are firmly against dividing up our forces to defend all positions and putting up resistance at every place for fear that our territory might be lost and our pots and pans smashed, since this can neither wipe out the enemy forces nor hold cities or localities.

Comrade Mao Tse-tung has provided a masterly summary of the strategy and tactics of people's war: You fight in your way and we fight in ours; we fight when we can win and move away when we can't.

In other words, you rely on modern weapons and we rely on highly conscious revolutionary people; you give full play to your superiority and we give full play to ours; you have your way of fighting and we have ours. When you want to fight us, we don't let you and you can't even find us. But when we want to fight you, we make sure that you can't

13 Mao Tse-tung, "The Present Situation and Our Tasks," *Selected Works*, Eng. ed., FLP, Peking, 1961, Vol. IV, p. 161.

get away and we hit you squarely on the chin and wipe you out. When we are able to wipe you out, we do so with a vengeance; when we can't, we see to it that you don't wipe us out. It is opportunism if one won't fight when one can win. It is adventurism if one insists on fighting when one can't win. Fighting is the pivot of all our strategy and tactics. It is because of the necessity of fighting that we admit the necessity of moving away. The sole purpose of moving away is to fight and bring about the final and complete destruction of the enemy. This strategy and these tactics can be applied only when one relies on the broad masses of the people and such application brings the superiority of people's war into full play. However superior he may be in technical equipment and whatever tricks he may resort to, the enemy will find himself in the passive position of having to receive blows, and the initiative will always be in our hands.

We grew from a small and weak to a large and strong force and finally defeated formidable enemies at home and abroad because we carried out the strategy and tactics of people's war. During the eight years of the War of Resistance Against Japan, the people's army led by the Chinese Communist Party fought more than 125,000 engagements with the enemy and put out of action more than 1,700,000 Japanese and puppet troops. In the three years of the War of Liberation, we put eight million of the Kuomintang's reactionary troops out of action and won the great victory of the people's revolution.

Adhere to the Policy of Self-Reliance

The Chinese people's War of Resistance Against Japan was an important part of the Anti-Fascist World War. The victory of the Anti-Fascist War as a whole was the result of the common struggle of the people of the world. By its participation in the war against Japan at the final stage, the Soviet army under the leadership of the Communist Party of the Soviet Union headed by Stalin played a significant part in bringing about the defeat of Japanese imperialism. Great contributions were made by the peoples of Korea, Viet Nam, Mongolia, Laos, Cambodia, Indonesia, Burma, India, Pakistan, Malaya, the Philippines, Thailand and certain other Asian countries. The people of the Americas, Oceania, Europe and Africa also made their contribution.

Under extremely difficult circumstances, the Communist Party of Japan and the revolutionary forces of the Japanese people kept up their valiant and staunch struggle, and played their part in the defeat of Japanese fascism.

The common victory was won by all the peoples, who gave one another support and encouragement. Yet each country was, above all, liberated as a result of its own people's efforts.

The Chinese people enjoyed the support of other peoples in winning both the War of Resistance Against Japan and the People's Liberation War, and yet victory was mainly the result of the Chinese people's own efforts. Certain people assert that China's victory in the War of Resistance was due entirely to foreign assistance. This absurd assertion is in tune with that of the Japanese militarists.

The liberation of the masses is accomplished by the masses themselves — this is a basic principle of Marxism-Leninism. Revolution or people's war in any country is the business of the masses in that country and should be carried out primarily by their own efforts; there is no other way.

During the War of Resistance Against Japan, our Party maintained that China should rely mainly on her own strength while at the same time trying to get as much foreign assistance as possible. We firmly opposed the Kuomintang ruling clique's policy of exclusive reliance on foreign aid. In the eyes of the Kuomintang and Chiang Kai-shek, China's industry and agriculture were no good, her weapons and equipment were no good, nothing in China was any good, so that if she wanted to defeat Japan, she had to depend on other countries, and particularly on the U.S.-British imperialists. This was completely slavish thinking. Our policy was diametrically opposed to that of the Kuomintang. Our Party held that it was possible to exploit the contradictions between U.S.-British imperialism and Japanese imperialism, but that no reliance could be placed on the former. In fact, the U.S.-British imperialists repeatedly plotted to bring about a " Far Eastern Munich " in order to arrive at a compromise with Japanese imperialism at China's expense, and for a considerable period of time they provided the Japanese aggressors with war matériel. In helping China during that period, the U.S. imperialists harboured the sinister design of turning China into a colony of their own.

Comrade Mao Tse-tung said: "China has to rely mainly on her own efforts in the War of Resistance." [14] He added, "We hope for foreign aid but cannot be dependent on it; we depend on our own efforts, on the creative power of the whole army and the entire people." [15]

Self-reliance was especially important for the people's armed forces and the Liberated Areas led by our Party.

The Kuomintang government gave the Eighth Route and New Fourth Armies some small allowances in the initial stage of the anti-Japanese war, but gave them not a single penny later. The Liberated Areas faced great difficulties as a result of the Japanese imperialists' savage attacks and brutal " mopping-up " campaigns, of the Kuomintang's military encirclement and economic blockade and of natural calamaties. The difficulties were particularly great in the years 1941 and 1942, when we were very short of food and clothing.

What were we to do? Comrade Mao Tse-tung asked: How has mankind managed to keep alive from time immemorial? Has it not been by men using their hands to provide for themselves? Why should we, their latter-day descendants, be devoid of this tiny bit of wisdom? Why can't we use our own hands?

The Central Committee of the Party and Comrade Mao Tse-tung put forward the policies of " ample food and clothing through self-reliance " and " develop the economy and ensure supplies," and the army and the people of the Liberated Areas accordingly launched an extensive production campaign, with the main emphasis on agriculture.

Difficulties are not invincible monsters. If everyone co-operates and fights them, they will be overcome. The Kuomintang reactionaries thought that it could starve us to death by cutting off allowances and imposing an economic blockade, but in fact it helped us by stimulating us to rely on our own efforts to surmount our difficulties. While launching the great campaign for production, we applied the policy of " better troops and simpler administration " and economized in the use of manpower and

14 Mao Tse-tung, " Interview with Three Correspondents from the Central News Agency, the *Sao Tang Pao* and the *Hsin Min Pao*," *Selected Works*, Vol. II.
15 Mao Tse-tung, " We Must Learn to Do Economic Work," *Selected Works*, Vol. III.

material resources; thus we not only surmounted the severe material difficulties and successfully met the crisis, but lightened the people's burden, improved their livelihood and laid the material foundations for victory in the anti-Japanese war.

The problem of military equipment was solved mainly by relying on the capture of arms from the enemy, though we did turn out some weapons too. Chiang Kai-shek, the Japanese imperialists and the U.S. imperialists have all been our "chiefs of transportation corps." The arsenals of the imperialists always provide the oppressed peoples and nations with arms.

The people's armed forces led by our Party independently waged people's war on a large scale and won great victories without any material aid from outside, both during the more than eight years of the anti-Japanese war and during the more than three years of the People's War of Liberation.

Comrade Mao Tse-tung has said that our fundamental policy should rest on the foundation of our own strength. Only by relying on our own efforts can we in all circumstances remain invincible.

The peoples of the world invariably support each other in their struggles against imperialism and its lackeys. Those countries which have won victory are duty bound to support and aid the peoples who have not yet done so. Nevertheless, foreign aid can only play a supplementary role.

In order to make a revolution and to fight a people's war and be victorious, it is imperative to adhere to the policy of self-reliance, rely on the strength of the masses in one's own country and prepare to carry on the fight independently even when all material aid from outside is cut off. If one does not operate by one's own efforts, does not independently ponder and solve the problems of the revolution in one's own country and does not rely on the strength of the masses, but leans wholly on foreign aid — even though this be aid from socialist countries which persist in revolution — no victory can be won, or be consolidated even if it is won.

The International Significance of Comrade Mao Tse-tung's Theory of People's War

The Chinese revolution is a continuation of the Great October Revolution. The road of the October Revolution is the common road for all people's revolutions. The Chinese revolution and the October Revolution have in common the following basic characteristics: (1) Both were led by the working class with a Marxist-Leninist party as its nucleus. (2) Both were based on the worker-peasant alliance. (3) In both cases state power was seized through violent revolution and the dictatorship of the proletariat was established. (4) In both cases the socialist system was built after victory in the revolution. (5) Both were component parts of the proletarian world revolution.

Naturally, the Chinese revolution had its own peculiar characteristics. The October Revolution took place in imperialist Russia, but the Chinese revolution broke out in a semi-colonial and semi-feudal country. The former was a proletarian socialist revolution, while the latter developed into a socialist revolution after the complete victory of the new-democratic revolution. The October Revolution began with armed uprisings in the cities and then spread to the countryside, while the Chinese revolution

429

won nation-wide victory through the encirclement of the cities from the rural areas and the final capture of the cities.

Comrade Mao Tse-tung's great merit lies in the fact that he has succeeded in integrating the universal truth of Marxism-Leninism with the concrete practice of the Chinese revolution and has enriched and developed Marxism-Leninism by his masterly generalization and summation of the experience gained during the Chinese people's protracted revolutionary struggle.

Comrade Mao Tse-tung's theory of people's war has been proved by the long practice of the Chinese revolution to be in accord with the objective laws of such wars and to be invincible. It has not only been valid for China, it is a great contribution to the revolutionary struggles of the oppressed nations and peoples throughout the world.

The people's war led by the Chinese Communist Party, comprising the War of Resistance and the Revolutionary Civil Wars, lasted for twenty-two years. It constitutes the most drawn-out and most complex people's war led by the proletariat in modern history, and it has been the richest in experience.

In the last analysis, the Marxist-Leninist theory of proletarian revolution is the theory of the seizure of state power by revolutionary violence, the theory of countering war against the people by people's war. As Marx so aptly put it, " Force is the midwife of every old society pregnant with a new one." [16]

It was on the basis of the lessons derived from the people's wars in China that Comrade Mao Tse-tung, using the simplest and the most vivid language, advanced the famous thesis that " political power grows out of the barrel of a gun." [17]

He clearly pointed out:

> The seizure of power by armed force, the settlement of the issue by war, is the central task and the highest form of revolution. This Marxist-Leninist principle of revolution holds good universally, for China and for all other countries.[18]

War is the product of imperialism and the system of exploitation of man by man. Lenin said that " war is always and everywhere begun by the exploiters themselves, by the ruling and oppressing classes." [19] So long as imperialism and the system of exploitation of man by man exist, the imperialists and reactionaries will invariably rely on armed force to maintain their reactionary rule and impose war on the oppressed nations and peoples. This is an objective law independent of man's will.

In the world today, all the imperialists headed by the United States and their lackeys, without exception, are strengthening their state machinery, and especially their armed forces. U.S. imperialism, in particular, is carrying out armed aggression and suppression everywhere.

What should the oppressed nations and the oppressed people do in the face of wars of aggression and armed suppression by the imperialists and their lackeys? Should they submit and remain slaves in perpetuity? Or should they rise in resistance and fight for their liberation?

[16] Karl Marx, *Capital*, Eng. ed., Foreign Languages Publishing House, Moscow, 1954, Vol. I, p. 751.
[17] Mao Tse-tung, " Problems of War and Strategy," *Selected Works*, Vol. II.
[18] *Ibid*.
[19] V. I. Lenin, " The Revolutionary Army and the Revolutionary Government," *Collected Works*, Eng. ed., FLPH, Moscow, 1962, Vol. VIII, p. 565.

Comrade Mao Tse-tung answered this question in vivid terms. He said that after long investigation and study the Chinese people discovered that all the imperialists and their lackeys " have swords in their hands and are out to kill. The people have come to understand this and so act after the same fashion." [20] This is called doing unto them what they do unto us.

In the last analysis, whether one dares to wage a tit-for-tat struggle against armed aggression and suppression by the imperialists and their lackeys, whether one dares to fight a people's war against them, is tantamount to whether one dares to embark on revolution. This is the most effective touchstone for distinguishing genuine from fake revolutionaries and Marxist-Leninists.

In view of the fact that some people were afflicted with the fear of the imperialists and reactionaries, Comrade Mao Tse-tung put forward his famous thesis that " the imperialists and all reactionaries are paper tigers." He said,

All reactionaries are paper tigers. In appearance, the reactionaries are terrifying, but in reality they are not so powerful. From a long term point of view, it is not the reactionaries but the people who are really powerful.[21]

The history of people's war in China and other countries provides conclusive evidence that the growth of the people's revolutionary forces from weak and small beginnings into strong and large forces is a universal law of development of class struggle, a universal law of development of people's war. A people's war inevitably meets with many difficulties, with ups and downs and setbacks in the course of its development, but no force can alter its general trend towards inevitable triumph.

Comrade Mao Tse-tung points out that we must despise the enemy strategically and take full account of him tactically.

To despise the enemy strategically is an elementary requirement for a revolutionary. Without the courage to despise the enemy and without daring to win, it will be simply impossible to make revolution and wage a people's war, let alone to achieve victory.

It is also very important for revolutionaries to take full account of the enemy tactically. It is likewise impossible to win victory in a people's war without taking full account of the enemy tactically, and without examining the concrete conditions, without being prudent and giving great attention to the study of the art of struggle, and without adopting appropriate forms of struggle in the concrete practice of the revolution in each country and with regard to each concrete problem of struggle.

Dialectical and historical materialism teaches us that what is important primarily is not that which at the given moment seems to be durable and yet is already beginning to die away, but that which is arising and developing, even though at the given moment it may not appear to be durable, for only that which is arising and developing is invincible.

Why can the apparently weak new-born forces always triumph over the decadent forces which appear so powerful? The reason is that truth is on their side and that the masses are on their side, while the reactionary

---

[20] Mao Tse-tung, " The Situation and Our Policy After the Victory in the War of Resistance Against Japan," *Selected Works*, Eng. ed., FLP, Peking, 1961, Vol. IV, pp. 14–15.

[21] Mao Tse-tung, " Talk with the American Correspondent Anna Louise Strong." *Selected Works*, Eng. ed., FLP, Peking, 1961, Vol. IV, p. 100.

classes are always divorced from the masses and set themselves against the masses.

This has been borne out by the victory of the Chinese revolution, by the history of all revolutions, the whole history of class struggle and the entire history of mankind.

The imperialists are extremely afraid of Comrade Mao Tse-tung's thesis that "imperialism and all reactionaries are paper tigers." and the revisionists are extremely hostile to it. They all oppose and attack this thesis and the philistines follow suit by ridiculing it. But all this cannot in the least diminish its importance. The light of truth cannot be dimmed by anybody.

Comrade Mao Tse-tung's theory of people's war solves not only the problem of daring to fight a people's war, but also that of how to wage it.

Comrade Mao Tse-tung is a great statesman and military scientist, proficient at directing war in accordance with its laws. By the line and policies, the strategy and tactics he formulated for the people's war, he led the Chinese people in steering the ship of the people's war past all hidden reefs to the shores of victory in most complicated and difficult conditions.

It must be emphasized that Comrade Mao Tse-tung's theory of the establishment of rural revolutionary base areas and the encirclement of the cities from the countryside is of outstanding and universal practical importance for the present revolutionary struggles of all the oppressed nations and peoples, and particularly for the revolutionary struggles of the oppressed nations and peoples in Asia, Africa and Latin America against imperialism and its lackeys.

Many countries and peoples in Asia, Africa and Latin America are now being subjected to aggression and enslavement on a serious scale by the imperialists headed by the United States and their lackeys. The basic political and economic conditions in many of these countries have many similarities to those that prevailed in old China. As in China, the peasant question is extremely important in these regions. The peasants constitute the main force of the national-democratic revolution against the imperialists and their lackeys. In committing aggression against these countries, the imperialists usually begin by seizing the big cities and the main lines of communication, but they are unable to bring the vast countryside completely under their control. The countryside, and the countryside alone, can provide the broad areas in which the revolutionaries can manoeuvre freely. The countryside, and the countryside alone, can provide the revolutionary bases from which the revolutionaries can go forward to final victory. Precisely for this reason, Comrade Mao Tse-tung's theory of establishing revolutionary base areas in the rural districts and encircling the cities from the countryside is attracting more and more attention among the people in these regions.

Taking the entire globe, if North America and Western Europe can be called "the cities of the world," then Asia, Africa and Latin America constitute "the rural areas of the world." Since World War II, the proletarian revolutionary movement has for various reasons been temporarily held back in the North American and West European capitalist countries, while the people's revolutionary movement in Asia, Africa and Latin America has been growing vigorously. In a sense, the contemporary world revolution also presents a picture of the encirclement of cities by the rural areas. In the final analysis, the whole cause of world revolution hinges on the revolutionary struggles of the Asian, African and Latin American peoples who make up the overwhelming majority of the world's population. The socialist countries should regard it as their internationalist duty to support the people's revolutionary struggles in Asia, Africa and Latin America.

The October Revolution opened up a new era in the revolution of the oppressed nations. The victory of the October Revolution built a bridge between the socialist revolution of the proletariat of the West and the national-democratic revolution of the colonial and semi-colonial countries of the East. The Chinese revolution has successfully solved the problem of how to link up the national-democratic with the socialist revolution in the colonial and semi-colonial countries.

Comrade Mao Tse-tung has pointed out that, in the epoch since the October Revolution, anti-imperialist revolution in any colonial or semi-colonial country is no longer part of the old bourgeois, or capitalist world revolution, but is part of the new world revolution, the proletarian-socialist world revolution.

Comrade Mao Tse-tung has formulated a complete theory of the new-democratic revolution. He indicated that this revolution, which is different from all others, can only be, nay must be, a revolution against imperialism, feudalism and bureaucrat-capitalism waged by the broad masses of the people under the leadership of the proletariat.

This means that the revolution can only be, nay must be, led by the proletariat and the genuinely revolutionary party armed with Marxism-Leninism, and by no other class or party.

This means that the revolution embraces in its ranks not only the workers, peasants and the urban petty bourgeoisie, but also the national bourgeoisie and other patriotic and anti-imperialist democrats.

This means, finally, that the revolution is directed against imperialism, feudalism and bureaucrat-capitalism.

The new-democratic revolution leads to socialism, and not to capitalism.

Comrade Mao Tse-tung's theory of the new-democratic revolution is the Marxist-Leninist theory of revolution by stages as well as the Marxist-Leninist theory of uninterrupted revolution.

Comrade Mao Tse-tung made a correct distinction between the two revolutionary stages, i.e., the national-democratic and the socialist revolutions; at the same time he correctly and closely linked the two. The national-democratic revolution is the necessary preparation for the socialist revolution, and the socialist revolution is the inevitable sequel to the national-democratic revolution. There is no Great Wall between the two revolutionary stages. But the socialist revolution is only possible after the completion of the national-democratic revolution. The more thorough the national-democratic revolution, the better the conditions for the socialist revolution.

The experience of the Chinese revolution shows that the tasks of the national-democratic revolution can be fulfilled only through long and tortuous struggles. In this stage of revolution, imperialism and its lackeys are the principal enemy. In the struggle against imperialism and its lackeys, it is necessary to rally all anti-imperialist patriotic forces, including the national bourgeoisie and all patriotic personages. All those patriotic personages from among the bourgeoisie and other exploiting classes who join the anti-imperialist struggle play a progressive historical role; they are not tolerated by imperialism but welcomed by the proletariat.

It is very harmful to confuse the two stages, that is, the national-democratic and the socialist revolutions. Comrade Mao Tse-tung criticized the wrong idea of "accomplishing both at one stroke," and pointed out that this utopian idea could only weaken the struggle against imperialism and its lackeys, the most urgent task at the time. The Kuomintang reactionaries and the Trotskyites they hired during the War of Resistance deliberately confused these two stages of the Chinese revolution, proclaiming the "theory of a single revolution" and preaching so-called "socialism" without any Communist Party. With this preposterous theory they attempted to swallow up the Communist Party, wipe out any revolution and prevent the advance of the national-democratic revolution, and they used it as a pretext for their non-resistance and capitulation to imperialism. This reactionary theory was buried long ago by the history of the Chinese revolution.

The Khrushchev revisionists are now actively preaching that socialism can be built without the proletariat and without a genuinely revolutionary party armed with the advanced proletarian ideology, and they have cast the fundamental tenets of Marxism-Leninism to the four winds. The revisionists' purpose is solely to divert the oppressed nations from their struggle against imperialism and sabotage their national-democratic revolution, all in the service of imperialism.

The Chinese revolution provides a successful lesson for making a thoroughgoing national-democratic revolution under the leadership of the proletariat; it likewise provides a successful lesson for the timely transition from the national-democratic revolution to the socialist revolution under the leadership of the proletariat.

Mao Tse-tung's thought has been the guide to the victory of the Chinese revolution. It has integrated the universal truth of Marxism-Leninism with the concrete practice of the Chinese revolution and creatively developed Marxism-Leninism, thus adding new weapons to the arsenal of Marxism-Leninism.

Ours is the epoch in which world capitalism and imperialism are heading for their doom and socialism and communism are marching to victory. Comrade Mao Tse-tung's theory of people's war is not only a product of the Chinese revolution, but has also the characteristics of our epoch. The new experience gained in the people's revolutionary struggles in various countries since World War II has provided continuous evidence that Mao Tse-tung's thought is a common asset of the revolutionary people of the whole world. This is the great international significance of the thought of Mao Tse-tung.

Defeat U.S. Imperialism and Its Lackeys by People's War

Since World War II, U.S. imperialism has stepped into the shoes of German, Japanese and Italian fascism and has been trying to build a great American empire by dominating and enslaving the whole world. It is actively fostering Japanese and West German militarism as its chief accomplices in unleashing a world war. Like a vicious wolf, it is bullying and enslaving various peoples, plundering their wealth, encroaching upon their countries' sovereignty and interfering in their internal affairs. It is the most rabid aggressor in human history and the most ferocious common enemy of the people of the world. Every people or country in the world that wants revolution, independence and peace cannot but direct the spearhead of its struggle against U.S. imperialism.

Just as the Japanese imperialists' policy of subjugating China made it possible for the Chinese people to form the broadest possible united front against them, so the U.S. imperialists' policy of seeking world domination makes it possible for the people throughout the world to unite all the forces that can be united and form the broadest possible united front for a converging attack on U.S. imperialism.

At present, the main battlefield of the fierce struggle between the people of the world on the one side and U.S. imperialism and its lackeys on the other is the vast area of Asia, Africa and Latin America. In the world as whole, this is the area where the people suffer worst from imperialist oppression and where imperialist rule is most vulnerable. Since World War II, revolutionary storms have been rising in this area, and today they have become the most important force directly pounding U.S. imperialism. The contradiction between the revolutionary peoples of Asia, Africa and Latin America and the imperialists headed by the United States is the principal contradiction in the contemporary world. The development of this contradiction is promoting the struggle of the people of the whole world against U.S. imperialism and its lackeys.

Since World War II, people's war has increasingly demonstrated its power in Asia, Africa and Latin America. The peoples of China, Korea, Viet Nam, Laos, Cuba, Indonesia, Algeria and other countries have waged people's wars against the imperialists and their lackeys and won great victories. The classes leading these people's wars may vary, and so may the breadth and depth of mass mobilization and the extent of victory, but the victories in these people's wars have very much weakened and pinned down the forces of imperialism, upset the U.S. imperialist plan to launch a world war, and become mighty factors defending world peace.

Today, the conditions are more favourable than ever before for the waging of people's wars by the revolutionary peoples of Asia, Africa and Latin America against U.S. imperialism and its lackeys.

Since World War II and the succeeding years of revolutionary upsurge, there has been a great rise in the level of political consciousness and the degree of organization of the people in all countries, and the resources available to them for mutual support and aid have greatly increased. The whole capitalist-imperialist system has become drastically weaker and is in the process of increasing convulsion and disintegration. After World War I, the imperialists lacked the power to destroy the new-born socialist Soviet state, but they were still able to suppress the people's revolutionary movements in some countries in the parts of the world under their own rule and so maintain a short period of comparative stability. Since World War II, however, not only have they been unable to stop a number of countries from taking the socialist road, but they are no longer capable of holding back the surging tide of the people's revolutionary movements in the areas under their own rule.

U.S. imperialism is stronger, but also more vulnerable, than any imperialism of the past. It sets itself against the people of the whole world, including the people of the United States. Its human, military, material and financial resources are far from sufficient for the realization of its ambition of dominating the whole world. U.S. imperialism has further weakened itself by occupying so many places in the world, overreaching itself, stretching its fingers out wide and dispersing its strength, with its rear so far away and its supply lines so long. As Comrade Mao Tse-tung has said, "Wherever it commits aggression, it puts a new noose around its neck. It is besieged ring upon ring by the people of the whole world." [22]

When committing aggression in a foreign country, U.S. imperialism can only employ part of its forces, which are sent to fight an unjust war far from their native land and therefore have a low morale, and so U.S. imperialism is beset with great difficulties. The people subjected to its aggression are having a trial of strength with U.S. imperialism neither in Washington nor New York, neither in Honolulu nor Florida, but are fighting for independence and freedom on their own soil. Once they are mobilized on a broad scale, they will have inexhaustible strength. Thus superiority will belong not to the United States but to the people subjected to its aggression. The latter, though apparently weak and small, are really more powerful than U.S. imperialism.

The struggles waged by the different peoples against U.S. imperialism reinforce each other and merge into a torrential world-wide tide of opposition to U.S. imperialism. The more successful the development of people's war in a given region, the larger the number of U.S. imperialist forces that can be pinned down and depleted there. When the U.S. aggressors are hard pressed in one place, they have no alternative but to loosen their grip on others. Therefore, the conditions become more favourable for the people elsewhere to wage struggles against U.S. imperialism and its lackeys.

Everything is divisible. And so is this colossus of U.S. imperialism. It can be split up and defeated. The peoples of Asia, Africa, Latin America and other regions can destroy it piece by piece, some striking at its head and others at its feet. That is why the greatest fear of U.S. imperialism is that people's wars will be launched in different parts of the World, and particularly in Asia, Africa and Latin America, and why it regards people's war as a mortal danger.

U.S. imperialism relies solely on its nuclear weapons to intimidate people. But those weapons cannot save U.S. imperialism from its doom. Nuclear weapons cannot be used lightly. U.S. imperialism has been condemned by the people of the whole world for its towering crime of dropping two atom bombs on Japan. If it uses nuclear weapons again, it will become isolated in the extreme. Moreover, the U.S. monopoly of nuclear weapons has long been broken ; U.S. imperialism has these weapons, but others have them too. If it threatens other countries with nuclear weapons, U.S. imperialism will expose its own country to the same threat. For this reason, it will meet with strong opposition not only from the people elsewhere but also inevitably from the people in its own country. Even if U.S. imperialism brazenly uses nuclear weapons, it cannot conquer the people, who are indomitable.

However highly developed modern weapons and technical equipment may be and however complicated the methods of modern warfare, in the final analysis the outcome of a war will be decided by the sustained fighting of the ground forces, by the fighting at close quarters on battlefields, by the

[22] The Statement of Chairman Mao Tse-tung in Support of the People of the Congo (Leopoldville) Against U.S. Aggression, November 28, 1964.

political consciousness of the men, by their courage and spirit of sacrifice. Here the weak points of U.S. imperialism will be completely laid bare, while the superiority of the revolutionary people will be brought into full play. The reactionary troops of U.S. imperialism cannot possibly be endowed with the courage and the spirit of sacrifice possessed by the revolutionary people. The spiritual atom bomb which the revolutionary people possess is a far more powerful and useful weapon than the physical atom bomb.

Viet Nam is the most convincing current example of a victim of aggression defeating U.S. imperialism by a people's war. The United States has made south Viet Nam a testing ground for the suppression of people's war. It has carried on this experiment for many years, and everybody can now see that the U.S. aggressors are unable to find a way of coping with people's war. On the other hand, the Vietnamese people have brought the power of people's war into full play in their struggle against the U.S. aggressors. The U.S. aggressors are in danger of being swamped in the people's war in Viet Nam. They are deeply worried that their defeat in Viet Nam will lead to a chain reaction. They are expanding the war in an attempt to save themselves from defeat. But the more they expand the war, the greater will be the chain reaction. The more they escalate the war, the heavier will be their fall and the more disastrous their defeat. The people in other parts of the world will see still more clearly that U.S. imperialism can be defeated, and that what the Vietnamese people can do, they can do too.

History has proved and will go on proving that people's war is the most effective weapon against U.S. imperialism and its lackeys. All revolutionary people will learn to wage people's war against U.S. imperialism and its lackeys. They will take up arms, learn to fight battles and become skilled in waging people's war, though they have not done so before. U.S. imperialism like a mad bull dashing from place to place, will finally be burned to ashes in the blazing fires of the people's wars it has provoked by its own actions.

The Khrushchev Revisionists Are Betrayers of People's War

The Khrushchev revisionists have come to the rescue of U.S. imperialism just when it is most panic-stricken and helpless in its efforts to cope with people's war. Working hand in glove with the U.S. imperialists, they are doing their utmost to spread all kinds of arguments against people's war and, wherever they can, they are scheming to undermine it by overt or covert means.

The fundamental reason why the Khrushchev revisionists are opposed to people's war is that they have no faith in the masses and are afraid of U.S. imperialism, of war and of revolution. Like all other opportunists, they are blind to the power of the masses and do not believe that the revolutionary people are capable of defeating imperialism. They submit to the nuclear blackmail of the U.S. imperialists and are afraid that, if the oppressed peoples and nations rise up to fight people's wars or the people of socialist countries repulse U.S. imperialist aggression, U.S. imperialism will become incensed, they themselves will become involved and their fond dream of Soviet-U.S. co-operation to dominate the world will be spoiled.

Ever since Lenin led the Great October Revolution to victory, the experience of innumerable revolutionary wars has borne out the truth that a revolutionary people who rise up with only their bare hands at the outset finally succeed in defeating the ruling classes who are armed to the teeth. The poorly armed have defeated the better armed. People's armed forces, beginning with only primitive swords. spears, rifles and hand-grenades, have in the end defeated the imperialist forces armed with modern aeroplanes, tanks, heavy artillery and atom bombs. Guerrilla forces have ultimately defeated regular armies. "Amateurs" who were never trained in any military schools have eventually defeated "professionals" graduated from military academies. And so on and so forth. Things stubbornly develop, in a way that runs counter to the assertions of the revisionists, and facts are slapping them in the face.

The Khrushchev revisionists insist that a nation without nuclear weapons is incapable of defeating an enemy with nuclear weapons, whatever methods of fighting it may adopt. This is tantamount to saying that anyone without nuclear weapons is destined to come to grief, destined to be bullied and annihilated, and must either capitulate to the enemy when confronted with his nuclear weapons or come under the "protection" of some other nuclear power and submit to its beck and call. Isn't this the jungle law of survival par excellence? Isn't this helping the imperialists in their nuclear blackmail? Isn't this openly forbidding people to make revolution?

The Khrushchev revisionists assert that nuclear weapons and strategic rocket units are decisive while conventional forces are insignificant, and that a militia is just a heap of human flesh. For ridiculous reasons such as these, they oppose the mobilization of and reliance on the masses in the socialist countries to get prepared to use people's war against imperialist aggression. They have staked the whole future of their country on nuclear weapons and are engaged in a nuclear gamble with U.S. imperialism, with which they are trying to strike a political deal. Their theory of military strategy is the theory that nuclear weapons decide everything. Their line in army building is the bourgeois line which ignores the human factor and sees only the material factor and which regards technique as everything and politics as nothing.

The Khrushchev revisionists maintain that a single spark in any part of the globe may touch off a world nuclear conflagration and bring destruction to mankind. If this were true, our planet would have been destroyed time and time again. There have been wars of national liberation throughout the twenty years since World War II. But has any single one of them developed into a world war? Isn't it true that the U.S. imperialists' plans for a world war have been upset precisely thanks to the wars of national liberation in Asia, Africa and Latin America? By contrast, those who have done their utmost to stamp out the "sparks" of people's war have in fact encouraged U.S. imperialism in its aggressions and wars.

The Khrushchev revisionists claim that if their general line of "peaceful coexistence, peaceful transition and peaceful competition" is followed, the oppressed will be liberated and "a world without weapons, without armed forces and without wars" will come into being. But the inexorable fact is that imperialism and reaction headed by the United States are zealously priming their war machine and are daily engaged in sanguinary suppression of the revolutionary peoples and in the threat and use of armed force against independent countries. The kind of rubbish peddled by the Khrushchev revisionists has already taken a great toll of lives in a number of countries. Are these painful lessons, paid for in blood, still insufficient? The essence of the general line of the Khrushchev revisionists is nothing other than the demand that all the oppressed peoples and nations and all the countries which have won independence should lay down their arms and place themselves at the mercy of the U.S. imperialists and their lackeys who are armed to the teeth.

"While magistrates are allowed to burn down houses, the common people are forbidden even to light lamps." Such is the way of the imperialists and reactionaries. Subscribing to this imperialist philosophy, the Khrushchev revisionists shout at the Chinese people standing in the forefront of the fight for world peace: "You are bellicose!" Gentlemen, your abuse adds to our credit. It is this very " bellicosity " of ours that helps to prevent imperialism from unleashing a world war. The people are "bellicose" because they have to defend themselves and because the imperialists and reactionaries force them to be so. It is also the imperialists and reactionaries who have taught the people the arts of war. We are simply using revolutionary "bellicosity" to cope with counter-revolutionary bellicosity. How can it be argued that the imperialists and their lackeys may kill people everywhere, while the people must not strike back in self-defence or help one another? What kind of logic is this? The Khrushchev revisionists regard imperialists like Kennedy and Johnson as "sensible" and describe us together with all those who dare to carry out armed defence against imperialist aggression as "bellicose." This has revealed the Khrushchev revisionists in their true colours as the accomplices of imperialist gangsters.

We know that war brings destruction, sacrifice and suffering on the people. But the destruction, sacrifice and suffering will be much greater if no resistance is offered to imperialist armed aggression and the people become willing slaves. The sacrifice of a small number of people in revolutionary wars is repaid by security for whole nations, whole countries and even the whole of mankind; temporary suffering is repaid by lasting or even perpetual peace and happiness. War can temper the people and push history forward. In this sense, war is a great school.

When discussing World War I, Lenin said,

> The war has brought hunger to the most civilized countries, to those most culturally developed. On the other hand, the war, as a tremendous historical process, has accelerated social development to an unheard-of degree. [23]

He added,

> War has shaken up the masses, its untold horrors and suffering have awakened them. War has given history momentum and it is now flying with locomotive speed. [24]

If the arguments of the Khrushchev revisionists are to be believed, would not that make Lenin the worst of all "bellicose elements"?

[23] V. I. Lenin, "For Bread and Peace," Collected Works, Eng. ed., Progress Publishers, Moscow, 1964, Vol. XXVI, p. 386.
[24] V. I. Lenin, "The Chief Task of Our Day," Collected Works, Eng. ed., Progress Publishers, Moscow, 1965, Vol. XXVII, p. 162.

In diametrical opposition the Khrushchev revisionists, the Marxist-Leninists and revolutionary people never take a gloomy view of war. Our attitude towards imperialist wars of aggression has always been clear-cut. First, we are against them, and secondly, we are not afraid of them. We will destroy whoever attacks us. As for revolutionary wars waged by the oppressed nations and peoples, so far from opposing them, we invariably give them firm support and active aid. It has been so in the past, it remains so in the present and, when we grow in strength as time goes on, we will give them still more support and aid in the future. It is sheer day-dreaming for anyone to think that, since our revolution has been victorious, our national construction is forging ahead, our national wealth is increasing and our living conditions are improving, we too will lose our revolutionary fighting will, abandon the cause of world revolution and discard Marxism-Leninism and proletarian internationalism. Of course, every revolution in a country stems from the demands of its own people. Only when the people in a country are awakened, mobilized, organized and armed can they over-throw the reactionary rule of imperialism and its lackeys through struggle ; their role cannot be replaced or taken over by any people from outside. In this sense, revolution cannot be imported. But this does not exclude mutual sympathy and support on the part of revolutionary peoples in their struggles against the imperialists and their lackeys. Our support and aid to other revolutionary peoples serves precisely to help their self-reliant struggle.

The propaganda of the Khrushchev revisionists against people's war and the publicity they give to defeatism and capitulationism tend to demoralize and spiritually disarm revolutionary people everywhere. These revisionists are doing what the U.S. imperialists are unable to do themselves and are rendering them great service. They have greatly encouraged U.S. imperialism in its war adventures. They have completely betrayed the Marxist-Leninist revolutionary theory of war and have become betrayers of people's war.

To win the struggle against U.S. imperialism and carry people's wars to victory, the Marxist-Leninists and revolutionary people throughout the world must resolutely oppose Khrushchev revisionism.

Today, Khrushchev revisionism has a dwindling audience among the revolutionary people of the world. Wherever there is armed aggression and suppression by imperialism and its lackeys, there are bound to be people's wars against aggression and oppression. It is certain that such wars will develop vigorously. This is an objective law independent of the will of either the U.S. imperialists or the Khrushchev revisionists. The revolutionary people of the world will sweep away everything that stands in the way of their advance. Khrushchev is finished. And the successors to Khrushchev revisionism will fare no better. The imperialists, the reactionaries and the Khrushchev revisionists, who have all set themselves against people's war, will be swept like dust from the stage of history by the mighty broom of the revolutionary people.

*   *   *

Great changes have taken place in China and the world in the twenty years since the victory of the War of Resistance Against Japan, changes that have made the situation more favourable than ever for the revolution-ary people of the world and more unfavourable than ever for imperialism and its lackeys.

When Japanese imperialism launched its war of aggression against China, the Chinese people had only a very small people's army and a very small revolutionary base area, and they were up against the biggest military despot of the East. Yet even then, Comrade Mao Tse-tung said that the Chinese people's war could be won and that Japanese imperialism could be defeated. Today, the revolutionary base areas of the peoples of the world have grown to unprecedented proportions, their revolutionary movement is surging as never before, imperialism is weaker than ever, and U.S. imperialism, the chieftain of world imperialism, is suffering one defeat after another. We can say with even greater confidence that the people's wars can be won and U.S. imperialism can be defeated in all countries.

The peoples of the world now have the lessons of the October Revolution, the Anti-Fascist War, the Chinese people's War of Resistance and War of Liberation, the Korean people's War of Resistance to U.S. Aggression, the Vietnamese people's War of Liberation and their War of Resistance to U.S. Aggression, and the people's revolutionary armed struggles in many other countries. Provided each people studies these lessons well and creatively integrates them with the concrete practice of revolution in their own country, there is no doubt that the revolutionary peoples of the world will stage still more powerful and splendid dramas in the theatre of people's war in their countries and that they will wipe off the earth once and for all the common enemy of all the peoples, U.S. imperialism, and its lackeys.

The struggle of the Vietnamese people against U.S. aggression and for national salvation is now the focus of the struggle of the people of the world against U.S. aggression. The determination of the Chinese people to support and aid the Vietnamese people in their struggle against U.S. aggression and for national salvation is unshakable. No matter what U.S. imperialism may do to expand its war adventure, the Chinese people will do everything in their power to support the Vietnamese people until every single one of the U.S. aggressors is driven out of Viet Nam.

The U.S. imperialists are now clamouring for another trial of strength with the Chinese people, for another large-scale ground war on the Asian mainland. If they insist on following in the footsteps of the Japanese fascists, well then, they may do so, if they please. The Chinese people definitely have ways of their own for coping with a U.S. imperialist war of aggression. Our methods are no secret. The most important one is still mobilization of the people, reliance on the people, making everyone a soldier and waging a people's war.

We want to tell the U.S. imperialists once again that the vast ocean of several hundred million Chinese people in arms will be more than enough to submerge your few million aggressor troops. If you dare to impose war on us, we shall gain freedom of action. It will then not be up to you to decide how the war will be fought. We shall fight in the ways most advantageous to us to destroy the enemy and wherever the enemy can be most easily destroyed. Since the Chinese people were able to destroy the Japanese aggressors twenty years ago, they are certainly still more capable of finishing off the U.S. aggressors today. The naval and air superiority you boast about cannot intimidate the Chinese people, and neither can the atom bomb you brandish at us. If you want to send troops, go ahead, the more the better. We will annihilate as many as you can send, and can even give you receipts. The Chinese people are a great, valiant people. We have the

441

courage to shoulder the heavy burden of combating U.S. imperialism and to contribute our share in the struggle for final victory over this most ferocious enemy of the people of the world.

It must be pointed out in all seriousness that after the victory of the War of Resistance Taiwan was returned to China. The occupation of Taiwan by U.S. imperialism is absolutely unjustified. Taiwan Province is an inalienable part of Chinese territory. The U.S. imperialists must get out of Taiwan. The Chinese people are determined to liberate Taiwan.

In commemorating the 20th anniversary of victory in the War of Resistance Against Japan, we must also point out in all solemnity that the Japanese militarists fostered by U.S. imperialism will certainly receive still severer punishment if they ignore the firm opposition of the Japanese people and the people of Asia, again indulge in their pipe-dreams and resume their old road of aggression in Asia.

U.S. imperialism is preparing a world war. But can this save it from its doom? World War I was followed by the birth of the socialist Soviet Union. World War II was followed by the emergence of a series of socialist countries and many nationally independent countries. If the U.S. imperialists should insist on launching a third world war, it can be stated categorically that many more hundreds of millions of people will turn to socialism; the imperialists will then have little room left on the globe; and it is possible that the whole structure of imperialism will collapse.

We are optimistic about the future of the world. We are confident that the people will bring to an end the epoch of wars in human history. Comrade Mao Tse-tung pointed out long ago that war, this monster, "will be finally eliminated by the progress of human society, and in the not too distant future too. But there is only one way to eliminate it and that is to oppose war with war, to oppose counter-revolutionary war with revolutionary war." [25]

All peoples suffering from U.S. imperialist aggression, oppression and plunder, unite! Hold aloft the just banner of people's war and fight for the cause of world peace, national liberation, people's democracy and socialism! Victory will certainly go to the people of the world!

Long live the victory of people's war!

DOCUMENT 31

Vice-Premier Ch'en Yi's September 29, 1965 Press Conference: China Is Determined to Make All Necessary Sacrifices for the Defeat of U.S. Imperialism

Complete Text
[*Peking Review*, Vol. VIII, No. 41 (October 8, 1965), pp. 7–14]

On the Sino-Indian Boundary Question

India must cease its intrusions and harassments. The question of the Chinese territory occupied by India will have to be thoroughly settled. There is a limit to China's forbearance.

---

[25] Mao Tse-tung, "Problems of Strategy in China's Revolutionary War," *Selected Works*, Eng. ed., FLP, Peking, 1965, Vol. I, p. 182.

Answering a question about the Sino-Indian border issue raised by the editor of the *Voice of Revolution* of the Congo (Brazzaville), Vice-Premier Ch'en Yi said: In its note of September 16, the Chinese Government demanded that India dismantle the 56 aggressive military works she had built within Chinese territory on the China-Sikkim border and withdraw the intruding Indian troops. The China-Sikkim boundary is the boundary between China and Sikkim and does not fall within the scope of the Sino-Indian boundary. It has long been delimited. India not only regards Sikkim as her protectorate, but has gone to the length of intruding into Chinese territory across the China-Sikkim boundary. It was her right as a sovereign state and entirely reasonable for China to lodge the protest and raise the demands in her note to the Indian Government. We had shown forbearance for several years. Knowing that it was in the wrong, the Indian Government withdrew all the intruding Indian troops and demolished a part of the aggressive military works upon receiving our notification. That was a good thing, and it was wise of them to do so. If India had failed to do so, the Chinese Government would have been entitled to act in self-defence, drive out the intruders and destroy the aggressive military works.

Along the Sino-Indian boundary of several thousand kilometres, Indian troops have crossed the line of actual control at many other places and carried out harassing raids. India is still occupying over 92,000 square kilometres of Chinese territory in the eastern, western and middle sectors of the Sino-Indian border. The Indian Government should understand that there is a limit to our forbearance, that it must cease its intrusions and harassments and that the question of Chinese territory occupied by it will have to be thoroughly settled.

On the Indian-Pakistan Conflict

If the Indian troops resume the aggressive war against Pakistan China will certainly give Pakistan moral and material support.

A correspondent of the London *Daily Express* asked what assistance the Chinese Government would give Pakistan with the resumption of the conflict between India and Pakistan. Vice-Premier Ch'en Yi said: The fact is that Pakistan is the victim of aggression and India the aggressor. Recently Indian troops have continued to launch attacks in the Lahore area. We do not wish to see the aggravation of the situation, and we hope that the Indian side knows how to restrain itself. If the situation is aggravated, it is certain that the Chinese Government and people will give moral and material support to Pakistan. Relying on the support of the United States, the Soviet Union and Britain, the Indian Government wants to do whatever it pleases, but that can frighten nobody. We hope that it will come to its senses.

India's aggression against Pakistan is not in the interest of the Indian people. I believe that the great Indian people of more than 400 million wish to live in peace with the other Afro-Asian peoples and unite with them in opposing imperialism and old and new colonialism. It is regrettable that the Indian leaders have failed to reflect this wish, but instead have perpetrated aggression by relying on foreign forces, and particularly on U.S. imperialism. Such an adventurist policy is bound to fail, and indeed it has already failed. If it is not altered, it will continue to meet with failure.

On Trade Relations between China and West Germany

A West German *D.P.A.* correspondent asked on what conditions China would enter into official trade relations with West Germany. Vice-Premier Ch'en Yi said: At present, China already has trade relations with West Germany. But conditions are not ripe for the establishment of official trade relations. In close collaboration with the United States, West Germany is restoring militarism and posing a threat to the security of Europe. West Germany has not given up her plan of annexing the German Democratic Republic. In these circumstances, China cannot enter into any official trade relations with West Germany.

There exists a traditional friendship between the people, the workers, peasants, scientists and intellectuals, of West Germany and the Chinese people. We hope that this friendship will develop.

On Sharing Nuclear Knowledge

The most important task for the Afro-Asian countries today is to shake off imperialist control. The just struggle of Afro-Asian countries against imperialism and colonialism is the best atom bomb.

A London *Times* correspondent asked whether China was prepared to share her nuclear knowledge with any of the developing countries.

In reply, Vice-Premier Ch'en Yi first commented on the western countries' practice of dividing nations into the "developed" and the "under-developed." He said: The western countries have shown a superiority complex by claiming themselves to be "developed" while degrading some other countries by calling them "under-developed." I do not agree with these terms. Now they promote the so-called under-developed countries by describing them as developing countries. So far as China is concerned, we are not grateful for that. The facts over the past three centuries show that the so-called developed countries have developed by exploiting the colonies, while the so-called under-developed countries remain undeveloped as a result of imperialist and colonialist exploitation. No rigid line should be drawn by classifying certain countries as developed and some others as under-developed. We hold that, politically, the Asian, African and Latin American countries which persist in opposing imperialism and colonialism are advanced, while the West European and North American imperialist countries are backward. Economically, we do not believe that the people of Asia, Africa and Latin America will for ever remain backward and that Western Europe and North America will for ever be in the van technically. The people of Asia, Africa and Latin America will overtake the industrially advanced countries within a few decades, once they shake off the control of imperialism and old and new colonialism and start to build their countries by relying on their own efforts. The history of New China over the past 16 years provides a most vivid evidence. China has achieved great successes in national construction mainly through the united efforts of the government and the people, through self-reliance, hard work and the exploitation of her own resources. So far there has not been any country in the world which can change its state of backwardness by merely relying on foreign aid.

Vice-Premier Ch'en Yi said: There are two aspects to the question of nuclear co-operation. As for the peaceful use of atomic energy and the building of atomic reactors, China has already been approached by several countries, and China is ready to render them assistance; as for the request for China's help in the manufacture of atom bombs, this question is not realistic.

In my opinion, the most important task for the Afro-Asian countries today is to shake off imperialist control politically, economically and culturally and develop their own independent economy. This task is an acute struggle and its accomplishment will take quite a few years. Any country with a fair basis in industry and agriculture and in science and technology will be able to manufacture atom bombs, with or without China's assistance. China hopes that Afro-Asian countries will be able to make atom bombs themselves, and it would be better for a greater number of countries to come into possession of atom bombs.

In our view, the role of atom bombs should not be over-stressed. The United States has been brandishing the atom bomb for atomic blackmail over the past twenty years, but it has failed. The just struggle of Afro-Asian countries against imperialism and colonialism is the best atom bomb.

On U.S. War of Aggression in Viet Nam

The so-called unconditional discussions proposed by Johnson are a fraud. If anybody tries to mediate on the Viet Nam question without making any distinction between the aggressor and the victim of aggression, his effort will objectively help U.S. imperialism.

A correspondent of the *Viet Nam News Agency* raised two questions:

(1) Since the beginning of 1965, while repeatedly proposing peace talks on the Viet Nam question, the United States has been launching military attacks and has increased the number of its troops in south Viet Nam to 130,000. It has employed various types of modern weapons on the battlefield and kept on escalating the war. What is your comment on these actions of the United States? And what is your comment on the stand taken by the Democratic Republic of Viet Nam?

(2) The United States attempts to bring about peace talks through the United Nations. U.S. aggression in Viet Nam is a matter which concerns the Geneva Conference nations only and has nothing to do with the United Nations. What comment could you make on this?

In reply, Vice-Premier Ch'en Yi said: The comrade correspondent from Viet Nam has asked me to comment on the actions of the U.S. Government. I think the best comment has already been made by the Vietnamese people on the south Viet Nam battlefield and in their fight against air attacks in north Viet Nam. By defeating the special war launched by U.S. imperialism, the Vietnamese people have given the best answer and the best comment.

U.S. imperialism has attempted, by bombing the north, to force the people of south Viet Nam to stop fighting and the whole of Viet Nam to give in. The Vietnamese people have not given in, and this is the best answer. The Vietnamese people's heroic struggle has won them the respect of the people of the world. The Chinese people have boundless admiration for the struggle of the Vietnamese people.

Some people believe that the Vietnamese people can defeat U.S. imperialism, while others do not. The fact is that the United States is the aggressor; although its military forces are not small, they are scattered all over the world in all those places it has occupied. Therefore, the forces it can use in Viet Nam are after all limited, and it is in an inferior position there. Viet Nam is a small country with a population slightly over 30 million, but she is waging a just war against aggression, the people of the whole country are united as one in resolute resistance to U.S. imperialism, and so she is in a superior position. This war will definitely end in victory for Viet Nam and defeat for U.S. imperialism.

The so-called unconditional discussions proposed by Johnson are a fraud. Its aim is to carve up Viet Nam, perpetuate U.S. occupation of south Viet Nam and turn it into a permanent puppet country of the United States. These are the terms set by Johnson for peace talks. All those who work for peace talks without knowing the truth about Viet Nam should give the matter serious thought. Johnson's scheme of peace talks is absolutely unacceptable to the Vietnamese people. How can the Vietnamese people tolerate the continued division of their motherland? The Viet Nam question can only be settled on the basis of the five-part statement of the South Viet Nam National Front for Liberation and the four-point proposition of the Government of the Democratic Republic of Viet Nam. In short, the U.S. troops must withdraw from Viet Nam completely and the Vietnamese people should be free to settle their own problems.

If anybody tries to mediate on the Viet Nam question without making any distinction between right and wrong, between the aggressor and the victim of aggression, his effort will objectively help U.S. imperialism, whatever his subjective wishes may be. The only way to attain peace in Viet Nam and the whole of Indo-China is to stand on the side of the Vietnamese people and oppose U.S. aggression until the U.S. aggressors get out of Viet Nam.

Some people say that the United States has not yet exhausted its strength. I say that the strength of the Vietnamese people has not been exhausted either, nor has that of the people of the world who support the Vietnamese people. Why should one only see the strength of the United States?

As for the United Nations, there is almost no difference between it and the United States. The United Nations is a tool of the United States, while the United States is the overlord of the United Nations. This is an objective and irrefutable fact.

True, there has been some change in the United Nations. The United Nations used to be the exclusive tool of the United States, and now it has become the tool of a few big powers, primarily the United States. The U.N. headquarters in New York has become the political bargaining place for a few big powers.

The United Nations has been discredited under the exclusive control of the United States; it can fare no better under the control of several big powers, primarily the United States.

It will only be advantageous to the United States if the United Nations should meddle in the Viet Nam question. As I know, the Vietnamese Government and people are firmly against this. The United Nations has no right to interfere in the Viet Nam question.

The future of Viet Nam must be decided by the Vietnamese people themselves, by President Ho Chi Minh, Premier Pham Van Dong and President Nguyen Huu Tho, and it admits of no foreign interference. The

Chinese people unreservedly stand on the side of the Vietnamese people until U.S. imperialism is defeated.

Vice-Premier Ch'en Yi answered six questions raised by the Japanese correspondents stationed in Peking from various newspapers, news agencies and broadcasting stations.

On the Second African-Asian Conference

The African-Asian Conference must openly denounce U.S. imperialism, No representative of the United Nations should be admitted to the conference. China firmly opposes Soviet participation in the conference. The convening of the African-Asian Conference in Algeria cannot be linked with her internal affairs, in which no foreign state should interfere.

Vice-Premier Ch'en Yi said: The African-Asian Conference is a meeting of the heads of state or government of the more than sixty African and Asian countries which have won independence. If this conference can develop the Bandung spirit and discuss the questions of fighting imperialism and colonialism and of the national-liberation movement of the world, I believe it will be of great significance in international life. The conference should support the people of Viet Nam, Laos, the Congo (Leopoldville), the Dominican Republic, Angola, Mozambique, Portuguese Guinea, South Africa, the Arab people of Palestine, and the people of South Yemen, Malaya, Singapore and North Kalimantan in their struggles against the aggression of the imperialists, colonialists and neo-colonialists headed by the United States. The Chinese Government has always stood for holding the conference along these lines and making it a success.

U.S. imperialism dislikes this conference very much and is trying to sabotage it by every means. It is anticipated that the first item on the agenda after the opening session will be the condemnation of U.S. imperialism for its aggressions throughout the world. If this is done, the Bandung spirit will be raised to a new level. If it fails to make an open denunciation of U.S. imperialism but only opposes imperialism and colonialism in general terms, then it will not have much significance.

Recently, a cabinet minister of a certain country told me that some newly independent countries could not openly denounce U.S. imperialism at the African-Asian Conference because of their need for U.S. aid to solve the bread question. On the other hand, some other Afro-Asian countries hold that the first and foremost task of the African-Asian Conference is to denounce U.S. imperialism, otherwise there will be no sense in convening the conference. These two tendencies are now engaged in a struggle. China firmly sides with those that stand for condemnation of U.S. imperialism. This position of China's will never change. For without adopting resolutions condemning U.S. imperialism, the African-Asian Conference will disappoint the people of Asia, Africa and Latin America. To hold such a conference would be a waste. As for the bread question, it is my view that if one relies on U.S. aid, one will get less and less bread, while by relying on one's own efforts one will get more and more. So far as certain countries are concerned, the more they denounce U.S. imperialism, the more bread they will probably get from it, otherwise they will not get any. Such is the character of U.S. imperialism — bullying the weak-kneed and fearing the strong.

I have told the leaders of some Afro-Asian countries: since many Afro-Asian countries are receiving aid and loans from the United States and other countries, thus incurring ever-increasing burdens, it may be advisable to adopt a resolution at the African-Asian Conference declaring the cancellation of all debts which Afro-Asian countries owe to the United States. If this can be done, the debts owed to China may also be cancelled. They said this was a very good idea and could be considered.

In order to sabotage the African-Asian Conference, the imperialists are trying to hook it up with the United Nations. The Bandung Conference has enjoyed high prestige among the people of the world precisely because, having nothing to do with the United Nations, it was free from U.N. influence and contributed to the anti-imperialist and anti-colonialist cause of the people of the world independently and outside the United Nations. If the conference is to be linked with the United Nations, it will be tantamount to discarding the Bandung spirit. The Chinese Government is firmly against this.

To invite a representative of the United Nations or anyone from it to the African-Asian Conference would mean, in effect, to bring the United States into the conference. Is it not ludicrous to invite agents of U.S. imperialism to an anti-imperialist conference?

The Chinese Government is resolutely against the participation of U Thant, Secretary-General of the United Nations, in the African-Asian Conference. Everybody is clear about the role U Thant is playing. He is not the head of the United Nations; the head of the United Nations is the United States. Not being the head of any Afro-Asian state, what qualifications has he to participate in the African-Asian Conference?

The United Nations has excluded China for 16 years. China cannot sit together with its representative. The Chinese Government does not force other countries to boycott U.N. meetings, nor should others force us to sit together with a representative of the United Nations. Otherwise, it would be running counter to the Bandung spirit. Joint struggle against imperialism is possible only when no one imposes his will on others. The invitation for U Thant to attend the African-Asian Conference was issued before Ben Bella's fall. I am thankful to President Houari Boumedienne because he showed sympathy with China's stand and said he would try to find a solution to this problem.

The Chinese Government categorically states that no representative of the United Nations should be admitted to the African-Asian Conference.

As for inviting the Soviet Union to the African-Asian Conference, the Chinese Government is firmly opposed to it. Whether historically or politically, the Soviet Union is by tradition a European country, and there is no reason for its participation in the African-Asian Conference. The Soviet Union did not ask for participation in the First Asian-African Conference. At that time, Prime Minister Nehru openly declared that the Soviet Union, a European country, was not to be invited. Last year, India demanded Soviet participation, but the 22 countries failed to reach agreement, which means in effect the rejection of the demand for Soviet participation in the African-Asian Conference. Khrushchev stated last year that the Soviet Union would not put forward its request, if its participation would not conduce to Afro-Asian solidarity.

This question was already closed and should no longer exist. It was only recently, after the new leaders of the Soviet Union received the support and encouragement of the United States, India, Tito and some other countries that they raised this question anew.

The question now is whether we should uphold the Bandung spirit and have the heads of the independent Afro-Asian countries meet and proclaim independent political views to promote the further progress of the anti-imperialist and anti-colonialist struggle in Asia and Africa, or whether we should submit to the unreasonable demand of a big power to gatecrash into the African-Asian Conference. The Chinese Government is firmly opposed to Soviet participation in the African-Asian Conference.

Some U.S. and other western newspapers declare outright that injection of the Soviet Union into the African-Asian Conference is the only way to offset the influence of China. The real implication of these words is that injection of the Soviet Union is the only way to water down the influence of the African-Asian Conference in opposing U.S. imperialism, colonialism and neo-colonialism. This is a major issue of principle, on which there can be no compromise or concession.

China is not afraid of an all-round debate with the Soviet Union. The injection of the Soviet Union into the African-Asian Conference will mean nothing more than the opening of a new battlefront in the struggle against modern revisionism.

Vice-Premier Ch'en Yi said: Algeria is the host country of the Second African-Asian Conference. Some people hesitate to go to Algiers for the conference because they have reservations about the new Algerian Government. We hold that the change of leadership in Algeria is her internal affair in which no foreign state should interfere. One should not link the convening of the African-Asian Conference in Algeria with her internal affairs. To do so would be running counter to the Bandung spirit.

Vice-Premier Ch'en Yi said: Another important question which the African-Asian Conference should discuss is how the Afro-Asian countries are to free themselves from imperialist control and develop their national economy independently.

The more foreign aid with conditions attached a country receives, the more difficult will it be for her to stand up. This is like drinking poison to quench one's thirst.

Before liberation, China was wholly controlled by the United States, and it was with political, economic and military aid from the United States that Chiang Kai-shek collapsed. And the situation in New China has become still better after she thoroughly embarked on a path of self-reliance upon the stoppage of all aid by Khrushchev. A country's economy will gain vigour in a few years' time, if she makes up her mind to stop relying on foreign aid, carries on construction with her own efforts and resources and turns out the products she needs. So long as this path is followed with determination, all Afro-Asian countries can solve their own economic problems, because they have all got a certain foundation for economic development.

Of course, on the above basis, Afro-Asian countries need to help supply each other's wants and aid each other on the principle of equality and mutual benefit. Such aid is not harmful but helpful. However, it is only of secondary importance. The point of primary importance is to rely on one's own efforts in national construction instead of being dependent on others. The Second African-Asian Conference will have more far-reaching significance than the first one if it can adopt a resolution for the building of independent national economies by the Afro-Asian countries through self-reliance and for their mutual economic co-operation on terms of equality and mutual benefit.

In brief, we should make a success of the conference. Otherwise, it would be better for the conference to be postponed until conditions are ripe than to drag everybody together to make a hotchpotch. The African-Asian Conference is a matter for all the Afro-Asian countries, and not for China alone. China has nothing to ask from the African-Asian Conference, and it is not that she cannot do without it. China stresses that the conference should support the anti-imperialist struggles of all peoples, but this is her wish and does not mean that she wants to gain anything from the conference.

The African-Asian Conference must be made a success. If there are assurances that it will be a success, the Chinese Government is for its convocation. Without such assurances, the Chinese Government is in favour of waiting till the conditions are ripe.

On the Restoration of China's Legitimate Rights in the United Nations

If the present U.N. General Assembly restores China's legitimate rights, the question remains unsolved. The U.N. should cancel its resolution condemning China and the Democratic People's Republic of Korea as aggressors and adopt a resolution condemning the United States as the aggressor. The U.N. Charter must be reviewed and revised jointly by all countries, big and small; all independent states should be included in the United Nations; and all imperialist puppets should be expelled.

Concerning the question of restoring to China her legitimate rights in the United Nations, which was raised by the Japanese correspondents, Vice-Premier Ch'en Yi said: The United Nations has long been controlled by the United States and has today become a place where two big powers, the United States and the Soviet Union, conduct political transactions. This state of affairs has not changed although dozens of Afro-Asian and peace-loving countries have made no small amount of efforts in the United Nations. China need not take part in such a United Nations.

During the U.S. war of aggression against Korea, the United Nations adopted a resolution naming China as an aggressor. How can China be expected to take part in an international organization which calls her an aggressor? Calling China an aggressor and then asking the aggressor to join, would not the United Nations be slapping its own face?

The question now is how to reform the United Nations in accordance with the purposes and principles of its Charter and to free it from the control of the United States and other big powers. If the task of reforming the United Nations cannot be accomplished, conditions will no doubt gradually ripen for the establishment of a revolutionary United Nations.

Will the present U.N. General Assembly adopt a resolution expelling the elements of the Chiang Kai-shek clique and restoring China's legitimate rights? I think this is impossible as the United Nations is now controlled by the United States. If things really turn out that way, the question would still remain unsolved.

The United Nations must rectify its mistakes and undergo a thorough reorganization and reform. It must admit and correct all its past mistakes. Among other things, it should cancel its resolution condemning China and the Democratic People's Republic of Korea as aggressors and adopt a resolution condemning the United States as the aggressor; the U.N. Charter must be reviewed and revised jointly by all countries, big and small; all independent states should be included in the United Nations; and all imperialist puppets should be expelled.

For more than ten years, many countries have in the United Nations firmly demanded the expulsion of the representatives of the Chiang Kai-shek clique and the restoration of China's legitimate rights. China is always grateful for this just and friendly action.

On Kuomintang-Communist Co-Operation

The Japanese correspondents asked about the possibility of co-operation between the Kuomintang and the Chinese Communist Party. Vice-Premier Ch'en Yi said: At present there are Revolutionary Committees of the Kuomintang in the provinces and municipalities as well as in Peking, which are co-operating very well with the Communist Party. New China is a country in which eight democratic parties co-operate with the Communist Party and are led by it. We welcome Mr. Li Tsung-jen's participation in this co-operation. Chiang Kai-shek and Chiang Ching-kuo are also welcome to join in this co-operation as Mr. Li Tsung-jen has done. Taiwan Province and any individual or group in Taiwan are welcome to come back to the embrace of the motherland and join in this co-operation. Only one condition is required: To break away from U.S. imperialist control and be loyal to the motherland. There are no other conditions. In my view, the possibility of Kuomintang-Communist co-operation is great and is moreover increasing.

On Sino-Japanese Relations

The Japanese correspondents asked about the prospects of Sino-Japanese relations. Vice-Premier Ch'en Yi replied: A lot has been said on this question by leaders of our country, so I will only give a brief answer here. If the present Japanese Government stops tailing after the United States, pursues an independent policy and renounces its anti-Chinese policy, possibilities will increase for the normalization of Sino-Japanese relations. At present the Sato Cabinet is politically following the U.S. anti-Chinese policy, while economically it wants to reap gains from Sino-Japanese trade. Such a policy is self-contradictory and cannot help normalize Sino-Japanese relations. It is up to Japan to remove this obstacle. Out of consideration for the traditional friendship between the great nations and peoples of China and Japan, the Chinese Government is willing to carry on trade between the two countries on the present level, but it is impossible to expand it.

The Japanese nation is full of promise, and the Japanese people love peace. They demand the liquidation of U.S. imperialist control and the dismantling of U.S. bases in Japan. We have deep sympathy with their demands.

On China's Third Five-Year Plan

The Japanese correspondents asked about China's Third Five-Year Plan. Vice-Premier Ch'en Yi said: Next year our country will commence its

Third Five-Year Plan. During the Second Five-Year Plan, our country met with great difficulties in its national construction because of natural disasters, the blockade imposed by the U.S. imperialists and the stoppage of aid by Khrushchev. After three years of readjustment, there has been an all-round turn for the better in the situation, and our industrial and agricultural production has entered a new stage of development, a stage of general upsurge. We shall have a good harvest this year, but there still are natural disasters. It will take decades — 30 to 50 years more of efforts to build up China's industry, agriculture and national defence and raise them to a higher level.

We have laid the foundation for building an independent, integrated and modern economic system, but many problems remain to be solved. In science and technology, the world's advanced levels have been reached in some branches, but in some others only the average levels, and there are still a number of gaps. We are optimistic about China's development, but there are still many difficulties to be surmounted.

In China, too, there are revisionists and people who have illusions about U.S. imperialism. Some people are in the process of remoulding themselves, and some have not yet remoulded themselves. But these elements play no role in the making of China's policies and exercise no influence among the people. China is stable.

On China's Development of Nuclear Weapons

The Japanese correspondents asked about the development of nuclear weapons in China. Vice-Premier Ch'en Yi said: China has exploded two atom bombs. I know this and so do you. A third atom bomb may be exploded. As to the time of its explosion, please wait for our communique. Atomic technology and delivery technology are, of course, rather complicated, but Chinese, Asians and Africans certainly can all master them, if efforts are made.

China does not decide her foreign policies according to whether or not she has got atom bombs. We are ready to enter into friendly co-operation with still more countries in order to oppose imperialism and colonialism, isolate U.S. imperialism and safeguard world peace.

We reaffirm that all countries, big and small, should come together and agree on the destruction of atom bombs and on the prohibition of the use, manufacture, stockpiling and testing of nuclear weapons. China is manufacturing atom bombs in order to liquidate them and for the purpose of self-defence. China has pledged never to be the first to use atom bombs. Our nuclear weapons will only be used for defence.

On the Delimitation of the Sino-Mongolian Boundary

A correspondent from the Hongkong paper *Chin Pao* asked: The relationship between Outer Mongolia and China proper is closer than that between Tibet and China proper, whether viewed historically or from the standpoint of race, colour and culture. Tibet is part of China's territory, and all the more so is Outer Mongolia. Such being the case, why is it that the delimitation of the Sino-Mongolian boundary should have taken place?

In reply, Vice-Premier Ch'en Yi said: Tibet and the Mongolian People's Republic are two different matters, which should not be mentioned in the same breath. The Mongolian People's Republic proclaimed independence in 1924 following a revolution, whereas Tibet has always been a part of China's territory.

In 1945 Chiang Kai-shek's government concluded a treaty with the Government of the Soviet Union recognizing the Mongolian People's Republic. After its founding, New China succeeded to the commitment and recognized Mongolia as a socialist country. It is only natural and nothing strange for China and Mongolia to delimit the boundary between them in a friendly way.

There are Han chauvinists in China, who have always refused to recognize the Mongolian People's Republic. We are opposed to such Han chauvinism. Since its founding, New China has provided the Mongolian People's Republic with large amounts of aid. In recent years, the leading group of Mongolia has been following the Khrushchev revisionists in opposing China. But we do not cancel our aid to it on this account, because our New China is guided by Marxism-Leninism and Mao Tse-tung's thought, and we are not Khrushchev revisionists. It is for the Mongolian people themselves to decide whether co-operation with China is more in their interests. We do not impose our will on them.

On the U.S. Use of Hongkong as a Base for its Aggressive War in Viet Nam

Answering questions put by the correspondents of the Hongkong *Cheng Wu Pao, The Hongkong Evening News* and *The Global Digest* about the use of Hongkong by the United States in its war of aggression against Viet Nam, Vice-Premier Ch'en Yi said: The fact that Britain and the Hongkong authorities allow the United States to use Hongkong as a base for aggression against Viet Nam has caused the anxiety of the local inhabitants. The Chinese Government considers the question not only one of using Hongkong as a base for aggression against Viet Nam but also of preparing to use it in future as a base for aggression against China. The Chinese Government is firmly opposed to this. This action of the British Government is most stupid. We hope that it will choose a wiser course in its own interests. Otherwise, China will take measures when necessary.

The U.S. wilful expansion of its war of aggression in Viet Nam and Britain's course of action in regard to " Malaysia " — all this is certainly not merely directed against Viet Nam or Indonesia, but against China as well. U.S. imperialism has never concealed its global strategy, which aims at the domination of the whole world. U.S. troops are going to Hongkong not simply for vacation. Mr. Wilson, the British Prime Minister, has declared that Britain is not giving up any of its strongholds and military bases east of the Suez. The U.S. and British imperialists are not in full agreement on some concrete measures in the Viet Nam war, but they have no fundamental difference when it comes to the question of consolidating the world colonial system. It is possible that the United States may extend the war to China's mainland. In that event, what grounds are there for thinking that the British and other imperialists will not return to their former colonies in Asia and Africa? That is why the struggles of the people of the world against imperialism and colonialism, and particularly against U.S. imperialism and its followers, form an integral whole. The people of the world should maintain sharp vigilance and support each other in these struggles.

The heroic struggle of the Vietnamese people is not merely their own affair, but a contribution to the worldwide struggle against imperialism and colonialism. If war should spread to China, she will put up staunch resistance and will be determined to defeat U.S. imperialism.

China sees not just the question of Taiwan, the question of Hongkong and the question of Macao, each on its own; what we see is the global strategy of U.S. imperialism. One must be prepared to wage a worldwide struggle before U.S. imperialism can be defeated. Will the imperialists allow the socialist countries in Eastern Europe and the Soviet Union to live in security? The Khrushchev revisionists place implicit trust in what U.S. imperialism says, and they will sooner or later come to grief for it.

Khrushchev said that, instead of liberating Hongkong and Macao herself, China was making other Asians and Africans fight imperialism and colonialism and pull chestnuts out of the fire for China. This is a malicious provocation. Khrushchev wanted to dictate China's policy. Our reply is: China's policy must be decided by China herself and not by the Khrushchev revisionists.

If the U.S. imperialists are determined to launch a war of aggression against us, they are welcome to come sooner, to come as early as tomorrow, We will take all necessary measures to defeat them. By then, the war will have no boundaries.

The Chinese people are ready to make all necessary sacrifices in the fight against imperialism. It is up to the U.S. President and the Pentagon to decide whether the United States wants a big war with China today. We cherish no illusions about U.S. imperialism. We are fully prepared against U.S. aggression. If the U.S. imperialists are determined to launch a war of aggression against us, they are welcome to come sooner, to come as early as tomorrow. Let the Indian reactionaries, the British imperialists and the Japanese militarists come along with them! Let the modern revisionists act in co-ordination with them from the north! We will still win in the end. The great Soviet people and the Communist Party of the Soviet Union will not allow their leaders to take such a criminal decision. Who will meet with destruction — the U.S. imperialists or the people of the world? It can be said with certainty that the U.S. imperialists will perish, while the people of the whole world will win liberation. As a Chinese saying goes, good will be rewarded with good, and evil with evil; if the reward is not forthcoming, it is because the time has not arrived; and when the time arrives, one will get all the reward he deserves!

In the struggle against U.S. imperialism, constant vacillation without a final determination will only lead to defeat and not to victory.

In the Korean war, the United States had a trial of strength with the peoples of Korea and China, and now it is having a trial of strength with the heroic Vietnamese people. The United States admits that such trials of strength are very much to its disadvantage. To us and to the people of the whole world, such trials of strength have great advantages; they have united the entire Vietnamese people and the entire Chinese people, and pushed the world anti-imperialist and anti-colonialist struggle to a new stage.

For sixteen years we have been waiting for the U.S. imperialists to come in and attack us. My hair has turned grey in waiting. Perhaps I will not have the luck to see the U.S. imperialist invasion of China, but my children may see it, and they will resolutely carry on the fight. Let no correspondent think that I am bellicose. It is the U.S. imperialists who are brutal and vicious and who bully others too much. They are bullying the Chinese, the Koreans, the Vietnamese, the Khmers, the Laotians, the Indonesians, the Congolese and the Dominicans. Even their ally France is being bullied by them. Those who are bullied by them have risen against them and become friends of China. This is of the United States' own making.

Should the U.S. imperialists invade China's mainland, we will take all necessary measures to defeat them. By then, the war will have no boundaries. It is the United States, and not China, that will have broken down the boundaries. We are willing to respect boundaries, but the United States wilfully violates boundaries and drives in wherever it likes. With the defeat of U.S. imperialism, the time will come when imperialism and colonialism will be really liquidated throughout the world. The ideal is bound to come true with the world truly becoming a community of nations with different social systems coexisting peacefully. China is ready to make all the necessary sacrifices for this noble ideal. She will never take the modern revisionist position of betraying Marxism-Leninism and proletarian internationalism.

The choice now is either to re-impose colonial shackles on the people of various countries in accordance with the global strategy of U.S. imperialism so as to subject them to enslavement and plunder, or to wage resolute struggles to defeat U.S. imperialism and put an end to the colonial system according to the will of the people, who dare to fight and dare to oppose imperialism, so that countries with different social systems can truly coexist peacefully throughout the world. One has to choose either of the two alternatives. The modern revisionist way of seeking ease and comfort at the expense of principles is a blind alley. China is ready to make her contribution to the struggle against U.S. imperialism and old and new colonialism.

DOCUMENT 32

Refutation of the New Leaders of the CPSU on " United Action "

by the Editorial Departments of *Jen-min Jih-pao* and *Hung Ch'i*
(November 11, 1965)

Excerpt

[*Peking Review*, Vol. VIII, No. 46 (November 12, 1965), pp. 10–21, at pp. 12–21]

The Khrushchev Revisionists Have Undermined the Common Basis of Unity

. . . .

The essence of the Khrushchev revisionist theory and line, which the new leaders of the CPSU are persisting in and developing further, is to protect imperialist rule in the capitalist world and restore capitalism in the socialist world.

Between the Marxist-Leninists and the Khrushchev revisionists there is a difference of fundamental line, a major difference between what is right and what is wrong. In the circumstances, how can there be " a common ideology" and "a common programme" between the Marxist-Leninists and the Khrushchev revisionists? How can there be a common basis for unity? In the circumstances, the relation between the Khrushchev revisionists and ourselves is certainly not one in which "what binds us together is much stronger than what divides us," as alleged by the new leaders of the CPSU; on all the fundamental issues of the present epoch the relation is one of sharp opposition; there are things that divide us and nothing that unites us, things that are antagonistic and nothing that is common.

Since there is such a difference of fundamental line, the achievement of unity requires either that we discard Marxism-Leninism and follow their revisionism, or that they renounce revisionism and return to the path of Marxism-Leninism. These are the only alternatives. It is impermissible and indeed utterly wrong if we take an equivocal or vague position on such a sharp question.

Are we expected to follow the new leaders of the CPSU in order to achieve unity under their revisionist programme? Wouldn't that mean that we must join them in betraying Marxism-Leninism, in putting down the people's revolutions in various countries and in acting as accomplices of the imperialists? It goes without saying that we will never do so.

Are we expected to look on and remain completely silent without criticizing, exposing and opposing the new leaders of the CPSU, while they are betraying all the fundamental principles of Marxism-Leninism, striving for Soviet-U.S. collaboration to dominate the world and opposing the people's revolutions in various countries? Wouldn't that mean that we must also abandon Marxism-Leninism, act as their ally in opposing the people's revolutions and become the accomplice of imperialism? It goes without saying that we will never do that either.

If the new leaders of the CPSU really want unity with the Marxist-Leninists, they must change their revisionist line and honestly admit their mistakes. They must publicly and solemnly admit before the Communists and the people of the world that their Khrushchev revisionism, great-power chauvinism and splittism are wrong, publicly admit that the revisionist line and programme decided upon at the 20th and the 22nd Congresses of the CPSU are wrong, and publicly guarantee not to repeat the errors of Khrushchev revisionism. Is it possible that they will do all this?

The antagonism between Marxism-Leninism and Khrushchev revisionism is a class antagonism between the proletariat and the bourgeoisie; it is the antagonism between the socialist and the capitalist roads and between the line of opposing imperialism and that of surrendering to it. It is an irreconcilable antagonism.

As Lenin said, "Unity is a great thing and a great slogan. But what the workers' cause needs is the *unity of Marxists*, not unity between Marxists, and opponents and distorters of Marxism." [13]

United Action Is Impossible with Those Who Transpose Enemies and Friends

The new leaders of the CPSU argue that even if there are differences of theory and line, these can be put aside and that "united action" should be taken and "unity against the enemy" achieved in practical struggle against imperialism.

[13] V. I. Lenin, "Unity," *Collected Works*, Eng. ed., Progress Publishers, Moscow, 1964, Vol. XX, p. 232.

The sharpest difference of theory and line between Marxism-Leninism and Khrushchev revisionism concerns precisely the question of handling our relations with enemies and friends, in other words, the question of whether to oppose or unite with imperialism, and above all the question of whether to oppose or unite with U.S. imperialism. This difference is decisive for all the most important practical actions in the international class struggle. How can it possibly be put aside in favour of an unprincipled unity that does not distinguish between enemies and friends?

The reactionary nature of Khrushchev revisionism is expressed in concentrated form in the line of Soviet-U.S. collaboration for the domination of the world. The Khrushchev clique completely transposed enemies and friends; it regarded U.S. imperialism, the arch enemy of the people of the world, as its closest friend, and the Marxist-Leninists of the world, including those of the Soviet Union, as its principal enemy.

It was precisely on this question that Khrushchev revealed himself as a renegade. It was on this question that the Marxist-Leninists of the whole world waged the sharpest struggle against the Khrushchev revisionists. And it was on this question that the Khrushchev revisionists were spurned by the revolutionary people of the world.

How have the new leaders of the CPSU acted on this question? Have they changed the line of Soviet-U.S. collaboration for world domination? Have they stopped transposing enemies and friends? Have they changed from being a force allied with U.S. imperialism to one opposing it?

The facts show they have not.

Let us consider the facts:

ONE. Immediately after taking office, the new leaders of the CPSU extolled Johnson as " sensible " and " moderate." They have continued to proclaim that the Soviet Union and the United States are two super-powers on which the fate of the world depends, that " there are sufficiently broad areas for co-operation " between them, and that " there are still many unutilized potentialities." [14] Even after the rabid expansion by U.S. imperialism of its war of aggression in Viet Nam, they have kept on stressing their desire for the " development and improvement of relations with the United States of America." At times they find it necessary to talk about a tendency towards a " freeze " in Soviet-U.S. relations, but behind the scenes they are stepping up their secret diplomacy and their deals with the United States.

TWO. The signing of the partial nuclear test ban treaty by the Soviet Union, the United States and Britain was an important landmark in Khrushchev's alliance with the United States against China. Not only have the new leaders of the CPSU accepted this legacy, but with this treaty as a basis they are actively plotting new deals with the United States for the " prevention of nuclear proliferation " and similar so-called " disarmament " measures in an effort to maintain the monopoly of the two nuclear overlords, the Soviet Union and the United States, against China and all other independent countries.

THREE. U.S. imperialism has been using the United Nations as a tool for opposing the revolutions of the people of the world. Catering to U.S. imperialism, Khrushchev used the United Nations as a stock exchange for the domination of the world by two great powers, the Soviet Union and

[14] A. A. Gromyko, Speech at the Plenary Session of the 19th General Assembly of the United Nations, December 7, 1964.

the United States. The new leaders of the CPSU have continued this reactionary policy. They have again brought up Khrushchev's proposal for a standing U.N. armed force. They voted in the United Nations for a " ceasefire " and for the realization of " national reconciliation " in the Congo (L), and they also voted for the " ceasefire " in the Dominican Republic. Wherever the people rise up in armed struggle against U.S. imperialism or win victories in such struggle, and wherever U.S. imperialism suffers defeats and finds itself in a predicament, the new leaders of the CPSU hurriedly come forward to help it out. Together with the U.S. imperialists, they are using the United Nations to attack, weaken and divide the forces opposing imperialism, colonialism and neo-colonialism, and to save, strengthen and extend U.S. imperialist positions. They serve as a fire-brigade for U.S. imperialism trying to stamp out the flames of revolution.

On April 7 this year, together with his proposal for " unconditional discussions " on the question of Viet Nam, Johnson publicized the scheme for " the international development of Southeast Asia " in order to undermine the struggle against U.S. imperialism waged by the people of Viet Nam and the other Southeast Asian countries and to step up economic infiltration, and he expressed the hope that the Soviet Union would join in. The United States regards the establishment of the " Asian Development Bank " as a means of putting this scheme into practice. In response to Johnson's call, the new leaders of the CPSU went so far as to send a delegation to Bangkok in October to sit together with delegations from the United States, Japan, and such puppet cliques as the Chiang Kai-shek gang, south Korea and " Malaysia " and take an active part in preparing for the establishment of the " Asian Development Bank." Such is the ardour of the new leaders of the CPSU for united action with U.S. imperialism.

FOUR. The new leaders of the CPSU have taken over and expanded the enterprises of the firm of Kennedy, Nehru and Khrushchev which Khrushchev worked hard to establish. They have carried further their alliance against China with the Indian reactionaries who are controlled by the U.S. imperialists. During Shastri's visit to the Soviet Union, they granted India aid to the tune of U.S. $900 million in one go, which is more than all the loans Khrushchev extended to India in nine years. They have speeded up their plans for military aid to India and are working hand in glove with the United States to help India's arms expansion, so that the Indian reactionaries are able to use Soviet-made weapons against China and other neighbouring countries.

Recently, during India's armed aggression against Pakistan and also in connection with the Sino-Indian boundary question, the new leaders of the CPSU revealed in all its ugliness their support of the aggressor and their alliance with the United States and India against China. The Soviet Union and the United States joined in an anti-China chorus both inside and outside the United Nations. In September 1965, in statements on the armed conflict between India and Pakistan, TASS attacked China by insinuation, and *Pravda* even openly sided with India against China on the Sino-Indian boundary question. People will recall that it was precisely with a TASS statement on the Sino-Indian boundary question that Khrushchev started his public attacks on China in September 1959. But his attacks pale into insignificance in comparison with those of the present leaders of the CPSU. They have discarded even the small fig-leaf

Khrushchev used in order to feign neutrality. Small wonder that the U.S. imperialists are gleefully hailing a " new era " in U.S.-Soviet co-operation.

The new leaders of the CPSU are able to deceive people because they sometimes make a few verbal attacks on U.S. imperialism. Why do they have to do this? The answer is that this meets the need of the U.S. imperialists as well as the revisionists themselves. The Khrushchev revisionists have to give the appearance of opposing the United States in order to render effective help to U.S. imperialism, hoodwink the masses and sabotage revolution. Otherwise, they could not play this deceptive role, and that would not be to the advantage of U.S. imperialism. Minor attacks in words but major help in deeds — such is the way the new leaders of the CPSU serve U.S. imperialism.

Some people ask, why is it that the Marxist-Leninists and the revolutionary people cannot take united action with the new leaders of the CPSU, yet can unite with personages from the upper strata in the nationalist countries, and strive for united action with them in the anti-imperialist struggle, and can even exploit the contradictions among the imperialist countries in the struggle against the United States?

The reason is that in the contemporary world opposition to or alliance with U.S. imperialism constitutes the hallmark for deciding whether or not a political force can be included in the united front against the United States.

In Asia, Africa and Latin America, with the exception of the lackeys of imperialism, personages from the upper strata in many nationalist countries desire in varying degrees to oppose imperialism, colonialism and neocolonialism headed by the United States. We should co-operate with them in the anti-imperialist struggle.

In the imperialist countries which are in sharp contradiction with the United States, some monopoly capitalists follow the U.S. imperialists, but there are also others who desire in varying degrees to oppose the United States. In the struggle against the United States, the people of the world can take united action with the latter on some questions and to a certain degree.

The crux of the matter is that, so far from opposing U.S. imperialism, the new leaders of the CPSU are allying themselves and collaborating with it to dominate the world. They have thus set themselves in opposition to the united front against U.S. imperialism. If they really opposed U.S. imperialism and did so by actual deeds we would readily take united action with them. But their so-called opposition to U.S. imperialism is only verbal and not genuine. We must tell them the truth: So long as their line of Soviet-U.S. collaboration against world revolution remains unchanged, and so long as they do not abandon their alliance with U.S. imperialism and reaction, we absolutely refuse to take any " united action " with them. We absolutely refuse to serve as a pawn in their secret diplomacy with U.S. imperialism or help them cover up their assistance to U.S. imperialism in suppressing the peoples' revolution in various countries.

The New Leaders of the CPSU Are Taking United Action with the United States on the Question of Viet Nam

The new leaders of the CPSU never weary of saying that, however serious the differences between them, Communists must take " united action " on the question of Viet Nam at this urgent juncture in the Vietnamese people's struggle against the United States.

Since the new leaders of the CPSU have destroyed the basis of inter-national proletarian unity, and since they transpose enemies and friends and persist in the line of Soviet-U.S. collaboration for world domination, is it still possible for the Marxist-Leninist parties to take united action with them on the question of Viet Nam?

At a time when the U.S. imperialists are committing rabid aggression against Viet Nam, all Communist Parties and socialist countries should as a matter of course take a unanimous stand and firmly support the Vietnamese people's just struggle to smash this aggression. The point is that the stand taken by the revisionist leadership of the CPSU on the question of Viet Nam is inseparable from their revisionist programme and line, and is contrary to the principled stand required of a Marxist-Leninist party.

When Khrushchev was in power, the revisionist leadership of the CPSU openly sided with U.S. imperialism and opposed and undermined the revolutionary struggle of the Vietnamese people against U.S. aggression. They alleged that " any small ' local war ' might spark off the conflagration of a world war." [15] Using this absurd argument to frighten and intimidate all peoples engaged in revolutionary armed struggle, they openly refused to support and aid the Vietnamese people in their anti-U.S. struggle. When the struggles of the Vietnamese and the Laotian peoples against U.S'. imperialism grew acute, their policy on the question of Indo-China was one of " disengagement." In July 1964, they indicated the desire of the Soviet Government to resign from its post as one of the two co-chairmen of the Geneva conference. Soon afterwards, when the U.S. imperialists engineered the Bac Bo Gulf incident, Khrushchev went so far as to concoct the slander that the incident was provoked by China.

The situation in Viet Nam developed directly contrary to the wishes of the Khrushchev revisionists. The Vietnamese people won victory after victory in their revolutionary anti-U.S. struggle, while the U.S. aggressors grew hard pressed. The new leaders of the CPSU came to realize that it was no longer advisable to copy Khrushchev's policy of " disengagement " in its totality. So they switched to the policy of involvement, that is, of getting their hand in.

The policy of involvement and the policy of disengagement are essentially the same. Both are products of Khrushchev revisionism and both are designed to meet the needs of U.S. imperialism.

The U.S. imperialists urgently need to extinguish the roaring flames of the Vietnamese people's revolution. And so do the Khrushchev revisionists because they want to carry out their line of Soviet-U.S. collaboration for world domination. When Khrushchev was following the policy of " dis-engagement," he was acting in close co-ordination with John F. Kennedy. And now that the new leaders of the CPSU are following the policy of involvement, they are similarly acting in tacit agreement and close collaboration with Lyndon B. Johnson.

Please consider the following facts:

In January 1965 the U.S. imperialists asked the Soviet Government to use its influence to have the Government of the Democratic Republic of Viet Nam accept two conditions: (1) stop supporting south Viet Nam, and first of all stop supplying it with guns; and (2) stop the attacks on cities

[15] N. S. Khrushchev, Talk at a Press Conference in Vienna, July 8, 1960.

in south Viet Nam. Faithfully obeying the orders of the U.S. imperialists, the new leaders of the CPSU officially transmitted to the Democratic Republic of Viet Nam these preposterous demands, which were aimed at forcing the Vietnamese people into unconditional surrender.

The new leaders of the CPSU have been busy running errands for the U.S. aggressors, who are anxious to find a way out of their predicament in Viet Nam. When Kosygin, Chairman of the Council of Ministers of the USSR, passed through Peking on his visit to Viet Nam in February 1965 and exchanged views with Chinese leaders, he stressed the need to help the United States "find a way out of Viet Nam." This was firmly rebutted by the Chinese leaders. We expressed the hope that the new leaders of the CPSU would support the struggle of the Vietnamese people and not make a deal with the United States on the question of Viet Nam. Kosygin expressed agreement with our views and stated that they would "not bargain with others on this issue." However, the new leaders of the CPSU soon went back on their promise.

Johnson wanted to play his fraudulent game of "unconditional discussions." So the new leaders of the CPSU put forward the idea of "unconditional negotiations." On February 16 this year, the day after Kosygin's return to Moscow, the Soviet Government officially put before Viet Nam and China a proposal to convene a new international conference on Indo-China without prior conditions, which in fact was advocacy of "unconditional negotiations" on the Viet Nam question. On February 23, disregarding the stand which the Vietnamese Government had taken against this proposal and without waiting for a reply from China, the new leaders of the CPSU discussed the question of calling the above-mentioned international conference with the President of France through the Soviet Ambassador to France.

Johnson's fraud of "unconditional discussions" met with a stern rebuff from the Government of the Democratic Republic of Viet Nam. The new leaders of the CPSU then began publicly to insinuate that negotiations could be held if only the United States stopped its bombing of north Viet Nam. They engaged in vigorous activities in the international field with a view to putting this project into effect. In communications to certain fraternal Parties, they said explicitly that they favoured negotiations with the United States on condition it stopped bombing north Viet Nam. They also said that ways and means should be sought to settle the Viet Nam question through negotiations. And sure enough, not long afterwards Johnson came out with the manoeuvre of "the temporary suspension of bombing."

After these plots of "unconditional negotiations" and of "stopping the bombing and holding negotiations" were foiled, the new leaders of the CPSU began to collaborate with the Indian reactionaries and the Tito clique — both lackeys of U.S. imperialism — as brokers on the question of Viet Nam. In their prescription for this question there was only mention of the cessation of U.S. bombing of north Viet Nam, only abstract talk about the implementation of the Geneva agreements but no mention of the fact that the crucial point in the implementation of these agreements is the complete withdrawal of the U.S. aggressor troops from Viet Nam. In addition, the new leaders of the CPSU have been engaged in secret diplomatic activities. In a nutshell, their purpose is to help the United States to bring about "peace talks" by deception, "peace talks" which could go on indefinitely and also allow the United States to hang on in south Viet Nam indefinitely.

To curry favour with U.S. imperialism, the new leaders of the CPSU went to the length of brutally suppressing demonstrations in the Soviet Union opposing U.S. imperialism and supporting Viet Nam which were held by students from Viet Nam, China and other Asian, African and Latin American countries.

Particularly noteworthy is the fact that last April the new leaders of the CPSU let Khrushchev emerge from limbo to talk with Western correspondents. In that interview, he advocated " peaceful coexistence " and attacked the Vietnamese people's struggle against U.S. aggression, alleging that "trouble starts with small things like Viet Nam and ends with disaster." [16] This was not accidental. It shows that, like Khrushchev, the new leaders of the CPSU are afraid that the so-called " minor trouble," that is, the question of Viet Nam, may spoil their fond dreams of Soviet-U.S. collaboration.

The new leaders of the CPSU are doing exactly what Khrushchev did before them, namely, pulling the Viet Nam question into the orbit of Soviet-U.S. collaboration. Since they are co-operating so closely with the U.S. imperialists in united action, it is of course impossible for Marxist-Leninists to join in and take " united action " with them.

At bottom, the new leaders of the CPSU are clamouring for " united action " on the Viet Nam question because this slogan is highly deceptive and is apt to create the illusion that it is still possible to have "unity against U.S. imperialism " with the new leaders of the CPSU who are intent on Soviet-U.S. collaboration for world domination. They do so in order to worm their way into the anti-U.S. front and carry out their policy of involvement in the service of U.S. imperialism.

Look at the trick of " aid " to Viet Nam the new leaders of the CPSU are playing and you will understand the real nature of their policy of involvement more clearly.

We have invariably held that it is the bounden proletarian-internationalist duty of all countries in the socialist camp to aid the fraternal Vietnamese people. The Vietnamese people who are standing in the forefront of the struggle against U.S. imperialism have every right and reason to demand and receive aid from every socialist country. China is helping the Vietnamese people to the best of her ability. We have stated on many occasions that if the Soviet Union genuinely wants to help the Vietnamese people in their struggle against U.S. aggression, the greater and more practical the aid the better. But what have the new leaders of the CPSU done? Whether in quantity or quality, their aid to Viet Nam is far from commensurate with the strength of the Soviet Union. They have ulterior motives in giving a certain amount of aid — they are trying to hoodwink the people at home and abroad, to keep the situation in Viet Nam under their control, to gain a say on the Viet Nam question and to strike a bargain with U.S. imperialism on it.

The U.S. imperialists appreciate the trick being played by the new leaders of the CPSU. They know full well that it is to their advantage for the new leaders of the CPSU to get involved in the Viet Nam question. Far from objecting to " aid " to Viet Nam from the new leaders of the

[16] " Mr. K. Speaks," *Daily Express*, April 6, 1965.

CPSU, they welcome it. The U.S. authorities have made it clear that Soviet involvement in the Viet Nam question is preferable to Soviet non-involvement. It has been pointed out in a U.S. magazine that "eventually, an arrangement might be contrived involving the stationing of Soviet troops in north Viet Nam . . . while American troops remain in south Viet Nam," and that "one of the paradoxical advantages of more direct Soviet military involvement would be the establishment of a direct American-Soviet bargaining relationship in this area." [17] In fact, the new leaders of the CPSU have disclosed the details of their so-called " aid " to Viet Nam to the Americans through various channels. On this matter, too, they are taking united action with the U.S. imperialists.

Furthermore, the new leaders of the CPSU have been using their " aid " to Viet Nam as a pretext for wantonly vilifying China, and have been assiduously spreading the lie that "China obstructed the transit of Soviet military equipment for Viet Nam." The truth is that we have always honoured our agreements and done our utmost speedily to transport to Viet Nam all military *matériel* in transit which was furnished by the Soviet Union with the concurrence of the Vietnamese comrades. By these fabrications and slanders, the new leaders of the CPSU have supplied further proof that they stop at nothing in order to ally themselves with the United States against China.

Marxist-Leninists must penetrate the appearance of things to get at their essence. Having carefully observed the actions of the new leaders of the CPSU on the question of Viet Nam over the past year, we can only reach the following conclusion : In calling so vehemently for " united action " on the Viet Nam question and trying by every means to bring about a summit conference of the Soviet Union, Viet Nam and China and an international meeting of the socialist countries and the fraternal Parties, the new leaders of the CPSU have no other purpose in mind than to deceive the world, to tie the fraternal countries to the chariot of Soviet-U.S. collaboration for world domination, to use the question of Viet Nam as an important counter in their bargaining with the United States, and to isolate and attack the Chinese Communist Party and all the other fraternal Parties which uphold Marxism-Leninism.

Things could not be clearer. If we were to take united action on the question of Viet Nam with the new leaders of the CPSU who are pursuing the Khrushchev revisionist line, wouldn't we be helping them to deceive the people of the world? Wouldn't we be helping them to bring the question of Viet Nam within the orbit of Soviet-U.S. collaboration? Wouldn't we be joining them in betraying the revolutionary cause of the Vietnamese people? Wouldn't we be joining them in attacking the Chinese Communist Party and all the other Marxist-Leninist parties? Wouldn't we be joining them in serving as accomplices of U.S. imperialism? Of course, we shall do nothing of the sort.

" United Action," So Called, Is a Means of Promoting Splittism

The clamour raised by the new leaders of the CPSU for " united action " is an attempt both to conceal and to carry on their great-power chauvinism

[17] Zbigniew Brzezinski, " Peace, Morality and Vietnam," *The New Leader*, April 12, 1965.

and splittism under the cover of hypocritical words. They claim to have "made a number of major moves" to promote unity and improve the relations between fraternal Parties and Soviet-Chinese relations. Let us look at the steps they have actually taken.

The March Moscow meeting which will remain for ever infamous was convened by the new leaders of the CPSU under the slogan of "united action." Khrushchev revisionism and splittism had in effect divided the international communist movement, and the March meeting, which the new leaders of the CPSU called regardless of all consequences, was an extremely grave step to bring about an open split. Since that meeting, they have taken a number of other steps in continuation of this divisive line.

The new leaders of the CPSU have conducted a feverish campaign against the Chinese Communist Party throughout their Party and among the entire Soviet People. They have organized meetings in offices, schools factories and villages to hear anti-Chinese speeches, wantonly attacking and vilifying China. Some of these speeches were made in the presence of Chinese comrades. They have been busy sending emissaries to many countries for the sole purpose of engaging in anti-Chinese activity and of spreading all sorts of anti-Chinese slanders. In international organizations and international activities they stop at nothing in pushing their anti-Chinese schemes.

The new leaders of the CPSU are continuing Khrushchev's anti-Albanian policy. Although in Japan they have met with serious set-backs in their criminal effort to support Yoshio Shiga and other renegades from the Japanese Communist Party in collusion with the U.S. imperialists and the Japanese reactionaries, they remain unreconciled and are continuing their counter-revolutionary sabotage and subversion against the Japanese Communist Party. They are also continuing their attacks on the Indonesian Communist Party, the Communist Party of New Zealand and other fraternal Parties which uphold Marxism-Leninism, and are carrying on various kinds of sabotage and subversion against them.

While continuing the practice of subjecting other Communist Parties and socialist countries to pressure, sabotage and subversion, the new leaders of the CPSU are also employing the more insidious stratagems of trying to woo them, buy them over, deceive them and sow dissension among them. They take the Chinese Communist Party, which firmly opposes Khrushchev revisionism, as the main target of their concentrated attacks, and they are trying to isolate it.

In the international mass organizations, the new leaders of the CPSU, using the slogan of "united action," continue to push their capitulationist line of not opposing the United States and not supporting revolution and their work of splitting anti-imperialist unity. They repeat Khrushchev's despicable stock tricks at the meetings of these international organizations, rely on behind-the-scene manipulation as well as open trouble-making and even resort to such ludicrous tactics as banging tables and stamping their feet.

In the name of "united action" the revisionist leadership of the CPSU is vainly trying to recover its position as the "father party," so that it may continue to wield the baton and compel the other Communist Parties and socialist countries to do this today and that tomorrow. Actually, however, its former power and prestige are gone beyond recall. Today, the new leaders of the CPSU and their followers are drawn together by self-interest, each seeking his own ends. The baton of the new leaders is less and less effective.

Facts have shown that if the Communists of a particular country accept the hodge-podge of revisionism, great-power chauvinism and splittism of the leaders of the CPSU, the country's revolutionary cause is impaired and undermined, its Communist Party becomes corrupted, goes downhill and degenerates, and both the country and Party find themselves beset with difficulties and at the mercy of others. On the other hand, those who firmly resist and oppose this hodge-podge find themselves in a quite different and much better position. This is as true today as it was before.

One of the purposes of the new leaders of the CPSU in advocating "united action" is to stop the open polemics. They want to gag the Marxist-Leninists and prevent the latter from exposing and criticizing them, so as to be free to carry out Khrushchev revisionism.

How can such a thing be possible? The present great debate has most vividly and clearly revealed what is decadent and dying and what represents the direction of future development and victory in the international communist movement. Khrushchev revisionism has been refuted down to the last point, and this poisonous weed has been converted into good fertilizer on the fields of world revolution. Truth becomes clearer through debate; the more the polemics, the higher the level of revolutionary consciousness and the greater the degree of revolutionary vigour. We shall certainly carry the debate to the finish and draw a clear line between what is right and what is wrong on the major problems. Failure to do so would be extremely harmful to the revolutionary cause of the people of the world and to the cause of opposing imperialism and defending world peace.

Another purpose of the new leaders of the CPSU in advocating "united action" is to stop what they call "factional activities" by the Marxist-Leninist parties. They want to strangle the Marxist-Leninist forces which are fighting to rebuild revolutionary proletarian parties or establish new ones, and to prevent the Chinese Communist Party and other Marxist-Leninist parties from supporting these newborn revolutionary forces.

In many countries, the Marxist-Leninists have broken with the revisionist cliques and either rebuilt Marxist-Leninist parties and organizations or founded new ones. This is the inevitable outcome of the practice of revisionism, great-power chauvinism and splittism by the leaders of the CPSU; it is the inevitable outcome of the struggle between the Marxist-Leninists and the revisionists in those countries and of the regrouping of the Communist Parties of those countries have forbidden their members to internationally and domestically.

Bowing to the baton of Khrushchev revisionism the leading groups in the revolutionary forces under conditions of deepening class struggle both do what the imperialists and reactionaries fear most, and only allowed them to do what is to the liking of the imperialists and reactionaries or is at least tolerable to them. Whoever acts differently is attacked, disciplined or expelled. Such being the case, the staunch Marxist-Leninists in those Parties are left with no alternative but to break with the revisionist leading groups, and the founding and growth of genuine revolutionary Marxist-Leninist parties and organizations become inevitable.

Revolution, the fight against imperialism and the fight against revisionism all have right on their side. Beyond all doubt, it is perfectly right to discard these decaying old revisionist groups and build new revolutionary parties.

We resolutely support all the forces in the world that persevere in Marxism-Leninism and revolution. It is our lofty proletarian-internationalist duty to strengthen our united action with all the Marxist-Leninist forces in the world.

"United Action," So Called, Is a Slogan to Deceive the Soviet People

The new leaders of the CPSU claim that the socialist countries have "a socio-economic system of the same type" and share the "common goal of building socialism and communism." This is one more reason they cite in their clamour for "united action."

This is throwing dust in people's eyes. Following in Khrushchev's footsteps, the new leaders of the CPSU are bringing about the further degeneration of the Soviet Union towards capitalism in the name of realizing "communism." Like Khrushchev, they use the slogan of "the state of the whole people" to abolish the dictatorship of the proletariat in the Soviet Union, thus making the Soviet state degenerate into an instrument for the rule of the privileged bourgeois stratum over the Soviet people. Like Khrushchev, they use the slogan of "the party of the entire people" to alter the proletarian character of the Communist Party of the Soviet Union and turn it into a party serving the interests of the privileged bourgeois stratum.

In their appraisal of Stalin, the new leaders of the CPSU pretend to be somewhat different from Khrushchev. But this is only an attempt to allay the resentment of the broad masses of the people and Party members in the Soviet Union. Far from criticizing Khrushchev's mistake in completely negating Stalin, they have followed him in describing the period of Stalin's leadership as "the period of the personality cult." They have sponsored the publication of numerous articles and literary and other works which keep on besmirching all aspects of the great Marxist-Leninist Stalin, the dictatorship of the proletariat and the socialist system.

Taking advantage of the state power they wield, the new leaders of the CPSU have centred their efforts on undermining the economic base of socialism, socialist ownership by the whole people and socialist collective ownership, and on setting up and developing a new system of exploitation and fostering and supporting the new bourgeoisie, thus accelerating the restoration of capitalism.

The report on the problems of industry by Kosygin, Chairman of the Council of Ministers of the USSR, at the recent plenary session of the Central Committee of the CPSU and the resolution which it adopted marked a big step along the road of the restoration of capitalism in the Soviet economy.

Through a Party resolution and government decrees, the new leaders of the CPSU have confirmed the experiments initiated in the Khrushchev period as a result of which socialist enterprises owned by the whole people degenerate into enterprises of a capitalist nature, and they have spread these experiments throughout the country. The key feature of the "new

466

system" of industrial management they have instituted is to enforce the capitalist principle of profit and to make profit-seeking the basic motive force of production in the enterprises through the "enhancement of economic incentives." In the name of widening the enterprises' right to self-management, they have scrapped a series of important quotas formerly set by the state for the enterprises in accordance with the plan, substituting capitalist free competition for socialist planned economy. They have vested in the managers the power to hire and fire workers, fix the level of wages and bonuses and freely dispose of large funds, thus turning them into virtual masters of the enterprises, who are able to bully and oppress the workers and usurp the fruits of their labour at will. In reality, this means restoring capitalism, replacing socialist ownership by the whole people with ownership by the privileged bourgeois stratum, and converting the socialist enterprises in the Soviet Union step by step into capitalist enterprises of a special type. This is by no means a "new creation"; it has been copied and developed from the old "experience" of the Tito clique in restoring capitalism in Yugoslavia.

It is elementary Marxism-Leninism that the system of management comes within the sphere of the relations of production and is an expression of the system of ownership. Under the guise of reforming the system of management, the new leaders of the CPSU have undermined the very foundation of the system of ownership by the whole people. This is exactly what the Tito clique of Yugoslavia did. Having a guilty conscience, the new leaders of the CPSU cry out that those who talk about the "bourgeois transformation" of the Soviet economy are "bourgeois ideologists" and "our enemies." [18] This is what the Tito clique said too. Such protestations are like the sign, "There is no silver buried here," put up by the man in the legend over the place where he hid his money.

In the countryside, too, the new leaders of the CPSU are accelerating the growth of capitalism, developing the private economy, enlarging the private plots, increasing the number of privately raised cattle, expanding the free market and encouraging free trading. They are using a variety of economic and administrative measures to encourage and foster the growth of a new kulak economy, sabotaging and disintegrating all aspects of the socialist collective economy.

Khrushchev wrought alarming havoc in Soviet agriculture. After taking office, the new leaders of the CPSU boasted that they had worked out "a scientifically based programme for an immediate and sharp rise in agricultural production." [19] But a year later, Soviet agriculture still remains in a mess, creating untold difficulties in the lives of the Soviet people. The new leaders of the CPSU are now laying the entire blame on the fallen Khrushchev. In fact, these serious troubles are precisely the outcome of their own intensified application of Khrushchev revisionism.

Facts show that the replacement of Khrushchev by these new leaders has been merely a change of personalities in the revisionist dynasty — just as all reactionary ruling classes have to change horses in order to maintain their rule. Although Khrushchev himself has fallen, the leading group of

---

[18] A. N. Kosygin, "On Improving Industrial Management, Perfecting Planning, and Enhancing Economic Incentives in Industrial Production," *Moscow News*, Supplement, October 2, 1965.

[19] "In Lenin's Way, with Scientific Accuracy," editorial in *Sovietskaya Russia*, March 28, 1965.

the CPSU is still the same old Khrushchev crowd; organizationally, it remains basically unchanged, and whether ideologically, politically, theoretically or in the realm of policy, theirs is still the same old Khrushchev revisionist stuff.

As Lenin pointed out, "opportunism is no chance occurrence, sin, slip, or treachery on the part of individuals, but a social product of an entire period of history." [20] It is inevitable that Khrushchev revisionism will exist as long as the social basis and the class roots which gave birth to it remain and as long as the privileged bourgeois stratum exists.

Because they are the political representatives of the privileged bourgeois stratum in the Soviet Union, just as Khrushchev was, the new leaders of the CPSU pursue domestic and foreign policies which are not proletarian but bourgeois, not socialist but capitalist. Like Khrushchev, they are in a position of antagonism to the Soviet people, who constitute more than 90 per cent of the Soviet population, and they are encountering ever stronger dissatisfaction and opposition on the part of the Soviet people.

When the new leaders of the CPSU loudly assert that the socialist countries have a "socio-economic system of the same type," they do so with the aim of covering up their restoration of capitalism in the Soviet Union, of preventing us from unmasking them, and of setting the Soviet people against China.

In our view, when a revisionist clique emerges and a capitalist come-back occurs in a socialist country, all the Marxist-Leninists in the world are duty-bound to expose and struggle against these things; this is the only correct and principled stand. The only way to serve the fundamental interests of the great Soviet people and to give them genuine support is resolutely to expose the fact that the revisionist leadership of the CPSU is restoring capitalism in the USSR.

If we should cease exposing and combating the domestic and external revisionist policies of the new leaders of the CPSU, if we should abandon our principled stand and take so-called "united action" with them, that would suit them very well. It would help them to hoodwink the Soviet people. It would hinder rather than support the Soviet people's struggle to defend the fruits of their socialist revolution; it would hinder rather than support the Soviet people's struggle against Khrushchev revisionism without Khrushchev.

Comrade Mao Tse-tung has often said to comrades from fraternal Parties that if China's leadership is usurped by revisionists in the future, the Marxist-Leninists of all countries should likewise resolutely expose and fight them, and help the working class and the masses of China to combat such revisionism. Taking the same stand, we consider it our bounden proletarian-internationalist duty firmly to expose the revisionist leadership of the CPSU to draw a clear line between ourselves and them, and to persist in the struggle against Khrushchev revisionism.

Persevere in the Struggle Against Khrushchev Revisionism

A fierce struggle is going on between the revolutionary people of the world on the one hand and the imperialists headed by the United States

---

[20] V. I. Lenin, "The Collapse of the Second International," *Collected Works*, Eng. ed., Progress Publishers, Moscow, 1964, Vol. XXI, p. 247.

and their lackeys on the other. The characteristic of the present world situation is that with the daily deepening of the international class struggle, a process of great upheaval, great division and great reorganization is taking place. The revolutionary movement of the people of the world is surging vigorously forward. Imperialism and all other decadent reactionary forces are putting up a wild death-bed fight. Drastic divisions and realignments of political forces are taking place on a world scale.

The revolutionary forces of the people of the world have surpassed the reactionary forces of imperialism. The advances of the revolutionary movement of the people of the world is the main current in the present situation. The people's revolutionary struggles in all countries will certainly triumph, while imperialism, reaction and modern revisionism will step by step descend to their doom. This is the inevitable trend of world history which no decadent reactionary force can change. But imperialism and reaction will not fall unless you strike them down, and modern revisionism, too, will not collapse unless you fight it. Before being overthrown and eliminated, they will invariably collaborate and, using different tactics, do all they can to hurl desperate attacks on the revolutionary forces. Thus, along with the growth and deepening of the revolutionary movement, there is an adverse counter-revolutionary current. The course of international development is unavoidably filled with contradictions and conflicts; there are bound to be zigzags and reversals. In all countries the people's revolutionary struggles necessarily advance in the form of waves.

As the struggle against the United States reaches a crucial phase, U.S. imperialism needs the services of Khrushchev revisionism all the more acutely. Hence it is inevitable that the struggle against Khrushchev revisionism must sharpen.

In the course of combating Khrushchev revisionism, there is bound to be a certain unevenness in the degree of people's understanding of the struggle. This kind of phenomenon becomes particularly conspicuous when the struggle becomes sharp. That is both natural and inevitable. Lenin said that when astonishingly abrupt changes took place, people "who were suddenly confronted with extremely important problems could not long remain on this level. They could not continue without a respite, without a return to elementary questions, without a new training which would help them 'digest' lessons of unparalleled richness and make it possible for incomparably wider masses again to march forward, but now far more firmly, more consciously, more confidently and more steadfastly." [21] Just such a situation exists at present.

As the struggle against Khrushchev revisionism becomes sharper and deeper, a new process of division will inevitably occur in the revolutionary ranks, and some people will inevitably drop out. But at the same time hundreds of millions of revolutionary people will stream in.

Faced with a complex situation of this kind, Marxist-Leninists must never abandon or slur over principles, but must take a clear stand, uphold revolutionary principles and persevere in the struggle against Khrushchev revisionism. Only in this way can the unity of the revolutionary forces be strengthened and expanded.

At present, the task facing all the Marxist-Leninist parties is to draw a clear line of demarcation both politically and organizationally between

[21] V. I. Lenin, "Certain Features of the Historical Development of Marxism," *Collected Works*, Eng. ed., F.L.P.H., Moscow, 1963, Vol. XVII, p. 42.

themselves and the revisionists, who are serving U.S. imperialism, and to liquidate Khrushchev revisionism in order to welcome the high tide of revolutionary struggle against U.S. imperialism and its lackeys.

In the final analysis, in all parts of the world including the Soviet Union, the masses of the people, who constitute the overwhelming majority of the population, and the overwhelming majority of Communists and cadres want revolution and are upholding or will uphold Marxism-Leninism. They are steadily awakening and joining the ranks of the struggle against imperialism and revisionism. It is certain that over 90 per cent of the world's population will become more closely united in the fight against imperialism, reaction and modern revisionism.

All the Communist Parties and all the socialist countries will eventually unite on the basis of Marxism-Leninism and proletarian internationalism and take united action in the struggle against imperialism. As Lenin told the old-line revisionists, the proletariat will sooner or later unite and eventually win on a world scale, "only it is moving and will move, is proceeding and will proceed, against you, it will be a victory over you." [22]

Unless the new leaders of the CPSU stop practising Khrushchevism without Khrushchev, admit and correct their mistakes and genuinely return to the revolutionary path of Marxism-Leninism, it is absolutely out of the question to expect the Marxist-Leninists to abandon the struggle against Khrushchev revisionism.

With power and to spare, we must not cease the pursuit
Or halt in mid-course for the sake of idle laurels.

This couplet summarizes an extremely important historical lesson. The Marxist-Leninists and all the other revolutionary people of the world must continue their victorious pursuit and carry the struggle against Khrushchev revisionism through to the end!

DOCUMENT 33

The International Duty of the Communists of All Countries

(November 28, 1965)

Complete Text

[Editorial, *Pravda*, November 28, 1965, p. 1, quoted from *CDSP*, Vol. XVII, No. 47 (December 15, 1965), pp. 3–5]

A sharp, relentless struggle, never ceasing for a moment, for social progress and the advancement of the great revolutionary cause is going on in the modern world. The forces of socialism, the international Communist, workers' and national-liberation movement, and the forces of democracy and peace are waging a vigorous offensive against the positions of imperialism and are pressing it back step by step. This offensive has the most diverse forms and is being waged on various sectors — political, economic, ideological. The historic struggle of socialism against imperialism

---

[22] V. I. Lenin, "Imperialism and the Split in Socialism," *Collected Works*, Eng. ed., Progress Publishers, Moscow, 1964, Vol. XXIII, p. 111.

is determining the solution of the fundamental problems of the life of mankind.

How will the development of the world revolutionary process proceed henceforth? Will the exploitation and oppression of man by man long remain in part of the world, will room be left for diktat and coercion in the international arena? At what price will the social progress of mankind be achieved? Will there or will there not be a world thermonuclear war? All these questions are at the center of attention of present-day society.

The answer to them is supplied by the practice of the struggle of the world system of socialism, the national-liberation movement, the struggle of the working class of the capitalist countries and above all its Communist vanguard. This answer is realistically embodied in their remarkable victories in the almost half a century that has elapsed since the October Revolution.

Each of the three great revolutionary forces of the present day operates in specific conditions, solves the tasks facing it with its own methods and means. But their interests lie in the same plane, they have the same common enemy — imperialism. Success on any sector of the anti-imperialist struggle advances the entire revolutionary front. Herein lies an objective basis for the joint action, mutual assistance and cooperation of all revolutionary forces.

Experience has clearly shown that unity of action of the revolutionary forces ensures the best conditions for promoting the construction of a new society in the socialist countries, for new victories of the national-liberation movement, for strengthening the independence of the new national states and their advance along the path of social progress, that it enables the international workers' movement to deliver increasingly telling blows against the class enemy, creates the possibility of checking the aggressive forces of imperialism and preventing a world thermonuclear war. It is precisely the unity of action of all anti-imperialist forces that will ensure the ultimate triumph of peace, democracy, national independence and socialism over war, reaction, colonialism and imperialism. As Lenin pointed out, " without a voluntary striving toward alliance and unity on the part of the proletariat and subsequently of all the working masses of all countries and nations of the entire world, the cause of victory over capitalism cannot be successfully concluded " (" Works," fourth [Russian] edition, Vol. XXXI, p. 128).

The nucleus of the solidarity of the revolutionary forces of the present day is the unity of action of the Communist and workers' parties. This is particularly true in our times, when the Communist movement has become the most influential political force of the present day, when the scope of the historical tasks facing it has greatly expanded and their complexity increased.

The unity of the workers' parties never came by itself, automatically. It has been achieved as a result of long, patient and persistent work, as a result of struggle against revisionist and dogmatic distortions of Marxism, on the basis of the affirmation in the revolutionary workers' movement of ideas and principles conforming to the vital needs of the epoch.

It is well known how implacably and consistently V. I. Lenin fought against right-wing opportunism and its attempts to revise the revolutionary principles of creative Marxism, how he unmasked its striving to hurl back the workers' movement. This struggle was aimed at rallying the healthy forces of the social-democratic movement, at helping the masses to get rid of opportunistic illusions and pursue a course toward their unity on the principled basis of scientific communism.

In the years preceding and following the October Revolution, Lenin carried out immense theoretical work to show what great harm left-wing opportunism and sectarianism do to the workers' movement. The book " ' Left-Wing ' Communism, an Infantile Disorder " and many of Lenin's other works helped the Communist Parties to define their tasks correctly, taught fraternal parties to resolve differences that might arise in the spirit of Communist Party spirit and proletarian internationalism.

In the new historical conditions, the Communist and workers' parties continue to work persistently and patiently, in Leninist fashion, at strengthening the unity of all Communists of the world. The Moscow conferences of 1957 and 1960 are a remarkable example of this. By profoundly analyzing changes that have taken place in the world, by advancing a number of new ideas that develop Marxist-Leninist theory and enrich the strategy and tactics of the workers' movement, the Communist Parties created conditions for achieving the close unity of the revolutionary forces.

The Declaration and Statement of the fraternal parties agreed upon and jointly adopted at the Moscow conferences are a principled basis on which their cooperation in various forms may successfully develop. " The Communist and workers' parties," the Moscow Statement of 1960 says, " are constantly educating the working people in a spirit of socialist internationalism and implacability toward all manifestations of nationalism and chauvinism. The solidarity and unity of the Communist and workers' parties and the peoples of the socialist countries and their fidelity to Marxist-Leninist teaching are the main source of the strength and invincibility of each socialist country and of the socialist camp as a whole."

Here are stressed both the very necessity for solidarity and its ideological-political platform, fidelity to our great revolutionary teaching, which is being developed collectively by all detachments of the Communist movement and is being constantly enriched by the experience of the revolutionary struggle of the masses.

On the basis of the ideas of the Declaration and the Statement, important new successes have been achieved in recent years in the peoples' struggle for peace, national independence, democracy and socialism. It must be recognized, however, that the enormous possibilities for the further development of our revolutionary cause that now exist have not been fully realized. The effectiveness of joint actions by the revolutionary forces has been in substantial measure weakened and undermined by differences that have arisen within the Communist movement.

The overwhelming majority of fraternal parties stand firmly on the positions of the general line of the Communist movement defined by the Moscow conferences of 1957 and 1960. Certain parties have taken their own positions, which differ radically from the general platform of Communists.

In these circumstances, this majority of Marxist-Leninist parties favors the closing of the ranks of the Communist and the entire liberation movement, despite the existing differences, and the waging of a resolute struggle against the common imperialist enemy on the basis of a policy of unity of action. The CPSU and other Marxist-Leninist parties are in fact pursuing this policy, dealing imperialism one blow after another and striving to organize joint actions directed at putting an end to imperialist aggression, at defending the rights of the peoples fighting for freedom.

Such an approach conforms to the supreme interests of all the revolutionary forces — the interests of the struggle against the common enemy. It also furthers the improvement of mutual understanding among the Communists of various countries, the maturing of the necessary conditions and an atmosphere conducive to the overcoming of the differences that have arisen.

This approach has found its expression in the decisions and actions of the overwhelming majority of fraternal parties and in the documents of the March consultative meeting.

The Marxist-Leninist parties are devoting increasing attention to actions aimed at consolidating the Communist ranks. The growing mutual understanding and cooperation that are forged in the course of joint anti-imperialist actions find strength and development in expanding contacts and in bilateral and multilateral meetings of representatives of fraternal parties.

Of great significance in this connection were such international actions of Communists as the meeting of representatives of all the fraternal parties of the countries of Latin America, the Brussels conference of representatives of the Communist Parties of Western Europe, and the exchange of views among representatives of almost 40 parties in Prague on the occasion of the 30th anniversary of the Seventh Comintern Congress. All these meetings took place in a spirit of unity and, in discussing their specific questions, fully affirmed the principles of the 1957 and 1960 international forums of Communist Parties.

The CPSU, together with other Marxist-Leninist parties, guided by the supreme interests of the revolutionary cause, is sparing no effort to overcome the difficulties that have arisen in the Communist movement. The CPSU and its Central Committee have done and are doing everything within their power to ensure a normalization of relations between the USSR and China, between our two parties. In the course of the past year the CPSU Central Committee has more than once proposed to the Chinese leadership the carrying out of joint moves on the most important specific questions, the development of relations on the state level and the solution of many disputed problems.

Demonstrating its good will, its striving for the solidarity of all revolutionary forces, our party has for more than a year now refrained from open polemics. It has done so not because it has nothing to say. Reared by Lenin, the CPSU has waged throughout its history and continues to wage a resolute struggle against nationalism, dogmatism and revisionism, for the solidarity of Communists on the principled basis of the revolutionary theory of Marxism. It has always been implacable toward any opportunists who, donning various masks, including the mask of " superrevolutionaries," have tried to divert the Communist movement from the correct course and thereby weaken its struggle for the cause of the working class.

In refraining from polemics, the CPSU Central Committee has proceeded from the supreme interests of the international Communist movement, the interests of the struggle against imperialism. In conditions of the intensified activity of the imperialist forces, the aggravation of differences within the ranks of the Communists and the stirring up of open polemics play into the hands of the class enemy and are exploited by him to strike blows against the liberation movement.

Unfortunately, the endeavors of the CPSU and other Marxist-Leninist parties to ensure the unity of action of Communists have met with no positive response from the leaders of the Communist Party of China.

Of course, unity of action cannot be imposed upon anyone by force. But the interests of each party, of each socialist country objectively coincide with and cannot be counterposed to the common interests of the Communist movement and the socialist commonwealth. And if one proceeds not in words but in deeds from the interests of the struggle for socialism, then one cannot fail to recognize that, whatever serious differences separate certain detachments of the great Communist army, renunciation of concerted action in the struggle against the common enemy weakens their positions, leads to errors and miscalculations and can do serious harm to our common cause.

A policy of frustrating unity of action, a course of intensifying attacks on the Marxist-Leninist parties is harmful to the entire international Communist and liberation movement. It has a negative effect on the activities of the fraternal parties of the capitalist countries, which are waging a struggle in difficult conditions against the class enemy. It does great harm to the international democratic organizations, creates an unhealthy atmosphere in their work. It considerably complicates the liberation struggle of the peoples and the consolidation of all anti-imperialist forces. This schismatic course inflicts especially heavy blows on those fraternal parties and peoples which, like the Workers' Party of Vietnam and the Vietnamese people, are in the forefront of the armed struggle against the imperialist aggressors and are therefore in particular need of the support of a united socialist camp and a united world Communist movement.

Renunciation of joint action is particularly dangerous in the case of parties that are in power in socialist states. The socialist system is the chief gain of the revolutionary forces, their principal stronghold in the struggle against imperialism. It is the chief factor ensuring mankind's unswerving advance along the path of social progress. To undermine the unity of the socialist countries in the face of the intensified activity of the imperialist forces means in essence deliberately to weaken the revolutionary front, deliberately to encourage the enemies of peace, democracy and socialism.

The clear and precise position of the Marxist-Leninist parties favoring unity of action is now being in fact opposed by a course of political and organizational demarcation, a course of splitting the Communist movement. Proclamation of this course is accompanied by violent attacks on the Soviet Union, carried out in the spirit of the worst models of anticommunist propaganda.

Ever since the victory of the October Socialist Revolution of 1917, the spearhead of imperialist policy has invariably been aimed against our policy. The reasons for this are clear. In the Soviet Union, with its mighty economic base and armed forces, the enemies of peace, democracy and socialism rightly see the chief obstacle to the implementation of their plots against the peoples. Through the decades the Soviet people, under the leadership of the Communist Party, denying themselves many things, have built this economic base in order to ensure the growth of the people's well-being and culture, to strengthen our country's defense capacity and to fulfill as successfully as possible the great internationalist mission imposed by history on the state of the first socialist revolution.

In their efforts to denigrate and slander the Soviet Union, our bourgeois adversaries try to cast doubts upon the prospects of the revolutionary reconstruction of society, to discredit and debase what is brightest for the Communist movement, what is dearest to the working people of the entire world — the gains of socialism.

What a gift for imperialist propaganda are the actions of those who consider it compatible with the conscience of a Communist to repeat the slanderous fabrications of the ideologists of imperialism regarding the "capitalist degeneration" of the Soviet state and who even go so far as to call for organizational demarcation from the basic forces that are carrying out the historic mission of building a new socialist and communist society, that are waging a decisive battle against imperialism.

The great Lenin taught Communists to ask, in appraising a particular political course or a particular action, the question: "Who benefits by it?" Who benefits today by attacks on the Soviet Union and other socialist countries, on the Marxist-Leninist parties that are waging a heroic struggle against the class enemy in the capitalist countries? Who benefits by a course of political and organizational demarcation, a splitting of the Communist ranks? The answer to these questions could not be clearer. Such attacks, such a course are of benefit only to the imperialists, the enemies of the cause of peace, democracy, national liberation and socialism.

One cannot but see that such actions are capable of doing great harm first of all to their initiators themselves. Indeed, from whom do they intend to demarcate themselves and against whom do they intend to unite? In substance, what is involved is demarcation from the overwhelming majority of Marxist-Leninist parties that uphold the positions of the Declaration of 1957 and the Statement of 1960, demarcation from the overwhelming majority of detachments of the liberation movement that favors unity of action in the struggle against imperialism.

The vitally important questions of the struggle against imperialism imperatively demand joint actions by the Communist Parties of the socialist countries and other anti-imperialist forces. Today there is such a question, the attitude toward which is the touchstone of a principled approach to the fulfillment of the supreme revolutionary duty.

The whole world is now following with emotion the heroic struggle of the people of Vietnam against the American aggressors. In these conditions, the decisive test of how a particular Communist Party fulfills its internationalist duty is the support it gives to the just cause of the Vietnamese people.

The Soviet Union is giving and will continue to give all the necessary aid to the heroic Vietnamese people. The Communist Party of the Soviet Union and our people are sacredly fulfilling their internationalist duty. The leaders of the Workers' Party and the government of the Democratic Republic of Vietnam have many times praised this aid highly. Thus quite recently, in connection with the 48th anniversary of the October Socialist Revolution, Prime Minister Pham Van Dong of the Democratic Republic of Vietnam said: "The CPSU, the Soviet government and the Soviet people are extending resolute and active support to the just struggle of the entire Vietnamese people against American imperialism, are supporting the correct position of the DRV and the National Liberation Front of South Vietnam, are rendering all possible assistance to the DRV in strengthening its defense capacity and economy."

Other fraternal parties have also launched vigorous action in support of Vietnam and for curbing the imperialist aggressors. Direct material aid on the part of socialist countries, the solidarity movement, the collection of funds, the organization of pressure on reactionary governments that send their troops to Vietnam — such are the forms of activity of the parties and the methods of struggle they are employing.

But however great in itself the aid given to the Vietnamese people by individual detachments of the Communist movement, the effectiveness of this aid depends largely on the coordination of the efforts of the fraternal parties and the socialist countries.

Events of recent months have convincingly shown that imperialism is trying to exploit the weakening of the solidarity of the Communist ranks. And anyone who renounces cooperation and rejects proposals for joint actions against the aggressor is impeding the struggle of the Vietnamese people and helping the aggressor.

The present-day Communist movement was founded by the great Lenin. He laid down its principled ideological and organizational foundations. The CPSU and other Marxist-Leninist parties sacredly observe Lenin's behest that the great questions of the workers' struggle for their liberation be resolved by implementing in fact " the unity of the class struggle of the workers for communism throughout the world " (" Works," fourth edition, Vol. XXXI, p. 244). This unity has already brought great victories to the revolutionary cause. And to come out against it today, to call for a split means to act contrary to the interests of the revolution, to take up arms against Lenin, to renounce the Leninist heritage.

The objective nature of the identity of the interests and goals of all revolutionary forces of the present day predetermines in the final analysis the inevitability of the collapse of any attempts to undermine the unity of the ranks of the world Communist movement. As the Statement of 1960 says, " A resolute defense of the unity of the international Communist movement on the basis of the principles of Marxism-Leninism and proletarian internationalism and the prevention of any actions that could undermine that unity are necessary conditions for victory in the struggle for national independence, democracy and peace, for the successful accomplishment of the tasks of socialist revolution and of the building of socialism and communism."

The CPSU has stood and continues to stand firmly for ensuring the solidarity of the Communist ranks, of all revolutionary forces. It has striven and always will strive for such solidarity on the principled basis of Marxism-Leninism, regarding as of paramount importance the interests of the common struggle against imperialism and its policy of reaction and aggression, for the triumph of the cause of communism.

Our party has never entered into any kind of compromise at the expense of principles. It has waged and always will wage an implacable struggle against any opportunism, against all who distort the great teaching of Marxism-Leninism. It will always continue firmly to pursue the Leninist course which ensures success in the building of communism and contributes to the advance of our entire common revolutionary cause.

This course has been tested by life and corresponds to the vital needs of the country, the fundamental interests of all strata of Soviet society —

workers, peasants, intelligentsia — and therefore meets with their unanimous approval and boundless support. The Soviet people warmly approve the foreign policy of the CPSU aimed at creating the most favorable international conditions for the building of communism in our country, at the close solidarity and cooperation of all the countries of the socialist commonwealth, at all-round support for the liberation movement of the peoples, the strengthening of peace and peaceful coexistence between states with different social systems.

The socio-political and ideological unity of all Soviet people, their solidarity around the Communist Party, its Central Committee and its Leninist line as defined by the decisions of its Congresses and the CPSU Program, is the source of the power and invincibility of the Land of Soviets and an earnest of the successful solution of the tasks facing us.

Throughout its long and arduous, but glorious and great, history, the world revolutionary movement has undergone many trials and overcome many difficulties. Each time it has emerged from these difficulties still further strengthened and made wiser by experience. There can be no doubt that the present difficulties as well, borne of attempts to introduce dissension in its ranks, will also be successfully overcome. A pledge of this is the vast experience collectively accumulated by the fraternal parties and the steadfast will of all revolutionaries toward unity of action in the struggle against imperialism, for the great ideals of peace and socialism.

DOCUMENT 34

Some Aspects of the Unity of Socialist Countries at the Present Time [1]

by Václav Kotyk

Complete Text

[*Slovanský Přehled* (Prague), No. 5, 1965, quoted from Radio Free Europe (Munich), East Europe Research and Analysis, *Czechoslovak Press Survey*, No. 1723 (325), December 2, 1965, pp. 3–22, as revised by Laurence Newman]

No one in the socialist world and in the international Communist movement will deny the essential need for and the importance of the unity of the countries of the world socialist system.[2] To put it more precisely — no one denies it in words. However, although all Communist and Workers' Parties of the socialist countries uphold the strengthening of the unity of the socialist countries as the goal of their policies, we encounter contradictions, weakening the unity and strength of socialism as a world system, in

---

[1] This study examines in detail some of the opinions expressed in an article in No. 5, 1964, of this periodical, " The Question of the Unity of the Countries of the World Socialist System."

[2] A. Novotný, in his speech on the occasion of the 20th anniversary of the liberation of Czechoslovakia, emphasized in this connection that " the unity of the socialist countries, the unity of the international Communist movement, and the unity of all revolutionary forces of the present are of decisive importance for the maintenance of peace and the freedom of the peoples and also for the success of further revolutionary changes in the world." (*Rudé Právo*, May 9, 1965.)

the relations of the socialist countries and Communist and Workers' Parties, as well as in the opinions regarding the essence, form, and methods of this strengthening of unity. Thus, verbal declarations, however sincere they may be, are not in themselves sufficient for the unity of the countries of the world socialist system to materialize.

What do we mean by unity of the socialist countries, and what is the specific substance of this unity? We very often find this demand for the unity of the socialist countries in literature and in documents, but only seldom do we discern efforts to explain what this unity really means and to study the unity of the socialist countries as an ever-developing category. The starting point for such studies could be theoretical conclusions about the relations of the socialist countries and the subjective and objective factors forming and influencing these relations on the one hand, and the historical experience of almost 20 years of development of the world socialist system, on the other hand.

The development of the world socialist system in recent years has demonstrated that the efforts to consolidate the unity of the socialist countries and to define the concept and substance of this unity, cannot be divorced from the objective conditions for the development of the world socialist system and that the general theoretical ideas regarding this unity cannot be separated from the specific historical conditions governing their implementation. In a word, in politics one cannot aim at something for which suitable conditions do not exist, i.e., one cannot implement a definite, concrete concept of unity that would be in conflict with the existing conditions under which world socialism is developing. On the contrary, such a concept must be based on the real conditions that prevail and on the possibilities existing in the current phase of development of world socialism, and it must not be based on subjective wishes.

*   *   *

The development of the world socialist system indicates that conflicting viewpoints dividing the Communist and Workers' Parties of the socialist countries are no accident and due to purely subjective factors alien to socialism, but that these conflicting viewpoints are due to far-reaching objective causes chiefly arising, first of all, from the distinct differences in the economic level of the individual socialist countries, from the uneven pace of their economic, political, and ideological development, and from other specific conditions of their historical development, socialist construction, and international position. This diversity of conditions also produces differences and a variety of forms as far as the approach and tactics of the individual Communist and Workers' Parties are concerned, and it is the reason why differences in the standpoints of the different Communist and Workers' Parties are not only possible, but, under the currently prevailing conditions of the development of world socialism, even inevitable.

The diversity of the specific objective conditions under which the individual Communist and Workers' Parties operate and which is the key to understanding the causes leading to disputes between the socialist countries, can be easily documented by many facts. In this context, let us remember the almost abysmal differences in the economic level of the individual socialist countries, which are bound to influence the viewpoints of the Communist and Workers' Parties regarding this question or another. Moreover, it will be a very long time before these differences are overcome. Very marked differences also exist in the objective international position of the individual socialist countries. In addition to common interests, factors governed by the specific position of the individual socialist countries also make themselves very strongly felt in their foreign policies. Different problems are given priority in the foreign political activities of each of these countries. Furthermore, the course of the revolutionary process in the individual countries and the forms and methods of the struggle of the individual Parties for political power also have their marked specific features in each instance. Socialist forms now come into being under conditions that are entirely different from the conditions already existing in the socialist state, and apparently this will also continue to be the case in the future. It is not only impossible but also contrary to the interests of the further development of world socialism to try and press this complicated and many-sided process, a process that in essence is immeasurably rich, into the existing ideological categories and into the existing forms of cooperation and organizational structure of the socialist world.

Thus, in the current phase of the development of the world socialist system, objective conditions exist which make it possible not only for differences of opinions to arise between the Communist and Workers' Parties of the socialist countries regarding this question or the other but also for different concepts to be adopted by them regarding the role of world socialism and the paths of its future development.[3] The decisive, specific objective conditions under which the individual Communist and Workers' Parties operate have a clear bearing on their subjective approach to various questions. However, the depth and extent of these conflicts cannot be explained by factors of an objective nature alone. That is to say, if objective conditions were the sole factors engendering disputes between the socialist countries, no other alternative would exist. At the same time, the development of world socialism demonstrates that the degree to which an objectively conditioned possibility of a conflict arising really erupts into a conflict largely depends on the subjective factor, i.e., on the policies of the Communist and Workers' Parties, and that the forms of and methods for resolving such conflicts often depend exclusively on the subjective factor.

However, from the aspect of the causes of disputes arising between socialist countries, factors of an objective nature are of prime importance. From this aspect it is also necessary to regard the current problems of the world socialist system as the expression of a specific development phase of world socialism and not as a retrogressive step in comparison with the "golden age of unity" of the fifties. Incidentally, a more thorough analysis would confirm how profoundly specific objective conditions influenced the policies of the individual Communist and Workers' Parties

---

[3] This fact was referred to more than once in the documents of a number of Communist and Workers' Parties in recent years. For instance, it is mentioned in the letter dated July 14, 1963 and addressed by the CPSU Central Committee to the party organizations and to all Communists in the USSR, which speaks of the different conditions under which the fraternal parties work. It says: "It is not surprising that in these circumstances the fraternal parties may develop different approaches to the solution of this or that problem." (*For the Unity of the International Communist Movement* [Prague, 1963], p. 217.) [*Pravda*, July 14, 1963, quoted from William E. Griffith, *The Sino-Soviet Rift* (Cambridge, Mass.: The M.I.T. Press, 1964), p. 323.— Ed.]

in this period (for instance, the collectivization of agriculture in the individual socialist countries, the question of the political trials, etc.), not to speak of the methods used for strengthening their unity and of the defensive and static concept of this unity. Undoubtedly, the unity of the socialist countries was also an expression of certain objective conditions in the first half of the fifties; however, these objective conditions were largely — even if not exclusively — inherent in the development of international conditions and were due to circumstances outside the world socialist system. Simplified ideas about the relations among the socialist countries also played their part in creating these conditions. The current development, under conditions that differ greatly from the situation in the first half of the fifties, has overcome these simplified ideas, according to which the victory of socialism in the individual countries and the bringing of the workers' class, essentially an international class, to power, would lead to new relations between states and nations and to the elimination of all major differences of opinion and disputes among them.[4] Incidentally, the interpretation of the relations between the socialist countries in the 1960 Moscow Statement of Communist and Workers' Parties was also marked by this simplified idea, when stating that "there are no objective causes in the nature of the socialist system for contradictions and conflicts between the peoples and states belonging to it," and that its development contributes to states and nations increasingly closing their ranks and to accentuating every aspect of their cooperation.[5] However, practice has proved that the development of the world socialist system does not take this simplified course, that the process of this development is far more complicated than had ever been assumed in Marxist literature, and that the establishment of relations of a new type is also not the automatic result of big social, economic, and political changes in the individual countries but a complicated, drawn-out, and protracted process.[6]

Hence, in view of the current objective conditions of the development of the world socialist system, the efforts of the socialist countries to achieve unity cannot be based on the elimination of the differences in the policies of the individual Communist and Workers' Parties but in their recognition.[7]

---

[4] Quite logically, similar ideas appeared in the opinions of Communist theorists even prior to the forming of the world socialist system, i.e., at a time when no practical experience about relations between socialist states was available. In this connection, I would refer to N. Bukharin's essay "Imperialism and Communism," published in 1936 in the American periodical *Foreign Affairs*, in which he assumed that no conflict of interests could exist between socialist states; see: *The Soviet Union 1922–1962: A Foreign Affairs Reader* (New York, 1963), p. 151.

[5] *Nová Doba*, No. 50, 1960, Supplement, p. 7. [*Pravda*, December 6, 1960, and *CDSP*, Vol. XII, No. 48 (December 28, 1960), p. 6; quoted from G. F. Hudson, Richard Lowenthal, and Roderick MacFarquar, *The Sino-Soviet Dispute* (New York: Praeger, 1961), p. 185.— Ed.]

[6] At certain times, the influence of social economic changes on the political stability of the countries concerned was reappraised in the practical policies of some socialist countries, in the sphere of relations as well as from the aspect of the internal development of socialism.

[7] In this connection V. I. Lenin said in his work *The Teething Troubles of Leftism*: " As long as national and state differences exist among peoples and countries — and these differences will continue to exist for a very long time even after the dictatorship of the proletariat has been establishd on a world scale — the unity of international tactics of the Communist working class movement of all countries demands, not the elimination of variety, not the abolition of national differences (that is a foolish dream at the present moment), but such an application of the *fundamental* principles of Communism (Soviet power and the dictatorship of the proletariat) as will *correctly*

The current conditions under which the world socialist system is developing require the independence and freedom of movement of the individual Communist and Workers' Parties not only in the organizational sense but also as far as the forming of ideological positions and the formulation of their internal and foreign policies are concerned. Today the unity of the socialist countries is possible only when based on the existence of some differences in the standpoints of the Communist and Workers' Parties, differences that correspond to the different situations and degree of development of the countries concerned. Hence it is necessary to discard the fiction of unity as an absolute identity of views of the Communist and Workers' Parties, and efforts to strengthen their unity must be consistently based on the specific conditions of the development of the world socialist system and of the individual socialist countries.

Therefore, the basic problem today does not consist in the efforts to attain absolute identity in the views of the Communist and Workers' Parties but in the efforts to find and create forms and methods of discussion and of settling disputes, which will make it possible to preserve their unity of approach to fundamental questions and which will respect the independence and the different conditions of the work of the individual Parties at the same time.[8] Therefore, the question of forms and methods of discussion, the question of forms and methods by which disputes can be settled, and the establishment of norms for relations among the socialist countries, corresponding to the current conditions of development, these are the key questions of today for the world socialist system. Thus the issue is not so much the disputes between socialist countries themselves, which are inevitable in a sense, as — because such disputes are inevitable — the methods for resolving disputes and norms for relations between socialist countries. The general secretary of the League of Communists of Yugoslavia, J. B. Tito, touched upon this issue in his speech of May 18, 1963 on current questions of the international Communist movement:

> The most recent experience has shown that copying and mechanically transferring certain forms of discussion from the past, when communist parties were not in power, can only do harm under conditions where these parties are responsible for the destiny of their own countries. Similarly, practice indicates that certain classical forms for reconciling points of view cannot contribute to an understanding of problems. We are therefore faced with the task of studying previous experiences and forms of cooperation and of finding better forms which suit the present degree of development of socialism, the responsibility of individual

modify these principles in *certain particulars*, correctly adapt and apply them to national and national-state differences." (V. I. Lenin, *Collected Works*, Vol. 31, pp. 86–87.) [Quoted from V. I. Lenin, " *Left-Wing* " *Communism, an Infantile Disorder*, pamphlet (New York: International Publishers, 1940), p. 73.— Ed.]

8 L. I. Brezhnev, the First Secretary of the CPSU Central Committee, clearly formulated this standpoint in his speech on the occasion of the 47th anniversary of the Great October Socialist Revolution when he said: " The attention given by each socialist country to the experience of building the new society in other countries is understandable. At the same time, we consider that it would be wrong to force the experience of any one party and country on other parties and countries. The choice of various methods, forms and means of socialist construction is the sovereign right of each people. We proceed from the fact that individuality in ways of building socialism should by no means hinder the development of friendly relations among the fraternal socialist countries." (*Rudé Právo*, November 7, 1964.) [*Pravda*, November 7, 1964, quoted from *CDSP*, Vol. XVI, No. 43 (November 18, 1964), p. 6.— Ed.]

communist parties and the needs of continued consolidation of socialism in its entirety.[9]

The fact that the development of the world socialist system has outgrown the existing forms of relations and discussions between the Communist and Workers' Parties is one of the reasons why disputes have reached such proportions and make themselves so strongly felt.

If we devote all this attention to the study of the diversity of the specific objective conditions of the development of the socialist countries that constitute the world socialist system, we are doing so because, among other things, this aspect, which is so important today, was largely neglected in past years. Yet no one denies that, in addition to differences of opinion, decisive common interests of the socialist countries, based on the general laws of socialist construction, also exist and that these common interests of socialism as a whole are the base on which the efforts to strengthen and develop the unity of the socialist countries are founded. The representatives of 19 Communist and Workers' Parties who participated in the consultative meeting in Moscow, March 1–5, 1965, expressed their conviction in the communiqué issued at the end of this conference that

> what unites the Communist Parties is much stronger than what dis-
> unites them at a given moment. Even given the existence of disagreements
> concerning the political line and many important problems in theory
> and tactics, it is fully possible and necessary to strive for unity of action
> in the struggle against imperialism, in the cause of comprehensive support
> for the liberation movement of the peoples in the struggle for universal
> peace and the peaceful coexistence of states with different social
> systems — regardless of whether the countries involved are large or
> small — in the struggle for the vital interests and historical tasks of the
> working class. Joint action in the struggle for these common goals is the
> most correct path for overcoming the existing differences.[10]

In connection with the efforts to strengthen the unity of the countries of the world socialist system, it is possible to form some theoretical and practical conclusions based on the experience gained to date from the development of world socialism.

First of all, no country and no Party must be excluded from the socialist community for the sole reason that this Party has adopted standpoints that differ from those adopted by other Communist and Workers' Parties, or even adopted by the majority of these Parties. No country and Party can be excluded from the socialist community even if the great majority of Parties is convinced that the standpoints of the former are incorrect and non-Marxist. This does not mean that incorrect standpoints of one Party or another cannot be criticized.[11] The contrary is true. However, what matters are the forms and methods of this criticism and the fact that the individual socialist countries are objectively parts of

[9] J. B. Tito, *Pozitsiya SKJ po Vazhnym Mezhdunarodnym Voprosam* (Belgrade, 1963). [*Borba*, May 19, 1963.— Ed.]

[10] *Rudé Právo*, March 10, 1965. [*Pravda*, March 10, 1965, quoted from *CDSP*, Vol. XVII, No. 9 (March 24, 1965), p. 7.— Ed.]

[11] The Moscow Statement says: "When a Party wants to clear up questions relating to the activity of another fraternal Party, its leadership approaches the leadership of the Party concerned; if necessary, they hold meetings and consultations." (*Nová Doba*, No. 50, 1960, Supplement, p. 15.) [*Pravda*, December 6, 1960, and *CDSP*, Vol. XII, No. 49 (January 4, 1961), p. 7; quoted from Hudson, Lowenthal, and MacFarquar, *op. cit.*, p. 204.— Ed.]

the world socialist system and not because they subjectively wish it.[12] The fact that this Party or the other has adopted different, and even incorrect, standpoints must not lead to conclusions about the country concerned having a nonsocialist character, etc. For instance, in spite of the ideological differences of opinion that exist between the majority of the Communist and Workers' Parties and the League of Communists of Yugoslavia regarding some questions, an objective analysis of the internal economic and political processes in Yugoslavia confirms that Yugoslavia has always been a socialist country, a country with numerous specific features of socialist construction, a country whose socialist character cannot be denied in spite of all reservations. From this aspect, the acceptance of the Marxist character of the social order in Yugoslavia is not only of fundamental importance for the relations of this socialist country or the other to Yugoslavia but also for the relations between socialist countries in general. The incorrect viewpoints of the Albanian Party of Labor also do not mean that Albania has ceased to be a socialist country. This is also generally valid for all other Communist and Workers' Parties.

An objective and unprejudiced approach to an appraisal of the internal processes and foreign policies of this country or the other — and at the present time this is the only possible approach — also excludes any form of pressure being brought to bear on countries and Parties that have adopted different standpoints, even if these viewpoints are entirely incorrect in the opinion of the majority of the other Parties, and this approach permits settlements of disputed questions only on the basis of discussions, noninterference, and independence. Recent experience has also confirmed that the leadership of this Party or the other cannot be coerced by any form of pressure to change its incorrect viewpoints and its policies, unless this were the pressure of the requirements of the objective development, or the pressure of the people of the country concerned. At the same time, it is necessary that mutual discussions should be conducted without rude and insulting formulations, without superficial judgments in specific questions, and with respect for the opinions of the adversary.[13] At the time of the cult, every disagreement became an irreconcilable conflict, " a dereliction of principles," a rift. However, if a disagreement leads to a rift, the possibility of discussion ceases to exist. Open discussion, a free exchange of views, and an incessant search are needed for a creative expansion of Marxism and for the strengthening of unity on this basis. In his reference to the results of the 22nd Congress of the CPSU, Palmiro Togliatti recalled in this connection that

> our movement has today become so great, so extensive, and holds so many and such diverse positions, that it is unthinkable that we can be harmed by a comparison of opinions that do not coincide always and

[12] I believe that one must distinguish between the world socialist system, of which objectively all countries building socialism are parts, and the socialist camp, of which not all socialist countries are a part. These two terms must not be assumed to be identical.

[13] The representatives of the Communist and Workers' Parties who convened in Moscow in 1965 regarded it as " useful to continue the exchange of opinions on important contemporary questions of common interest in a comradely form, without mutual attacks." (*Rudé Právo*, March 10, 1965.) [*Pravda*, March 10, 1965, quoted from *CDSP*, Vol. XVII, No. 9 (March 24, 1965), p. 8.— Ed.]

in every respect, provided that the fundamental principles of our doctrine and of proletarian internationalism are not violated.[14]

The present conditions of development of the world socialist system therefore demand the promotion of every form of contact between the Communist and Workers' Parties, the search for new forms of cooperation that would make possible the achievement of unity under the present conditions. It was this problem to which the Moscow conference paid its main attention. The communiqué emphasizes in this connection that " in the struggle for the resolution of the tasks common to the whole Communist movement, it is expedient to use all possibilities and paths, bilateral and multilateral meetings of the representatives of the fraternal parties and other forms of party communication and exchanges of opinion." [15]

The interests of the unity of the socialist countries demand that the differences of opinions among Communist and Workers' Parties not be allowed to lead to an interruption of relations, of their state, economic, and cultural contacts. It would be theoretically wrong and would lead to harmful practical results if we were to identify Party relations with the international relations among the socialist countries, if we were to deduce from the unavoidable conflicts of opinion in ideological questions between the Communist and Workers' Parties the necessity of transferring these conflicts onto the plane of cooperation among the socialist states. This is fully confirmed by the development of the world socialist system. It is understandable that the differences of opinion among the Communist and Workers' Parties must influence to some extent other spheres of relations among the socialist countries, that it is difficult to draw a perfect line between practical politics and ideological conflicts, and thus that relations between states are deeper and more harmonious when there is an identity of views among the Parties than when there are conflicts. Therefore upon the identity or difference of opinion in fundamental contemporary questions may depend — and actually does depend — the intensity and extent of mutual relationships and the character of Party contacts but not their existence — as long as the common interests of socialism are respected. The interest of unity excludes any form of pressure, any subordination of the weaker Party to the stronger one, any creation of a mechanical and formal unity, as well as mutual isolation or elimination of mutual cooperation.

One condition of unity and of its consolidation is adherence to the principle of equality and noninterference with the internal affairs of the other Communist and Workers' Parties and socialist countries. It is therefore a question of adhering to the fundamental principles of relations among the socialist countries; the importance of these principles was emphasized by the 20th Congress of the CPSU, by the documents issued by the Communist and Workers' Parties during the period following the 20th Congress [16] and in the agenda documents regarding the Moscow

14 *Pravda*, November 16, 1961. [*L'Unità*, November 11, 1961, quoted from Alexander Dallin, ed., with Jonathan Harris and Grey Hodnett, *Diversity in International Communism* (New York: Columbia University Press, 1963), p. 420.— Ed.]

15 *Rudé Právo*, March 10, 1965. [*Pravda*, March 10, 1965, quoted from *CDSP*, Vol. XVII, No. 9 (March 24, 1965), p. 7.— Ed.]

16 In this connection, one should recall the declaration of the government of the USSR of October 30, 1956 on the foundations of the further development of friendship and cooperation between the USSR and the other socialist countries; the declaration emphasizes that the countries of the socialist camp can build mutual relations " only

conference of the Communist and Workers' Parties.[17] Emphasis should be put not on a formal proclamation of these principles but on their consistent application in the practical politics of the Communist and Workers' Parties and of the governments of the individual socialist countries, especially those that occupy an objectively important place in the development of the world socialist system. The upholding of sovereignty and equality of the countries of the socialist system signifies in practical politics respect for the laws, order, and traditions existing in the socialist countries, respect for the leading Party and government bodies to whom the people of the country entrusted their development, and respect for the existing state frontiers between socialist countries.[18] Without respecting these elementary principles the unity of socialist countries cannot be achieved. At the same time, it is well known that the relations among the socialist countries, being relations of a new type, are not based on the principle of equality and noninterference alone and that their characteristic feature is the principle of mutual fraternal help.[19] Jiří Hendrych drew attention to this principle in his speech on the occasion of the 95th anniversary of V. I. Lenin's birthday. Hendrych said that no progress in cooperation could be achieved without a full understanding of the problems of the other partners and that pettiness must be excluded from mutual cooperation.[20] At present the principle of unity of the national and international interests is stressed as one of the fundamental principles governing the relations among the socialist countries.

From the point of view of the realization of these principles, development after the 20th Congress has gone a long way. The Information Bureau was abolished when it came into conflict with the needs of the Communist movement due to its structure and also to its activities. Bilateral contacts have become the basic form of relations; they enable the Communist and Workers' Parties to get acquainted with mutual problems. The Leninist thesis on the various ways to socialism and the various forms of organizing socialist society was fully re-established by the 20th Congress. The principles of equality and noninterference, which were often violated during the period of the cult of personality, were established in the relations of the socialist countries, thanks to the CPSU. The efforts to normalize relations with Yugoslavia, the well-known declaration of the Soviet government of October 30, 1956 regarding the

on the principles of complete equality, of respect for territorial integrity, state independence and sovereignty, and of noninterference in one another's internal affairs." (*Documents of Soviet Foreign Policy, 1945–1961* [Prague, 1962], p. 113.) [*Pravda*, October 31, 1956, and *CDSP*, Vol. VIII, No. 40 (November 14, 1956), pp. 10–11; quoted from Paul E. Zinner, ed., *National Communism and Popular Revolt in Eastern Europe* (New York: Columbia University Press, 1956), p. 486.— Ed.]

[17] *Nová Doba*, No. 50, 1960, addenda, p. 7.

[18] *Izvestiya*, May 31, 1964.

[19] The principles governing the relations between the socialist countries were formulated thoroughly in the Declaration of the Communist and Workers' Parties of the Socialist Countries of November 1957: "The socialist countries base their relations on the principles of complete equality, respect for territorial integrity and state independence and sovereignty, and non-interference in one another's affairs. These are important principles but they do not exhaust the essence of relations among the socialist countries. Fraternal mutual aid is an integral part of these relations. The principle of socialist internationalism finds effective expression in this mutual aid." [*Pravda*, November 22, 1957, quoted from *CDSP*, Vol. IX, No. 47 (January 1, 1958), p. 4.— Ed.]

[20] *Rudé Právo*, April 22, 1965.

relations with other socialist countries, and the negotiations between the USSR and Poland in October 1956 — all these steps were clear expressions of the desire of the CPSU and the Soviet government to eliminate energetically and definitely the existing flaws in the relations among the socialist countries. At the initiative of the CPSU the Leninist concept of relations among the Communist and Workers' Parties was restored, and the reference to the CPSU as the leading Party of the Communist movement was eliminated with final validity. Naturally, this does not change anything as regards the position of the CPSU as a Party with rich experience in socialist and Communist building of society.

However, unity among socialist countries is incompatible with both the nationalist tendencies [21] that have been apparent recently within the world socialist movement and the trend toward hegemony of certain forces. If any one of the Communist Parties refused to give up such trends, if for any reason it would be unwilling to overcome the existing differences, a restoration of unity would be impossible. Unity among socialist countries is the concern of all the Communist and Workers' Parties; in this process a particularly important place is taken by the biggest and most influential Communist Party of our time.[22] The strengthening of unity cannot be a unilateral process. It anticipates a sincere effort of all the Parties. It is impossible to quote Marxism-Leninism all the time and at the same time refuse to take any real steps aimed at the restoration of unity.

A true, not just a formal, unity of the socialist countries can be established only on the basis of a Marxist appraisal of the contemporary situation (as a matter of fact the very answer to the question what is and what is not a Marxist viewpoint is often a complicated identification process), on the basis of the tasks facing the Communist and Workers' Parties, on the basis of adherence to the principles of socialist internationalism. Unity among the countries of the world socialist system can definitely not be built on a compromise between Marxist and dogmatic views, on some illusions as to the possibility of overcoming the differences by compromise.[23] Permanent unity among the socialist countries cannot be built on the basis of some momentary and temporary events in the international situation, i.e., on the basis of factors outside the limits of the socialist system itself. Naturally, this does not signify that the influence of these outside factors upon the development and upon the very substance of unity among the socialist countries should be underestimated. The menace by the imperialist forces, the aggravating international tension that we witness today in connection with U.S. aggression in Vietnam, force the Communist and Workers' Parties to concentrate to a much larger degree on their common interests, on the common defense against the imperialist forces. On the other hand, it is this very imperialist danger that again underlines the vital importance of unity for the preservation of

---

[21] It is no accident that the Moscow Statement of 1960 reacted at length to the expressions of nationalism and national narrow-mindedness.

[22] Today these are primarily — though not exclusively — the CPSU and the CCP.

[23] That there were certain illusions can be deduced from the words of the Moscow Statement of 1960 that " Imperialists, renegade and revisionist hopes of a split within the socialist camp are built on sand and doomed to failure. All the socialist countries cherish the unity of the socialist camp like the apple of their eye." (*Nová Doba*, No. 50, 1960.) [*Pravda*, December 6, 1960, and *CDSP*, Vol. XII, No. 48 (December 28, 1960), p. 6; quoted from Hudson, Lowenthal, and MacFarquar, *op. cit.*, p. 184.— Ed.]

independence and thus for the guarantee of socialist progress in all the socialist countries. The emphasis on the common interest of socialism apparent in the current policy of some of the Communist and Workers' Parties to a greater degree than used to be the case in previous discussions within the Communist movement cannot be considered to be accidental.

In a situation where conflicting views among the Communist and Workers' Parties are not only a possible but an inevitable aspect of the development of world socialism, any unity of action of the Communist and Workers' Parties in the socialist countries depends to a *decisive* extent on adherence to such norms of relationship, to such forms and methods of discussion that will make possible, even in the prevailing situation, a common stand of the socialist countries on current problems. In the light of the present objective conditions in the development of the world socialist system, the question of the common interests of the socialist countries, the question of "what binds us together will be seen, though on a somewhat different level." No doubt there exists a common interest of all the socialist countries in the defense of socialism against the attacks of the imperialist forces, a common interest in the further advance of socialism in the world, etc. There exist at the same time profound differences, for example in the foreign policy concept of the relationship toward the nonsocialist world, in the intepretation of the concept of peaceful coexistence and its place in the further development of the world socialist revolution. Under these conditions it would be a mistake to believe that the expression of the existence of common interests must be automatically a common viewpoint on every problem within the sphere of this common interest. The objectively existing interest of all the socialist countries in the further strengthening and expanding of the socialist forces in the world by no means brings about an identity of views on the methods, forms, and concepts of the continued fight for socialism and of the further development of the world socialist revolution.

In this connection the question arises, in what area is an agreement possible, as well as the need to delimit the scope of these concrete questions wherein the common interest is accompanied by the corresponding social points of view. A number of problems will remain in which the actual standpoints of the Communist and Workers' Parties differ, notwithstanding the fundamental common interest of socialism. If the existing objective conditions do not permit the Communist and Workers' Parties to find common viewpoints on all the fundamental problems there certainly is no reason to believe that no forms of discussion or methods of solving differences could be found that would make possible a common front of the Communist and Workers' Parties in some questions while respecting the independence and the difference in conditions in the individual Parties. In the common interest of socialism, the practical activity of the individual Parties should be such as not to widen the gulf and not to dramatize the existing differences and, on the other hand, to permit a common stand wherever conditions for it exist. This is the mark of a subjective factor of an internationalist attitude.

*   *   *

In the present situation, the fundamental problem of the policy of the Communist and Workers' Parties is the harmonization of the national interests still existing under socialism with the interests of the world

487

socialist system as a whole, the harmonization of the interests of any individual socialist country with the fundamental interests of the world socialist system. It is a question of solving the conflict between the national and the supranational, the latter being of an objective character. Differences are natural in every situation, and thus also in the question of the unity among socialist countries. Overcoming these differences is the moving force of all progress. They must therefore be seen not only in a negative light but also in the light of the necessity for a constant creative progress of the theory and political practice of Marxism. Discussion within the Communist movement has, apart from its negative aspects, also positive ones. They not only attest a new stage in the development of world socialism but also call forth and make it possible to formulate more clearly the goals and methods of the fight for socialism, and create the conditions for the development of Marxist thought and its creative application in today's specific concrete conditions. It requires a scientific knowledge of the world socialist system. It was the current aspects of the development of world socialism that were not paid sufficient attention in the past; unfortunately only the existence of differences of opinion has demonstrated with due urgency the importance of the scientific research done in the countries of the world socialist system.

As long as the policy of an individual Party respects the principles of internationalism, i.e., as long as it does not approach the common problems and tasks of socialism from its own " problem Number One," the variety of conditions and the ensuing variety of views need not lead to deep-seated conflicts. After all, the fundamental problems facing the whole of humanity and the world socialist system today, namely the question of peace or war, of the liberation of nations from poverty and backwardness, etc., cannot be solved within the framework of regional policy, be it European, Asiatic, or any other; even less can they be solved from the standpoint of the interests of the individual socialist countries. There are situations in which viewpoints that are fully acceptable in the light of the narrow national standpoint are in conflict with the interests of the socialist system as a whole. These common interests of socialism are the true criterion of the internationalist attitude of each Party. The possibility of a conflict among socialist countries appears only whenever there is a violation of the dialectical unity of national and international interests, i.e., whenever the views and the policy of a subjective factor reflect objective reality wrongly, whenever they are an expression of an insufficient knowledge of this experience or situation.

In the course of implementing the principles of socialist internationalism it is possible to encounter in the policy of the Communist and Workers' Parties signs of the question of relations between the national and international being handled wrongly. National narrow-mindedness manifests itself sometimes in the attempts to generalize, attach absolute validity to, and submit to other Parties ideas founded on certain historical particularities of one country and its difficulties based upon its specific situation, and present them as the only true Marxist views. This can occur at a time when these misconceptions that have grown out of the objective and specific conditions of one or another country contradict the nature of our era and of the contemporary laws of social development and of the world socialist system, which the international Communist movement has elaborated.

Although in theory nobody denies the unity of national and international interests, the organic connection of the interests and needs of one country with the interests and needs of socialism as a whole is one of the most complicated problems of practical politics in the Communist and Workers' Parties of the socialist countries. This is accentuated by the fact that there are attempts to exploit the difficulties in the relationships among the socialist countries toward impairment of their unity; this we have witnessed in the form of the various political and economic concepts appearing in the Western world. However, no social process has ever materialized without difficulties; thus it could hardly be expected that a process as complicated as that of creating historically completely new relations among countries and nations will be devoid of difficulties. Contrary to the past, when everything seemed much simpler, the contemporary conditions for the international approach of the Communist and Workers' Parties of the socialist countries are greatly challenged as concerns the problems of internal structure and mutual relations.

Although in the past the problems of international cooperation among the socialist countries were emphasized and interpreted chiefly from the propagandistic point of view, today these questions constitute the core of the political activity of the Communist and Workers' Parties. The line of the 20th Congress alone can form the theoretical foundation of the unity of the socialist countries; this has been emphasized many times in the documents and declarations of the majority of the Communist and Workers' Parties. Under the present conditions, it is our duty not only to defend this line but also to help to create a Marxist concept of world socialism and its unity, corresponding to the present and constantly changing conditions.

Selected Bibliography

Brzezinski, Zbigniew K. *The Soviet Bloc: Unity and Conflict.* 2nd ed. New York: Frederick A. Praeger, 1961.

The standard work on bloc politics through 1960, with an excellent epilogue on the rift in the revised edition. A new, revised edition will be published in 1967.

——. "Threat and Opportunity in the Communist Schism," *Foreign Affairs,* Vol. XL, No. 3 (Apr. 1963), pp. 513–526.

An excellent estimate, with policy recommendations.

Charles, David A. "The Dismissal of Marshal P'eng Teh-huai," *The China Quarterly,* No. 8 (Oct.–Dec. 1961), pp. 63–76.

The basic and reliable account.

Crankshaw, Edward. *The New Cold War: Moscow v. Pekin.* Harmondsworth, Eng.: Penguin, 1963.

Valuable, as are his articles, for disclosure of unpublished Sino-Soviet exchanges, particularly at the November 1960 81-party meeting.

Dallin, Alexander, ed., with Jonathan Harris and Grey Hodnett. *Diversity in International Communism.* New York: Columbia University Press, 1963.

A voluminous documentary study, covering all Communist parties, on the Twenty-Second Party Congress and its aftermath, up to April 1963.

Dallin, Alexander. "Long Divisions and Fine Fractions," *Problems of Communism,* Vol. XI, No. 2 (Mar.–Apr. 1962), pp. 7–16.

The best analysis of the situation in international communism at the beginning of 1962.

Doolin, Dennis J. *Territorial Claims in the Sino-Soviet Conflict.* Stanford, Cal.: The Hoover Institution, 1965.

An excellent annotated collection of documents.

Griffith, William E. *Albania and the Sino-Soviet Rift.* Cambridge, Mass: The M.I.T. Press, 1963.

Detailed analysis, with documents, of Albania's role in the rift, through November 1962.

Griffith, William E., ed. *Communism in Europe,* Vol. 1. Cambridge, Mass.: The M.I.T. Press, 1964.

——. *Communism in Europe,* Vol. 2. Cambridge, Mass.: The M.I.T. Press, 1966.

Symposia on Eastern and Western European Communist parties and their interaction with the Sino-Soviet rift.

491

Griffith, William E. *The Sino-Soviet Rift*. Cambridge, Mass.: The M.I.T. Press, 1964.

Detailed analysis, with documents, of Sino-Soviet relations, 1963–1964.

———. "The November 1960 Moscow Meeting: A Preliminary Reconstruction," *The China Quarterly*, No. 11 (July–Sept. 1962), pp. 38–57; reprinted in Walter Laqueur and Leopold Labedz, eds. *Polycentrism*. New York: Frederick A. Praeger, 1962, pp. 107–126.

Now needs to be supplemented; see Griffith, *The Sino-Soviet Rift, op. cit.*, p. 19, note 14.

Honey, P. J. *Communism in North Vietnam*. Cambridge, Mass.: The M.I.T. Press, 1963.

A detailed study of the North Vietnamese party's role in the rift.

Hudson, Geoffrey, Richard Lowenthal, and Roderick MacFarquhar, *The Sino-Soviet Dispute*. New York: Frederick A. Praeger, 1961.

Analyses and documents of the rift up to early 1961.

Labedz, Leopold, ed. *International Communism after Khrushchev*. Cambridge, Mass.: The M.I.T. Press, 1965.

The most recent and best symposium on the impact of the rift throughout international communism.

London, Kurt, ed. *Unity and Contradiction*. New York: Frederick A. Praeger, 1963.

A 1962 collection of essays by leading authorities on the rift and its background.

Lowenthal, Richard. *World Communism since Stalin*. New York: Oxford University Press, 1964.

A collection of excellent articles. Particularly valuable for Soviet-Yugoslav relations.

———. "The Rise and Decline of International Communism," *Problems of Communism*, Vol. XII, No. 2 (Mar.–Apr. 1963), pp. 19–32.

———. "The World Scene Transformed," *Encounter*, Vol. XXI, No. 4 (Oct. 1963), pp. 3–10.

———. "The Prospects for Pluralistic Communism," in Milorad M. Drachkovitch, ed. *Marxism in the Modern World*. Stanford, Cal.: Stanford University Press, 1965, pp. 225–274.

Among the best analyses of the rift and its effects.

Mehnert, Klaus. *Peking and Moscow*. New York: G. F. Putnam, 1963.

The best historical background of the rift.

Scalapino, Robert A., ed. *The Communist Revolution in Asia*. Englewood Cliffs, N.J.: Prentice-Hall, 1965.

The best and most up-to-date symposium on Asian communism.

Seton-Watson, Hugh. "The Great Schism," *Encounter,* Vol. XV, No. 5 (May 1963), pp. 61–70.

One of the best brief analyses.

Zagoria, Donald S. *The Sino-Soviet Conflict.* Princeton, N.J.: Princeton University Press, 1962.

The best detailed book-length treatment, up to the Twenty-Second CPSU Congress; now needs to be supplemented by material which has become available, cited in Griffith, *The Sino-Soviet Rift, op. cit.,* p. 19, note 14.

The most useful regular analyses of current Sino-Soviet and international Communist developments are produced in Munich by analysts of Radio Free Europe, notably Fritz Ermath, Richard Rockingham Gill, and Joseph C. Kun, and of Radio Liberty, particularly Christian Duevel.

Index